WILEY

The Complete Guide to

AUDITING STANDARDS

AND OTHER PROFESSIONAL STANDARDS FOR ACCOUNTANTS

2008

**Subscriber
Update
Service**

BECOME A SUBSCRIBER!
Did you purchase this product from a bookstore?

If you did, it's important for you to become a subscriber. John Wiley & Sons, Inc. may publish, on a periodic basis, supplements and new editions to reflect the latest changes in the subject matter that you *need to know* in order stay competitive in this ever-changing industry. By contacting the Wiley office nearest you, you'll receive any current update at no additional charge. In addition, you'll receive future updates and revised or related volumes on a 30-day examination review.

If you purchased this product directly from John Wiley & Sons, Inc., we have already recorded your subscription for this update service.

To become a subscriber, please call **1-877-762-2974** or send your name, company name (if applicable), address, and the title of the product to:

mailing address: **Supplement Department**
                                   John Wiley & Sons, Inc.
                                   One Wiley Drive
                                   Somerset, NJ 08875

e-mail: **subscriber@wiley.com**
fax: **1-732-302-2300**
online: **www.wiley.com**

For customers outside the United States, please contact the Wiley office nearest you:

Professional & Reference Division
John Wiley & Sons Canada, Ltd.
22 Worcester Road
Etobicoke, Ontario M9W 1L1
CANADA
Phone: 416- 236-4433
Phone: 1-800-567-4797
Fax: 416-236-4447
Email: canada@jwiley.com

John Wiley & Sons Australia, Ltd.
33 Park Road
P.O. Box 1226
Milton, Queensland 4064
AUSTRALIA
Phone: 61-7-3859-9755
Fax: 61-7-3859-9715
Email: brisbane@johnwiley.com.au

John Wiley & Sons, Ltd.
The Atrium
Southern Gate, Chichester
West Sussex, PO19 8SQ
ENGLAND
Phone: 44-1243 779777
Fax: 44-1243 775878
Email: customer@wiley.co.uk

John Wiley & Sons (Asia) Pte. Ltd.
2 Clementi Loop #02-01
SINGAPORE 129809
Phone: 65-64632400
Fax: 65-64634604/5/6
Customer Service: 65-64604280
Email: enquiry@wiley.com.sg

WILEY

The Complete Guide to
AUDITING STANDARDS
AND OTHER PROFESSIONAL STANDARDS FOR ACCOUNTANTS

2008

Nick A. Dauber   Marc H. Levine

Anique Ahmed Qureshi   Joel G. Siegel

WILEY

JOHN WILEY & SONS, INC.

For general information on our other products and services or technical support, please contact our Customer Care Department within the United States at 800-762-2974, outside the United States at 317-572-3993 or fax 317-572-4002.

Wiley also publishes its books in a variety of electronic formats. Some content that appears in print may not be available in electronic books. For more information about Wiley products, visit our Web site at http://www.wiley.com.

Library of Congress Cataloging-in-Publication Data:

Wiley, the complete guide to auditing standards, and other professional standards for accountants, 2008 / Nick A. Dauber

    p. cm.

Includes index.

ISBN 978-0-470-18397-7 (pbk.)

    1. Auditing – Standards – United States – Handbooks, manuals, etc. 2. Accounting – Standards – United States – Handbooks, manuals, etc. I. Dauber, Nicky A. II. John Wiley & Sons. III. Title: Complete guide to auditing standards, and other professional standards for accountants. IV. Title: Guide to auditing standards, and other professional standards for accountants. V. Title: Auditing standards, and other professional standards for accountants.

    HF5616.U5W559 2008

    657.02'1873—dc22   2008002755

Printed in the United States of America

10   9   8   7   6   5   4   3   2   1

DEDICATED TO

KAREN J. DAUBER
Loving wife and dear friend

KATIE AND MICHAEL DAUBER
Precious children

MARGIE, MARC AND SUSAN DAUBER
Loving and wonderful mother, father, and sister

SHAHEEN QURESHI
Loving wife

AQSA N. QURESHI AND YASEEN A. QURESHI
Wonderful children

MOHAMMAD RAFIQUE QURESHI AND ZAKIA QURESHI
Loving parents

CAROL LEVINE
Dedicated wife and friend

REVA, DANIEL AND SORI LEVINE
Loving children

YAAKOV LEVINE
Loving Grandson

TESSIE and SAMUEL LEVINE
Dearly departed Mother and Father

ROBERTA M. SIEGEL
Loving wife, colleague and best friend

CONTENTS

PREFACE

The Complete Guide to Auditing Standards and Other Professional Standards for Accountants 2008 is written primarily to help auditors and certified public accountants (CPAs) apply and comply with authoritative auditing and other professional standards. It represents a comprehensive, up-to-date compendium of current auditing standards, including the requirements of the Public Company Accounting Oversight Board (PCAOB), established under the Sarbanes-Oxley Act. The PCAOB now requires that the audit report state that the audit engagement was conducted in accordance with its standards rather than, as previously, with generally accepted auditing standards (GAAS).

The book emphasizes practical applications to implement audit and other professional standards and requirements.

We cover

Auditing Standards of the PCAOB
Statements on Auditing Standards (SAS)
Statements on Standards for Attestation Engagements (SSAE)
Statements on Standards for Accounting and Review Services (SSARS)
Interpretations of SAS, SSARS, and SSAE
Statements on Consulting Services
Statements on Quality Control
Statements on Standards for Tax Services (SSTS)
Statements on Personal Financial Planning
Statement on Standards for Valuation Services

The text covers all the topics an auditor must know about

Audit reports:

General standards
Fieldwork standards

Standards of reporting:

Special reports
Internal control
Compliance auditing

Application of agreed-upon procedures:

Letters for underwriters
Attestation engagements
Accounting and review services
Filings under federal securities statutes
Interim financial information
Statistical sampling

We intend the book to be a valuable reference for not only accounting and auditing professionals but also for persons who must interact with auditors, such as company managers, bank loan officers, suppliers, current and potential investors, and workers at governmental audit agencies such as the Securities and Exchange Commission. The book explains the standards and their requirements fully, in clear language, using technical terminology only where necessary. Our goal was to write a practical and effective "how to" guide. So, throughout, we have tried to make this book quick to read, easy to follow, comprehensive, and useful.

Constant changes in auditing mean that auditors and CPAs, both internal and external, must constantly work to stay current if they are to avoid serious consequences. Mistakes in the application of authoritative standards can have disastrous effects on investors (stockholders), creditors, regulatory bodies, management, and employees. Corporate failures such as Enron and WorldCom, with their legal problems due to improper auditing techniques, are evidence of the crucial importance of this book. The book brings professionals the most recent developments and emerging issues and helps them understand and apply these new audit standards.

The tools and techniques covered can be adopted outright or modified as needed. Checklists, charts, diagrams, report forms, schedules, tables, exhibits, illustrations, examples, practice aids, and step-by-step instructions add to the practicality of the book. The costs and benefits of various auditing approaches are discussed and answers to common questions are provided.

Accounting and auditing students and candidates preparing for the CPA exam will also benefit from this book. We hope they will keep this book handy for easy reference and daily use.

Any ambiguous situation or problem may be solved by referring to the comprehensive index. Corporate managers, internal auditors, and external auditors who closely adhere to the material, suggestions, and recommendations in this book should greatly minimize their legal exposure.

ABOUT THE AUTHORS

Nick Dauber, MS, CPA, is an accounting practitioner, specializing in auditing and taxation. Prior to starting his practice almost 25 years, ago, he was an audit and tax manager at a CPA firm.

Mr. Dauber is also an instructor of Auditing and Taxation at Queens College of the City University of New York. He was the president of Person/Wolinsky CPA Review Courses and has instructed over 100,000 CPA exam candidates during the past 28 years. Mr. Dauber was the writer of the review course's auditing and taxation material and served as the editor of the law and financial accounting material.

In 1992, Mr. Dauber was named Professor of the Year at Queens College and was the recipient of the Golden Apple Award bestowed by the Golden Key National Honor Society. He has also served as an award-winning lecturer in auditing and taxation for the Foundation for Accounting Education at the New York State Society of CPAs as well as for the American Institute of Certified Public Accountants.

Mr. Dauber has served as a book reviewer for major book publishers, and has published articles in many professional accounting journals including *The CPA Journal (New York), Massachusetts CPA, Virginia Accountant Quarterly, and National Public Accountant.*

Books that Mr. Dauber has authored include *The Vest-Pocket CPA* (John Wiley & Sons), *Corporate Controller's Handbook of Financial Management* (CCH), and *Barron's How to Prepare for the CPA Exam.* He has also been a contributor to professional books in accounting and auditing.

Anique Ahmed Qureshi, PhD, CPA, CIA, is professor of accounting and information systems at Queens College of the City University of New York and a consultant on accounting, auditing, and information systems. Dr. Qureshi has written ten books published by South-Western, Aspen, Prentice-Hall, Glenlake, and the American Management Association. His articles have appeared in accounting and information systems journals, including *The CPA Journal, Internal Auditing, National Public Accountant, International Journal of Computer Applications in Technology,* and the *Journal of Business Research.*

Marc H. Levine, PhD, CPA, is professor of accounting, Queens College of the City University of New York, and a financial accounting and auditing consultant. He was previously associated with Deloitte and Touche, CPAs. He has written seven books, including the WG&L Audit Manual (Warren, Gorham, and Lamont) and *GAAP 1994 to 2008, Handbook of Policies and Procedures* (CCH), and more than 55 articles on auditing and financial accounting topics. His articles have been published in *The CPA Journal, Journal of Corporate Accounting and Finance, Practical Accountant, National Public Accountant, Massachusetts CPA Review, Cost and Management,* and *Management Accountant,* among others.

Joel G. Siegel, PhD, CPA, is a self-employed certified public accountant and professor of Accounting at Queens College of the City University of New York. He previously worked as an auditor for the Defense Department of the United States, and Price Waterhouse Coopers, LLP. Dr. Siegel has acted as a consultant in accounting and auditing to many organizations, including Citicorp, International Telephone and Telegraph, United Technologies, The American Institute of CPAs, and Person/Wolinsky CPA Review Courses.

Dr. Siegel is author of 65 books and 275 articles on accounting and auditing topics. His books have been published by South-Western, International Publishing, Glenlake, Prentice-Hall, Aspen Law and Business, Richard Irwin, McGraw-Hill, Probus, Macmillan, Harper

Collins, John Wiley & Sons, Barron's American Management Association, and the American Institute of CPAs.

His articles have been published in many accounting, auditing, and financial journals including *EDP Auditing, The CPA Journal Practical Accountant, National Public Accountant, Ohio Public Accountant, Massachusetts CPA Review, Michigan CPA, Virginia Accountant Quarterly, Today's CPA* (Texas Society of CPAs), *Delaware CPA, Financial Executive, Financial Analysts Journal,* and the *Journal of Corporate Accounting and Finance.*

Dr. Siegel was the recipient of the Outstanding Educator of America Award. He is listed in *Who's Where among Writers* and *Who's Who in the World.* He has served as chairperson of the National Oversight Board.

WILEY

The Complete Guide to
AUDITING
STANDARDS
AND OTHER PROFESSIONAL
STANDARDS FOR
ACCOUNTANTS

2008

PART 1

AUDITING STANDARDS
OF THE PCAOB

PCAOB 1 REFERENCES IN AUDITORS' REPORTS TO THE STANDARDS OF THE PUBLIC COMPANY ACCOUNTING OVERSIGHT BOARD

An audit report on the financial statements of a public company regulated by the PCAOB should (1) be titled "Report of Independent Registered Public Accounting Firm," (2) refer to "the standards of the Public Company Accounting Oversight Board (United States)," (3) not include any reference to generally accepted auditing standards, and (4) include the city and state (or country, if a non-US auditor) from which the audit report is issued. A sample standard report follows:

Report of Independent Registered Public Accounting Firm

We have audited the accompanying balance sheet of [*company name*] as of (at) [*date*] and the related statements of income, retained earnings, and cash flows for the year then ended. These financial statements are the responsibility of the Company's management. Our responsibility is to express an opinion on these financial statements based on our audit.

We conducted our audit in accordance with the standards of the Public Company Accounting Oversight Board (United States). Those standards require that we plan and perform the audit to obtain reasonable assurance about whether the financial statements are free of material misstatement. An audit includes examining, on a test basis, evidence supporting the amounts and disclosures in the financial statements. An audit also includes assessing the accounting principles used and significant estimates made by management, as well as evaluating the overall financial statement presentation. We believe that our audit provides a reasonable basis for our opinion.

In our opinion, the financial statements referred to above present fairly, in all material respects, the financial position of [*company name*] as of (at) [*date*], and the results of its operations and its cash flows for the year then ended in conformity with accounting principles generally accepted in the United States of America.

[*Signature*]

[*City and State or Country*]

[*Date*]

Guidance for modifying the standard report applicable to financial statements of a public company regulated by the PCAOB may be found in AU Section 508.

PCAOB 3 AUDIT DOCUMENTATION

INTRODUCTION

AS 3 supersedes SAS 96, *Audit Documentation*, and provides general guidance for documentation that should be prepared and retained for engagements performed according to the Public Company Accounting Oversight Board ("PCAOB") standards.

Audit documentation is the written record that supports the auditor's representations and conclusions. Documentation serves as a basis for review and is used to plan and perform the engagement. It includes records of planning and performing the work, as well as a record of the procedures performed and evidence obtained. Audit documentation is sometimes referred to as workpapers or working papers.

Audit documentation must be prepared for each engagement conducted according to the standards of the PCAOB. It must be sufficiently detailed and clear. Audit documentation may be in the form of memoranda, confirmations, correspondence, schedules, audit programs, and letters of representation. Audit documentation may be kept on paper, in electronic files, or in other media.

Audit documentation should show compliance with the PCAOB standards. For every relevant assertion, the documentation should support the basis for the auditor's conclusions. The documentation should also show that the underlying accounting records have been reconciled with the financial statements.

REQUIREMENTS

Audit documentation must provide enough information so that an experienced auditor with no connection to the engagement is able (AS 3, paragraph 6)

1. To understand the nature, timing, extent, and results of the procedures performed, evidence obtained, and conclusions reached.
2. To determine who performed the work and the date such work was completed as well as who reviewed the work and the date of such review.

Significant findings or items contradicting the auditor's final conclusions must be documented. For instance, any procedures performed to resolve differences in the professional judgment of the engagement team members should be documented.

The auditor should consider additional documentation if, after the documentation completion date, the auditor has persuasive evidence that due to lack of documentation, procedures may not have been performed or evidence may not have been obtained. The auditor should comply with the provisions of AU Section 390, *Consideration of Omitted Procedures after the Report Date*, if the auditor is unable to determine whether sufficient evidence was obtained.

The documentation should identify specific items that were inspected, including confirmations, tests of details, tests of operating effectiveness of controls, and walkthroughs.

For audit samples the documentation should include identifying characteristics of items selected.

Audit documentation should be kept of items such as auditor independence, staff training and proficiency, and client acceptance and retention policy. All significant findings or issues in an engagement should be documented. If appropriate, cross-referencing to other available supporting audit documentation may be done. Audit documentation must be kept for at least seven years.

All audit documentation should be complete before the audit report release date. All auditing procedures performed to obtain evidence should be documented. A complete and final set of audit documentation should be ready within 45 days

1. After the report release date,
2. From the date that fieldwork was substantially completed, or
3. From the date the engagement ended, if the engagement was not completed.

While audit documentation must not be deleted or discarded after the documentation completion date, it is permissible to add information to the documentation. Any information added should clearly indicate

1. The date the information was added,
2. The name of the person who prepared the additional documentation, and
3. The reason for adding it.

WORK PERFORMED BY OTHER AUDITORS

For work performed by another auditor, the auditor issuing the report must review and retain the following if the primary auditor will not be referencing the work of the secondary auditor:

1. Engagement completion documents.
2. A list of significant fraud risk factors, how the auditor addressed those risks, and the procedures performed.
3. Significant findings or issues that are inconsistent with or contradict the final conclusions.
4. Findings affecting consolidated accounts in the consolidated financial statements.
5. Information enabling the reconciliation of the financial statement amounts audited by the other auditor to the information underlying the consolidated financial statements.
6. A schedule of audit adjustments, including a description of the nature and cause of each misstatement.
7. Significant deficiencies and material weaknesses in internal control over financial reporting.
8. Letters of representations from management.
9. Matters communicated to the audit committee.

However, if the auditor decides to make reference in the audit report to the work of the other auditor, the auditor issuing the report does not need to perform the procedures above. Instead the auditor should refer to AU Section 543, *Part of Audit Performed by Other Independent Auditors.*

PCAOB 4 REPORTING ON WHETHER A PREVIOUSLY REPORTED MATERIAL WEAKNESS CONTINUES TO EXIST

Effective Date: February 6, 2006

INTRODUCTION

When an entity reports a material weakness in its internal control over financial reporting, the management may engage the auditor to ensure that the material weakness does not exist prior to the next annual audit. The auditor's objective is to obtain reasonable assurance as to whether the previously reported material weakness still exists. The auditor's opinion specifically relates to the existence of the identified material weakness and is not an opinion on the effectiveness of internal control over financial reporting, nor is the opinion meant to update the previous opinion on the effectiveness of internal control over financial reporting. The auditor should obtain and evaluate evidence to ascertain whether controls were appropriately designed and were operating effectively.

AS 4 (paragraph 7) states that an auditor may report on whether a previously reported material weakness continues to exist only if management

1. Accepts responsibility for the effectiveness of internal controls.
2. Evaluates the effectiveness of the specific control(s) that it believes addresses the material weakness, using the same control criteria that management used for its most recent annual assessment of internal control over financial reporting and management's stated control objective.
3. Asserts that the specific control(s) are effective in achieving its objectives.
4. Supports its assertion with sufficient evidence, including documentation.
5. Presents a written report to accompany the auditor's report.

STANDARDS OF PCAOB

The auditor must comply with the standards of the PCAOB in performing an engagement to report on whether a previously reported material weakness continues to exist; this includes

1. Planning the engagement.
2. Obtaining an understanding of internal control over financial reporting.
3. Testing and evaluating whether a material weakness continues to exist, including using the work of others.
4. Forming an opinion on whether a previously reported material weakness continues to exist.

The engagement must be adequately planned and assistants properly supervised. The engagement must be performed by individuals having adequate technical proficiency as an auditor. An independence in mental attitude must be maintained by the auditor and due professional care exercised.

The auditor must evaluate management's assertion that controls related to a material weakness were designed and operated effectively. If the auditor finds that there is not sufficient evidence to support management's assertion, the auditor cannot complete the engagement to report on whether a previously reported material weakness continues to exist.

The management should select an appropriate date for its assertion that a previously reported material weakness no longer exists. The auditor should evaluate whether to use the work performed by others. The auditor should modify the nature, timing, or extent of work the auditor would perform if relying upon the work of others.

The auditor should obtain written representations from management. Management may conclude that a previously reported material weakness no longer exists because its severity has been significantly reduced. In the written representation, management should (AS 4, paragraph 44)

1. Acknowledge its responsibility for establishing and maintaining effective internal control over financial reporting;
2. State that it has evaluated the effectiveness of the specified controls using the specified control criteria and management's stated control objective(s);
3. State its assertion that the specified controls are effective in achieving the stated control objective(s) as of a specified date;
4. State its assertion that the identified material weakness no longer exists as of the same specified date;
5. State that it believes that its assertions are supported by sufficient evidence;
6. Describe any material fraud and any other fraud that, although not material, involves senior management or management or other employees who have a significant role in the company's internal control over financial reporting and that has occurred or come to management's attention since the date of management's most recent annual assessment of internal control over financial reporting; and
7. State whether there were, subsequent to the date being reported on, any changes in internal control over financial reporting or other factors that might significantly affect the stated control objective(s) or indicate that the identified controls were not operating effectively as of, or subsequent to, the date specified in management's assertion.

The written representations should be signed by those with responsibility for the company's internal control over financial reporting. Failure to obtain written representation, including management's refusal to furnish the representations, constitutes a scope limitation, necessitating the auditor to disclaim opinion or withdraw from the engagement.

AUDITOR'S REPORT

The auditor's report on whether a previously reported material weakness continues to exist must include the following elements (AS 4, paragraph 51):

1. A title that includes the word *independent*.
2. A statement that the auditor has previously audited and reported on management's annual assessment of internal control over financial reporting as of a specified date based on the control criteria, as well as a statement that the auditor's report identified a material weakness.

3.   A description of the material weakness.

4.   An identification of management's assertion that the identified material weakness in internal control over financial reporting no longer exists.

5.   An identification of the management report that includes management's assertion, such as identifying the title of the report (if the report is titled).

6.   A statement that management is responsible for its assertion.

7.   An identification of the specific controls that management asserts to address the material weakness.

8.   An identification of the company's stated control objective that is achieved by these controls.

9.   A statement that the auditor's responsibility is to express an opinion on whether the material weakness continues to exist as of the date of management's assertion based on his or her auditing procedures.

10. A statement that the engagement was conducted in accordance with the standards of the Public Company Accounting Oversight Board (United States).

11. A statement that the standards of the Public Company Accounting Oversight Board require that the auditor plan and perform the engagement to obtain reasonable assurance about whether a previously reported material weakness continues to exist at the company.

12. A statement that the engagement includes examining evidence supporting management's assertion and performing such other procedures the auditor considered necessary in the circumstances and that the auditor obtained an understanding of internal control over financial reporting as part of his or her previous audit of management's annual assessment of internal control over financial reporting and updated that understanding as it specifically relates to changes in internal control over financial reporting associated with the material weakness.

13. A statement that the auditor believes the auditing procedures provide a reasonable basis for his or her opinion.

14. The auditor's opinion on whether the identified material weakness exists (or no longer exists) as of the date of management's assertion.

15. A paragraph that includes the following statements:

     a.   That the auditor was not engaged to and did not conduct an audit of internal control over financial reporting as of the date of management's assertion, the objective of which would be the expression of an opinion on the effectiveness of internal control over financial reporting, and that the auditor does not express such an opinion, and

     b.   That the auditor has not applied auditing procedures sufficient to reach conclusions about the effectiveness of any controls of the company as of any date after the date of management's annual assessment of the company's internal control over financial reporting, other than the controls specifically identified in the auditor's report, and that the auditor does not express an opinion that any other controls operated effectively after the date of management's annual assessment of the company's internal control over financial reporting.

16. A paragraph stating that, because of its inherent limitations, internal control over financial reporting may not prevent or detect misstatements and that projections of any evaluation of the effectiveness of specific controls or internal control over financial reporting overall to future periods are subject to the risk that controls may become inadequate because of changes in conditions, or that the degree of compliance with the policies or procedures may deteriorate.

17. The manual or printed signature of the auditor's firm.
18. The city and state (or city and country, in the case of non-US auditors) from which the auditor's report has been issued.
19. The date of the auditor's report.

The auditor should modify the standard report if any of the following exist:

1. Material weaknesses previously reported but not addressed by the auditor's opinion.
2. A significant subsequent event that occurred.
3. Additional information in management's report about whether material weaknesses continue to exist.

While an auditor is not permitted to issue a qualified opinion, the auditor may issue a disclaimer of opinion due to a scope limitation. The auditor may also elect not to report on whether a material weakness continues to exist and withdraw from the engagement. If the auditor does not issue a report, the auditor must still communicate his conclusions that the material weakness continues to exist to the audit committee.

APPENDIX A

ILLUSTRATIVE REPORTS ON WHETHER A PREVIOUSLY REPORTED MATERIAL WEAKNESS CONTINUES TO EXIST

EXAMPLE A-1. ILLUSTRATIVE AUDITOR'S REPORT FOR A CONTINUING AUDITOR EXPRESSING AN OPINION THAT A PREVIOUSLY REPORTED MATERIAL WEAKNESS NO LONGER EXISTS

Report of Independent Registered Public Accounting Firm

We have previously audited and reported on management's annual assessment of XYZ Company's internal control over financial reporting as of December 31, 200X, based on [*identify control criteria, e.g., "criteria established in Internal Control—Integrated Framework issued by the Committee of Sponsoring Organizations of the Treadway Commission (COSO)"*]. Our report, dated [*date of report*], identified the following material weakness in the Company's internal control over financial reporting:

[*Describe material weakness*]

We have audited management's assertion, included in the accompanying [*title of management's report*], that the material weakness in internal control over financial reporting identified above no longer exists as of [*date of management's assertion*] because the following control(s) addresses the material weakness:

[*Describe control(s)*]

Management has asserted that the control(s) identified above achieves the following stated control objective, which is consistent with the criteria established in [*identify control criteria used for management's annual assessment of internal control over financial reporting*]: [*state control objective addressed*]. Management also has asserted that it has tested the control(s) identified above and concluded that the control(s) was designed and operated effectively as of [*date of management's assertion*]. XYZ Company's management is responsible for its assertion. Our responsibility is to express an opinion on whether the identified material weakness continues to exist as of [*date of management's assertion*] based on our auditing procedures.

Our engagement was conducted in accordance with the standards of the Public Company Accounting Oversight Board (United States). Those standards require that we plan and perform the engagement to obtain reasonable assurance about whether a previously reported material weakness continues to exist at the company. Our engagement included examining evidence supporting management's assertion and performing such other procedures as we considered necessary in the circumstances. We obtained an understanding of the company's internal control over financial reporting as part of our previous audit of management's annual assessment of XYZ Company's internal control over financial reporting as of December 31, 200X, and updated that understanding as it specifically relates to changes in internal control over financial reporting associated with the material weakness described above. We believe that our auditing procedures provide a reasonable basis for our opinion.

In our opinion, the material weakness described above no longer exists as of [*date of management's assertion*].

We were not engaged to and did not conduct an audit of internal control over financial reporting as of [*date of management's assertion*], the objective of which would be the expression of an opinion on the effectiveness of internal control over financial reporting. Accordingly, we do not express such an opinion. This means that we have not applied auditing procedures sufficient to reach conclusions about the effectiveness of any controls of the company as of any date after December 31, 200X, other than the control(s) specifically identified in this report. Accordingly, we do not express an opinion that any other controls operated effectively after December 31, 200X. Because of its inherent limitations, internal control over financial reporting may not prevent or detect misstatements. Also, projections of any evaluation of the effectiveness of specific controls or internal control over financial reporting overall to future periods are subject to the risk that controls may become inadequate because of changes in conditions or that the degree of compliance with the policies or procedures may deteriorate.

[*Signature*]

[*City and State or Country*]

[*Date*]

EXAMPLE A-2. ILLUSTRATIVE AUDITOR'S REPORT FOR A SUCCESSOR AUDITOR EXPRESSING AN OPINION THAT A PREVIOUSLY REPORTED MATERIAL WEAKNESS NO LONGER EXISTS

Report of Independent Registered Public Accounting Firm

We were engaged to report on whether a previously reported material weakness continues to exist at XYZ Company as of [*date of management's assertion*] and to audit management's next annual assessment of XYZ Company's internal control over financial reporting. Another auditor previously audited and reported on management's annual assessment of XYZ Company's internal control over financial reporting as of December 31, 200X, based on [*identify control criteria; e.g., "criteria established in Internal Control—Integrated Framework issued by the Committee of Sponsoring Organizations of the Treadway Commission (COSO)"*]. The other auditor's report, dated [*date of report*], identified the following material weakness in the Company's internal control over financial reporting:

[*Describe material weakness*]

We have audited management's assertion, included in the accompanying [title *of management's report*], that the material weakness in internal control over financial reporting identified above no longer exists as of [*date of management's assertion*] because the following control(s) addresses the material weakness:

[*Describe control(s)*]

Management has asserted that the control(s) identified above achieves the following stated control objective, which is consistent with the criteria established in [*identify control criteria used for management's annual assessment of internal control over financial reporting*]: [*state control objective addressed*]. Management also has asserted that it has tested the control(s) identified above and concluded that the control(s) was designed and operated effectively as of [*date of management's assertion*]. XYZ Company's management is responsible for its assertion. Our responsibility is to express an opinion on whether the identified material weakness continues to exist as of [*date of management's assertion*] based on our auditing procedures.

Our engagement was conducted in accordance with the standards of the Public Company Accounting Oversight Board (United States). Those standards require that we plan and perform the engagement to obtain reasonable assurance about whether a previously reported material weakness continues to exist at the company. Our engagement included obtaining an understanding of internal control over financial reporting, examining evidence supporting management's assertion, and performing such other procedures as we considered necessary in the circumstances. We believe that our auditing procedures provide a reasonable basis for our opinion.

In our opinion, the material weakness described above no longer exists as of [*date of management's assertion*].

We were not engaged to and did not conduct an audit of internal control over financial reporting as of [*date of management's assertion*], the objective of which would be the expression of an opinion on the effectiveness of internal control over financial reporting. Accordingly, we do not express such an opinion. This means that we have not applied auditing procedures sufficient to reach conclusions about the effectiveness of any controls of the company other than the control(s) specifically identified in this report. Accordingly, we do not express an opinion that any other controls operated effectively. Because of its inherent limitations, internal control over financial reporting may not prevent or detect misstatements. Also, projections of any evaluation of the effectiveness of specific controls or internal control over financial reporting overall to future periods are subject to the risk that controls may become inadequate because of changes in conditions or that the degree of compliance with the policies or procedures may deteriorate.

[*Signature*]

[*City and State or Country*]

[*Date*]

EXAMPLE A-3. ILLUSTRATIVE AUDITOR'S REPORT FOR A CONTINUING AUDITOR EXPRESSING AN OPINION ON ONLY ONE PREVIOUSLY REPORTED MATERIAL WEAKNESS WHEN ADDITIONAL MATERIAL WEAKNESSES PREVIOUSLY WERE REPORTED

Report of Independent Registered Public Accounting Firm

We have previously audited and reported on management's annual assessment of XYZ Company's internal control over financial reporting as of December 31, 200X, based on [*identify control criteria; e.g., "criteria established in* **Internal Control—Integrated Framework** *issued by the Committee of Sponsoring Organizations of the Treadway Commission (COSO)"*]. Our report, dated [*date of report*], identified the following material weakness in the Company's internal control over financial reporting:

[*Describe material weakness*]

We have audited management's assertion, included in the accompanying [*title of management's report*], that the material weakness in internal control over financial reporting identified above no longer exists as of [*date of management's assertion*] because the following control(s) addresses the material weakness:

[*Describe control(s)*]

Management has asserted that the control(s) identified above achieves the following stated control objective, which is consistent with the criteria established in [*identify control criteria used for management's annual assessment of internal control over financial reporting*]: [*state control objective addressed*]. Management also has asserted that it has tested the control(s) identified above and concluded that the control(s) was designed and operated effectively as of [*date of management's assertion*]. XYZ Company's management is responsible for its assertion. Our responsibility is to express an opinion on whether the identified material weakness continues to exist as of [*date of management's assertion*] based on our auditing procedures.

Our engagement was conducted in accordance with the standards of the Public Company Accounting Oversight Board (United States). Those standards require that we plan and perform the engagement to obtain reasonable assurance about whether a previously reported material weakness continues to exist at the company. Our engagement included examining evidence supporting management's assertion and performing such other procedures as we considered necessary in the circumstances. We obtained an understanding of the company's internal control over financial reporting as part of our previous audit of management's annual assessment of XYZ Company's internal control over financial reporting as of December 31, 200X, and updated that understanding as it specifically relates to changes in internal control over financial reporting associated with the material weakness described above. We believe that our auditing procedures provide a reasonable basis for our opinion.

In our opinion, the material weakness described above no longer exists as of [*date of management's assertion*].

We were not engaged to and did not conduct an audit of internal control over financial reporting as of [*date of management's assertion*], the objective of which would be the expression of an opinion on the effectiveness of internal control over financial reporting. Accordingly, we do not express such an opinion. This means that we have not applied auditing procedures sufficient to reach conclusions about the effectiveness of any controls of the company as of any date after December 31, 200X, other than the control(s) specifically identified in this report. Accordingly, we do not express an opinion that any other controls operated effectively after December 31, 200X.

Our report on management's annual assessment of XYZ Company's internal control over financial reporting, dated [*date of report*], [*attached or identify location of where the report is publicly available*] identified additional material weaknesses other than the one identified in this report. We are not reporting on those other material weaknesses and, accordingly, express no opinion regarding whether those material weaknesses continue to exist after [*date of management's annual assessment; e.g., December 31, 200X*]. Because of its inherent limitations, internal control over financial reporting may not prevent or detect misstatements. Also, projections of any evaluation of the effectiveness of specific controls or internal control over financial reporting overall to future periods are subject to the risk that controls may become inadequate because of changes in conditions or that the degree of compliance with the policies or procedures may deteriorate.

[*Signature*]

[*City and State or Country*]

[*Date*]

PCAOB 5 AN AUDIT OF INTERNAL CONTROL OVER FINANCIAL REPORTING THAT IS INTEGRATED WITH AN AUDIT OF FINANCIAL STATEMENTS

Effective Date: November 15, 2007.

INTRODUCTION

An Audit of Internal Control over Financial Reporting that is integrated with an Audit of Financial Statements (AS 5) was issued by the Public Company Accounting Oversight Board (PCAOB, or the "Board") and approved by the Securities and Exchange Commission on July 25, 2007. AS 5 is effective for audits of internal control over financial reporting required by Section 404(b) of the Sarbanes-Oxley Act of 2002. Independent auditors engaged to audit the financial statements are required to comply with the AS 5 standard when performing their auditing engagements.

AS 5 establishes the requirements for performing an audit of management's assessment of the effectiveness of internal control over financial reporting. Management's assessment is integrated with an audit of the financial statements.

Effective internal control over financial reporting exists when there are no material weaknesses. The auditor must obtain reasonable assurance that no material weaknesses exist in internal control over financial reporting. The auditor satisfies this objective by obtaining and evaluating evidence. Even when financial statements are not materially misstated, there may be one or more material weaknesses in internal controls over financial reporting.

DEFINITIONS

AS 5 defines *internal control over financial reporting* as follows:

A process designed by, or under the supervision of, the company's principal executive and principal financial officers, or persons performing similar functions, and effected by the company's board of directors, management, and other personnel, to provide reasonable assurance regarding the reliability of financial reporting and the preparation of financial statements for external purposes in accordance with generally accepted accounting principles and includes those policies and procedures that

- *Pertain to the maintenance of records that, in reasonable detail, accurately and fairly reflect the transactions and dispositions of the assets of the company.*

- *Provide reasonable assurance that transactions are recorded as necessary to permit preparation of financial statements in accordance with generally accepted accounting principles, and that receipts and expenditures of the company are being made only in accordance with authorizations of management and directors of the company.*
- *Provide reasonable assurance regarding prevention or timely detection of unauthorized acquisition, use or disposition of the company's assets that could have a material effect on the financial statements.*

A *control deficiency* exists when the design or operation of a financial control does not allow management, or its employees, to prevent or detect misstatements on a timely basis, while performing their normal duties.

1. A deficiency in *design* exists when either

    a. A necessary control is missing, or
    b. An existing control is improperly designed and does not meet the control objective.

2. A properly designed control could have a deficiency in *operation* when it does not operate as designed, or the individual performing the control lacks either the qualifications or the authority to perform the control properly.

A *material weakness* is a deficiency or a combination of deficiencies that result when there is a reasonable possibility that a material misstatement in the financial statements will not be prevented or detected on a timely basis. In other words, as expressed by the terminology in SFAS 5, *Accounting for Contingencies*, the likelihood that a material misstatement will not be prevented or detected is either *reasonably possible* or *probable*.

A *significant deficiency* is a control deficiency or combination of control deficiencies that is less severe than a material weakness but important nonetheless.

The "reasonable person" standard is used to determine if a misstatement is considered *inconsequential*. In other words, would a reasonable person conclude that a misstatement is immaterial to the financial statements either individually or when aggregated with other misstatements. A misstatement would be considered as being more than inconsequential if a reasonable person is unable to conclude that a misstatement is immaterial to the financial statements either individually or when aggregated with other misstatements.

The auditor should consider if compensating controls were effective before determining that a significant deficiency or material weakness exists. It is possible for well-designed *preventive* controls that are operating as designed to be nonetheless unable to prevent a misstatement. Overlapping *detective* controls can be especially useful in such situations. Effective internal control over financial reporting will generally include a combination of preventive and detective controls.

FRAMEWORK USED BY MANAGEMENT TO CONDUCT ITS ASSESSMENT

The assessment by management of the effectiveness of a company's internal control over financial reporting must be based on an appropriate recognized framework. This generally means the use of the Committee of Sponsoring Organizations (COSO) framework in the United States. The COSO of the Treadway Commission has published a report, *Internal Control—Integrated Framework,* that provides management with an appropriate framework for making financial assessments. This report is generally referred to as the COSO report. Other suitable frameworks have been published in other countries and may be used. While different countries may have different frameworks, the basic form of these frameworks should be similar to that of COSO, and the auditor should be able to apply the guidance framework in a reasonable manner.

REASONABLE ASSURANCE

The concept of reasonable assurance is essential in the auditor's assessment about the effectiveness of internal control over financial reporting. While *reasonable* assurance provides a high level of assurance, it falls short of *absolute* assurance.

INTEGRATING THE AUDIT

The audit of internal control over financial reporting should be integrated with the audit of the financial statements. While the objectives of the audits are not the same, the auditor must plan and perform the work to achieve the objectives of both audits simultaneously. The process of obtaining sufficient evidence to support a control risk assessment of low will generally permit the auditor to reduce the amount of work necessary to give an opinion on the financial statement.

PLANNING THE AUDIT

The audit should be properly planned, and assistants should be supervised. AS 5 (paragraph 9) specifies the following as factors that may be important to the company's financial statements and its internal control over financial reporting:

1. Knowledge of the company's internal control over financial reporting that was obtained during any other engagements performed by the auditor.
2. External industry practices affecting the way the company operates, such as

    a.   Financial reporting practices,
    b.   Economic conditions,
    c.   Laws and regulations, and
    d.   Technological changes.

3. Internal business practices relating to the company's organization, operating characteristics, and capital structure.
4. Extent of recent changes, if any, in the company, its operations, or its internal control over financial reporting.
5. Auditor's preliminary judgments about materiality, risk, and other factors relating to the determination of material weaknesses.
6. Control deficiencies previously communicated to the audit committee or management.
7. Legal or regulatory matters of which the company is aware.
8. Type and extent of available evidence related to the effectiveness of the company's internal control over financial reporting.
9. Preliminary judgments about the effectiveness of internal control over financial reporting.
10. Public information about the company relevant to the evaluation of the likelihood of material financial statement misstatements and the effectiveness of the company's internal control over financial reporting.
11. Knowledge about risks related to the company evaluated as part of the auditor's client acceptance and retention evaluation.
12. Relative complexity of the company's operations.

FRAUD CONSIDERATIONS

The auditor should evaluate controls specifically designed to reduce the risk of fraud. The auditor should consider AU Section 316, *Consideration of Fraud in a Financial Statement Audit.* Generally, the auditor evaluates the same controls during the audit of internal control over financial reporting as controls in a financial statement audit. The auditor should alter the nature, timing, or extent of procedures if the auditor identifies deficiencies in controls designed to prevent and detect fraud during the audit of internal control over financial reporting.

USING THE WORK OF OTHERS

The auditor may use the work of others, including internal auditors, to alter the nature, timing, or extent of the work. The auditor should evaluate the work performed by others by

1. Evaluating the nature of the controls subjected to the work of others
2. Evaluating the competence and objectivity of the individuals who performed the work: the auditor should not use the work of individuals with low objectivity regardless of competence. Moreover, the auditor should not use the work of individual with low competence, regardless of objectivity.
3. Testing the work of others to evaluate the quality and effectiveness of the work performed

As the control risk increases, the greater is the need for the auditor to perform independently rather than relying on the work of others.

MATERIALITY CONSIDERATIONS

The auditor should apply the concept of materiality in auditing internal control over financial reporting. The materiality considerations are essentially the same when auditing internal control over financial reporting as when auditing financial statements. The auditor uses materiality in determining whether a deficiency or combination of deficiencies in controls is a significant deficiency or a material weakness.

USING A TOP-DOWN APPROACH

Auditors should use a top-down approach to auditing internal controls over financial reports. A top-down approach requires the auditor to understand the overall risks to internal control over financial reporting at the financial statement level. The auditor next considers entity-level controls and delves deeper to significant accounts and disclosures that may be materially misstated. Finally, the auditor verifies any signs of risk and performs tests of the controls in appropriate areas in response to the assessed risk of misstatement for each relevant assertion.

Entity-level controls include controls related to the control environment and controls over management override. Entity-level controls also include controls over the company's risk assessment process, controls to monitor the result of operations, controls to monitor other controls, controls over period-end financial reporting and risk management practices.

The control environment is critical for effective internal controls. The auditor should consider management's integrity, ethical values, philosophy, and operating style. The auditor should also consider the role of the board or audit committee in exercising its oversight responsibilities.

The auditor should especially consider controls over period-end financial reporting process. More specifically, what procedures are used

1. To enter transaction totals into the general ledger,
2. For the selection and application of accounting policies,
3. For processing journal entries,
4. For recurring and nonrecurring adjustments to the financial statements, and
5. For the preparation of the financial statements and related disclosures.

Relevant assertions for significant accounts and disclosures should be identified. Included in the financial statement should be assertions about its

1. Existence or occurrence,
2. Completeness,
3. Valuation or allocation,
4. Rights and obligations, and
5. Presentation and disclosure.

Risk factors include

1. Size and composition of the account,
2. Susceptibility to misstatement due to error or fraud,
3. Level of activity and complexity,
4. Type of account,
5. Accounting and reporting issues,
6. Exposure to losses in the account,
7. Possibility of contingent liabilities,
8. Related-party transactions, and
9. Changes from prior period in account or disclosure characteristics.

The auditor should understand the likely sources of potential misstatements. This is achieved by

1. Understanding the flow of transactions,
2. Identifying critical points within the entity's process where a misstatement could arise, and
3. Identifying controls that management has implemented to address potential misstatement, to prevent or detect unauthorized purchase, to use or dispose of an entity's assets.

The auditor should perform a walk-through for each major class of transactions by tracing a transaction from origination through the company's information systems to the company's financial reports. Walk-throughs confirm and provide evidence for the following:

1. The auditor's understanding of the process flow of transactions.
2. The auditor's understanding of the design of controls identified for all five components of internal control over financial reporting, including those related to the prevention or detection of fraud.
3. The auditor's understanding of the process as complete by determining whether all points in the process at which misstatements related to each relevant financial statement assertion that could occur have been identified.
4. The auditor's understanding of the effectiveness of the design of controls.
5. The auditor's understanding of whether controls have been placed in operation.

The entire process of initiating, authorizing, recording, processing, and reporting individual transactions and controls for each of the significant processes identified should be addressed by walk-throughs.

At each important stage during the walk-through, the auditor should inquire of the company's personnel about their understanding of what is required by the company's prescribed procedures and controls. The auditor should evaluate whether the processing procedures are performed as intended and on a timely basis. The auditor should be especially alert and take notice of exceptions to the company's prescribed procedures and controls.

The auditor may carry documentation concerning walk-throughs forward each year, updating the document for changes. The auditor should evaluate the effect on related accounts if there have been significant changes in the process flow of transactions.

TESTING CONTROLS

The auditor should select relevant controls for testing based on which controls, either individually or in combination, address the assessed risk of misstatement. When testing controls, the auditor's aim is to determine the effectiveness of controls by testing whether the control are operating as designed. Auditors test controls by performing a variety of procedures including

1.   Inquiry of appropriate personnel,
2.   Observation of operations,
3.   Inspection of documents and records, and
4.   Walk-throughs.

When the auditor identifies deviations from an entity's controls, the auditor should determine the effect of the deviation on assessed risk. Some types of control tests are considered more effective than others. The effectiveness of testing from least effective to most effective is as follows:

1.   Inquiry.
2.   Observation.
3.   Inspection of relevant documentation.
4.   Reperformance of a control.

Testing controls over a greater period of time provides more evidence of effectiveness than over a shorter period of time. Also performing tests closer to the date of management's assessment provides more evidence than those performed earlier in the year. Even better evidence is obtained as a control is tested more extensively. When the auditor tests controls at an interim date, additional evidence should be obtained about the operation of the controls for the remaining period.

In subsequent year audits, the auditor should use the knowledge previously obtained to make a risk assessment and modify the nature, timing, and extent of procedures as appropriate. This may allow the auditor to reduce testing in subsequent audits. Benchmarking strategy may be used for automated application controls. The auditor should vary the nature, timing, and extent of testing and introduce unpredictability into testing.

EVALUATING IDENTIFIED DEFICIENCIES

The auditor must evaluate identified control deficiencies and determine whether the deficiencies, individually or in combination, are material weaknesses as of the date of management's assessment. The auditor is not required to search for deficiencies that are less severe than a material weakness.

This evaluation should include both quantitative and qualitative factors. The auditor should consider

1. The likelihood that the deficiency, individually or in combination, could cause a misstatement in an account balance or disclosure, and
2. The potential magnitude of the misstatement.

The severity of the deficiency depends on the possibility that the controls will fail to prevent or detect misstatements of an account balance or disclosure and the magnitude of the misstatement. The severity of a deficiency does not depend on whether a misstatement has actually occurred.

The auditor should evaluate the interaction of controls. Some controls may depend on the functioning of other controls. When evaluating the magnitude of the potential misstatement, the auditor should recognize that while the maximum amount that an account balance or total of transactions can be overstated is generally the recorded amount, there is no limit on the amount of potential understatement.

The auditor should consider the degree of assurance and the level of detail that a prudent official would require in order to obtain reasonable assurance that the transactions are recorded as necessary and in conformity with generally accepted accounting principles. Typically, inadequate documentation of the design of financial controls and the absence of sufficiently documented evidence are considered control deficiencies, and the auditor has to determine their significance.

The auditor should consider the effect of compensating controls in determining whether a control deficiency is a material weakness.

AS 5 (paragraph 69) gives the following items as indicators of material weaknesses in internal controls:

1. Identification of fraud, whether or not material, on the part of senior management.
2. Restatement of previously issued financial statements to reflect the correction of a material misstatement.
3. Identification by the auditor of a material misstatement of financial statements in the current period in circumstances that indicate that the misstatement would not have been detected by the company's internal control over financial reporting.
4. Ineffective oversight of the company's external financial reporting and internal control over financial reporting by the company's audit committee.

WRAPPING-UP

The auditor should evaluate evidence from all sources when forming an opinion on internal control over financial reporting, including the results of the auditor's evaluation of the design and tests of operating effectiveness of controls. The auditor should evaluate the adequacy of the presentation of the elements required by the SEC of management. The auditor may form an opinion on the effectiveness of internal controls over financial reporting only when there have been no scope restrictions on the auditor's work. If there was a scope limitation, the auditor must disclaim an opinion or withdraw from the engagement.

The auditor should obtain written representations from management (AS 5, paragraph 75)

1. Acknowledging management's responsibility for establishing and maintaining effective internal control over financial reporting.
2. Stating that management has performed an evaluation and made an assessment of the effectiveness of the company's internal control over financial reporting and specifying the control criteria.
3. Stating that management did not use the auditor's procedures performed during the audits of internal control over financial reporting or the financial statements as part

of the basis for management's assessment of the effectiveness of internal control over financial reporting.

4. Stating management's conclusion, as set forth in its assessment, about the effectiveness of the company's internal control over financial reporting based on the control criteria as of a specified date.

5. Stating that management has disclosed to the auditor all deficiencies in the design or operation of internal control over financial reporting identified as part of management's evaluation, including separately disclosing to the auditor all such deficiencies that it believes to be significant deficiencies or material weaknesses in internal control over financial reporting.

6. Describing any fraud resulting in a material misstatement to the company's financial statements and any other fraud that does not result in a material misstatement to the company's financial statements but involves senior management or management or other employees who have a significant role in the company's internal control over financial reporting.

7. Stating whether control deficiencies identified and communicated to the audit committee during previous engagements have been resolved, and specifically identifying any that have not.

8. Stating whether there were, subsequent to the date being reported on, any changes in internal control over financial reporting or other factors that might significantly affect internal control over financial reporting, including any corrective actions taken by management with regard to significant deficiencies and material weaknesses.

If the auditor is unable to obtain written representations from management, there is then a sufficient scope limitation to preclude an unqualified opinion. The auditor must either withdraw from the engagement or disclaim the audit opinion if management limits the scope of the audit.

The auditor should consider the effects of management's refusal on other representations obtained by the auditor. AU Section 333, *Management Representations,* provides additional guidance on this subject.

All material weaknesses and significant deficiencies identified during the audit should be communicated to the management and audit committee in writing prior to the issuance of the auditor's report on internal control over financial reporting.

The company's audit committee has a critical function within the control environment and monitoring components of internal control over financial reporting. The audit committee can set a positive tone from top management and can challenge the company's activities in the financial arena. The auditor should assess the effectiveness of the audit committee as part of understanding and evaluating the control environment and the monitoring components of internal control over financial reporting. If the auditor concludes that the audit committee is ineffective, the auditor must communicate that conclusion in writing to the board of directors.

REPORTING ON INTERNAL CONTROL

The auditor's report on the audit of internal control over financial reporting must include the following elements (AS 5, paragraph 85)

1. A title that includes the word independent.

2. A statement that management is responsible for maintaining effective internal control over financial reporting and for assessing the effectiveness of internal control over financial reporting.

3. An identification of management's report on internal control.
4. A statement that the auditor's responsibility is to express an opinion on the company's internal control over financial reporting based on the audit results.
5. A definition of internal control over financial reporting as stated in AS 5 (Appendix, paragraph A5).
6. A statement that the audit was conducted in accordance with the standards of the Public Company Accounting Oversight Board (United States);
7. A statement that the standards of the Public Company Accounting Oversight Board require that the auditor plan and perform the audit to obtain reasonable assurance about whether effective internal control over financial reporting was maintained in all material respects.
8. A statement that an audit includes obtaining an understanding of internal control over financial reporting, assessing the risk that a material weakness exists, testing and evaluating the design and operating effectiveness of internal control based on the assessed risk, and performing such other procedures as the auditor considered necessary in the circumstances.
9. A statement that the auditor believes the audit provides a reasonable basis for a concluding opinion.
10. A paragraph stating that because of inherent limitations, internal control over financial reporting may not prevent or detect misstatements and that projections of any evaluation of effectiveness to future periods are subject to the risk that controls may become inadequate because of changes in conditions, or that the degree of compliance with the policies or procedures may deteriorate.
11. The auditor's opinion on whether the company maintained, in all material respects, effective internal control over financial reporting as of the specified date, based on the control criteria.
12. The manual or printed signature of the auditor's firm.
13. The city and state (or city and country, in the case of non-US auditors) from which the auditor's report has been issued.
14. The date of the audit report.

SEPARATE OR COMBINED REPORTS

The auditor may choose to issue a combined report or separate reports. A combined report contains both an opinion on the financial statement and an opinion on internal control over financial reporting.

The following is an example of a combined report expressing an unqualified opinion on financial statements and an unqualified opinion on internal control over financial reporting (AS 5, paragraph 87):

Report of Independent Registered Public Accounting Firm

[*Introductory paragraph*]

We have audited the accompanying balance sheets of W Company as of December 31, 20X8 and 20X7, and the related statements of income, stockholders' equity and comprehensive income, and cash flows for each of the years in the three-year period ended December 31, 20X8. We also have audited W Company's internal control over financial reporting as of December 31, 20X8, based on [*identify control criteria; e.g., "criteria established in **Internal Control—Integrated Framework** issued by the Committee of Sponsoring Organizations of the Treadway Commission (COSO)"*]. W Company's management is responsible for these financial statements, for maintaining effective internal control over financial reporting, and for its assessment of the effectiveness of internal control over financial reporting, included in the accompanying [*title of manage-*

ment's report]. Our responsibility is to express an opinion on these financial statements and an opinion on the company's internal control over financial reporting based on our audits.

[*Scope paragraph*]

We conducted our audits in accordance with the standards of the Public Company Accounting Oversight Board (United States). Those standards require that we plan and perform the audits to obtain reasonable assurance about whether the financial statements are free of material misstatement and whether effective internal control over financial reporting was maintained in all material respects. Our audits of the financial statements included examining, on a test basis, evidence supporting the amounts and disclosures in the financial statements, assessing the accounting principles used and significant estimates made by management, and evaluating the overall financial statement presentation. Our audit of internal control over financial reporting included obtaining an understanding of internal control over financial reporting, assessing the risk that a material weakness exists, and testing and evaluating the design and operating effectiveness of internal control based on the assessed risk. Our audits also included performing such other procedures as we considered necessary in the circumstances. We believe that our audits provide a reasonable basis for our opinions.

[*Definition paragraph*]

A company's internal control over financial reporting is a process designed to provide reasonable assurance regarding the reliability of financial reporting and the preparation of financial statements for external purposes in accordance with generally accepted accounting principles. A company's internal control over financial reporting includes those policies and procedures that (1) pertain to the maintenance of records that, in reasonable detail, accurately and fairly reflect the transactions and dispositions of the assets of the company; (2) provide reasonable assurance that transactions are recorded as necessary to permit preparation of financial statements in accordance with generally accepted accounting principles, and that receipts and expenditures of the company are being made only in accordance with authorizations of management and directors of the company; and (3) provide reasonable assurance regarding prevention or timely detection of unauthorized acquisition, use, or disposition of the company's assets that could have a material effect on the financial statements.

[*Inherent limitations paragraph*]

Because of its inherent limitations, internal control over financial reporting may not prevent or detect misstatements. Also, projections of any evaluation of effectiveness to future periods are subject to the risk that controls may become inadequate because of changes in conditions, or that the degree of compliance with the policies or procedures may deteriorate.

[*Opinion paragraph*]

In our opinion, the financial statements referred to above present fairly, in all material respects, the financial position of W Company as of December 31, 20X8 and 20X7, and the results of its operations and its cash flows for each of the years in the three-year period ended December 31, 20X8, in conformity with accounting principles generally accepted in the United States of America. Also in our opinion, W Company maintained, in all material respects, effective internal control over financial reporting as of December 31, 20X8, based on [*identify control criteria; e.g., "criteria established in* **Internal Control—Integrated Framework** *issued by the Committee of Sponsoring Organizations of the Treadway Commission (COSO)"*].

[*Signature*]

[*City and State or Country*]

[*Date*]

If the auditor chooses to issue separate reports, the following paragraph must be added to the auditor's report on the financial statements:

We also have audited, in accordance with the standards of the Public Company Accounting Oversight Board (United States), W Company's internal control over financial reporting as of December 31, 20X8, based on [*identify control criteria*] and our report dated [*date of report, which should be the same as the date of the report on the financial statements]* expressed *[include nature of opinions].*

The auditor should also add the following paragraph to the report on internal control over financial reporting:

We also have audited, in accordance with the standards of the Public Company Accounting Oversight Board (United States), the [identify financial statements] of W Company and our report dated *[date of report, which should be the same as the date of the report on the effectiveness of internal control over financial reporting]* expressed *[include nature of opinion].*

Both reports should be dated the same, since the auditor cannot audit internal control over financial reporting without also auditing the financial statements. The date of the auditor report should not be earlier than the date on which the auditor finally had in hand sufficient competent evidence to support the audit opinion.

MATERIAL WEAKNESSES

If the auditor identifies one or more material weaknesses, the auditor must express an adverse opinion on the company's internal control over financial reporting (unless there is a restriction on the scope of engagement). When expressing an adverse opinion due to a material weakness, the report must include

1. A definition of the material weakness, and
2. A statement that the material weakness has been identified and an identification of the material weakness is described in management's assessment.

The auditor should determine the effect of an adverse audit opinion on internal control over the financial statements. The auditor should also disclose whether the audit opinion on the financial statements was affected by an adverse opinion toward internal control over financial reporting.

SUBSEQUENT EVENTS

The auditor should inquire of management and obtain written representations about changes in internal control over financial reporting or other factors that occur subsequent to the date of audit but before the date of the auditor's report. The auditor should inquire about (AS 5, paragraph 94)

1. Relevant internal audit (or similar functions, e.g., loan review in a financial institution) reports issued during the subsequent period,
2. Independent auditor reports (if other than the auditor's) of deficiencies in internal control,
3. Regulatory agency reports on the company's internal control over financial reporting, and
4. Information about the effectiveness of the company's internal control over financial reporting obtained through other engagements.

AU Section 560, *Subsequent Events,* provides additional guidance about subsequent events for financial statement audits; this information may also be helpful to the auditor when auditing internal controls over financial reporting.

PART 2

AUDITING

110 RESPONSIBILITIES AND FUNCTIONS OF THE INDEPENDENT AUDITOR

SOURCES OF STANDARDS

SAS 1, *Codification of Auditing Standards and Procedures*
SAS 78, *Consideration of Internal Control in a Financial Statement Audit: An Amendment to Statement on Auditing Standards No. 55*
SAS 99, *Consideration of Fraud in a Financial Statement Audit*

SUMMARY

This section states that the objective of an audit of financial statements is to enable an independent auditor to express an opinion as to the fairness of presentation, in all material respects, of an entity's financial position, results of operations, and cash flows in conformity with GAAS. The section also distinguishes between the responsibilities of management and of the auditor.

MANAGEMENT RESPONSIBILITIES

1. Management is responsible, in general, for the preparation and fairness of presentation of the financial statements and specifically for adopting sound accounting policies.
2. Establishing and maintaining effective internal control over financial reporting (see AU Section 319 for a complete discussion of internal control).

AUDITOR RESPONSIBILITIES

An auditor is responsible for planning and performing an audit to obtain reasonable, though not absolute, assurance about whether the financial statements are free of material misstatement, which may be caused by error (see AU Section 312), fraud (see AU Section 316), and certain illegal acts (see AU Section 317).

An auditor is also responsible for expressing an opinion on the fairness of presentation of the financial statements. It should be readily apparent that, out of responsibility to the profession, an auditor should

1. Possess the professional qualifications (education, experience, and certification) required of an independent auditor.
2. In performing an audit, adhere to the generally accepted auditing standards established by the AICPA.
3. Comply with the Code of Professional Conduct and its rules therein promulgated by the AICPA.

AUDITOR SUGGESTIONS

An auditor may, but is not required to, make suggestions to management about the form and content of the financial statements. Unless precluded by government regulation, an auditor may even draft the financial statements, based on information furnished by management during the audit.

120 DEFINING PROFESSIONAL REQUIREMENTS IN STATEMENTS ON AUDITING STANDARDS

SOURCE OF STANDARDS

SAS 102, *Defining Professional Requirements in Statements on Auditing Standards*

INTRODUCTION/SUMMARY

This section clarifies terminology concerning audit "requirements."

PROFESSIONAL REQUIREMENTS

An *unconditional requirement*, included in a Statement on Auditing Standards, means that the auditor is required to comply with the requirement in all cases. The phrases *"must"* and *"is required"* are indicative of an unconditional requirement.

A *presumptively mandatory requirement*, on the other hand, means that, under normal conditions the auditor is required to comply with the requirement. However, in rare circumstances the auditor may depart from a presumptively mandatory requirement, provided the auditor documents the justification for the departure and how alternative procedures performed were sufficient. The phrase *"should"* indicates a presumptively mandatory requirement.

EXPLANATORY MATERIAL

Explanatory material is text included in a Statement on Auditing Standards that provides additional explanation and guidance on a professional requirement or identifies and describes other audit procedures or actions. It should be noted that the words *"may, might, and could"* are used in the context of explanatory material.

150 GENERALLY ACCEPTED AUDITING STANDARDS

SOURCES OF STANDARDS

SAS 95, *Generally Accepted Auditing Standards*
SAS 98, *Omnibus Statement on Auditing Standards (2002)*
SAS 105, *Amendments to Statement on Auditing Standards No. 95, Generally Accepted Auditing Standards*
SAS 113, *Omnibus Statement on Auditing Standards – 2006*

SUMMARY

Because an auditor is required to plan, perform, and report the results of a financial statement audit in accordance with generally accepted auditing *standards* (GAAS), GAAS is concerned with measuring the quality of the audit and the objectives to be attained during an audit. Auditing *procedures* are the procedures the auditor performs during the course of the audit to achieve specific audit objectives.

AUDITING STANDARDS

There are 10 GAAS classified into three categories:

1. General standards
2. Standards of fieldwork
3. Standards of reporting

GENERAL STANDARDS

The first general standard requires that the auditor possess adequate technical training and proficiency in order to perform the audit.

The second general standard requires the maintenance of independence in mental attitude concerning all matters pertaining to the audit.

The third general standard requires that the auditor exercise due professional care in performing the audit and preparing the audit report thereon.

STANDARDS OF FIELDWORK

The first fieldwork standard requires the auditor to adequately plan the audit and, if assistants are utilized, to properly supervise them.

The second fieldwork standard requires the auditor to obtain a sufficient understanding of the entity and its environment, including its internal control, to assess the risk of material misstatement of the financial statements whether due to error or fraud, and to design the nature, extent, and timing of further audit procedures.

The third fieldwork standard calls for the auditor to obtain sufficient appropriate audit evidence to afford a reasonable basis for expressing an opinion on the financial statements being audited.

STANDARDS OF REPORTING

The first reporting standard requires the audit report to specifically state whether the financial statements are presented in conformity with generally accepted accounting principles.

The second reporting standard requires the audit report to include identification of circumstances in which there is a lack of consistency in accounting principles between accounting periods.

The third reporting standard requires the audit report to state if informative disclosures in the financial statements are not reasonably adequate.

The fourth reporting standard requires the auditor to express, in the audit report, an opinion regarding the fairness of the financial statements taken as a whole. Alternatively, if an opinion cannot be expressed, an assertion to this effect (i.e., a disclaimer of opinion) must be included in the report. When disclaiming an opinion, the audit report must state the reasons that preclude the expression of an opinion. (Whenever an auditor's name is associated with financial statements, the report must clearly indicate the character of the auditor's work and the degree of responsibility undertaken by the auditor.)

INTERPRETATIVE PUBLICATIONS

An auditor should adhere to the recommendations on how to apply Statements on Auditing Standards (SASs) contained in the following publications:

1. Interpretations of SASs issued by the Auditing Standards Board of the AICPA
2. The AICPA Audit and Accounting Guides
3. Appendices to the SASs
4. AICPA Auditing Statements of Position

An auditor who departs from the recommendations in authoritative interpretive publications must be prepared to explain how the audit report otherwise complies with the SAS provisions referenced in the above-mentioned publications.

NONAUTHORITATIVE PUBLICATIONS

To facilitate understanding and application of SASs, an auditor may seek guidance from the following nonauthoritative publications:

1. The *Journal of Accountancy*, published by the AICPA
2. Other professional journals, such as publications of a state society of certified public accountants
3. The *CPA Letter*, published by the AICPA
4. Textbooks
5. Continuing professional education course materials
6. Audit programs and checklists

161 THE RELATIONSHIP OF GENERALLY ACCEPTED AUDITING STANDARDS TO QUALITY CONTROL STANDARDS

SOURCES OF STANDARDS

SAS 25, *The Relationship of Generally Accepted Auditing Standards to Quality Control Standards*
SAS 98, *Omnibus Statement on Auditing Standards – 2002*

SUMMARY

This section states that pursuant to Statement on Quality Control Standards 2, *System of Quality Control for a CPA Firm's Accounting and Auditing Practice*, a firm of independent auditors must establish and maintain a system of quality control for its audit practice. The quality control system should provide reasonable, though not absolute, assurance that auditing firm personnel comply with auditing standards.

Quality control standards apply to the conduct of the auditor's practice—how the auditor runs the business. *Auditing* standards apply to the conduct of actual audit engagements. While there typically is some interrelationship between the two types of standards, deficiencies in or instances of noncompliance with quality controls do not necessarily mean that the firm has departed from the auditing standards.

201 NATURE OF THE GENERAL STANDARDS

210 TRAINING AND PROFICIENCY OF THE INDEPENDENT AUDITOR

220 INDEPENDENCE

230 DUE PROFESSIONAL CARE IN THE PERFORMANCE OF WORK

SOURCES OF STANDARDS

SAS 1, *Codification of Auditing Standards and Procedures*

SAS 69, *The Meaning of "Present Fairly in Conformity with Generally Accepted Accounting Principles"*

SAS 99, *Consideration of Fraud in a Financial Statement Audit*

SAS 103, Audit Documentation

SAS 104, *Amendment to SAS No. 1, Codification of Auditing Standards and Procedures ("Due Professional Case in the Performance of Work")*

SUMMARY

These four sections provide guidance to an auditor in connection with the general standards under the GAAS enumerated in AU Section 150, define professional skepticism, and discuss the concept of reasonable assurance.

SECTION 201 *NATURE OF THE GENERAL STANDARDS*

This section states that the general standards are personal and relate strictly to an auditor's qualifications and the quality of the work performed. The general standards do not relate to the actual fieldwork and the auditor's reporting.

SECTION 210 *TRAINING AND PROFICIENCY OF THE INDEPENDENT AUDITOR*

This section makes it clear that adequate technical training and proficiency as an auditor should be based on a combination of experience and formal education, including continued understanding of new accounting and auditing pronouncements. Further, the practitioner charged with final responsibility for an audit must be able to exercise seasoned judgment and review the work and judgment of subordinates.

SECTION 220 *INDEPENDENCE*

This section states that independence requires that an auditor be impartial and act without bias toward the client. This will ensure that the public maintains confidence in the profession. In order to be independent, an auditor must be intellectually honest. This is commonly known as independence in fact. An auditor must also be *recognized* as independent. This is commonly known as independence in appearance.

To maintain independence, an auditor should adhere to the AICPA's Code of Professional Conduct and any requirements of the Securities and Exchange Commission. The AICPA Code of Professional Conduct affirms that an auditor must be free of any obligation to or interest in the client, its management, or its owners.

SECTION 230 DUE PROFESSIONAL CARE IN THE PERFORMANCE OF WORK

This section states that due professional care requires that an auditor observe the standards of fieldwork and reporting. An auditor should

1. Possess "the degree of skill commonly possessed" by other auditors and
2. Exercise this skill with reasonable care and diligence.

Due professional care requires the exercise of professional skepticism. Throughout the conduct of an audit engagement, an auditor must have a questioning mind and critically assess the evidence obtained. An attitude of professional skepticism means that an auditor should not presume that management is completely honest or dishonest. An auditor should never be satisfied with less than persuasive evidence.

The exercise of professional skepticism means that an auditor should obtain reasonable, not absolute, assurance that the financial statements are free of material misstatements caused by error or fraud. Being required only to obtain reasonable assurance, an auditor is not an insurer or guarantor of the fairness of the presentation of the financial statements. (It should be understood that "reasonable assurance" is defined as a "high level of assurance.")

310 APPOINTMENT OF THE INDEPENDENT AUDITOR

SOURCES OF STANDARDS

SAS 1, *Codification of Auditing Standards and Procedures*
SAS 45, *Omnibus Statement on Auditing Standards – 1983*
SAS 83, *Establishing an Understanding with the Client*
SAS 89, *Audit Adjustments*
SAS 108, *Planning and Supervision (amends or supersedes the four Sources of Standards listed above)*

SUMMARY

This section discusses the appointment of the independent auditor, with special attention to the timing of the appointment and the understanding with the client that should be established.

TIMING OF APPOINTMENT

Early appointment is considered beneficial because it enables the auditor to

1. Properly plan the audit,
2. Expedite the performance of the auditing procedures, and
3. Determine the extent to which auditing procedures can be performed before the balance sheet date.

Waiting to appoint the auditor until near or after the year-end date can jeopardize the conduct of an audit that is sufficient to support an unqualified opinion. Before accepting such an engagement, an auditor should discuss with the client whether the audit limitations might be overcome. For example, if engaged after a client has performed a year-end physical inventory, an auditor may be able to observe a physical count after year-end. If the auditor is satisfied with the count, that the client has strong internal control over inventory and that the client maintains accurate perpetual inventory records, the auditor can roll back the inventory amount to the balance sheet date.

ESTABLISHING AN UNDERSTANDING WITH THE CLIENT

To reduce the risk of misinterpretation by either party about the needs and expectations of the other, the auditor should establish an understanding with the client about the services to be performed for each engagement that covers

1. The objectives of the engagement,
2. The responsibilities of management, and
3. The limitations of the engagement.

An auditor should not accept an engagement unless an understanding with the client has been established. The auditor should document the understanding in the working papers (audit documentation), in the form of an engagement letter. The understanding should generally cover the following matters:

1. The objective of the audit, which is namely to express an opinion on the financial statements. However, an auditor may decline to express an opinion or decline to issue a report if the audit cannot be completed.
2. Management's responsibility for

    a. The financial statements;
    b. Establishing and maintaining effective internal control;
    c. Complying with all laws and regulations;
    d. Making all financial records and related information available to the auditor;
    e. Providing the auditor with a representation letter at the end of the audit (see AU Section 333);
    f. Adjusting the financial statements to correct material misstatements; and
    g. Affirming in the representation letter that the effects of any uncorrected misstatements aggregated by the auditor are immaterial, both individually and in the aggregate, to the financial statements taken as a whole.

3. The auditor's responsibility for conducting the audit in accordance with GAAS; the auditor is required to obtain reasonable rather than absolute assurance about whether the financial statements are free of material misstatements caused by error or fraud.
4. In connection with the client's internal control

    a. The auditor is required to obtain an understanding of internal control sufficient to plan the audit and determine the nature, extent, and timing of substantive procedures. However, the audit is not designed to provide assurance about internal control.
    b. While the auditor is responsible for communicating internal control related matters identified in an audit (see AU Section 325) to those charged with governance, the audit is not designed to identify control deficiencies.

5. Terms of the engagement, such as timing, assistance of client personnel, fees, and billing.
6. Arrangements relating to the use of specialists (see AU Section 336) and internal auditors (see AU Section 322).
7. Arrangements involving a predecessor auditor (see AU Section 315).
8. Additional services to be provided and the arrangements for these.
9. Any limitation of or other arrangements regarding the liability of the auditor or the client (e.g., agreement to indemnify the auditor for liability arising from known misrepresentations to the auditor by management).
10. Conditions under which others may be granted access to audit working papers (documentation).

311 PLANNING AND SUPERVISION

SOURCES OF STANDARDS

GAAS

SAS 108, *Planning and Supervision*

Interpretation of AU 311, *Communications between the Auditor and Firm Personnel Responsible for Nonaudit Services*

Audit Strategy Planning Questionnaire (focus queries adapted from the Appendix of SAS 108)

ADDITIONAL NON-GAAS PROFESSIONAL GUIDANCE

Practitioner Checklists (adapted from the AICPA Audit and Accounting Manual).

SUMMARY

In accordance with the first standard of fieldwork, the auditor must adequately plan the audit and supervise any assistants. Planning and supervision is an ongoing process that begins with the engagement acceptance and continues throughout the audit as evidence is accumulated in support of the audit opinion. GAAS requires the auditor to develop an overall strategy for the conduct, organization, and staffing of the audit.

The extent, nature, and timing of planning will vary with the size and complexity of the entity being audited. Primary planning variables include the auditor's experience with and understanding of the entity, its environment, and internal control. A paramount planning consideration is the auditor's assessment of the risk of material misstatement based on the audit members' understanding of these attributes. In addition the performance of audit procedures may uncover evidence causing the auditor to revise the previously established audit strategy.

Planning and supervision functions may be delegated to other members of the audit team by the auditor with final responsibility for the audit. Individuals of the audit team other than the individual(s) with final responsibility are referred to as "assistants." The general term "auditor," however, will be used to refer to either of the two aforementioned individuals.

GAAS GUIDANCE

PLANNING CONSIDERATIONS

Appointment of the Auditor

Clearly, an early engagement appointment enables the auditor to have sufficient time to properly plan prior to the onset of the balance-sheet date. However, an auditor may accept an engagement near or after the close of the fiscal year. If the latter occurs, the auditor must ascertain whether an audit and expression of an unqualified opinion is possible. If it is not, then the auditor should make the client aware that a qualified opinion or disclaimer may have to be rendered.

Obtaining an Understanding with the Client

The auditor must reach an understanding with the client regarding the services to be performed on an engagement. The understanding should be documented in a written communication. Using a written medium minimizes any chance of misinterpretation by either the auditor or client. In general, the understanding should include: the objectives of the engagement; management's responsibilities relating to the audit; the auditor's responsibilities; and the limitations of the engagement. However, it is important to note that certain other engagements (audits of recipients of governmental financial assistance, application of agreed-upon procedures to specified elements, accounts, or items of a financial statement, etc.) may require different objectives.

The following statements are examples of items that might be included in an understanding with a client regarding the audit of an entity's financial statements:

1. The objective of the audit to be performed is the expression of an opinion on the financial statements.
2. Management has the sole responsibility for the financial statements of the entity as well as the selection and application of the accounting policies being used.
3. Management has the responsibility for establishing programs and controls to prevent and detect fraud.
4. Management has the responsibility for ensuring that the entity is in compliance with all laws and regulations that exist relating to its activities.
5. Management has responsibility for establishing and maintaining effective internal control over the entity's financial reporting.
6. Management has the sole responsibility for all financial records and related information made available to the auditor.
7. Management will provide the auditor with a representation letter at the end of the audit confirming certain representations made to the auditor by the client during the audit.
8. The responsibility for conducting the audit in accordance with GAAS lies with the auditor. This includes (a) obtaining reasonable rather than absolute assurance about whether the financial statements are free from material misstatement regardless of whether caused by error or fraud (i.e. a material misstatement may remain undetected) and (b) indicating that the audit is not designed to detect any error or fraud that is immaterial to the financial statements. If the auditor is unable to complete the audit or unable to form an opinion, then that auditor may decline to express an opinion or decline to issue a report on the financial statements.
9. An audit is not designed to provide assurance on the internal control of the entity nor to determine if any significant deficiencies exist. Nevertheless, the auditor is responsible for making sure that those charged with the entity's governance are aware of any significant deficiencies that become apparent during the audit.
10. Management has the responsibility for adjusting the financial statements to correct material misstatements and for affirming that the effects of any uncorrected misstatements aggregated during the current audit, both individually and in the aggregate, are immaterial to the financial statements taken as a whole.

All of the aforementioned should be communicated to the client in writing in an engagement letter.

Additional matters that may be included in the understanding with the client consist of the following:

11. The overall audit strategy that will be followed.
12. The use of specialists or internal auditors that will be needed.
13. The need for the involvement of a predecessor auditor.
14. Billing and fees.
15. Any restriction or constraint on the liability of the auditor or the client, such as indemnification to the auditor for liability arising from obtaining misrepresentations by management.
16. Any circumstances where access to audit documentation may be granted to others.
17. An enumeration of any services that will be provided by the auditor relating to regulatory requirements.
18. Any other services that will be provided during the engagements. For example, accounting assistance and preparation of tax services.

Getting Started—Preliminary Engagement Activities

The auditor must plan the audit to ensure that

1. He or she has the ability and necessary independence needed for successful performance and completion.
2. There are no management integrity issues.
3. The client completely understands the terms of the engagement and there are no misunderstandings.

To meet these objectives, the following activities should be performed by auditor from the start of the engagement:

- Procedures relating to the continuance of the client relationship and audit engagement and
- Evaluation of the auditor's compliance with ethical requirements including independence.

These activities should occur before performing any significant activities for the audit engagement. In addition they should be reevaluated throughout the audit as conditions and circumstances change. If an engagement is continuing, then auditor-client communication should occur shortly after the completion of the previous audit. Communication is especially important when events or situations surface that can negatively affect the auditor's ability to plan and perform the audit engagement in a way that acceptably reduces the level of audit risk. More discussion of these considerations can be found in Quality Control Standards (QC), Section 20, System of Quality Control for a CPA Firm's Accounting and Auditing Practice. An analysis of Section 20 may be found on page 455 of this volume.

Parameters for Planning the Overall Audit Strategy

General considerations. Some points to consider in establishing the overall audit strategy are as follows:

1. Ascertain the overall characteristics (scope) of the engagement, such as the basis of reporting, industry-specific reporting requirements, and locations of the entity.
2. Determine the timing of the audit such as the deadlines for interim and final reporting, and key dates for expected communications with management and persons with governance responsibilities.

3.   Ascertain the following important considerations that will affect the current audit. These include

   a.   Materiality levels.
   b.   Areas where there may be a higher level of material misstatement (preliminary identification).
   c.   Material locations and account balances to be audited (preliminary identification).
   d.   Determination of evidence regarding the operating effectiveness of the client's internal control.
   e.   Identification of any recent developments relating to the entity, such as in the industry sector to which it belongs, reporting considerations affecting the entity.
   f.   Experience gained from previous engagements of the entity.

The Audit Strategy Planning Questionnaire and Practitioner Checklists at the end of this section may prove helpful in establishing an overall audit strategy.

The development of an audit strategy allows the auditor to determine the resources that will be needed for the following areas:

- Use of experienced audit professionals for specific content areas and areas of high risk.
- Need for additional experts or specialists on matters of complexity and specialization.
- Number of audit personnel needed for such areas as the inventory count at important locations and the need for review of other auditors' work.
- Number of audit hours budgeted to areas of high risk.
- When audit personnel are to be assigned, whether they are needed at interim audit periods or at certain cutoff dates.
- How audit personnel are to be supervised and managed. For example, when will team briefing and debriefing meetings take place? Will partner and manager reviews occur at the client's or auditor's office? Should there be quality control reviews on the engagement?

In an audit of a small entity, the overall audit strategy can, generally, be expected to be uncomplicated. Coordination and communication among audit team members is clearer and simpler than in a large entity. The auditor of a small entity may be a sole practitioner. Planning for the audit of this entity may consist of nothing more than a memo prepared by the sole practitioner at the end of the previous audit. The audit may be based on an audit documentation review, with highlighting of areas that have been updated and modified in the current period based on recent discussions with the owner-manager.

The Audit Plan

The audit plan is developed by the auditor to document the audit procedures that will be performed so that the audit risk can be kept to an acceptably low level. The audit plan is much more detailed than the audit strategy. It contains an enumeration of the nature, timing, and extent of audit procedures that the audit team will perform. The audit team performs these procedures in pursuance of audit evidence needed to establish a level of audit risk that is sufficiently low to be deemed acceptable. This documentation represents an evidential record of the planning and performance of auditing that will be done. Although the audit plan is usually derived from the audit strategy they are not necessarily separate or sequential. Instead, they should be viewed as being closely interrelated in that changes in one will frequently result in changes to the other.

The audit plan should include a description of the following:

1. The nature, timing, and extent of planned risk assessment procedures needed to assess the risks of material misstatement of the financial statements of the entity being audited.
2. The nature, timing, and extent of further planned audit procedures for each material class of transactions, account balances, and disclosure. Parameters regarding further planned audit tests are described in Section 318, *Performing Audit Procedures in Response to Assessed Risks and Evaluating the Audit Evidence Obtained.* The auditor's decision to test the operating effectiveness of controls, as well as the nature, timing, and extent of planned substantive procedures is a function of his or her response to the assessment of risk and evidence derived.
3. Any other audit procedures needed to be performed for the engagement by the auditor that are in accordance with GAAS, such as direct communication with the legal counsel of the audited entity.

Will Specialized Skills Be Needed in Performing the Audit?

The auditor must ascertain whether specialized skills will be needed to perform the audit. For example, a business valuations person or tax specialist may be required. The specialist may be either on the auditor's staff or may be an outside professional. If such a person is part of the auditor's staff, then the supervision of that individual by the auditor with final responsibility and his or her managers by upper managers is the same as for other assistants.

The auditor should also ascertain whether the use of an IT (information technology) professional will be necessary. Such an individual is generally needed to

- Determine the effect of IT on the audit.
- Understand the IT controls that exist or
- Design and perform tests of IT controls or substantive tests.

The following should be considered in determining whether an IT professional is needed on the audit team:

1. The degree of complexity of the entity's system and IT controls.
2. The degree to which data is shared among the entity's systems.
3. The extent that the entity participates in electronic commerce.
4. The degree of use of emerging technologies.
5. The importance of audit evidence only available in electronic form.
6. The existence of new systems and changes made to existing systems of the entity.

Typically the following responsibilities are assigned to the IT professional on the audit:

- Investigation of how the entity's data and transactions are initiated, authorized, recorded, processed, and reported by making queries of the entity's IT personnel.
- Determination of how the entity's IT controls are designed.
- Inspection of systems documentation.
- Observation of the operation of IT controls and
- Performance of tests of IT controls.

Communicating with those persons charged with governance. GAAS requires the auditor to provide an overview of the planned scope and timing of the audit to those responsible for the governance of the entity. For more information on this topic, see Section 380, *The Auditor's Communication with Those Charged with Governance.*

Other Matters to be Considered in an Initial Audit Engagement

General considerations:

1. Perform procedures for the acceptance of the audit engagement and client relationship. For specific details, see QC Section 20, System of Quality Control for a CPA Firm's Accounting and Auditing Practice.
2. Where there has been a change of auditors, engage in the necessary communication with the previous auditor described in Section 315, *Communications between Predecessor and Successor Auditors*

Considerations relating to the overall audit strategy and audit plan. The following procedures are nothing more than an expansion of the standard planning activities that are normally done at the beginning of any recurring audit. However, they are important and need to be followed in this situation because the auditor does not have any previous experience with a first-time client.

1. Make arrangements to fully review the previous auditor's documentation of the prior period's audit.
2. Fully plan the procedures that need to be followed so that sufficient audit evidence can be aggregated regarding the appropriateness of the client's opening balances.
3. Make sure that competent, capable firm audit personnel are assigned on the engagement to deal with anticipated risks and contingencies.
4. Perform other audit procedures required by the audit firm's quality control for an initial audit engagement. For example, the audit firm may require the intervention of a senior firm member or partner to review the proposed audit strategy prior to beginning the performance of audit procedures.

PERFORMING SUPERVISORY FUNCTIONS

Supervision consists of managing and directing the work of assistants and determining whether they are successfully accomplishing the objectives of the audit.

Supervisory activities generally consist of

- Instructing and administrating assistants.
- Keeping abreast of significant issues encountered during the audit.
- Reviewing the work performed by assistant accountants.
- Mediating any arguments and differences of opinion that may surface among audit personnel.

In general, the amount of supervision that is needed in any given situation is a function of: (1) the complexity of the work being performed by the assistants; (2) the qualifications of the assistants; and (3) the assistants' knowledge of the of the industry and client's business.

Additional Considerations Relating to Performing Supervisory Functions

The auditor with final responsibility for the audit should advise the members of his or her audit team of the need to maintain a questioning mind and be professionally skeptical in aggregating evidence during the audit. Audit team members should be fully cognizant of the susceptibility of the financial statements of the entity to material misstatement due to error or fraud and how risks facing the business may affect the audit.

Assistants performing work on the audit should be advised of the following, by the auditor with final responsibility or his or her representatives, before the outset of the audit as well as during its performance:

1. The objectives of the audit procedures to be performed.
2. Matters affecting the nature, timing, and extent of audit procedures they will be performing. For example, assistants should be apprised of how the characteristics of the business the entity operates in may affect their assignments.
3. Any accounting and auditing issues the assistants believe significantly relate to the financial statements or the auditor's report must be brought to the attention of the supervisory members of the audit team so their significance can be assessed.
4. Any difficulties encountered during the audit, such as resistance on the part of the client in responding to an audit inquiry or providing information that has been requested or missing documentation that cannot be explained by the client, should be brought to the attention of the appropriate individuals in the firm.

The partner with final responsibility or his or her supervisory audit personnel should fully review the work performed by each assistant making sure the work was adequately performed and documented. The review should also include an evaluation of the findings reached by the assistants relative to the conclusions to be presented in the audit report.

If disagreements related to accounting and auditing issues arise during the audit that an assistant believes are significant, the assistant has the responsibility of bringing these issues to the attention of supervisory personnel on the audit. In fact there may be differences in opinion among the members of the audit team regarding these issues. Supervisory personnel of the audit should be fully aware of the procedures that should be followed when such differences arise among audit personnel Assistants should be able to document their disagreements with conclusions reached when they believe that it may be necessary to disassociate themselves from the conclusion(s) or action(s) taken by other audit personnel on the audit team.

INTERPRETATIONS OF AU 311: PLANNING AND SUPERVISION

Interpretation 1, *Communications between the Auditor and Firm Personnel Responsible for Nonaudit Services,* deals with the issue of nonaudit services performed by the audit firm for the entity being audited and what the auditor should do in planning a discussion with audit firm personnel responsible for these services.

The interpretation states that the auditor should consider the nature of nonaudit services that have been performed (tax planning, recommendations on the cost-accounting systems, etc.) and ascertain whether these services might affect the entity's financial statements or the performance of the audit. If the nonaudit services are found to have implications for the audit, then this needs to be discussed with the personnel of the firm that performed the services, and a determination should be made how the scope of the audit will be affected. The auditor may also choose to review the workpapers that were prepared for the nonaudit engagement in making a determination of the potential effect on the audit.

AUDIT STRATEGY PLANNING QUESTIONNAIRE

FOCUS QUERIES THAT SHOULD BE CONSIDERED IN ESTABLISHING THE OVERALL AUDIT STRATEGY

The following queries will help the auditor focus not only on matters affecting the overall audit strategy but also on the detailed audit plan that can be used. The queries are classified into three categories: (1) engagement scope considerations; (2) reporting objectives, timing of the audit and required communications; and (3) scope of the audit. This questionnaire is adapted from the Appendix of Section 311.

Engagement Scope Considerations

1. What is the basis of reporting the information to be audited? Must reconciliations to another basis of reporting be prepared?
2. Are there any industry-specific reporting requirements that must be adhered to? For example, reports required by industry regulators.
3. What are the locations to be included in the audit? How many are there? Which ones will be audited by other auditors?
4. What is the nature of the control relationship between the parent and its subsidiaries? Does this reconcile with how the entity being audited is to be consolidated?
5. What type of divisions or subsidiaries of the company to be audited exist? Will the audit of these entities require any specialized professional expertise?
6. Is the reporting currency different from the dollar? Will there be a need for currency translation of the financial statements being audited?
7. Is there a need for statutory or regulatory audit requirements (e.g., audits of states local governments or nonprofit organizations)?
8. Will the work of the internal auditors of the entity be available to the auditor? What will be the extent of reliance on such work?
9. Does the entity being audited make use of service organizations? Can the auditor obtain evidence concerning the design or operation of controls performed by them?
10. What is the expected use of audit evidence obtained in prior audits? For example, may evidence related to test of controls and risk assessment procedures be accessed?
11. What will be the effect of information technology on the audit procedures to be performed? For example, how will technology affect the availability of data? What is the expected use of computer-assisted audit techniques on the engagement?
12. Will it be possible to coordinate the expected coverage and timing of audit work with any reviews of interim financial information?
13. Will it be possible to discuss matters that may affect the audit with the audit firm personnel responsible for performing other services for the entity being audited?
14. Will entity data and client personnel be available to the audit team when needed?

Reporting Objectives, Timing of the Audit, and Required Communications

As part of the planning process, the auditor must determine the reporting objectives of the engagement, the timing of the audit, and required audit communications. In pursuance of these considerations, the following queries should be considered:

1. What is the entity's reporting timetable including interim periods?
2. What are the expected types and timing of reports to be issued as well as other communications (both written and oral) related to the audit? These include the auditor's report, management letters, and required communications with those charged with governance. These matters should also be discussed with management.
3. What are the expected deliverables from the audit?
4. When and how often should meetings between the auditor and management take place regarding the status of the audit work?
5. When should the auditors of the other locations of the engagement communicate so a clear understanding is reached regarding the expected types and timing of reports as well as other related information? What should the form of these communications take?

6. What is the expected nature and timing of communications among audit team members? When should team meetings be timed? When should the review of work performed by members of the audit team take place?
7. Are there any other expected communications with third parties as a result of performing the audit? Are there any statutory or contractual reporting responsibilities?

Scope of the Audit

The auditor should consider the following queries concerning materiality in establishing the scope of the audit:

1. Materiality considerations

    *   What are the materiality parameters for the current engagement?
    *   What are the materiality parameters for the auditors of the other locations?
    *   What are the firm's procedures for reevaluating the materiality parameters as audit procedures are performed?
    *   What are the material locations and account balances of the current engagement?

2. What audit areas manifest a higher risk of material misstatement? Will they be clearly identified to the members of the audit team?
3. What is the effect of assessed risk of material misstatement on the scope, supervision, and review at the overall financial statement level?
4. With respect to the selection of the audit team members, will personnel with greater experience be assigned to areas where there may be greater risks of material misstatement?
5. In budgeting for the engagement, will a sufficient amount of time be set aside for areas which indicate a higher risk of material misstatement?
6. Will an emphasis on a questioning mind and the exercise of a strong sense of professional skepticism in gathering and evaluating evidence on the part of members of the audit team throughout the audit be supported by the partner in charge and other supervisory personnel?
7. Will the results of previous audits involving the evaluation of the entity's internal control operating effectiveness and identified weaknesses be taken into consideration? Will it be determined that these problems were addressed?
8. Is it apparent and clear that a managerial commitment to the design and operation of internal control exists?
9. Will an analysis of the volume of transactions to be audited be made so that it may be determined whether it is more effective to rely on the entity's internal control?
10. Is the importance of internal control to the successful operation of the business evident throughout the entity?
11. Have there been any significant business developments affecting the entity during the period? These include changes in information technology and business processes; changes in key management positions; and any acquisitions, mergers, and divestitures.
12. Have there been any significant industry developments during the period? These may include changes in industry regulations or changes in reporting requirements.
13. Has there been any significant change in GAAP that would affect the way the entity accounts for and reports its transactions?
14. Have there been any other significant developments affecting the entity? For example, has there been any change in the legal environment in which the entity operates?

PRACTITIONER CHECKLISTS

FORM 1—PLANNING PROGRAM CHECKLIST

Procedures Completed By:_____ **Ref. No.**_____

1. Contact the client's managers, board of directors, or audit committee for the following information relating to the audit engagement?

   Type   _____
   Scope   _____
   Timing   _____

2. Find out the types of reports to be rendered on the engagement? For example, are reports to be filed with the SEC, on consolidated financial statements, etc.?

3. Are all members of the audit team familiar with the client's operations such as: products and services, production methods, and locations of operations?

4. Do all audit team members fully understand the nature of the audit and the potential intricacies that may be encountered [relating to] the client's assets, liabilities, revenues, gains, expenses, and loss accounts? This may be determined, for example, by reviewing

   - Last year's working papers (if this is a continuing engagement),
   - Financial statements from prior years, and
   - The chart of accounts in the context of the client's business and industry.

5. What decisions have been made by the board of directors, stockholders, and other important company committees about the financial statements? Has the company fully followed through on these decisions?

6. Are all members of the audit team familiar with the client's current accounting policies and procedures? For example, all audit team members should have an understanding of

   - How the client records and classifies transactions,
   - How decisions about transaction classification are made, and
   - How information for financial statement note disclosures is gathered and prepared.

7. Do all audit team members fully understand not only the current professional pronouncements that apply to the audit but also any guidance that might have just been released?

8. Question firm personnel about items on the financial statements that are likely to need audit adjustments?

9. Which client personnel will be responsible for helping accumulate information and prepare data for the audit?

10. If a predecessor accountant reported on a previous set of financial statements, has the client granted permission for the predecessor to discuss relevant matters with the auditor?

11. Ascertain to what extent will specialists, consultants, internal auditors, and other personnel need to participate in the audit.

12. How does work performed by internal auditors and any reports they prepared affect the scope of the audit and work performed by the auditor?

13. Discuss with knowledgeable members of the client's staff the following items and their likely effect on the current audit:

    a. Current accounting or reporting problems.
    b. Changes made in accounting principles since the last audit.
    c. Work of the internal audit staff.
    d. Modifications in the way information is processed, including technology changes.
    e. Resolution of issues raised in last year's management letter.
    f. Significant changes in client personnel.
    g. When important audit-related activities will take place, such as

        (1) Preliminary audit work,
        (2) Observation of inventory procedures, and
        (3) Confirmation of accounts receivable.

    h. How much audit-related assistance the client will provide.
    i. The accessibility to client records that will be needed for audit purposes.

14. Are there any type I or type II subsequent events disclosures that require adjustments to the financial statements or notes?

15. Have any components of the client company been reported on by other accountants that the auditor may decide to rely on?

FORM 2—PERSONNEL AND SUPERVISION PROGRAM CHECKLIST

Procedures	*Completed by:*	*Ref. No:*
1. Prepare a time budget for each area so that audit personnel requirements for the engagement are known and work may be scheduled.		
2. Before the engagement begins, obtain approval from the partner-in-charge of the proposed time budget.		

3. Recruit the firm personnel needed to ensure the success of the engagement, taking into account the following factors:
• Size and difficulty of the engagement.
• Special knowledge, proficiency, and expertise needed.
• Time requirements of the work and availability of firm personnel.
• Training and preparation of assistant accountants assigned to the engagement. Make sure all assistants have reviewed:
  • Last year's workpapers, if this is a continuing engagement;
  • Financial statements from prior years;
  • Current GAAP and GAAS pronouncements that relate to the engagement; and
  • The time allocated to their audit area on the approved time budget.		

4. Instruct all assistant accountants to notify the accountant in charge of the engagement of any significant problems that arise during the audit.		

		Completed *by:*	Ref. *No:*
	Procedures		
5.	Instruct all assistants on firm policy regarding professional disagreements that may arise, including notifying the accountant in charge and documenting the matter.		
6.	Enumerate all supervisory activities that should be incorporated into this program that relate to the engagement at hand.		

312 AUDIT RISK AND MATERIALITY

SOURCE OF STANDARDS

SAS 107, *Audit Risk and Materiality in Conducting an Audit*

INTRODUCTION/SUMMARY

Audit risk and materiality affect the nature, timing, and extent of auditing procedures, as well as the evaluation of those results. They affect the application of generally accepted auditing standards. In particular, audit risk and materiality affect the standard of fieldwork and reporting.

AUDIT RISK

Audit risk is the risk that the auditor may unknowingly fail to appropriately modify his or her opinion on financial statements that are materially misstated. (AU 312.02) In other words, audit risk refers to the probability that the auditor will issue an inappropriate opinion on the financial statements.

The auditor should plan the audit so that audit risk is limited to a level acceptable for expressing an opinion on the financial statements, based on the auditor's professional judgment. Audit risk may be assessed in quantitative or qualitative terms.

Audit risk always exists. Even when audits are well planned and carefully performed, an auditor is at best only able to obtain reasonable assurance. The nature of audit evidence is such that absolute assurance that material misstatements are detected is not possible. Furthermore the characteristics of fraud make it impossible to obtain absolute assurance.

MATERIALITY

The auditor's consideration of materiality is a matter of professional judgment. Financial Accounting Standards Board Statement of Financial Accounting Concepts 2, *Qualitative Characteristics of Accounting Information,* defines materiality as follows:

> *The magnitude of an omission or misstatement of accounting information that, in the light of surrounding circumstances, makes it probable that the judgment of a reasonable person relying on the information would have been changed or influenced by the omission or misstatement.*

SEC Regulation S-X (Rule 1-02) defines materiality as follows:

> *The term "material," when used to qualify a requirement for the furnishing of information as to any subject, limits the information required to those matters about which an average prudent investor ought reasonably be informed.*

In *Escott v. BarChris Construction Corp* (283 F. Supp. 643 [S.D.N.Y. 1968]), the court reaffirmed the definition above by stating that materiality was affected by that amount that would influence the decision making of an "average prudent investor." Other court cases have also referred to judgment by a "reasonable shareholder" or "informed investor." The general consensus appears to be that materiality would affect the judgment of an average informed user about financial statements. The standard is not aimed toward a naive layperson or an expert.

Users of financial statements are assumed to (SAS 107 Paragraph 6):

1. Have appropriate knowledge of business and economic activities,
2. Study the financial statements with due diligence,
3. Understand the concept of materiality, and
4. Understand that use of estimates and professional judgment about future events results in inherent uncertainties.

Misstatements may be classified as *known* or *likely*. *Known* misstatements are specific misstatements identified during the audit. These misstatements arise from the incorrect selection or misapplication of accounting principles or misstatements/misinterpretation of facts. *Likely* misstatements arise from differences in the judgment of auditors and management concerning accounting estimates. *Likely* misstatements also result from extrapolations about the population from audit evidence based on sampling.

Materiality has both quantitative and qualitative aspects. A quantitatively immaterial amount may nonetheless be material due to qualitative factors. For instance, a bribe of an immaterial amount may lead to a material liability to the entity. Bribing of individuals also has a direct effect on the integrity of management. If there are questions about management's integrity, the auditor needs to assess the pervasiveness of the problem. Frequent small and immaterial unintentional mistakes could cumulatively have a material effect on the financial statements.

Generally, potential misstatements in more liquid asset accounts (cash, marketable securities, inventory) are considered more important than misstatements in less liquid accounts (fixed assets). Also, what is material to the financial statements of a particular entity might change from one period to another; the amount of materiality may change from year to year because of fluctuations in income, sales, assets, or some other factor. The following qualitative factors may be relevant to the audit:

1. The potential effect of the misstatement on trends, especially trends in profitability.
2. A misstatement that changes a loss into income, or vice versa.
3. The effect of the misstatement on segment information, for example, the significance of the matter to a particular segment important to the future profitability of the entity; the pervasiveness of the matter on the segment information; and the impact of the matter on trends in segment information, all in relation to the financial statements taken as a whole.
4. The potential effect of the misstatement on the entity's compliance with loan covenants, other contractual agreements, and regulatory provisions.
5. The existence of statutory or regulatory reporting requirements that affect materiality thresholds.
6. A misstatement that has the effect of increasing management's compensation, for example, by satisfying the requirements for the award of bonuses or other forms of incentive compensation.
7. The sensitivity of the circumstances surrounding the misstatement, for example, the implications of misstatements involving fraud and possible illegal acts, violations of contractual provisions, and conflicts of interest.
8. The significance of the financial statement element affected by the misstatement, for example, a misstatement affecting recurring earnings as contrasted to one involving a nonrecurring charge or credit, such as an extraordinary item.

9. The effects of misclassifications, for example, misclassification between operating and nonoperating income or recurring and nonrecurring income items or a misclassification between fundraising costs and program activity costs in a not-for-profit organization.

10. The significance of the misstatement or disclosures relative to known user needs, for example

    a. Of earnings and earnings per share to public-company investors and the equity amounts to private-company creditors,

    b. Of misstatement on the calculation of purchase price in a transfer of interests (buy/sell agreement), and

    c. Of misstatements of earnings when contrasted with expectations.

11. The definitive character of the misstatement; for example, the precision of an error that is objectively determinable as contrasted with a misstatement that unavoidably involves a degree of subjectivity through estimation, allocation, or uncertainty.

12. The motivation of management with respect to the misstatement; for example, an indication of a possible pattern of bias by management when developing and accumulating accounting estimates, or a misstatement precipitated by management's continued unwillingness to correct weaknesses in the financial reporting process.

13. The existence of offsetting effects of individually significant but different misstatements.

14. The likelihood that a misstatement that is currently immaterial will have a material effect in future periods because of a cumulative effect, for example, that builds over several periods.

15. The cost of making the correction; for example, it may not be cost-beneficial for the client to develop a system that calculates a basis to record the effect of an immaterial misstatement. On the other hand, if management appears to have developed a system to calculate an amount that represents an immaterial misstatement, it may reflect a motivation of management.

16. The risk that possible additional undetected misstatements would affect the auditor's evaluation.

Auditors use several factors in determining materiality. The usual practice is to use the relative size of a potential misstatement to some base to decide on materiality. For instance, an amount in the range of 5% to 10% of net income is often considered material. Potential misstatements on the balance sheet may be tied to current assets or total assets.

Auditors generally do not use absolute size to determine materiality. An absolute amount of $100,000 may be highly material to one entity and totally immaterial to another entity. However, an auditor may determine that some absolute large amount will always be considered material. An absolute amount criterion for determining materiality is rarely used by auditors.

The concept of materiality recognizes that some items, either individually or in the aggregate, affect fair presentation of financial statements. The auditor's standard report represents the auditor's opinion that the financial statements taken as a whole are not materially misstated.

Auditors generally place extra importance on detection of misstatements in financial statements that will be widely distributed, such as those of publicly held companies. Similarly auditors may be more cautious about detecting misstatements when an important event, such as approval of a major loan or merger, is taking place. One reason for this is the auditor's own legal liability for potentially material misstatements. The auditor will also have stricter materiality standards for items where there is uncertainty about future outcome.

ERROR AND FRAUD

Misstatements in financial statements can result from errors or fraud. A misstatement may consist of any of the following:

1. A difference between the amounts, classification, or presentation of a reported financial statement element, account, or item and the amount, classification, or presentation that would have been reported under generally accepted accounting principles.
2. The omission of a financial statement element, account, or item.
3. A financial statement disclosure that is not presented in accordance with generally accepted accounting principles.
4. The omission of information required to be disclosed in accordance with generally accepted accounting principles.

The auditor's responsibility is to plan the audit to obtain reasonable assurance that material misstatements, individually or in the aggregate, in the financial statements are detected. The auditor has no responsibility to detect misstatements whether caused by error or fraud that are not material to the financial statements.

Error refers to unintentional misstatements or omissions of amounts or disclosures in the financial statements. Errors may involve

1. Mistakes in gathering or processing data from which financial statements are prepared,
2. Unreasonable accounting estimates arising from oversight or misinterpretation of facts, or
3. Mistakes in the application of accounting principles relating to amount, classification, manner of presentation, or disclosure.

Unlike errors, which are unintentional misstatements, fraud involves intentional acts. Auditors are primarily interested in discovering fraudulent acts that may cause a misstatement of financial statements. Two broad types of fraudulent misstatements are relevant to the auditor's consideration:

1. Misstatements arising from fraudulent financial reporting.
2. Misstatements arising from misappropriation of assets.

AU Section 316, *Consideration of Fraud in a Financial Statement Audit,* discusses these two types of misstatements in detail.

It is important to note that the auditor's responsibility is simply to obtain reasonable assurance that the financial statements are free from material misstatement. No distinction is made whether the misstatement is caused by error or by fraud.

A distinction is made, however, in the way auditors are required to respond to the misstatement. In general, an isolated immaterial error is considered insignificant to the audit. In contrast, anytime fraud is detected, the auditor should consider the integrity of the management and the employees and possible consequences of the fraud on other aspects of the audit.

CONSIDERATIONS AT THE FINANCIAL STATEMENTS LEVEL

Audit risk and materiality have a direct effect on auditor's judgment concerning the sufficiency and appropriateness of evidence that is used to determine the fair presentation of financial statements. The auditor should consider audit risk and materiality in (SAS 107, paragraph 11)

1. Determining the extent and nature of risk assessment procedures;

2. Identifying and assessing the risks of material misstatement;
3. Determining the nature, timing, and extent of audit procedures; and
4. Evaluating evidence and determining fair presentation of financial statements.

When planning the audit, the auditor is required to exercise, for audit purposes, some preliminary judgment about materiality levels. This judgment may be quantified, but numbers are not required.

The nature, timing, and extent of audit planning affects both audit risk and materiality. Audit risk and materiality considerations vary with

1. The size and complexity of the entity,
2. The auditor's experience with the entity, and
3. The auditor's knowledge of the entity's business.

Auditors assess the risk of material misstatement during the planning stages of the audit. In considering audit risk, the auditor is required to specifically assess the risk of material misstatement of the financial statements due to fraud. In addition the auditor should consider the entity's internal controls. An understanding of the controls may increase or decrease the auditor's concern about the risk of material misstatement.

If the auditor concludes that there is a significant risk of material misstatements in the financial statements, the auditor should consider (AU 312.16)

1. Modifying the nature, timing, or extent of audit procedures;
2. Assigning appropriate audit staff; and
3. Requiring appropriate levels of supervision.

The auditor may need to expand the audit procedures or modify the procedures to obtain more persuasive evidence. The auditor may also need to modify the timing of the audit procedures by applying them closer to year-end. Generally, higher-risk audit engagements require more experienced audit staff. Greater supervision is also needed under such circumstances.

The auditor should consider the extent of auditing procedures that will need to be performed for an entity that operates out of multiple locations or has multiple components. The auditor should consider the following factors regarding the selection of a particular location or component:

1. The nature and amount of assets and transactions executed at the location or component;
2. The degree of centralization of records or information processing;
3. The effectiveness of the control environment, particularly with respect to management's direct control over the exercise of authority delegated to others and its ability to effectively supervise activities at the location or component;
4. The frequency, timing, and scope of monitoring activities by the entity or others at the location or component; and
5. Judgments about materiality of the location or component.

The auditor's judgment affects both the appropriate levels of audit risk and materiality. The auditor must evaluate whether the financial statements taken as a whole are free of material misstatement.

The auditor sets an overall materiality level for the financial statements taken as a whole.

CONSIDERATIONS AT THE INDIVIDUAL ACCOUNT-BALANCE, CLASS-OF-TRANSACTIONS, OR DISCLOSURE LEVEL

There is an inverse relationship between audit risk and materiality.

A decrease in the level of audit risk (i.e., the auditor wants greater assurance that financial statements are not materially misstated), while keeping other factors constant, would require the auditor to do one or more of the following (AU 312.17):

1. Select a more effective auditing procedure.
2. Perform auditing procedures closer to year-end.
3. Increase the extent of a particular auditing procedure.

Audit risk must be considered at the individual account-balance, class-of-transactions, and disclosure level. Such consideration helps in determining the scope of the audit procedures. The auditor should consider the risk of overstatement and understatement at the relevant assertion level.

At the account-balance, class-of-transactions, and disclosure level, the audit risk consists of (AU 312.20)

1. The risk (both the inherent risk and the control risk) that the balance, class, or disclosure and related assertions contain misstatements (whether caused by error or fraud) that could be material to the financial statements when aggregated with misstatements in other balances, classes, or disclosure; and
2. The risk (detection risk) that the auditor will not detect such misstatements.

The relationship between inherent risk (IR), control risk (CR), detection risk (DR), and audit risk (AR) is defined by the following model:

$$AR = IR \times CR \times DR$$

More specifically, inherent risk, control risk, and detection risk are defined as follows (AU 312.21):

1. *Inherent risk* is the susceptibility of an assertion to a material misstatement, assuming that there are no related controls.
2. *Control risk* is the risk that if a material misstatement occurs in an assertion, it will not be prevented or detected on a timely basis by the entity's internal control.
3. *Detection risk* is the risk that the auditor will not detect a material misstatement that exists in an assertion.

INHERENT RISK

Inherent risk relates to the nature of certain assertions to be more susceptible to material misstatements than other assertions. Some examples are as follows:

1. Cash is more susceptible to theft than land.
2. There is a greater possibility of misstatement in amount involving complex calculations than simple calculations.
3. There is greater inherent risk in accounts consisting of accounting estimates by management than in accounts whose values may be calculated through more routine means.
4. An entity operating in a high-tech environment may have a higher inherent risk. For instance, inventory in such an environment is more susceptible to obsolescence and thereby a greater likelihood that the inventory may be overstated.
5. Lack of sufficient working capital to continue operations.
6. Declining industry characterized by a large number of business failures.

CONTROL RISK

Control risk is a measure of the auditor's assessment of the likelihood that misstatements will not be prevented or detected by the entity's internal controls. Control risk is a function of the effectiveness of the design and operation of internal control. Due to the inherent limitations of internal controls, such as collusion or management override, control risk can never be completely eliminated.

DETECTION RISK

Detection risk is a measure of risk that the audit evidence will fail to detect misstatements. Detection risk is a function of the effectiveness of auditing procedures and how the procedures are applied by the auditor. Detection risk exists because auditors generally use sampling techniques and do not examine 100% of the account balance or a class of transactions. It can be due to nonsampling issues as well, and this risk will exist even if the auditor was able to examine 100% of the balance or class. Nonsampling issues include

1. Selection of an inappropriate auditing procedure,
2. Misapplication of an appropriate procedure, and
3. Misinterpretation of audit results.

Uncertainties generated by nonsampling issues can be minimized, though not necessarily eliminated, by proper planning, training and supervision. Implementing appropriate quality control standards also helps in minimizing such uncertainties.

RISK RELATIONSHIPS

The standard audit risk model was discussed previously. Risk of material misstatement (RMM) is the product of inherent risk (IR) and control risk (CR). Detection risk (DR) is the product of a test of details risk (TD) and substantive analytical procedures risk (AP). The audit risk model may also be written as

$$AR = RMM \times DR$$

Both inherent risk and control risk exist independently of the audit of financial statements. In contrast, audit procedures affect detection risk. Detection risk has an inverse relationship to inherent and control risk. The greater the inherent and control risk the auditor believes exists, the lesser is the detection risk that can be accepted. The converse is also true.

Assessment of inherent risk for an assertion is a matter of the auditor's professional judgment. Professional judgment is also involved in assessing control risk. It is based on the auditor's evaluation of evidence that supports the effectiveness of internal control in preventing or detecting misstatements in financial statement assertions.

Based on the auditor's judgment, the auditor might make a separate or a combined assessment of inherent risk and control risk. Auditors are required to appropriately document the basis for their assessment of inherent and control risk, separately or in combination using

1. Questionnaires,
2. Checklists,
3. Instructions,
4. Material used to obtain the understanding of internal control and the performance of appropriate tests of controls (for control risk only), and
5. Other similar materials.

The detection risk that can be accepted increases as the auditor's assessment of inherent risk and control risk decreases. However, the auditor cannot rely on assessments of inherent risk and control risk to the exclusion of a through examination of account balances and classes of transactions.

As audit procedures are performed, the auditor may come across information that differs substantially from the information that was used to plan the audit. As new evidence is obtained, the auditor may modify the nature, timing, and extent of other planned procedures. In such a situation the auditor may reconsider which audit procedures are to be performed.

DETERMINING MATERIALITY FOR THE OVERALL FINANCIAL STATEMENT WHEN PLANNING THE AUDIT

The materiality level is *not* a threshold below which identified misstatements are necessarily considered immaterial. The auditor should consider qualitative factors when establishing an overall audit strategy.

In determining materiality, the auditor often selects a percentage of some benchmark. The following factors should be considered in selecting an appropriate benchmark (AU 312.28):

1. Elements of financial statements, such as assets or income.
2. Financial statement items where users' attention should be focused.
3. Nature of the entity, its size, its industry, its type of ownership, and its financial structure.

Prior periods' financial statements with budgets and forecasts should be considered by the auditor in determining materiality. Consideration should be given to macroeconomic factors as well as industry-specific factors. Auditors' understanding of user needs and expectations affect the materiality determination. For instance, user expectations may differ based on the inherent uncertainty associated with particular financial statement items.

MATERIALITY FOR PARTICULAR ITEMS OF LESSER AMOUNTS THAN THE MATERIALITY LEVEL DETERMINED FOR THE FINANCIAL STATEMENTS

It is possible for misstatements of certain items of lesser amounts than the materiality level to influence economic decisions taken by the company. Low amounts are often associated with low materiality of an item in the financial statement.

TOLERABLE MISSTATEMENT

Tolerable misstatement (TM), also known as tolerable error, is the maximum error in a population that the auditor is willing to accept.

CONSIDERATIONS AS THE AUDIT PROGRESSES

Auditor's judgment about materiality for planning purposes is often different than when evaluating audit findings. As the audit progresses, the auditor generally becomes aware of additional qualitative and quantitative factors. If the auditor determines initial judgment about materiality to be inappropriate, related level of tolerable misstatement should be reconsidered. This could also affect the nature, timing and extent of remaining audit procedures.

The auditor should never assume that identified misstatements are isolated occurrences. Circumstances surrounding the occurrence of the misstatement may suggest the need to revise overall audit strategy.

COMMUNICATION OF MISSTATEMENTS TO MANAGEMENT

All known and likely misstatements that are identified, other than trivial ones, should be communicated to the appropriate level of management in a timely manner. The auditor should distinguish between known and likely misstatements. Management should adjust known misstatements, including the effect of prior period misstatements. If the management decides not to correct some or all of the identified misstatements, the auditor should obtain an understanding of management's reasons for not making the correction and its implications for the auditor's report.

EVALUATING AUDIT FINDINGS

The auditor should consider, both individually and in the aggregate, the effects of misstatements that are not corrected by the entity. As discussed previously, both qualitative and quantitative factors should be considered when evaluating the effects of misstatements. When aggregating misstatements, the auditor should include not just "known misstatements" (the amount of misstatements specifically identified) but also the "likely misstatements" (the auditor's best estimate of the total misstatements in the account balances or classes of transactions that were examined). Auditors should aggregate likely misstatements to evaluate whether in relation to individual amounts or the totals, the financial statements as a whole have become materially misstated. The auditor should not ignore qualitative factors when making the evaluation.

Analytical procedures are used by auditors to identify potential misstatements and their approximate magnitude. If the auditor is unable to estimate the approximate magnitude of potential misstatements identified by analytical procedures, other procedures should be utilized to enable the auditor to estimate the likely misstatement.

The auditor should evaluate whether management's accounting estimates are supported by the audit evidence and whether the estimated amounts included in the financial statements are reasonable. If the auditor believes the estimated amounts are not reasonable, the auditor should treat the difference between that estimate and the closest reasonable estimate as a likely misstatement.

The auditor should further consider if management's accounting estimates are systematically biased. The auditor should be aware that management's estimates may be clustered at either end of the auditor's range of acceptable amounts, indicating a possible bias on the part of management.

Even if estimates included in the financial statements are individually reasonable, the management may be trying to introduce some type of a systematic bias. If each accounting estimate included in the financial statements was individually reasonable, but the effect of the difference between each estimate and the estimate best supported by the audit evidence was to increase income, the auditor should reconsider the estimates taken as a whole.

The auditor should also consider likely misstatements from prior periods. Past likely misstatements may not have been corrected by the entity because those misstatements might not have caused the financial statements to be materially misstated. However, the misstatements from the prior period could have an effect on the current period. If the auditor believes the current period financial statements to be materially misstated due to prior period misstatement, the auditor should include in the aggregate the effect on current period's financial statements of those prior-period likely misstatements.

After accumulating and evaluating sufficient evidential matter, the auditor may conclude that the misstatements are so many that the financial statements are materially misstated. In such a case, the auditor should request management to correct the misstatements. If a material misstatement is not corrected, the auditor should consider the implications for the audit, that the cumulative effect of immaterial misstatements on the balance sheet will have a material effect on future financial statements. The auditor should also be aware that the there is always a possibility of other undetected material misstatements. If the auditor is concerned that the risk of additional undetected material misstatements is unacceptably high, the auditor should perform additional procedures to reduce the risk of material misstatement to an acceptable level.

DOCUMENTATION

The nature and effect of aggregated misstatements should be documented. The auditor also should document whether the aggregated misstatements cause the financial statements to be materially misstated.

The levels of materiality and tolerable misstatement, as well as any changes made to those levels, should be documented. The documentation should note how the levels were initially determined and why changes were made. All known and likely misstatements identified by the auditor that have been corrected by management should be documented.

Uncorrected known and likely misstatements should be summarized. An assessment by the auditor about the effects of uncorrected misstatements, individually or in the aggregate, on the financial statements should be documented. When documenting, it should be possible to separately determine the effects of known and likely misstatements, including uncorrected misstatements identified in prior periods.

315 COMMUNICATIONS BETWEEN PREDECESSOR AND SUCCESSOR AUDITORS

SOURCES OF STANDARDS

GAAS

SAS 84, *Communications between Predecessor and Successor Auditors*
SAS 93, *Omnibus Statement on Auditing Standards*

NON-GAAS PROFESSIONAL GUIDANCE

Practice Alert 97-3, *Changes in Auditors and Related Topics*

SUMMARY

AU Section 315 provides guidance on the communications that are required when a client changes auditors. The predecessor auditor is the auditor who reported on the most recent audited financial statements or who was engaged to perform an audit but did not complete it and has resigned, declined reappointment, or is being or has been terminated. The successor auditor is the auditor who has accepted or is deciding whether to accept an engagement to audit the financial statements of an entity in accordance with GAAS but has not yet communicated with the predecessor about this.

AU Section 315 discusses not only the communications that should occur between predecessor and successor auditors during a transition but also communications when the successor discovers misstatements in the financial statements that were reported on by the predecessor.

GAAS GUIDANCE

PRELIMINARY CONSIDERATIONS FOR A CHANGE OF AUDITORS

In general, the successor auditor is responsible for communication between predecessor and successor auditors. Whether the communication is oral or written, it should be held in confidence whether or not the successor accepts the engagement. Even after making a proposal for an audit engagement, the successor should not accept the position until the communications required by AU Section 315 take place.

If more than one auditor is currently considering an audit engagement, the predecessor should not be expected to respond to inquiries potential successors might have until the client has selected the successor auditor. Final acceptance by the successor, however, is always subject to what is learned in the communication with the predecessor auditor.

Required Preengagement Communications

In deciding whether to accept an engagement, a successor auditor must make inquiries of the predecessor. To do this, it is necessary for the auditor to ask the prospective client's permission to make inquiries of the predecessor auditor before final acceptance. Under the Code of Professional Ethics, if a prospective client authorizes the predecessor auditor to respond fully to inquiries made by the prospective successor, confidential information obtained on the audit may be disclosed. The prospective client may, however, set limitations on areas that the predecessor may respond to, or deny permission to respond altogether. The successor auditor must consider the reasons for limitation or denial in deciding whether to accept the engagement.

AU Section 315 notes that inquiries made by the successor auditor must be specific and reasonable. They should cover

1. Any disputes the predecessor auditor had with the client over accounting principles, auditing procedures, or other audit-related matters;
2. Discussions the predecessor had with the client's audit committee, board of directors, board of trustees, or the owner in owner-managed entities about fraud and illegal acts of the client.
3. Communications to management and those charged with governance regarding significant deficiencies and material weaknesses in internal control.
4. Matters relating to the integrity of management.
5. The predecessor's analysis of what circumstances precipitated the change of auditors.
6. Any other reasonable inquiries that the potential successor might consider helpful in making a decision about the engagement.

The potential successor should also seek the prospective client's permission to have access to the predecessor's working papers in order to make a thorough review. It is a good idea to obtain a formal consent letter from the client like the following to avoid any confusion about the content of communications between predecessor and successor auditors.

FORM 1

Client's Consent to Communication between
Predecessor and Successor Auditors

[*Date*]
[*Name of company*]
[*Address of company*]

This writing documents your consent to allow [*name of successor*], as successor independent auditors, access to our working papers for our audit of the December 31, 20X1 financial statements of [*name of company*]. In addition this letter documents your consent to us to respond fully to the inquiries of [*successor auditor*]. The review of our working papers is undertaken for the purpose of obtaining an understanding about [*name of company*] and information about our audit to assist [*successor auditor*] in planning the audit of the December 31, 20X2 financial statements of [name of company].

Please confirm your consent by signing and dating a copy of this letter and returning it to us.

The form of the letter that we will provide [*successor auditor*] regarding the use of the working papers is attached.

Sincerely,
[*Predecessor auditor*]

_____

[*Signature of representative*]

Accepted:
[*Name of company*]

_____

[*Signature of representative*]

FORM 2

Successor Auditor's Acknowledgment Letter on Use of the Working Papers

[*Date*]
[*Name of successor auditor*]
[*Address of successor auditor*]

We have previously audited the December 31, 20X1 financial statements of [*name of company*] in accordance with generally accepted auditing standards and rendered a report on those financial statements. No auditing procedures have been performed since the report date. You have requested access to our working papers in connection with that audit. Our firm has been authorized by [*name of the company*] to allow you to review those working papers.

Because the performance of our audit was not performed or planned with the intent of your request, it is possible that items that may be of interest to you may not be specifically addressed. We make no representations as to the appropriateness or adequacy of the information in our working papers for your purposes. Clearly, our professional judgment and assessment of the audit risk and materiality for our audit may be different from that which you would have chosen.

It is known that the purpose of your review is to obtain information about the [*name of company*] and that our working papers and results will hopefully assist you in planning your 20X2 audit of the [*name of company*]. Access to our working papers is predicated on this objective.

We will provide you with copies of those working papers that you request that provide factual information about [*name of company*]. Any copies of working papers or other information derived therefrom will be subject to your normal policy of retention and confidential client information. Furthermore you agree, if a third party should request access to your working papers for your audit of [*name of company*], to obtain our permission before allowing access to our working papers or information derived therefrom. In addition you agree to obtain any releases on our behalf that you obtain from such a third party. Also you agree to apprise and provide us with a copy of any subpoena, summons, or other court order for access to your working papers that might include copies of our working papers or information derived therefrom.

We ask that you confirm your agreement with these considerations by signing and dating a copy of this letter and returning it to us.

Sincerely,
[*Name of predecessor auditor*]

_____

[*Signature of representative*]

Accepted:
[*Name of successor auditor*]

_____ Date: _____
[*Signature of representative*]

Other Limitations on Access That May Be Included in Acknowledgment Letters

The predecessor may be willing to grant extensive access if the successor is willing to give restrictive assurances about use of the working papers. To illustrate, the following limitations on the use of the working papers may be required by the predecessor auditors if the successor is given broader access for the working paper review:

- With respect to the review of the predecessor's working papers, the successor agrees not to comment, orally or in writing, about whether the work performed by the predecessor auditor in the audit engagement of the client was performed in accordance with GAAS.

- The successor auditor agrees not to use the audit procedures or their results as documented in the predecessor's working papers as evidence in rendering an opinion for the period that the successor has agreed to render an opinion on (except where allowed by AU Section 315).
- The successor auditor agrees not to provide expert testimony or litigation support services or accept any engagement that requires comments on the quality of the predecessor's audit.

Once Permission Is Granted

If permission is granted, the predecessor decides which working papers are to be shown and copied for the successor auditor. Usually the predecessor will be willing to speak or meet with the successor auditor for a discussion and exchange of information. The following areas of the working papers are generally made available:

- Documentation of the audit planning that took place.
- Documentation of the client's internal control system.
- Audit results.
- Analysis of balance sheet accounts.
- Analysis of income statement accounts.
- Documentation of any continuing contingencies.
- All other matters of continuing accounting and auditing significance.

IMPACT OF OPENING BALANCES AND CONSISTENCY OF ACCOUNTING PRINCIPLES ON OPINIONS ON CURRENT FINANCIAL STATEMENTS

The successor auditor must obtain sufficient appropriate audit evidence to ascertain the impact of the client's opening balances and the consistency of its accounting principles in order to establish a starting point for expressing an opinion on current financial statements. How the auditor uses the audit evidence derived is a matter of professional judgment, but AU Section 315 notes that the evidence needed may be drawn from several sources:

1. Last audited financial statements.
2. Predecessor's auditor report on last audited financial statements.
3. Inquiries made by the successor about the predecessor audit.
4. Successor's review of the predecessor's working papers for the last audited financial statements. This review may influence the nature, timing, and extent of audit procedures that the successor may perform on the opening balances to determine the consistency of accounting principles.
5. Successor's current audit work performed on opening balances and transactions of prior periods. For example, by testing the collections of cash relating to material year-end accounts receivable in the early part of the new period, the auditor is gathering evidence about their existence at period's end. Auditing sales and shipping documents of inventory sold in the early part of the year adds to the credibility of the client's inventory realizability at the period's end.

The successor may choose to rely significantly on evidence gathered from inquiries of the predecessor auditor, as well as from a review of the working papers and the predecessor's report on the prior period financial statements. However, in reporting on the current period financial statements, the successor should make no reference at all to the influence of the report or work of the predecessor; the opinion on current financial statements is totally the responsibility of the successor auditor.

REAUDITING AND REREPORTING ON FINANCIAL STATEMENTS

An auditor may be asked to audit and report on the previously audited financial statements. This engagement is known as a reaudit. The following guidelines should be followed in accepting and performing a reaudit. They are obviously very similar to the guidelines about communication between predecessor and successor auditors.

1. In making inquiries of the predecessor, the successor should clearly communicate that the purpose is to help the successor decide whether to accept a reaudit engagement.
2. If the reaudit engagement is accepted by the successor auditor, then the planning of the audit may be a function of inquiries of the predecessor and review of the predecessor's report and working papers.
3. The successor is entirely responsible for the nature, timing, and extent of the work to be performed on a reaudit.
4. A reaudit should be planned and performed in accordance with GAAS.
5. The successor should assume no responsibility related to work performed by the predecessor, and should not issue a report related to that work that might imply divided responsibility between successor and predecessor auditors.
6. The predecessor should not be considered a specialist or internal auditor as defined by GAAS.
7. The successor may have audited the financial statements of the entity for the current period. If the successor has been asked to reaudit financial statements for a preceding period or periods, the results of the current audit should be helpful in planning and performing the reaudit.
8. If the successor cannot obtain sufficient appropriate audit evidence in a reaudit engagement, any opinion should be qualified or disclaimed on that ground.
9. GAAS requires that an auditor observe or make test counts at the reaudit date, though clearly this is not possible for the successor. The successor should determine that these procedures were done by the predecessor by reviewing the predecessor's working papers and making queries as needed. The successor should also observe or perform some physical counts of inventory at a date subsequent to the reaudit period, perhaps as part of the current audit, as well as testing inventory transactions. The tests should include tests of prior inventory transactions, review of prior inventory counts, and tests of inventory reasonability using the gross profit test, retail method, or another inventory estimating technique.

MISSTATEMENTS FOUND IN REAUDITED FINANCIAL STATEMENTS

A successor auditor who has reason to believe that the financial statements reported by the predecessor auditor may require revision should take the following actions:

1. The successor should attempt to resolve the problem by asking the client to inform the predecessor of the circumstances and arrange a meeting of the three parties to decide what to do.
2. The successor should clearly communicate to the predecessor all evidence discovered of a possible misstatement of the financial statements reported on by the latter. With this information the predecessor may be able to fully follow the procedures enumerated in AU Section 561, *Subsequent Discovery of Facts Existing at the Date of the Auditor's Report.*
3. If the successor is dissatisfied with how this problem was resolved or if the client refuses to inform the predecessor that there is a problem, the successor should con-

sider the effect of this on the current engagement and decide whether to resign from the engagement.

NON-GAAS PROFESSIONAL GUIDANCE

PRACTICE ALERT 97-3, CHANGES IN AUDITORS AND RELATED TOPICS

NOTE: The information that follows is based on the findings of the SEC Practice Section Professional Issues Task Force. Although it has not yet been approved or disapproved by any AICPA committee, it is provided here as an additional source of practical guidance.

In determining whether to take on a new client, it is imperative that the successor auditor confer with the client's former auditor, who is an invaluable source of information about the acceptability of the client. For example, the successor can find out whether there were any disagreements between the client and the predecessor about auditing procedures, accounting principles, the integrity of management, or any other relevant matter.

The successor auditor has the responsibility for initiating the dialogue with the predecessor. The successor should ask permission from the prospective client to make inquiries of the predecessor before the engagement is accepted. The client should permit the predecessor to respond to such inquiries without qualification. If the client authorizes only a qualified communication or blocks the inquiry altogether, the successor should ascertain the reasons and consider choosing not to accept the engagement.

PA 97-3 notes that the predecessor should respond fully to the inquiries of the successor, but there may be circumstances where the predecessor may decide that it is not in his or her best interest to do so, because of pending litigation with the client, disciplinary proceedings, or other such matters. The successor auditor should carefully consider these circumstances in deciding whether to accept the engagement.

316 CONSIDERATION OF FRAUD IN A FINANCIAL STATEMENT AUDIT

SOURCES OF STANDARD

SAS 99, *Consideration of Fraud in a Financial Statement Audit*
SAS 113, *Omnibus Statement on Auditing Standards—2006*

INTRODUCTION/SUMMARY

Management is responsible for designing and implementing controls to prevent, deter and detect fraud. AU 110.03 (Responsibilities and Functions of the Internal Auditor) states

> *Management is responsible for adopting sound accounting policies and for establishing and maintaining internal control that will, among other things, initiate, record, process, and report transactions (as well as events and conditions) consistent with management's assertions embodied in the financial statements.*

The auditor's responsibility for considering fraud when planning an audit is stated in AU 110.02 as follows:

> *The auditor has a responsibility to plan and perform the audit to obtain reasonable assurance about whether the financial statements are free of material misstatement, whether caused by error or fraud.*

DESCRIPTION AND CHARACTERISTICS OF FRAUD

Fraud is a legal concept, and auditors do not have the professional expertise to make such a legal determination. Instead, auditors are interested in acts that cause a material misstatement of the financial statements. The basic difference between fraud and error is that in fraud the misstatements are intentional. AU Section 316.05 defines fraud as

> *An intentional act that results in a material misstatement in financial statements that are the subject of an audit.*

Auditors are concerned about two types of fraud/misstatements.

1. Misstatements arising from fraudulent financial reporting.
2. Misstatements arising from misappropriation of assets.

PROFESSIONAL SKEPTICISM

The auditor should exercise professional skepticism when considering the risk of material misstatement due to fraud. The auditor should recognize that regardless of past experience with the entity or the auditor's belief about management's honesty and integrity, a material misstatement due to fraud could be present.

Discussion among Engagement Personnel

AU 316.14 states that members of the audit team should discuss the potential for material misstatement due to fraud. The discussion should include

1. An exchange of ideas or "brainstorming" among the audit team members about

    a. How the entity's financial statements might be susceptible to material misstatement due to fraud,
    b. How management could perpetrate and conceal fraudulent financial reporting, and
    c. How assets of the entity could be misappropriated;

2. Importance of maintaining professional skepticism throughout the audit.

INFORMATION NEEDED TO IDENTIFY RISKS OF MATERIAL MISSTATEMENT DUE TO FRAUD

Inquiring of Management and Others within the Entity

The auditor should inquire of management about (AU 316.20)

1. Management's knowledge of fraud or suspected fraud;
2. Allegations of fraud or suspected fraud;
3. Risks of fraud in the entity;
4. Programs and controls established to mitigate fraud risks;
5. Entity with multiple locations:

    a. The nature and extent of monitoring of locations and
    b. Locations for which risk of fraud may be more likely to exist;

6. Communication with employees about business practices and ethical behavior.

The auditor should inquire whether management has reported to the audit committee about the entity's internal control ability to prevent, deter, or detect material misstatements due to fraud. The auditor should also inquire of the audit committee about the risks of fraud and whether fraud is suspected.

The auditor should inquire of internal audit personnel about the risks of fraud, including any procedures that have been performed to identify or detect fraud. The auditor should also inquire of internal auditors whether they encountered fraud or suspected fraud.

The auditor should direct inquiries to others within the entity to include

1. Employees at all levels of authority,
2. Employees not directly involved in financial reporting,
3. Employees involved in initiating, recording, or processing complex or unusual transactions, and
4. In-house legal counsel.

Management is generally in a unique position to perpetrate fraud. Management may directly or indirectly manipulate accounting records. Management can also override controls. Management may sometimes try to conceal fraud through collusion. Auditors should use professional judgment in corroborating management's responses resolving inconsistencies.

SAS 109, *Understanding the Entity and its Environment and Assessing the Risks of Material Misstatement,* requires the auditor to identify and assess the risk of material misstatement at both

1. The financial statement level, and

2. The relevant assertion level with respect to

    a. Classes of transactions,
    b. Account balances, and
    c. Disclosures.

SAS 110, *Performing Audit Procedures in Response to Assessed Risks and Evaluating the Audit Evidence Obtained,* requires the auditor to determine overall responses to address the assessed risk of material misstatement at the financial statement level. The auditor should design and perform audit procedures to respond to the assessed risks of material misstatement at the financial statement and relevant assertion levels.

ANALYTICAL PROCEDURES

AU Section 329, *Analytical Procedures,* requires analytical procedures to be performed in planning the audit. The auditor should consider unusual or unexpected relationships in identifying the risks of material misstatement due to fraud. The auditor should perform analytical procedures for the revenue accounts. Since analytical procedures generally use data aggregated at a high level, analytical procedures can only direct the auditor's attention to whether a material misstatement of the financial statements exists. The results of analytical procedures cannot be conclusive; the results should be considered along with other information obtained by the auditor.

FRAUD RISK FACTORS

Fraud generally occurs when three conditions are present:

1. Management or employees have an incentive or are under pressure.
2. Circumstances exist that provide an opportunity for fraud to be perpetrated.
3. Individuals involved are able to rationalize committing a fraudulent act.

Specific examples of fraud risk factors for Fraudulent Financial Reporting and Misappropriation of Assets are identified by AU 316.85 (Appendix: Examples of Fraud Risk Factors):

FRAUDULENT FINANCIAL REPORTING

Incentives/Pressures

1. Financial stability or profitability is threatened by economic, industry, or entity operating conditions, such as (or as indicated by)

    a. High degree of competition or market saturation, accompanied by declining margins.
    b. High vulnerability to rapid changes, such as changes in technology, product obsolescence, or interest rates.
    c. Significant declines in customer demand and increasing business failures in either the industry or overall economy.
    d. Operating losses making the threat of bankruptcy, foreclosure, or hostile takeover imminent.
    e. Recurring negative cash flows from operations or an inability to generate cash flows from operations while reporting earnings and earnings growth.
    f. Rapid growth or unusual profitability, especially compared to that of other companies in the same industry.

New accounting, statutory, or regulatory requirements

2. Excessive pressure exists for management to meet the requirements or expectations of third parties due to the following:

   a. Profitability or trend level expectations of investment analysts, institutional investors, significant creditors, or other external parties (particularly expectations that are unduly aggressive or unrealistic), including expectations created by management in, for example, overly optimistic press releases or annual report messages.

   b. Need to obtain additional debt or equity financing to stay competitive—including financing of major research and development or capital expenditures.

   c. Marginal ability to meet exchange listing requirements or debt repayment or other debt covenant requirements.

Perceived or real adverse effects of reporting poor financial results on significant pending transactions, such as business combinations or contract awards

3. Information available indicates that management or the board of directors' personal financial situation is threatened by the entity's financial performance arising from the following:

   a. Significant financial interests in the entity.

   b. Significant portions of their compensation (for example, bonuses, stock options, and earn-out arrangements) being contingent upon achieving aggressive targets for stock price, operating results, financial position, or cash flow.

Personal guarantees of debts of the entity

4. There is excessive pressure on management or operating personnel to meet financial targets set up by the board of directors or management, including sales or profitability incentive goals.

Opportunities

The nature of the industry or the entity's operations provides opportunities to engage in fraudulent financial reporting that can arise from the following:

1. Significant related-party transactions not in the ordinary course of business or with related entities not audited or audited by another firm.

2. A strong financial presence or ability to dominate a certain industry sector that allows the entity to dictate terms or conditions to suppliers or customers that may result in inappropriate or non-arm's-length transactions.

3. Assets, liabilities, revenues, or expenses based on significant estimates that involve subjective judgments or uncertainties that are difficult to corroborate.

4. Significant, unusual, or highly complex transactions, especially those close to period-end that pose difficult "substance over form" questions.

5. Significant operations located or conducted across international borders in jurisdictions where differing business environments and cultures exist.

6. Significant bank accounts or subsidiary or branch operations in tax-haven jurisdictions for which there appears to be no clear business justification.

There is ineffective monitoring of management as a result of the following:

1. Domination of management by a single person or small group (in a nonowner-managed business) without compensating controls.

2. Ineffective board of directors or audit committee oversight over the financial reporting process and internal control.

There is a complex or unstable organizational structure, as evidenced by the following:

1. Difficulty in determining the organization or individuals that have controlling interest in the entity.
2. Overly complex organizational structure involving unusual legal entities or managerial lines of authority.
3. High turnover of senior management, counsel, or board members.

Internal control components are deficient as a result of the following:

1. Inadequate monitoring of controls, including automated controls and controls over interim financial reporting (where external reporting is required).
2. High turnover rates or employment of ineffective accounting, internal audit, or information technology staff.
3. Ineffective accounting and information systems, including situations involving reportable conditions.

Attitudes/Rationalizations

Risk factors reflective of attitudes/rationalizations by board members, management, or employees that allow them to engage in and/or justify fraudulent financial reporting may not be susceptible to observation by the auditor. Nevertheless, the auditor who becomes aware of the existence of such information should consider it in identifying the risks of material misstatement arising from fraudulent financial reporting. For example, auditors may become aware of the following information that may indicate a risk factor:

1. Ineffective communication, implementation, support, or enforcement of the entity's values or ethical standards by management or the communication of inappropriate values or ethical standards.
2. Nonfinancial management's excessive participation in or preoccupation with the selection of accounting principles or the determination of significant estimates.
3. Known history of violations of securities laws or other laws and regulations, or claims against the entity, its senior management, or board members alleging fraud or violations of laws and regulations.
4. Excessive interest by management in maintaining or increasing the entity's stock price or earnings trend.
5. A practice by management of committing to analysts, creditors, and other third parties to achieve aggressive or unrealistic forecasts.
6. Management failing to correct known reportable conditions on a timely basis.
7. An interest by management in employing inappropriate means to minimize reported earnings for tax-motivated reasons.
8. Recurring attempts by management to justify marginal or inappropriate accounting on the basis of materiality.
9. The relationship between management and the current or predecessor auditor is strained, as exhibited
   a. Frequent disputes with the current or predecessor auditor on accounting, auditing, or reporting matters;
   b. Unreasonable demands on the auditor, such as unreasonable time constraints regarding the completion of the audit or the issuance of the auditor's report;

  c. Formal or informal restrictions on the auditor that inappropriately limit access to people or information or the ability to communicate effectively with the board of directors or audit committee; and

  d. Domineering management behavior in dealing with the auditor, especially involving attempts to influence the scope of the auditor's work or the selection or continuance of personnel assigned to or consulted on the audit engagement.

MISAPPROPRIATION OF ASSETS

Incentives/Pressures

Personal financial obligations may create pressure on management or employees with access to cash or other assets susceptible to theft to misappropriate those assets. Adverse relationships between the entity and employees with access to cash or other assets susceptible to theft may motivate those employees to misappropriate those assets. For example, adverse relationships may be created by

1. Known or anticipated future employee layoffs;
2. Recent or anticipated changes to employee compensation or benefit plans; and
3. Promotions, compensation, or other rewards inconsistent with expectations.

Opportunities

Certain characteristics or circumstances may increase the susceptibility of assets to misappropriation. For example, opportunities to misappropriate assets increase when there are

1. Large amounts of cash on hand or processed;
2. Inventory items that are small in size, of high value, or in high demand;
3. Easily convertible assets, such as bearer bonds, diamonds, or computer chips; and
4. Fixed assets that are small in size, marketable, or lacking observable identification of ownership.

Inadequate internal control over assets may increase the susceptibility of misappropriation of those assets. For example, misappropriation of assets may occur because there are

1. Inadequate segregation of duties or independent checks;
2. Inadequate management oversight of employees responsible for assets (e.g, inadequate supervision or monitoring of remote locations);
3. Inadequate job applicant screening of employees with access to assets;
4. Inadequate recordkeeping of assets;
5. Inadequate system of authorization and approval of transactions (e.g., in purchasing);
6. Inadequate physical safeguards over cash, investments, inventory, or fixed assets;
7. Lack of complete and timely reconciliations of assets;
8. Lack of timely and appropriate documentation of transactions (e.g., credits for merchandise returns);
9. Lack of mandatory vacations for employees performing key control functions;
10. Inadequate management understanding of information technology, which enables information technology employees to perpetrate a misappropriation; and
11. Inadequate access controls over automated records, including controls over and review of computer systems event logs.

Attitudes/Rationalizations

Risk factors reflective of employee attitudes/rationalizations that allow them to justify misappropriations of assets are generally not susceptible to observation by the auditor. Nevertheless, the auditor who becomes aware of the existence of such information should consider it in identifying the risks of material misstatement arising from misappropriation of assets. For example, auditors may become aware of the following attitudes or behavior of employees who have access to assets susceptible to misappropriation:

1. Disregard for the need for monitoring or reducing risks related to misappropriations of assets.
2. Disregard for internal control over misappropriation of assets by overriding existing controls or by failing to correct known internal control deficiencies.
3. Behavior indicating displeasure or dissatisfaction with the company or its treatment of the employee.
4. Changes in behavior or lifestyle that may indicate assets have been misappropriated.

IDENTIFYING RISKS THAT MAY RESULT IN A MATERIAL MISSTATEMENT DUE TO FRAUD

The identification of a risk of material misstatement due to fraud involves consideration of the following:

1. The type of risk that can exist

   a. Fraudulent financial reporting, or
   b. Misappropriation of assets.

2. The magnitude/materiality of the risk.
3. The likelihood of the risk.
4. The pervasiveness of the risk

   a. Within the financial statements as a whole, or
   b. Relating to a particular assertion, account, or class of transactions.

ASSESSING IDENTIFIED RISKS

When obtaining an understanding of internal controls, the auditor should consider whether entity programs and controls to identify risks of material misstatement due to fraud are properly designed and operating.

RESPONDING TO THE RESULTS OF THE ASSESSMENT

The auditor should maintain an attitude of professional skepticism when obtaining and evaluating audit evidence. This includes

1. Designing additional or different auditing procedures to obtain more reliable evidence, and
2. Obtaining corroboration of management's representations and explanations.

If the auditor concludes that application of auditing procedures will not sufficiently address the risks of material misstatement due to fraud, the auditor should withdraw from the engagement.

For specifically identified risks, the auditor should change the nature, timing, and extent of auditing procedures. The auditor may obtain additional corroborative evidence. The auditor may modify the timing of substantive tests. For example, tests may be performed at or near the end of the reporting period. The auditor may increase the sample size or perform more detailed analytical procedures.

When considering the risk of misappropriation of assets, the auditor will usually focus on account balances more susceptible to misappropriation and potential misstatement. The auditor will also direct attention to the risk of management override of controls.

Journal entries and other adjustments often provide evidence of fraud. Financial statements may be materially misstated due to

1. Recording inappropriate or unauthorized journal entries, or
2. Making adjustments or reclassifying accounts on financial statements but not making associated journal entries.

Inappropriate or unauthorized journal entries and adjustments usually are

1. Made to unrelated or infrequently used accounts,
2. Made by unauthorized individuals, or
3. Recorded at the end of the period or as postclosing entries with little or no explanation or description.

The auditor also should review significant accounting estimates used in the prior year to determine whether management's estimates indicate potential bias. With the benefit of hindsight the auditor may be better able to assess potential management bias in making current-year estimates. If the auditor determines that management is potentially biased in making accounting estimates, the auditor should consider whether such a bias represents a risk of a material misstatement due to fraud.

The auditor should evaluate the rationale for significant or unusual transactions. Such analysis may indicate that management has entered into the transactions to engage in fraudulent financial reporting or conceal misappropriation of assets. The auditor should consider (AU 316.67)

1. Transactions that are overly complex,
2. Management's discussion for transactions with the audit committee or board of directors,
3. Management's selection of a particular accounting treatment without regard to the underlying economics of the transaction,
4. Transactions involving unconsolidated related parties, and
5. Transactions involving previously unidentified related parties.

EVALUATING AUDIT EVIDENCE

The auditor should assess the risks of material misstatement due to fraud throughout the audit. Auditor should consider (AU Section 316.68)

1. Discrepancies in the accounting records, including

    a. Transactions not recorded completely or timely.
    b. Unsupported or unauthorized balances or transactions.
    c. Last-minute adjustments that significantly affect financial results.
    d. Evidence of unauthorized access to systems and records.
    e. Tips or complaints about alleged fraud.

2. Conflicting or missing evidential matter, including

    a. Missing documents.
    b. Documents that appear to have been altered.

    c. Unavailability of other than photocopied or electronically transmitted documents when documents in original form are expected to exist.

    d. Significant unexplained items on reconciliations.

    e. Inconsistent, vague, or implausible responses from management or employees arising from inquiries or analytical procedures.

    f. Unusual discrepancies between the entity's records and confirmation replies.

    g. Missing inventory or physical assets of significant magnitude.

    h. Unavailable or missing electronic evidence, inconsistent with the entity's record retention practices or policies.

    i. Inability to produce evidence of key systems development and program change testing and implementation activities for current year system changes and deployments.

3. Problematic or unusual relationships between the auditor and management, including

    a. Denial of access to records, facilities, certain employees, customers, vendors, or others from whom audit evidence might be sought.

    b. Undue time pressures imposed by management to resolve complex or contentious issues.

    c. Complaints by management about the conduct of the audit or management intimidation of audit team members, particularly in connection with the auditor's critical assessment of audit evidence or in the resolution of potential disagreements with management.

    d. Unusual delays by the entity in providing requested information.

    e. Unwillingness to facilitate auditor access to key electronic files for testing through the use of computer-assisted audit techniques.

    f. Denial of access to key IT operations staff and facilities, including security, operations, and systems development personnel.

    g. An unwillingness to add or revise disclosures in the financial statements to make them more complete and transparent.

The auditor performs analytical procedures to identify unusual or unexpected relationships that may indicate a risk of material misstatement due to fraud. The auditor should also consider how management and others within the organization responded to inquiries about analytical relationships. Vague, implausible, or inconsistent responses may indicate that there is a potential problem.

If the auditor concludes that fraud-related misstatements exist, but the misstatements are not material to the financial statements, the auditor should evaluate the implications. The auditor would be especially concerned if the matter involves higher level management. This may be indicative of a more pervasive problem and has implications about the integrity of management.

If the auditor concludes that fraud-related misstatement exists and that its effect may be material, the auditor should (AU 316.77)

1. Attempt to obtain additional evidential matter to assess the likelihood of material fraud and its effect on the financial statements.

2. Consider the implications for other aspects of the audit.

3. Discuss the matter with management that is at least one level above those involved and with the audit committee.

4. Suggest that the client consult with legal counsel, if necessary.

COMMUNICATING ABOUT POSSIBLE FRAUD

If the auditor concludes that fraud may exist, the auditor should bring it to the attention of an appropriate level of management or audit committee, as necessary. The auditor should have an understanding with the audit committee about communicating misappropriations perpetrated by lower level employees.

If the auditor concludes that fraud-related risks of material misstatement have continuing control implications, the auditor should consider whether these risks represent reportable conditions that should be communicated to senior management and the audit committee. Generally, the auditor has no responsibility to, nor should the auditor, disclose possible fraud to parties other than the entity's senior management and its audit committee.

The auditor's ethical and legal responsibilities would ordinarily preclude the auditor from taking actions that involve parties other than the audit committee and senior management. The auditor may, however, disclose information to parties outside the entity under the following circumstances:

1. To comply with legal and regulatory requirements.
2. To a successor auditor when the successor makes inquiries in accordance with AU Section 315, *Communications between Predecessor and Successor Auditors.*
3. In response to a subpoena.
4. To a funding agency or other specified agency in accordance with requirements for the audits of entities that receive governmental financial assistance.

The auditor will probably want to consult with legal counsel before discussing such matters with parties outside the entity.

DOCUMENTING THE AUDITOR'S CONSIDERATION OF FRAUD

AU 316.83 requires the auditor to document the following:

1. Discussion among engagement personnel in planning the audit about the susceptibility to fraud, including

    a. How and when the discussion occurred,
    b. The audit team members who participated, and
    c. The subject matter discussed.

2. Procedures performed to obtain information necessary to identify and assess the risks of material misstatement due to fraud.
3. Specific risks of material misstatement identified and the auditor's response to those risks.
4. Risk of improper revenue recognition.
5. Results of procedures performed to address the risk of management override of controls.
6. Other conditions and analytical relationships leading to additional procedures.
7. Nature of fraud-related communication with the management, audit committee, and others.

317 ILLEGAL ACTS BY CLIENTS

SOURCE OF STANDARDS

SAS 54: *Illegal Acts by Clients*

See 9317 for interpretation of this section.

INTRODUCTION/SUMMARY

Illegal acts mean violations of laws or governmental regulations. Personal misconduct by the clients' personnel, misconduct that is unrelated to business activities, is not considered illegal acts in the context of AU Section 317. Illegal acts, within the context of AU Section 317, consist of acts by management or employees of the entity under audit acting on behalf of the entity.

Generally, an auditor lacks the professional competence to determine whether an act is illegal. An auditor's expertise is in accounting and auditing. While the auditor's training and experience may provide a reasonable basis for recognizing some acts by the client as illegal, the ultimate determination as to the legality of a particular act would generally require the advice of a lawyer or a determination by a court of law.

The auditor is more likely to recognize violations of laws and regulations that have a direct and material effect on the financial statements. AU Section 317.05 states

> *The auditor's responsibility to detect and report misstatements resulting from illegal acts having a direct and material effect on the determination of financial statement amounts is the same as that for misstatements caused by error or fraud as described in AU Section 110,* **Responsibilities and Functions of the Independent Auditor**.

Most entities are affected by a variety of laws or regulations including

1. Securities trading.
2. Occupational safety and health.
3. Food and drug administration.
4. Environmental protection.
5. Equal employment.
6. Price-fixing or other antitrust violations.

CONSIDERING THE POSSIBILITY OF ILLEGAL ACTS

Certain illegal acts have a direct and material effect on the financial statements. Other illegal acts may be regarded as having material but indirect effects on financial statements. An audit generally provides no assurance that illegal acts will be detected or contingent liabilities will be disclosed. However, if specific information comes to the auditor's attention concerning illegal acts that may have a material indirect effect on the financial statements, the auditor should apply procedures to ascertain whether an illegal act has occurred.

AUDIT PROCEDURES IN ABSENCE OF EVIDENCE OF POSSIBLE ILLEGAL ACTS

Generally, an audit does not include specific procedures to detect illegal acts. Nevertheless, the auditor should make inquiries of management about compliance with laws and regulations. The auditor should also obtain written representations from management concerning the absence of violations or possible violations of laws or regulations. The auditor should also inquire about

1. The entity's policies to prevent illegal acts, and
2. The directives issued by the client and representations obtained from management concerning compliance with laws and regulations.

SPECIFIC INFORMATION CONCERNING POSSIBLE ILLEGAL ACTS

When applying audit procedures, the auditor may come across specific information concerning possible illegal acts. AU 317.09 lists the following relevant items:

1. Unauthorized transactions, improperly recorded transactions, or transactions not recorded in a complete or timely manner in order to maintain accountability for assets.
2. Investigation by a governmental agency, an enforcement proceeding, or payment of unusual fines or penalties.
3. Violations of laws or regulations cited in reports of examinations by regulatory agencies that have been made available to the auditor.
4. Large payments for unspecified services to consultants, affiliates, or employees.
5. Sales commissions or agents' fees that appear excessive in relation to those normally paid by the client or to the services actually received.
6. Unusually large payments in cash, purchases of bank cashiers' checks in large amounts payable to bearer, transfers to numbered bank accounts, or similar transactions.
7. Unexplained payments made to government officials or employees.
8. Failure to file tax returns or pay government duties or similar fees that are common to the entity's industry or the nature of its business.

AUDIT PROCEDURES IN RESPONSE TO POSSIBLE ILLEGAL ACTS

Upon becoming aware of a possible illegal act, the auditor should attempt to obtain an understanding of the act, the circumstances surrounding it, and the potential effect on the financial statements. Inquires should be made of management at least one level above those involved. If management is unable to provide satisfactory answers, the auditor should consult with the client's legal counsel or other specialists knowledgeable about such matters.

The auditor should also consider applying some additional procedures.

1. Examining support documents, such as invoices, canceled checks, and agreements and comparing the amounts with accounting records.
2. Confirming the information concerning the possible illegal act with the other party to the transaction or with intermediaries, such as banks or lawyers.
3. Determining whether the transaction has been properly authorized.
4. Finding whether other similar transactions or events have occurred and ways to identify them.

THE AUDITOR'S CONSIDERATION OF FINANCIAL STATEMENT EFFECT

If the auditor concludes on the basis of evidence obtained as well as consultation with legal counsel that an illegal act has or is likely to have occurred, the auditor should consider the effect on the financial statements as well as the implications for other aspects of the audit.

Both qualitative and quantitative factors should be considered in evaluating the materiality of an illegal act. For example, AU 312.11, *Audit Risk and Materiality in Conducting an Audit*, states

> *An illegal payment of an otherwise immaterial amount could be material if there is a reasonable possibility that it could lead to a material contingent liability or a material loss of revenue.*

The auditor should consider the contingent effects of an illegal act in the financial statements, including fines and penalties. Loss contingencies resulting from illegal acts should be evaluated and reported like other loss contingencies.

COMMUNICATION WITH THE AUDIT COMMITTEE

The audit committee, or others with equivalent authority and responsibility, should be adequately informed about illegal acts that come to the auditor's attention. The auditor does not have responsibility to communicate matters that are obviously inconsequential to the audit committee. However, it would be prudent to reach an agreement with the audit committee about how small inconsequential items should be communicated.

If senior management is involved in an illegal act, the auditor should communicate directly with the audit committee. While the communication may be either oral or written, the auditor should document any oral communication. The communication with the audit committee should describe

1. The act.
2. The circumstances of its occurrence.
3. The effect on the financial statements.

Remedial actions taken by senior management should also be communicated to the audit committee. Possible remedial actions include

1. Disciplinary action against involved personnel.
2. Restitution.
3. Adoption of preventive or corrective policies and procedures.
4. Modifications of certain control activities.

EFFECT ON THE AUDITOR'S REPORT

If an illegal act has a material effect on the financial statements, the auditor should ask the management to adjust the financial statements or appropriately disclose the facts. If the illegal act is neither properly accounted for nor disclosed, the auditor should express, depending on the materiality, a qualified opinion or an adverse opinion on the financial statements. If there is some type of a client-restricted scope limitation and the auditor is unable to obtain sufficient evidential matter about possible material illegal acts, the auditor should generally disclaim an opinion.

The auditor should withdraw from the engagement if the client is unwilling to accept the auditor's modified report. When withdrawing from the engagement, the auditor should provide the reasons for withdrawal in writing to the audit committee or the board of directors. Withdrawal from the engagement may also be necessary when the client does not take remedial actions that the auditor considers necessary.

Generally, an auditor has no responsibility to disclose illegal acts to parties other than the client's senior management and its audit committee or board of directors. In general, unless the matter affects the auditor's opinion on the financial statements, disclosure of illegal acts to external parties is a violation of the auditor's ethical or legal obligation of confidentiality. AU 317.23 states that the auditor, in the following circumstances, has a duty to notify outside parties:

1. When the entity reports an auditor change under the appropriate securities law on Form 8-K.
2. To a successor auditor when the successor makes inquiries in accordance with AU Section 315, *Communications between Predecessor and Successor Auditors.*
3. In response to a subpoena.
4. To a funding agency or other specified agency in accordance with requirements for the audits of entities that receive financial assistance from a government agency.

It would be prudent for the auditor to consult legal counsel before disclosing or discussing illegal acts with parties outside the client.

RESPONSIBILITIES IN OTHER CIRCUMSTANCES

Sometimes an auditor may be involved in an engagement where it is accepted that the auditor has a responsibility for detecting illegal acts. A typical case would be audits of governmental units in accordance with the Single Audit Act of 1984. In that case the auditor tests and reports on the entity's compliance with certain laws and regulations.

Another case where the auditor may accept a greater responsibility for detecting illegal acts may be the rare engagement whereby a corporation's board of directors engages an auditor to apply agreed-upon procedures in order to report on compliance with the corporation's code of conduct.

318 PERFORMING AUDIT PROCEDURES IN RESPONSE TO ASSESSED RISKS AND EVALUATING THE AUDIT EVIDENCE OBTAINED

SOURCE OF STANDARDS

SAS 110, *Performing Audit Procedures in Response to Assessed Risks and Evaluating the Audit Evidence Obtained*

INTRODUCTION/SUMMARY

The auditor is required to assess the risk of material misstatement (RMM) according to SAS 107, *Audit Risk and Materiality in Conducting an Audit*. RMM is the auditor's combined assessment of inherent risk and control risk. Auditors are required to perform audit procedures to respond to assessed RMM.

OVERALL RESPONSES

The auditor's assessment of RMM is affected by the auditor's understanding of the control environment. An effective control environment allows the auditor to have greater confidence about the reliability of internally generated audit evidence. This allows the auditor, for instance, to perform tests at interim date rather than at period end.

The auditor's overall responses to the assessed RMM include

1. Maintaining professional skepticism in gathering and evaluating audit evidence.
2. Assigning more experienced staff.
3. Using specialists.
4. Greater supervision of staff.
5. Element of unpredictability in selection of further audit procedures.
6. Changes in nature, timing, and extent of further audit procedures.
7. Increase the number of locations to be included in the audit scope.

The effectiveness of the control environment has a significant bearing on whether the auditor will employ a primarily substantive approach or a combined approach that uses tests of controls as well as substantive procedures.

AUDIT PROCEDURES RESPONSIVE TO RISKS OF MATERIAL MISSTATEMENT AT THE RELEVANT ASSERTION LEVEL

There should be a clear linkage between audit procedures and the risk of material misstatement at the relevant assertion level for each class of transactions, account balance, and disclosure. The higher the auditor's assessment of risk, the more reliable and relevant the evidence must be to satisfy the auditor's objectives. Evidence about the accuracy and completeness of data generated by the entity's information system should be obtained.

Tests of controls or substantive procedures may be performed at an interim date or at period end. The higher the RMM, the more likely it is that the auditor will perform the procedures at the end of period or at unpredictable/unannounced times. Certain procedures may only be performed at or after the period end date.

The extent or quantity of audit procedures is determined by the auditor's judgment. The auditor should consider the assessed risk of material misstatement, the tolerable misstatement, and the degree of assurance desired. Generally, sampling is used to achieve audit objectives.

Tests of controls should be performed if controls are expected to be effective in preventing or detecting a material misstatement in a relevant assertion. When testing controls, the auditor should obtain evidence about how controls were applied at relevant times during the period under audit. If substantially different controls were used at various times, the auditor should consider each time period separately.

Tests of controls may be designed to be performed concurrently with test of details. When performing these dual-purpose tests, the auditor should consider how the outcome of the test of controls may affect the extent of substantive procedures to be performed.

If misstatements are not identified by a substantive procedure, the auditor cannot conclude that controls related to relevant assertion being tested are effective. A material misstatement that is detected by the auditors, but not identified by the entity, should be considered as at least a significant deficiency. It may also be a strong indicator of a material weakness in internal controls that should be communicated to management.

When evidence about the operating effectiveness of controls is obtained during an interim period, consideration should be given to what further evidence is needed for the remaining period. If the auditor plans to use audit evidence about the effectiveness of controls that was obtained in a prior period, the auditor should evaluate whether changes have occurred subsequent to the prior audit. If the auditor plans to rely on controls that have changed since last tested, the auditor should test the effectiveness of the controls in the current audit.

If the controls have not changed since the last audit, the auditor should plan on testing the operating effectiveness of such controls once in every third year in an annual audit. As a rule, the higher the risk of material misstatement, or the greater the reliance auditor plans on placing on the internal control, the shorter the time elapsed between testing the effectiveness of controls.

The more the auditor plans on relying on the operating effectiveness of controls, the more the auditor should increase the extent of test of controls. The auditor should also increase the extent of testing of controls as the rate of expected deviation increases. In some instances the expected rate of deviation may be too high to obtain evidence that will sufficiently reduce the control risk. Tests of controls would then be inappropriate.

IT processing is inherently consistent and will operate consistently unless program modifications are made. In such instances the auditor may be able to limit testing to a few control operations. Once the auditor determines that automated controls are working effectively, the auditor should perform tests to determine that the controls continue to work as intended, especially if changes are made to the program.

SUBSTANTIVE PROCEDURES

Substantive procedures include tests of details of classes of transactions, account balances, disclosures, and substantive analytical procedures. Substantive procedures are used to detect material misstatements at the relevant assertion level.

The auditor should design and perform substantive procedures for all relevant assertions regardless of assessed risk of material misstatement, since the auditor's assessment is judgmental. Moreover internal controls have inherent limitations such as management override of controls.

The auditor's substantive procedure should consist of agreeing financial statements to the underlying accounting records. The auditor should also examine material journal entries and adjustments made while preparing the financial statements. The nature and complexity of the entity's financial reporting system and the associated risk of material misstatement will influence auditor's examination of journal entries and other adjustments.

The auditor should perform specific substantive procedures to address any significant assessed risk of material misstatement at the relevant assertion level. Substantive analytical procedures are generally appropriate when there is a large volume of predictable transactions. Tests of details are generally used to obtain evidence about account balances, including the existence and valuation assertion.

The auditor should consider the following when designing substantive analytical procedures (AU 318.57):

1. The suitability of using substantive analytical procedures for a given assertion.
2. The reliability of other internal and external data that may be used to determine expectations about recorded amounts or ratios.
3. The possibility of identifying material misstatement at a required level of assurance.
4. The acceptable level of differences in recorded amounts and expected value.

In many instances substantive procedures are performed at an interim date. Then the auditor should perform additional substantive tests to cover the remaining period. Performing substantive procedures at an interim date increases the risk that misstatements may remain unidentified at period end. If the auditor has identified risks of misstatement due to fraud, the auditor may address those risks by changing the timing of audit procedures.

Audit evidence from prior period substantive procedures provides little or no evidence for the current period audit. Performance of substantive procedures in a prior period audit and the evidence gathered from such procedures is therefore not considered sufficient to reduce detection risk to an acceptably low level for the current period.

Coordination of the timing of audit procedures is important. For instance, audit procedures may need to be coordinated for related-party transactions and balances. Or, audit procedures over readily negotiable assets are coordinated with procedures related to cash, bank accounts, and loans.

ADEQUACY OF PRESENTATION AND DISCLOSURE

The auditor should evaluate whether the financial statements are presented appropriately. This includes appropriate classification and description of information in conformity with generally accepted accounting principles. The auditor should consider whether management has disclosed all information as appropriate for the audit.

EVALUATING THE SUFFICIENCY AND APPROPRIATENESS OF THE AUDIT EVIDENCE OBTAINED

The audit of financial statements is a cumulative and iterative process. The auditor should evaluate the risk of material misstatement after performing audit procedures. This may result in the auditor obtaining additional evidence or in modifying the timing, nature, or extent of further audit procedures. AU 318.75 describes the following factors as affecting the sufficiency and appropriateness of audit evidence:

1. Significance of the potential misstatement in the relevant assertion and the likelihood of its having a material effect, individually or aggregated with other potential misstatements, on the financial statements.
2. Effectiveness of management's responses and controls to address the risks.
3. Experience gained during previous audits with respect to similar potential misstatements.
4. Results of audit procedures performed, including whether such audit procedures identified specific instances of fraud or error.
5. Source and reliability of available information.
6. Persuasiveness of the audit evidence.
7. Understanding of the entity and its environment, including its internal control.

If the auditor believes that sufficient appropriate evidence has not been obtained with respect to a material financial statement assertion, the auditor should obtain additional evidence. If it is not possible to obtain additional evidence, then the auditor should express a qualified opinion or a disclaimer of opinion.

AU 318.77 specifies the following documentation requirements:

1. The overall responses to address the assessed risks of misstatement at the financial statement level.
2. The nature, timing, and extent of the further audit procedures.
3. The linkage of those procedures with the assessed risks at the relevant assertion level.
4. The results of the audit procedures.
5. The conclusions reached with regard to the use in the current audit of audit evidence about the operating effectiveness of controls that was obtained in a prior audit.

APPENDIX

ILLUSTRATIVE FINANCIAL STATEMENT ASSERTIONS AND EXAMPLES OF SUBSTANTIVE PROCEDURES ILLUSTRATIONS FOR INVENTORIES OF A MANUFACTURING COMPANY

This appendix from SAS 110 illustrates the use of assertions in designing substantive procedures. It does not illustrate tests of controls. The illustrated examples are not intended to be all-inclusive, nor are they expected to illustrate all of the procedures that would be applied in an audit.

Illustrative assertions about account balances	*Examples of substantive procedures*
Existence	
Inventories included in the balance sheet physically exist.	• Physical examination of inventory items. • Obtaining confirmation of inventories at locations outside the entity. • Inspection of documents relating to inventory transactions between a physical inventory date and the balance sheet date.
Inventories represent items held for sale or use in the normal course of business.	• Inspecting perpetual inventory records, production records, and purchasing records for indications of current activity. • Reconciling items in the inventory listing to a current computer-maintained sales catalog and subsequent sales and delivery reports using computer-assisted audit techniques (CAATs). • Inquiry of production and sales personnel. • Using the work of specialists to corroborate the nature of specialized products.
Rights and Obligations	
The entity has legal title or similar rights of ownership to the inventories.	• Examining paid vendors' invoices, consignment agreements, and contracts. • Obtaining confirmation of inventories at locations outside the entity.
Inventories exclude items billed to customers or owned by others.	• Examining paid vendors' invoices, consignment agreements, and contracts. • Inspecting shipping and receiving transactions near year-end for recording in the proper period.
Completeness	
Inventory quantities include all products, materials, and supplies on hand.	• Observing physical inventory counts. • Analytically comparing the relationship of inventory balances to recent purchasing, production, and sales activities. • Inspecting shipping and receiving transactions near year-end for recording in the proper period.

Illustrative assertions about account balances	*Examples of substantive procedures*

Completeness

Inventory quantities include all products, materials, and supplies owned by the company that are in transit or stored at outside locations.

- Obtaining confirmation of inventories at locations outside the entity.
- Analytically comparing the relationship of inventory balances to recent purchasing, production, and sales activities.

Inventory listings are accurately compiled and the totals are properly included in the inventory accounts.

- Inspecting shipping and receiving transactions near year-end for recording in the proper period.
- Examining the inventory listing for inclusion of test counts recorded during the physical inventory observation.
- Reconciliation of all inventory tags and count sheets used in recording the physical inventory counts using CAATs.
- Recalculation of inventory listing for clerical accuracy using CAATs.
- Reconciling physical counts to perpetual records and general ledger balances and investigating significant fluctuations using CAATs.

Valuation and Allocation

Inventories are properly stated at cost (except when market is lower).

- Examining paid vendors' invoices and comparing product prices to standard cost buildups.
- Analytically comparing direct labor rates to production records.
- Recalculation of the computation of standard overhead rates.
- Examining analyses of purchasing and manufacturing standard cost variances.

Slow-moving, excess, defective, and obsolete items included in inventories are properly identified.

- Examining an analysis of inventory turnover.
- Analyzing industry experience and trends.
- Analytically comparing the relationship of inventory balances to anticipated sales volume.
- Walk-through of the plant for indications of products not being used.
- Inquiring of production and sales personnel concerning possible excess, or defective or obsolete inventory items.
- Logistic and distribution business process (e.g., cycle time, volume of returns, or problems with suppliers).

Inventories are reduced, when appropriate, to replacement cost or net realizable value.

- Inspecting sales catalogs or industry publications for current market value quotations.
- Recalculation of inventory valuation reserves.
- Analyzing current production costs.
- Examining sales after year-end and open purchase order commitments.

Illustrative assertions about presentation and disclosure	*Examples of substantive procedures*

Rights and Obligations

The pledge or assignment of any inventories is appropriately disclosed.

- Obtaining confirmation of inventories pledged under loan agreements.

Completeness

The financial statements include all disclosures related to inventories specified by generally accepted accounting principles.

- Using a disclosure checklist to determine whether the disclosures included in generally accepted accounting principles were made.

Understandability

Inventories are properly classified in the balance sheet as current assets.

- Examining drafts of the financial statements for appropriate balance sheet classification.

Disclosures related to inventories are understandable.

- Reading disclosures for clarity.

Accuracy and Valuation

The major categories of inventories and their bases of valuation are accurately disclosed in the financial statements.

- Examining drafts of the financial statements for appropriate disclosures.
- Reconciling the categories of inventories disclosed in the draft financial statements to the categories recorded during the physical inventory observation.

319 UNDERSTANDING THE ENTITY AND ITS ENVIRONMENT AND ASSESSING THE RISKS OF MATERIAL MISSTATEMENT

INTRODUCTION/SUMMARY

The second standard of fieldwork specifically requires the auditor to obtain an understanding of the entity's internal controls sufficient to plan the audit. The second standard of fieldwork states

> *The auditor must obtain a sufficient understanding of the entity and its environment, including its internal control, to assess the risk of material misstatement of the financial statements whether due to error or fraud, and to design the nature, timing, and extent of further audit procedures.*

The auditor is required to perform audit procedures to obtain an understanding of the entity, its environment, and its internal controls. The auditor uses this understanding to identify and assess risk of material misstatement and in performing audit procedures. Obtaining an understanding of the entity and its environment is a continuous ongoing process of gathering, updating and analyzing information.

RISK ASSESSMENT PROCEDURES

To obtain an understanding of the entity and its environment, the auditor is required to perform risk assessment procedures. These include

1. Inquiries of management and others within the entity.
2. Analytical procedures.
3. Observation and inspection.

Understanding the following factors will help the auditor understand the entity and its environment:

1. Industry, regulatory, and other external factors.
2. Nature of the entity.
3. Objectives and strategies and the related business risks that may result in a material misstatement of the financial statements.
4. Measurement and review of the entity's financial performance.
5. Internal control, which includes the selection and application of accounting policies.

Auditor is not permitted to simply assess control risk at "maximum" without support; instead, auditor must perform risk assessment procedures to support the risk assessment. The auditor will typically inquire of those outside the organization, such as external legal counsel, and obtain and review information from sources such as banks, rating agencies, and trade journals.

The auditor should apply analytical procedures to assist in planning the audit and to identify high risk areas. Analytical procedures may uncover unusual transactions or amounts or trends.

Inquiries of management and others may be supported by audit procedures such as

1. Observation and inspection of entity's activities and operations.
2. Inspection of documents, records and internal control manuals.
3. Reading minutes of board of directors' meetings.
4. Reading reports prepared by management.
5. Visiting entity's facilities and plants.
6. Performing a walkthrough, including tracing transactions through the entity's information system.

The auditor may use information about the entity and its environment that was obtained in a prior period audit. Under such circumstances the auditor should determine whether changes have occurred and the effect of those changes and their relevance.

The auditor should explicitly assess the risk of material misstatement due to fraud. Fraud risk factors may be due to either fraudulent financial reporting or misappropriation of assets.

DISCUSSION AMONG THE AUDIT TEAM

The engagement team should discuss the susceptibility of the financial statements to material misstatement. This discussion should be part of the planning process and should be documented. Generally, it would be efficient for this discussion to occur concurrently with discussion about fraud risk as required by SAS 99. In multilocation audits, multiple discussions may take place with key members of the audit team.

The aim of the discussion is to provide more experienced team members an opportunity to share their insights with others on the team. The discussion should emphasize the need to exercise professional skepticism. Auditor should be alert to conditions that may indicate a material misstatement. The auditor should also be rigorous in following up on such indications.

UNDERSTANDING THE ENTITY AND ITS ENVIRONMENT

The auditor should obtain an understanding of the entity and its environment by considering both the external industry and regulatory controls and the internal company measurement and controls of financial performance.

Industry, Regulatory, and Other External Factors

Auditor should consider industry conditions such as the competitive environment, technological developments, use of long-term contracts, and regulatory environment. Auditor should understand the nature of the entity's operations, ownership and capital structure, and governance. An entity with a complex structure may have several subsidiaries in multiple locations. There may be issues concerning allocation of goodwill or its impairment.

Objectives and Strategies

The auditor should understand the objective and strategies of the entity, including business risks that may result in material misstatement of the financial statements. Objectives are the overall plans for the entity and strategies are the operational approaches used to achieve its objectives.

While the auditor is expected to understand the business risk, the auditor does not have a responsibility to identify all business risks. Business risk has financial consequences; however, not all business risk will give rise to the risk of material misstatement.

Smaller entities may not formally set their objective and strategies, or manage business risk. Under such circumstances the auditor will obtain an understanding primarily through inquiries of management and by observation.

Measurement and Review of Financial Performance

Auditors should obtain an understanding of an entity's performance measures. Performance measures may motivate the management to take actions to misstate financial statements.

Internal Control

The auditor should obtain an understanding of the five components of internal control to identify potential misstatements, and design test of controls and substantive procedures. This understanding of internal controls consists of five components.

1. The *control environment* sets the tone for the entity as a whole and is the foundation for all other components of internal controls.
2. *Risk assessment* involves identifying and analyzing relevant risk so that the entity's objectives may be achieved.
3. *Control activities* are the policies and procedures that are used to ensure that the management's directives are carried out.
4. The *information and communication* component is used to identify, collect, and exchange relevant data to enable the entity to carry out its activities.
5. The *monitoring* component is used to assess and evaluate the quality of internal controls.

The control environment is the base or foundation for all other components. The entity's objectives are attained through risk assessment and control activities. Information needed to attain the entity's objectives is communicated throughout the entity, and the entire process is monitored.

The division of controls into the five components is a conceptual model that facilitates understanding. From the auditor's perspective, the model is useful in determining which specific aspects affect financial statement assertions, and therefore the auditor's ability to form judgments about those assertions.

This understanding should be documented by describing the design of the controls relevant to financial statement audit and assessing whether the controls are functioning as intended. The auditor needs to assess the level of control risk and document the findings. In a financial audit, control risk is the risk that internal controls will not prevent or detect material misstatements in the financial statements. This risk directly affects the scope of the auditor's work.

When assessing control risk, the auditor is most concerned with controls that affect the reliability of financial statements. However, other controls are also frequently relevant to an audit. For instance, controls that affect an entity's compliance with governmental regulations may be relevant to the audit if failure to comply could have a direct and material effect on the financial statements. Often controls to safeguard assets also meet both reporting and operational objectives. The auditor's consideration of controls in such a situation is often limited to controls that are relevant to reliable financial reporting. Controls concerned with excessive usage or wastage may not be relevant for a financial auditor. Most controls relating to operational efficiency or effectiveness of managerial decision making are not relevant to an audit and generally will not be included in the auditor's assessment of control risk.

There are inherent limitations to the effectiveness of internal control. Several factors may reduce or eliminate the effectiveness of internal controls including

1. Human error or mistakes in judgment,
2. Collusion among individuals, and
3. Management's override of controls.

Internal controls are affected by both quantitative and qualitative estimates. They are also affected by judgments made by management about the cost–benefit relationship of an entity's controls. The cost of an entity's internal control should not exceed the benefits that are expected to be derived.

While the cost–benefit relationship should be considered in designing internal controls, it is frequently impossible to precisely and accurately measure the costs and benefits associated with controls. In light of the inherent limitations as well as cost–benefit considerations, internal controls are meant to provide reasonable, but not absolute assurance that the objectives of the controls will be met.

INTERNAL CONTROL COMPONENTS

CONTROL ENVIRONMENT

The control environment sets the tone of an organization, influencing the control consciousness of its people. Control environment is the foundation for all other components of internal control, providing discipline and structure. The auditor should consider the collective effect on the control environment of strengths and weaknesses in various control environment factors. The control environment may be seen as an umbrella that covers risk assessment, control activities, information and communication, and monitoring.

An organization's top management can create an environment that encourages its employees to be control conscious. This in turn enhances the quality of other internal control components. Conversely, the effectiveness of controls may be reduced and the risk of fraud increased with a poor control environment. Knowledge about the control environment gives the auditor insight into the management's and board of directors' attitudes toward internal controls.

When evaluating the controls, the auditor should concentrate on the substance of the controls rather than their form; controls established by the management may not be followed or acted upon. The control environment is the foundation for all other components of internal control. Control environment factors include the following:

1. Integrity and ethical values.
2. Commitment to competence
3. Board of directors or audit committee participation.
4. Management's philosophy and operating style.
5. Organizational structure.
6. Assignment of authority and responsibility.
7. Human resource policies and practices.

Integrity and Ethical Values

The effectiveness of internal controls is directly affected by the integrity and ethical values of the individuals who create, administer, and monitor the controls. If the management establishes ethical standards, communicates them to the employees, and leads by its own example, it will create an environment that is conducive to ethical behavior.

Commitment to Competence

Competence refers to the knowledge and skills required to accomplish an individual's job responsibilities. If employees are not competent, they will not know what is expected of them and will not be able to carry out their tasks. Their work quality will suffer because they are more likely to make mistakes. Controls may not be followed simply because employees may not understand what is expected of them. Competent employees are committed to quality. Management can enhance quality by hiring employees capable of performing their duties and by providing employees with appropriate training.

Board of Directors or Audit Committee Participation

The oversight function of the board of directors and audit committees is a critical factor in the control environment. An effective board and audit committee would decrease the possibility of management overriding internal controls. It reduces the likelihood of management engaging in illegal acts, misappropriating resources, or engaging in other activities exposing the entity to unwarranted risks. An effective board is independent of management and actively scrutinizes management's activities. The board should not shy from asking management difficult questions.

The presence of an audit committee is an especially important factor in the control environment. Audit committees serve as a direct link between the board and the external as well as internal auditors. This allows auditors and board members to discuss matters concerning the integrity of management and other similar issues. Presence of the audit committee is a sign that the board is monitoring management activities.

Management's Philosophy and Operating Style

Management, through its actions, can signal to employees about the importance or lack of importance of internal controls. For instance, management can set unrealistic financial targets and encourage employees to take aggressive actions to meet those targets.

Organizational Structure

Key areas of responsibility and authority are defined by the organizational structure. It provides a framework for planning, executing, controlling, and monitoring operations.

Assignment of Authority and Responsibility

Authority and responsibility for operating activities are usually assigned by following business practice policies on the delegation of authority and responsibilities, and reporting relationships and authorization hierarchies.

Human Resource Policies and Practices

The quality of internal control is directly affected by the quality of personnel. An organization should have policies and procedures for hiring, training, and evaluating employees. There should be a sufficient number of employees, and the employees should have the resources to adequately carry out their responsibilities.

RISK ASSESSMENT

Risk assessment is the entity's identification and analysis of relevant risks to the achievement of its objectives. Management's risk assessment forms a basis for determining how the risks should be managed.

All entities encounter a variety of risks. Management must determine what types of risks to take and what steps need to be taken to contain those risks. From a financial reporting perspective, there are business risks concerning an entity's ability to record, process, summarize, and report financial data consistent with management assertions in the financial statements.

Common factors that can affect an entity's business risk include

1. Changes in accounting principles or new pronouncements.
2. Significant changes to the entity's information systems.
3. Significant changes in personnel.
4. Corporate restructuring.
5. Significant expansion into new areas or product lines or acquisition of foreign operation.
6. Changes in regulatory environment.
7. Changes in operating environment, such as increased competition from major competitors.

The auditor's assessment of risk is distinct from management's risk assessment. The auditor is primarily concerned about the risk of issuing an inappropriate opinion on the entity's financial statement. As part of auditor's risk assessment, the auditor should consider how management

1. Estimates the various business risks,
2. Evaluates the likelihood that the risk will occur, and
3. Takes actions to address these risks.

It is acceptable if management determines not to take any action to address an identified risk. In some instances the cost to avoid the risk may not be worth the expense associated with the risk.

CONTROL ACTIVITIES

Control activities are policies and procedures that are used to ensure that the management's directives are carried out. In other words, control activities policies and procedures are used to ensure that necessary actions are taken to address the risks involved in achieving the entity's objectives.

Control activities may be automated or manual. The objectives may be at organizational or functional levels. Audit-related control activities may be classified into the following categories:

1. Performance reviews.
2. Information processing.
3. Physical controls.
4. Segregation of duties.

Performance review controls check the performance of individuals or processes in a system. For instance, actual performance may be compared with budgeted or forecasted performance. Unusual relationships between financial and operating data may also be analyzed.

Information processing controls are used to ensure the accuracy, completeness, and authorization of transactions. There are two broad categories of information processing controls: general controls and application controls. General controls affect the overall control environment. They also include controls over data and network centers. Controls over software development, acquisition, and maintenance are also classified as general controls.

Application controls are specific to a computer program or application. Application controls typically consist of controls over data input, processing, and output. These controls are concerned with validity, completeness, and valuation of internal control objectives.

Application controls may be incorporated in an IT system or performed by individuals. When application controls are performed by individuals, they are referred to as user controls. The efficacy of user controls depends on both the accuracy of the information produced and the effectiveness of the individual review of the information.

Physical controls are used to physically secure assets. This includes having secure facilities where assets are stored, or limiting access to computer programs and data files. Segregation of duties controls requires separating three functions.

1. Authorization of transactions.
2. Recording of transactions.
3. Custody of assets.

Independent check of these functions enhances accountability and reduces the possibility of misappropriation of assets. The use of IT affects the way that control activities are implemented. For instance, in an IT-based information system, segregation of duties often is achieved by implementing security controls. For this reason, it is necessary to separate IT (information technology) duties from the user departments. In an IT environment, the traditional separation of the three functions is not possible or even necessary. The computer program can play a significant role in the authorization and recording of transactions.

INFORMATION AND COMMUNICATION

Information and communication systems support the identification, capture, and exchange of information in a form and time frame that enable people to carry out their responsibilities. The accounting system is one part of the information system relevant to financial reporting objectives. The accounting system, whether automated or manual, is used to capture transactions data, including events and conditions. The quality of the information system significantly affects management's ability to prepare reliable financial reports. It also affects management's ability to take appropriate action to control the entity's activities. Communication involves developing an understanding of roles and responsibilities with respect to internal controls over financial reporting.

The auditor must obtain an understanding of the information system with respect to financial reporting objectives. In particular, the auditor must understand the following:

1. The classes of transactions in the entity's operations which are significant to the financial statements.
2. The procedures, both automated and manual, by which transactions are initiated, recorded, processed, and reported from their occurrence to their inclusion in the financial statements.
3. The related accounting records, whether electronic or manual, supporting information, and specific accounts in the financial statements involved in initiating, recording, processing, and reporting transactions.
4. How the information system captures other events and conditions that are significant to the financial statements.
5. The financial reporting process used to prepare the entity's financial statements, including significant accounting estimates and disclosures.

The auditor should understand the procedures an entity uses to prepare financial statements and related disclosures, including an understanding of how misstatements may occur. This includes the following procedures:

Procedures used to enter transaction totals into the general ledger

1. An IT system can, for instance, automatically transfer information from transaction processing systems to general ledger or financial reporting systems.
2. Automated processes and controls may be used in IT systems to reduce the risk of error, but such controls may not prevent an individual from inappropriately overriding the controls.
3. Without an adequate audit trail being maintained by the IT system, there may be little or no visible evidence of inappropriate intervention.

Procedures used to initiate, record, and process journal entries in the general ledger

1. Journal entries that are required on a recurring basis such as sale, purchase, and cash disbursement transactions.
2. Recording accounting estimates made by management such as changes in the estimate of uncollectible accounts receivable.
3. The use of nonstandard journal entries to record infrequent or unusual transactions, such as business combinations.

Other procedures used to record recurring and nonrecurring adjustments to the financial statements

1. Other procedures, such as consolidating adjustments, report combinations, and reclassifications that are not part of the formal journal entries.

MONITORING

Monitoring is a process that assesses the quality of internal control performance over time. Monitoring involves assessing the design and operation of the controls. Management needs to monitor controls to know whether the controls are operating as intended. If warranted, controls should be modified as circumstances change. In addition to management, the internal auditors and other personnel with the organization are frequently involved in monitoring. For example, customer service representative handling complaints from customers may be able to provide feedback about problems or illustrate areas in need of improvement.

The independent auditor needs to obtain sufficient knowledge of the major activities the entity uses to monitor internal control over financial reporting.

Discussion with management is an important way to obtain information about the types of monitoring activities an entity uses, and how those activities are used to modify internal controls when required.

In particular, the external auditor should consider the effects of the internal audit function when auditing financial statements. The internal audit department, especially for larger organizations, is critical for effective monitoring. The internal audit department must be independent of both the operating and accounting departments, and it should report to the highest level within the organization, ideally to either top management or the audit committee of the board of directors.

APPLICATION OF THE INTERNAL CONTROL
COMPONENTS TO SMALL AND MIDSIZED ENTITIES

The five components of internal control are applicable to entities of all sizes. However, the way they are configured within an entity depend on several factors including

1. The entity's size.
2. The entity's organization and ownership characteristics.
3. The nature of the entity's business.
4. The diversity and complexity of operations.
5. The entity's legal and regulatory environment.
6. The nature and complexity of the systems, including the use of service organizations.

Small and midsized entities may implement the internal control components differently than larger entities. For instance, the control environment may emphasize integrity and ethical behavior through oral means or by example, rather than through a written formal code of conduct. Smaller organization also may not have any independent or outside members on the board of directors.

The risk assessment process at a smaller entity is likely to be less formal and less structured For example, the financial reporting objective may not be formally established, but rather implicitly recognized in smaller organizations. Direct personal involvement by management with employees and others is likely to be a prime source of risk assessment information.

Similar to risk assessment, control activities tend to be less formal in smaller entities. Moreover certain types of control activities may not be relevant in smaller entities. For instance, management might retain the authority for approving credit, authorizing significant purchases, and other material activities. This can provide strong control over those activities without necessitating more detailed control activities. Appropriate segregation of duties is often more difficult in smaller organizations. Smaller companies should still make an attempt to segregate duties. However, if that is not possible, management/owners should play an active role in performing or overseeing incompatible activities to minimize negative effects and achieve control objectives.

Information systems in small or midsized organizations are also likely to be less formal than in larger organizations. Their value to the company, however, is just as significant. Smaller entities may not have extensive descriptions of accounting procedures or written policies. Communication channels may be less formal and information will go through fewer levels. In most instances, management presence will be greater.

Monitoring activities of smaller entities is also more likely to be informal. This function may normally be performed as a part of the overall management of the entity's operations. Management's direct involvement in operations often will be important in identifying significant variances from expectations and errors or inaccuracies in the financial data.

EFFECT OF INFORMATION TECHNOLOGY ON INTERNAL CONTROL

The use of IT can enhance internal controls by replacing manual controls, which are subject to human error, with automated controls, which may be processed consistently. The use of IT can also create new risks unique to an electronic environment. Almost every entity, including the smallest of businesses, now uses a computerized accounting system. Computers can sometimes give auditors false confidence. Auditors may mistakenly assume that because the information was generated through a computer, it must be accurate. Reliance on untested computer programs can be dangerous. Auditors must realize that computers are programmed by individuals. There may be unintentional programming errors or intentional unauthorized modifications to the computer program. Such errors or mistakes tend to be material because computers will process transactions, whether correct or incorrect, on a consistent basis.

All five components of internal control may be affected by the use of IT. The use of IT has an effect on how transactions are initiated, recorded, processed and reported. Controls in an IT environment often consist of a combination of automated and manual controls. Manual controls may

1. Be independent of IT controls.
2. Rely on information produced by IT controls.
3. Be limited to monitoring the effective functioning of IT controls, and to handle exceptions.

Most entities will have a mix of manual and automated controls consistent with the nature and complexity of the entity's IT environment. IT provides potential benefits of effectiveness and efficiency for an entity's internal control because it enables an entity to

1. Consistently apply predefined business rules and perform complex calculations in processing large volumes of transactions or data;
2. Enhance the timeliness, availability, and accuracy of information;
3. Facilitate the additional analysis of information;
4. Enhance the ability to monitor the performance of the entity's activities and its policies and procedures;
5. Reduce the risk that controls will be circumvented; and
6. Enhance the ability to achieve effective segregation of duties by implementing security controls in applications, databases, and operating systems.

IT poses specific risks to an entity's internal control, including

1. Reliance on systems or programs that are inaccurately processing data, processing inaccurate data, or both;
2. Unauthorized access to data that may result in destruction of data or improper changes to data, including the recording of unauthorized or nonexistent transactions or inaccurate recording of transactions;
3. Unauthorized changes to data in master files;
4. Unauthorized changes to systems or programs;
5. Failure to make necessary changes to systems or programs;
6. Inappropriate manual intervention; and
7. Potential loss of data.

DEVELOPING AN UNDERSTANDING OF INTERNAL CONTROLS

Auditors are required to obtain a sufficient understanding of an entity's internal controls for planning purposes. A sufficient understanding enables the auditor to

1. Determine whether the controls are effectively designed.
2. Identify misstatements that may occur because of design weaknesses.
3. Consider the risk associated with misstatements.
4. Design substantive tests to detect misstatements.

In developing the understanding, the auditor evaluates the design of relevant controls and whether they are being utilized. The auditor needs to determine how the controls are supposed to operate and whether the entity has actually placed them in operation. The aim of the auditor is to be able to restrict substantive testing by relying on certain relevant controls.

The understanding of internal controls required for planning is obtained through a variety of actions, including

1. Reviewing prior years' working papers for continuing engagements,
2. Updating and evaluating the auditor's prior experience with the entity,

3. Reading documentation concerning policies and procedures,
4. Examining documents and records,
5. Making inquiries of entity's personnel,
6. Observing personnel in the performance of their duties, and
7. Performing a "walk-through" of a few transactions.

Except for the initial audit, the auditor has a wealth of information obtained from previous audits. Generally, systems and controls do not change significantly from year to year. This allows the auditor to simply update and carry the information into the current working papers. Reviewing prior years' working papers can greatly help the auditor in assessing the likelihood of material misstatements in current year's financial statements. In the absence of a change, control weaknesses from the prior year are likely to continue in the current year. Similarly, if controls were found to be effective last year and there have not been significant changes in personnel or procedures, this gives the auditor considerable information in planning substantive tests for the current year.

Most large entities have extensive written policies and procedures. This includes items such as organizational chart, accounting manual, systems manual, and corporate code of ethics and conduct. Auditors will read this information and discuss issues with the entity's personnel to ensure a complete and accurate understanding.

Examining documents and records, both in paper and electronic form, can provide the auditor with a better understanding of the entity's controls, as well as provide evidence about control policies and procedures that have been placed in operation. The auditor should also observe entity activities and operation and perform a walk-through of at least a few transactions. The auditor should observe the entity's personnel in the performance of their duties.

EVALUATING INTERNAL CONTROL DESIGN EFFECTIVENESS

After obtaining an understanding of the controls, the auditor evaluates the effectiveness of the design to assess whether the controls, if operating as intended, will achieve the control objectives. In other words, are controls designed to ensure that transactions are authorized and processed completely and recorded accurately, and that assets are protected.

DOCUMENTING THE UNDERSTANDING OF INTERNAL CONTROLS

The understanding of the internal controls may be documented in the form of questionnaires, narratives, and flowcharts. Auditors generally will not use both narratives and flowcharts to document the same internal control system. Narratives and flowcharts are both intended to describe the flow of documents and records in an accounting system. In some instances, however, the auditor may feel that a combination is best. The decision to use one or the other or a combination of both is based primarily on the relative cost of preparation and the ease of documenting the understanding in the current and subsequent years.

INTERNAL CONTROL QUESTIONNAIRES

Internal control questionnaires are the most efficient means of gathering information about the controls. A series of questions about the controls in each audit area is listed. The questions may be open- or close-ended.

Generally, the close-ended questions elicit a "yes" or "no" response, where the "yes/no" indicates the presence or absence of a control. The auditor may answer "N/A" (not applicable) for questions that do not apply to this specific entity. A more open-ended questionnaire may be used to focus the auditor's attention onto certain control objectives.

The primary advantage of using a questionnaire is the ability to thoroughly cover each audit area. It is also an efficient way of delegating responsibility to junior audit team members. Internal control questionnaires are a desirable way of reminding the auditor of the different types of controls that should exist. The primary disadvantage of questionnaires is that they do not provide an overall view of the controls in the system being examined. A standard internal control questionnaire may also be inapplicable to certain audit clients.

Flowcharts

Flowcharts are a symbolic, diagrammatic, or pictorial representation of the entity's documents and their flow within the organization. Flowcharts depict a significant class of transactions from inception to processing to disposition.

The primary advantage of a flowchart is that it provides a concise overview of the entity's system. It is useful as an analytical tool in the auditor's evaluation of controls. With the aid of computer software, it is easy to create and update flowcharts. Flowcharts are easier from the user's perspective as it is generally easier to follow a diagram than it is to read narrative descriptions. Flowcharts may be especially helpful for subsequent year auditors in understanding and updating the system.

A properly prepared flowchart of an accounting system and related controls has certain characteristics. It shows the origin of every document and record in the system. It shows where the documents come from and how they are generated. It shows where all processing takes place, by department, individual job function or computer program, as well as the frequency of operations. It shows details of significant accounting procedures and control activities, including segregation of duties and monitoring activities. The disposition of every document and record should also be shown. It shows what ultimately happens to the documents: the documents are filed, mailed or sent outside, shredded or otherwise destroyed.

The flowchart indicates controls relevant to assessing control risk. Information in flowcharts is frequently organized by areas of responsibility within the system. For instance, segregation of duties may be shown by indicating which job functions are responsible for authorizing or recording transactions. The flow of transactions is generally from top-left to bottom-right.

Narratives

Narratives are written descriptions of the entity's internal controls. A properly prepared narrative has the same elements as a flowchart. It should show the origin and disposition of every document and record in the system. It should also show where processing takes place. The narrative should describe controls relevant to assessing control risk.

Narratives generally are not as effective as flowcharts in describing the characteristics of a system. In particular, narratives are not as effective at showing separation of duties. Narratives may be more difficult for subsequent year auditors to understand and update. Narratives may also not be as effective in providing an overview of the entire system. However, narratives are often a cost-effective way of documenting unsophisticated internal controls.

A narrative memorandum is often sufficient if the auditor decides to assess control risk at maximum (100%) and intends to place no reliance on internal controls to restrict substantive testing.

ASSESSING CONTROL RISK

Control risk should be assessed in terms of financial statement assertions. These assertions are part of the account balance, transaction class, and disclosure components of financial statements. The risk of material misstatement in financial statement assertions consists of the following three risks:

1. *Inherent risk:* Inherent risk is the susceptibility of an assertion to a material misstatement, provided that there are no related controls.
2. *Control risk:* Control risk is the risk that a material misstatement that could occur in an assertion will not be prevented or detected on a timely basis by the entity's internal control.
3. *Detection risk:* Detection risk is the risk that the auditor will not detect a material misstatement that exists in an assertion.

Auditability of Entity

After obtaining an understanding of controls, the auditor should make a *preliminary* assessment of control risk. Before making a preliminary assessment of control risk, the auditor should consider several factors. The auditor should consider the *integrity of management* and the *adequacy of financial records*. Both factors affect the auditability of the entity.

The auditor may be unable to perform procedures or rely on management's representation if management lacks integrity. Lack of integrity has a direct effect on the reliability of evidence. Similarly, if the accounting records are deficient, audit evidence may not be reliable. So it may be impossible to perform an audit.

Preliminary Assessment

The preliminary assessment of control risk is generally made for each transaction-related audit objective for each major class of transaction. The risk assessment is the auditor's expectation that the controls will neither prevent *material misstatements* from occurring nor *detect or correct* them after they have occurred. The auditor may assess control risk at maximum and follow a primarily substantive audit strategy or the auditor may assess control risk below maximum and follow a reliance audit strategy. Auditors may use subjective expressions such as *high*, *moderate*, or *low* to assess the control risk. Or, the auditors may make a numerical assessment such as 30 or 80%.

The auditor should consider the following factors in determining whether control risk should be assessed at the maximum level or at a lower level:

1. The nature of the assertion.
2. The volume of transactions or data related to the assertion.
3. The nature and complexity of the systems, including the use of IT, by which the entity processes and controls information supporting the assertion.
4. The nature of the available evidence, including audit evidence that is available only in electronic form.

If control risk is assessed below the maximum level, the auditor will take the following three steps:

1. Identify specific controls relevant to specific assertions.
2. Perform tests of controls.
3. Conclude on the assessed level of control risk.

Management's attitude toward internal control is a critical factor in the auditor's preliminary assessment of control risk. If the management does not take controls seriously, it is doubtful that a detailed analysis of control activities will be useful. It will probably be best to assess control risk at maximum. When the control risk is assessed at maximum, the assessment should be documented and substantive tests should be performed.

In contrast, if management has a positive attitude toward controls, the auditor should examine the specific policies and procedures in place. When the control risk is assessed below maximum, the auditor should identify the specific controls that will be relied on. The auditor should consider that the controls could have a pervasive effect on multiple assertions. On the other hand, some controls may affect only single assertions.

An internal control weakness may be defined as the absence of adequate controls. Control weaknesses directly increase the probability of misstatements in the financial statements. To identify and evaluate control weaknesses, the auditor starts by first identifying existing controls. Next the auditor should identify which controls, if any, are missing. If controls are missing, what specific types of misstatements may occur? Finally, are there any compensating controls that offset previously identified weaknesses? Controls may be either directly or indirectly related to an assertion. The more direct the relationship, the greater is the likelihood that the control will be more effective in reducing control risk for that assertion.

Tests of Controls

Tests of controls are performed to provide evidence to support the lower level of control risk. Tests of controls are concerned with assessing how controls were applied, the consistency with which they were applied, and by whom they were applied. The following procedures are commonly used to test controls:

1. Observation of application of controls and control-related activities.
2. Reperformance by auditor of entity procedures.
3. Inquiry of appropriate entity personnel.
4. Inspection of documents, records and reports in both electronic and paper form.
5. Walk-through of transactions.

Many controls leave a documentary trail, and inspection of documents and records can provide evidence that documents are properly completed. Observation of control-related activities is appropriate for testing those controls, such as segregation of duties that may not leave documentary evidence. For some controls there is documentary evidence, but the evidence is insufficient for the auditor's purpose of assessing control risk. In such instances auditors will generally reperform control activities to determine whether the expected results are obtained. If reperformance does not result in misstatements, the auditor has greater confidence that the procedures are operating as intended. While making inquiries of the entity's personnel is not a strong source of evidence concerning the effectiveness of operation of controls, it is nonetheless a useful source of evidence.

The amount of evidence the auditor needs to accumulate to test controls depends on the desired assessed level of control risk. For a lower assessed level of control risk, a larger sample size will be needed and more extensive tests of controls will be performed. The extent of testing may be reduced if evidence from the prior years' audit indicates that the controls were working effectively and are still working effectively. For instance, the auditor may use a smaller sample size to test such controls. Tests of controls should ideally be applied to transactions for the entire audit period. If it is impractical to do so, and the testing will be for a period less than the entire audit period, the auditor should ascertain that controls did not change during the period that was not tested. If changes occurred, the auditor should obtain evidence about the nature and extent of such changes.

Many of the above-mentioned procedures are also used to obtain an understanding of controls, not just to test them. While a conceptual distinction is made between the "understanding" phase and "preliminary control assessment" phase, most auditors proceed through the two phases almost simultaneously, rather than as two separate and independent phases. Both phases include inquiry, documentation, and observation.

A key difference between the two phases is that procedures to obtain an understanding are applied to all relevant controls, whereas tests of controls are applied only to key controls where the assessed control risk is below maximum.

Another important difference is that procedures to obtain an understanding are performed on only a few transactions, usually at a given point in time. Tests of controls, on the other hand, are applied to a much larger sample size, across the entire period under audit.

Manual and Automated IT Controls

Control compliance is often affected by whether the control is performed manually or electronically. Manually performed controls are subject to human errors and mistakes. In contrast, as long as they are effectively designed, electronic controls can be automatically applied on a consistent basis. Auditors are frequently able to reduce the extent of testing when automated IT controls are in place. When significant transaction data are only available in an electronic form, the auditor may be unable to rely solely on substantive tests to support financial statement assertions. Under such circumstances the auditor may have to perform a more extensive test of controls to obtain sufficient evidence for financial statement assertions.

Concluding on the Assessed Level of Control Risk

Auditors will use results from the test of controls to revise the preliminary assessed level of control risk. Based on the audit risk model, the auditor uses the revised assessed level of control risk and the assessed level of inherent risk as well as acceptable audit risk to determine the acceptable level of detection risk.

The acceptable level of detection risk is used to determine the nature, extent, and timing of the substantive test. If the tests of controls are consistent with the auditor's preliminary assessment of control risk, there is no need to modify the nature, extent, and timing of substantive tests. On the other hand, if the tests of controls do not support the preliminary assessment, the assessed level of control risk will be increased, and the nature, extent and timing of substantive tests will have to be modified. The auditor is required to document the basis for reaching the conclusion concerning the assessed level of control risk.

The auditor should consider the characteristics of evidence in determining the assessed level of control risk. In general, the lower the assessed level of control risk, the greater the assurances that must be provided by evidence that the relevant controls are designed and operating effectively. Moreover, as the acceptable level of detection risk decreases, the assurance provided from substantive tests should increase. Auditors will often do one or more of the following to get greater assurance:

1. Change the nature of substantive tests from a less effective to a more effective procedure, such as using tests directed toward independent parties outside the entity rather than tests directed toward parties or documentation within the entity.
2. Change the timing of substantive tests, such as performing them at year-end rather than at an interim date.
3. Change the extent of substantive tests, such as using a larger sample size.

Documenting the Assessed Level of Control Risk

The auditor must document on the audit conclusions about the assessed level of control risk. The documentation should include the basis for concluding that the effectiveness of the design and operation of controls supports that assessed level. The type of documentation is based on

1. The assessed level of control risk.
2. The nature of the entity's internal control.
3. The nature of the entity's documentation of internal control.

Further Reduction in the Assessed Level of Control Risk

The auditor may want to further reduce the assessed level of control risk for certain assertions after having obtained an understanding of the internal controls. The auditor should consider if additional evidence to support a further reduction is available and whether it would be efficient to perform a test of controls. The auditor should consider whether additional evidence to support reduction in the assessed level of control risk would require more effort than the substantive tests for that assertion.

EVIDENCE TO SUPPORT THE ASSESSED LEVEL OF CONTROL RISK

Auditors must obtain sufficient evidence to support the assessed level of control risk. The sufficiency of evidence is left to the auditor's judgment. Evidence is affected by several factors, including

1. The source of evidence,
2. The timeliness of evidence, and
3. Existence of other evidence.

These factors substantially affect the degree of assurance provided by evidence. These factors also influence the nature, timing, and extent of the tests of controls that the auditor applies to obtain evidence. The auditor normally uses techniques such as inquiry, observation, and reperformance. Different test of controls are effective under different circumstances.

In general, evidence obtained directly by the auditor, such as through observation, provides more assurance than evidence obtained indirectly, such as through inquiry. Of course, the auditor should be aware that observing the application of a control may be performed very differently when the auditor is present than when the auditor is not present. Moreover inquiry alone will generally not provide sufficient evidence, and additional corroborating evidence will be required to support the conclusion about the effectiveness of the design or operation of that control.

Timeliness of evidence concerns when evidence is obtained and the relevant audit period. Certain types of evidence, such as evidence obtained through observations, pertain only to the specific point in time when the procedure was performed. Such evidence may be insufficient for the entire period under audit. Generally, the auditor must supplement such evidence with other evidence pertaining to the entire audit period.

The auditor should also consider evidence gathered in prior audits. To evaluate the significance of such evidence on the current audit, the auditor should consider

1. The significance of assertions involved;
2. The specific controls that were evaluated;
3. The design and operation of those controls;
4. The amount of time that has elapsed since the original evaluation; and
5. Changes subsequent to the prior audit that have occurred in internal control, including changes in policies, procedures, and personnel.

The auditor will generally have to evaluate various types of evidence that relate to the same assertion. The auditor must determine the combined effect of these various types of assertions. Often the various types of evidence support the same conclusion about the design or operation of a control and the degree of assurance provided increases. Conversely, when the various types of evidence lead to different conclusions about the design or operation of controls, the assurance provided by the evidence decreases.

The auditor should also consider the interrelationship of an entity's control environment, risk assessment, control activities, information and communication, and monitoring. An ineffective control environment for an otherwise effective control is likely to lead the auditor to reduce the assurances provided by evidence. For instance, the effectiveness of automated controls in a computer program is likely to be questioned if the control environment is ineffective and unauthorized changes to the computer program are possible. In such an environment the auditor will likely need additional evidence about the design and operation of that computer program for the audit period.

LIMITATIONS OF AN ENTITY'S INTERNAL CONTROL

Well-designed internal controls, at best, can only provide reasonable assurance that an entity's control objectives are being met. Several factors limit the effectiveness of internal controls, including

1. Errors in human judgment/decision making.
2. Collusion by two or more individuals.
3. Management override of internal controls.

Internal controls are affected by management's assessment of cost–benefit criteria. The cost of controls should not exceed the expected benefits to be derived from the controls. While conceptually the cost–benefit consideration is easy to understand, it is usually difficult to implement because precise measurements of costs and benefits is often not possible.

322 THE AUDITOR'S CONSIDERATION OF THE INTERNAL AUDIT FUNCTION IN AN AUDIT OF FINANCIAL STATEMENTS

SOURCE OF STANDARDS

GAAS

SAS 65, *The Auditors' Consideration of the Internal Audit Function in an Audit of Financial Statements*

SUMMARY

This section provides the auditor with guidance on the work of the internal auditors and its use in an audit performed in accordance with GAAS. At the beginning of an audit engagement the auditor is required to obtain an understanding of the client's internal controls both as a basis for planning the audit and for determining the nature, timing, and extent of the tests to be performed. As part of this assessment the auditor must consider the client's internal audit function (if it exists). Since an important aspect of many internal audit functions is to review, assess, and monitor controls, the work of the internal auditor may be significantly useful to the external auditor. The outside auditor may also choose to use the internal auditors' work directly in performing the audit.

For these reasons AU Section 322 requires that the external auditor obtain an understanding of the internal audit function, assess the objectivity and competence of the internal auditors, assess the extent and effect of the internal auditor's work on the audit, and take into account other considerations discussed in this section.

GAAS GUIDANCE

LEARNING AND UNDERSTANDING THE INTERNAL AUDIT FUNCTION

A highly important function of the internal audit staff is to test the performance of the client's controls throughout the year to ascertain how effective their design and operation are. Thus the work of the internal auditor clearly affects the audit. In order to learn about and functionally understand the entity's internal audit function, the outside auditor should make inquiries in the following areas:

- The magnitude of the internal audit work including the nature, timing and extent of the procedures used. Review of the internal audit plan would be appropriate.

- The published professional standards of The Institute of Internal Auditors and the General Accounting Office. These represent the professional standards developed for the practice of internal auditing in the United States.
- Limitations on the scope of activities of the internal auditors.
- Accessibility of internal audit documents and records.
- Status of the internal audit function within the company as described in the organization chart. To what hierarchical level do the internal auditors report?
- Information about the company's internal audit objectives and aims as enumerated in the corporate charter, goals statement, and other written company documents.

The Relevance of Internal Audit Activities to the Audit of an Entity's Financial Statements

In order to assess the relevance of internal audit activities to the audit of the entity's financial statements, AU Section 322 suggests the following activities be considered:

- Determine the scope of internal audit activities by reviewing completed internal audit reports.
- Look at the internal audit activities that outside auditors previously relied on by reviewing prior year's working papers.
- Determine how much resources have been allocated to financial versus operating activities.

In general, accounting activities are relevant when they generate data about activities and controls relating to the initiation, recording, processing, and reporting of financial data in the financial statements, and when they generate data about potential misstatements relating to these functions.

Evaluation of the Learning and Understanding Phase

Once the internal audit function is learned and understood, the auditor must determine which internal audit functions are relevant to the audit of the financial statements. This determination influences the nature, timing, and extent of the audit activities that will be performed. If the decision is that the internal audit functions are not relevant to the financial statement audit, the auditor should not continue any internal audit exploratory activities unless assistance will be requested from the internal auditor. (More will be said about requesting assistance below.)

Based simply on cost–benefit considerations, the decision may be made to stop viewing the work of the internal auditor as relevant to audit activities even if some internal audit functions do affect the audit. However, if the auditor decides that the work of the internal audit staff would efficiently influence the performance of substantive tests in the audit, AU Section 322 requires that the auditor assess the competence and objectivity of the internal auditors so that their work may be relied on.

COMPETENCE AND OBJECTIVITY OF THE INTERNAL AUDIT STAFF

Before relying on the work of the entity's internal auditor staff, the auditor must evaluate their competence and objectivity. The following areas should be reviewed in evaluating competence:

- Professional certifications attained and continuing education courses taken.
- Audit programs, procedures, and policies used in performance of their work.
- The extent of professional experience and education.

- Assignment of jobs to internal auditors.
- Supervisory and evaluation procedures.

In determining the objectivity of the internal auditors, the following four queries need answers:

1. Does the internal audit staff report to an individual in the corporate hierarchy of sufficient rank to ensure that their assessments, findings, and conclusions will be adequately considered? That is, have suggestions made by the internal auditors in the past been heeded or ignored?
2. Does the internal audit staff have access to the audit committee and board of directors?
3. Does the audit committee and the board involve themselves in the hiring and interviewing of internal auditors?
4. Are there rules to ensure that conflict of interest is minimized? For example, to insure that their objectivity has not been compromised, internal auditors should be precluded from auditing areas where they recently worked or where they will be assigned to after their internal audit function tasks are over. Nor should they be assigned to areas where relatives and close friends are working.

After accumulating the information described, it is necessary to conclude whether the internal auditors are sufficiently competent and objective so that the auditor may rely on their work to influence the audit. Testing should be done so that the determination is measured and objective. The extent of the testing required should be a function of how much reliance the auditor intends to place on the work of the internal audit staff. The following activities can be effective:

- Assess the aggregate of information gathered from past experience and interactions with the entity's internal audit function.
- Examine any outside quality control reviews of the entity's internal audit activities.
- Interview management about the competence and objectivity of the internal auditors.

After gathering this information, assess the internal audit staff's competence and objectivity using the parameters discussed above and in the light of published professional internal auditing practice standards, such as those of the Institute of Internal Auditors and General Accounting Office.

AREAS WHERE INTERNAL AUDIT WORK AFFECTS THE AUDIT

AU Section 322 describes three areas where the work of the internal auditing staff affects the audit. These include procedures relating to the following areas:

- Understanding the internal control of the entity.
- Risk assessment.
- Substantive testing.

Each of these areas will now be discussed in greater detail.

Understanding the Internal Control System

AU Section 319 requires the auditor obtain an understanding of all the components of an entity's internal control so that the audit may be properly planned. Since a primary function of the internal auditor is to review, assess, and monitor controls, studying the procedures performed by them will significantly assist the auditor in this task. The auditor may want to review such documents as flowcharts, narratives, internal control checklists, and manuals that have been prepared by the client's internal audit staff in assessing controls in the entity's operating areas. The auditor may also want to rely on ongoing tests the internal auditors perform to determine that the controls are working as intended or are appropriately modified when they are not meeting their objectives.

Assessment of Risk

An entity's control system significantly affects its account balances, classes of transactions, and virtually all assertions presented in the financial statements. The auditor's appraisal of the internal control system influences the assessment of the risk of material misstatement at the financial-statement level, which in turn affects the entire audit strategy. As a component of the control system, the work of the internal auditors may significantly affect auditor decisions about procedures to be performed. That is, the internal audit function affects not only the auditor's evaluation of material misstatement but also the auditor's decisions about the nature, timing, and extent of the audit procedures to be performed.

At the account balance or class-of-transaction level, control risk is the risk that a material misstatement might not be prevented or detected by the internal control system. The auditor assesses this risk for financial statement assertions and tests the controls when supporting control risk assessments are below the highest level. The work of the internal auditors may be of significant assistance here. The results of their tests may show that the controls in place are both well designed and working as intended. For example, their tests may show that disbursements of cash for the purchase of merchandise on credit (bona-fide payables) are only made after all underlying documentation has been carefully compared by personnel to prove that only merchandise that was needed, ordered, received, and billed is paid for. The effectiveness of the internal auditor's tests will allow the independent auditor to rely on them in modifying the nature, timing, and amount of testing that will have to be done.

Substantive Tests

The independent auditor may find that internal audit staff has performed important substantive tests that can be directly used in the audit. For example, internal auditors carefully check aging schedules of accounts receivable to ensure that an appropriate amount of allowance is recorded so that accounts receivable are properly stated at net realizable value. For investments, internal auditors carefully review the current values of owned securities to ensure that the client's trading and available-for-sale investment portfolios are properly stated at fair values in accordance with GAAP. By relying on this and other work performed by the internal auditors, the auditor can modify the amount of work that would otherwise have to be done.

EXTENT OF RELIANCE ON INTERNAL AUDIT PROCEDURES BY THE INDEPENDENT AUDITOR

In deciding on how much of the work of the internal auditor to use, the auditor must consider the following factors:

1. The materiality of the account balance or class of transaction being audited. The more material the account or class of transactions, the less the auditor should depend on the work of the internal auditor.
2. The risk of material misstatement (inherent and control risk) of financial statement assertions and the degree of subjectivity of the audit evidence being used to support the assertions being tested. Both the risk of material misstatement and the degree of subjectivity are also directly related to the need for the auditor to perform separate tests and rely less on the work of the internal auditor. For example, where there is a high risk of material misstatement or highly subjective audit evidence in areas like

contingency transactions, subsequent events, uncertainties, and others that use accounting estimates in the valuation of assets and liabilities, substantive tests performed by the internal auditor alone would not relieve the independent auditor of the responsibility to do substantive tests of accounts and transactions. Where the risk of material misstatement or the subjectivity of audit evidence is low, as with the existence of cash, prepaid expenses, or additions to fixed assets, then the auditor may choose to rely more on the work performed by the internal auditors or even choose to rely entirely on their work.

Once it is decided that the work of the internal auditor will influence the procedures performed by the independent auditor, it is important that they coordinate their activities to maximize time and maximize efficiency. The auditor should therefore

- Meet periodically with the internal audit staff during the audit to insure that all their efforts are being coordinated properly;
- Schedule the performance of internal audit work so that the work requested is done in time to be available when it is needed;
- Ensure that information from the internal audit staff and access to their workpapers is available when needed;
- Maintain open lines of communication to the internal audit staff so that any problems that may arise may be quickly resolved; and
- Review any pertinent reports prepared by the internal auditors.

EVALUATING THE EFFECTIVENESS OF THE INTERNAL AUDITOR'S WORK

The independent auditor needs to evaluate the quality and effectiveness of the internal auditor's work in order to decide on the audit procedures that need to be performed. This evaluation is a function of the following queries:

- Is the scope of the internal auditor's work adequate to meet the objectives of the outside audit?
- Were the procedures followed in internal audit programs adequate to meet the needs of the external auditor?
- Were the internal auditors' working papers properly prepared? Were the audit procedures performed properly and fully documented? Was the preparation of the working papers fully reviewed and supervised?
- Were the audit conclusions in line with the evidence derived from the procedures that were performed?
- Were the audit reports in line with the evidence collected?
- Were the results of the independent auditor's tests of the internal audit work (including tests of balances, transactions, and controls) and other audit evidence gathered consistent with the results of the internal auditor?
- Do the independent auditor's tests demonstrate that the work of the internal auditor is of high quality and effective?

REQUESTING DIRECT AUDIT ASSISTANCE FROM THE INTERNAL AUDITORS

During the course of the audit the independent auditor may ask the internal auditor to perform some audit work such as substantive tests, tests of controls, or even obtaining an understanding of the entity's internal control system. When such direct assistance is requested and provided, the independent auditor should take the following actions:

1. Assess the objectivity and competence of internal auditors.
2. Supervise, review, evaluate, and test the work performed.

3. Inform the internal auditors when they provide direct assistance about

   a. Their responsibilities when performing audit procedures in an independent audit;
   b. The objectives of the procedures they are about to perform;
   c. Situations that they may come upon that might influence the nature, timing, and extent of the audit procedures that will be performed; and
   d. Immediately bringing to the attention of the independent auditor any important accounting and auditing issues they identify.

324 SERVICE ORGANIZATIONS

SOURCES OF STANDARDS

SAS 70, *Service Organizations*
SAS 78, *Consideration of Internal Control in a Financial Statement Audit: An Amendment to Statement on Auditing Standards No. 55*
SAS 88, *Service Organizations and Reporting on Consistency*
SAS 98, *Omnibus Statement on Auditing Standards—2002*

SUMMARY

This section provides guidance in connection with the audit of the financial statements of an entity that uses services from another organization (a "service organization") that make up part of its information system. Such services are considered part of an entity's information system if they affect any of the following:

1. How the entity's transactions are initiated.
2. The accounting records, supporting information, and specific accounts in the financial statements that are involved in the processing and reporting of the entity's transactions.
3. The accounting processing used from the initiation of the transactions to their inclusion in the financial statements, including electronic methods used to transmit, process, maintain, and access information.
4. The financial reporting process used to prepare financial statements, inclusive of significant accounting estimates and disclosures.

Examples of service organizations are

1. Electronic data processing service centers.
2. Bank trust departments that invest and service assets for employee retirement plans.
3. Mortgage bankers that service the mortgages of others.

The section does not apply to circumstances that limit the services to execution of transactions authorized by the client such as the processing of checking account transactions by a bank.

EFFECT OF USE OF A SERVICE ORGANIZATION ON A USER ORGANIZATION'S INTERNAL CONTROL

The significance of the service organization's controls depends on the type of services it provides, primarily the nature and materiality of the transactions it processes and the degree of interaction between service and user organizations.

If there is a high interaction between their activities, it may be practicable for the user organization to implement effective controls for the transactions.

PLANNING THE AUDIT

In planning the audit, the auditor of the user organization should learn all about the controls placed in operation not just by the entity but also by organizations whose services are part of the entity's information system. To do so, the user auditor should consider all available information concerning the service organization's internal controls, including

1. Technical manuals.
2. Contracts between user and service organizations.
3. Reports on the service organization's controls by internal auditors, service auditors, or regulatory authorities.
4. Previous experience with the service organization.

If an independent auditor for the user encounters a restriction on the scope of the audit and is unable to obtain sufficient evidence to achieve the audit objectives, the auditor should express a qualified opinion or disclaim an opinion on the financial statements.

ASSESSING THE USER ORGANIZATION'S CONTROL RISK

To assess control risk at below the maximum level for assertions related to controls at the service organization, the user's auditor should obtain the report of the service auditor, if available, on controls in place and tests of operating effectiveness.

The user's auditor should be satisfied about the service auditor's professional reputation as a basis for relying on the report. If no report of the service auditor is available, the user's auditor or the service auditor may have to perform tests of controls at the service organization.

REPORTS ISSUED BY SERVICE AUDITORS

The auditor for the service organization may issue two types of reports on internal controls.

1. Reports on controls placed in operation.
2. Reports on controls placed in operation and tests of operating effectiveness.

REPORT ON CONTROLS PLACED IN OPERATION

While this type of report may be useful to a user auditor in planning the audit, it is not intended to give the auditor a basis for the assessment of control risk below the maximum level. Such a report should contain a disclaimer of opinion on the operating effectiveness of controls.

The contents of this type of report should

1. Refer to the applications, services, products, or other aspects of the service organization that are covered.
2. Describe the scope and nature of the procedures performed by the service auditor.
3. Identify the party specifying the control objectives.
4. State the purpose of the service auditor's engagement.
5. Include a disclaimer of opinion on the operating effectiveness of the controls.
6. Include an opinion as to whether the description of the controls presents fairly, in all material respects, the relevant aspects of the service organization's controls that were in operation as of a specific date.
7. Include an opinion as to whether the described controls were suitably designed to provide reasonable, though not absolute, assurance that internal control objectives would be achieved if the described controls were complied with satisfactorily.

8. Include a statement regarding inherent limitations on the effectiveness of internal control and a caveat about projecting the evaluation to future periods.
9. Identify the intended users of the report.

A sample report follows.

To XYZ Service Organization:

We have examined the accompanying description of controls related to the _____application of XYZ Service Organization. Our examination included procedures to obtain reasonable assurance about whether (1) the accompanying description presents fairly, in all material respects, the aspects of XYZ Service Organization's controls that may be relevant to a user organization's internal control as it relates to an audit of financial statements, (2) the controls included in the description were suitably designed to achieve the control objectives specified in the description, if those controls were complied with satisfactorily, and (3) such controls had been placed in operation as of_____. The control objectives were specified by_____. Our examination was performed in accordance with standards established by the American Institute of Certified Public Accountants and included those procedures we considered necessary in the circumstances to obtain a reasonable basis for rendering our opinion.

We did not perform procedures to determine the operating effectiveness of controls for any period. Accordingly we express no opinion on the operating effectiveness of any aspects of XYZ Service Organization's Controls, individually or in the aggregate.

In our opinion, the accompanying description of the aforementioned application presents fairly, in all material respects, the relevant aspects of XYZ Service Organization's controls that have been placed in operation as of_____. Also, in our opinion, the controls, as described, are suitably designed to provide reasonable assurance that the specified control objectives would be achieved if the described controls were complied with satisfactorily.

The description of controls at XYZ Service Organization is as of _____ and any projection of such information to the future is subject to the risk that, because of change, the description may no longer portray the controls in existence. The potential effectiveness of specific controls at the Service Organization is subject to inherent limitations and, accordingly, errors and fraud may occur and not be detected. Furthermore the projection of any conclusion, based on our findings, to future periods is subject to the risk that changes may alter the validity of such conclusions.

This report is intended solely for use by the management of XYZ Service organization, its customers, and the independent auditors of its customers_____.

REPORT ON CONTROLS PLACED IN OPERATION AND TESTS OF OPERATING EFFECTIVENESS

This type of report may be useful to a user auditor in planning the audit and may also provide a basis for the auditor to reduce the assessment of control risk to below the maximum level of control risk.

This type of report should

1. Refer to the applications, services, products, or other aspects of the service organization covered.
2. Describe the scope and nature of procedures performed by the service auditor.
3. Identify the party specifying the control objectives.
4. State the purpose of the service auditor's engagement.
5. Include an opinion as to whether the description of the controls presents fairly, in all material respects, the relevant aspects of the service organization's controls that were in operation as of a specific date.
6. Include an opinion as to whether the described controls were suitably designed to provide reasonable, though not absolute, assurance that internal control objectives would be achieved if the controls were complied with satisfactorily.
7. Refer to a description of tests of controls at the service organization.

8. State the period covered by the report of the service auditor.
9. Include an opinion as to whether the tested controls were operating with sufficient effectiveness to provide reasonable, though not absolute, assurance that the pertinent control objectives were achieved.
10. Indicate that the relative effectiveness and significance of specific service organization controls and their effect on the assessment of control risk at the organization depend on interaction with controls and other factors relevant to the user organization.
11. State that no procedures have been performed to assess control risk at the user organization.
12. Include a statement about inherent limitations on the effectiveness of internal control and a caveat about projecting the evaluation to future periods.
13. Identify the intended users of the report.

A sample report follows.

To XYZ Service Organization:

We have examined the accompanying description of controls related to the _____ application of XYZ Service Organization. Our examination included procedures to obtain reasonable assurance about whether (1) the accompanying description presents fairly, in all material respects, the aspects of XYZ Service Organization's controls that may be relevant to a user organization's internal control as it relates to an audit of financial statements, (2) the controls included in the description were suitably designed to achieve the control objectives specified in the description, if those controls were complied with satisfactorily, and (3) such controls had been placed in operation as of _____. The control objectives were specified by _____. Our examination was performed in accordance with standards established by the American Institute of Certified Public Accountants and included those procedures we considered necessary in the circumstances to obtain a reasonable basis for rendering our opinion.

In our opinion, the accompanying description of the aforementioned application presents fairly, in all material respects, the relevant aspects of XYZ Service Organization's controls that have been placed in operation as of _____. Also, in our opinion, the controls, as described, are suitably designed to provide reasonable assurance that the specified control objectives would be achieved if the described controls were complied with satisfactorily.

In addition to the procedures we considered necessary to render our opinion as expressed in the preceding paragraph, we applied tests to specific controls, listed in Schedule X, to obtain evidence about their effectiveness in meeting the control objectives, described in Schedule X, during the period from _____ to _____. The specific controls and the nature, timing, extent, and results of the tests are listed in Schedule X. This information has been provided to user organizations of XYZ Service Organization and to their auditors to be taken into consideration, along with information about the internal control at user organizations, when making assessments of control risk for user organizations. In our opinion, the controls that were tested, as described in Schedule X, were operating with sufficient effectiveness to provide reasonable, but not absolute, assurance that the control objectives specified in Schedule X were achieved during the period _____ to _____.

The relative effectiveness and significance of specific controls at XYZ Service Organization and their effect on assessments of control risk at user organizations are dependent on their interaction with controls and other factors present at individual user organizations. We have performed no procedures to evaluate the effectiveness of controls at individual user organizations.

The description of controls at XYZ Service Organization is as of _____ and any projection of such information to the future is subject to the risk that, because of change, the description may no longer portray the controls in existence. The potential effectiveness of specific controls at the Service Organization is subject to inherent limitations and, accordingly, errors and fraud may occur and not be detected. Furthermore, the projection of any conclusion, based on our findings, to future periods is subject to the risk that changes may alter the validity of such conclusions.

This report is intended solely for the use by management of XYZ Service organization, its customers, and the independent auditors of its customers.

325 COMMUNICATION OF INTERNAL CONTROL RELATED MATTERS IDENTIFIED IN AN AUDIT

SOURCES OF STANDARDS

SAS 112, *Communicating Internal Control Related Matters Identified in an Audit*

SUMMARY

This section describes an auditor's responsibilities concerning the identification and communication of internal control related matters observed during a financial statement audit. An auditor may find deficiencies in a client's internal control that might be of interest to management and those charged with governance. These deficiencies are commonly known as significant deficiencies and material weaknesses.

DEFINITIONS

A *control deficiency* exists when the design or operation of an internal control does not allow management or other employees performing their normal assigned functions, to prevent or detect financial statement misstatements on a timely basis.

A *significant deficiency* is a control deficiency, or combination of control deficiencies, that adversely affect the entity's ability to initiate, authorize, record, process, or report financial data reliably in accordance with generally accepted accounting principles such that there is more than a remote likelihood that a more than inconsequential financial statement misstatement will not be prevented or detected.

A *material weakness* is a significant deficiency, or combination of significant deficiencies, that results in more than a remote likelihood that a material financial statement misstatement will not be prevented or detected.

The phrase *more than inconsequential* is the threshold for evaluating the significance of a control deficiency. A misstatement is considered to be inconsequential if a reasonable person would conclude, after considering the possibility of further undetected misstatements, that the misstatement, either individually or when aggregated with other misstatements, would clearly be immaterial to the financial statements. Whether a misstatement is inconsequential is a matter of professional judgment, which should be based on both quantitative and qualitative factors.

EVALUATING CONTROL DEFICIENCIES
IDENTIFIED AS PART OF THE AUDIT

While an auditor is not required to specifically search for control deficiencies, the auditor is required to evaluate identified control deficiencies and determine whether they are significant deficiencies or material weaknesses.

The auditor should be aware that the absence of identified material financial statement misstatements does not imply that there are no significant deficiencies or material weaknesses. Potential for material misstatement governs.

Examples of control deficiencies that are generally considered to be at least significant deficiencies and are likely to be material weaknesses include

1. Poor financial reporting and internal control oversight.
2. Restatement of prior period financial statements to correct one or more material misstatements.
3. An ineffective internal audit function.
4. Lack of compliance with pertinent regulations.
5. Material or immaterial fraud perpetrated by senior management.
6. An ineffective internal control environment.

COMMUNICATION—FORM, CONTENT, AND TIMING

If an auditor concludes that identified control deficiencies are significant deficiencies or material weaknesses, then the auditor is required to communicate the control deficiencies in writing to management and those charged with governance (see AU Section 380).

An auditor is required to communicate significant deficiencies and material weaknesses previously communicated if not yet remediated. The written communication may be made by referring to the written communication (and the date of that communication) previously issued.

The issuance of the written communication should generally coincide with the audit report release date (i.e., the date that the auditor grants the entity permission to use the auditor's report on the financial statements), but in no event should the communication be made later than 60 days after the report release date. Earlier communication may be important and need not be in writing.

The written communication of significant deficiencies and material weaknesses should

1. State that the purpose of the audit was to express an opinion on the financial statements, but not to express an opinion on the effectiveness of the entity's internal control over financial reporting.
2. State that the auditor is not expressing an opinion on the effectiveness of internal control.
3. Define *control* deficiency, significant *deficiency* and, where relevant, *material weakness*.
4. Identify significant deficiencies and, if applicable, material weaknesses.
5. State that the communication is intended solely for the information and use of management, those charged with governance, and others within the organization and is not intended to be and should not be used by anyone other than these specified parties (reference to a government authority is permissible); and
6. The auditor may, but is not required to, include additional statements regarding the general inherent limitations of internal control, including the possibility of management override.

It should be noted that an auditor may issue a communication stating that no material weaknesses were identified during the audit for submission to governmental authorities. However, the auditor should not issue a written communication stating that no significant deficiencies were identified.

ILLUSTRATIVE REPORT

The sample report may be used by an auditor to advise management and those charged with governance that one or more significant deficiencies and/or material weaknesses have been identified.

In planning and performing our audit of the financial statements of Kate Company as of and for the year ended December 31, 20XX, in accordance with auditing standards generally accepted in the United States of America, we considered Kate Company's internal control over financial reporting (internal control) as a basis for designing our auditing procedures for the purpose of expressing our opinion on the financial statements, but not for the purpose of expressing an opinion on the effectiveness of the Company's internal control. Accordingly, we do not express an opinion on the effectiveness of the Company's internal control.

Our consideration of internal control was for the limited purposes described in the preceding paragraph and would not necessarily identify all deficiencies in internal control that might be significant deficiencies or material weaknesses. However, as discussed below, we identified certain deficiencies in internal control that we considered to be significant deficiencies [and other deficiencies that we considered to be material weaknesses].

A control deficiency exists when the design or operation of a control does not allow management or employees, in the normal course of performing their assigned functions, to prevent or detect misstatements on a timely basis. A significant deficiency is a control deficiency, or a combination of control deficiencies, that adversely affects the entity's ability to initiate, authorize, record, process, or report financial data reliably in accordance with generally accepted accounting principles such that there is more than a remote likelihood that a misstatement of the entity's financial statements that is more than inconsequential will not be prevented or detected by the entity's internal control. We consider the following deficiencies to be significant deficiencies in internal control:

[*Describe the significant deficiencies that were identified.*]

[A material weakness is a significant deficiency, or combination of significant deficiencies, that results in more than a remote likelihood that a material misstatement of the financial statements will not be prevented or detected by the entity's internal control. We believe that the following deficiencies constitute material weaknesses.]

[*Describe the material weaknesses that were identified.*]

This communication is intended solely for the information and use of management, [*identify the body or individuals charged with governance*], others within the organization, and [*identify any specified governmental authorities*] and is not intended to be and should not be used by anyone other than these specified parties.

The auditor may, but is not required to, include additional wording regarding the general inherent limitations of internal control, including the possibility that management may override the entity's internal controls.

The appendix to AU Section 325 presents the following examples of circumstances that may be control deficiencies, significant deficiencies, or material weaknesses.

DEFICIENCIES IN THE DESIGN OF CONTROLS

1. Inadequate design of internal control over the preparation of the financial statements being audited.
2. Inadequate design of internal control over a significant account or process.

3. Inadequate documentation of the components of internal control.
4. Insufficient control consciousness within the organization, for example, the tone at the top and the control environment.
5. Absent or inadequate segregation of duties within a significant account or process.
6. Absent or inadequate controls over the safeguarding of assets, (this applies to controls that the auditor determines would be necessary for effective internal control over financial reporting).
7. Inadequate design of information technology (IT) general and application controls that prevent the information system from providing complete and accurate information consistent with financial reporting objectives and current needs.
8. Employees or management who lack the qualifications and training to fulfill their assigned functions. For example, in an entity that prepares financial statements in accordance with generally accepted accounting principles, the person responsible for the accounting and reporting function lacks the skills and knowledge to apply generally accepted accounting principles in recording the entity's financial transactions or preparing its financial statements.
9. Inadequate design of monitoring controls used to assess the design and operating effectiveness of the entity's internal control over time.
10. The absence of an internal process to report deficiencies in internal control to management on a timely basis.

FAILURES IN THE OPERATION OF INTERNAL CONTROL

1. Failure in the operation of effectively designed controls over a significant account or process, for example, the failure of a control such as dual authorization for significant disbursements within the purchasing process.
2. Failure of the information and communication component of internal control to provide complete and accurate output because of deficiencies in timeliness, completeness, or accuracy, for example, the failure to obtain timely and accurate consolidating information from remote locations that is needed to prepare the financial statements.
3. Failure of controls designed to safeguard assets from loss, damage, or misappropriation. This circumstance may need careful consideration before it is evaluated as a significant deficiency or material weakness. For example, assume that a company uses security devices to safeguard its inventory (preventive controls) and also performs periodic physical inventory counts (detective control) timely in relation to its financial reporting. Although the physical inventory count does not safeguard the inventory from theft or loss, it prevents a material misstatement of the financial statements if performed effectively and timely. Therefore, given that the definitions of material weakness and significant deficiency relate to likelihood of misstatement of the financial statements, the failure of a preventive control such as inventory tags will not result in a significant deficiency or material weakness if the detective control (physical inventory) prevents a misstatement of the financial statements. Material weaknesses relating to controls over the safeguarding of assets would only exist if the company does not have effective controls (considering both safeguarding and other controls) to prevent or detect a material misstatement of the financial statements.
4. Failure to perform reconciliations of significant accounts. For example, accounts receivable subsidiary ledgers are not reconciled to the general ledger account in a timely or accurate manner.

5. Undue bias or lack of objectivity by those responsible for accounting decisions, for example, consistent understatement of expenses or overstatement of allowances at the direction of management.
6. Misrepresentation by client personnel to the auditor (an indicator of fraud).
7. Management override of controls.
8. Failure of an application control caused by a deficiency in the design or operation of an IT general control.

326 EVIDENTIAL MATTER

SOURCES OF STANDARDS

SAS 106, *Audit Evidence*

INTRODUCTION/SUMMARY

Independent auditors spend a significant amount of time gathering and evaluating evidential matter in order to render an opinion on the entity's financial statements. The third standard of fieldwork, as amended by SAS 105, *Generally Accepted Auditing Standards* (amendment to SAS 95), states

> The auditor must obtain sufficient appropriate audit evidence by performing audit procedures to afford a reasonable basis for an opinion regarding the financial statements under audit.

SAS 106, *Audit Evidence*, describes the concept of audit evidence as follows (paragraph 2):

> *Audit evidence* is all the information used by the auditor in arriving at the conclusions on which the audit opinion is based and includes the information contained in the accounting records underlying the financial statements and other information.

CONCEPT OF AUDIT EVIDENCE

Evidence to support the financial statements consists of both the underlying accounting data and corroborating information. Accounting records consist of a variety of items, including checks, invoices, contracts, general and subsidiary ledgers, worksheets, and disclosures. While accounting data alone cannot be considered sufficient, audit evidence is necessary, and an opinion on financial statements should not be issued without it. Corroborating information includes

1. Checks.
2. Records of electronic fund transfers.
3. Invoices.
4. Contracts.
5. Minutes of meetings.
6. Confirmations and other written representations by knowledgeable people.
7. Information obtained by the auditor from inquiry, observation, inspection, and physical examination.
8. Other information developed by, or available to, the auditor.

For some entities the accounting data and corroborating evidence may only be available in an electronic form. Electronic evidence may exist only at a certain point in time. The auditor should consider the time period during which information is available when determining the nature, timing, and extent of substantive testing and possibly tests of controls.

The underlying accounting data are generally tested through

1. Analysis and review.
2. Retracing steps in the accounting process.
3. Recalculation.
4. Reconciling.

The performance of such procedures may signal to the auditor that the accounting records are internally consistent, which is useful in determining the fairness of the financial statements.

Management has the responsibility for preparing financial statements based on the entity's accounting records. The auditor obtains evidence by testing the accounting records to determine that the accounting records are internally consistent and agree to the financial statements.

Accounting records alone are not sufficient appropriate audit evidence, and other evidence should be obtained through procedures such as inquiry, observation, and inspection. Furthermore, auditor should read the minutes of meetings and obtain confirmations from third parties if necessary.

SUFFICIENT APPROPRIATE AUDIT EVIDENCE

Sufficiency refers to the quantity of audit evidence, whereas *appropriateness* refers to its quality. Appropriate evidence is both relevant and reliable. The quantity of evidence needed is affected by the risk of misstatement and the quality of such evidence. Sufficiency and appropriateness are interrelated; more evidence does not necessarily compensate for lower quality.

The reliability of audit evidence is affected by its nature, source, and is circumstance dependent. In general (SAS 106, paragraph 8)

1. Audit evidence is more reliable when it is obtained from knowledgeable independent sources outside the entity;
2. Audit evidence that is generated internally is more reliable when the related controls imposed by the entity are effective;
3. Audit evidence obtained directly by the auditor (e.g., observation of the application of a control) is more reliable than audit evidence obtained indirectly or by inference (e.g., inquiry about the application of a control);
4. Audit evidence is more reliable when it exists in documentary form, whether paper, electronic, or other medium (e.g., a contemporaneously written record of a meeting is more reliable than a subsequent oral representation of the matters discussed); and
5. Audit evidence provided by original documents is more reliable than audit evidence provided by photocopies or facsimiles.

The quantity and type of evidential matter required is ultimately a matter of the auditor's judgment. Generally, the auditor has to rely on evidence that is persuasive rather than convincing. It is unlikely that an auditor will be convinced beyond all doubt concerning all aspects of the statements being audited. Because of economic constraints, an auditor's opinion must be formed within a reasonable length of time and at reasonable cost. However, the difficulty and expense in testing an item is not a valid reason for omitting that test.

ASSERTIONS IN OBTAINING AUDIT EVIDENCE

Management is responsible for the fair presentation of financial statements. Management should make several assertions in the financial statements and related disclosures regarding the

1. Recognition.
2. Measurement.
3. Presentation.
4. Disclosure of information.

SAS 106 (paragraph 15) defines three categories of assertions:

1. Assertions about classes of transactions and events for the period under audit

    a. *Occurrence.* Transactions and events that have been recorded have occurred and pertain to the entity.
    b. *Completeness.* All transactions and events that should have been recorded have been recorded.
    c. *Accuracy.* Amounts and other data relating to recorded transactions and events have been recorded appropriately.
    d. *Cutoff.* Transactions and events have been recorded in the correct accounting period.
    e. *Classification.* Transactions and events have been recorded in the proper accounts.

2. Assertions about account balances at the period end

    a. *Existence.* Assets, liabilities, and equity interests exist.
    b. *Rights and obligations.* The entity holds or controls the rights to assets, and liabilities are the obligations of the entity.
    c. *Completeness.* All assets, liabilities, and equity interests that should have been recorded have been recorded.
    d. *Valuation and allocation.* Assets, liabilities, and equity interests are included in the financial statements at appropriate amounts and any resulting valuation or allocation adjustments are appropriately recorded.

3. Assertions about presentation and disclosure

    a. *Occurrence and rights and obligations.* Disclosed events and transactions have occurred and pertain to the entity.
    b. *Completeness.* All disclosures that should have been included in the financial statements have been included.
    c. *Classification and understandability.* Financial information is appropriately presented and described and disclosures are clearly expressed.
    d. *Accuracy and valuation.* Financial and other information is disclosed fairly and at appropriate amounts.

The auditor must determine, for each significant class of transactions, the account balance, the presentation and disclosure, and the relevance of each financial statement assertion. In making this determination, the auditor should consider the source of likely potential misstatements by evaluating (SAS 106, paragraph 19)

1. The nature of the assertion;
2. The volume of transactions or data related to the assertion; and
3. The nature and complexity of the systems, including the use of information technology, by which the entity processes and controls information supporting the assertion.

AUDIT PROCEDURES FOR OBTAINING AUDIT EVIDENCE

The auditor should develop a specific audit objective with respect to each relevant assertion. The auditor should consider which procedures to perform, the timing of those procedures, and which items to select for applying those procedures.

The auditor is required to perform risk assessment audit procedures. This requires the auditor to obtain an understanding of the entity and its environment. Internal controls should be evaluated and the risk of material misstatement assessed. Tests of controls should be performed to test the operating effectiveness of controls in preventing or detecting material misstatements at the relevant assertion level. Substantive procedures including tests of details of classes of transactions, account balances, disclosures, and analytical procedures should be performed to detect material misstatements at the relevant assertion level. The nature and timing of audit procedures may be affected by the fact that certain data are only available at a specific time or that data may only be available in a specific format (e.g., electronic).

The auditor should use the types of audit procedures described below when performing risk assessment procedures, tests of controls, or substantive procedures.

INSPECTION OF RECORDS OR DOCUMENTS

Inspection consists of examining all types of documents on any type of media. Inspection does not involve vouching or tracing. The nature and source of documents affects its reliability. For internally generated documents, the effectiveness of related controls also affects reliability. Various financial statement assertions are addressed through inspection. For instance, examining stock certificates provides evidence of the existence of an asset but not necessarily its value.

INSPECTION OF TANGIBLE ASSETS

This type of evidence is use most frequently for cash, securities, inventory, and property and equipment. Physical examination of tangible assets generally provides appropriate evidence about the existence assertion but not necessarily about its valuation, or rights and obligations assertion.

OBSERVATION

Observation generally consists of looking at client activities to gain an understanding of who performs them, when they are performed, and how they are performed. Observation is used to gather evidence about activities that may not leave an audit trail. Observation satisfies all financial statement assertions. However, it is unlikely to be sufficient by itself and corroborating evidence is generally necessary. Observation of the counting of inventory is generally performed in all audits.

INQUIRY

Inquiry consists of seeking information of all types from knowledgeable individuals. The auditor should consider the knowledge, objectivity, experience, responsibility, and knowledge of the individual being questioned. Inquiry may

1. Concern financial or nonfinancial data;
2. Be oral or written, and the response to inquiry may be oral or written; and
3. Involve individuals inside or outside the audit client.

Written *Management Representations* are an example of inquiries. Inquiry alone does not generally provide sufficient appropriate audit evidence, and corroborating evidence is particularly important. Inquiries alone are insufficient for testing the operating effectiveness of controls. Inquiries are useful in providing evidence for all the financial statement assertions.

CONFIRMATION

Confirmation is a type of inquiry where generally written representation of information is obtained directly from a third party. Generally, accounts receivable are confirmed directly with debtors. Confirmations may also be used to get evidence about the absence of certain conditions. Confirmations provide evidence about existence and rights and obligations assertions.

RECALCULATION

Recalculation consists primarily of checking the mathematical accuracy of documents and records. It is typically performed using CAAT to check the accuracy of the summarization of a file.

REPERFORMANCE

The auditor independently executes procedures or controls either manually or through use of CAAT.

ANALYTICAL PROCEDURES

Analytical procedures use comparisons and relationships between financial and nonfinancial data to identify significant or unusual items. Analytical procedures satisfy all financial statement assertions and are required on all audits. In some instances, analytical procedures alone may be sufficient evidence testing small balances. However, in most instances, analytical procedures alone are insufficient and additional evidence is necessary to meet the requirements of sufficient appropriate evidence.

328 AUDITING FAIR VALUE MEASUREMENTS AND DISCLOSURES

SOURCE OF STANDARDS

GAAS

SAS 101, *Auditing Fair Value Measurements and Disclosures*
SAS 113, *Omnibus Statement on Auditing Standards—2006*

SUMMARY

Fair value measurements of assets, liabilities, and components of equity may be generated from the initial recording of transactions or from changes in their values over time. GAAP requires that in certain situations, changes in fair value be disclosed in net income and in other comprehensive income. Other audit outcomes may also occur from the measurement and disclosure of fair value.

AU Section 328 establishes audit guidance and standards on auditing the fair value measurements and disclosures contained in financial statements. Other audit procedures may also provide information about the measurement and disclosure of fair value.

GAAS GUIDANCE

Fundamental Issues of Fair Value Measurement and Disclosures

GAAP requires that certain items in the financial statement be measured and disclosed at their fair values. *Fair value* is defined as

> *the amount at which that asset (or liability) could be bought (or incurred) or sold (or settled)*
> *in a current transaction between willing parties, that is, other than in a forced or liquidation*
> *sale. (Statement of Financial Accounting Concepts No. 7)*

In requiring measurement of fair value, GAAP requires that observable market prices be used to the greatest extent possible. Fair value measurements for which market prices are not observable are inherently imprecise because they are assumptions about future conditions, transactions, or events whose outcome is uncertain and will therefore be subject to change. Because consideration of such assumptions is based on information available at the time of the audit, the auditor is not responsible for predicting future conditions, transactions, or events that, had they been known at the time of the audit, could have had a significant effect on management's actions or management's assumptions about fair value measurements and disclosures.

In determining the fair value measurements and related disclosures that will be included in the client's financial statements, management needs to make several important determinations. Management must

- Establish the accounting and financial reporting processes for determining fair value measurements and disclosures.
- Select the valuation methods that will be used.
- Identify, explain, and support significant assumptions used in determining fair value measurements and disclosures.
- Prepare the valuation.
- Ensure the presentation and disclosure of fair value measurements comply with GAAP.

The actual measurement of fair value will vary in complexity with the item whose value is being measured. For example, where investments are bought and sold in active markets, there is reliable information available on the prices at which trades occur. Clearly, the published price quotations in an active market are the best evidence of their fair value. However, the process is much more difficult for a complex derivative financial instrument where management may have to estimate fair value based on current information available (see below). The instrument may not even have a current market price.

If no market prices are observable, GAAP requires that the valuation methods used incorporate assumptions that marketplace participants would use in their estimates of fair value whenever such information is obtainable without undue cost and effort. AU Section 328 notes that if information about market assumptions is not available, the client may use its own assumptions as long as there are no contrary data indicating that different assumptions should be used. These parameters apply only to fair value accounting estimates. Fair value may also be estimated through the use of a valuation method that, for example, might discount future estimated cash flows.

UNDERSTANDING THE ENTITY'S PROCESS FOR DETERMINING FAIR VALUE MEASUREMENTS AND RELATED CONTROLS AND RISK ASSESSMENT ASSOCIATED WITH IT

Management is responsible for designing the accounting and financial reporting process that will determine the entity's fair value measurements. The process for determining fair value measurements may range from the simplistic and highly reliable to more sophisticated mechanisms using intricate calculations that may be tainted with uncertainty and subjectivity.

In order to plan the nature, timing, and extent of audit procedures to be performed, GAAS requires that the auditor understand how the entity obtains its fair value measurements as well as the related controls and assessment of risk associated with the measurements. In doing this, AU Section 328 suggests that the following areas be considered:

1. The role of information technology in the process of fair value measurements and disclosure.
2. The expertise and experience of those persons who help generate fair value measurements.
3. Controls relating to the process of measuring fair value; for example, data controls and segregation of duties between those committing the entity to the transactions and those responsible for doing the value.
4. The extent to which the entity employs specialists to obtain fair value measurements and disclosures.

5. The breadth and width of accounts or transactions that require fair value measurements or disclosures regardless of where the transactions originated (e.g., routine and recurring transactions vs. unusual ones).

6. The use of a service organization to provide fair value measurements or the data that supports the measurements (if so, see AU Section 324, *Service Organizations*).

7. The assumptions used by management in determining fair value.

8. The process used to formulate and apply management's assumptions. Did management use available market information to develop these assumptions?

9. The documentation that supports management's assumptions about fair value measurements.

10. What processes, if any, used to monitor changes in management's assumptions in determining fair value.

11. The reliability of security procedures and change controls including approval processes for valuation models and information systems related to the determination of fair value.

12. The controls relating to the consistency, timeliness, and reliability of the data used in valuation models.

The risk of material misstatement and the determination of the nature, timing, and extent of audit procedures are predicated on the auditor's understanding of the entity's processes and controls. There is a direct relationship between the risk of material misstatement and the complexity of the accounting and reporting requirements for fair value measurements.

Since fair value determinations often require management to make subjective judgments and increase with the complexity of the measurement, the possibility of management override of controls becomes an issue. (See AU Section 316, *Consideration of Fraud in a Financial Statement Audit.*) The auditor must then consider the inherent limitations of internal control in assessing control risk.

FAIR VALUE MEASUREMENTS AND CONFORMITY WITH GAAP

In ascertaining whether the client's fair value measurements and disclosures in the financial statements are in conformity with GAAP, the auditor should consider the following areas:

- Assets or liabilities requiring fair value measurements.
- Disclosures describing the basis for the fair value measurements and any significant uncertainties related to these measurements.

In making an assessment of fair value conformity and adequacy of the related accounting, the auditor should utilize

- An understanding of the GAAP requirements,
- Knowledge of the client's business and industry, and
- Knowledge of the results of other audit procedures.

The auditor's knowledge of the client's business and industry is particularly important where the asset or liability or the valuation method is highly complex. AU Section 328 states

> The measurement of the fair value of some items, for example "in process research and development" or intangible assets acquired in a business combination, may involve special considerations that are affected by the nature of the entity and its operations. Also, the auditor's knowledge of the business, together with the results of other audit procedures, may help identify assets for which management should assess the need to recognize an impairment loss under applicable GAAP. (AU Section 328.16)

The auditor should also evaluate the client's courses of action and ability to generate information related to fair value measurements, fair value presentation and disclosure, and how fair value changes are reported in the financial statements. Questions should be raised about the client's fair value process and related supportive evidence obtained in the following areas:

- Management's track record in making sure its stated intentions for assets or liabilities are carried out.
- Management's written plans and other documentation, including budgets and minutes relating to fair value considerations.
- Management's stated reasons for choosing a particular course of action.
- Management's ability to carry out a particular course of action given the entity's economic circumstances including contractual commitments.

LACK OF OBSERVABLE MARKET PRICES

Often no market prices will be observable, so the entity will have to estimate amounts using a valuation method. The auditor must determine whether the method of measurement is appropriate. The evaluation requires

- Understanding management's rationale for selecting a particular method;
- Discussing with management its reasons for selecting the valuation method; and above all
- Using professional judgment.

In acquiring an understanding of the reasons for choosing the valuation method, the auditor should determine whether

- The valuation method is appropriate given what is being valued;
- The valuation method is suitable to the business, industry, and environment in which the entity operates; and
- Management has chosen the method by applying the required GAAP. That is, does GAAP support the method selected in the circumstances at hand?

The auditor should ascertain whether management has investigated the different range of fair value measurements that can be generated from the different valuation methods available. If so, the auditor should determine how management reached its conclusions about which valuation method to use. The auditor should also evaluate whether the method chosen for determining fair value measurements was applied consistently. It is possible that consistent application of valuation methods is not appropriate given changes in the environment or circumstances, or changes in accounting principles. On the other hand, management may simply have decided to change valuation methods. If so, the auditor must decide whether the new method is more appropriate than the old, whether the change is supported by a change in GAAP requirements, or whether new circumstances have presented themselves.

USE OF A SPECIALIST

The auditor has to decide whether a specialist is necessary to audit the client's fair value measurements. In doing so, the auditor must first decide on who, if not the auditor, has the necessary skill and knowledge to plan and perform procedures related to fair values. If the decision is to use a specialist, the auditor should consider the guidance in AU Section 336, *Using the Work of a Specialist.*

Through discussions with the specialist or by reading the report of the specialist, the auditor must ascertain whether the specialist's understanding of the definition of fair value and the method the specialist will use to determine fair values are consistent with those of management and with GAAP. AU Section 328 says, for example, that the method used by a specialist for estimating the fair value of real estate or a complex derivative may not be consistent with the measurement principles specified in GAAP.

TESTING FAIR VALUE MEASUREMENTS AND DISCLOSURES

The auditor's tests of the entity's fair value measurements and disclosures are a function of the assessed risk of material misstatement. The procedures the auditor plans to perform vary significantly in their nature, timing, and extent because of both the wide range of possible fair value measurements (from relatively simple to complex) and the variances in the risk of material misstatement associated with the overall process for determining fair values.

Substantive tests of a client's fair value measurements may involve

- Testing management's significant assumptions, valuation models, and the data used to develop fair value measurements and disclosures;
- Confirming the entity's measurements through independent fair value estimates; and
- Reviewing subsequent events and transactions to ensure fair value measurement and disclosure accuracy.

The auditor must assess the complexity of the fair value measurement. Complexities may differ due either to the nature of the items being measured or to the valuation methods used. For example, AU Section 328 states that in the absence of quoted prices in an active market, an estimate of a security's fair value may be based on the discounted cash flow valuation method or the transactions valuation method.

The more complex a measurement, the more uncertain is its reliability. This increased uncertainty may be due to

- The number of complex assumptions associated with the measurement,
- Increased subjectivity of assumptions,
- Lack of objective data due to the use of highly subjective factors,
- The length of the forecast period, and/or
- More uncertainty about future occurrences or outcomes of events underlying the assumptions used.

As noted, the nature, timing, and extent of the audit procedures to be performed on fair value measurements and disclosures are a function of the auditor's understanding of the process management used for measuring fair value as well as his or her assessment of the risk of material misstatement. Auditors should consider these three possibilities in preparing audit procedures for this area:

1. The client's fair value measurements were made at a date that does not coincide with the date when the entity is required to measure and report the information in its financial statements. The auditor should investigate whether management has taken into account the effect of events, transactions, and changes in conditions that occurred between the date of the measurement and the reporting date.
2. Collateral may be a significant consideration in measuring the fair value of an investment or evaluating its carrying amount. In general, collateral is commonly assigned for certain types of investments in debt instruments. GAAP requires that such investments be measured at fair value or be evaluated for impairment. The auditor's responsibility is to obtain competent audit evidence of the existence, value, rights, and access to or transferability of such collateral. The auditor should also determine whether all appropriate liens have been filed and whether there are appropriate disclosures about the collateral.

3. It may be necessary to perform additional audit procedures to be satisfied with fair value measurement(s). AU Section 328 suggests that an auditor may choose, for example, to inspect an asset to obtain information about its current physical condition that may be relevant to its fair value. In another situation, inspection of a security may reveal a restriction on its marketability and thus on its fair value.

The auditor must test the significant assumptions, the underlying data, and the valuation model supporting the entity's fair value measurements and disclosures.

In determining the nature, timing, and extent of the audit procedures to be performed in measuring and disclosing fair value, the auditor must thoroughly understand the process management used to determine fair value. The basic question is whether the client's process is reliable. To do this, the auditor must test management's significant assumptions, underlying data, and valuation model. In pursuing this end, the following questions should be asked:

1. Are management's assumptions relating to fair value reasonable and consistent with market data? Was fair value measured using an appropriate model? Was information that was reasonably available at the time used by management to derive fair value?

2. Has the client's process been tested by comparing fair value measurements determined in prior periods to the results for the current period? Have variances from the prior period fair value measurements resulted from changes in market or economic circumstances?

3. Did the assumptions used by management in measuring fair value, taken individually and as a whole, provide a reasonable basis for the fair value measurements and disclosures in the financial statements?

4. In complex valuation methods, what important assumptions were made? For example, a complex valuation method might consist of valuation methods that employ a combination of estimates of expected future cash flows together with estimates of the future values of assets or liabilities discounted to the present. Has the auditor fully investigated the significant assumptions underlying the valuation methods? Are the assumptions reasonable and consistent with current market information?

5. Are management's assumptions on which fair value measurements are based generally supported by both internal and external sources of evidence? How reliable are these sources of evidence including related historical and market information?

6. Just which fair value related assumptions does management consider significant? Generally, significant assumptions cover matters that materially affect the fair value measurement and may include those

    • Sensitive to variation or uncertainty in amount or nature (e.g., AU Section 328 notes that assumptions about short-term interest rates may be less susceptible to significant variation than those about long-term interest rates); and
    • Susceptible to misapplication or bias.

7. How sensitive are the valuations to changes in significant assumptions, including market conditions? Management should use techniques such as sensitivity analysis, when possible, to help identify particularly sensitive assumptions. If management has not done this, the auditor should think about employing such techniques to identify those assumptions.

8. Do management's assumptions and factors, taken as a whole and individually, provide a reasonable basis for the fair value measurements? (AU Section 328 suggests that because assumptions are often interdependent they need to be internally con-

sistent.) A particular assumption that may seem reasonable in isolation may not be reasonable when used in conjunction with other assumptions.

9. Are the assumptions on which the fair value measurements are based individually and taken as a whole both realistic and consistent with

   - The general economic environment of the country, the specific industry of which the entity is a part, and the entity's specific economic circumstances;
   - The plans of the entity (these include management's specific objectives and strategies);
   - The entity's past experience;
   - Existing market information;
   - Assumptions made in prior periods;
   - Assumptions used by management in making other accounting estimates used for the financial statement accounts as well as other matters relating to the financial statements; and
   - Cash flow risk, including variability in the amount and timing of cash flows and related effects on the discount rate?

10. Is the client reliance (if any) on historical financial information in the development of fair value measurement assumptions justified? The historical information used might not be representative of future conditions or events. For example, management may engage in new activities or circumstances may change.

11. What model did the entity use to measure fair value? Were the assumptions underlying the model's use reasonable? Was the model appropriate considering the entity's circumstances? AU Section 328 illustrates this point by noting that it may be inappropriate to use discounted cash flows for valuing an equity investment in a start-up enterprise if there are no current revenues on which to base the forecast of future earnings or cash flows. Note that for items valued by the entity using a valuation model, the auditor does not function as an appraiser and is not expected to substitute a personal judgment for that of management.

12. How accurate, complete, and relevant are the data used to prepare the fair value measurements including any information used by a specialist?

    Were the fair value measurements properly determined using objective data and management's assumptions? The auditor should test the data used to develop fair value measurements and disclosures. AU Section 328 suggests that the tests might include

    - Procedures like verifying the source of the data;
    - Mathematical recomputation of inputs; and
    - Review of information for internal consistency (i.e., testing whether the information is consistent with management's intent and ability to carry out specified courses of action).

USING INDEPENDENT ESTIMATES TO CORROBORATE FAIR VALUES

To corroborate management's fair value measurements, the auditor may generate independent estimates using a proprietary model. The auditor may apply this model using management's assumptions (after a full evaluation of these assumptions) or personal assumptions in order to compare the results with management's fair value measurements. However, if the auditor makes any assumptions, the auditor must also fully understand management assumptions to ensure that the auditor's independent estimates take into consideration all significant variables considered by management Afterward the auditor should evaluate any significant differences between the auditor's and management's estimates and test the data that management used to measure fair value.

USING SUBSEQUENT EVENTS AND TRANSACTIONS TO CORROBORATE FAIR VALUES

The auditor may choose to use events and transactions that occur after the balance sheet date but before the date of the auditor's report as evidence of fair value measurement. AU Section 328 notes, for example, that sale of an investment shortly after the balance sheet date would provide qualitative supporting evidence for fair value measurements as of the balance sheet date. When there is such substantiation, the audit procedures just described may need to be minimized or need not be performed at all. However, the auditor must be aware of the possibility that the subsequent events or transactions used may reflect changes in circumstances occurring after the balance sheet date (e.g., the prices of actively traded marketable securities may change). If so, subsequent events and transactions are not competent evidence of the balance sheet fair value measurement. In using subsequent or transactions to substantiate fair value measurements, the auditor should make sure to use only events or transactions that reflect the same circumstances as existed at the balance sheet date.

FAIR VALUE DISCLOSURES

The Financial Accounting Standards Board (FASB) requires the disclosure of fair values in financial statements for many reasons. An important one is that such disclosure enhances the relevance of the financial statements to users wanting to assess the entity's performance and financial position. In this context GAAS requires that the auditor evaluate whether the fair value disclosures conform with GAAP. In addition to the fair value information required under GAAP, some entities also choose to disclose voluntary additional fair value information in the notes to the financial statements.

In auditing required and voluntary fair value measurements and related note disclosures for GAAP conformity, the following guidance should be followed:

1. The auditor must obtain competent audit evidence that the valuation principles used in measuring fair value conform to GAAP.
2. The valuation principles being used should be applied consistently.
3. The method of estimation and significant assumptions used must be adequately disclosed.
4. There should be adequate disclosures about fair value information in the financial statements. In evaluating adequacy, the auditor should make sure there is sufficient disclosure about fair value measurements that are highly uncertain. That is, the auditor must make sure that users are sufficiently informed about any such uncertainty.
5. There may be occasions when a client omits fair value information required by GAAP because it may not be practical to determine such values with adequate reliability. If so, the auditor must evaluate whether the financial statements are materially misstated.
6. The fair value measurements and disclosures conform with GAAP evaluated in the context of the financial statements taken as a whole (see AU Section 312.36 through AU Section 312.41).

MANAGEMENT REPRESENTATIONS

GAAS requires written representations as part of the audit of an entity's financial statements (see AU Section 333). The auditor should therefore obtain written representation from management about the reasonableness of significant assumptions underlying fair value measurements and disclosures—such as statements about whether management intends to carry out specific courses of action that are relevant to the use of fair value measurements and disclosures.

AU Section 328 notes that management representations about fair value measurements and disclosures should include statements about

1. The appropriateness of

   a. The measurement methods used,
   b. Related assumptions used in determining fair value, and
   c. Consistency in application (of the methods used);

2. The completeness and adequacy of disclosures related to fair values; and
3. The use of subsequent events as a basis for necessary adjustments to the fair value measurements and disclosures in the financial statements.

COMMUNICATION WITH AUDIT COMMITTEES

Fair value measurements are considered sensitive accounting estimates because of their significance to financial statements and because of the possibility that future events affecting them may differ markedly from management's current judgments. AU Section 380, *Communication with Audit Committees*, requires that the entity's audit committee be informed about both the process used by management in formulating such sensitive accounting estimates and the basis for the auditor's conclusions about their reasonableness.

AU Section 328 suggests that the auditor should consider communicating the following fair value considerations to the audit committee:

- The nature of the significant assumptions used in measuring fair value.
- The degree of subjectivity involved in formulating the assumptions.
- The relative materiality of the items being measured at fair value to the financial statements as a whole.

The nature and form of the actual communication to the entity's audit committee should be determined by the guidance in AU Section 380.

329 ANALYTICAL PROCEDURES

SOURCES OF STANDARDS

SAS 56, *Analytical Procedures*
SAS 96, *Audit Documentation*

INTRODUCTION/SUMMARY

Analytical procedures are defined by AU Section 329 as evaluations of financial information made by a study of plausible relationships among both financial and nonfinancial data. An assumption behind analytical procedures is that plausible relationships among data are expected to continue unless known conditions provide evidence to the contrary. Analytical procedures range from simple data comparisons to the complex multivariate models.

The auditor should have an understanding of analytical procedures as well as their limitations. Analytical procedures generally require knowledge of the client and the operating environment. The relationships used in analytical procedures and the types of data analyzed require comparisons with expectations.

Analytical procedures are normally used at three stages in the audit.

1. Analytical procedures are used in the planning stage to assist the auditor in planning the nature, timing, and extent of other auditing procedures. Some analytical procedures are required to be performed in the planning stage. Analytical procedures at the planning stage help the auditor identify significant matters requiring special consideration. Typically aggregated data at a high level is used in the planning stage.
2. Analytical procedures may also be used during the testing phase of an audit as a substantive test to obtain evidential matter about particular assertions related to account balances or classes of transactions.
3. Analytical procedures are required at the final or review phase of the audit. They serve as an overall review of the financial information in the final review stage of the audit. They are used at this stage to help the auditor take a final objective look at the financial statements for material misstatements.

AU 329.05 gives the following examples of sources of information for developing expectations about analytical procedures:

1. Financial information for comparable prior period(s) giving consideration to known changes.
2. Anticipated results, budgets, or forecasts, including extrapolations from interim or annual data.
3. Relationships among elements of financial information within the period.
4. Information regarding the industry in which the client operates.
5. Relationships of financial information with relevant nonfinancial information.

ANALYTICAL PROCEDURES IN PLANNING THE AUDIT

Analytical procedures are applied in the planning phase to assist the auditor in planning the nature, timing, and extent of auditing procedures that will be used to obtain evidential matter. The analytical procedures used at this stage are meant to improve the auditor's understanding of the client's business and the environment. These procedures also help in identifying vulnerable areas.

Analytical procedures in the planning phase generally use data aggregated at a high level. The sophistication, extent, and timing of the procedures vary widely based on the size and complexity of the client. Analytical procedures used in planning the audit may use both financial data and relevant nonfinancial information.

ANALYTICAL PROCEDURES USED AS SUBSTANTIVE TESTS

Substantive tests include

1.   Tests of details.
2.   Analytical procedures.

The auditor may use either one or both types of substantive tests. The auditor will normally make the decision about which procedures to use to achieve a particular audit objective based on the expected effectiveness and efficiency of the procedures. For certain assertions, analytical procedures are highly effective in providing assurance, whereas for other assertions, tests of details may be more efficient or effective.

The expected effectiveness and efficiency of an analytical procedure in identifying potential misstatements depends on several factors, including (AU329.11)

1.   The nature of the assertion,
2.   The plausibility and predictability of the relationship,
3.   The availability and reliability of the data used to develop the expectation, and
4.   The precision of the expectation.

NATURE OF ASSERTION

Analytical procedures are especially effective and efficient when

1.   Potential misstatements would not be apparent from an examination of the detailed evidence, and/or
2.   Detailed evidence is not readily available.

PLAUSIBILITY AND PREDICTABILITY OF THE RELATIONSHIP

The more stable the environment, the more predictable the relationship. An unstable or dynamic environment will make the analysis difficult. Income statement accounts tend to foster a more predictable relationship than relationships involving only balance sheet accounts. Relationships are generally less predictable where transactions show significant management discretion. The auditor should be aware that data may sometimes appear to be related when in fact it is not. Moreover an unexpected relationship can sometimes provide valuable information when properly analyzed.

AVAILABILITY AND RELIABILITY OF DATA

Data may not always be available for the auditor to develop expectations in applying analytical procedures. The reliability of the data depends on several factors including the sources of data, the conditions under which the data were gathered, and other information about the data. The following factors influence the auditor's consideration of the reliability of data (AU 329.16):

1. Whether the data were obtained from external independent sources or from internal potentially biased sources.
2. Whether sources within the entity were independent of those who are responsible for the amount being audited.
3. Whether there were adequate and reliable controls in the environment under which data were developed.
4. Whether the data were subjected to audit testing in the current or prior year.
5. Whether the expectations were developed using data from a variety of sources.

PRECISION OF THE EXPECTATION

The expectation should be precise enough to enable the auditor to detect potential material misstatements. The precision of the expectation depends on several factors, including the detail of the data being used to develop the expectations. For example, monthly amounts will generally be more effective than annual amounts in detecting material misstatements. Financial relationships can also be affected by a variety of factors. Effective identification of precise factors that significantly affect the relationship is generally necessary to achieve the desired level of assurance. It is possible that material misstatement may be obscured by offsetting factors.

INVESTIGATION AND EVALUATION OF SIGNIFICANT DIFFERENCES

When using analytical procedures for substantive testing purposes, the auditor should consider the magnitude of difference from the expectation that can be accepted without further inquiry. Significant unexpected differences should be investigated by the auditor. Frequently the auditor does this by making inquiries of management. Management responses should be corroborated with other evidential matter. If the difference cannot be explained, additional evidence about the assertion should be obtained by performing other audit procedures.

DOCUMENTATION OF SUBSTANTIVE ANALYTICAL PROCEDURES

When analytical procedures are used as a substantive test, the auditor should document the following (AU 329.22):

1. The expectation and the development of the expectation.
2. Results of the comparison/ratio analysis.
3. Additional auditing procedures performed due to significant unexpected differences.

ANALYTICAL PROCEDURES USED IN THE OVERALL REVIEW

Analytical procedures are used at the final review stage to identify areas where additional evidence might be needed. The auditor would generally read the financial statements and notes at this stage. The auditor should also consider

1. If there is sufficient evidence to explain unusual or unexpected fluctuations identified in the planning or substantive testing stage of the audit, and
2. If there are any new unusual or unexpected fluctuations that were not previously discovered.

330 THE CONFIRMATION PROCESS

SOURCES OF STANDARDS

GAAS

SAS 67, *The Confirmation Process*

ADDITIONAL NON-GAAS PROFESSIONAL GUIDANCE

AICPA Audit and Accounting Audit Manual
Practice Alert 03-1, *Audit Confirmations*

SUMMARY

AU Section 330 provides guidance about the use of confirmations. It recasts previous confirmation guidance into concepts of audit risk assessment, financial statement assertions, skepticism, and related variables that were not required before. It also highlights areas where the auditor must be especially careful in using confirmations, warning particularly against overreliance. The confirmation of accounts receivable has been a generally accepted auditing procedure since the McKesson & Robbins debacle catapulted its use to a preeminent position in the late 1930s, but empirical studies, practitioner interpretations, and peer reviews make it clear that auditors from time to time overrely on confirmations for audit evidence.

AU Section 330 rectifies this problem by using audit risk assessment in determining the audit procedures to be applied, including whether confirmations should be used at all. It also enumerates factors that influence the reliability of confirmations as well as the alternative procedures that must be performed when confirmation replies are not received and gives guidance on evaluation of results.

GAAS GUIDANCE

THE CONFIRMATION PROCESS

NOTE: At the end of this section there are a number of forms that will be useful to the practitioner in the confirmation process.

The process of confirming data consists of requesting information from a third party about an item relating to an assertion on the financial statements of a client company. The process encompasses the following:

- Confirmation selection;
- Confirmation request design;
- Communication to the third party;
- Third-party response to the confirmation; and
- Evaluation of the confirmed information, or lack of it, in terms of audit objectives and reliability.

The quality of evidence derived from information from third parties about financial statement assertions made by management is reliable. AU Section 326, Audit Evidence, describes this in the following way:

> *Audit evidence is more reliable when it is obtained from knowledgeable independent sources outside the entity.*

HOW DOES THE AUDITOR'S ASSESSMENT OF AUDIT RISK RELATE TO THE PERFORMANCE OF CONFIRMATION PROCEDURES?

In general, the auditor uses audit risk assessment to determine the audit procedures to be used in a given situation. The audit risk model is discussed in AU Section 312. Section 312 discusses how the assessment of inherent risk and control risk determines the acceptable level of detection risk enabling the auditor to design an audit program to achieve a suitably low level of audit risk. It is the auditor's assessment of the latter that allows him or her to ascertain the audit procedures that will be required. Confirmation procedures are one of these.

The auditor performs confirmation procedures to obtain evidence from third parties about financial statement assertions made by management. The greater the combined assessed level of inherent risk and control risk, the greater assurance the auditor needs from the performance of substantive tests relating to a given financial statement assertion. As a result, the auditor will be required to design tests which will provide more or different evidence about the assertion. For example, if the level of combined assessed inherent and control risk has increased, the auditor might choose to use confirmations rather than tests of documents or parties within the entity. Alternatively, he or she might choose to use confirmation procedures with these tests rather than in place of them.

In general, if an entity has executed unusual or complex transactions, it is not uncommon for there to be high levels of inherent and control risk. Combined high levels of assessed inherent and control risk together with unusual or complex transactions usually signal the need for the auditor to confirm the transactions with other parties in addition to examining any documentation that the entity might have. For example, if the auditor ascertains that the level of inherent and control risk for a client relating to an unusual sale at the end of the entity's fiscal period is elevated, then clearly the auditor should confirm that sales transaction and its details.

In general, the auditor must ascertain whether the performance of confirmation procedures reduces the audit risk for a financial assertion to an acceptably low level. In making this determination the following should be considered: (1) the materiality of the account balance and (2) the auditor's assessment of the applicable inherent and control risk assessment. If it is decided that more than confirmations are needed, additional substantive procedures should be performed to insure that there is sufficient satisfactory audit evidence. For example, with respect to the completeness and existence assertions of accounts receivable, it may be necessary for the auditor to perform sales cutoff tests in addition to confirming accounts receivable in order to achieve an acceptably low level of audit risk.

Correspondingly, if the combined assessed level of inherent and control risk is low, then the auditor requires less assurance from the performance of substantive tests to verify a conclusion about the client's financial statement assertion. As a result, the auditor may change the nature of the tests to be performed from a more costly but effective test to those that are less costly and less effective. To illustrate, if the combined assessed level of inherent and control risk over the existence of cash is low, it would be acceptable for the auditor to decide not to confirm cash balances but rather limit his or her tests to inspecting the client's bank statements.

USING CONFIRMATIONS TO TEST FINANCIAL STATEMENT ASSERTIONS

AU Section 326 categorizes financial statement assertions into five groups

1. Existence or occurrence.
2. Completeness.
3. Rights and obligations.
4. Valuations or allocation.
5. Presentation and disclosure.

Although confirmations may be designed to test any one of these assertions, they are most effective in testing for existence and rights and obligations and less effective for the completeness and valuation assertions. For those assertions that are not well addressed by the confirmation process, other audit procedures should be used in combination with or in lieu of confirmations. For example, with respect to completeness, although a confirmation might not prove highly effective in detecting an understatement in accounts payable, if properly designed, it can be of some use.

AU Section 330 indicates that success in addressing the completeness assertion depends in part on the population from which the auditor selects the items to be tested. To illustrate, when testing for the completeness assertion of a client's accounts payable balance, the appropriate population should be a list of vendors, receiving documents, or disbursements rather than the amounts recorded in the accounts payable subsidiary ledger. This will make it possible to detect any accounts payable amounts that may not appear in the ledger. Some confirmation forms were not designed to explicitly test for completeness, so the auditor should not depend on these forms to detect information about account balances not listed.

The confirmation process consists of designing the confirmation request, performing confirmation procedures, and evaluating the results. In accordance with AU Section 230, *Due Professional Care in the Performance of Work*, the auditor must exercise reasonable professional skepticism throughout this process, and never be satisfied with less than persuasive evidence even when there is an assumption of unquestionable client honesty.

Confirmation Design

The confirmation should be customized to insure that the evidence collected is reliable and satisfies audit objectives. Satisfaction relates to the assertions being tested (previously discussed). Reliability is predicated on the following factors:

- The type of confirmation request used.
- The audit firm's prior experience on the audit.
- The type of information being confirmed.
- The respondent.

Type of confirmation request. Confirmations may be positive, blank, or negative. Positive confirmations require that respondents specifically note whether they agree or disagree with the data on the confirmation. The blank form does not furnish any information but asks the respondent to fill in the data required. Negative confirmations require a response only if the respondent disagrees with the information provided.

Positive confirmations provide direct audit evidence when they are returned, but there is a clear risk that an individual may sign and return the confirmation without actually authenticating the accuracy of the data. To reduce that risk, an auditor may choose to send out a blank confirmation to increase the probability of an accurate response. Because the recipient must obtain the information required before sending back the confirmation, the blank form is considered more reliable than those that carry the information to be verified. However, the use of blank forms usually has a lower response rate because they require additional action on the part of the respondent. Still, by performing additional audit procedures, the effect of the lower response rate may be mitigated.

Negative confirmations are the least reliable. If a negative confirmation is not returned, what conclusion should the auditor reach? Did the respondent choose to ignore the confirmation request and not return it or should it be considered a correct response? Offsetting this consideration is their lower cost. Negative confirmations are cheaper than positive confirmations because they do not require second requests and subsequent review. If a positive confirmation is not returned, second requests are almost always sent out, with appropriate follow-up.

AU Section 330 notes that negative confirmations may be used when

1. The combined assessed level of inherent and control risk is low (there is a low susceptibility to misstatement or the auditor has concluded that there is a low probability that internal controls will not detect or prevent misstatement);
2. There is a large number of small balances; and
3. The auditor has no reason to believe that the recipients of the requests will not give consideration to the confirmation requests. For example, the auditor determines from the previous auditor that response rates in prior years were very high. The current auditor would have no reason to believe that recipients would not give the due consideration to current confirmation mailings.

Negative confirmations may also be used, for example, in populations where the probability of widespread misstatements is minimal and conscientious review of the confirmations sent can be expected. For example, if these criteria have been satisfied in an audit of a financial institution, an auditor might choose to use negative confirmations at the end of the year when confirming demand deposits accounts. The confirmations might be sent to customers with the customers' year-end statements.

Negative confirmations may also be used in conjunction with positive confirmations. For example, in auditing the accounts receivable balance, positive confirmations might be used to verify the more material customer account balances and negative confirmations less material ones. In all cases, however, the choice of confirmation type and the extent of its use is a matter of the auditor's judgment.

Returned negative confirmations clearly provide important evidence relating to, for example, an account receivable balance, but if a confirmation is not returned, the auditor should not conclude that the customer received the confirmation and determined that the data were correct. It may be that the customer's address is currently unknown.

The firm's prior experience on the audit. In determining how much reliance to place on confirmation procedures, the firm's prior experience on the audit of this or a similar client should be considered. For example, an auditor may want to identify the degree of misstatements in prior years, the response rate experienced, and the existence of inaccurate information conveyed on the confirmation. If the confirmation results for a prior year were unreliable, or if the response rates were significantly lower than should be expected, the auditor should consider alternative procedures for obtaining reliable audit evidence. For example, in auditing accounts receivable, an auditor might consider examining subsequent cash collections on account, reviewing duplicate sales invoices, or corresponding with the client as possible alternative procedures.

The type of information being confirmed. In designing the confirmation process, the auditor must consider what types of information respondents can confirm. This will affect both the response rate and the quality of the evidence obtained. For example, in designing the confirmation to be used in an audit of the mortgage division of a financial institution, the auditor should ascertain whether debtor respondents can readily determining the balance of their loan at a given point in time. They may be able to easily confirm how current their periodic payments are and what the amount is, but they may be uncertain about the principal balance outstanding as of the audit date. Thus the confirmation should not ask about this.

The items to be confirmed are a function of the auditors' understanding of the client's arrangements and transactions with confirmation respondents. The auditor should analyze the essence of these activities in deciding what to include in the confirmation request. For example, an auditor who believes that there is a significant risk that there may be oral modification to a written agreement may want to confirm not only the details of the agreement but also whether there have been oral modifications.

Auditor's knowledge of the respondent. The design of the confirmation should also relate to the auditor's knowledge of the respondent. For example, the auditor should only send a confirmation to an individual known to be competent and knowledgeable about the information to be confirmed. AU Section 330 states that the auditor's knowledge of the respondent's objectivity, neutrality, competence, ability, and willingness to respond should all be considered not only in designing the confirmation request but also in evaluating the results and determining the need for additional auditing procedures. These considerations and the discovery of questionable transactions (e.g., unusual transactions at year-end) may increase the auditor's professional skepticism about respondents. If so, the auditor may want to reevaluate the efficacy of sending a confirmation request.

PERFORMING CONFIRMATION PROCEDURES

In performing confirmation procedures, the following guidance should be followed:

1. The auditor must maintain control of the confirmation request and return response through direct communication with the respondent. This will ensure that the result will not be biased as a result of interception. Internal auditors (see AU Section 322, *The Auditor's Consideration of the Internal Audit Function in an Audit*) may help in the control process.

2. If a positive confirmation is used, a second, and perhaps even a third, request should be sent to respondents who have not replied.

3. If an auditor receives oral confirmation of an assertion, it should be documented in the workpapers. If the information conveyed is significant, the respondent should be asked to follow up with a written confirmation.

4. If a confirmation is submitted as a facsimile, to reduce the risk of an inappropriate source and increase the validity of the confirmation, the auditor should verify the source and contents of the facsimile response by calling the sender.

Follow-up on Nonresponses

When responses to positive confirmations have not been received, the auditor should apply alternative auditing procedures to keep audit risk acceptably low. The procedures should depend on the account balance and assertion being tested. For example, in accounts receivable, alternative procedures enable the auditor to ascertain that for accounts not confirmed, the balances existed and were properly stated. Alternative procedures include matching subsequent cash receipts with the balances being paid, verifying that sales invoices were issued and billed to customers, checking shipping documents to prove that goods were actually sent out, and reviewing other documentation for evidence of balance existence on the balance sheet date.

The confirmation procedure is used less for accounts payable than for accounts receivable. In this situation, the auditor primarily searches for balances and transactions that have been omitted or may be misstated. To test for these conditions, alternative procedures might consist of examination of subsequent cash disbursements, correspondence from third parties, confirmations sent to active vendors for which there is no balance at the audit date, and other procedures to test for completeness or understatement.

AU Section 330 notes that alternative accounting procedures may not be necessary even if the auditor has not received responses to positive confirmation requests under the following conditions:

1. There are no unusual or systematic patterns to the nonresponses (e.g., all nonresponses related to year-end transactions appear not to be fictitiously created by the client to overstate the accounts receivable control balance).
2. When projecting the probabilistic amount of overstatement from the nonresponses and all other unadjusted differences, the total does not influence the auditor's decision regarding material misstatement.

Confirmation Procedure Evaluation

After confirming account balances and transactions and performing any necessary alternative procedures, the combined evidence gathered must be evaluated. AU Section 330 recommends that in doing the evaluation the auditor assess

- The overall reliability of the confirmation procedures and alternative procedures performed.
- The effect of confirmation exceptions received, both quantitative and qualitative;
- Any evidence produced from other procedures; and
- The need to generate additional evidence.

Once this has been done, the auditor may decide that the data gathered through all the tests performed were not sufficient and may decide to

- Request additional confirmations, and
- Perform additional tests on transactions and balances, and use analytical review procedures until the requisite satisfaction is obtained.

Generally Accepted Auditing Procedure: Confirmation of Accounts Receivable

Important considerations in confirmation of accounts receivable under GAAS are as follows:

- Confirmation of accounts receivable is a Generally Accepted Auditing Procedure.
- Accounts receivable (and other receivables that require confirmation, such as notes receivable from customers) is defined for this purpose as claims against an entity's customers that were generated from the sale of goods and services, and a financial institution's loans.
- AU Section 330 presumes that during an audit, accounts receivable will be confirmed unless one or more of the following applies:

1. The accounts receivable are immaterial.
2. Based on prior experience with this or similar clients, the auditor knows that confirmation requests will generate a response rate that is either inadequate or unreliable; the use of confirmations is therefore deemed not to be useful.
3. The auditor concludes that the combined assessed level of inherent and control risk is low and that the evidence provided by analytical procedures and other substantive tests of details are sufficient to reduce audit risk to a sufficiently low level that the use of confirmations is not necessary.

If one or more of these three conditions exists and the auditor decides not to use confirmations in examining accounts receivable, the auditor must fully document the reason for this decision in the workpapers of the engagement.

Controlling Correspondence During the Receivable Confirmation Process (Nonauthoritative)

Here are some helpful hints to keep correspondences under control.

1. Have clients prepare all cover letters and confirmation requests on their own letterhead.
2. Keep copies of the cover letter and confirmation for second requests, current workpaper documentation, and any subsequent engagement.
3. Before confirmation requests are mailed out, compare the names and addresses on the requests to the client's records, and compare the balances shown on the confirmations to those in the client's subsidiary ledger.
4. Control the entire mailing procedure process from the stuffing of requests into envelopes through their transfer to the local post office.
5. The confirmation request envelopes that are mailed should have the auditor's post office or postal box number designated as the return address so that any undeliverable requests will be returned directly to the auditor, not the client. If client envelopes are used, attach an auditor's label to each envelope to accomplish this goal.
6. To expedite the return of confirmation requests, have the client include prepaid reply envelopes with the request letter. If confirmation replies are being returned from many different audits, it may be helpful to code the reply envelopes so that they can be separated by engagement before they are opened. If a client objects to the use of an auditor's name and address on the reply envelope, it may be sent to a client's post office box as long as the box is under the full control of the auditor, who should make arrangements with the post office personnel to forward replies received to the auditor after control of the box is relinquished.
7. Control receipt of responses so that the entire confirmation process is deemed independent of the client.

PRACTITIONER CONFIRMATION FORMS AND EXHIBITS

FORM 1. POSITIVE CONFIRMATION

[Use client's letterhead for this form]
[Date]
[Insert customer name and address here]

Dear Gentlemen/Ladies:

As part of the audit of our financial statements, our auditors request that you carefully review the accuracy of your account balance as of the close of business *[insert date]*. If the amount of indebtedness to us indicated below is correct, please indicate this by placing an X in the space provided. If it is incorrect, please indicate the amount you believe is the correct amount of indebtedness and explain the difference in the space provided.

Please note that no payments are to be sent to our auditors. Upon completing this form, please sign, date, and mail it directly to our auditors in the self-addressed envelope provided.

Thank you for your consideration in this matter.

Yours truly,

[Signature and title of client]

Date:_____

The amount owed us as of the close of business on [*insert date here*] is $_____.

I agree with this amount_____.

I disagree with this amount. The balance should be $_____. The difference is due to the following reasons:

[Please insert lines for explanation here]

_____

_____

_____

_____

_____

_____

_____

_____

The same form may be used for second or third confirmation requests by simply stamping it as such.

FORM 2. NEGATIVE CONFIRMATION

The following may be attached to, stamped on, or pasted on the customer's statement.

Audit Confirmation Request

Please carefully review this statement and communicate any discrepancies directly to our auditors in the envelope included for your convenience.

[Name of Auditors]

[Address of Auditors]

If no response is forthcoming, it will be assumed to be correct by our auditors.
Please do not send any payments to our auditors.

FORM 3. ACCOUNTS RECEIVABLE CONTROL SCHEDULE

Date of Confirmation Mailings: FIRST REQ:_____   SECOND REQ:_____ THIRD REQ:_____

Date of Confirmation Receipt

Confirmation Number	Name of Respondent	First Request	Second Request	Third Request
1. _____	_____	_____	_____	_____
2. _____	_____	_____	_____	_____
3. _____	_____	_____	_____	_____
4. _____	_____	_____	_____	_____
5. _____	_____	_____	_____	_____

FORM 4. ACCOUNTS RECEIVABLE STATISTICAL SUMMARY

	Number of Accounts	Percent	Dollar Amount	Percent of Dollar Amount
Total Confirmations Sent				
Positive				
Negative				
Not Confirmed				
Total Accounts Receivable				

	Number of Accounts	Percent	Dollar Amount	Percent of Dollar Amount
Results				
Positive Confirmations:				
No Exceptions Reported				
Exceptions Reported:				
Exceptions Reconciled				
Exceptions Not Reconciled				
Total Exceptions Reported				
Nonreplies				
Alternative Procedures on Nonreplies				
Total Positive Confirmations				
Negative Confirmations:				
No Exceptions Reported				
Exceptions Reported				
Exceptions Reconciled				
Exceptions Not Reconciled				
Total Exceptions Reported				
Nonreplies				
Total Negative Confirmations				
Accounts Not Sent				

FORM 5. AUDIT GUIDANCE CHECKLIST—CONFIRMATIONS OF ACCOUNTS RECEIVABLE

Completed By:_____ Ref. No. _____

1. Get an aged trial balance schedule of accounts receivable (A/R) from the client.
2. Check the accuracy of the entire aged trial balance schedule and trace the amount to the general ledger A/R account balance and A/R subsidiary ledger balance.
3. To insure that all A/R accounts are represented, trace a sample of accounts in the aged trial balance to the subsidiary ledger and a sample of subsidiary ledger accounts to the aged trial balance.
4. Select those A/R balances that will be confirmed, using a statistical or nonstatistical plan, from the trial balance.
5. Prepare the confirmation requests and control their mailing.
6. Trace returned confirmations to the A/R trial balance.
7. Investigate all returned confirmation replies that indicate differences. Examine these differences and reconcile them to their reported balances.
8. Attempt to remail as many of the returned confirmations as possible by getting corrected addresses for those confirmations that were returned.
9. Mail second request confirmations to those accounts that were not responded to. If necessary, mail out third requests.
10. For those accounts for which responses were not received, apply the following alternative procedures:

    - Review cash payments received from customers and match client remittance advices sent by client.
    - Examine underlying documentation to ensure a sale of goods and services took place (e.g., purchase order, invoice, receiving report, etc).

11. Post the dates confirmations were sent out and the date responses were received to an A/R control schedule (see Form 3).
12. Summarize all confirmation results in a statistical summary (see Form 4).

ADDITIONAL PROFESSIONAL GUIDANCE (NONAUTHORITATIVE)

PRACTICE ALERT 03-1, AUDIT CONFIRMATIONS (UPDATED)

This Practice Alert (PA) represents the views of the members of the Professional Issues Task Force (PITF) and has not been approved by any technical committee of the AICPA. Although it is based on existing professional literature, the experience of members of the task force, and information provided by certain AICPA member firms to their own professional staff, it is considered nonauthoritative. In general, PAs are intended to help the auditor understand and apply Statements on Auditing Standards. In applying this guidance, the auditor should be satisfied that it is both appropriate and relevant to the circumstances of the audit. This PA was fully reviewed by the AICPA Audit and Attest staff and deemed to be appropriate.

Introduction

The purpose of this alert is to provide additional guidance to practitioners on the use of confirmations. Audit confirmations can be effectively used to obtain evidence from third parties when auditing many accounts and areas. PA 03-1 enumerates the areas where confirmations are most commonly used:

- Accounts receivable,
- Notes receivable,
- Inventory,
- Consigned merchandise,
- Construction and production contracts,
- Investment securities,
- Market values,
- Accounts payable,
- Notes payable,
- Lines of credit,
- Account balances and other information from financial institutions,
- Other actual and contingent liabilities,
- Related-party transactions, and
- Unusual transactions.

Improving Confirmation Response Rates

To improve confirmation response rates

1. The auditor should make sure that the information being requested is confirmable and that the respondent is motivated to reply. For example, customers may be more likely to respond if the confirmation is sent with their monthly statement. Respondent motivation is also enhanced if outstanding invoices and unapplied credits constituting the account balance are sent with the request.

2. If a balance consists of complex computations, it may be difficult for a recipient to respond to (e.g., interest calculations on a mortgage balance). Instead, the auditor might ask the respondent to verify specific components of the contract so that the auditor can do the calculations necessary to confirm the balance. For example, the respondent might be asked to corroborate the interest rate, original balance, number of installments, and date of last payment so that the proper balance may be computed.

3. If the auditor determines that it would be more prudent to ask certain respondents to confirm their understanding of certain information rather than providing the in-

formation with the request, an open confirmation should be sent. This type of confirmation is particularly appropriate when the auditor does not require authentication of amounts but rather the confirmation of the terms of a transaction.

4. Make sure that the organization being audited is clearly identified on the confirmation.
5. Try to send the confirmation to a particular individual who will be accountable for the response, rather than to a group or committee or other general unit.
6. Make sure that the confirmation is clearly worded and not confusing.
7. Ask the client to hand-sign the confirmation. Doing so increases the familiarity of the transaction and generally increases the response rate.
8. Set response deadlines to emphasize the urgency of the request.
9. If necessary, send second and third confirmation requests out to the respondent.
10. If necessary, call the client to get oral verification of the information, and then ask that written confirmation be sent in.

Useful Hints Relating to Negative and Positive Confirmations

The following important considerations relating to the use of positive and negative confirmations are discussed in PA 03-1:

- *Positive confirmations* require the recipient to respond directly to the auditor, stating whether he or she agrees with the information presented on the confirmation. Although this form will provide evidence only if the respondent replies to the confirmation, it is more reliable, in general, than a negative confirmation.
- *Negative confirmations* require the respondent to reply only if he or she disagrees with the information presented. If a response to a negative confirmation request is not received, the auditor makes the assumption that the respondent not only received the confirmation but also agreed with the information it presented. Thus, in using negative confirmations, an auditor places a significant amount of reliance on the absence of a reply. In this sense, negative confirmations are less reliable than positive confirmations.

Section 330.20 notes that negative confirmation may be used to reduce the audit risk to an acceptable low level when the following three conditions exist:

1. The combined assessed level of inherent and control risk is low.
2. The population being tested is made up of only a large number of small balances.
3. There is no basis to believe that the recipients of the requests are unlikely to give them valid consideration. This conclusion may be based on the results of positive confirmation procedures performed on the engagement or similar engagements in past years.

In any situation the auditor may choose to send positive confirmations to some respondents and negative confirmations to others. If only negative confirmations are used, more should be sent than if positive confirmations had been used. If negative confirmations are used, the auditor should use other substantive audit procedures to supplement them. For non-responding parties to whom positive confirmations were sent

- Send second and third requests, if necessary, either oral or written; and
- Report any returned confirmations that were undelivered to a client official who is independent of the area being confirmed.

When a respondent disagrees with the information presented on a positive confirmation, the auditor should attempt to resolve the exception. The exception should be evaluated for both qualitative and quantitative implications. If an exception cannot be resolved or other audit procedures indicate that the exception may represent a misstatement, the auditor should do the following in order to reduce audit risk to an acceptably low level:

1. Ascertain the reason for the misstatement.
2. Impute the misstatement to the entire population being tested to ascertain whether additional audit evidence is necessary to reduce the risk of material misstatement to an acceptably low level. In doing this imputation, the auditor should also consider any other misstatements included in the sample being analyzed.
3. Consider the possibility that there may have been fraud. (Clearly, an extensive investigation would be required before it could be determined that fraud has occurred.) The auditor in this case is advised to follow the guidance in AU Section 316, *Consideration of Fraud in a Financial Statement Audit.*
4. Report to a client official who is not directly responsible for or associated with the accounts or information subject to the confirmation all unreconciled misstatements.
5. Consider whether the confirmation response indicating the misstatement should be reported to the audit committee.

Electronic Confirmations

Electronic confirmations or the use of an electronic confirmation process is not prohibited by Section 330. In fact, Auditing Interpretation 1 of Section 330 specifically states that properly controlled electronic communications may be considered a reliable form of audit evidence. Inherent in this statement is the realization that in general, confirmation with a third party is not without some risk of interception, alteration, or fraud. Although electronic confirmation improves the paper confirmation process by reducing the risk of human intervention and misdirection, it is still burdened with the risk that the confirmed information could be compromised, altered, or be the object of fraud.

If the auditor uses electronic confirmations, the auditor should consider the reliability of this information as audit evidence. This includes the risk that

1. The confirmation may not be from the proper source.
2. The responding party may not be the authorized respondent.
3. The transmission's integrity may have been compromised.

If the auditor plans to rely on an electronic confirmation process that is in place with a confirmation respondent, the auditor should obtain an assurance trust services report or another auditor's report that the process has the appropriate design and operating effectiveness regarding electronic and manual confirmation controls. These reports should address these risks. However, if they do not, then the auditor must perform additional tests in order to obtain satisfaction that the aforementioned risks are reduced to an acceptably low level.

Interpretation 1 of Section 330 notes that electronic confirmations may be considered sufficient and valid confirmation responses if the auditor is satisfied that

- The electronic process is secure and properly controlled, and
- The confirmation is directly from a third party who is the authorized respondent.

Several ways are available to validate the sender of electronic information and the authorization of the respondent to confirm the information. For example, encryption, electronic digital signatures, and procedures to verify the Web site authenticity all perform these functions and enhance the security of the electronic confirmation process. A brief explanation of these processes follows:

- *Encryption.* This is the process of encoding electronic data so it cannot be read without a second party employing a second matching encryption key. Encryption reduces the chance that unintended intervention in a communication will occur.
- *Digital signatures.* The use of the encryption of codes, text, or other means can ensure that only the true signer of the document has attached the appropriate signature. The signature and its characteristics are uniquely linked to the signer. Digital computer programs create a unique signature as well as authenticity confirmation checking at a later date.
- *Web site authenticity programs.* These programs use mathematical algorithms and other means to monitor data or a Web site to ensure that content has not been altered or changed without proper authorization. For example, Webtrust or VeriSign certifications could be attached to Web sites to indicate that the information is protected and has not been tampered with.

Confirmations Received by Fax or Electronically

The auditor should validate all confirmations received by fax or electronically (by e-mail). They may be validated by performing the following steps:

1. After receiving the fax or e-mail, verify the source and contents of the response with the sender by telephone.
2. Request that the sender mail the original confirmation directly to the auditor. The auditor should always communicate directly with the confirmation recipient.
3. Document all procedures performed in the audit workpapers.

Requests Not to Confirm Information

On occasion, management may ask that the auditor not confirm certain balances or information. It is important that the auditor determine the basis for such requests. The following six guidance points may be helpful:

1. The usual reason provided for not confirming a balance or other audit information is that there is a dispute with the customer. However, be aware that this reason may be a diversion to prevent the auditor from confirming an inappropriate transaction. The existence of a dispute is not an acceptable reason for not confirming information with a customer.
2. Do not rely on a management request not to confirm certain information. Challenge the client's reasons for not confirming and seek evidence corroborating the client's contention.
3. Under certain circumstances an auditor may decide to accept a request not to seek external confirmation of information. The auditor should then perform alternative auditing procedures to obtain audit satisfaction.
4. If a request not to confirm is made, the auditor may want to include a schedule of such accounts in the client's representation letter with the reasons for the request.
5. If the auditor determines that management's request not to confirm certain balances is reasonable—and (a) there is no limitation on the scope of work to be performed and (b) the auditor is able to obtain audit satisfaction by using alternative audit procedures, then a reference in the auditor's report to omission of the confirmation process or the use of alternative audit procedures is not necessary.
6. If, on the other hand, the auditor determines that management's request not to confirm certain balances is unreasonable and creates restrictions that significantly limit the scope of work to be performed, the auditor should add a disclaimer or withdraw

from the engagement altogether. PA 03-1 suggests that the auditor also consult with legal counsel about the matter.

Use of Alternative Procedures

After an account, transaction, event, etc., has been chosen for confirmation, it should be confirmed or tested using alternative methods to obtain the audit evidence necessary to reduce audit risk to an acceptable low level. Included in the population to be subjected to alternative procedures are

- Nonresponses to positive confirmations.
- Positive or negative confirmations that were returned as undeliverable.
- Accounts that were selected but not confirmed at the client's request.

Section 330 sanctions the omission of alternative procedures to nonresponding positive confirmations in limited circumstances. This occurs if the following criteria are satisfied:

- Unusual qualitative factors or systematic characteristics related to nonresponses have not been identified by the auditor.
- In testing for overstatements, the total of nonresponses projected as a 100% misstatement to the population when added to the sum of all other unadjusted differences does not affect the auditor's determination regarding whether the financial statements are materially misstated.

Notwithstanding the aforementioned considerations, the auditor should be careful in deciding not to perform alternative procedures even though unusual factors or systematic characteristics have not surfaced and items that were projected as 100% misstatements indicate underlying causes of other misstatements that would not be identified.

Alternative procedures performed on an entity's accounts receivable, for example, might consist of an examination of its

1. Cash receipts records,
2. Remittance advices or other evidence of subsequent collection,
3. Shipping records,
4. Evidence of receipt of goods by the customer,
5. Invoices, and
6. Customer correspondences.

The assessed risk of material misstatement, the nature of the account balance or other information the auditor attempted to confirm, and the availability of audit evidence all determine the nature and extent of alternative procedures to be performed. In order to reduce audit risk to an acceptably low level, the auditor should perform a combination of alternative procedures because, in general, the evidence obtained through the use of confirmations is more credible than that obtained internally. As always, the auditor should maintain an appropriate level of skepticism regarding why no response was received.

Using Client Personnel in the Confirmation Process

To increase the efficiency of the audit, an auditor may decide to use client personnel to help examine differences and nonresponses to confirmations. This is done while the auditor maintains control of the audit confirmation process (from mailing through confirmation receipt). Client personnel can help by doing the following activities:

- Accumulate and list data.
- Reconcile book and reported amounts for the auditor's follow-up and evaluation.
- Accumulate documents for the auditor's inspection.

- Investigate exceptions, under the supervision of the auditor, who will also inspect them on a test basis. Throughout this process the auditor should always maintain control over the confirmations by keeping the original reply and giving the client a copy.

Using Confirmations for Different Accounts and Areas of the Audit

The following is specific confirmation guidance relating to several important accounts and areas of the audit of the financial statement.

Confirmation of accounts receivable. Accounts receivable include

1. Claims against customers from the sale of goods and services in the normal course of business, and
2. A financial institution's loans.

The confirmation of accounts receivable in an audit is a generally accepted auditing procedure. There is a presumption that the auditor will always confirm a client's accounts receivable in an audit unless one of the following is true:

- The client's accounts receivable are immaterial to its financial statements.
- The use of confirmations will be ineffective.
- The auditor's combined assessed level of inherent and control risk is low, and this assessed level, in conjunction with the evidence expected to be provided by analytical procedures or other substantive tests of details, is sufficient to reduce audit risk to an acceptable low level for the applicable financial statements assertions.

An auditor who decides not to confirm a client's accounts receivable must provide evidence that the use of confirmations would be ineffective. The decision not to confirm as well as the evidence supporting this conclusion should be fully documented in the auditor's working papers. A reason not to confirm might be based on past experience with this client or similar engagements. The auditor, in this case, believes that the response rate to confirmation would be inadequate or the responses are expected or known to be unreliable. In other situations, the auditor might decide not to confirm because certain entities have a known policy of not responding to confirmation requests. The federal government, for example, might be one such entity.

When the auditor decides not to confirm accounts receivable because the auditor believes that the procedure would be ineffective, getting audit risk reduced to an acceptably low level may require that either a combination of alternative procedures be performed or the performance of alternative procedures to a larger number of items than would have been confirmed.

It should be noted that the performance of alternative audit confirmation procedures may be difficult to perform if the entity uses electronic systems and as a result shipping documents, and the like, may not be accessed.

Confirmation of terms of unusual or complex agreements or transactions. Terms of unusual or complex agreements or transactions should be confirmed by the auditor. The confirmation of terms, for example, can easily be directly done with the confirmation of balances or can be done separately. The confirmation of details should be directed to individuals of the entity who would be familiar with such matters. For example, such individuals might include

1. Executives in the sales department.
2. The chief financial officer.
3. The chief operating officer.
4. The chief executive officer.

AU Section 316, *Consideration of Fraud in a Financial Statement Audit*, requires that an auditor presume that there is a risk of material misstatement due to fraud relating to revenue recognition Therefore, he or she should carefully evaluate revenue transactions to determine conformity with GAAP. The auditor should also confirm the terms of transactions and the absence of any side agreements. The necessity of using confirmations in this situation increases if any of the following circumstances surface:

1. Altered dates on contracts or shipping documents (these may indicate the possibility of fraud).
2. Significant sales volume at or near the end of the reporting period.
3. Use of unorthodox or nonstandard contracts or contract clauses.
4. Lack of evidence of customer acceptance.
5. Existence of extended payment terms or nonstandard installment receivables.
6. Lack of involvement by the accounting or finance department in sales transactions or in monitoring the activity of distributors.
7. Unusual volume of sales to distributors or retailers.
8. Sales, other than sales of software, with commitments for future upgrades.
9. Use of letters of authorization rather than signed contracts or agreements.
10. High volume of sales with significant uncertainties and obligations for the seller associated with them.
11. High pressure from upper management to increase revenues and earnings.
12. High volume of sales to resellers (value added) and distributors that lack financial strength.
13. Existence of bill-and-hold transactions.
14. Existence of terms that cause ever-increasing receivable balances; customers who seem to think that they do not have to make payments until the merchandise they purchase is resold to end users.
15. Use of linked transactions or contracts.

Confirmation of accounts payable. Confirmation of accounts payable consists of confirming accounts with an entity's suppliers so that the existence and completeness of its payables can be established. Confirmation of accounts payable is also used to detect the existence of "linked" or "round-trip" transactions. These transactions occur when an entity enters into a sales transaction with a customer but sends all or some of the sales proceeds back to the customer in an ostensible bonafide purchase transaction, usually in a different accounting period. This type of transaction is not uncommon in those industries where revenue recognition is emphasized instead of income. To detect it, the auditor confirms balances with major suppliers and/or customers with which the entity has recorded sales and purchases.

Confirmation of accounts payable has been shown to be effective in many other situations as well. For example, it may be used in the following circumstances:

- Accounts payable balances show a zero or small balance at year-end but were relatively active all period long.
- There is a risk of unprocessed and unrecorded vendor invoices and control over payables and cash disbursements is poor.
- There is a risk of unrecorded liabilities and/or inappropriate accounting because of industry practices, among these Internet businesses, real estate, software companies, energy, and telecommunications.
- Complex business transactions generate situations where there may be unrecorded accounts (e.g., may exist) combinations, royalty contracts, and the like.

Form of accounts payable confirmation. Since a primary objective in the audit of accounts payable is discovering whether there are unrecorded liabilities, the use of blank confirmation forms has been found to be the most effective way of uncovering these items. The respondent should be asked to supply the auditor with a listing of all the components of the client's accounts payable balance as well as information on equal exchange transactions (e.g., quid pro quo) that the client may have participated in and left unrecorded or improperly recorded.

To obtain a satisfactory degree of confidence from the confirmation of liabilities relating to suppliers, the auditor should do the following:

1. Review the client documents for confirmable balances and transactions:

    a. Accounts payable subsidiary ledger,
    b. Suppliers' invoice files, and
    c. Supplier disbursement records.

2. Obtain from client personnel a list of major suppliers for accounts payable confirmation.
3. Maintain and update the list of major client suppliers in the permanent file of the working papers.
4. Determine whether there are other suppliers (e.g., advertising suppliers, construction contractors, equipment suppliers, suppliers with known or suspected disputed balances, or other major suppliers of services) from which confirmation of accounts payable balances should be obtained.
5. Perform alternative procedures for suppliers whose receivable information was not obtainable through the confirmation process or who should have been selected for confirmation and were not. Alternative procedures consist of examining payment documents after the confirmation date to identify unrecorded items that should have been accrued as a liability as of the confirmation date. These groups include

    a. Suppliers who did not reply to the confirmation request and from whom accounts payable statements are not available,
    b. Suppliers with a large payable balance who were not included in the list of confirmable balances, and
    c. Suppliers with unusually small balances who were not included in the list of confirmable balances.

Confirmation of Related-Party Transactions

Because of the risk of fraud in transactions involving related parties and variable interest entities (e.g., Enron fiasco), the auditor must perform audit procedures to identify related party transactions. The auditor should strive, in this endeavor, to learn and fully understand the essence of all related-party relationships involving the entity under audit.

To gain a comprehensive understanding of these type of transactions, the auditor should confirm

- The transaction amount(s) and terms with the other parties to the transaction.
- Guarantees and other significant data with the other parties to the transaction.
- Significant information with intermediaries such as banks, guarantors, agents, and attorneys. This may generate the most reliable source of audit evidence in that management may be part of both sides of the related-party transaction.
- Unusual transactions.

Alternatives to Confirmation

Given the ever-increasing use of new technology in an audit, it is sometimes difficult for an auditor to ascertain whether GAAS is being satisfied. For example, PA 03-1 discusses the ability of the current day auditor to directly access data held by a third party concerning a client's account balance. An auditor, for example, can now make online inquiries about a client's bank balance or other related information using the client's personal identification number (pin).

Although such information is obviously competent evidential matter and very similar to confirmed data, it does not technically meet the definition of a confirmation. AU Section 330, *The Confirmation Process* (Paragraph 4), defines the confirmation process as follows:

> *Confirmation is the process of obtaining and evaluating a direct communication from a third party in response to a request for information about a particular item affecting financial statement assertions.*

From this definition it can be seen that a bona fide confirmation requires that the auditor make a direct request for information from a third party who should reply directly to the auditor. Making on-line inquiries regarding a client account balance does not satisfy GAAS confirmation requirements, and thus is classified as an alternative auditing procedure.

331 INVENTORIES

SOURCES OF STANDARDS

GAAS

SAS 1, *Section 313 Inventories*
SAS 43, *Omnibus Statement on Auditing Standards*
SAS 67, *The Confirmation Process*

ADDITIONAL NON-GAAS PROFESSIONAL GUIDANCE

Practice Alert 94-2, Auditing Inventories—Physical Observations
Practice Alert 01-2, Audit Considerations in Times of Economic Uncertainty

SUMMARY

Observing inventories is a generally accepted auditing procedure. If it is decided not to physically observe the inventory of a client on an engagement, the burden of justifying this decision rests with the auditor. It is important to note that this section relates only to the observation of inventories, not to other important auditing procedures related to inventories.

GAAS GUIDANCE

GUIDELINES FOR THE OBSERVATION OF INVENTORY

Under GAAS, if inventory quantities are determined by means of a physical count that took place as of the balance sheet date or within a reasonable time before or after that date, the auditor must

1. Be present during the count and observe the client's inventory-taking process,
2. Make test counts of inventory, and
3. Make inquiries of the client in order to assess both the effectiveness of the client's count and the reliance that can be placed on the representations made regarding its inventories. If necessary, tests of intervening transactions should be performed.

If the client maintains perpetual inventory records that are periodically checked by physical counts, the observation may be performed either during or after the end of the period being examined.

A client may use statistical sampling techniques to determine end-of-the period inventory quantities. The auditor must make sure that these techniques are reliable, statistically valid, are properly applied, and produce reasonable results.

In general, observation, test counts, inquires, and other inventories must all be performed so that the auditor can be confident about the client's inventory-taking procedures and representations about the current quantities and condition of its inventory. Most important, under GAAS, tests of the accounting records alone are not sufficient for the auditor to be satisfied as to current quantities. AU Section 331 emphasizes this in the following guidance:

> It will always be necessary for the auditor to make, or observe, some physical counts of the inventory and apply appropriate tests of intervening transactions. This should be coupled with inspection of the records of any client's counts and procedures relating to the physical inventory on which the balance-sheet inventory is based.

Financial Statements of the Current Period and Periods for Which There Are No Observations and Test Counts

An auditor may be asked to perform an audit on financial statements of the current period that includes one or more periods in which he or she did not observe the physical inventory procedure and did not make any test counts of inventory. Assuming that the auditor is able to observe the inventory-taking process in the current period, then through testing prior transactions, estimating past inventory balances using the gross profit method, and reviewing prior test counts, he or she would be able to rely on the client's assertions about prior inventory balances.

Inventories in Public Warehouses

GAAS requires direct confirmation from warehouse workers or other custodians of client inventories that are held in public warehouses. An auditor must also apply one or more of the following procedures if inventories represent a large part of the client's current or total assets so that there is reasonable assurance of its existence.

1. If possible, observe the client's physical count of inventory in the warehouse.
2. Determine whether the warehouser's control procedures are acceptable in terms of, for example, the custody of goods and pledging of warehouse receipts (if applicable) by obtaining a report from an independent auditor. It is also possible for the auditor to obtain assurance of the reliability of the warehouser by applying alternative procedures at the warehouse.
3. Confirm information about warehouse receipts from lenders if receipts have been pledged as collateral.
4. Test the client's procedures for reviewing the functioning of the warehouser.

Form 1 illustrates a confirmation of inventories held in a public warehouse.

FORM 1. CONFIRMATION OF INVENTORIES HELD IN A PUBLIC WAREHOUSE

[Use Client's Letterhead for This Form]

[Date]
[Insert custodian's name and address here]

Dear Gentlemen/Ladies:

As part of the audit of our financial statements, our auditors request that you confirm to them the accuracy of quantities of inventory held by you but owned by us at _____.
We are enclosing a listing of the inventory held by you that is shown on our records.
In addition, please also respond to the following:

- If your count of the inventory differs from the quantities shown on the list provided, please indicate an explanation of the discrepancies that exists.
- What method did you use to ascertain the quantities of inventory that you are confirming (e.g., by counting, weighing)?

- Were negotiable or nonnegotiable warehouse receipts issued? If so, do you know if any of these have been pledged or assigned?
- Are any amounts owed to you as of _____?
- Are there any liens against our inventory?

Please respond to the aforementioned questions in a separate letter.

A stamped, self-addressed envelope is enclosed for your convenience. Please mail your response directly to our auditors.

Thank you for your consideration in this matter.

Sincerely,

_____

[Client's name and signature]

Form 2 shows an audit guidance checklist for observing inventory.

FORM 2. AUDIT GUIDANCE CHECKLIST—OBSERVATION OF INVENTORY

[Completed by/Date/Comments]

Preliminary Considerations

1. Prior to the date of the physical count, meet with client representatives and review the procedures that they will follow to obtain an accurate physical count of the inventory. Suggest appropriate modifications as needed.
2. Make sure the client's physical arrangement ensures that an accurate count can be taken. For example, provision should be made so that goods are not allowed to be moved or produced during the count (double counting).
3. Verify that goods that the client does not have title are segregated and not counted.
4. Goods that are owned by the client that are at other locations during the count (consigned goods, goods in transit, etc.) should be determined and included in the physically counted inventory.
5. Determine the need for the services of a specialist during the count.

Observing the Physical Count of Inventory

1. On the day of the physical count of inventory, make sure that the client has made provision for the items discussed in the preliminary considerations (see Preliminary Considerations Nos. 2, 3, and 4. If not, make suggestions for modification before the onset of the count.
2. Visit the receiving and shipping department to get the cut-off numbers of the last receiving report and shipping advice issued before the physical count of inventory. These numbers will be used to test the appropriateness of the client's cutoff after the count. Also make sure these departments do not ship or receive goods during the count.
3. Sample items of inventory, and visually check all items, to see that they are properly tagged or included on count sheets. Make sure that the control numbers on these documents are accounted for.
4. Observe the client's physical counting process. In doing so, make sure that the count procedures previously discussed with the client are being properly adhered to. (See Preliminary Considerations No. 1.)
5. Make test counts of inventory. Trace this information to the inventory count tickets and count sheets. Choose items on the count sheets, locate and count the inventory, and verify the accuracy of the posted numbers. In each case, also verify the accuracy of the description of item, location, and so on.
6. During the count, observe that the count ticket clearly indicates that an item is counted. This minimizes the possibility of exclusion or duplication.
7. Throughout the count, check for items on the warehouse or production floor, that were not counted. Inquire why these items were excluded.

8. Throughout the physical count, be sensitive to the movement of inventory that could cause possible double counting. Make note of this in the work papers and discuss it with the client.

9. Throughout the physical count, be alert for obsolete, damaged, or old inventory that may be a candidate for write-down or write-off.

10. Prepare a summary of the adequacy of the physical count to be included in the workpapers.

Considerations after the Physical Count

1. Trace a sample of the client's counts as recorded on the inventory tags or count sheets to the inventory count summary sheets. Do the same for the auditor test counts made during the count. Also trace quantities from the summary sheets to the count tickets or count sheets generated during the physical count to ensure that the summary includes only quantities that were physically counted.

2. If the client maintains perpetual records, trace a sample of physically counted items as shown on the tags or count sheets to and from the client's inventory count summary sheets as described in item 1 to ensure that the counted numbers are being used in the perpetual records determining the recorded inventory balance. Where there is a discrepancy between the perpetual record and the physical quantity counted, make sure that the client adjusted its perpetual records to the physically counted quantities.

3. Test that the client has made a proper cutoff with respect to the physical observation count. For example, items that were sold before the physical count date (as indicated by testing a small number of shipping advices prepared before the last shipping advice generated before the count; see the second item in the checklist Observing the Physical Count of Inventory) should not have been included in the physical count. They should be accounted for as a sale in the period under audit. Also test those items sold out after the physical count that were included in the physical count. For a small number of receiving reports that are dated before the physical count date (see the second item in the checklist Observing the Physical Count of Inventory), make sure that inventory items were both counted and recorded as bona fide purchases of inventory.

ADDITIONAL NON-GAAS PROFESSIONAL GUIDANCE

PRACTICE ALERT (PA) 94-2, AUDITING INVENTORIES—PHYSICAL OBSERVATIONS

The information that follows is based on the findings of the SEC Practice Section Professional Issues Task Force. It has not been approved or disapproved by any committee of the AICPA. It is provided here as an additional source of guidance for the practitioner.

Inventory Fraud

The independent auditor should be aware of fraud schemes and techniques that have been perpetrated by client personnel to companies' physical inventories. PA 94-2 enumerates the following examples of such fraud:

- Mislabeled boxes that contain scrap, obsolete, or lower-value materials.
- Inventory that has been consigned, rented, or traded in for which credits have not been granted.
- Hollow squares in a group of stacked goods or empty boxes similarly placed.
- Inventory accounts that have been directly increased or altered for items that were not test-counted by the auditor.
- Computer programs that generate fraudulent physical quantity tabulations.
- Water added to liquid inventory substances and other dilutive practices so that the inventory seems greater than it really is but is less valuable.

- Inventory counts and compilations manipulated at client locations that the auditor has not visited.
- Double-counted inventory that is "in transit" between locations.
- Items included in inventory that have been sold but not yet shipped to a customer (sometimes known as "bill and hold sales").
- Work-in-process inventory classified as finished inventory and overstating the stage of completion of work-in-process.
- False confirmations of inventory that is held by others.
- Inventory physically moved so that it will be counted at two locations.
- Physical inventory reconciled to falsified amounts in the general ledger.

Thwarting Fraud during the Inventory Observation Process

There are many ways an auditor can successfully thwart fraud during the client's inventory observation process. The following considerations should be heeded:

Planning Procedures

1. Everyone on the audit team should clearly understand the client's business, products, computer information applications, and controls. In addition, they should be well versed in the client's inventory count procedures, data summarizing, pricing, and cut-off procedures. This is particularly important when a client plans to count inventory at a date other than that of the financial statements or at various dates. Clearly, this increases the risk of inventory misstatement. An auditor who believes that the client's internal controls are poor should suggest that the inventory be taken at the end of the client's fiscal period.
2. When senior and experienced audit team members are familiar with and understand the client's overall business (computer applications, inventory procedures, business systems), they can better plan how to observe the client's inventory count. For example, if there is a material amount of in-process inventory, assigning experienced auditors to the count will ensure that there is minimum difficulty in ascertaining the degree of completion and valuation of the goods. If a client's inventory consists of sophisticated, complex goods, it may be necessary to assign more senior people to the count to ensure that the observation is not fraught with fraud.
3. Proper planning is particularly important if it is necessary to use the personnel of another office of the auditing firm or if another CPA firm is participating. It is only through planning that the auditor will be assured that others will fully understand the audit steps that must be followed, the scope of the count, the client's internal controls related to the count and how much reliance to place on them, the cutoff procedures that will be used, and any risks relating to the count.

The Actual Physical Count

1. Performing test counts throughout the client's inventory, especially in areas that are hard to count, will reduce the risk of duplicate or fictitious inventory and otherwise prevent misstatement. In general, inventory fraud is more prevalent in areas not test-counted by auditors.
2. Client personnel are sometimes utilized in making test counts. To reduce risk, the auditor may want to do the following:

    a. Record the details of inventory counts made by the client and not test or counted by the auditor as evidence that the final listing is composed of inventory actually counted by the client.

    b.   Make test counts that the client is not aware of to ensure that the inventory is being properly counted.

    c.   Maintain strict control over the audit work papers to ensure that the client is not aware of what test counts are being done.

3.   As a matter of general practice, during the observation of a client's inventory the auditor should open some of the packages or boxes counted by client personnel to make sure that the goods inside match their description. The auditor should always be on the lookout for empty boxes and "hollow squares" (spaces between stacks of boxes) to make sure the inventory counted fully exists. Units of measure on inventory count sheets or tags should be logical and make sense in the circumstances. The auditor should maintain control over the test counts as follows:

4.   Establish a policy of analyzing tags and count sheets for unusual amounts, unreasonably large quantities, large extended values, and curious descriptions. All such items should be scrutinized for validity. Items that fall into these categories that were not test-counted earlier should be counted.

5.   Make sure that the client controls inventory tags and count sheets so that no fraudulent information may be included in the count data. The client should have internal control procedures that ensure that the final inventory listing consists only of bona fide inventory data. Make sure these controls are working as prescribed.

6.   Analyze the final inventory listing to identify areas of additional audit review.

7.   During the test count, incorrect client counts may be discovered. Evaluate the situation and, if needed, increase the number of test counts or augment other audit procedures. In particular, it may be necessary to recount the work of count teams responsible for the errors found. Recounts of other inventory areas may also be required.

Multiple Inventory Locations

Frequently the inventory of audit clients is situated in multiple locations. It is important for the auditor to be aware of all such locations to make sure all inventory is included in the final tally. It is also possible for the client to shift inventory so that fraudulent double counting occurs. The following techniques may minimize the possibility of double counting:

1.   Have the client take physical inventory at all locations at the same time to help minimize the possibility of inventory shifting.

2.   If the auditor cannot observe the physical count of inventory at some material client locations, advise the client that observations at some locations will take place without advance notice. This possibility hopefully will minimize any inventory manipulation.

3.   Perform alternative auditing procedures at those sites to detect possibilities of inventory fraud or misstatements. Such alternatives might include trend analysis of inventory to sales levels, year-to-year inventories by locations, and so forth.

Consignment Inventory

Clearly, all items counted as part of the client's inventory should be owned by the client as of the balance sheet date. To ensure that all inventory on hand is the property of the client, the auditor should do the following:

1.   Review and test the client's controls and procedures for identifying, segregating, and excluding consignment goods.

2. To test the validity of consignment inventory that has been identified by the client, accumulate the following information to make sure these goods were not included in the client's inventory count:

   a. Description of the goods,
   b. Quantities,
   c. Serial numbers, and
   d. Shipping advice numbers.

In auditing goods that have been consigned by the client to others (e.g., inventory stored at another location), GAAS generally require the auditor to obtain written confirmation of their existence from the custodian of the goods. If the amount of inventory involved is material, the auditor should also physically observe the custodian's count of the inventory, following the guidance of AU Section 331, *Inventories Held in Public Warehouses* (see the preceding section.)

Use of Specialists in the Physical Observation of Inventory

Often the auditor will need a specialist's help in the physical observation of the client's inventory. PA-92 notes that a specialist may be used to

- Measure quantities that are difficult to ascertain, such as stockpiled materials or mineral reserves;
- Value special-purpose inventory, such as high-technology equipment or materials, chemicals, works of art, or precious gems; and
- Measure the stage of completion of work in progress for long-term contracts.

If it is determined that the specialist engaged is in any way associated with the client, the auditor should perform additional tests to ensure that the specialist's findings are reasonable. The specialist's assumptions, methods, and findings should be tested. If necessary, the auditor may decide to use the services of another specialist who is entirely independent of the client.

Postobservation Considerations

When inventory is counted at a date other than the balance-sheet date, the same number of audit procedures have to be performed until the auditor can be satisfied about inventory quantity and quality increases. The nature and magnitude of such procedures depends on the following variables:

1. The business the client is engaged in.
2. The type of inventory being counted.
3. The inventory turnover period.
4. The inventory records kept by the client.
5. The strength of the client's internal controls related to inventory.
6. The interval of time between the observation and the balance sheet date.

If a client counts its inventory using a cycle count program or some other form of interim physical count, the additional risks require different controls and the performance of different audit tests. Greater guidance in this area may be found in Statement on Auditing Standard 45, *Omnibus Statement on Auditing Standards—1983,* "Substantive Tests Prior to the Balance Sheet Date."

To obtain audit satisfaction when inventory is counted at a date other than the balance sheet date, the auditor should test material items in the reconciliation of the physical inventory count to the general ledger. The reconciliation helps not only to determine fraud and other intentional misstatements but also to expose inadvertent errors made by the client. Analyzing items in the reconciliation is particularly important for locations where the auditor did not observe the physical count. In particular, goods in transit and inventory transfers between affiliates, locations, or departments should be fully evaluated to ascertain which items of inventory should be included and which should not.

PRACTICE ALERT (PA) 01-2, AUDIT CONSIDERATIONS IN TIMES OF ECONOMIC UNCERTAINTY

Clearly, skepticism is appropriate when the auditor attempts to corroborate management's financial statement assertions. Management's explanations should support the assertions and above all should make logical sense. If necessary, evidence should be obtained to substantiate management's explanations. The auditor may also decide to corroborate certain explanations in discussions with the audit committee or other members of the board.

Signs of increased accounting and reporting risk that should stimulate increased professional skepticism include the following inventory issues enumerated in PA 01-2:

1. Indications of excessive inventory, such as

   a. An unusual increase in inventory balances,
   b. Reduction in turnover, or
   c. Increased backlog or deterioration in inventories.

2. Difficulties in selling company products to consumers because they are not technologically attractive. Is there a viable market plan to sell the products? Will this venture likely to be profitable?

3. A material or unusual amount of sales cancellations and returns after the end of the year.

4. Declining prices and shrinking profits, causing inventory to be valued over market.

5. Indications of "channel stuffing."

6. Reduced manufacturing production causing an overcapitalization of inventory overhead rather than expensing the costs of excess capacity.

7. Unfavorable purchase commitments, sales commitments, or similar arrangements.

332 AUDITING DERIVATIVE INSTRUMENTS, HEDGING ACTIVITIES, AND INVESTMENTS IN SECURITIES

SOURCE OF STANDARDS

SAS 92, *Auditing Derivative Instruments, Hedging Activities and Investments in Securities*

INTRODUCTION/SUMMARY

AU Section 332 provides guidance on planning and performing auditing procedures for assertions about derivative instruments, hedging activities, and investments in securities. The five assertions are

1. Existence or occurrence.
2. Completeness.
3. Rights and obligations.
4. Valuation or allocation.
5. Presentation and disclosure.

This section is applicable to derivative instruments of all entities. Derivatives are defined by Financial Accounting Standards Board (FASB) Statement of Financial Accounting Standards 133, *Accounting for Derivative Instruments and Hedging Activities.* FASB Statement 133 states that a derivative is a financial instrument or other contract with all three of the following characteristics (AU 332.02):

1. It has one or more underlyings, and one or more notional amounts or payment provisions or both.
2. It requires either no initial net investment or an initial net investment that is smaller than would be required for other types of similar contracts.
3. It requires or permits net settlement that can readily be settled by a means outside the contract, or it provides for delivery of an asset that puts the recipient in a position not substantially different from a net settlement.

This section is applicable for hedging activities for which FASB 133 permits hedge accounting. Generally, an entity enters into a derivative transaction for the following reasons:

1. As an investment,
2. As a hedge of exposure to changes in fair value (fair value hedge),
3. As a hedge of exposure to variability in cash flows (cash flow hedge), and
4. As a hedge of foreign currency exposure.

This section applies to both debt securities and equity securities. The definition of debt security and equity security is that given in FASB 115, *Accounting for Certain Investments in Debt and Equity Securities.* This debt or equity security, however, does not have to be subject to the requirements of FASB 115.

SPECIAL KNOWLEDGE TO PLAN AND PERFORM PROCEDURES

Special skills or knowledge may be needed to plan and perform auditing procedures for derivatives and securities. For instance, the auditor needs to obtain an understanding of an entity's information system for derivatives and securities. The auditor should understand how to apply GAAP for assertions about derivatives. Sometimes, derivatives have complex features that require specialized knowledge to evaluate the measurement and disclosure of the derivative. An understanding of risk management concepts may also be needed to assess inherent risk and control risk for derivatives used in hedging activities.

AUDIT RISK AND MATERIALITY

The auditor should design procedures to obtain reasonable assurance of detecting material misstatements of assertions about derivatives and securities. The auditor should consider both the inherent risk and control risk for these assertions.

Inherent Risk Assessment

Inherent risk is assessed for an assertion about a derivative or security by determining its susceptibility to a material misstatement in the absence of related controls. The following factors affect inherent risk:

1. An entity may enter into derivatives as hedges to minimize the risk of loss from changes in market conditions. It is possible that market conditions may change in an unexpected manner and that the hedge is ineffective. This increases inherent risk for certain assertions about the derivatives, since it may no longer be in conformity with GAAP.
2. Inherent risk may also increase due the complexity of the features of the derivative or security. Derivatives introduce greater complexity in measurement and disclosure issues.
3. There is greater inherent risk for derivatives that do not involve an initial exchange of cash. The risk is greater that these transactions may not be identified for valuation and disclosure considerations in accordance with GAAP.
4. The greater the experience of an entity with derivatives or securities the lower is the inherent risk for assertions.
5. Inherent risk is greater for certain assertions about embedded derivatives, since they are less likely to be identified by management.
6. Risk associated with various external factors may affect assertions about derivatives and security, including
   a. Credit risk,
   b. Market risk,
   c. Basis risk, and
   d. Legal risk.
7. Accounting guidance may not be available for newly developed forms of derivatives.
8. An entity relies significantly on external expertise or experts. For example, an entity may have to rely on a specialist to value derivatives.

9. As the number and subjectivity of GAAP-related assumptions increases, so does the inherent risk of material misstatement for certain assertions.

Control Risk Assessment

Obtaining an understanding of internal control. Auditors are required to obtain an understanding of internal control to identify the types and risk of potential material misstatement, perform test of controls if reliance is warranted, and design substantive tests. Common controls for an entity with extensive derivatives transactions include (AU 332.10)

1. Monitoring by staff that is independent of derivatives activities;
2. Senior management approval of derivative activity;
3. Senior management for divergences from approved derivatives strategies;
4. Transmittal of derivatives positions to the risk measurement systems;
5. Performance of reconciliations to ensure data integrity;
6. Derivatives traders, risk managers, and senior management to define constraints on derivatives activities and justify identified excesses;
7. Periodic review of controls and results of derivatives activities to determine whether controls are being effectively implemented; and
8. Review of limits in considering changes in strategy, risk tolerance of the entity, and market conditions.

According to AU 332.11, service organization's services are part of an entity's information system for derivatives and securities if they affect any of the following:

1. How the entity's derivatives and securities transactions are initiated.
2. The accounting records, supporting information, and specific accounts in the financial statements involved in the processing and reporting of the entity's derivatives and securities transactions.
3. The accounting processing involved from the initiation of those transactions to their inclusion in the financial statements, including electronic means (e.g., computers and electronic data interchange) used to transmit, process, maintain, and access information.
4. The process the entity uses to report information about derivatives and securities transactions in its financial statements, including significant accounting estimates and disclosures.

AU 332.12 gives the following examples of a service organization's services that would be part of an entity's information system:

1. The initiation of the purchase or sale of equity securities by a service organization acting as investment adviser or manager.
2. Services that are ancillary to holding an entity's securities such as

   a. Collecting dividend and interest income and distributing that income to the entity,
   b. Receiving notification of corporate actions,
   c. Receiving notification of security purchase and sale transactions,
   d. Receiving payments from purchasers and disbursing proceeds to sellers for security purchase and sale transactions, and
   e. Maintaining records of securities transactions for the entity.

3. A pricing service providing fair values of derivatives and securities through paper documents or electronic downloads that the entity uses to value its derivatives and securities for financial statement reporting.

AU 332.13 states that the following are examples of a service organization's services that would not be part of an entity's information system:

1. The execution by a securities broker of trades that are initiated by either the entity or its investment adviser.
2. The holding of an entity's securities.

Assessing control risk. The auditor should assess control risk after an understanding of internal control over derivatives and securities transactions has been obtained. The auditor should identify controls that may be relied on to prevent or detect material misstatements. Reliance on these controls allows the audit to assess control risk below maximum for assertions about derivatives and securities.

Substantive Procedures

The assessed levels of inherent risk and control risk for assertions about derivatives and securities are used to determine the nature, timing, and extent of the substantive testing. Some substantive tests provide evidence on multiple assertions. The auditor should consider whether the results of other audit procedures conflict with management's assertions about derivatives and securities.

Financial Statement Assertions

Existence or occurrence. Assertions about existence deal with whether the derivatives and securities reported in the balance sheet through recognition or disclosure exist at the date of the balance sheet. Assertions about occurrence concern whether derivatives and securities transactions reported in the financial statements actually exist or took place. Examples of substantive procedures for verifying the assertions about derivatives and securities include (AU 332.21)

1. Directly confirming the security with the issuer;
2. Directly confirming the security with the holder of the security, or confirming the derivative with the counterparty;
3. Obtaining a confirmation of settled transactions from the broker-dealer or counterparty;
4. Obtaining a confirmation of unsettled transactions from the broker-dealer or counterparty;
5. Physically inspecting the security or derivative contract;
6. Reading executed partnership or similar agreements;
7. Inspecting underlying agreements and other forms of supporting documentation for

   a. Amounts reported,
   b. Evidence precluding the sales treatment of a transfer, and
   c. Unrecorded repurchase agreements;

8. Inspecting supporting documentation for subsequent realization or settlement; and
9. Performing analytical procedures.

Completeness. The completeness assertion deals with matters opposite from those of the existence or occurrence assertion. The completeness assertion is concerned with the possibility of omission of the entity's derivatives and securities from being reported in the financial statements through recognition or disclosure. It also concerns whether all derivatives and securities transactions are reported in the financial statements. The assessed level of control risk will affect the extent of substantive procedures for the completeness assertion. Derivatives may not involve an initial exchange of tangible consideration. They may make it difficult to limit audit risk to an acceptable level if control risk is assessed at the maximum. Examples of substantive procedures for completeness assertions about derivatives and securities include (AU 332.22)

1. Inquiring of the counterparty to a derivative or the holder of a security for information about matters such as whether there are any side agreements or agreements to repurchase securities sold;
2. Inquiring of frequently used counterparties or holders with whom there are presently no derivatives or securities to confirm that status;
3. Identify embedded derivatives by inspecting financial instruments and other such agreements;
4. Inspecting documentation for activity in the subsequent period;
5. Performing appropriate analytical procedures;
6. Examining assets that have been removed to determine that the criteria for sales have been met; and
7. Reading other information, such as minutes of meetings of the board of directors or other committees.

Derivatives may not involve an initial exchange of tangible consideration. There may instead be a commitment to perform under a contract. Therefore the auditor should not rely exclusively on evidence from cash receipts and disbursements to test for the completeness assertion. The auditor should also inquire about operating activities where derivatives may have been used to hedge risk. An entity may also have converted interest bearing debt from fixed to variable, or vice versa, using derivatives. If service organizations are used to provide information systems for derivatives, the auditor should obtain evidential matter about the operating effectiveness of controls at the service organizations.

Contacting the service organization is important because there is always the possibility that the derivatives not requiring an initial exchange of tangible consideration were not recorded.

Rights and obligations. This assertion deals with the rights and obligations associated with derivatives and securities. AU 332.25 provides the following examples of substantive procedures for assertions about rights and obligations associated with derivatives and securities:

1. The auditor should inquire about and confirm significant terms and conditions with the counterparty to a derivative or the holder of a security. The auditor should also confirm the absence of any side agreements.
2. The underlying agreements and other forms of supporting documentation should be inspected.
3. The auditor should review minutes of meetings of the board of directors and read contracts and other agreements for evidence about rights and obligations. For instance, securities could have been pledged as collateral or securities sold with a commitment to repurchase them.

Valuation. The valuation assertion about the valuation of derivatives and securities deals with whether the amounts reported in the financial statements have been included at appropriate amounts in conformity with generally accepted accounting principles (GAAP). GAAP requires derivatives and securities to be valued at cost, the investee's financial results, or fair value. GAAP also requires disclosure about the value of a derivative or security. Impairment losses should be recognized in earnings prior to their realization.

Valuation based on cost. Securities may be valued at cost. The auditor may obtain evidence about the cost of securities by inspecting documentation supporting the purchase, confirming directly with the issuer or holder, and testing for discount or premium amortization. The auditor should evaluate management's conclusion about recognizing impairment losses for a decline in the security's fair value.

Valuation based on an investee's financial results. Securities may be valued based on an investee's financial results. This includes, but is not limited to, the equity method of accounting. When valuing securities based on the investee's financial results, the auditor should obtain sufficient evidence in support of the investee's financial results by reading the financial statements of the investee and the accompanying audit report. The auditor may also perform additional procedures if, in the auditor's judgment, additional evidential matter is warranted or the investee's financial statement have not been audited.

The auditor should consider the time lag in reporting between the date of the financial statements of the investor and that of the investee. The time lag in reporting should be consistent from period to period. If the time lag has a material effect on the entity's financial statements, the auditor should consider the effects of the lack of comparability. If the effect is material, an explanatory paragraph should be added to the auditor's report because of the change in reporting period.

The auditor should evaluate the need to recognize an impairment loss for a decline in the security's fair value below its carrying amount. The auditor should also consider material subsequent events which occur after the date of the investee's financial statements but before the date of the investor's audit report.

The auditor should consider evidence of material transactions between the entity and the investee. This will assist the auditor in determining

1. The propriety of eliminating unrealized profits and losses on transactions, and
2. The adequacy of disclosures about material related party-transactions.

Valuation based on fair value. Derivatives and securities may be valued based on their fair values. The method for determining fair value may depend on the nature of the entity and its industry. For instance, there may be differences due to price quotations from inactive markets, significant liquidity discounts, control premiums, and commissions or other costs. The auditor should determine whether GAAP specifies the method to be used and whether the entity has used that method to determine fair value.

Prices for derivatives and securities listed on national exchanges or over-the-counter markets are readily available and provide sufficient evidence of the fair value of the derivatives and securities.

If market price for derivative or securities is not available, it may be possible to get estimates of fair value from broker-dealers or other third-party sources. These sources may use a variety of valuation models, such as the Black-Scholes option pricing model. If the derivative or security is valued by the entity using a valuation model, the auditor should not substitute a personal judgment for that of the entity's management. The auditor is not expected to act as an appraiser. However, the auditor should assess the reasonableness and appropriateness of the model and whether the assumptions used are reasonable. The auditor may need to engage a specialist to assist in assessing the model. It is not appropriate to use a valuation model when GAAP requires that the fair value of a security be determined using market prices.

Impairment losses. An impairment loss for decline in fair value that is not temporary might require recognition in earnings. Determining whether losses are temporary requires the exercise of judgment. Some estimate about the probability of future events will be necessary. AU 332.47 identifies the following factors as likely to influence judgment concerning determination of impairment of loss:

1. Fair value is significantly below cost and

    a. The decline is attributable to adverse conditions specifically related to the security or to certain conditions in an industry or in a geographic area;
    b. The decline has existed for an extended period of time; and
    c. Management does not possess both the intent and the ability to hold the security for a period of time sufficient to allow for any anticipated recovery in fair value.

2. The security has been downgraded by a rating agency.
3. The financial condition of the issuer has deteriorated.
4. Dividends have been reduced or eliminated, or scheduled interest payments have not been made.
5. The entity recorded losses from the security subsequent to the end of the reporting period.

The auditor should consider whether management has reached an appropriate conclusion concerning the impairment loss. In other words, does the auditor's evidence corroborate or conflict with management's conclusion about loss impairment as well as the amount of impairment adjustment?

Presentation and disclosure. Assertions about presentation and disclosure are concerned with the appropriate classification, description, and disclosure of derivatives and securities in the entity's financial statements. The auditor should consider whether an appropriate accounting principle has been selected and applies. In addition the information presented should be classified and summarized in a reasonable manner. Information should be neither too detailed nor too condensed. For some derivatives and securities, GAAP might have certain requirements. For example, certain securities are classified into categories, such as held-to-maturity, based on management's intent and ability.

ADDITIONAL CONSIDERATIONS ABOUT HEDGING ACTIVITIES

AU 322.52 provides the following guidance about hedging activities:

To account for a derivative as a hedge, generally accepted accounting principles require management

1. At the inception of the hedge to designate the derivative as a hedge, and
2. Contemporaneously formally document

    a. The hedging relationship,
    b. The entity's risk management objective,
    c. The strategy for undertaking the hedge, and
    d. The method of assessing the effectiveness of the hedge.

To qualify for hedge accounting, generally accepted accounting principles require that management have an expectation, both at the inception of the hedge and on an ongoing basis, that the hedging relationship will be highly effective in achieving the hedging strategy.

For assertions based on management's intent and ability, GAAP requires consideration of whether (AU 332.55):

1. Debt securities classified as *held-to-maturity* depend on management's intent and ability to hold them to their maturity;
2. Equity securities reported using the *equity* method depend on management's ability to significantly influence the investee; and
3. Equity securities classified as *trading* or *available-for-sale* depend on management's intent and objectives in investing in the securities.

MANAGEMENT REPRESENTATIONS

The auditor should obtain written representations from management confirming management's intent and ability that affect assertions about derivatives and securities. This includes management's intent and ability:

1. To hold a debt security until its maturity, or
2. To enter into a forecasted transaction for which hedge accounting is applied.

Furthermore the auditor should obtain representations from management confirming other aspects of derivatives and securities transactions.

333 MANAGEMENT REPRESENTATIONS

SOURCES OF STANDARDS

GAAS

SAS 85, *Management Representations*
SAS 89, *Audit Adjustments*
SAS 99, *Consideration of Fraud in a Financial Statement Audit*
SAS 113, *Omnibus Statement on Auditing Standards—2006*
Interpretation of AU Section 333, *Management Representations on Violations and Possible Violations of Laws and Regulations.*
Illustrative Management Representation Letter (adapted from AU Section 333)
Illustrative Updating Management Representation (AU Section 333)

SUMMARY

AU Section 333 requires that the outside independent auditor obtain written representations from a client company when performing an audit in accordance with GAAS. In the normal course of performing an audit, management makes many oral and written representations to the auditor as a result of inquiries and investigative activities. Although these representations constitute audit evidence, they are not substitutes for auditing procedures that must be performed in order to generate an opinion on the financial statements under audit.

Written representations must be obtained from management for all financial statements and periods covered by the auditor's report. Management's refusal to furnish written representations is considered a limitation on the scope of the audit and the auditor must disclaim an opinion on the financial statements or withdraw from the engagement altogether.

GAAS GUIDANCE

The auditor must obtain written representations from management during the course of an audit performed in accordance with GAAS for the following reasons:

- Written representations confirm representations that were communicated either directly or indirectly from inquiries made by the auditor or from other audit activities performed.
- Written representations document the appropriateness of the communicated representations.
- Written representations ensure that miscommunications relating to the contents of any representations are minimized.

Written representations are an important part of the evidence an auditor gathers as part of an audit performed in accordance with GAAS, but they are in no way a substitute for performing the auditing procedures that are required to generate an opinion on the entity's financial statements. Rather, they complement those auditing procedures. For example, often, even when the auditing procedures performed indicate that disclosure in a particular area is complete, an auditor should obtain a written representation from management documenting the fact that it has no knowledge of any related transactions that should have been disclosed but were not.

On occasion, the use of auditing procedures might generate only a limited amount of evidence and needs to be supplemented with representational documentation. In some cases, obtaining hard sufficient supporting data is just not possible and therefore the use of written representations are an excellent additional source of documentation. For example, in auditing investments in securities, an auditor may want to confirm management's intent regarding the classification of the investments (trading, available-for-sale, and held-to-maturity) by asking for a representation letter rather than using auditing procedures that could produce only limited results given the intangible nature of intent.

On occasion, an auditor may find that management's representations contradict some of the evidence derived from other auditing procedures. The veracity of the management representations should then be more fully investigated so that the auditor can decide whether undue reliance is being placed on this form of evidence.

GAAS requires that management representations be in writing and cover all the financial periods being reported on. If a single period is being reported on, for example, then management's written representations should cover only that period. However, if comparative statements are being reported on, the representations should address all the periods covered by the auditor's report. (See sample representations letter, Form 1, at the end of this section.)

AU Section 333 notes that written representations should be obtained regarding management responsibility in the following categories:

Financial statement representations

1. Statement of responsibility by management regarding the fair presentation of the following financial statements:

   a. Balance sheet.
   b. Income statement.
   c. Statement of cash flows.

2. Management's conviction that the financial statements are fairly presented in accordance with GAAP.

Acknowledgments of completeness of information

1. Management should assert, in writing, that the following areas of information are complete and have been made available to the independent auditor:

   a. All financial documents and related records.
   b. All minutes of meetings of stockholders, directors, and committees of directors.
   c. Communications with regulatory agencies relating to deficiencies or non-compliance in reporting practices.
   d. Recorded transactions (i.e., there were no unrecorded transactions).

Recognition, measurement, and disclosure acknowledgements. Management acknowledges its responsibility for

1. The design and implementation of controls, programs, and other activities that ensure that fraud is prevented and detected.
2. Knowledge of fraud or suspected fraud related to the entity on the part of

   a. Management.
   b. Employees who are significantly involved in internal control.

    c.   Other individuals where the fraud could materially effect the entity's financial statements.

3.   The belief that the effects of any uncorrected misstatements in the financial statement discovered during the current engagement (relating to the latest period presented) are both individually and in the aggregate immaterial to the financial statements taken as a whole. (The representation letter or attachment to the letter should summarize those uncorrected financial statement misstatements.)

4.   Any ongoing plans or intentions that may affect the carrying value or classifications of assets or liabilities.

5.   Written or oral guarantees for which the entity may be contingently liable.

6.   Any allegations of fraud or suspected fraud or information relating to such allegations may affect the entity as a result of communications from

    a.   Employees.
    b.   Former employees.
    c.   Financial analysts.
    d.   Regulators.
    e.   Short sellers.
    f.   Others.

7.   Pending claims and assessments against the entity that the entity's counsel believes are likely to turn into assertions requiring disclosure in the notes to the financial statements as required by FASB Statement 5, *Accounting for Contingencies.*

8.   Other liabilities and gain or loss contingencies that FASB Statement 5 requires to be accrued or disclosed.

9.   Information about related parties and related-party transactions (including amounts receivable from and payable to related parties).

10.   Significant estimates and disclosures of material concentrations known to management that are required by Statement of Position 94-6, *Disclosures of Certain Significant Risks and Uncertainty.*

11.   Violations of law or possible violations of law or regulations that would require disclosure in the financial statements or would generate the recording of a loss contingency.

12.   Compliance with contractual agreements made by the company that may affect the financial statements.

13.   Pledging of bona fide title to assets, liens, or encumbrances on assets as collateral.

Subsequent Events Disclosures

1.   Management asserts that all subsequent-event information affecting the financial statements is fully presented (including activity that must be disclosed so that the financial statements are not viewed as being misleading).

THE REPRESENTATION LETTER

The following important considerations relating to the representation letter are emphasized in AU Section 333:

1.   Management's representations should cover matters relating to the industry, business, or environment in which the entity operates.

2.   Representations by management may be limited to matters that are, individually or collectively, material to the financial statements. Materiality levels may differ for different representations. Management and the independent auditor should agree on

what is material to the financial statements and should discuss this in the representation letter. Specifically

   a. Materiality should be discussed either qualitatively or quantitatively.

   b. Materiality considerations do not apply to representations not directly related to financial statement amounts, such as management's acknowledgement of its responsibility for fair presentation in the financial statements, the availability of all financial records and data, and availability of minutes of meetings of stockholders, directors, and committees of directors; and

   c. Materiality does not apply to management's acknowledgement of its responsibility for its employees regarding the design and implementation of programs and controls to prevent and detect fraud.

3. Written representations should be addressed directly to the auditor.

4. The representation letter should be dated as of the date of the auditor's report. This is important because the auditor is concerned with events occurring through the report date that may require financial statement adjustments or modifications of financial statement disclosures.

5. If the auditor's report is dual-dated, the auditor should obtain additional representations from management relating to the subsequent period. For more information regarding this matter, see AU Section 530, *Dating of the Independent Auditor's Report* (paragraph .05).

6. The letter should be signed by all those the auditor believes are responsible for and knowledgeable about the matters covered by the representations (i.e., CEO and CFO).

7. Although the current management team might not have been in charge during all the periods covered by the auditor's report, the auditor must still obtain written representations from them for all such periods. Which representations must be obtained will depend on the specific audit engagement and financial statement presentation.

8. An auditor may request written representations relating to the audit from individuals other than management of the client company; AU Section 333 gives the following illustrations of such circumstances:

   a. Representations about the completeness of the minutes of meetings of stockholders, directors, and committees of directors from the individual of the entity who is responsible for maintaining this information.

   b. Representations from the management of the parent company regarding a subsidiary for which an auditor is engaged to audit the financial statements without auditing the statements of the parent. The auditor may request representations on such matters as related parties and related-party transactions or the intention of the parent to continue financial support to the subsidiary.

9. In certain situations the auditor should obtain from the client company an updating representation letter (see Form 2 at end of section). This should occur when

   a. Information has come to the attention of management that would cause them to believe that a prior representation needs to be modified, and

   b. Events have occurred since the balance sheet date (subsequent events) of the latest financial statements that require adjustment to or additional disclosures in the financial statements.

Auditor's Recourse if Management Refuses to Furnish Written Representations

If management refuses to provide written representations, the auditor must view this as a limitation sufficient to block the rendering of an unqualified opinion. In this situation the auditor may either disclaim an opinion on the financial statements or withdraw from the engagement altogether. Alternatively, based on the representations that were not provided or on the nature and conditions of the refusal, the auditor may decide that a qualified opinion can be rendered.

If management has refused to provide some required representations, the auditor should also decide whether the representations (if any) that were provided can be relied upon. In some circumstances the auditor will have received representations concerning a matter for which the auditor was precluded from performing audit procedures that are necessary given how material they are to the financial statements. Even though the auditor did receive representations from management, the limitation on the scope of the audit requires that the auditor qualify this by an opinion or disclaim an opinion.

INTERPRETATION OF AU SECTION 333

INTERPRETATION 1, MANAGEMENT REPRESENTATIONS ON VIOLATIONS AND POSSIBLE VIOLATIONS OF LAWS AND REGULATIONS

AU Section 333 requires that written representations be obtained from management about violations of laws or regulations whose effects should be considered for disclosure in financial statements or as a basis for recording a loss contingency. Interpretation 1 notes that guidance on disclosure of litigation, claims, and assessments that may result from possible violations are provided in FASB Statement 5, *Accounting for Contingencies,* and in AU Section 317, *Illegal Acts by Clients.*

AU Section 333, in referring to the representation of "possible violations," does not include matters that go beyond the criteria for evaluating the disclosure requirements described in FASB Statement 5 and AU Section 317. The requirement for representation refers to matters that have come to management's attention and are significant enough that they should be considered in determining whether financial statement disclosures are necessary. Clearly, this is a matter of judgment. However, in asking management for a representation, the auditor is not asking them (management) to speculate on all legal challenges to its activities.

PRACTITIONER ILLUSTRATIVE MANAGEMENT REPRESENTATION LETTERS

FORM 1. ILLUSTRATIVE MANAGEMENT REPRESENTATION LETTER (ADAPTED FROM AU SECTION 333)

The following letter, which relates to an audit of financial statements prepared in conformity with generally accepted accounting principles, is presented for illustrative purposes only. The introductory paragraph should specify the financial statements and periods covered by the auditor's report, for example, "balance sheets of XYZ Company as of December 31, 19X1 and 19X0, and the related statements of income and retained earnings and cash flows for the years then ended." The written representations to be obtained should be based on the circumstances of the engagement and the nature and basis of presentation of the financial statements being audited.

*(The qualitative discussion of materiality used in this illustrative letter is adapted from FASB Statement of Financial Accounting Concepts 2, **Qualitative Characteristics of Accounting Information**.)*

[*Date*]
To [*Independent auditor*]

We are providing this letter in connection with your audit(s) of the [identification of financial statements] of [name of entity] as of [dates] and for the [periods] for the purpose of expressing an opinion as to whether the [consolidated] financial statements present fairly, in all material respects, the financial position, results of operations, and cash flows of [name of entity] in conformity with accounting principles generally accepted in the United States of America. We confirm that we are responsible for the fair presentation in the [consolidated] financial statements of financial position, results of operations, and cash flows in conformity with generally accepted accounting principles.

Certain representations in this letter are described as being limited to matters that are material. Items are considered material, regardless of size, if they involve an omission or misstatement of accounting information that, in the light of surrounding circumstances, makes it probable that the judgment of a reasonable person relying on the information would be changed or influenced by the omission or misstatement.

We confirm, to the best of our knowledge and belief, [as of (date of auditor's report),] the following representations made to you during your audit(s):

1. The financial statements referred to above are fairly presented in conformity with accounting principles generally accepted in the United States of America.
2. We have made available to you all:

    a. Financial records and related data.
    b. Minutes of the meetings of stockholders, directors, and committees of directors, or summaries of actions of recent meetings for which minutes have not yet been prepared.

3. There have been no communications from regulatory agencies concerning noncompliance with or deficiencies in financial reporting practices.
4. There are no material transactions that have not been properly recorded in the accounting records underlying the financial statements.
5. We believe that the effects of the uncorrected financial statement misstatements summarized in the accompanying schedule are immaterial, both individually and in the aggregate, to the financial statements taken as a whole.
6. We acknowledge our responsibility for the design and implementation of programs and controls to prevent and detect fraud.
7. We have no knowledge of any fraud or suspected fraud affecting the entity involving:

    a. Management;
    b. Employees who have significant roles in internal control; or
    c. Others where the fraud could have a material effect on the financial statements.

8. We have no knowledge of any allegations of fraud or suspected fraud affecting the entity received in communications from employees, former employees, analysts, regulators, short sellers, or others.
9. The company has no plans or intentions that may materially affect the carrying value or classification of assets and liabilities.
10. The following have been properly recorded or disclosed in the financial statements:

    a. Related-party transactions, including sales, purchases, loans, transfers, leasing arrangements, and guarantees, and amounts receivable from or payable to related parties.
    b. Guarantees, whether written or oral, under which the company is contingently liable.
    c. Significant estimates and material concentrations known to management that are required to be disclosed in accordance with the AICPA's Statement of Position 94-6, *Disclosure of Certain Significant Risks and Uncertainties.* [Significant estimates are estimates at the balance sheet date that could change materially within the next

year. Concentrations refer to volumes of business, revenues, available sources of supply, or markets or geographic areas for which events could occur that would significantly disrupt normal finances within the next year.]

11. There are no

    a. Violations or possible violations of laws or regulations whose effects should be considered for disclosure in the financial statements or as a basis for recording a loss contingency.

    b. Unasserted claims or assessments that our lawyer has advised us are probable of assertion and must be disclosed in accordance with Financial Accounting Standards Board (FASB) Statement 5, Accounting for Contingencies.

    c. Other liabilities or gain or loss contingencies that are required to be accrued or disclosed by FASB Statement 5.

12. The company has satisfactory title to all owned assets, and there are no liens or encumbrances on such assets nor has any asset been pledged as collateral.

13. The company has complied with all aspects of contractual agreements that would have a material effect on the financial statements in the event of non- compliance.

[Add any representations that are unique to the entity's business or industry.]

To the best of our knowledge and belief, no events have occurred subsequent to the balance-sheet date and through the date of this letter that would require adjustment to or disclosure in the aforementioned financial statements.

_____

[Name of chief executive officer and title]

_____

[Name of chief financial officer and title]

FORM 2. ILLUSTRATIVE UPDATING MANAGEMENT REPRESENTATION LETTER (ADAPTED FROM AU SECTION 333)

The *following letter is presented for illustrative purposes only. Management need not repeat all of the representations made in the previous representation letter. (See Form 1.)*

If matters exist that should be disclosed to the auditor, they should be indicated by listing them following the representation. For example, if an event subsequent to the date of the balance sheet has been disclosed in the financial statements, the final paragraph could be modified as follows: "To the best of our knowledge and belief except as discussed in Note X to the financial statements, no events have occurred...."

[*Date*]
To [*Auditor*]

In connection with your audit(s) of the [identification of financial statements] of [name of entity] as of [dates] and for the [periods], for the purpose of expressing an opinion as to whether the [consolidated] financial statements present fairly, in all material respects, the financial position, results of operations, and cash flows of [name of entity] in conformity with accounting principles generally accepted in the United States of America, you were previously provided with a representation letter under date of [date of previous representation letter]. No information has come to our attention that would cause us to believe that any of those previous representations should be modified.

To the best of our knowledge and belief, no events have occurred subsequent to [date of latest balance sheet reported on by the auditor] and through the date of this letter that would require adjustment to or disclosure in the aforementioned financial statements.

_____

[Name of chief executive officer and title]

_____

[Name of chief financial officer and title]

334 RELATED PARTIES

SOURCES OF STANDARDS

GAAS

SAS 45, *Omnibus Statement on Auditing Standards*
Interpretation of AU Section 334, *Exchange of Information Between the Principal and Other Auditor on Related Parties*
Interpretation of AU Section 334, *Examination of Identified Related-Party Transactions with a Component*
Interpretation of AU Section 334, *The Nature and Extent of Auditing Procedures for Examining Related-Party Transactions*
Interpretation of AU Section 334, *Management's and Auditor's Responsibilities with Regard to Related-Party Disclosures Prefaced by Terminology such as "Management Believes That"*

ADDITIONAL NON-GAAS PROFESSIONAL GUIDANCE:

Practice Alert 95-3, *Auditing Related Parties and Related-Party Transactions*

SUMMARY

AU Section 334 provides guidance on the procedures that are required to be followed in performing an audit of an entity's financial statements in accordance with GAAS in identifying related-party relations and transactions. In addition the pronouncement provides the accounting and disclosure requirements that the auditor must know concerning related-party activities. It is important to note that the procedural parameters enumerated in AU Section 334 should not be considered to be comprehensive nor should they be required to be followed in all audits.

RELATED-PARTY ACCOUNTING CONCEPTS

WHAT ARE RELATED-PARTY TRANSACTIONS?

Related-party transactions are simply transactions that occur between closely associated parties. However, because they involve business associates, they cannot be assumed to be carried out on an arm's-length basis, which is the required condition for competitive, free market operations. As a result GAAP (FASB Statement 57, *Related-Party Disclosures*) requires that financial statements include disclosure of material related party transactions besides compensation arrangements, expense allowances, and other such items with employees. The required disclosures should include a description of the nature of the relationship; a description of the transactions; the dollar amount of the transactions, including transactions for zero amounts or nominal amounts; and amounts due from or to related parties as of the date of each balance sheet presented. Transactions that are eliminated in the preparation of consolidated financial statements are not required to be disclosed.

FASB Statement 57 enumerates the following examples of related-party transactions. They include transactions between

- A parent company and its subsidiaries;
- Subsidiaries of a common parent;
- An enterprise and trusts for the benefit of employees, such as pensions and profit-sharing trusts that are managed by or under the trusteeship of the enterprise's management;
- An enterprise and its principal owners, management, or members of their immediate families; and
- Affiliates.

Transactions occurring in the normal course of business are frequently between related parties. Such transactions include

- Sales;
- Purchases;
- Transfers of realty and personal property;
- Services received or furnished including accounting, management, engineering, and legal services;
- Use of property and equipment by lease;
- Borrowings and lendings;
- Guarantees;
- Maintenance of bank balances as compensating balances for the benefit of another; and
- Intercompany billings based on allocations of common costs, and filings of consolidated tax returns.

In addition it must be noted that FASB Statement 57 provides that even transactions between related parties that were not recorded because no money was involved should be considered for disclosure. For example, assume that an entity accepts services from a related party and does not record the transaction because it was not charged for the service. The transaction in this situation would still be considered a related-party transaction.

GAAS GUIDANCE

ACCOUNTING DISCLOSURES

In general, GAAP does not require that related-party transactions be accounted for differently than transactions that would be accounted for that involve parties that are unrelated. GAAP always emphasizes substance over form, and this principal should be carefully followed in accounting for related-party transactions. In this regard the adequacy of disclosure should be considered paramount.

CIRCUMSTANCES THAT MAY INDICATE THE EXISTENCE OF RELATED PARTIES

The following circumstances may indicate the existence of related parties:

1. Making loans with no scheduled terms regarding their repayment.
2. Exchanging property for similar property in a nonmonetary transaction.
3. Selling real estate at an amount that significantly differs from its appraised value.

4. Borrowing or lending at an interest-free basis or at a rate of interest that is significantly below or above the prevailing market rate of interest at the time of the transaction.

Related-Party Audit Procedures

During the course of an audit the auditor should be aware of the possible existence of material related party transactions that may affect the financial statements or require disclosure by FASB 57, since such transactions relate to common ownership or management control relationships despite the casual nature of some related-party transactions. A related-party transaction or disclosure may be uncovered by following the audit procedures that are normally performed in an audit in accordance with GAAS. In addition specifically designed procedures may be performed to increase the probability of their discovery. However, the performance of these procedures cannot provide complete assurance that all related-party transactions will be revealed.

The scope of the audit procedures to be performed regarding the existence of related-party transactions should be designed by the auditor based on the following considerations:

1. Management responsibilities and the relationship of each component to the total entity.
2. Controls over management activities.
3. The business purpose served by each component of the entity.
4. The business structure and style of operations. (Generally, these considerations are predicated on the ability of the entity's managers, product diversification, geographical location, and tax and legal considerations. However, occasionally business structure and operating style are intentionally designed to hide related-party transactions.)

In addition the auditor should be cognizant of the following conditions that may have precipitated the occurrence of related-party transactions:

1. The need for a continued favorable earnings record so that the price of a company's stock can be supported.
2. An overly positive earnings forecast.
3. Continued dependence on a single or relatively few products, customers, or transactions for the success of the company.
4. The existence of a large number of business failures in a declining industry in which the entity is a part.
5. Excess capacity.
6. Insufficient working capital or credit to continue the business.
7. High magnitude of litigation especially between stockholders and management.
8. High susceptibility to the risk of obsolescence, especially if the company is in a high-technology industry.

AUDIT PROCEDURES THAT TEST FOR THE EXISTENCE OF UNDISCLOSED RELATED PARTIES

Related-party transactions on the part of the reporting entity involving investor–investee, parent–subsidiary, or other close business relationships require a careful review by the auditor so that proper GAAP disclosure requirements may be satisfied. However, uncovering the existence of any unknown relationships may require the use of other, more precisely designed audit procedures. Such procedures include the following steps:

1. Appraise the company's procedures for identifying and appropriately accounting for related-party transactions.

2. Make inquiries of management regarding the names of all related parties and ascertain whether there were any transactions with these parties during the period under audit.

3. Obtain the entity's SEC and other regulatory agencies' filings and review them for the names of all related parties and for other businesses in which officers and directors occupy directorships or other management positions.

4. Examine the entity's prior year's working papers for the names of identified related parties.

5. Examine material investment transactions that were executed during the period under audit to ascertain whether their nature and magnitude created related parties.

6. Ascertain the names of all pension and other trusts established for the benefit of employees and the names of their officers and trustees. These individuals are considered related parties under FASB Statement 57, *Related-Party Disclosures.*

7. Examine the entity's stockholder listings of closely held companies so that principal stockholders may be identified.

8. Explore existing "related entity" relationships and the extent of management's involvement in these transactions by making inquiries of the related entity's predecessor, principal, or other auditors regarding their knowledge of such associations.

PROCEDURES THAT ASSIST THE AUDITOR IN IDENTIFYING RELATED-PARTY TRANSACTIONS AND PREVIOUSLY UNDETERMINED RELATED-PARTY RELATIONSHIPS

1. Analyze information about material transactions that might have been authorized or discussed by the board of directors, the executive, or an operating committees of the entity by reviewing the minutes of their meetings.

2. Review conflict-of-interests statements that have been filed with the company by its managers. These statements are filed by managers of an entity with the board of directors of the company and indicate any relationships that may exist between the reporting individual and the parties that transact business with the company.

3. Carefully review the magnitude and nature of business transacted with major customers, suppliers, borrowers, and lenders to ascertain whether previously undisclosed relationships exist.

4. Ascertain whether compensating bank balances were maintained for or by related parties by reviewing confirmations of compensating balance arrangements.

5. Communicate the names of known related parties to all auditors who perform segments of the audit or audit and report separately on the accounts of related components of the entity so that they may be aware of any related-party transactions that may have occurred during their audits.

6. Carefully review the accounting records for large, unusual, or nonrecurring transactions or balances, especially those that were recognized at or near the end of the reporting period.

7. Check for the existence of related parties or related-party transactions by examining invoices from law firms that have performed regular or special services for the entity.

8. Determine whether guarantees relating to loans receivable and payable exist by reviewing the confirmations of these items. When guarantees do in fact exist, ascertain the relationship of the guarantor to the reporting entity to see if the former is a related party whose relationship requires disclosure.

9. Determine whether accounting, management, or other services are being provided for at no charge (e.g., or is being paid for by a major stockholder).

10. Determine the existence of material related-party transactions by reviewing proxy and other material filed with the SEC and other reports that could have been filed with other regulatory agencies.

LEARNING THE PURPOSE, NATURE, AND EXTENT OF IDENTIFIED RELATED-PARTY TRANSACTIONS AND THEIR EFFECT ON THE FINANCIAL STATEMENTS

The auditor must obtain satisfaction regarding the purpose, nature, and extent of material related-party transactions and their effect on the financial statement of the reporting entity. This determination extends beyond a mere inquiry of management. GAAS requires that the auditor obtain sufficient, appropriate audit evidence in support of any related-party transaction. In order to accomplish this, the auditor must consider performing the following audit procedures:

1. Determine an understanding of the "true" substance of the transaction. That is, the transactions must make business sense. If the auditor lacks the specialized knowledge or experience to understand a particular transaction, the auditor should seek advice from those individuals who are familiar with such a transaction.
2. Ascertain whether the transaction under scrutiny has been approved by the board of directors of the entity or other officials whose approval was required.
3. Test the amounts to be disclosed in the financial statements or that are being considered for disclosure for reasonableness.
4. Inspect and confirm items of collateral, and test and check their transfer ability and value.
5. Examine invoices, executed copies of agreements, contracts, receiving reports, shipping receipts, and related documents.
6. Audit intercompany account balances as of concurrent dates (even if the fiscal years differ). Auditors for those entities that have participated in related-party transactions should exchange important relevant information that may require disclosure.

EXTENDED AUDIT PROCEDURES REQUIRED BY GAAP WHEN AN AUDITOR BELIEVES THAT A FULL UNDERSTANDING OF THE RELATED PARTY TRANSACTION IS REQUIRED.

GAAS requires that extended audit procedures be performed (which ordinarily would not be performed) when an auditor believes that a related-party transaction needs to be more fully understood so that an adequate financial statement disclosure may be presented. Arrangements for the performance of these procedures should be approved in advance by the entity being audited. The related (extended) audit procedures are as follows:

1. Intermediaries to the related-party transaction should be consulted with. These parties include banks, guarantors, agents, or attorneys. Obtaining information from these parties enables the auditor to obtain a better under standing of the transaction.
2. In pursuance of related-party transaction information, data should be collected regarding the financial status of the other party or parties associated with the entity's uncollected balances, guarantees, and other obligations. This data may be derived from audited financial statements, unaudited financial statements, tax returns, taxing authorities, financial publications, and credit agencies. The auditor must ascertain not only the degree of assurance that is needed in this situation, but also whether the documentary evidential matter collected in this manner satisfies this assurance.
3. If the auditor deems questionable the relationship of unfamiliar customers, suppliers, or other business enterprises with which the client company has transacted a

material amount of business, he or she should refer to financial publications, trade journals, credit agencies, and other informational sources to obtain audit satisfaction regarding that party.

4. The auditor should inspect all material evidence possessed by the related party or parties of the transaction(s) so that a full understanding of the transaction(s) can be obtained.

5. Confirm the amount of the transactions and their terms (including guarantees and other related data) with the other party(ies) to the related-party transaction.

FINANCIAL STATEMENT DISCLOSURE AUDIT CONSIDERATIONS

FASB Statement 57, *Related-Party Disclosures,* requires that the notes of an entity's financial statements include for each material related-party transaction (or aggregation of similar such transactions) certain disclosures. These disclosures were enumerated at the beginning of the chapter (see "What are Related-Party Transactions?"). With respect to such disclosures the auditor should be able to respond affirmatively to the following audit queries:

1. Has sufficient, competent, evidential matter been obtained to enable the auditor to fully understand the relationship that exists between the parties in question?

2. Has the effect of the related-party transaction(s) on the financial statements been ascertained?

3. Has all the available information that has been evaluated concerning the related party or control relationship (common ownership or management control relationships) satisfied the auditor that there is adequate financial statement disclosure?

4. Has the following been considered? FASB Statement 57 specifies that if a note includes a representation regarding a related-party transaction(s), it should not in any way imply that such a transaction(s) was executed on terms equivalent to that which would occur from an independent arm's-length transaction. Of course, if it can be substantiated that the related-party transaction occurred on an arm's-length basis, then this fact should be disclosed. However, if management includes such a representation that the auditor deems to be unsubstantiated by management, then the auditor should express a qualified or adverse opinion on the financial statements (based on the materiality of the transaction) because of the departure from GAAP.

INTERPRETATIONS OF AU SECTION 334, *RELATED PARTIES*

INTERPRETATION NO. 4, EXCHANGE OF INFORMATION BETWEEN THE PRINCIPAL AND OTHER AUDITORS ON RELATED PARTIES

AU Section 334 notes that the auditor should always be aware of the possibility of material related-party transactions and make appropriate inquiries regarding that possibility. As a result the auditor should make inquiries of other auditors of related entities concerning their knowledge of existing relationships and the extent of management's involvement in these relationships. Interpretation 4 specifies when the principal auditor should make these inquiries. The inquiry of the principal auditor and other auditors regarding the names of known related parties and related information should take place at an early stage of the audit.

INTERPRETATION NO. 5, EXAMINATION OF IDENTIFIED RELATED-PARTY TRANSACTIONS WITH A COMPONENT

AU Section 334 requires an auditor to apply necessary procedures to obtain satisfaction concerning the effect of identified related-party transactions on the financial statements. This interpretation focuses on obtaining satisfaction when there is a principal auditor–other auditor relationship and the principal auditor must obtain satisfaction involving not only the component (i.e., the financial statements of the entity) under audit but also other components (i.e., the financial statements of other entities comprising the consolidated unit) being audited by other auditors.

Interpretation 5 states that the audit procedures may sometimes have to be applied to the accounting records of components of an entity that are being audited by another. The principal auditor may choose to perform the required procedures alone or may ask the other auditor to perform them. If circumstances arise indicating the possibility of the existence of related-party transactions and the primary auditor determines that access to the other auditor's work papers is needed to clarify his understanding of the effects of those transactions on the financial statements, then such access should be made available.

INTERPRETATION NO. 6, THE NATURE AND EXTENT OF AUDITING PROCEDURES FOR EXAMINING RELATED-PARTY TRANSACTIONS

This interpretation discusses the extent of tests that need to be performed to identify related-party transactions to ensure that they are adequately disclosed and do not contain misstatements when, taken together with other errors in the other balances and transactions, would have a material effect on the financial statements. In auditing related-party transactions (or any account balance or category of transactions), the auditor must determine the appropriate audit risk and design and then perform the required substantive tests. In an audit of related-party transactions, the assessment of risk level is generally higher than other types of transactions. The reason for this is that the participants of related-party transactions are frequently motivated by more sensitive circumstances than are the case for usual business transactions. The greater the risk assessment, the greater is the amount of resulting substantive testing that must be performed. In assessing the appropriate risk level of a related-party transaction, it is imperative that the auditor know why this related-party transaction occurred. When were the parties to the transaction motivated to execute it? Does the transaction make good business sense? An auditor must be familiar with the specialized transactions of the business being audited to be able to make such an assessment. If the auditor does not have this required knowledge, the auditor should consult with an individual who has such information. In order to fully understand the essence of the related-party transaction(s), the auditor may have to obtain evidential matter relating to the transaction, obtain the audited or unaudited financial statements of the related party, or actually audit the related party's financial statements.

The interpretation also notes that the auditor should obtain representations from the senior management and its board of directors whether they or any related party engaged in transactions with the entity during the period. This is in addition to the specific procedures delineated in AU Section 334 regarding the existence of related-party transactions.

INTERPRETATION NO. 7, MANAGEMENT'S AND AUDITOR'S RESPONSIBILITIES WITH REGARD TO RELATED-PARTY DISCLOSURES PREFACED BY TERMINOLOGY SUCH AS "MANAGEMENT BELIEVES THAT"

If management discloses a related-party transaction in its financial statements (based on terms that would exist in an arm's-length transaction) and prefaces the representation with the expression "Management believes that" or "It is the Company's Belief that," does this terminology change management's responsibility to fully explain and corroborate the representation? Interpretation 7 notes that FASB Statement 57, *Related-Party Transactions,* states that there shall be no implication of a related-party transaction being executed on terms that would exist in an arm's-length transaction unless such representation can be substantiated. Using prefaces, such as "Management believes that" or "It is the Company's belief that," does not mitigate management's responsibility to validate such representations.

If management includes such phraseology, which implies that a related-party transaction had been consummated on terms equivalent to an ongoing arm's-length transaction and management has not fully convinced the auditor of this fact, then the auditor is required under AU Section 334 to express a qualified or adverse opinion, based on the materiality of the transaction, because of a departure from GAAP, Clearly, an auditor should never assume that a related-party transactions was executed on the same basis as an independent arm's-length transaction. Such representations must be fully substantiated.

ADDITIONAL NON-GAAS PROFESSIONAL GUIDANCE

PRACTICE ALERT (PA) 95-3, AUDITING RELATED PARTIES AND RELATED-PARTY TRANSACTIONS

NOTE: The information that follows is based on the findings of the SEC Practice Section Professional Issues Task Force. It has not been approved or disapproved by any committee of the AICPA. It is provided here as an additional source of practical guidance for the practitioner.

The identification of related party and related transactions is a very important activity in the audit of an entity's financial statements. There are several reasons for this. For example

- GAAP requires that an entity's financial statements disclose all material related-party transactions as well as certain control relationships;
- Inadequate related-party transaction disclosure increases the potential for misleading and erroneous financial statements; and
- Undisclosed related parties have been shown to facilitate the occurrences of fraudulent financial reporting and misappropriation of assets.

Related parties and related-party transactions can cause difficulties for an auditor. The following highlights some considerations related to this issue:

- Related-party transactions cannot always be identified. For example, transactions with an unknown related party may take the form of a series of unnoticeable, immaterial transactions that would only draw audit attention when considered in the aggregate.
- Although the auditor performs audit tests under GAAS to identify the existence of related parties and related-party transactions, the primary means of identifying such activity is management's disclosure of it. That is, the auditor primarily relies on management to identify all related party and related-party transactions.
- An entity's internal control system may not be able to identify related-party transactions.

PA 95-3 enumerates the following occurrences that may indicate the existence of undisclosed transactions with related parties:

1. Sales transactions were recorded that require repurchase, resulting in the negation of part or all of the revenue that was recognized on the sale.
2. Loans were made to parties that clearly do not have the ability to repay them.
3. Services or goods were purchased (from an ostensibly related party) at virtually no cost to the entity.
4. Borrowing took place from a party, executed at below market rates of interest.

5. Loans were made to a party for an apparent bona fide purpose that were written off soon after as being uncollectible.
6. Payments were made for services at highly inflated prices or for services that were never rendered.
7. An entity making a sale to another party fully funded the other party to the transaction. Effectively, the sale is without substance.
8. Purchases of assets were made at prices in excess of the goods' fair market value.
9. Interest was accrued at above market rates of interest of loans made to certain parties.
10. Money was provided to a debtor of the company to be used to repay a loan or receivable that had already been deemed to be uncollectible.
11. Sales of goods were made to a related party at below going market prices. The related party, in turn, sold the goods to a customer at higher bona fide prices and retained the difference.

SUMMARY OF CONSIDERATIONS RELATED TO DISCOVERING RELATED PARTIES AND RELATED-PARTY TRANSACTIONS

1. Identifying and determining the existence of related-party and related-party transactions is a significant part of the audit.
2. Throughout the audit, the auditor should maintain an awareness of events that may indicate the existence of related party and related-party transactions (see enumeration of occurrences that may indicate the existence of undisclosed related-party transactions [above]).
3. By fully investigating all related-party activities, the auditor is assured that any related-party transactions that the entity has been involved with will be properly accounted for and disclosed in the financial statements. Such disclosures will provide users with relevant and important information in their decision-making activities.

336 USING THE WORK OF A SPECIALIST

SOURCES OF STANDARDS

GAAS

SAS 73, *Using the Work of a Specialist*

Interpretation of AU Section 336, *The Use of Legal Interpretations as Evidential Matter to Support Management's Assertion that a Transfer of Financial Assets Has Met the Isolation Criterion in Paragraph 9(a) of Financial Accounting Standards Board Statement No. 140*

ADDITIONAL NON-GAAS PROFESSIONAL GUIDANCE

Practice Alert 02-2, *Use of Specialists*

SUMMARY

AU Section 336 provides guidance to an auditor who uses the work of a specialist in performing an audit in accordance with GAAS. The section defines a specialist as a "person (or firm) possessing special skills or knowledge in a particular field other than accounting or auditing." Specialists can be used in a myriad of situations. They are generally needed when a unique competence is required to check on the corrections of assertions of the client. For example, an actuary might be required to verify the assumptions underlying an entity's pension and postretirement funding, entries, and disclosures. In the area of inventory, engineering specialists might be called in to ascertain the degree of completion of sophisticated machinery (medical, electronic, biological, etc.) or to estimate its replacement cost as of a given date. A geologist might be called to determine the extent of a client's oil reserves. Specialists may also be appraisers, environmental consultants, and lawyers. A lawyer may be engaged to interpret a contractual agreement as well as to handle many other law-related functions.

The parameters of using the work of a specialist by the auditor as comprehensively enumerated in AU Section 336 are described in the following sections. The Interpretation of AU Section 336 on the use of legal interpretations to support management regarding whether a transfer of financial assets has met the isolation criterion of FASB Statement 140 follows the discussion on AU Section 336.

GAAS GUIDANCE

WHEN SHOULD THE GUIDANCE OF AU SECTION 336 BE USED?

AU Section 336 should be applied in the following situations:

1. A specialist is hired by an auditor who uses the specialist's findings as audit evidence to evaluate material assertions in the financial statements.

2. A specialist employed by an auditing firm is hired as an advisor by the management of the company being audited. The auditor uses that specialist's work as audit evidence to evaluate material assertions in the financial statements.

3. A specialist is employed or engaged by management and the auditor uses the specialist's work as audit evidence to evaluate material assertions in the financial statement.

SITUATIONS WHERE AN AUDITOR MAY CHOOSE TO USE THE SERVICES OF A SPECIALIST

During an audit an auditor may realize that the skill or knowledge of a specialist is needed for the performance of substantive tests. AU Section 336 denotes situations where an auditor may decide to use the services of a specialist:

- Valuing functions:

  1. Special-purpose inventories,
  2. High-tech materials and equipment,
  3. Pharmaceuticals,
  4. Financial products that are complex,
  5. Artwork, and
  6. Real estate.

- Ascertaining quantity and/or condition for assets:

  1. Minerals,
  2. Mineral reserves, and
  3. Stockpiles of stored materials.

- Utilizing special measuring techniques and/or methods:

  1. Determining employee pension benefit obligations and related disclosures, and
  2. Ascertaining loss reserves in the insurance industry.

- Interpreting information:

  1. Technical requirements,
  2. Agreements in the form of contracts or other legal documents, and
  3. Regulations.

WHAT QUALIFICATIONS MUST A SPECIALIST POSSESS?

Before an auditor engages a specialist, AU Section 336 requires that the auditor evaluate the specialist's qualifications in the following ways:

1. Check the magnitude and quality of the individual's past work experience.
2. Review the person's professional certifications, licenses, and other assessments of competence in the relevant field of expertise.
3. Check with individuals and organizations that should be familiar with the person's reputation and professional standing.

The auditor should also familiarize his or herself with the nature of the work to be performed (or already performed) by the specialist. This means obtaining an understanding of

1. Any relationship of the client to the specialist, especially any circumstances that might impair the specialist's independence. (The impairment of objectivity is dis-

cussed in more detail below under "Independence of the Specialist Relative to the Client.")

2. The scope and goals of the specialist's work.
3. The suitability of using the specialist's work in evaluating assertions in the financial statements. The auditor should directly communicate to the specialist how the specialist's work will be used. That is, the specialist should be cognizant of the purpose of the work. Reciprocally, the auditor should make sure that the work of the specialist will be able to support the assertions being tested.
4. The methods or assumptions on which the specialist's work is based.
5. How those methods or assumptions compare with those used in preceding periods.
6. The conclusions of the specialist and their effect on the assertions of the financial statements.

RELYING ON THE FINDINGS OF THE SPECIALIST

After the specialist's findings are submitted, the auditor should perform procedures to determine whether the findings can be used. These include

1. Learning and understanding the techniques and suppositions on which the work of the specialist work was predicated,
2. Testing the data provided to the specialist, and
3. Ascertaining whether the specialist's results support the assertions in the financial statement being tested.

After performing these procedures, the auditor must decide whether to use the work of the specialist. If it is determined that the results derived by the specialist are unreasonable, additional procedures need to be performed. If the auditor concludes that the findings of the specialist are unacceptable, then the auditor should seek the opinion of another specialist. Under normal circumstances, however, the auditor would use the specialist's findings.

INDEPENDENCE OF THE SPECIALIST RELATIVE TO THE CLIENT

The auditor must ascertain that the client is independent of the specialist and cannot control or significantly influence the latter. For example, the auditor should make sure that there are no relationships, such as family, ownership, employment, or contractual rights (including related-party transactions), between the client and specialist that could impair the specialist's objectivity. If there are no such relationships, the auditor should be able to place high reliability on the findings of the specialist.

If there is a relationship between client and specialist, the auditor must assess whether the objectivity of the specialist might be impaired. In these circumstances additional tests must be performed on the specialist's approaches and conclusions to determine that the outcomes reached were warranted and do not require reevaluation by another professional.

EFFECT ON THE AUDITOR'S REPORT

If the conclusions reached by the specialist support the related assertions in the financial statement of the client, the auditor may conclude that there is sufficient appropriate audit evidence on which to base an unqualified opinion. However, the auditor should make no reference to the work or conclusions of the specialist in the report. Such a reference might imply that a more thorough effort was made by the auditor than was agreed-on or that there is a qualification of opinion or division of responsibility with respect to the work done.

If the specialist's findings do not support the assertions in the financial statements (i.e., there is in fact a material discrepancy), AU Section 336 requires that the auditor perform additional auditing procedures that will provide evidence that will resolve the conflict. It may be necessary for the auditor to obtain an opinion from another specialist to help resolve the discrepancy. The auditor may ultimately decide that the matter cannot be reasonably resolved at all. In such a case, the auditor should either qualify or disclaim an opinion on the financial statements because of a scope limitation. These opinion modifications are necessary because the auditor has been precluded from obtaining sufficient competent evidence relating to a material assertion in the financial statements.

If the auditor chooses to perform additional auditing procedures, perhaps even engaging another specialist to resolve the discrepancy between the specialist's findings and client's financial statement assertions, the auditor may determine that the client's financial statements are not in conformity with GAAP. The auditor must then express a qualified or adverse opinion.

INTERPRETATION OF AU SECTION 336, *USING THE WORK OF A SPECIALIST*

THE USE OF LEGAL INTERPRETATIONS AS EVIDENTIAL MATTER TO SUPPORT MANAGEMENT'S ASSERTION THAT A TRANSFER OF FINANCIAL ASSETS HAS MET THE ISOLATION CRITERION IN PARAGRAPH 9(A) OF FINANCIAL ACCOUNTING STANDARDS BOARD FASB STATEMENT NO. 140

FASB Statement 140 requires that if a transferor of financial assets sells the assets, total control must be surrendered before the transfer may be considered a bona fide sale. Although several requirements must be satisfied in accounting for transfers and servicing of financial assets, a significant consideration is whether the isolation criterion has been met. FASB Statement 140 requires that the transferred assets are to be beyond the reach of the transferor and its creditors, even in bankruptcy or other receivership.

An important component of this interpretation is auditor guidance in determining whether to use the work of a legal specialist (generally the client's internal or external attorney who is knowledgeable about these matters) to help provide competent evidence to determine compliance with the isolation criterion. The interpretation discusses the following considerations regarding this matter:

1. Routine transfers of financial assets that do not result in any continuing involvement by the transferor do not require assistance from a legal specialist.
2. The use of a legal specialist may be appropriate for transfers that have complex legal structures, such as continuing involvement by the transferor and other considerations that make it difficult to ascertain whether isolation has occurred.
3. Legal opinions relating to transfers occurring over an extended period of time may require periodic updates to ensure that there have been no subsequent changes in the law.
4. Management may be asked to obtain an update on the prior structure if a transferor executes a new sale of financial assets that management determines to be comparable to a prior one to ensure that no new changes in the law have occurred.

If it is decided to use the services of a legal specialist, the auditor must evaluate the appropriateness and suitability of the specialist's legal opinion. Salient guidelines for this are as follows:

1. Does the legal specialist have experience with and knowledge of the United States Bankruptcy Code and other federal, state, or foreign laws, as well as knowledge of

the area of financial assets transfers and the isolation criterion of FASB Statement 140?

2. Do the legal specialist's findings support management's assertion regarding isolation? If so, it may be assumed that sufficient competent evidence has been obtained.
3. Does any limitation, disclaimer of opinion, or facts or circumstances that do not relate to the isolation criterion affect the reasoned legal opinion generated by the specialist? Such limitations might not provide sufficient competent evidence that a transfer of assets complies with FASB Statement 140.
4. Are any hypothetical transactions on which the specialist's conclusions are based different from the transactions under scrutiny? They would not provide competent supportive evidence.

Any legal opinions generated by specialists that are restricted solely to either the client or to parties other that the auditor are, in general, not acceptable audit evidence.

Another important area in the interpretation provides guidance for the auditor when the legal response of the specialist does not provide the appropriate supportive evidence regarding the transfer of financial assets. Included in this category are potentially supportive legal opinions that are being restricted by the specialist and are therefore unavailable for the auditor's use. If the legal opinion issued does not provide sufficient supportive evidence regarding the transfer, the auditor should not consider the sale of financial assets to be in conformity with GAAP and must issue a qualified or an adverse opinion. If the auditor is unable to get access to a potentially supportive legal opinion because of restrictions imposed by the legal specialist, the auditor should consider this a scope limitation and issue a qualified opinion or disclaim an opinion altogether.

ADDITIONAL NON-GAAS PROFESSIONAL GUIDANCE

PRACTICE ALERT (PA) 02-2, USE OF SPECIALISTS

NOTE: The information that follows is based on the findings of the SEC Practice Section Professional Issues Task Force but has not yet been approved or disapproved by any committee of the AICPA. It is provided here as an additional source of practical guidance.

Should a Specialist Be Used?

In deciding whether to use a specialist, the auditor must determine if specialized knowledge will be needed to substantiate management's assertions. No engagement should ever be accepted by an independent auditor unless it is certain that the requisite level of understanding regarding the audit and audit-related information can be obtained either directly or indirectly through the services of a specialist.

Employment or Engagement of a Specialist

A specialist hired by an audit firm is subject to the firm's independence requirements. It is not necessary for the auditor to check the qualifications of an internal specialist at the onset of an audit. This was done at the time of employment by the audit firm as part of its personnel verification process of its professional employees' education and licensing requirements.

It is important for the auditor to know who the specialist is working for. If the specialist was hired by the accounting firm and is functioning as part of the audit team, AU Section 336 does not apply but AU Section 311, *Planning and Supervision,* does because the specialist requires the same supervision as any assistant accountant. AU Section 311 is also followed if the accounting firm hires an actuary pension specialist to help determine whether the pension and actuarial computations of its clients are correct. On the other hand, if the client hires the accounting firm to perform pension work and the auditor later relies on and uses this information as part of the audit, the auditor should rely on AU Section 336 as well as most of PA 02-2.

Using a specialist as part of the audit team has several advantages—including reduction of audit risk for the auditing firm, because the specialist is familiar with the firm's professional policies, and maximizing the knowledge and talent of the specialist on an audit, because audit team members are familiar with the specialist's qualifications as well as how to best apply them to the audit.

An auditor who engages an outside specialist should

- Reach an understanding with the specialist about the scope of the engagement that the specialist is hired for,
- Document in writing any arrangement with the specialist as well as the engagement understanding should be documented in writing,
- Discuss the methods and assumptions used by the specialists, and
- Determine whether the specialist's findings are consistent with those of other specialists that are employed or engaged by the client.

Clearly, a specialist that is engaged by a client is not independent of the client. However, it is only the requirement of objectivity that really matters. A specialist engaged by a client need not be independent but must be objective. An auditor who believes the specialist's objectivity may be impaired should engage another specialist or perform additional audit procedures on the specialist's assumptions, methods, or findings to ascertain whether they are reasonable.

Confirming the Terms of the Specialist's Engagement

If an auditor decides to use the findings of a specialist, the following terms related to the specialist's engagement should be clarified:

1. The specialist's relationship with the client.
2. The assumptions and methods that the specialist uses.
3. The consistency of those assumptions and methods with those used in the prior period and by other industry specialists.
4. Compliance of the specialist with the auditor's requirements.
5. The scope and objectives of the work of the specialist.
6. The auditor's intended use of the specialist's work.
7. The appropriateness of the specialist's work given its intended use.
8. What information is supplied by the client to the specialist (so that the auditor can ascertain what must be tested as part of the audit).
9. An outline of the items the report of specialist should cover and the form and content of the findings.
10. The extent of the specialist's access to client files and records.
11. Any nonclient information that the specialist intends to use.
12. Maintenance of client confidentiality.
13. Any additional information or documentation that may be required to support the auditor's procedures and ultimate report.

Audit Procedures Relating to the Work of the Specialist

An auditor who chooses to use the findings of a specialist should perform the following audit procedures:

- Obtain a confirmation directly from the specialist regarding the nature and scope of the engagement.

- Obtain an understanding of the methods and assumptions used by the specialist.
- Ascertain whether the source data used by the specialist are reliable. If they are not, the specialist's findings will not be accurate, which will adversely affect the audited financial statements.
- Corroborate the source data (both accounting and nonaccounting) that the client gave to the specialist, using the following procedures:

  1. Ask whether the specialist is satisfied with the accuracy of the source data.
  2. Perform tests to determine if the data are relevant and reliable.

  For example, if the specialist was consulting on a pension plan actuarial computation, the auditor might want to verify the actual return on the client's plan assets submitted to the specialist by deducting the fair value of the plan assets at the beginning of the period from their fair value at the end of the period and by deducting from that amount the difference between contributions made to the plan and benefits paid during the same period. In verifying an unrecognized prior- service computation in a pension calculation, an auditor may want to check the number of employees and their expected dates of retirement that were provided to the specialist by comparing the information to the client's personnel database.

- Evaluate whether the specialist's findings support the financial statements.

  For example, in an illustration in PA 02-2 a specialist actuary decides that an automobile insurance company should reduce the amount of loss reserves that it maintains relative to the percentage that it maintained last year. An auditor who knows that the loss experience of insurance companies in that state has actually increased may decide the actuary's findings are unreasonable, choosing either to perform additional audit procedures to achieve audit satisfaction with respect to the specialist findings or to seek the opinion of another specialist. If, after taking such actions, the auditor is still uncomfortable with the results, the auditor's report should be qualified or an opinion disclaimed because of a scope limitation.

- If the client has decided to engage a specialist, the auditor should consider including a representation about this in the client representation letter. The following example from PA 02-2 is an illustration of how it might be phrased:

  We assume responsibility for the findings of specialists in evaluating the [*describe assertion*] and have adequately considered the qualifications of the specialists in determining the amounts and disclosures used in the financial statements and underlying accounting records. We did not give nor cause any instructions to be given to specialists with respect to the values or amounts derived in an attempt to bias their work, and we are not otherwise aware of any other matters that have an impact on the objectivity of the specialists.

GUIDANCE RELATED TO USING DIFFERENT TYPES OF SPECIALISTS

INFORMATION TECHNOLOGY (IT) SPECIALISTS

IT specialists are generally employed or engaged by an audit firm. Guidance in their use is enumerated in AU Section 311, *Planning and Supervision, and SAS 94, The Effect of Information Technology on the Auditor's Consideration of Internal Control in a Financial Statement Audit*. Some salient issues relating to this guidance follow:

Should an IT Specialist Be Used on an Audit?

To ascertain whether an IT specialist is needed, the following should be considered:

1. Evaluate the degree of complexity of the client's systems and IT controls as well as how they are used.
2. Determine how much audit evidence is available only in electronic form.
3. Ascertain the client's use of cutting-edge, emerging technologies.

4. Ascertain the extent to which data are shared.
5. Determine the changes that the client has made to existing systems and whether new systems have been put into operation.
6. Determine the extent to which the client participates in electronic commerce.

How Can the IT Specialist Assist the Audit Team?

The extent of the IT specialist's participation in an audit is a function of the following variables:

1. The complexity of the IT used by the client in its transactional cycles.
2. Control risk assessments.
3. IT skills available on the audit engagement.

The IT specialist may assist the audit team in the following functions:

1. Preliminary review of the client's computer processing system.
2. Performing

   a. Tests of controls: design and implementation,
   b. Substantive tests of client-based IT systems, and
   c. Computer-assisted audit techniques.

3. Interpreting tests results.
4. Preparing internal control and management letters and other client communications.
5. Analyzing the IT files according to audit parameters used to identify transactions that indicate the possibility of irregularities for the following audit tests and investigative activities:

   a. Revenue and other cutoff testing,
   b. Examining and reviewing purchase ledger transactions,
   c. Testing for duplicate invoices,
   d. Testing for correct payroll rates and deductions by matching payments to payroll master files,
   e. Searching for unusual payroll payments,
   f. Searching for payments to specific individuals,
   g. Segmenting payments by magnitude and reviewing all unusual items,
   h. Performing ratio analysis,
   i. Testing accounts receivable and payable aging schedules, and
   j. Examining payments by vendor or invoice numbers.

6. Performing digit analysis: The IT specialist can be particularly helpful in using mathematical concepts, equations, and formulas to investigate irregularities in data sets. Digit analysis consists of identifying number duplication, excessive round numbers, identical or closely identical entries in data subsets, and so forth.

Responsibilities of the Auditor Who Uses an IT Specialist

There is no transfer of responsibility for information technology from the auditor to an IT specialist used on an audit. Even when an IT specialist is part of the audit group, the auditor is still responsible for

1. Ascertaining (in conjunction with the IT specialist) what objectives must be met in reviewing the client's computer processing system and what audit procedures need to be performed,
2. Reviewing the work of the IT specialist,
3. Participating as necessary in the work being performed,

4. Evaluating the audit risk and strategies and modifying any audit procedures that must be performed, and
5. Ensuring that all IT issues relating to the audit are documented in the workpapers.

Business Valuation Specialists

When valuations related to purchase price allocations and related impairment tests follow (FASB Statement 141 [Revised 2007], *Business Combinations;* FASB Statement 142, *Goodwill and Other Intangible Assets*) after a business combination, a business valuation specialist should be used. This is especially true when the valuation and impairment tests have a material impact on the company's financial statements. It does not matter whether the business valuation specialist is internal or external. The auditor should also perform audit procedures to determine whether the specialist's findings support client assertions in the financial statements.

337 INQUIRY OF A CLIENT'S LAWYER CONCERNING LITIGATION, CLAIMS, AND ASSESSMENTS

SOURCE OF STANDARD

SAS 12, *Inquiry of a Client's Lawyer Concerning Litigation, Claims, and Assessments*

See section 9337 for interpretations of this section.

INTRODUCTION/SUMMARY

The Statement of Financial Accounting Standards 5, *Accounting for Contingencies,* sets forth the financial accounting and reporting requirements for loss contingencies, including those arising from litigation, claims, and assessments. The auditor's responsibility is to obtain sufficient evidential matter by considering the following factors (AU 337.04):

1. The existence of a condition, situation, or set of circumstances indicating an uncertainty as to the possible loss to an entity arising from litigation, claims, and assessments.
2. The period in which the underlying cause for legal action occurred.
3. The degree of probability of an unfavorable outcome.
4. The amount or range of potential loss.

AUDIT PROCEDURES

An entity's management is the primary source of information about litigation, claims, and assessments. Management generally has direct knowledge about such matters. Therefore the auditor should (AU 337.05)

1. Inquire of the management about policies and procedures for identifying, evaluating, and accounting for litigation, claims, and assessments;
2. Obtain from management a description and evaluation of litigation, claims, and assessments that existed

   a. At the date of the balance sheet being reported on, and
   b. During the period from the balance-sheet date to the date the information is furnished;

3. Have management identify matters that have been referred to legal counsel;
4. Have management provide assurance that they have disclosed all such matters required to be disclosed by Statement of Financial Accounting Standards 5;
5. Examine all documents, particularly correspondence and invoices from lawyers, concerning litigation, claims, and assessments; and
6. Obtain client's permission to communicate with the client's lawyer.

Auditors usually do not have expertise in law to make judgments concerning litigation, claims, and assessments. Therefore the auditor generally requests the client's management to send a letter of inquiry to their lawyers. The auditor will also generally perform procedures such as reading minutes of meetings of directors, reading contracts and other legal documents, obtaining bank confirmations, and inspecting other documents for possible guarantees by the client.

INQUIRY OF A CLIENT'S LAWYER

The client's senior management is the primary source of evidence concerning litigation, claims, and assessments. The auditor uses a letter of audit inquiry to the client's lawyer to corroborate the information furnished by management. The inquiry may be directed to the client's in-house general counsel or legal department. However, if external legal counsel is involved, evidential matter obtained from in-house counsel is not a substitute for information from external counsel. It is not acceptable for the external counsel to refuse to furnish the information to the auditor.

AU 337.09 states that the matters that should be covered in a letter of audit inquiry include, but not be limited to, the following:

1. The date of the audit.
2. Identification of the company and subsidiaries, if any.
3. A list prepared by management or counsel that describes and evaluates pending or threatened litigation, claims, and assessments.
4. A list prepared by management describing and evaluating probable unasserted claims and assessments that, if asserted, would have at least a reasonable possibility of an unfavorable outcome, where a lawyer has devoted substantive attention on behalf of the entity either in the form of legal consultation or representation.
5. A statement by the client acknowledging matters involving unasserted possible claims or assessments where the lawyer has formed a professional conclusion requiring disclosure.
6. A request that the lawyer specifically identify the nature of and reasons for any limitation on the legal response.

The lawyer should have either represented the entity in a legal matter or been consulted by the entity, and the lawyer should have devoted substantive attention to the matter on behalf of the company. For each item on the list, the lawyer should either furnish the following information or explain why the lawyer's views differ from those of management:

1. A description of the matter, the progress to date, and the intended action of the entity.
2. An evaluation of the probability of an unfavorable outcome and, if possible, an estimate of the amount or range of potential loss.
3. A report listing omissions in the list provided by management concerning pending or threatened litigation, claims, and assessments. If management's list is complete, the lawyer should make a statement affirming that fact.

The lawyer should be requested to comment on any matters of consultation. In particular, the lawyer should describe or evaluate matters in which the lawyer's views differ from those of the management. The lawyer should advise the client and consult with the client concerning the disclosure requirements of Statement of Financial Accounting Standards 5.

The auditor does not need to inquire about matters that are not material. Of course, the auditor and the client should have an understanding of what constitutes materiality.

In some instances the auditor may request a conference with the client's counsel. The conference may offer an opportunity for a more detailed discussion than would be possible through a written inquiry. A conference may be especially useful when discussing matters concerning unsettled points of law, the effect of uncorroborated information, or other complex judgments. The auditor should document conclusions reached concerning the accounting requirements.

The lawyer may be required by a lawyer's Code of Professional Responsibility to resign if the client disregards the lawyer's advice concerning financial accounting and reporting for litigation, claims, and assessments. When the client changes lawyers or a lawyer resigns, the auditor should consider inquiring about the reasons of the change or resignation.

LIMITATIONS OF THE LAWYER'S RESPONSE

A lawyer may limit a response to

1. Matters to which the lawyer has given substantive attention in the form of legal consultation or representation; or
2. Matters that are individually or collectively material to the financial statements, as long as the lawyer and auditor have reached an understanding on materiality.

If a lawyer refuses to respond to the inquiry letter either in writing or orally, this would be a scope limitation sufficient to preclude an unqualified opinion. A lawyer may be unable to respond because of inherent uncertainties in evaluating litigation, claims, and assessments. The lawyer might not have competence to judge the likelihood of an unfavorable outcome. Moreover historical data concerning similar litigation may not be relevant or available. Similarly the potential amount of loss may vary widely at different stages of litigation. Thus it may not be possible for the lawyer to form a conclusion with respect to such matters.

Under such circumstances the auditor ordinarily will conclude that the financial statements are affected by uncertainty concerning the outcome of a future event that is not susceptible to reasonable estimation. AU 508, *Reports on Audited Financial Statements,* Paragraphs 45 to 49, provide additional guidance.

ILLUSTRATIVE AUDIT INQUIRY LETTER TO LEGAL COUNSEL

The following example of an audit inquiry letter is given in AU Section 337A:

In connection with an audit of our financial statements at [*balance sheet date*] and for the [*period*] then ended, management of the Company has prepared, and furnished to our auditors [*name and address of auditors*], a description and evaluation of certain contingencies, including those set forth below involving matters with respect to which you have been engaged and to which you have devoted substantive attention on behalf of the Company in the form of legal consultation or representation. These contingencies are regarded by management of the Company as material for this purpose [*management may indicate a materiality limit if an understanding has been reached with the auditor*]. Your response should include matters that existed at [*balance sheet date*] and during the period from that date to the date of your response.

Pending or Threatened Litigation [*excluding unasserted claims*]

[*Ordinarily the information would include (1) the nature of the litigation, (2) the progress of the case to date, (3) how management is responding or intends to respond to the litigation, e.g,, to contest the case vigorously or to seek an out-of-court settlement, and (4) an evaluation of the likelihood of an unfavorable outcome and an estimate, if one can be made, of the amount or range of potential loss.*]

Please furnish to our auditors such explanation, if any, that you consider necessary to supplement the foregoing information, including an explanation of those matters as to which your views may differ from those stated and an identification of the omission of any pending or threatened litigation, claims, and assessments or a statement that the list of such matters is complete.

Unasserted Claims and Assessments [considered by management to be probable of assertion, and that, if asserted, would have at least a reasonable possibility of an unfavorable outcome]

[*Ordinarily management's information would include: (1) the nature of the matter, (2) how management intends to respond if the claim is asserted, and (3) an evaluation of the likelihood of an unfavorable outcome and an estimate, if one can be made, of the amount or range of potential loss.*]

Please furnish to our auditors such explanation, if any, that you consider necessary to supplement the foregoing information, including an explanation of those matters as to which your views may differ from those stated.

We understand that whenever, in the course of performing legal services for us with respect to a matter recognized to involve an unasserted possible claim or assessment that may call for financial statement disclosure, if you have formed a professional conclusion that we should disclose or consider disclosure concerning such possible claim or assessment, as a matter of professional responsibility to us, you will so advise us and will consult with us concerning the question of such disclosure and the applicable requirements of Statement of Financial Accounting Standards 5. Please specifically confirm to our auditors that our understanding is correct.

Please specifically identify the nature of and reasons for any limitation on your response.

[The auditor may request the client to inquire about additional matters, e.g., unpaid or unbilled charges or specified information on certain contractually assumed obligations of the company, e.g., guarantees of indebtedness of others.]

339 AUDIT DOCUMENTATION

SOURCE OF STANDARDS

SAS 103, *Audit Documentation.*
SAS 113, *Omnibus Statement on Auditing Standards—2006*

See section 9339 for interpretations of this section.

SUMMARY

The type, content, form, and quantity of audit documentation are a matter of the auditor's judgment. Documentation should be prepared and maintained in a form that meets the needs of an engagement. Documenting audit procedures, evidence gathered, and conclusion reached is essential in every audit. The auditor should be aware that certain Statements on Auditing Standards (SAS) contain specific documentation requirements.

Audit documentation is the primary support for the auditor's report and is used as an aid in conducting and supervising the audit. Documentation provides primary support for

1. The representation that the auditor performed the audit in accordance with generally accepted auditing standards, and
2. The opinion expressed, or the assertion that an opinion cannot be expressed.

Documentation assists the audit team in planning and performing the audit. For instance, documentation assists auditor new to the audit engagement. Documentation also assists in supervising the work as well as quality control.

The nature, timing, extent, and results of auditing procedures performed and the evidence obtained should be documented. The process of preparing complete documentation enhances the quality of an audit. Documentation should show which team member(s) performed the work and which team member(s) reviewed the work. The documentation should also show that the accounting records agree with the financial statements or other information.

CONTENT OF AUDIT DOCUMENTATION

Audit documentation may be stored in electronic form, paper form, or other media and includes items such as

1. Abstracts or copies of entity documents;
2. Abstracts or copies of significant contracts or agreements;
3. Analyses;
4. Audit programs;
5. Commentaries prepared or obtained by the auditor;
6. Checklists;
7. Correspondence, including emails;
8. Letters of confirmation and representation;

9.   Issues memoranda;
10. Schedules of work the auditor performed; and
11. Summary of significant findings or issues.

When documentation is transferred from paper to another media, the auditor should ensure that the copy is faithful in form and content to the original paper document. The auditor should also be aware that there may be legal, regulatory, or other reasons to keep the original paper documents.

There is no need to retain in audit documentation

1.   Superseded drafts of working papers and financial statements; and
2.   Previous versions of documents corrected or updated due to typographical or other errors, or documents reflecting incomplete or preliminary thinking.

THE NATURE AND EXTENT OF DOCUMENTATION

The auditor should ask the following questions in determining the nature and extent of documentation:

1.   What is the risk of material misstatement associated with the assertion, account or class of transactions?
2.   What is the extent of judgment involved in performing the work and evaluating the results?
3.   What is the nature of the auditing procedure?
4.   What is the significance of the evidence relative to the assertion being tested?
5.   What are the nature and extent of exceptions identified?

The auditor should document all significant audit findings. The documentation should specify what actions were taken by the auditor, including what additional evidence was obtained by the auditor. The basis for reaching the final conclusion should also be documented. Significant audit findings or issues that should be documented include

1.   Matters regarding the appropriate selection, application, and consistency of accounting principles:

a.   How is the accounting for complex or unusual transactions determined?
b.   How are estimates and uncertainties accounted for?

2.   Audit procedure results indicating material misstatement in the financial statements or disclosures;
3.   Unusually large modification in the application of auditing procedures;
4.   Unusual difficulty in applying necessary auditing procedures;
5.   Findings suggesting a modification of the auditor's report; and
6.   Audit adjustments.

When documenting significant findings/issues, the auditor should note issues discussed, and when and with whom the discussion took place. The auditor should also document information that contradicts with or is inconsistent with the auditor's final conclusions regarding significant findings or issues. This does not mean that the auditor needs to retain documentation that is incorrect or superseded. However, the auditor should document how the contradictions or inconsistencies were addressed, what types of procedures were performed, and who was consulted. Differences in professional judgment among member of the audit team and/or others consulted should also be documented.

IDENTIFICATION OF PREPARER AND REVIEWER

When documenting the nature, timing, and extent of audit procedures, the auditor should include

1. Who performed and reviewed the work, and
2. The date the work was completed and reviewed.

It is not necessary for each piece of working paper to include evidence of review; it is sufficient that it be clear from the documentation who reviewed specified elements of the audit work and when the review was performed.

DOCUMENTATION OF SPECIFIC ITEMS TESTED

Procedures performed, including tests of controls and substantive, should be documented. Documentation should also include identifying characteristics of specific items tested.

DEPARTURES FROM SAS

The auditor must justify any departure from presumptively mandatory requirements of Generally Accepted Auditing Standards. Auditor should document the alternative procedures performed and how those procedures were sufficient to achieve the objectives of the presumptively mandatory requirement.

REVISIONS AFTER THE DATE OF AUDITOR'S REPORT

The auditor's report should not be dated earlier than the date on which sufficient appropriate audit evidence has been obtained. Frequently the report release date will be the date that the auditor delivers report to the entity.

NEW INFORMATION

Guidance in AU Section 390, *Consideration of Omitted Procedures After the Report Date,* should be followed if the auditor believes certain procedures were omitted. Furthermore the auditor should follow guidance given in AU Section 561, *Subsequent Discovery of Facts Existing at the Date of the Auditor's Report,* upon becoming aware of new information.

On becoming aware of new information or realizing certain procedures were omitted, the auditor should make appropriate changes. The auditor should document when and by whom changes were made and reviewed, the specific reasons for the changes, and the effects, if any, of the changes on auditor's conclusions.

The auditor has two options for dating the auditor's report when a disclosed event occurs subsequent to the original date of the auditor's report but before the issuance of financial statements:

1. Use dual dating.
2. Or date the report as of the later date.

With dual dating, the auditor's responsibility for events occurring after the original report date is limited to the specific event disclosed. In contrast, dating the report as of the later date extends auditor's responsibility for all subsequent events till the date of the report.

ASSEMBLING AND COMPLETING THE AUDIT FILE

Assembly of the final audit file should be done on a timely basis, but no later than 60 days after the report release date. Prior to the documentation completion date, the auditor may make changes such as complete the documentation and assembly of the audit evidence, delete or discard superseded documentation, sign off on the file completion checklists, and add information received after the date of the auditor's report. The release date of the report should be recorded in the audit documentation.

MODIFICATIONS AFTER THE DOCUMENTATION COMPLETION DATE

The auditor must not delete or discard documentation after the documentation completion date until the specified retention period has elapsed. If modifications are necessary, the amendments may be noted along with when and by whom the changes were made and reviewed, reasons for the changes, and the effects on the auditor's conclusions.

OWNERSHIP AND CONFIDENTIALITY OF AUDIT DOCUMENTATION

Audit documentation is owned by the auditor. This right is sometimes recognized by state statutes. Audit documentation should not be considered either a substitute for or a part of the client entity's accounting records. It is the auditor's responsibility to retain the documentation for a reasonable period of time, at least five years from the report release date, sufficient to meet legal and regulatory requirements. Auditor should be aware that statues, regulations, and other policies may mandate a longer retention period.

The auditor must maintain confidentiality of client information. The auditor also has an obligation to prevent unauthorized access, modification, or deletion to the documentation. Auditor should ensure that reasonable and appropriate controls exist for recording when and by whom documentation was created, changed, or reviewed. Auditors also have a responsibility to protect the integrity of information, especially when information is shared electronically.

AUDIT DOCUMENTATION REQUIREMENTS IN OTHER SAS

Specific documentation requirements are included in several other Statements on Auditing Standards (SAS). For instance, AU Section 310 requires the accountant to document the understanding with the client. Individual SAS statements should be consulted to understand each statements specific requirement. This section (AU Section 339) does not in any way modify or change the requirements in the individual SAS statements.

341 ABILITY OF THE ENTITY TO CONTINUE AS A GOING CONCERN

SOURCES OF STANDARDS

SAS 59, *The Auditor's Consideration of an Entity's Ability to Continue as a Going Concern*

SAS 64, *Omnibus Statement on Auditing Standards—1990*

SAS 77, *Amendments to Statements on Auditing Standards No. 22, Planning and Supervision; No. 59, The Auditor's Consideration of an Entity's Ability to Continue as a Going Concern; and No. 62, Special Reports*

SAS 96, *Audit Documentation*

SAS 113, *Omnibus Statement on Auditing Standards*

SAS 114, *The Audition's Communication with Those Changed with Governance*

Interpretation of AU Section 341, *Eliminating a Going-Concern Paragraph from a Reissued Report.*

SUMMARY

When an audit of an entity's financial statements is conducted in accordance with GAAS, there is a presumption that the entity is a going concern. Although no entity will last forever, in accordance with GAAP, it is assumed that the entity will endure long enough to pay its debts, fulfill its commitments, and meet its long-term goals. If current evidence suggests that this going-concern assumption is no longer viable and the entity must be liquidated, the firm must value its assets at net realizable value (what will be received in an outright sale) and its liabilities must be shown in the order of payment in accordance with law. Evidence that might indicate that an entity will not be able to continue as a going concern is its inability to satisfy its debts as they come due without, for example, having to sell operating assets, restructure its obligations, or revise its operations. AU Section 341 gives guidance on the responsibility of the independent auditor conducting an audit in accordance with GAAS when there appears to be substantial doubt about the ability of the entity to operate as a going concern.

GAAS GUIDANCE

THE RESPONSIBILITY OF THE AUDITOR TO ASCERTAIN WHETHER SUBSTANTIAL DOUBT EXISTS

GAAS requires that the auditor ascertain from the audit procedures performed on the financial statement whether there is substantial doubt about the entity's ability to continue as a going concern for a reasonable period (not to exceed one year) beyond the date of the audited financial statements. The auditor's evaluation should be based on gathered knowledge of any relevant conditions and events that exist at or have occurred prior to the date of the auditor's report. The following factors should be considered in making this evaluation:

1. Evidence gathered in planning and performing audit procedures indicates that there may be substantial doubt about the entity's ability to continue as a going concern for a reasonable amount of time. The auditor may decide that additional information must be gathered to support or negate this position.
2. An auditor who believes that there is substantial doubt should

    a. Ascertain what management is currently doing to improve this situation, and
    b. Evaluate whether management's plans are reasonably likely to be effective in mitigating the inability to maintain going-concern status.

3. If, after considering management's plans, the auditor still believes that there is substantial doubt about going-concern status, the auditor should

    a. Ensure the disclosures about this circumstance in the entity's financial statements are adequate, and
    b. Include an explanatory paragraph after the opinion paragraph about this belief.

4. If an auditor determines that substantial doubt does not exist, then he or she may want to consider whether any disclosure is needed at all. However, the absence of such a disclosure does not provide assurance of an entity's ability to continue as a growing concern.

At the same time the absence of such a disclosure when the entity has ceased to exist (within a reasonable period after the date of the financial statements) should not imply that the auditor performed inadequately.

EVIDENCE OF SUBSTANTIAL DOUBT REGARDING CONTINUING AS A GOING CONCERN

GAAP does not require the auditor to perform special procedures to identify evidence of doubt about an entity's ability to continue as a going concern. Procedures satisfying normal audit objectives should be adequate to detect evidence that might imply doubt about the entity's ability to continue as a going concern. However, the auditor should always be sensitive to evidence that implies a going-concern issue. AU Section 341 enumerates several procedures that might identify such issues:

- Review subsequent events.
- Obtain information, preferably through confirmation about the details of maintaining or obtaining financial support.
- Review compliance with the terms of debt and loan agreements.
- Review analytical procedures.
- Read the minutes of meetings of the following groups:

    - Board of directors,
    - Committees of the board of directors, and
    - Stockholders.

- Question the entity's legal counsel about litigation, claims, and assessments involving the company.

CONDITIONS THAT MAY INDICATE GOING-CONCERN PROBLEMS

The following areas of concern are derived from the procedures enumerated in the previous section, and other audit procedures may raise substantial doubt in the mind of an auditor about the entity's ability to continue as a going concern:

Negative Trends That Have Materialized

1. Recurring operating losses
2. Working capital deficiencies
3. Negative cash flows from operating activities
4. Adverse key financial ratios

Other Indications of Possible Financial Difficulties

1. Dividend arrearages on preferred stock
2. Restructuring of debt
3. Noncompliance with statutory capital requirements
4. Defaults on loans
5. Denial of credit from suppliers
6. Attempting to dispose of a substantial amount of assets to raise cash
7. Constantly seeking new sources or methods of financing

Internal Considerations

1. Managerial dependence on the success of a single project to raise cash
2. Need to revise operations to increase productivity and efficiency
3. Work stoppages or other labor difficulties
4. Long-term commitments that do not make economic sense

External Occurrences

1. Legal proceedings that involve the entity
2. New legislation or other regulatory considerations that might adversely affect the entity's ability to operate profitably
3. Loss of an important franchise, license, or patent
4. Loss of a principal supplier or customer
5. Underinsured or uninsured coverage for such events as a drought, earthquake, or flood

EVALUATING MANAGEMENT'S PLANS FOR DEALING WITH THE GOING-CONCERN ISSUE

After considering all the possible events described above, the auditor may decide that there is substantial doubt about the ability of the enterprise to continue as a going concern. At this point the auditor must review what management has done or plans to do to resolve this situation. The auditor must evaluate the likelihood that such plans will reduce for a reasonable period the existing doubt about the firm's ability to maintain its going-concern status. The auditor should raise the following questions about management's plans and actions:

Disposal of Assets

1. Has management stopped making asset disposal-type transactions, such as pledging assets in loan agreements or encumbrances against assets?
2. Is the marketability of assets that are scheduled for sale being reviewed?
3. Are the effects of such sales and disposals being studied?

Borrowing Money or Restructuring Debt

1. Is management thoroughly reviewing the availability of debt financing, such as lines of credit, factoring, or sale-leaseback of assets?
2. Are there plans or an intent to restructure debt to guarantee loans?

3. Has management explored the effect of their restrictions on additional borrowings and the availability of collateralized assets on their plans for borrowing?

Reducing or Delaying Expenditures

1. Has management studied the feasibility of initiating plans to

    a. Reduce overhead or administrative expenditures?
    b. Postpone maintenance or research and development projects?
    c. Lease rather than purchase assets?

2. Has management analyzed the effects of reducing or delaying these expenditure?

Increase Ownership Equity

1. Has management initiated plans to increase the entity's ownership equity?
2. Has management committed to reduce any current dividend requirement?
3. Has management accelerated cash distributions from affiliates or other investors? Have they succeeded with these collections?

ADDITIONAL CONSIDERATIONS

In evaluating management's plans, the auditor should concentrate on those elements that are most important in reducing any substantial doubt about the client's ability to continue as a going concern. The auditor should obtain as much evidence as possible to overcome this doubt. When prospective financial information is essential to management's plans and actions for dealing with the problem, the auditor might find it helpful to concentrate on the adequacy of those underlying assumptions that are

- Material to the prospective financial statements,
- Associated with a high degree of risk,
- Susceptible to change, and
- Inconsistent with the entity's prior experience and track record.

In addition the following audit procedures may be helpful:

1. Read the entity's prospective financial statement and related information.
2. Obtain information about the underlying assumptions for the prospective financial statements.
3. Compare prospective financial information presented in prior periods with actual results.
4. Compare prospective financial information for the current period to results achieved to date.

While gathering evidence of this type, the auditor may come upon factors whose effects were not included in the prospective financial statements. The auditor should apprise management of this situation and ask that management revise the prospective financial statements to reflect these changes.

FINANCIAL STATEMENT DISCLOSURES

Under GAAS when there is substantial doubt about the entity's ability to continue as a going concern, the auditor must disclose

- The causal factors that gave rise to the substantial doubt,
- The effects of these factors,
- Management's evaluation of the significance of these factors and any mitigating conditions and events that may exist,

- The potential that operations might be discontinued,
- Management's plans to deal with the doubts about the entity's ability to continue as a going concern, and
- Specific information about the recoverability of assets and classification of recorded assets or amounts or classification of liabilities.

EFFECTS ON THE AUDITOR'S REPORTS

After carefully considering all the conditions and events that may raise doubt about the entity's ability to continue as a going concern, including management's plans to deal with the issue, the auditor may decide that substantial doubt does exist. If so, the auditor's report must be modified. SAS 64 gives the following illustration of the explanatory paragraph (following the opinion paragraph) that should be included in the auditor's report describing uncertainty about the entity's ability to continue as a going concern. This paragraph should include the phrase "Substantial doubt about its (the entity's) ability to continue as a going concern" or similar wording that includes the terms substantial doubt and going concern.

> The accompanying financial statements have been prepared assuming the company will continue as a going concern. As indicated in Note [X] to the financial statements, the company has suffered recurring losses from operations and has a net capital deficiency that raises substantial doubt about its ability to continue as a going concern. Management's plans in regard to these matters are also described in Note [X]. The financial statements do not include any adjustments that might result from the outcome of this uncertainty.

An auditor may decide that the disclosures in the notes about the entity's ability to continue as a going concern are insufficient. As a departure from GAAP, this requires the auditor to issue an "except for" qualified opinion or an adverse opinion.

After considering all related conditions and events, the auditor may also decide that substantial doubt about the going-concern issue does not exist. In this situation the auditor's report does not have to be modified.

An auditor who is also reporting on comparative financial statements should realize that substantial going-concern doubt in the current period does not in any way imply that such doubt existed in any prior period. Therefore the auditor's report on the financial statements of those prior periods need not be modified. Finally, if comparative financial statements are presented in which there was substantial doubt expressed in a prior period that no longer exists in the current period, the explanatory paragraph describing the uncertainty relating to the prior period is not repeated on the current statements.

COMMUNICATION WITH THOSE CHARGED WITH GOVERNANCE

If, after aggregately considering all the conditions, events, and management's plans, the auditor decides that substantial doubt about the entity's ability to continue as a going concern for a reasonable period of time remains, the auditor should communicate the following to those charged with governance:

1. The nature of the events or conditions identified.
2. The possible effect on the entity's financial statements and adequacy of related disclosures in the financial statements.
3. The effects on the auditor's report.

DOCUMENTING SUBSTANTIAL DOUBT

If the auditor decides after considering all the events and conditions that have been identified that there could be substantial going-concern doubt, this should be fully documented in the working papers. AU Section 341 specifies that the following be documented:

- The conditions or events that caused the auditor to determine that there is a going-concern problem.
- The plans management has devised to overcome the adverse effects of the conditions or effects causing the going-concern problem.
- The audit procedures performed and the evidence collected in ascertaining details of management's plans to overcome the going-concern problem.
- The effects of the causal conditions or events and the adequacy of the entity's disclosure of these considerations if the auditor believes that the substantial going-concern doubt was not alleviated by management's plans to overcome it.
- Assuming the substantial doubt was alleviated, the conclusion about the need for disclosure of the conditions and events that caused the belief that there was a going-concern problem on the first place.
- The auditor's evaluation of the need to include an explanatory paragraph in the audit report. For example, if the auditor determines that the entity's disclosure about its ability to continue as a going concern is inadequate, the determination of whether to express either a qualified or adverse opinion based on this departure from GAAP should be documented.

INTERPRETATION OF AU SECTION 341

INTERPRETATION NO. 1, ELIMINATING A GOING-CONCERN EXPLANATORY PARAGRAPH FROM A REISSUED REPORT

An auditor may have issued an audit report on the financial statements of an entity that included a paragraph communicating substantial doubt considerations about the entity's ability to continue as a going concern for a reasonable period of time. If the conditions that gave rise to such doubt have been resolved (e.g., the entity received much-needed financing), should the auditor reissue the report without the going-concern explanatory paragraph that was in the original report?

Interpretation 1 states that an auditor has no obligation to reissue the report without the going-concern paragraph that appeared in the original report but may choose to do so. If that choice is made, the following procedures should be performed:

1. Audit the transaction or event that initiated the request to reissue the report without the going-concern explanatory paragraph.
2. Perform the audit procedures enumerated in Paragraph 12 of AU Section 560, *Subsequent Events,* at or near the date of reissuance. GAAS requires this so that the auditor can determine whether the occurrence of any subsequent events may require adjustments or disclosures for fair presentation in accordance with GAAP.
3. At the date of reissuance, review:

   a. The conditions and events that indicated a going-concern problem,
   b. Management's plans to deal with the problem, and
   c. The effects of the going-concern problem on the financial statements of the entity.

In addition to the aforementioned considerations, the auditor should also perform any and all procedures that the auditor considers important. Based on the aggregated information collected, the entity's going-concern status should be reassessed.

342 AUDITING ACCOUNTING ESTIMATES

SOURCES OF STANDARDS

GAAS

SAS 57, Auditing Accounting Estimates
SAS 113, Omnibus Statement on Auditing Standards—2006

SUMMARY

AU Section 342 provides guidance on obtaining and evaluating sufficient appropriate audit evidence supporting client accounting estimates in an audit of financial statements in accordance with GAAS. It describes an accounting estimate as "an approximation of a financial statement element, item, or account."

Accounting estimates are often included in historical financial statements for the following reasons, as given in AU Section 342:

- The measurement of some amounts or the valuation of some accounts is uncertain, pending the outcome of future events.
- Relevant data concerning events that already occurred cannot be accumulated on a timely, cost-effective basis.

Accounting estimates included in financial statements being audited are the responsibility of management. GAAS requires that the auditor evaluate management's estimates within the context of the financial statements as a whole. All estimates are sensitive to potential bias relating to subjective factors affecting the inherent estimating process.

GAAS GUIDANCE

WHAT ARE ACCOUNTING ESTIMATES?

AU Section 342 notes that in financial statements, accounting estimates measure the effects of past business transactions or events or the present status of an asset or liability. The following are some examples of areas of the financial statements which utilize accounting estimates:

- *Receivables.* Uncollectible receivables; allowance for loan pledges.
- *Inventories.* Obsolete inventory; net realizable value of inventories with respect to expected future selling prices and future costs.
- *Financial instruments.* Valuation of securities; trading versus investment security classifications.
- *Productive facilities, natural resources, and intangibles.* Useful lives and residual values; depreciation and amortization methods.
- *Accruals.* Property and casualty insurance company loss reserves; compensation plans and deferred plans.

- *Revenues.* Airline passenger revenue; subscription income.
- *Contracts.* Revenue to be earned; costs to be incurred.
- *Leases.* Initial direct costs; executory costs.
- *Litigation.* Probability of loss; amount of loss.
- *Rates.* Annual effective tax rate for interim reporting purposes; imputed interest rates on receivables and payables.
- *Miscellaneous areas.* Fair values in nonmonetary exchanges; interim period costs in interim reporting; current amounts in personal financial statements. (AU Section 342, Appendix)

RESPONSIBILITY FOR PREPARING AND EVALUATING ESTIMATES

Management has the responsibility for preparing accounting estimates for the financial statements. Estimates should be based on objective information. However, they should also take into account subjective factors. For example, management predicates its judgment of the future on the knowledge and objective experience it has of current and past events as well as its subjective expectations of likely future conditions.

The auditor has the responsibility of evaluating the reasonableness of the accounting estimates made by management in terms of the financial statement taken as a whole. This is difficult for two reasons: (1) The subjective nature of accounting estimates makes them difficult to control. (2) There is always a risk of bias entering into an accounting estimate even when entity personnel try their hardest to be objective. That is why professional skepticism is always appropriate when an auditor evaluates accounting estimates.

PREPARATION OF ACCOUNTING ESTIMATES

Preparing reasonable accounting estimates generally require that management follow the procedures enumerated below; the auditor should be familiar with them although management may apply them only informally:

1. Ascertain situations in which accounting estimates will be needed.
2. Determine the factors that influence the preparation of estimates.
3. Predicate estimates on relevant, reliable information.
4. Prepare assumptions that reflect management decisions about the likelihood of future events and situations.
5. Prepare estimated amounts based on the aforementioned procedures.
6. Ensure that the estimated amounts have been prepared in conformity with GAAP.

CONTROLLING MISSTATEMENTS IN ACCOUNTING ESTIMATES

Internal control procedures increase the likelihood that the accounting estimates used by the entity will not be misstated. AU Section 342 enumerates several important aspects of internal control procedures that contribute to this objective:

1. Management must emphasize the need for accurate accounting estimates.
2. All accounting estimates should be based on relevant, reliable, comprehensive information.
3. Only qualified entity personnel should prepare accounting estimates.
4. All accounting estimates should be reviewed and approved by the appropriate levels of management. The review should include the following areas:

    a. Sources of factors affecting the estimates.
    b. Assumptions underlying the estimates.
    c. Reasonableness of those assumptions.

      d.   Use of the work of specialists to generate the estimates.

      e.   Changes that must be made to previous methods to arrive at current estimates.

5.   To ensure the reliability of the estimating process, estimates from past years should be compared to present results.

6.   Management must ascertain that the estimates generated this period are consistent with the entity's plans and objectives.

In addition to these accounting estimate internal controls, the auditor should ensure that all accounting estimates are reasonable and are presented in conformity with GAAP (which includes appropriate disclosure), and that all estimates that could be material to the entity's financial statements have been identified and included.

INCLUSION OF ALL NECESSARY ACCOUNTING ESTIMATES IN THE FINANCIAL STATEMENTS

In determining whether the client has identified all the accounting estimates that should be included in the financial statements, the auditor must consider

- The industry or industries in which the entity operates,
- How the entity conducts its business,
- New accounting pronouncements that relate to the entity, and
- Other external factors.

The auditor should review all the assertions management has made in the financial statements to determine whether any additional estimates are needed.

AU Section 342 suggests that the auditor should also evaluate the following considerations that might suggest the need for accounting estimates; this information may surface as a result of the performance of other audit functions:

1.   Changes that were made or are being planned including changes in business tactics, in the business itself, or in the industry in which the business operates.

2.   Important information related to ongoing litigation, claims, and assessments (see AU Section 337, *Inquiry of a Client's Lawyer Concerning Litigation, Claims, and Assessments*) and other contingencies.

3.   Data derived from the minutes of meetings of the board of directors, stockholders, and important committees.

4.   Changes in the way information is accumulated.

5.   Data from reviewing important:

      a.   Supervisory reports and correspondence, and

      b.   Regulatory examination reports.

Auditors should also ask management about any other circumstances or situations that might signal the need for additional accounting estimates.

ARE THE ACCOUNTING ESTIMATES REASONABLE?

GAAS requires that the auditor evaluate for reasonableness accounting estimates that are material to the financial statements. An important part of this evaluation is comparing present estimates to past estimates and to industry experiences. It is equally important that the auditor focus on key factors and assumptions (relating to the estimates) that are

1.   Sensitive to variations,

2.   Deviations from historical patterns,

3.   Significant to the accounting estimates, and

4.   Subjective and sensitive to misstatement and bias.

The auditor may also choose to obtain written representations from management about these key factors and assumptions.

Ways to Evaluate the Reasonableness of Accounting Estimates

There are three approaches an auditor may use in evaluating the reasonableness of an accounting estimate. These may be used alone or in combination. A description of each one follows along with the related auditing procedures that should be used in executing the approach:

Analyze the Process Management Used to Develop the Estimate

1. Ascertain what controls, if any, there are over the client's accounting estimates and whether these controls are being complied with.
2. Determine what considerations, information, and factors management used to formulate the assumptions underlying the accounting estimates.
3. Determine that the data gathered in support of the assumptions underlying the accounting estimates are relevant, reliable, and complete.
4. Determine that the assumptions underlying the accounting estimates are consistent with
   a. Each other,
   b. Supporting data,
   c. Relevant historical data, and
   d. Industry data.
5. Find out whether changes in the business, the industry, or both affected the assumptions underlying the estimates and what their influence was.
6. Find out how the firm's objectives, goals, and plans may have influenced the assumptions underlying the accounting estimates; review the supporting documentation for accuracy. Does the documentation support the assumptions?
7. Determine whether the historical data used in formulating the assumptions underlying the estimates are reliable and consistent with data from the period under audit.
8. Ascertain whether it may be necessary to use specialists to analyze some of the assumptions.
9. Test the assumptions, factors, and data through test computations to determine whether the accounting estimates were properly prepared.

Establish Expectations

To ensure reasonableness, the auditor should independently establish an expectation of what each estimate should be based on a professional understanding of the entity's industry, business, client circumstances, and other relevant factors. The auditor should then compare the expected estimate with the client's estimates to make sure the latter are reasonable. For example, assume that a client book publisher estimates the amount of returns for its publications each period. The auditor can test these estimates by looking at industry data for book returns of the same type of subject. If the results are similar, the auditor will have more confidence that the client's estimates are reasonable.

Review Subsequent Transactions and Events

Another way to ascertain whether the client's estimates are reasonable is to test transactions and events that occur after the balance-sheet date but before the date of the auditor's report to see if they support the estimates. For example, assume management believes a customer whose payment is 90 days overdue will ultimately fully pay and not default (the account is considered material). This positive belief is based on the customer's past payment history and special current circumstance for not being able to make payments. The client has accordingly adjusted its allowance for doubtful accounts to a lesser amount than it would have been if the account was considered nearly fully uncollectible as part of its estimate of the net realizable value of its accounts receivable. After year-end the customer, as the client expected, pays the account in full. In this situation the review of subsequent transactions clearly showed that the client's estimate was correct. Through this sort of transactional (hindsight) analysis, the auditor was able to test the entity's estimates for reasonableness.

Reasonableness of Estimates in Terms of the Financial Statements Taken as a Whole

An auditor must evaluate whether estimates are reasonable with respect to the financial statement taken as a whole. The guidelines for the evaluation are given in AU Section 312, *Audit Risk and Materiality in Conducting an Audit* (Paragraph .56), as follows:

- Accounting estimates are not considered accurate with certainty. Therefore, if an auditor finds the difference between the amount estimated by the entity in the financial statements and that supported by audit evidence is not significant, the client's estimate should not be viewed as a likely misstatement.
- If, on the other hand, the auditor deems that the amount estimated in the financial statements by the entity is unreasonable, the difference should be treated as a likely misstatement.

INTERPRETATIONS OF AU SECTION 342, AUDITING ACCOUNTING ESTIMATES

INTERPRETATION 1, PERFORMANCE AND REPORTING GUIDANCE RELATED TO FAIR VALUE DISCLOSURES

This interpretation relates to the auditor's responsibilities when entities are disclosing required or both required and voluntary fair value financial information. FASB Statement 107, Disclosures about Fair Value of Financial Instruments, requires all entities to disclose the fair value of financial instruments that can be estimated. Some entities disclose only the information required by FASB Statement 107; others voluntarily disclose the fair value of other areas (e.g., assets and liabilities) that go beyond the No. 107 requirements. What are the responsibilities of the auditor in this situation?

The interpretation notes that in auditing both required and voluntary fair value information, the auditor should obtain enough competent evidence to derive assurance about

1. The acceptability and consistency of the valuation principles being used and whether they are supported by appropriate documentation, and
2. Proper disclosure of the methods of estimation and the assumptions relating to the fair value information.

These assurances must be satisfied. If they cannot be, the auditor must decide whether there is a material departure from GAAP.

Parameters to Be Followed by the Auditor When Only the Required Information of FASB Statement 107 Is Disclosed in the Financial Statements

The auditor should adhere to the following guidance only if he or she is sure that the client's fair value disclosures:

- Consist only of those required by Statement 107.

- Were determined in accordance with Statement 107.
- Were obtained by methods that were consistently applied.
- Are supported by appropriate documentation.
- Include disclosure of the methods of estimation and significant assumptions underlying the estimates.

If the foregoing criteria were followed:

1. The auditor may issue a standard unqualified opinion when the entity discloses in its basic financial statements the information required by Statement 107 (assuming no other modifications are necessary).
2. When management uses its best estimate of fair value when quoted market values are lacking and the range of possible fair values used is material, the auditor should add an emphasis-of-matter paragraph describing the nature and possible range of such information.
3. If the required fair value disclosures were not presented in the entity's financial statements, the auditor must determine whether these statements materially depart from GAAP.

Parameters to Be Followed by the Auditor When Voluntary Information Is Presented in Addition to Required Information in Accordance with FASB Statement 107

The auditor may audit the voluntary fair value information presented in financial statements only if the following two requirements are satisfied:

1. The measurement and disclosure criteria used to prepare the fair value information disclosed in the financial statements are deemed reasonable.
2. The voluntary information is reliable; competent persons, such as auditors, using the same measurement and disclosure criteria would obtain materially similar results.

If the voluntary information does not satisfy these requirements, the auditor may not accept an engagement to audit this information. When voluntary fair value disclosures are used they supplement the required disclosures. The information generated may constitute either a complete balance sheet (the fair value of all material items in the balance sheet is presented) or a less than complete balance sheet:

Complete presentation. If the audited disclosures constitute a complete balance sheet presentation, the auditor should express an opinion on the fair value presentation and include a paragraph that

- Indicates that the fair value financial statements are the responsibility of management and were audited,
- Describes what the fair value information intends to convey and designates the note containing the basis of the presentation,
- Indicates that the fair value presentation need not be in conformity with GAAP, and
- Incorporates the auditor's opinion on fair value presentation.

An illustration of such a paragraph is shown below:

> We have also audited in accordance with auditing standards generally accepted in the United States of America the supplemental fair value balance sheet of ABC Company as of December 31, 20XX. As described in Note X, the supplemental fair value balance sheet has been prepared by management to present relevant financial information that is not provided by the historical-cost balance sheets and is not intended to be a presentation in conformity with generally accepted accounting principles. In addition, the supplemental fair value balance sheet does not purport to present the net realizable, liquidation, or market value of ABC Company as a whole. Furthermore, amounts ultimately realized by ABC Company from the disposal of assets may vary significantly

from the fair values presented. In our opinion, the supplemental fair value balance sheet referred to above presents fairly, in all material respects, the information set forth therein as described in Note X. (AU Section 9342.06)

Less than complete presentation. If the audited fair value disclosures do not constitute a complete balance sheet presentation but are on the face of the financial statements or in the notes to the financial statement, the auditor may issue a standard unqualified opinion without referring to the disclosures in the report. If, on the other hand, the audited disclosures are in a supplemental schedule or exhibit, GAAS requires that a paragraph be added to the report. The following is an example of the wording of such a paragraph:

> Our audit was conducted for the purpose of forming an opinion on the basic financial statement taken as a whole. Supplemental schedule X (or Exhibit X) containing audited fair value disclosures is presented for purposes of additional analysis is not a required part of the basic financial statements. Such information has been subjected to auditing procedures applied in the audit of the basic financial statements and, in our opinion, is fairly stated in all material respects in relation to the basic financial statements taken as a whole. (AU Section 551.12)

Unaudited Fair Value Voluntary Disclosures

In some situations the auditor may be faced with unaudited fair value voluntary disclosures that are either included in auditor-submitted documents or in client-prepared documents. The information may be unaudited because the auditor

1. Was not engaged to audit the voluntary information, and
2. Was unable to audit the fair value information because the information did not satisfy the measurement and disclosure requirement that they be reasonable and reliable (see above).

Unaudited voluntary disclosures in an auditor-submitted document. When unaudited voluntary fair value disclosures in an auditor-submitted document are located on the face of the financial statements, in the notes, or on a supplemental schedule to the basic financial statements, they should be labeled "unaudited" and the auditor should disclaim an opinion on them. The wording of such a disclaimer may be found in AU Section 551.13.

Unaudited voluntary disclosures in a client-prepared document. When unaudited voluntary fair value disclosures in a client-prepared document are located on the face of the financial statements, in the notes, or in a supplemental disclosure, they should be labeled "unaudited." When they are not presented in any of these locations, the auditor should follow the guidance in AU Section 550, Other Information in Documents Containing Audited Financial Statements.

350 AUDIT SAMPLING

SOURCE OF STANDARDS

SAS 39, *Audit Sampling*
SAS 43, *Omnibus Statement on Auditing Standards*
SAS 45, *Omnibus Statement on Auditing Standard—1983*
SAS 111, *Amendment to Statement on Auditing Standards No. 39, "Audit Sampling"*

See section 9350 for interpretations of this section.

INTRODUCTION/SUMMARY

AU 350.01 defines *audit sampling* as

> The application of an audit procedure to less than 100 percent of the items within an account balance or class of transactions for the purpose of evaluating some characteristic of the balance or class.

Auditors may use either statistical or nonstatistical sampling. Statistical sampling allows the auditor to

1. Design an efficient sample,
2. Measure the sufficiency of the evidential matter and quantify sampling risk, and
3. Statistically evaluate the sample results.

The primary disadvantage of statistical sampling is the additional costs incurred in

1. Training auditors,
2. Designing samples to meet the statistical requirements, and
3. Selecting items to be examined.

Professional judgment is required in both statistical and nonstatistical approaches when planning, performing, and evaluating samples. The third standard of fieldwork requires that

> Sufficient competent evidential matter is to be obtained through inspection, observation, inquiries, and confirmations to afford a reasonable basis for an opinion regarding the financial statements under audit.

Both statistical and nonstatistical approaches to audit sampling can provide sufficient evidential matter. The auditor's selection between the two depends on their relative cost and effectiveness.

The concept of sufficiency is related primarily to the design and size of the audit samples. The competence of evidential matter is a matter of auditing judgment. Competence is not affected by the design and evaluation of the audit sample.

UNCERTAINTY AND AUDIT SAMPLING

Audit risk is the uncertainty inherent in applying audit procedures. Audit risk includes both sampling risk and nonsampling risk. Sampling risk arises when the result of tests lead the auditor to reach a conclusion different from the conclusions that would have been reached if all the items had been considered. Sampling risk is inversely related to sample size. As the sample size increases, the sampling risk decreases.

All aspects of audit risk other than sampling risk are encompassed in nonsampling risk. Even if a procedure is applied to all transactions or balances, the auditor may fail to detect a material misstatement due to nonsampling risk. Nonsampling risk arises due to

1. The possibility of selecting an inappropriate audit procedure, and/or
2. The auditor failing to recognize misstatements in the documents being examined.

Nonsampling risk can generally be reduced through adequate planning and supervision and proper conduct of a firm's audit practice.

SAMPLING RISK

When performing substantive testing, the auditor is concerned with two aspects of sampling risk:

1. *Risk of incorrect acceptance.* The risk that the auditor is willing to take of accepting a balance as correct when it is materially misstated.
2. *Risk of incorrect rejection.* The risk that the auditor is willing to reject a balance as materially misstated correct when it is correct.

When performing test of controls, the auditor is also concerned with two aspects of sampling risk:

1. *Risk of assessing control risk too low.* The risk that the auditor will accept a control as effective when the control risk based on the sample is less than the true operating effectiveness of the control.
2. *Risk of assessing control risk too high.* The risk that the auditor will reject a control as being ineffective when the control risk based on the sample is greater than the true operating effectiveness of the control.

The risk of incorrect rejection and the risk of assessing control risk too high affect the efficiency of the audit. The risk of incorrect acceptance and the risk of assessing control risk too low affect the effectiveness of the audit.

SAMPLING IN TESTS OF DETAILS

Planning Samples

When planning for test of details, the auditor should consider the following factors:

1. The relationship of the sample to the relevant audit objective.
2. Preliminary judgments about materiality levels.
3. The allowable risk of incorrect acceptance.
4. Characteristics of the population.

When planning for test of details, the auditor should consider tolerable misstatement. Tolerable misstatement is the amount of monetary misstatement that may exist without causing the financial statements to be materially misstated.

It is generally possible to reduce sample size by stratification. The actual number of items in a sample depends on

1. The tolerable misstatement,
2. The acceptable risk of incorrect acceptance, and
3. The characteristics of the population.

Sample Selection

The aim of sample selection is to obtain a sample in such a way that the sample is representative of the population. Sample selection should allow all items in the population to have a chance of being selected. Generally, some type of random selection system is used to obtain samples.

Performance and Evaluation

Appropriate audit procedures are applied to each item in the sample. Sometimes, the entity may be unable to locate supporting documentation. The auditor should consider the reasons for missing items and the implication it has in relation to assessing risks of material misstatement due to fraud, as well as the assessed level of control risk that is expected to be supported or the degree of auditor's reliance on management representations.

The auditor uses the results of the sample to project the total misstatement. The projected misstatement should take into account an allowance for sampling risk. The auditor should consider the qualitative aspects of the misstatements including

1. The nature and cause of misstatements, and
2. The possible relationship of the misstatements to other phases of the audit.

The auditor should also consider known misstatements from nonsampling applications.

SAMPLING IN TESTS OF CONTROLS

Planning Samples

The auditor should consider the following factors when planning an audit sample for test of controls:

1. The relationship of the sample to the objective of the test of controls.
2. The maximum rate of deviations from prescribed controls that would support the auditor's assessed level of control risk.
3. The auditor's allowable risk of assessing control risk too low.
4. Characteristics of the population, that is, the items comprising the account balance or class of transactions of interest.

The auditor obtains samples for tests of controls to evaluate the operating effectiveness of controls. Tolerable deviation rate is the maximum rate of deviations from the prescribed control that the auditor is willing to accept without altering the assessed level of control risk. While deviations from controls increase the risk of material misstatements, the deviations do not necessarily result in misstatements. Deviations would cause misstatements only if the deviations and the misstatements occurred on the same transactions.

The sample size for testing controls is determined by

1. The tolerable deviation rate,
2. The likely rate of deviations, and
3. The acceptable risk of assessing control risk too low

Sample Selection

The sample selected should be representative of the population. Sample selection should allow all items in the population to have a chance of being selected. Generally, some type of random selection system is used to obtain samples.

Performance and Evaluation

Appropriate auditing procedures should be applied to each sample item. If the estimated sample deviation rate is less than the tolerable deviation rate for the population, the auditor should consider the risk that such a result might be due to an unrepresentative sample. The auditor's professional judgment must be used in making the final evaluation.

The auditor should consider the qualitative aspects of the deviations, including

1. The nature and cause of the deviations, and
2. The possible relationship of the deviations to other phases of the audit.

380 THE AUDITOR'S COMMUNICATION WITH THOSE CHARGED WITH GOVERNANCE

SOURCES OF STANDARDS

GAAS

SAS 114, *The Auditor's Communication with Those Charged with Governance*
Practitioner Checklist: Requirements to Communicate with Those Charged with Governance in Other Statements on Auditing Standards besides Section 380 (from Appendix A of SAS 114)

SUMMARY

Section 380 discusses the GAAS guidance relating to the auditor's communication with those charged with governance with respect to an audit of an entity's financial statements. This guidance applies to audits of financial statements prepared either in accordance with GAAP or with a comprehensive basis of accounting other than GAAP. However, it does not establish standards regarding the auditor's communication with an entity's management or owner(s) unless they are charged with governance responsibilities.

Section 380 defines *those charged with governance* as the individual(s) with the responsibility for the entity's strategic direction and accountability. This includes supervising the entity's financial accounting process. In some cases those charged with governance have the final responsibility for approving the financial statements, in others, this rests with *management*. In general, *those charged with governance* include the *board of directors or audit committee* if the entity has such groups.

Management refers to the person(s) responsible for achieving the objectives of the entity set by *those charged with governance* and is empowered to establish policies and decisions needed to accomplish these objectives. In addition, management has the responsibility for the financial statements as well as designing, implementing, and maintaining effective control over financial reporting.

The auditor's communication with those charged with governance is important because it ensures there will be an effective and efficient two-way transfer of information between these two bodies. The guidance in this section provides the framework for such communication as well as enumerating the specifics that need to be communicated. Other requirements to be communicated with those charged with governance are noted in other Statements on Auditing Standards and are enumerated in a checklist at the end of this section.

In general, the auditor should communicate to those charged with governance all significant and relevant issues that he or she believes are relevant to overseeing the financial reporting process. The clear communication of the matters to be enumerated and discussed in this section is an integral part of every audit and is a required audit activity under GAAS.

GAAS GUIDANCE

INTRODUCTORY COMMUNICATION CONSIDERATIONS

Communication and effective interchange between those charged with governance and the auditor is very important. The auditor and those responsible for governance are responsible for establishing clear two-way communications regarding the following matters:

- Those charged with governance must understand the responsibilities of the auditor with respect to the audit of the financial statements.
- Those charged with governance are responsible for turning over to the auditor all information relevant to the audit.
- Timely observations from the audit relating to the financial accounting reporting process must be provided to those charged with governance.
- Although the auditor must maintain independence and objectivity, it is imperative that those charged with governance and the auditor maintain a constructive, effective working relationship so that all audit-related matters issues may be resolved.
- Those charged with governance are responsible for assisting the auditor in gaining an understanding of the entity and its environment, identifying important sources of audit evidence, and providing information about important transactions and events relating to the audit. All relevant information relating to these areas must be fully conveyed to the auditor by those charged with governance.
- It is the responsibility of those charged with governance as part of their financial overseeing responsibility to minimize the risks of material misstatement of the entity's financial statements.

It is important to note that management is also responsible for communicating governance issues to those charged with governance. Management is not relieved of this responsibility because of the auditor's communications.

LEGAL RESPONSIBILITIES

An auditor may be required to report certain matters to regulatory or enforcement governmental bodies that was communicated to those responsible for governance. For example, in certain situations, government auditing standards require that illegal acts, fraud, violations of parts of contracts or grants, and abuse must be reported by auditors to parties outside the audited entity. In some rare situations, an auditor is precluded from communicating information even to those charged with governance or others within the entity, for fear that such communication may prejudice a future investigation of an actual or suspected illegal act. The auditor, under these circumstances, may want to obtain additional legal advice relating to this matter.

WHO ARE THOSE CHARGED WITH GOVERNANCE?

The auditor must ascertain who the individuals within the entity charged with governance are so that a communication connection may be established. The composition of the governing unit varies with the entity. Usually it consists of individuals who are a part of the board of directors. However, it may also consist of persons who are outside and not part of the entity, such as exists with some governmental agencies. In other cases, the governing unit may consist of individuals who are part of management. In others, governance and managerial individuals would never be the same.

In general, the governing unit is composed of a collective body consisting of one or more of the following forms:

- Board of directors
- Supervisory board
- Partners
- Proprietors
- Management committee
- Trustees
- Owner/manager (one person)
- Audit committee (subgroup of the board of directors)

Because of the entity's structure, it may not be possible to identify the individuals with whom the auditor is to communicate regarding governance matters. This may be due to the governance structure of the entity not being formally defined, as in the case of family-owned entities, some not-for-profit organizations, and some governmental entities. The auditor may find it helpful, in such situations, to refer to section 314, *Understanding the Entity and Its Environment and Assessing the Risks of Material Misstatement,* to determine whom to communicate with regarding governance considerations. When the auditor cannot identify the persons with whom to communicate regarding governance considerations, the auditor and the client should agree on the specific individual(s) within the entity who can be relied on for this information.

Communicating with the Entity's Audit Committee or Comparable Subgroup Charged with Governance

An audit committee or comparable subgroup charged with governance (with a different name) exists in many entities today. In seeking to fulfill the responsibility to communicate with those charged with governance, a primary activity for the auditor is to communicate with the entity's audit committee, where one exists. Positive governance protocol requires the auditor to

1. Have access to the entity's audit committee whenever needed,
2. Meet with members of the audit committee periodically, and
3. Meet with the audit committee without management at least once a year.

The auditor must decide whether communication with the audit committee, related subgroup, or individual satisfactorily fulfills the auditor's responsibility to communicate with those responsible for governance. In making this determination, the auditor should consider the following:

1. The responsibilities of the audit committee or subgroup and overall governing body.
2. The information to be communicated.
3. Whether the audit committee or subgroup has the ability to take action based on the information conveyed to them and provide the auditor with additional explanations as needed.
4. Whether there are any conflicts of interest that may exist between the audit committee and other members of the governing committee.
5. Whether the auditor should communicate the information that the auditor has discovered directly to the governing body. The auditor always retains the right to directly communicate information or findings to the governing body and may indicate so in the engagement letter. The decision to directly communicate with the govern-

ing body is a function of the auditor's determination that data he or she has communicated to the audit committee or subgroup was effectively communicated to the governing unit of the entity.

COMMUNICATIONS WITH MANAGEMENT

Management has executive responsibility for the conduct of the entity's operations and for its financial statements. To that end many matters must be discussed with management during the course of an audit including information which will be communicated to those who have governance responsibilities. As a matter of course the auditor may always want to first discuss with management or the entity's audit committee matters that should be communicated to those charged with governance. These preliminary discussions will give the auditor a chance to obtain clarity relating to important facts and issues and enable management and/or the internal audit staff to provide expanded details and explanations regarding these issues before conveying this information to those charged with governance. The auditor should always use discretion in discussing matters with management. For example, it would be inappropriate for the auditor to discuss matters relating to management's competency and integrity with management.

Communications When Those Charged with Governance Are All Involved in the Management of the Entity

If those charged with governance are all involved in the management of the company, then the communications to management as discussed in the prior section is required only once. They need not be communicated to those same persons again in their governance role. However, care must be taken that the communication to the person(s) who has (have) responsibility for financial reporting fully informs all those charged with governance.

WHAT SHOULD BE COMMUNICATED BY THE AUDITOR TO THOSE CHARGED WITH GOVERNANCE RESPONSIBILITIES?

The following matters should be communicated by the auditor to those charged with governance:

1. The responsibilities of the auditor under GAAS.
2. An overview of the planned scope and timing of the audit.
3. Findings from the audit that are significant.

Management's communication of these matters to those charged with governance may influence the form and timing of the auditor's communication. However, it does not relieve the auditor's responsibility to also communicate them. In addition this guidance does not in any way prevent the auditor from communicating any other matters to those charged with governance.

The aforementioned three considerations will now be fully discussed.

The Responsibilities of the Auditor under GAAS

Under GAAS the following auditor responsibility considerations should be communicated to those charged with governance:

1. The responsibility of the auditor for forming and expressing an opinion regarding whether the financial statements that have been prepared by management with the oversight of those charged with governance are presented fairly, in all material respects, in conformity with GAAP.

2. Management or those charged with governance are not relieved of their responsibilities as a result of the audit of the financial statements performed by the auditor.

These considerations may be communicated through the engagement letter or comparable form of contract as long as they are conveyed to those charged with governance.

The following should also be communicated by the auditor:

- The auditor is responsible for performing the audit in accordance with GAAS.
- The audit is designed to obtain reasonable, rather than absolute, assurance about whether the financial statements are free from material misstatement.
- An audit of the financial statements includes consideration of internal control over financial reporting as a basis for designing audit procedures that are deemed appropriate. However, this consideration is not for the purpose of expressing an opinion on the effectiveness of the entity's internal control over its financial reporting system.
- The auditor is responsible for communicating significant financial accounting audit matters that are relevant to the responsibilities of those charged with governance in overseeing the financial reporting process. However, GAAS does not require the auditor to design procedures that identify other matters to communicate with those charged with governance.
- In certain circumstances, the auditor is also responsible for communicating matters required by laws or regulations, by agreement with the entity or by requirements applicable to the engagement.

If an entity includes other information in documents containing audited financial statements, the auditor must communicate this responsibility to those charged with governance regarding such information as well as any audit procedures performed and results relating to the other information. Additional information relating to the auditor's responsibility for information prepared by management accompanying audited financial statements may be found in Section 550, *Other Information in Documents Containing Audited Financial Information;* Section 558, *Required Supplementary Information;* and Section 551, *Reporting on Information Accompanying the Basic Financial Statements in Auditor-Submitted Documents.*

Planned Scope and Timing of the Audit.

An overview of the planned scope and timing of the audit should be communicated to those charged with governance. However, the auditor must be careful not to compromise the effectiveness of certain detailed audit procedures by communicating their nature and timing to those charged with governance who, for example, are also involved in the management of the entity. Doing this will make the audit procedures too predictable.

Communication regarding the planned scope and timing of the audit provides the following benefits:

1. It enables those charged with governance to better understand the importance and relevance of the auditor's work to the former's financial oversight responsibilities including: (a) discussing issues of risk and materiality, and (b) identifying any areas where they may want the auditor to perform additional procedures.
2. It improves the auditor's understanding of the entity and its environment.

Matters that are communicated to those charged with governance by the auditor should include the following:

1. How significant risks of material misstatement, whether due to fraud or error, will be addressed by the auditor.
2. The auditor's approach to internal control deemed relevant to the audit (e.g., whether the auditor will express an opinion on the effectiveness of internal control over financial reporting).
3. Materiality considerations in planning and executing the audit, including focusing on factors considered instead of specific thresholds or amounts.
4. If an internal audit function exists in the entity, determination of the extent to which the auditor will use the work of the internal auditor as well as ascertaining how the external and internal auditor can work together most effectively.

Other planning matters that the auditor and those charged with governance should discuss include the following:

1. The views and opinions of those charged with governance regarding

    a. The individual(s) in the governance structure of the entity that the auditor should communicate with,
    b. Allocation of responsibilities between those charged with governance and management,
    c. The objectives and strategies of the entity including related business risks that may result in material misstatements,
    d. Areas of the audit that warrant particular attention as well as those they believe merit additional audit procedures to be performed,
    e. Communications with regulators regarding significant matters, and
    f. Any other matters that those charged with governance believe significantly relate to the audit of the financial statements.

2. The attitudes, beliefs, and actions of those charged with governance relating to

    a. The importance of the entity's internal control including how those charged with governance oversee its effectiveness, and
    b. The detection or the possibility of fraud.

3. The actions and responses of those charged with governance with respect to developments and changes in financial reporting, laws, accounting standards, corporate governance practices and related matters.
4. The actions and responses of those charged with governance in response to previous communications with the auditor.

It is important to note that the auditor has sole, unequivocal responsibility to determine the overall audit strategy and audit plan of the engagement, including the nature, timing, and extent of procedures necessary to obtain sufficient audit evidence. Although the communication with those charged with governance clearly assists the auditor in planning the scope and timing the audit, it does not in any way change or mitigate the auditor's responsibility.

Significant Findings from the Audit to Be Communicated to Those Charged with Governance

The following items from the audit should be communicated to those charged with governance:

1. The auditor's views about the qualitative considerations relating to the entity's significant accounting practices. These include

    a.   Accounting policies (appropriateness to circumstances of entity, initial selection of, changes in, effect of policies in controversial or emergency areas, etc.),

    b.   Accounting estimates (management's identification of estimates and the process for generating them, risk of material misstatements, possible management bias, disclosure of estimation uncertainty, etc.), and

    c.   Financial statement disclosures (issues and judgments in formulating sensitive financial statement disclosures, neutrality, consistency and clarity of disclosures, etc.).

2.   Any significant difficulties occuring during the audit.

3.   Any uncorrected misstatements other than those deemed trivial.

4.   Any disagreements that surfaced with management.

5.   Findings or issues that arose during the audit that the auditor believes would be relevant to those charged with governance in their oversight capacity of the financial reporting process.

The auditor should also communicate the following matters to those charged with governance unless the latter are all involved in managing the entity:

- Corrected, material misstatements that were brought to the attention of management as a result of the performance of audit procedures. Frequently recurring immaterial misstatements that have been corrected may indicate a bias in the preparation of the entity's financial statements and should also be communicated.

- Representations requested by the auditor from management: a copy of the representations letter given by management to the auditor should be provided to those charged with governance.

- Management's consultations with other accountants.

- Any significant issues from the audit that were discussed with management.

As part of the communication of significant findings, the auditor may request additional information from those charged with governance as part of the process of obtaining supportive audit evidence. For example, the auditor may request a confirmation from those charged with governance that their understanding of facts relating to certain transactions and events are all consistent.

Qualitative considerations relating to the entity's significant accounting practices. GAAP allows the entity to make judgments about its accounting policies and financial statement disclosures. GAAS requires that there be an open and constructive communication with those charged with governance about the entity's significant accounting practices, including comments from the auditor regarding their acceptability. The auditor, in this communication, for example, might indicate to those charged with governance why the auditor believes a significant accounting practice is not appropriate and, if necessary, request that a change be made. If the change is not made by the client, then the auditor must consider its effect on the financial statements of current and future years as well as on the auditor's report.

Difficulties Encountered during the Audit

Those charged with governance should be informed by the auditor of any significant difficulties encountered in working with management during the performance of the audit. Examples of significant difficulties include the following:

1.   Material delays in providing the auditor with required information.

2.   Being provided with an unusually brief time within which to complete the audit.

3.   Burdensome efforts required to obtain sufficient appropriate audit evidence.

4.   Expected information not made readily available to the auditor.

5. Managerial restrictions imposed on the auditor.
6. Unwillingness on the part of management to provide information to the auditor about plans for dealing with the adverse effects of conditions that caused the auditor to believe there is substantial doubt about the entity's ability to continue as a going concern.

The aforementioned may result in a scope limitation causing the auditor to modify his or her audit opinion.

MISSTATEMENTS THAT WERE NOT CORRECTED

Under Section 312, *Audit Risk and Materiality in Conducting an Audit,* the auditor is required to amass all nontrivial known and likely misstatements identified during the audit and communicate them to the appropriate level of management. In addition, the auditor should communicate with those charged with governance any uncorrected misstatements and their effects on the opinion in the auditor's report. The auditor should request their correction. In reporting the uncorrected misstatements to those charged with governance, the misstatements need to be reported individually. However, if there are a large number of small uncorrected misstatements, the auditor may communicate their number and overall monetary effect, rather than the details of each misstatement. If known and likely misstatements have not been corrected, the auditor should discuss the implications of such a failure with those charged with governance and indicate to them the effect on prior periods with respect to relevant classes of transactions, account balances or disclosures, and the financial statements as a whole. The implications in relation to future financial statements should be discussed as well.

DISAGREEMENTS WITH MANAGEMENT

Disagreements with management may occasionally arise during the course of an audit. Disagreements may occur, for example, over: the application of accounting principles to the entity's transactions and events; management's decisions relating to accounting estimates; the scope of the audit; disclosures to be included in the entity's financial statements; the wording of the auditor's report, etc. Any disagreements with management must be discussed with those charged with governance. The discussion should focus on whether the disagreement(s) was (were) satisfactorily resolved and about matters that individually or in the aggregate could significantly affect the entity's financial statement or auditor's report.

MANAGEMENT'S CONSULTATION WITH OTHER ACCOUNTANTS

On occasion, management may decide to consult with other accountants about accounting and auditing matters. When the auditor is aware of such consultations, he or she should discuss his or her views regarding the significant matters of the consultations with those charged with governance. Section 625, *Reports on the Application of Accounting Principles,* describes the circumstances in which the auditor should be informed of such consultations.

SIGNIFICANT ISSUES COMMUNICATED WITH MANAGEMENT

Any significant issues that were discussed or were the subject of correspondence with management should be communicated to those charged with governance. The following are examples of such issues:

1. Business conditions that affect the entity and plans and strategies that would affect the risks of material misstatement of the financial statements.

2. Discussions relating to the initial and/or recurring retention of the auditor, correspondences and discussions relating to the applications of accounting principles and auditing standards.

INDEPENDENCE CONSIDERATIONS

GAAS requires that the auditor be independent for all audits. In fact the auditor's report clearly affirms the auditor's independence. However, in certain circumstances, the auditor may decide that it is necessary to communicate to those charged with governance, circumstances or relationships that may be perceived as bearing on the auditor's independence, especially for public interest entities, such as

- Employee benefit and health and welfare plans subject to the Employee Retirement Income Security Act audit requirements;
- Governmental retirement plans;
- Entities or programs (including for-profit entities) subject to the Single Audit Act OMB Circular A-133 audit requirements and entities or programs subject to similar program oversight; and
- Financial institutions, credit unions, and insurance companies.

These relationships may be, for example, financial interests, business or family, or nonaudit services provided or expected to be provided. However, the auditor should also communicate that he or she has given significant consideration to the matter and has reached the conclusion that independence has not, in fact, been impaired. The form and timing of the communication relating to independence will be affected by the entity's governing structure and whether an audit committee exists. For example, in the situation where all those charged with governance are involved in the management of the company, the auditor may be satisfied that those charged with governance have all been notified as to the auditor's independence through their management activities or perhaps through other means such as the management letter.

THE COMMUNICATION PROCESS

ESTABLISHING A MUTUAL UNDERSTANDING

It is very important that the auditor reach an understanding with those charged with governance regarding the form, timing and expected general content of their communications. Effective two-way communication may be maximized if those charged with governance are apprised of the auditor's responsibilities, an overview of the planned scope and timing of the audit, and the expected general content of the communications. The first two considerations have already been discussed in prior parts of this section.

Other matters that will contribute to an effective two-way communication between auditor and those charged with governance include a discussion of the following objectives:

1. There should be a clear purpose of what will be communicated. When the auditor and those charged with governance know the purpose of the communication, they are in a better position to have a mutual understanding of the important issues to be conveyed as well as the expected actions that will arise from the communication process.
2. Know the form the communication will take.
3. Establish the individual(s) on the audit team and those who are charged with governance who will communicate with each other regarding relevant matters.

4. Emphasize that it is the expectation of the auditor that not only will there will be effective, two-way communication with those charged with governance but also that the latter will reciprocally communicate with the auditor regarding relevant matters. For example, considerations relevant to the audit that might be communicated include matters of strategic decisions that may significantly affect the nature, timing, and extent of audit procedures, the suspicion or detection of fraud, or concerns about the integrity or incompetence of senior management.
5. Emphasize that the process of taking action is the responsibility of both auditor and those charged with governance regarding each other's communications. This includes reporting back on matters communicated.

In general, the communication process will vary in accordance with the situation on hand. Variables to consider include

- Size and governance structure of the entity,
- How those charged with governance operate, and
- The auditor's view of the significance of matters to be communicated.

If communication between the auditor and those charged with governance is not adequate, it will clearly be difficult to establish an effective two-way communication for the audit.

WHAT FORMS SHOULD COMMUNICATION TAKE?

Significant findings from the audit should be communicated by the auditor to those charged with governance in writing when the auditor believes that oral communication would be inadequate. The communication need not include matters that were communicated and were resolved. Other communications, however, may be either oral or in writing.

Effective communication forms may consist of

- Formal presentations,
- Written reports,
- Other forms of written communications (e.g., engagement letter provided to those charged with governance), and
- Discussions (less formal communications).

The form of communication (oral versus writing, detailed presentation or summary, formal or informal presentation, etc.) are a function of many considerations. These include the following:

1. The significance of the matter being communicated.
2. Whether the matter has been resolved.
3. Whether management has previously communicated the matter.
4. The characteristics of the entity being audited including its size, operating structure, control environment, and legal structure.
5. Regulatory or legal requirements which may require written communication.
6. Expectations of those in charge of governance regarding periodic meetings or communications with the auditor.
7. The amount of expected dialogue and ongoing contact the auditor will have with those charged with governance.
8. Significant changes in the membership of the governing body.
9. If auditor does a special-purpose financial statement audit for the entity, whether or not he also will be auditing its general-purpose financial statements.

TIMING OF THE COMMUNICATIONS

It is imperative that the auditor communicate with those charged with governance on timely basis so that the latter may take appropriate action when needed. What constitutes appropriate timing in a given situation will vary with the circumstances at hand. For example, the significance and nature of the matter and action expected to be taken by those charged with governance should be considered.

The following should be considered by the auditor as part of the communication timing process:

- Planning matters should take place early in the audit engagement. In an initial audit, it should be part of the terms of the engagement.
- If significant problems are encountered during the audit, they should be conveyed as soon as possible so that those charged with governance may be able to assist the auditor in resolving the difficulties or reaching an acknowledgement that it is probable that a modified opinion may be necessary.

Other factors that the auditor may want to consider regarding the timing of the communications include

1. The size, operating structure, control environment, and legal structure of the entity.
2. Legal obligations that may exist which require that data be conveyed within a given amount of time.
3. Expectations of those charged with governance regarding periodic meetings or communications with the auditor.
4. Timely communications of material weaknesses so that appropriate remedial actions may be taken.
5. Special- and general-purpose financial statements both being audited by the auditor.

COMMUNICATION ADEQUACY

The two-way communication between the auditor and those charged with governance should be evaluated for adequacy by the auditor. Clearly, effective communication benefits both of these parties. However, if the communication is deemed not adequate, appropriate action must be taken to improve its effectiveness. Section 314, *Understanding the Entity and Its Environment and Assessing the Risks of Material Misstatement,* states that participation by those charged with governance, including their interaction with internal audit and external auditors, is an element of the entity's internal control environment. Inadequate communication between the auditor and those charged with governance may be indicative of an unsatisfactory control environment, which will have an effect on the auditor's assessment of the risks of material misstatements.

The auditor's evaluation of the adequacy of the communication with those charged with governance should be based on observations resulting from the performance of audit procedures for other purposes. Specific procedures for this evaluation do not need to be designed. Queries relating to the observations on which the auditor's evaluation should be based may consist of the following:

1. Have appropriate and timely actions been taken by those charged with governance in response to matters communicated by the auditor?
2. Are those charged with governance manifesting openness in their communications with the auditor?
3. Are those charged with governance willing and able to meet with the auditor without management present?

4. Are those charged with governance able to fully understand and act on matters communicated to them by the auditor? For example, are they willing to probe issues and question recommendations made to them?
5. Is the auditor having problems establishing a reciprocal understanding regarding the form, timing, and expected general content of communications with those charged with governance?
6. Does it appear that those charged with governance, who are also involved with managing the entity, are aware of how matters discussed with the auditor affect their broader governance responsibilities and management responsibilities?

If the two-way communication between auditor and those charged with governance has been deemed to be inadequate, there is a risk that the auditor has not successfully obtained all the audit evidence needed to form an opinion on the financial statements. It is important that the auditor consider the effect of this in the audit's assessment of the risks of material misstatements. The auditor should discuss this situation with those charged with governance. However, if resolution cannot be achieved, the following actions may need to be taken by the auditor:

1. Modify the audit opinion on the basis of a scope limitation.
2. Obtain legal advice about the consequences of alternative courses of action.
3. Communicate with third parties (e.g., a regulator) or a higher authority in the governance hierarchy outside the entity (e.g., shareholders in a general meeting, or a governmental agency responsible for certain governmental entities).
4. Withdraw from the engagement.

DOCUMENTING THE COMMUNICATION

When communications have been executed in accordance with this section orally, GAAS requires that the auditor document them. Section 339, *Audit Documentation,* requires that the auditor document any discussions of significant findings or issues (including responses) with management or others, including those charged with governance of the entity on a timely basis. When issues have been communicated in writing, a copy of the communication should be retained by the auditor. Documentation of an oral communication may include a copy of the minutes prepared by the entity, assuming those minutes have been deemed an appropriate record of the communication.

PRACTITIONER CHECKLIST

REQUIREMENTS TO COMMUNICATE WITH THOSE CHARGED WITH GOVERNANCE ENUMERATED IN OTHER STATEMENTS ON AUDITING STANDARDS BESIDES SECTION 380 (FROM APPENDIX A OF SAS 114)

The requirements to communicate with those charged with governance are included in several other Statements on Auditing Standards that the auditor should be familiar with in addition to Section 380. The following are an enumeration of these. The parameters of this section (Section 380) do not, in any way, change the requirements or guidelines enumerated below.

_____ (1) Paragraph .17 of Section 317, *Illegal Acts by Clients:* The auditor must communicate with the audit committee or others with equivalent authority and responsibility any illegal acts that come to the auditor's attention.
_____ (2) Paragraph .22 of Section 801, *Compliance Auditing Considerations in Audits of Governmental Entities and Recipients of Governmental Financial*

Assistance: The auditor must communicate with management and the audit committee or others with equivalent authority and responsibility when the auditor becomes aware, in an audit performed in accordance with GAAS, that the entity is subject to an audit requirement that may not be covered in the terms of the current engagement. In addition the aforementioned parties should be apprised that an audit performed in accordance with GAAS may not satisfy legal, regulatory, or contractual requirements that are currently applicable.

_____ (3) Paragraph .22 of Section 316, *Consideration of Fraud in a Financial Statement Audit:* The auditor must inquire directly of the audit committee (or at least its chair) any views about the risks of fraud and whether it currently has knowledge of any fraud or suspected fraud affecting the entity.

_____ (4) Paragraph .79 of Section 316, *Consideration of Fraud in a Financial Statement Audit:* The auditor must communicate with those charged with governance any fraud involving senior management and any fraud caused by senior management, or other employees, that causes a material misstatement of the financial statements. Also the auditor should reach an understanding with those charged with governance regarding the nature and extent of communications about misappropriations committed by lower level employees.

_____ (5) Paragraph .20 of Section 325, *Communicating Internal Control Related Matters Identified in an Audit:* The auditor must communicate in writing to management and those charged with governance any control deficiencies identified during the audit that are evaluated as being significant deficiencies or material weaknesses.

390 CONSIDERATION OF OMITTED PROCEDURES AFTER THE REPORT DATE

SOURCE OF STANDARDS

SAS 46, *Consideration of Omitted Procedures after the Report Date*

SUMMARY

An auditor has no responsibility to retrospectively review the audit work. However, engagements are subject to subsequent scrutiny by both peer review and internal inspection.

While there may be no indication that the audited financial statements are not presented fairly in conformity with the relevant basis of accounting, the auditor, after the report is issued, may conclude that one or more auditing procedures that should have been performed were inadvertently omitted. This is not the same as an auditor later becoming aware of facts that existed at the report date (see AU Section 561).

This section provides guidance in connection with the actions to be taken by the auditor who determines after the report date that he or she omitted a particular audit procedure.

ACTIONS TO BE TAKEN BY THE AUDITOR

After the date of the audit report, an auditor who determines that an audit procedure was omitted should assess the importance of the omitted procedure in terms of the auditor's present ability to support an opinion already expressed and decide whether alternative procedures performed compensated for the omitted procedure.

If the omission impairs the auditor's ability to support the original opinion and the auditor believes that there are or may be parties currently relying, or likely to rely, on the report, the auditor should promptly arrange to apply the omitted procedures or satisfactory alternatives.

If after application of those procedures the auditor becomes aware of facts that would have affected the report, the auditor should advise the client to

1. Disclose the facts to actual or potential statement users,
2. Issue revised statements, to be accompanied by a revised auditor's report,
3. Make suitable disclosure in new financial statements if they are about to be issued, and
4. Notify users or potential users if the effects on financial statements will take a long time to determine and advise them that revised statements will follow later.

If the client refuses to make appropriate disclosures, the auditor must notify the client that the auditor's report no longer holds and undertake to notify all other actual users, potential users, and regulatory bodies.

If the auditor cannot perform the omitted procedures or suitable alternatives, the auditor should consult with an attorney to determine an appropriate course of action and the auditor's responsibilities to the client, regulatory authorities, and other persons likely to rely on the report.

411 THE MEANING OF "PRESENT FAIRLY IN CONFORMITY WITH GENERALLY ACCEPTED ACCOUNTING PRINCIPLES"

SOURCES OF STANDARDS

SAS 69, *The Meaning of Present Fairly in Conformity with Generally Accepted Accounting Principles*
SAS 91, *Federal GAAP Hierarchy*
SAS 93, *Omnibus Statement on Auditing Standards—2000*

SUMMARY

An independent auditor's report contains an opinion about whether financial statements present fairly, in all material respects, the entity's financial position, results of operations, and cash flows in conformity with GAAP. The report must also identify the country of origin of those GAAP.

This section explains the meaning of the phrase "present fairly ... in conformity with generally accepted accounting principles."

GENERALLY ACCEPTED ACCOUNTING PRINCIPLES

Generally accepted accounting principles are the conventions, rules, and procedures needed to define accepted accounting practice at a given point in time. An auditor should consider whether substance of a transaction or an event differs from its form.

FAIRNESS OF PRESENTATION

An auditor should measure fairness of presentation within the framework of generally accepted accounting principles. The expression of the opinion as to fairness of presentation should be based on his judgment as to whether

1. The principles selected and applied have general acceptance;
2. The principles applied are appropriate in the circumstances;
3. The financial statements, including the notes, are informative;
4. The financial statements are classified and summarized in a reasonable way and are neither too detailed nor too condensed;
5. The underlying events are presented within limits that are reasonable and practical for financial statements.

GENERAL ACCEPTANCE

The principles selected and applied have general acceptance based on the following hierarchy of authority. Authority is highest in level one and depends on whether the entity is a nongovernmental entity, a state or local government entity, or a federal government entity.

Level One

1. *Nongovernmental entities.* FASB Statements of Financial Accounting Standards and Interpretations; Accounting Principles Board (APB) Opinions; and AICPA Accounting Research Bulletins.
2. *State and local governments.* Government Accounting Standards Board (GASB) Statements and Interpretations, as well as AICPA and FASB pronouncements if they have been made applicable to state and local governments by a GASB Statement or Interpretation.
3. *Federal governmental entities.* Federal Accounting Standards Advisory Board (FASAB) Statements and Interpretations, as well as AICPA and FASB pronouncements if they have been made applicable to federal governmental entities by a FASAB Statement or Interpretation.

Level Two

1. *Nongovernmental entities.* FASB Technical Bulletins, AICPA Industry Audit and Accounting Guides, and AICPA Statements of Position.
2. *State and local governments.* GASB Technical Bulletins and, if specifically made applicable to state and local governments by the AICPA and cleared by GASB, AICPA Industry Audit and Accounting Guides and AICPA Statements of Position.
3. *Federal entities.* FASAB Technical Bulletins and, if specifically made applicable to federal entities by the AICPA and cleared by the FASAB, AICPA Industry Audit and Accounting Guides and AICPA Statements of Position.

Level Three

1. *Nongovernmental entities.* Consensus positions of the FASB Emerging Issues Task Force and AICPA Practice Bulletins.
2. *State and local governments.* Consensus positions of the GASB Emerging Issues Task Force and AICPA Practice Bulletins, if specifically made applicable to state and local governments by the GASB.
3. *Federal entities.* AICPA AcSec Practice Bulletins, if specifically made applicable to federal governmental entities and cleared by the FASAB, and Technical Releases of the Accounting and Auditing Policy committee of the FASAB.

Level Four

1. *Nongovernmental entities.* AICPA accounting interpretations guides (Qs and As) published by the FASB staff, as well as general and industry practices that are widely recognized.
2. *State and local governments.* Implementation guides (Qs and As) published by the GASB staff, as well as widely recognized and prevalent practices.
3. *Federal entities.* Implementation guides published by the FASAB staff and practices widely recognized and prevalent in the federal government.

Level Five ("other accounting literature")

These sources should be considered only in the absence of sources identified in levels one through four.

1. *Nongovernmental entities.* Other accounting literature, including FASB Concepts Statements, AICPA Issue Papers, International Accounting Standards of the International Accounting Standards Committee, Governmental Accounting Standards Board (GASB) Statements, Interpretations, and Technical Bulletins, pronouncements issued by other professional associations or regulatory agencies, Technical Service Inquiries and Replies included in AICPA Technical Practice Aids, and accounting textbooks, handbooks, and articles.

2. *State and local governments.* Other accounting literature, including GASB Concepts Statements and pronouncements in levels one through four that were not made specifically applicable to state and local governments, FASB Concepts Statements, AICPA Issues Papers, International Standards of the International Accounting Standards Committee, pronouncements issued by other professional associations or regulatory agencies, Technical Service Inquiries and Replies included in AICPA Technical Practice Aids, and accounting textbooks, handbooks, and articles.

3. *Federal entities.* Other accounting literature, including FASB Concepts Statements, pronouncements in levels one through four that were not made specifically applicable to federal entities, FASB Concepts Statements, GASB Statements, Interpretations, Technical Bulletins, and Concepts Statements, AICPA Issues Papers, International Standards of the International Accounting Standards Committee, pronouncements issued by other professional associations or regulatory agencies, Technical Service Inquiries and Replies included in AICPA Technical Practice Aids, and accounting textbooks, handbooks, and articles.

APPROPRIATENESS

The principles applied should be appropriate in the circumstances; they must reflect the substance of transactions and events. When alternatives exist and no criteria have been established to differentiate their use, any form of guidance may be used as long as it adheres to the substance of the transaction.

420 CONSISTENCY OF APPLICATION OF GENERALLY ACCEPTED ACCOUNTING PRINCIPLES

SOURCES OF STANDARDS

SAS 1, *Codification of Auditing Standards and Procedures*
SAS 43, *Omnibus Statement on Auditing Standards*
SAS 88, *Service Organizations and Reports on Consistency*

SUMMARY

Consistency in the application of GAAP is needed to facilitate comparability of financial statements between two or more periods. Unless otherwise indicated in the auditor's report, the implication is that there is consistency in the application of accounting principles.

This section provides guidance about factors that may affect the comparability of financial statements and thus the auditor's report.

ACCOUNTING CHANGES AFFECTING CONSISTENCY

CHANGE IN ACCOUNTING PRINCIPLES

A material change in accounting principle between accounting periods, as from a declining-balance method of depreciation to the straight-line method, must be recognized by the inclusion in the auditor's report of an explanatory paragraph after the opinion paragraph (see AU Section 508 for additional guidance).

CHANGE IN REPORTING ENTITY

A change in reporting entity is a special type of change that results in financial statements that are, in effect, those of a different reporting entity. This commonly results when consolidated or combined financial statements succeed the financial statements of individual companies, or there is a change in the companies included in combined financial statements.

An auditor is not required to include an explanatory paragraph about consistency when there is a change in the reporting entity resulting from a transaction or event, or the creation, cessation, or complete or partial purchase or disposition of a subsidiary or other business unit.

However, a change in reporting entity that does not result from a transaction or event does require an explanatory paragraph about consistency in the auditor's report.

CORRECTION OF AN ERROR IN PRINCIPLE

An auditor must include an explanatory paragraph about consistency in the report if there is a change from a principle that is not generally accepted to one that is, even if the change was made to correct a mistake in the application of a principle. This modification is required even if the change is properly accounted for as the correction of an error.

CHANGE IN ESTIMATE

An auditor must include an explanatory paragraph about consistency in the report if there is a change in accounting principle that is inseparable from a change in accounting estimate.

CHANGE IN PRESENTATION OF CASH FLOWS

A change in an entity's policy for determining items to be treated as cash equivalents is considered a change in accounting principle. Such a change necessitates

1. Restatement of the prior period financial statements presented comparatively with those of the period reflecting the change, and
2. Inclusion of an explanatory paragraph about consistency in the auditor's report.

ACCOUNTING CHANGES NOT AFFECTING CONSISTENCY

Certain accounting changes do not affect consistency in the application of accounting principles. If they may have a material effect on the comparability of financial statements, they must be disclosed in the audit report. However, an auditor is not required to include an explanatory paragraph about consistency in the report. The following situations do not require the inclusion of the consistency modification:

1. A change in an accounting estimate for salvage value, inventory obsolescence, and uncollectible accounts receivable, and the like.
2. Correction of an error not involving an accounting principle, such as a mathematical mistake, an oversight, or misuse of facts at the time the financial statements were originally prepared.
3. A change in classification or a reclassification, as when the balance of long-term debt is reclassified as a current liability when the debt is to be liquidated in the current accounting period.
4. Adoption of accounting principles and policies for new transactions and events that is different in substance from transactions and events in a prior period.
5. A change in an accounting policy that has no material effect on the current period financial statements but that is expected to have a material effect on future financial statements. If such a change is not disclosed in the financial statements, the auditor should qualify the opinion.

FIRST-YEAR AUDITS

A successor auditor should adopt reasonable and practicable procedures to determine consistency in the application of accounting principles between periods. To be satisfied about consistency, a successor auditor may review client records and audit documentation prepared by predecessor auditors.

If client records are inadequate or there is a restriction on the scope of the audit, a successor auditor may not be satisfied about consistency or the validity of opening account balances. If that happens, an auditor may determine that a disclaimer of opinion on the current period financial statements is warranted.

SELECTED INTERPRETATIONS

IMPACT OF FIFO TO LIFO CHANGE IN COMPARATIVE FINANCIAL STATEMENTS (ISSUED IN JANUARY 1975; REVISED IN APRIL 1989)

An auditor is not required to include an explanatory paragraph about consistency in the audit report when a company presents comparative financial statements and the year of the FIFO-to-LIFO change is the earliest year presented. This type of change does not require inclusion of the cumulative effect of the change in the financial statements of the period of the change.

EFFECT OF ACCOUNTING CHANGES BY AN INVESTEE ON CONSISTENCY (ISSUED IN JULY 1980; REVISED IN JUNE 1993)

An auditor must include an explanatory paragraph about consistency in his report when there has been a change in accounting principle by an investee accounted for by the equity method.

EFFECT OF ADOPTION OF A NEW ACCOUNTING STANDARD THAT DOES NOT REQUIRE THE ENTITY TO DISCLOSE THE EFFECT OF THE CHANGE IN THE YEAR OF ADOPTION (ISSUED IN APRIL 2002)

If a new accounting standard necessitates a change in an accounting principle and, under the standard, disclosure of the change in the year of adoption is not required, an auditor need not independently determine the effect of the change. However, the auditor should determine whether it is necessary to include an explanatory paragraph about consistency in the audit report, based on

1. How material the cumulative effect of the change is, and
2. Whether the disclosure is voluntary.

In general, an explanatory paragraph is not warranted, but it would be necessary if either

1. The cumulative effect of the change is material, or
2. Disclosure is made in the financial statements that management believes that the effect of the change is or may be material in the year of adoption.

431 ADEQUACY OF DISCLOSURE IN FINANCIAL STATEMENTS

SOURCES OF STANDARDS

SAS 32, *Adequacy of Disclosure in Financial Statements*

SUMMARY

The third standard of reporting under GAAS says that informative disclosures in the financial statements are presumed to be reasonably adequate unless otherwise indicated in the auditor's report.

This section provides guidance on the possible need to modify the report due to a client's inadequate disclosure in financial statements.

REQUIRED REPORT MODIFICATION

An auditor should express a qualified or adverse opinion if management omits information from financial statements that GAAP requires. The auditor should provide the information in his report, if practicable.

Practicable means that the information is reasonably obtainable from the client's records and providing the information does not put the auditor in the position of a preparer of the information. It would thus not be practicable for an auditor to prepare a basic financial statement or segment information for inclusion in his audit report.

Although an auditor may participate in the preparation of a client's financial statements, the financial statements remain the representation of management. The auditor's participation does not require that his or her report be modified.

504 ASSOCIATION WITH FINANCIAL STATEMENTS

SOURCES OF STANDARDS

SAS 26, *Association with Financial Statements.*
SAS 72, *Letters for Underwriters and Certain Other Requesting Parties.*

See section 9504 for interpretations of this section.

SUMMARY

Any time an auditor's name is associated with financial statements, the accompanying report should clearly indicate the nature of the work performed and the degree of responsibility being assumed. The fourth standard of reporting requires either

1. An expression of opinion regarding the financial statements taken as a whole, or
2. An assertion to the effect that an opinion cannot be expressed.

The primary aim of the fourth reporting standard is to minimize misunderstanding by clearly stating the degree of responsibility the accountant is assuming.

AU 504.03 states

An accountant is associated with financial statements when he has consented to the use of his name in a report, document, or written communication containing the statements.

The accountant is also considered "associated" when the accountant prepares or assists in preparing the financial statements. The accountant is considered associated even though the accountant does not append his name to the statements. Even if the accountant participates in the preparation of financial statements, the statements are still representations of management. The management is ultimately responsible for their fair presentation in conformity with GAAP. An accountant may be associated with audited or unaudited financial statements.

DISCLAIMER OF OPINION ON UNAUDITED FINANCIAL STATEMENTS

When the accountant is associated with unaudited financial statements, a disclaimer of opinion is used to comply with the requirements of the fourth standard of reporting. AU 504.05 states that when an accountant is associated with the financial statements of a public entity, but has not audited or reviewed these statements, the accountant should issue a disclaimer of opinion using the following report format:

The accompanying balance sheet of X Company as of December 31, 19X1, and the related statements of income, retained earnings, and cash flows for the year then ended were not audited by us and, accordingly, we do not express an opinion on them.

[Signature and date]

This disclaimer may be placed directly on the financial statements, or it may be attached to the financial statements. Each page of the financial statements should also be clearly marked as "Unaudited." With a disclaimer of opinion, the accountant has no responsibility to apply procedures other than reading the financial statements for obvious material misstatements. In general, the accountant should not mention or describe any procedure that may have been applied. Describing such procedures might mistakenly lead the user to conclude that the financial statements have been audited or reviewed.

Anytime the accountant's name is included in client-prepared written communication containing financial statements of a public entity that have not been audited or reviewed, the accountant should ensure that the financial statements are clearly marked as "unaudited" and that there is a notation that the accountant is not expressing an opinion on the financial statements.

DISCLAIMER OF OPINION ON UNAUDITED FINANCIAL STATEMENTS PREPARED ON A COMPREHENSIVE BASIS OF ACCOUNTING

If the accountant is associated with unaudited financial statements of a public entity prepared in accordance with a comprehensive basis of accounting other than generally accepted accounting principles, the accountant should modify the identification of financial statements in the disclaimer of opinion. AU 504.07 provides the following example for a disclaimer of opinion on cash-basis statements:

> The accompanying statement of assets and liabilities resulting from cash transactions of XYZ Corporation as of December 31, 19X1, and the related statement of revenues collected and expenses paid during the year then ended were not audited by us and, accordingly, we do not express an opinion on them.
>
> [*Signature and date*]

The accountant should include in a note to the financial statements a description of how the basis of presentation differs from generally accepted accounting principles. The accountant may, but does not have to, state the monetary effect of such differences.

DISCLAIMER OF OPINION WHEN NOT INDEPENDENT

A disclaimer of opinion is also required when the accountant is not independent with respect to the client. The second general standard requires that "In all matters relating to the assignment, an independence in mental attitude is to be maintained by the auditor or auditors." For financial statements of nonpublic entities, the accountant should refer to the Statements on Standards for Accounting and Review Services for additional guidance.

When an accountant is not independent, the accountant should specifically state that he or she is not independent and issue a disclaimer of opinion. The accountant should not explain reasons for the lack of independence. The accountant also should not describe any procedures that may have been performed. Including the reasons why independence is lacking or describing procedures may confuse the user. An example of a report of a disclaimer of opinion due to lack of independence is as follows (AU 504.10) :

> We are not independent with respect to XYZ Company, and the accompanying balance sheet as of December 31, 19X1, and the related statements of income, retained earnings, and cash flows for the year then ended were not audited by us and, accordingly, we do not express an opinion on them.
>
> [*Signature and date*]

CIRCUMSTANCES REQUIRING A MODIFIED DISCLAIMER

An accountant who is aware that the unaudited financial statements on which the accountant is issuing a disclaimer of opinion are not in conformity with generally accepted accounting principles (include adequate disclosure) should proceed as follows:

1. The accountant should suggest that management make the appropriate revisions.
2. If the appropriate revisions are not made by management, the accountant should describe the client's noncompliance in the disclaimer of opinion. This description should be precise and explain the nature of the departure. If possible, the effects of the departure on the financial statements should be stated. Information necessary for adequate disclosure should also be presented. However, if management has elected to omit substantially all of the disclosures, the accountant should clearly indicate that in the report, but is not expected to include all the disclosure notes in the report.
3. If the client does not agree to the revisions or will not accept the accountant's modified disclaimer of opinion, the accountant should refuse to be associated with the statements and, if necessary, withdraw from the engagement.

REPORTING ON AUDITED AND UNAUDITED FINANCIAL STATEMENTS IN COMPARATIVE FORM

Filed with SEC

When unaudited financial statements are presented in comparative form with audited financial statements in documents filed with the Securities and Exchange Commission, such statements should be clearly marked as "unaudited." Such statements should not be referred to in the auditor's report.

Not Filed with SEC

When unaudited financial statements are presented in comparative form with audited financial statements in any other document, the unaudited financial statements should be clearly marked "unaudited." The accountant should also either

1. Reissue the report on the prior period, or
2. Modify the report on the current period by including a separate paragraph describing the responsibility assumed.

Prior Period Statements That Have Been Audited

AU 504.16 states that when the financial statements of the prior period have been audited and the report on the current period is to contain a separate paragraph, it should indicate

1. Which prior period financial statements were audited,
2. Date of the previous report,
3. Type of opinion expressed,
4. If the opinion was other than unqualified, the substantive reasons given, and
5. Whether no auditing procedures were performed after the date of the previous report.

The following example from AU 504.16 shows a sample separate paragraph:

> The financial statements for the year ended December 31, 19X1, were audited by us (other accountants) and we (they) expressed an unqualified opinion on them in our (their) report dated March 1, 19X2, but we (they) have not performed any auditing procedures since that date.

PRIOR PERIOD STATEMENTS ARE UNAUDITED

AU 504.17 states that when the financial statements of the prior period are unaudited and the report on the current period is to contain a separate paragraph, it should include

1. A statement of the service previously performed,
2. The date of the report on that service,
3. A description of any material modifications noted in that report, and
4. A statement that the service had less scope than an audit and does not provide the basis for the expression of an opinion on the financial statements taken as a whole.

When the financial statements are of a public entity, the separate paragraph should include

1. A disclaimer of opinion, or
2. A description of a review.

When the financial statements of a nonpublic entity were compiled or reviewed, the separate paragraph should describe the compilation or review. AU 504.17 gives the following example of a separate paragraph describing a review:

> The 20X1 financial statements were reviewed by us (other accountants) and our (their) report thereon, dated March 1, 20X2, stated we (they) were not aware of any material modifications that should be made to those statements for them to be in conformity with generally accepted accounting principles. However, a review is substantially less in scope than an audit and does not provide a basis for the expression of an opinion on the financial statements taken as a whole.

AU 504.17 gives the following example of a separate paragraph describing a compilation:

> The 20X1 financial statements were compiled by us (other accountants) and our (their) report thereon, dated March 1, 20X2, stated we (they) did not audit or review those financial statements and, accordingly, express no opinion or other form of assurance on them.

508 REPORTS ON AUDITED FINANCIAL STATEMENTS

SOURCES OF STANDARDS

SAS 58, *Reports on Audited Financial Statements*
SAS 64, *Omnibus Statement on Auditing Standards—1990*
SAS 79, *Amendment to Statement on Auditing Standards No. 58*
SAS 85, *Management Representations*
SAS 93, *Omnibus Statement on Auditing Standards—2000*
SAS 98, *Omnibus Statement on Auditing Standards—2002*

SUMMARY

This section applies to an auditor's reports on historical financial statements; it does not apply to unaudited financial statements, reports on incomplete financial information, or special reports. The fourth standard of reporting indicates that the auditor's report shall either contain an expression of opinion about the financial statements taken as a whole, or an assertion to the effect that an opinion cannot be expressed. When an overall opinion cannot be expressed, the reasons should be stated.

Where an auditor's name is associated with financial statements, the report should contain a clear-cut indication of the character of the audit, if any, and how much responsibility he is taking.

The fourth standard of reporting applies equally to a complete set of financial statements and to an individual financial statement, so the auditor may express an unqualified opinion on one financial statement while simultaneously expressing a qualified or adverse opinion or disclaimer of opinion on another. The introductory paragraph of the auditor's report should clearly identify the financial statements reported on.

If a statement of changes in stockholder's equity accounts is part of the basic financial statements, it should be referred to in the introductory paragraph of the report but need not be reported on in the opinion paragraph.

AUDITOR'S STANDARD REPORT

The basic elements of the auditor's standard report are as follows:

1. A title that includes the word "independent," (e.g., "Independent Auditor's Report").
2. An addressee, which may be the company, its board of directors, or the stockholders (partners, general partner, or proprietor if the entity is unincorporated).
3. An introductory paragraph that specifies that

    a. The financial statements identified in the report were audited,
    b. The financial statements are the responsibility of management, and

   c.   The auditor's responsibility is to express an opinion on the financial statements based on the audit.

4.   A scope paragraph that includes statements that

   a.   The audit was conducted in accordance with generally accepted auditing standards (GAAS) and the United States is the country of origin of those standards (e.g., "auditing standards generally accepted in the United States of America" or "US generally accepted auditing standards"), and

   b.   Those standards require that the auditor plan and perform the audit to obtain reasonable assurance that the financial statements are free of material misstatements.

   c.   An audit includes examining evidence, on a test basis, supporting the amounts and disclosures in the financial statements;

   d.   Assessing the accounting principles used; and significant estimates made by management; and

   e.   Evaluating the overall financial statement presentation.

   f.   The auditor believes that the audit provides a reasonable basis for an opinion.

5.   An opinion paragraph that includes an opinion as to whether the financial statements present fairly, in all material respects, the financial position of the company as of the balance sheet date and the results of its operations and its cash flows for the period then ended in conformity with GAAP. The opinion should identify the country of origin of the GAAP (e.g., "accounting principles generally accepted in the United States of America" or "US generally accepted accounting principles").

6.   A signature of the auditor's firm, which may be manual or printed.

7.   The date of the audit report (see AU Section 530).

The standard audit report covering a single year is as follows:

Sample Standard Independent Auditor's Report

Independent Auditor's Report

[Addressee]

     We have audited the accompanying balance sheet of X Company as of December 31, 20XX, and the related statements of income, retained earnings, and cash flows for the year then ended. These financial statements are the responsibility of the Company's management. Our responsibility is to express an opinion on these financial statements based on our audit.

     We conducted our audit in accordance with auditing standards generally accepted in the United States of America. Those standards require that we plan and perform the audit to obtain reasonable assurance about whether the financial statements are free of material misstatements. An audit includes examining, on a test basis, evidence supporting the amounts and disclosures in the financial statements. An audit also includes assessing the accounting principles used and significant estimates made by management, as well as evaluating the overall financial statement presentation. We believe that our audit provides a reasonable basis for our opinion.

     In our opinion, the financial statements referred to above present fairly, in all material respects, the financial position of X Company as of (at) December 31, 20XX, and the results of its operations and its cash flows for the year then ended in conformity with accounting principles generally accepted in the United States of America.

[Signature]

[Date]

Sample Standard Independent Auditor's Report on Comparative Financial Statements

Independent Auditor's Report

[*Addressee*]

We have audited the accompanying balance sheets of X Company as of December 31, 20X2 and 20X1, and the related statements of income, retained earnings, and cash flows for the years then ended. These financial statements are the responsibility of the Company's management. Our responsibility is to express an opinion on these financial statements based on our audits.

We conducted our audits in accordance with auditing standards generally accepted in the United States of America. Those standards require that we plan and perform the audit to obtain reasonable assurance about whether the financial statements are free of material misstatements. An audit includes examining, on a test basis, evidence supporting the amounts and disclosures in the financial statements. An audit also includes assessing the accounting principles used and significant estimates made by management, as well as evaluating the overall financial statement presentation. We believe that our audits provide a reasonable basis for our opinion.

In our opinion, the financial statements referred to above present fairly, in all material respects, the financial position of X Company as of (at) December 31, 20X2 and 20X1, and the results of its operations and its cash flows for the years then ended in conformity with accounting principles generally accepted in the United States of America.

[*Signature*]

[*Date*]

TYPES OF AUDIT REPORTS

UNQUALIFIED OPINION

In an unqualified opinion, the auditor states that the financial statements present fairly, in all material respects, the financial position, results of operations, and cash flows of the entity in conformity with US GAAP.

While not affecting an unqualified opinion, certain circumstances may require the addition of an explanatory paragraph or explanatory language to the audit report (see below).

QUALIFIED OPINION

In a qualified opinion, the auditor states that "except for" the effects of the matters to which the qualification relates, the financial statements present fairly, in all material respects, die financial position, results of operations, and cash flows of the entity in conformity with US GAAP.

ADVERSE OPINION

In an adverse opinion, the auditor states that the financial statements do not present fairly the entity's financial position, results of operations, and cash flows in conformity with US GAAP.

DISCLAIMER OF OPINION

In a disclaimer of opinion, the auditor states that he does not express an opinion on the financial statements.

EXPLANATORY LANGUAGE ADDED TO THE STANDARD REPORT

While not negating the unqualified opinion, certain circumstances may require an additional explanatory paragraph or at least explanatory language in the standard report.

OPINION BASED IN PART ON REPORT OF ANOTHER AUDITOR

(See AU Section 543)

When the auditor's report is based in part on the opinion of another auditor and the principal auditor decides to refer to the report of the other auditor, this fact should be disclosed in the introductory paragraph and the other auditor's report mentioned in the scope and opinion paragraphs.

Sample Independent Auditor's Report, Division of Responsibility

Independent Auditor's Report

We have audited the consolidated balance sheet of ABC Company and subsidiaries as of December 31, 20X2 and 20X1, and the related consolidated statements of income, retained earnings, and cash flows for the years then ended. These financial statements are the responsibility of the Company's management. Our responsibility is to express an opinion on these financial statements based on our audits. We did not audit the financial statements of B Company, a consolidated subsidiary, which statements reflect total assets of $_____and $_____as of December 31, 20X2 and 20X1, respectively, and total revenues of $_____and $_____for the years then ended. Those statements were audited by other auditors whose report thereon has been furnished to us, and our opinion expressed herein, insofar as it relates to the amounts included for B Company, is based solely upon the report of the other auditors.

We conducted our audits in accordance with auditing standards generally accepted in the United States of America. Those standards require that we plan and perform the audit to obtain reasonable assurance about whether the financial statements are free of material misstatements. An audit includes examining, on a test basis, evidence supporting the amounts and disclosures in the financial statements. An audit also includes assessing the accounting principles used and significant estimates made by management, as well as evaluating the overall financial statement presentation. We believe that our audits and the report of the other auditors provide a reasonable basis for our opinion.

In our opinion, based on our audits and the report of the other auditors, the consolidated financial statements referred to above present fairly in all material respects, the financial position of ABC Company and subsidiaries as of December 31, 20X2 and 20X1, and the results of their operations and their cash flows for the years then ended in conformity with accounting principles generally accepted in the United States of America.

DEPARTURE FROM A PROMULGATED ACCOUNTING PRINCIPLE

When the financial statements contain a material departure from GAAP, an auditor generally should not express an unqualified opinion, but if he can demonstrate that due to unusual circumstances, the financial statements would be misleading had they not departed from GAAP, an unqualified opinion is acceptable. However, it should contain a separate explanatory paragraph either preceding or following the opinion paragraph that clearly describes the departure, its approximate effects, if practicable, and the reasons that compliance with the principle would have been misleading.

Sample Paragraph Explaining a Departure from GAAP

As more fully described in Note X to the financial statements, the Company's treatment of deferred income taxes is at variance with Statement Number 109 of the Financial Accounting Standards Board (FASB). Had FASB Statement Number 109 been followed, net income for the year would have increased [decreased] by $_____ and retained earnings at December 31, 20XX increased [decreased] by $_____. In our opinion, compliance with FASB Statement Number 109 would result in a misleading presentation because _____.

LACK OF CONSISTENCY

The standard report implies that the auditor is satisfied that there have been no material changes in accounting principles that would affect the comparability of financial statements between accounting periods. When there is a change in accounting principle, the report should include an explanatory paragraph after the opinion paragraph that identifies the nature of the change and refers the reader to the note to the financial statements that discusses the change. For example:

> As discussed in Note B to the financial statements, the company changed its method of computing depreciation in 20XX.

The auditor's concurrence with the change in accounting principle is implicit in an unqualified audit report; an auditor who does not concur with the change should issue a qualified or adverse opinion.

The explanatory paragraph is generally required in reports on financial statements of subsequent years when the year of change is reported on, but no additional explanation is necessary if a change in accounting principle that does not require a cumulative effect adjustment (e.g., a change from first-in, first-out to last-in, first-out) is made at the beginning of the earliest period reported on. If an accounting change is accounted for by retroactive restatement of the financial statements affected, the explanation should be included only in the year of the change.

EMPHASIS OF A MATTER

An auditor may wish to emphasize a matter, such as an unusually important subsequent event, that is already disclosed in the financial statements. The explanatory language should be presented in a separate paragraph, either preceding or following the opinion paragraph—phrases like "with the foregoing explanation" should not be used in the opinion paragraph. Emphasis of a matter is not intended to negate an unqualified opinion.

DEPARTURES FROM UNQUALIFIED OPINIONS

SCOPE LIMITATIONS

Scope limitations, whether imposed by the client or by circumstances, may require the auditor to qualify or to disclaim an opinion. Scope limitations occur when there is not enough appropriate evidence or there are restrictions on the scope of the audit. Common scope limitations involve observation of physical inventory counts and confirmation of accounts receivable balances.

Significant client-imposed scope limitations should ordinarily cause the auditor to disclaim an opinion rather than qualify it.

An opinion qualified because of a scope limitation should describe the situation in a paragraph preceding the opinion paragraph and both the scope and opinion paragraphs should refer to the situation. The wording of the opinion paragraph should indicate that the qualification pertains to the possible effects on the financial statements, not to the scope limitation itself, and should use the word "except" or "exception" in a phrase like "except for" or "with the exception of."

Sample Independent Auditor's Report, Scope Limitation

Independent Auditor's Report

[Same introductory paragraph as in the standard report]

Except as discussed in the following paragraph, we conducted our audits in accordance with auditing standards generally accepted in the United States of America. Those standards require that we plan and perform the audit to obtain reasonable assurance about whether the financial statements are free of material misstatements. An audit includes examining, on a test basis, evidence supporting the amounts and disclosures in the financial statements. An audit also includes assessing the accounting principles used and significant estimates made by management, as well as evaluating the overall financial statements presentation. We believe that our audits provide a reasonable basis for our opinion.

We were unable to obtain audited financial statements supporting the Company's investment in a foreign affiliate stated at $_____ and $_____ at December 31, 20X2 and 20X1, respectively, or its equity in earnings of that affiliate of $_____ and $_____, which is included in net income for the years then ended, as described in Note X to the financial statements; nor were we able to satisfy ourselves as to the carrying value of the investment in the foreign affiliate or the equity in its earnings by other auditing procedures.

In our opinion, except for the effects of such adjustments, if any, as might have been determined to be necessary had we been able to examine evidence regarding the foreign affiliate investment and earnings, the financial statements referred to in the first paragraph above present fairly, in all material respects, the financial position of X Company as of (at) December 31, 20X2 and 20X1, and the results of its operations and its cash flows for the years then ended, in conformity with accounting principles generally accepted in the United States of America.

There are times when notes to financial statements may contain unaudited information (e.g., pro forma calculations) that should be subjected to auditing procedures. An auditor who is unable to do so should express a qualified opinion or a disclaimer of opinion. If the disclosures are not truly necessary for fair presentation of the financial statements (e.g., pro forma effects of a business combination or a subsequent event), they may be identified as unaudited or as not covered by the auditor's report.

UNCERTAINTIES

Uncertainties are matters that are expected to be resolved at a future date, at which time conclusive evidence concerning their outcome is likely to become available. Among common uncertainties are loss contingencies that may result from litigation, claims, and assessments (see AU Section 337).

Management is responsible for making the required disclosures as required by US GAAP and estimating the effect of future events on financial statements or determining that a reasonable estimate cannot be made. An audit includes assessing whether there is enough evidence to support management's analysis. The fact that there is no information related to the outcome of uncertainties does not necessarily mean that the evidential matter is not sufficient. The auditor's judgment about sufficiency is based on evidence that is or should be available.

If the auditor concludes that there is enough evidence to support management's assertions about matters involving uncertainties and their financial statement presentation and disclosure, a standard unqualified opinion ordinarily is appropriate.

If, on the other hand, there is enough evidence concerning uncertainties but it is not made available to the auditor, there is a scope limitation and a qualified opinion or a disclaimer of opinion is appropriate. It is well to be careful to distinguish such a scope limitation from a situation in which the auditor concludes that financial statements are materially misstated due to departures from GAAP as they relate to uncertainties. In the latter situation a qualified opinion or an adverse opinion is appropriate.

LIMITED REPORTING ENGAGEMENTS

Limited reporting engagements are common, as when an auditor is asked to report on one basic financial statement (e.g., the balance sheet) and not the others. These engagements do not involve scope limitations if the auditor has unlimited access to information underlying the basic financial statements and all procedures considered necessary in the circumstances are appropriately applied. These types of engagements have limited reporting objectives.

Sample Independent Auditor's Report on a Limited Engagement

Independent Auditor's Report

We have audited the accompanying balance sheet of X Company as of December 31, 20XX. This financial statement is the responsibility of the Company's management. Our responsibility is to express an opinion on this financial statement based on our audit.

We conducted our audit in accordance with auditing standards generally accepted in the United States of America. Those standards require that we plan and perform the audit to obtain reasonable assurance about whether the financial statements are free of material misstatements. An audit includes examining, on a test basis, evidence supporting the amounts and disclosures in the financial statements. An audit also includes assessing the accounting principles used and significant estimates made by management, as well as evaluating the overall financial statement presentation. We believe that our audit provides a reasonable basis for our opinion.

In our opinion, the balance sheet referred to above presents fairly, in all material respects, the financial position of X Company as of (at) December 31, 20XX, in conformity with accounting principles generally accepted in the United States of America.

DEPARTURE FROM A GENERALLY ACCEPTED ACCOUNTING PRINCIPLE

Financial statements that are materially affected by a departure from GAAP call for a qualified or an adverse opinion.

A qualified opinion based on a departure from GAAP should have an explanatory paragraph preceding the opinion paragraph that discloses

1. All the substantive reasons that caused the auditor to conclude that there has been a departure from GAAP, and if practicable,
2. The principal effects of the departure on the financial statements.

If the principal effects are not reasonably determinable, that should be stated. If the necessary disclosures are contained in a note to the financial statements, the auditor may refer to the note and shorten the explanatory paragraph. The opinion paragraph should contain both qualifying language and a reference to the explanatory paragraph.

A sample report is presented below.

Independent Auditor's Report

[Addressee]

[Same introductory and scope paragraphs as in the standard report]

The Company has excluded, from property and debt in the accompanying balance sheets, certain lease obligations that, in our opinion, should be capitalized in order to conform with accounting principles generally accepted in the United States of America. If these lease obligations were capitalized, property would be increased by $_____and $_____, long-term debt by $_____and $_____, retained earnings by $_____and $_____as of December 31, 20X2 and 20X1, respectively. Additionally, net income would be increased (decreased) by $_____ and $_____and earnings per share would be increased (decreased) by $_____and $_____, respectively for the years then ended.

In our opinion, except for the effects of not capitalizing certain lease obligations as discussed in the preceding paragraph, the financial statements referred to above present fairly, in all material respects, the financial position of X Company as of (at) December 31, 20X2 and 20X1, and the results of its operations and its cash flows for the years then ended in conformity with accounting principles generally accepted in the United States of America.

If the necessary disclosures are contained in a note to the financial statements, the explanatory paragraph may be shortened as follows:

As more fully described in Note X to the financial statements, the Company has excluded certain lease obligations from property and debt in the accompanying balance sheets. In our opinion, accounting principles generally accepted in the United States of America require that such obligations be included in the balance sheets.

INADEQUATE DISCLOSURE

When financial statements, including the notes, fail to disclose information required by GAAP, the auditor should express a qualified or an adverse opinion and, if practicable, the report should disclose the omitted information.

A qualified opinion issued due to inadequate disclosure follows.

Independent Auditor's Report

[*Same introductory paragraph as in the standard report*]

The Company's financial statements do not disclose (describe the nature of the omitted disclosures). In our opinion, disclosure of this information is required by accounting principles generally accepted in the United States of America.

In our opinion, except for the omission of the information discussed in the preceding paragraph...

OMISSION OF THE STATEMENT OF CASH FLOWS

When a balance sheet and income statement are presented but the statement of cash flows is omitted, the result is an incomplete presentation. In this circumstance the auditor generally should issue a qualified opinion, but is not precluded from expressing an adverse opinion. In any event, the auditor is not required to prepare the statement of cash flows to include in the report.

If the opinion is qualified, the auditor's report should

1. Not refer to the statement of cash flows in the introductory paragraph,
2. Include a separate paragraph describing the omission, and
3. Modify the opinion paragraph by adding the wording "except that the omission of a statement of cash flows results in an incomplete presentation as explained in the preceding paragraph."

Independent Auditor's Report

We have audited the accompanying balance sheets of X Company as of December 31, 20X2 and 20X1, and the related statements of income and retained earnings for the years then ended. These financial statements are the responsibility of the Company's management. Our responsibility is to express an opinion on these financial statements based on our audit.

[*Same scope paragraph as in the standard report*]

The Company declined to present a statement of cash flows for the years ended December 31, 20X2 and 20X1. Presentation of such statement summarizing the Company's operating, investing, and financing activities is required by accounting principles generally accepted in the United States of America.

In our opinion, except that the omission of a statement of cash flows results in an incomplete presentation as explained in the preceding paragraph, the financial statements referred to above present fairly, in all material respects, the financial position of X Company as of (at) December 31, 20X2 and 20X1, and the results of its operations for the years then ended in conformity with accounting principles generally accepted in the United States of America.

DEPARTURES FROM GAAP INVOLVING RISKS OR UNCERTAINTIES

Departures from GAAP that involve risks or uncertainties may result from

1. Inadequate disclosure,
2. Inappropriate accounting principles, and
3. Unreasonable accounting estimates.

If financial statements contain material departures, the auditor should qualify the opinion or express an adverse opinion.

ACCOUNTING CHANGES

An auditor should generally express a qualified opinion if

1. A newly adopted accounting principle is not a GAAP,
2. The method of accounting for the effect of the change does not conform to GAAP, or
3. Management has not given the auditor reasonable justification for making the change in accounting principle.

An auditor who determines that the effect of the change is sufficiently material should express an adverse opinion.

The following is an example of the report that might be issued if management has not given the auditor reasonable justification for an accounting change.

Independent Auditor's Report

[*Same introductory and scope paragraph as in the standard report*]

As disclosed in Note X to the financial statements, the Company adopted, in 20X2, the first-in, first-out method of accounting for its inventories, whereas it previously used the last-in, first-out method. Although use of the first-in, first-out method is in conformity with accounting principles generally accepted in the United States of America, in our opinion the Company has not provided reasonable justification for making this change, as is required by US generally accepted accounting principles.

In our opinion, except for the change in accounting principle discussed in the preceding paragraph, the financial statements referred to above present fairly, in all material respects, the financial position of X Company as of December 31, 20X2 and 20X1, and the results of its operations and cash flows for the years then ended in conformity with accounting principles generally accepted in the United States of America.

If the financial statements for the year of change are presented in comparison with a subsequent year's financial statements, the auditor should continue to disclose his reservations about the financial statements for the year of the change, but there is no requirement to qualify the opinion for the financial statements of the subsequent year.

It should be readily apparent that continued use in future years of an accounting principle that departs from GAAP should lead the auditor to express a qualified or an adverse opinion, depending on how material the departure is to the subsequent-year financial statements.

A qualified or an adverse opinion should also be given if an entity accounts for the effect of a change prospectively when GAAP require restatement or the inclusion of the cumulative effect of the change in the year of the change.

ADVERSE OPINIONS

An auditor should express an adverse opinion when, in his or her judgment, the financial statements taken as a whole are not presented fairly in conformity with GAAP.

An adverse opinion should include at least one explanatory paragraph preceding the opinion paragraph that discloses

1. All substantive reasons for the adverse opinion, and if practicable,
2. The principal effects on the financial statements of the subject matter leading to the adverse opinion.

If these effects cannot be reasonably determined, the audit report should so state.

Presented below is an illustrative auditor's report containing an adverse opinion.

Independent Auditor's Report

[Same introductory and scope paragraphs as in the standard report]

As discussed in Note X to the financial statements, the Company carries its property, plant and equipment accounts at appraisal values, and provides depreciation on the basis of such values. Further, the Company does not provide for income taxes with respect to differences between financial income and taxable income arising because of the use, for income tax purposes, of the installment method of reporting gross profit from certain types of sales. Accounting principles generally accepted in the United States of America require that property, plant, and equipment be stated at an amount not in excess of cost, reduced by depreciation based on such amount, and that deferred income taxes be provided.

Because of the departures from accounting principles generally accepted in the United States of America identified above, as of December 31, 20X2, and 20X1, inventories have been increased $_____and $_____by inclusion in manufacturing overhead of depreciation in excess of that based on cost; property, plant, and equipment, less accumulated depreciation, is carried at $_____and $_____in excess of an amount based on the cost to the Company; and deferred income taxes of $ and $_____have not been recorded; resulting in an increase of $_____and $_____in retained earnings and in appraisal surplus of $_____and $_____, respectively. For the years ended December 31, 20X2, and 20X1, cost of goods sold has been increased $ and $_____, respectively, because of the effects of the depreciation accounting referred to above and deferred income taxes of $_____and $_____have not been provided, resulting in an increase in net income of $_____and $_____, respectively.

In our opinion, because of the effects of the matters discussed in the preceding paragraphs, the financial statements referred to above do not present fairly, in conformity with accounting principles generally accepted in the United States of America, the financial position of X Company as of December 31, 20X2, and 20X1, or the results of its operations or its cash flows for the years then ended.

DISCLAIMER OF OPINION

An auditor generally issues a disclaimer of opinion when the auditor has not been able to perform an audit sufficient in scope to enable expression of an opinion. Thus a disclaimer of opinion is appropriate whenever the auditor encounters a significant limitation on the scope of the audit. A disclaimer of opinion is not appropriate when the auditor believes that the financial statements contain one or more material departures from GAAP.

When disclaiming an opinion because of a scope limitation, the auditor should state in a separate paragraph the reasons why the audit did not comply with GAAS. In the final paragraph of the report (the disclaimer of opinion paragraph), the auditor should state that the scope of the audit was not sufficient to warrant the expression of an opinion. To prevent misleading readers, it is important to omit the scope paragraph from the report.

Sample Disclaimer of Opinion

Independent Auditor's Report

We were engaged to audit the accompanying balance sheets of X Company as of December 31, 20X2, and 20X1, and the related statements of income, retained earnings, and cash flows for the years then ended. These financial statements are the responsibility of the Company's management.

[Scope paragraph – omitted]

The Company did not make a count of its physical inventory in 20X2 or 20X1, stated in the accompanying financial statements at $_____as of December 31, 20X2, and at $_____as of December 31,20X1. Further, evidence supporting the cost of property and equipment acquired prior to December 31, 20X1, is no longer available. The Company's records do not permit the application of other auditing procedures to inventories or property and equipment.

Since the Company did not take physical inventories and we were not able to apply other auditing procedures to satisfy ourselves as to inventory quantities and the cost of property and equipment, the scope of our work was not sufficient to enable us to express, and we do not express, an opinion on these financial statements.

PIECEMEAL OPINIONS

An auditor should not express an opinion about certain identified items in financial statements if the auditor has issued a disclaimer of opinion or an adverse opinion on the financial statements as a whole.

REPORTS ON COMPARATIVE FINANCIAL STATEMENTS

A continuing auditor should update the report on prior periods that are presented on a comparative basis with the current period. The auditor's report on comparative financial statements ordinarily should be dated as of the date on which the auditor has obtained sufficient appropriate audit evidence for the most recent audit.

An auditor may express a qualified or adverse opinion, disclaim an opinion, or include an explanatory paragraph with respect to the financial statements for one or more periods while issuing a different report on the other financial statements presented.

CHANGE IN OPINION ON PRIOR PERIOD FINANCIAL STATEMENTS

An updated opinion may differ from a previous one, as in the case where an auditor previously expressed a qualified or adverse opinion because of a departure from GAAP and the prior period financial statements have been restated in the current period to conform to GAAP.

In the updated report, the auditor should disclose all the substantive reasons for the different opinion in one or more separate explanatory paragraphs of the report. The explanatory paragraphs, preceding the opinion paragraph, should disclose the original date of the auditor's report, the type of opinion previously expressed, the circumstances that caused the opinion to differ, and the fact that the updated opinion does differ from the one previously expressed.

Independent Auditor's Report

[Same introductory and scope paragraph as in the standard report]

In our report dated March 1, 20X2, we expressed an opinion that the 20X1 financial statements did not fairly present financial position, results of operations, and cash flows in conformity with accounting principles generally accepted in the United States of America because of two departures from such principles: (1) the Company carried its property, plant, and equipment at appraisal values, and provided for depreciation on the basis of such values, and (2) the Company did not provide for deferred income taxes with respect to differences between income for financial reporting purposes and taxable income. As described in Note X, the Company changed its method of accounting for these items and restated its 20X1 financial statements to conform with accounting principles generally accepted in the United States of America. Accordingly, our present opinion on the 20X1 financial statements, as presented herein, is different from that expressed in our previous report.

In our opinion, the financial statements referred to above present fairly, in all material respects, the financial position of X Company as of (at) December 31, 20X2 and 20X1, and the results of its operations and its cash flows for the years then ended in conformity with accounting principles generally accepted in the United States of America.

PREDECESSOR AUDITOR'S REPORT REISSUED

A predecessor auditor may reissue or consent to the reuse of a previously issued report on the financial statements of a prior period when they are to be presented on a comparative basis with audited financial statements of a later period. Before doing so, to determine whether or not the previous report is still appropriate, the predecessor auditor should proceed as follows:

1. Read the current period financial statements.
2. Compare the prior period financial statements with those to be presented comparatively.
3. Obtain a management letter from the former client that clearly states

    a. Whether management is aware of any information that would lead them to believe that any previous representations require modification, or
    b. Whether any events have occurred after the balance sheet date of the latest prior-period financial statements reported on by the predecessor that would necessitate adjustment to or disclosure in those financial statements.

4. Obtain a representation letter from the successor auditor that clearly states whether the audit performed by the successor revealed any matters that might have a material effect on, or require disclosure in, the prior period financial statements.

If the predecessor auditor feels that the report as previously issued requires revision, the auditor should exercise professional judgment in making inquiries and choosing procedures to apply. The reissued report should use the date of the previous report unless the report required revision or the financial statements required restatement, in which cases dual dating is appropriate.

REPORT OF PREDECESSOR AUDITOR NOT PRESENTED

When the predecessor's audit report is not presented, the successor should state in the introductory paragraph the following:

1. That another auditor audited the financial statements of the prior period.
2. The date of the predecessor's report.
3. The type of report issued by the predecessor.

4. The reasons for an other-than-standard report.

Sample Report When the Predecessor's Report Is Not Presented

Independent Auditor's Report

We have audited the accompanying balance sheet of ABC Company as of December 31, 20X2, and the related statements of income, retained earnings, and cash flows for the year then ended. These financial statements are the responsibility of the Company's management. Our responsibility is to express an opinion on these financial statements based on our audit. The financial statements of ABC Company as of December 31, 20X1, were audited by other auditors whose report, dated March 31, 20X2, expressed an unqualified opinion on those statements.

[Same scope paragraph as in the standard report]

In our opinion, the 20X2 financial statements referred to above present fairly, in all material respects, the financial position of ABC Company as of (at) December 31, 20X2, and the results of its operations and its cash flows for the year then ended in conformity with accounting principles generally accepted in the United States of America.

In the event that the predecessor auditor's report was other than the standard report, the introductory paragraph might be modified as follows:

...were audited by other auditors whose report dated March 31, 20X2, on those statements included an explanatory paragraph that described the change in the Company's method of computing depreciation discussed in Note X to the financial statements.

If prior-period financial statements have been restated, the introductory paragraph should state that a predecessor's auditor reported on the financial statements before they were restated. If the successor auditor audited the adjustments, the following explanatory paragraph is appropriate:

We also audited the adjustments described in Note X that were applied to restate the 20X1 financial statements. In our opinion, such adjustments are appropriate and have been properly applied.

AUDITING INTERPRETATIONS

REPORT OF OUTSIDE INVENTORY-TAKING FIRM AS AN ALTERNATIVE PROCEDURE FOR OBSERVING INVENTORIES (ISSUED IN JULY 1975; REVISED IN OCTOBER 2000)

Because a count of inventory by an outside firm alone is not an acceptable substitute for the observation and test-checking of some physical counts, the auditor should verify the effectiveness of the counting procedures used by the inventory-taking firm by

1. Observing the inventory-taking firm's procedures and controls,
2. Making or observing some physical counts,
3. Recomputing, on a test basis, calculations of the inventory submitted, and
4. Applying any appropriate tests to the intervening transactions.

REPORTING ON FINANCIAL STATEMENTS PREPARED ON A LIQUIDATION BASIS (ISSUED IN DECEMBER 1984; LATEST REVISION IN OCTOBER 2000)

An auditor may report on financial statements prepared on a liquidation basis of accounting. An unqualified opinion may be expressed if the liquidation basis of accounting has been properly applied and the client's financial statements include adequate disclosures.

REFERENCE IN AUDITOR'S STANDARD REPORT TO MANAGEMENT'S REPORT (ISSUED IN JANUARY 1989)

The auditor's report should make no reference to a report issued by management, commonly included in an annual shareholder's report that states that the financial statements are the responsibility of management.

REPORTING AS SUCCESSOR AUDITOR WHEN PRIOR PERIOD AUDITED FINANCIAL STATEMENTS WERE AUDITED BY A PREDECESSOR AUDITOR WHO HAS CEASED OPERATIONS (ISSUED IN NOVEMBER 2002)

If prior period financial statements audited by a predecessor auditor who has ceased operations are presented for comparative purposes with current period financial statements, the successor auditor should modify the audit report to state that the predecessor has ceased operations; for example

> The financial statements of ABC Company as of December 31, 20X1, and for the year then ended were audited by other auditors who have ceased operations. Those auditors expressed an unqualified opinion on those financial statements in their report dated March 31, 20X2.

REFERENCES TO PCAOB STANDARDS IN AN AUDIT REPORT OF A NONISSUER (ISSUED IN JUNE 2004)

If an audit was conducted in accordance with both generally accepted auditing standards and the auditing standards of the Public Company Accounting Oversight Board, the auditor may, but is not required to, indicate in the audit report the compliance with both sets of standards. The audit report modification may also indicate that the auditor's consideration of internal control was to design audit procedures and was not sufficient to express an opinion on the effectiveness of internal control. Under these circumstances, the auditor may choose to modify the scope paragraph of the audit report as follows:

> We conducted our audit in accordance with generally accepted auditing standards as established by the Auditing Standards Board (United States) and in accordance with the auditing Standards of the Public Company Accounting Oversight Board (United States). Those standards require that we plan and perform the audit to obtain reasonable assurance about whether the financial statements are free of material misstatement.
>
> The Company is not required to have, nor were we engaged to perform, an audit of its internal control over financial reporting. Our audit included consideration of internal control over financial reporting as a basis for designing audit procedures that are appropriate in the circumstances, but not for the purpose of expressing an opinion on the effectiveness of the Company's internal control over financial reporting. Accordingly, we express no such opinion.
>
> An audit also includes examining, on a test basis, evidence supporting the amounts and disclosures in the financial statements, assessing the accounting principles used and significant estimates made by management, as well as evaluating the overall financial statement presentation. We believe that our audit provides a reasonable basis for our opinion.

530 DATING OF THE INDEPENDENT AUDITOR'S REPORT

SOURCES OF STANDARDS

SAS 1, *Codification of Auditing Standards and Procedures*
SAS 29, *Reporting on Information Accompanying the Basic Financial Statements in Auditor-Submitted Documents*
SAS 98, *Omnibus Statement on Auditing Standards—2002*
SAS 103, *Audit Documentation*

SUMMARY

In general, the auditor's report should be dated no earlier than the date on which the auditor has obtained sufficient appropriate audit evidence to support the opinion. The auditor has no responsibility to make inquiries or apply auditing procedures after the date of the audit report.

EVENTS AFTER COMPLETION OF FIELDWORK BUT BEFORE REPORT ISSUANCE

If a subsequent event (see AU Section 560) requires an adjustment to the financial statements but that event has not been disclosed, the audit report should normally be dated in accordance with the general rule above.

If such an event occurs after the original date of the auditor's report but before the issuance of the related financial statements, and the event is disclosed, the auditor may date the audit report as of the date of the event (i.e., the later date). Alternatively, the auditor may dual-date the audit report. In dual dating, the first date is the date of the original report and the second the date of the event. For example

April 1, 200X, except for Note K, as to which the date is April 15, 200X.

If there is a subsequent event requiring financial statement adjustment and the financial statements are not adjusted as required by GAAP, the auditor should generally qualify the opinion. If the failure to adjust the financial statements could mislead the readers, the opinion should be an adverse opinion.

If a subsequent event requiring disclosure is disclosed, either in a note to the financial statements or in the auditor's report, dual-dating is appropriate. If the disclosure is not made, the auditor should qualify the opinion or express an adverse opinion if the financial statements are misleading. In either circumstance the auditor may use dual dating or date the report as of the subsequent event.

REISSUANCE OF THE INDEPENDENT AUDITOR'S REPORT

A reissued audit report should generally be dated with the date of the original report. Under most circumstances the auditor has no responsibility to make inquiries or otherwise investigate about events that might have occurred between the original report date and the date of reissuance.

However, an auditor who does become aware of an event that occurred between the original report date and the date of reissuance should consider the need for disclosure in the financial statements or adjustment of the financial statements. If the auditor concludes that either action is necessary and the client complies with GAAP, the auditor may dual-date the report or date it as of the event.

An event that requires disclosure only may be marked by using the caption "Event (Un-audited) subsequent to the Date of the Independent Auditor's Report." The audit report should be dated with the date of the original report.

532 RESTRICTING THE USE OF AN AUDITOR'S REPORT

SOURCE OF STANDARDS

SAS 87, *Restricting the Use of an Auditor's Report*

SUMMARY

This section provides guidance for circumstances when the auditor restricts the use of reports issued pursuant to Statements on Auditing Standards. The section defines both "general-use" and "restricted-use" reports and specifies language for restricted-use reports.

GENERAL-USE AND RESTRICTED-USE REPORTS

General-use reports are auditors' reports that are not restricted to specified parties. Audit reports that express an opinion on financial statements prepared in conformity with GAAP or another comprehensive basis of accounting ordinarily are for general use.

Restricted-use reports are intended only for specified parties. A report may be restricted as to use due to

1. The purpose of the report,
2. The nature of the procedures performed,
3. Its basis or the assumptions used,
4. The extent to which the procedures performed are known or understood, and
5. The possibility that the report might be misunderstood when taken out of the context in which it was intended to be used.

An auditor's report should be restricted in the following circumstances:

1. The subject matter of the report or the presentation being reported on is based on measurement or disclosure criteria set out in contracts or regulations not in conformity with GAAP or another comprehensive basis of accounting.
2. The report is a by-product of a financial statement audit; namely it is based on results of procedures designed to enable the expression of an opinion on the financial statements taken as a whole, not to provide assurance on the specific subject matter of the report (see AU Section 325, *Communication of Internal Control Related Matters Noted in an Audit*; AU Section 380, *Communication with Audit Committees*; and AU Section 623, *Special Reports*).

REPORTING AS A BY-PRODUCT OF A FINANCIAL STATEMENT AUDIT

The use of by-product reports should be restricted to the client's audit committee, board of directors, management, others within the organization, and specified regulatory agencies, and, for reports on compliance with contracts, to the parties to the agreement.

COMBINED REPORTS

Use of a single combined report should be restricted to specified parties when the report covers some subject matter or presentations that require a restriction on use to specified parties and some that ordinarily do not require a restriction.

INCLUDING A SEPARATE RESTRICTED-USE REPORT IN THE SAME DOCUMENT WITH A GENERAL-USE REPORT

When a separate restricted-use report is part of a document that also contains a general-use report, the restricted-use report continues to be restricted and the general-use report continues to be for general use.

ADDING SPECIFIED PARTIES

In connection with by-product reports, an auditor should not agree to add other parties after the engagement is completed or during the course of the engagement.

With respect to reports on subject matter or a presentation based on measurement or disclosure criteria contained in contracts or regulations, an auditor may add other specified parties but should first consider the identity of the other parties and the intended use of the report. An auditor who agrees to add other parties should obtain affirmative knowledge (ordinarily in writing) of their understanding of

1.   The nature of the engagement,
2.   The measurement or disclosure criteria used, and
3.   The report.

Adding other parties after a report is issued is permissible and may be accomplished by reissuing the report, using the original report date, or by providing other written acknowledgment that the other parties have been added as specified parties. The written acknowledgment should state that no procedures were performed after the date of the report.

LIMITING DISTRIBUTION OF REPORTS

Although an auditor is not responsible for controlling a client's distribution of restricted-use reports, the auditor should consider informing the client that such reports are not intended for distribution to nonspecified parties, regardless of whether they are part of a document that contains a separate general-use report.

REPORT LANGUAGE—RESTRICTED USE

The following elements should be included in a separate paragraph at the end of a restricted-use report:

1.   A statement that the report is intended solely for the information and use of the specified parties.
2.   Identification of the parties to whom use is restricted.
3.   A statement that the report is not intended to be and should not be used by anyone other than the specified parties.

Sample Restricted-Use Language

This report is intended solely for the information and use of [*the specified parties*] and is not intended to be and should not be used by anyone other than these specified parties.

534 REPORTING ON FINANCIAL STATEMENTS PREPARED FOR USE IN OTHER COUNTRIES

SOURCE OF STANDARDS

SAS 51, *Reporting on Financial Statements Prepared for Use in Other Countries*

SUMMARY

This section gives guidance for the auditor engaged to report on the financial statements of a US entity that have been prepared in conformity with the accounting principles of another country for use outside the United States. It specifically addresses reporting alternatives.

The section might apply when

1. A US auditor is asked to report on financial statements of one or more US entities for inclusion in the consolidated financial statements of a non-USA parent,
2. A US entity has one or more non-US investors, or
3. A US entity wishes to raise capital in another country.

PURPOSE AND USE OF FINANCIAL STATEMENTS

When an auditor is engaged to report on the financial statements of a US entity that have been prepared in conformity with the accounting principles of another country for use outside the United States, before issuing an audit report, the auditor should have a clear understanding of, and obtain written representations from management regarding the purpose and uses of the financial statements.

GENERAL AND FIELDWORK STANDARDS

When auditing financial statements prepared in conformity with accounting principles generally accepted in another country, the auditor should perform the procedures that are necessary to comply with the general and fieldwork standards of US GAAS. However, the auditing procedures generally performed under US GAAS may need to be modified, depending on the other country's accounting principles. For example, the auditor may have to apply procedures to test revaluation adjustments when the other country's accounting principles require that certain assets be revalued to reflect the effects of inflation.

The auditor should clearly understand the accounting principles on which the financial statements are based. This can be done by

1. Reading the statutes and professional literature of the other country,
2. Consulting with others who are expert in the relevant accounting principles, and

3. Considering the standards established by the International Accounting Standards Committee.

COMPLIANCE WITH AUDITING STANDARDS OF ANOTHER COUNTRY

An auditor who is asked to apply the auditing standards of another country, when reporting on financial statements prepared in conformity with accounting principles generally accepted in that country, should comply with the general and fieldwork standards of that country in addition to US GAAS. If unfamiliar with the auditing standards of the other country, the auditor should read the authoritative literature of the country that details the standards. If necessary, the auditor should consult with experts in the standards.

REPORTING STANDARDS IN GENERAL

If financial statements prepared in conformity with accounting principles generally accepted in another country are prepared for use only outside the United States, the auditor may report using either a US-style report modified to report on the accounting principles of another country or the report form of the other country. These options are also available when there is limited distribution of the financial statements to US parties such as banks and institutional investors that deal directly with the entity as a way to discuss differences from US accounting principles.

REPORTING STANDARDS: DUAL FINANCIAL STATEMENTS

Financial statements prepared in conformity with accounting principles generally accepted in another country ordinarily are not useful to US users. If financial statements are needed for use both in another country and within the United States, the auditor may therefore report on two sets of financial statements, one prepared in conformity with accounting principles generally accepted for use outside the United States and the other prepared in accordance with US GAAP. In these circumstances the auditor may wish to modify one or both of the audit reports by adding a statement that another report has been issued on the financial statements. For example

> We also have reported separately on the financial statements of International Company for the same period presented in accordance with accounting principles generally accepted in [*name of country*]. (The significant differences between the accounting principles accepted in [*name of country*] and those generally accepted in the United States are summarized in Note X.)

If dual statements are not prepared, or if the financial statements prepared in conformity with accounting principles generally accepted in another country will have more than limited distribution in the United States, the auditor should report on them using the US standard form of report, modified as appropriate for departures from US GAAP.

US-STYLE MODIFIED REPORT

A US-style report may be modified when reporting on financial statements prepared in conformity with accounting principles generally accepted in another country that are intended for use only outside the United States. The modified report should include the following:

1. A title that includes the word *independent*.
2. An introductory paragraph that

    a. States that the identified financial statements were audited;

  b. Refers to the note to the financial statements describing the basis of presentation on which the auditor is reporting, including the nationality of the accounting principles; and

  c. States that the financial statements are the responsibility of the company's management and that the auditor's responsibility is to express an opinion on the financial statements based on the audit.

3. A scope paragraph that includes statements that

  a. The audit was conducted in accordance with auditing standards generally accepted in the United States of America and, if appropriate, with the auditing standards of the other country;

  b. Those standards require that the auditor plan and perform the audit to obtain reasonable assurance about whether the financial statements are free of material misstatements;

  c. An audit includes examining, on a test basis, evidence supporting the amounts and disclosures in the financial statements; assessing the accounting principles used and significant estimates made by management; evaluating the overall presentation of the financial statement;

  d. The auditor believes that the audit provides a reasonable basis for an opinion.

4. An opinion paragraph that states whether the financial statements are presented fairly in all material respects, in conformity with the basis of accounting described. If, in the auditor's judgment, the financial statements are not presented fairly, all substantive reasons that led the auditor to this conclusion should be disclosed in an explanatory paragraph preceding the opinion paragraph and the opinion paragraph should be modified. The modified opinion paragraph should refer to the explanatory paragraph.

5. If comparative financial statements are being reported on, and there is a lack of consistency in the application of the basis of accounting that materially affects the comparability of the financial statements, an explanatory paragraph should be added after the opinion paragraph. The explanatory paragraph should describe the change in accounting principle and refer to the note to the financial statements that describes the change and its effects on the statements.

6. A signature of the auditor's firm, which may be manual or printed.

7. The date of the audit report (see AU Section 530).

Sample US-Style Modified Report

Independent Auditor's Report

  We have audited the accompanying balance sheet of International Company as of December 31, 20XX, and the related statements of income, retained earnings, and cash flows for the year then ended which, as described in Note X, have been prepared on the basis of accounting principles generally accepted in [*name of country*]. These financial statements are the responsibility of the Company's management. Our responsibility is to express an opinion on these financial statements based on our audit.

  We conducted our audit in accordance with auditing standards generally accepted in the United States of America and in [*name of country*]. US standards require that we plan and perform the audit to obtain reasonable assurance about whether the financial statements are free of material misstatements. An audit includes examining, on a test basis, evidence supporting the amounts and disclosures in the financial statements. An audit also includes assessing the accounting principles used and significant estimates made by management, as well as evaluating the overall presentation of the financial statements. We believe that our audit provides a reasonable basis for our opinion.

In our opinion, the financial statements referred to above present fairly, in all material respects, the financial position of International Company as of (at) December 31, 20XX, and the results of its operations and its cash flows for the year then ended in conformity with accounting principles generally accepted in the [*name of country*].

REPORT FORM OF ANOTHER COUNTRY

As an alternative to using a modified US-style report, an auditor may use the standard report of another country if

1. Such a report would be used by the auditors in the other country under similar circumstances,
2. The auditor understands and is in a position to make the attestations contained in the report, and
3. The report identifies the other country if the auditor believes there is a risk that readers might misunderstand either the report or the financial statements because of their resemblance to those prepared in conformity with standards of the United States.

When using the standard report of another country, the auditor should be careful to comply with the reporting standards of the other country. The auditor should be aware that the audit report of the other country, even if similar in appearance to a US-style report, may suggest a different meaning and therefore require a different responsibility due to culture or custom. The auditor might also be required to provide explicit or implicit assurance of compliance with the law or otherwise require understanding of local law. Accordingly, the auditor needs to understand the auditor's legal responsibilities and should consider the need to consult with persons experienced in the audit reporting practices of the other country.

USE IN THE UNITED STATES

When reporting on financial statements prepared in conformity with accounting principles generally accepted in another country that will have more than limited distribution in the United States, the auditor should issue a US-style report that contains a qualified opinion or an adverse opinion if there is any departure from GAAP. The auditor may add an explanatory paragraph expressing an opinion on whether the financial statements are in conformity with the accounting principles of the other country.

AUDITING INTERPRETATION

FINANCIAL STATEMENTS FOR GENERAL USE ONLY OUTSIDE THE UNITED STATES IN ACCORDANCE WITH INTERNATIONAL ACCOUNTING STANDARDS AND INTERNATIONAL STANDARDS ON AUDITING (ISSUED IN MAY 1996)

An auditor practicing in the United States is permitted to report on the financial statements of a US entity prepared in conformity with International Accounting Standards for general use only outside the United States. The auditor should follow (1) the general and fieldwork standards under US GAAS and (2) any additional requirements of the International Standards on Auditing. The audit report may be in the form of a US-style report or the report specified in the International Standards.

543 PART OF AUDIT PERFORMED BY OTHER INDEPENDENT AUDITORS

SOURCES OF STANDARDS

SAS 1, *Codification of Auditing Standards and Procedures*
SAS 64, *Omnibus Statement on Auditing Standards—1990*

SUMMARY

This section provides guidance to help a principal auditor make a decision whether to use the work and reports of other auditors. It also describes the procedures to be performed and the reporting standards to be followed when part of the audit is performed by another auditor.

PRINCIPAL AUDITOR'S COURSE OF ACTION

An auditor may be engaged to report on an entity's financial statements when other auditors have audited the financial statements of one or more subsidiaries, divisions, branches, components, or investments included in the financial statements to be reported on.

In these circumstances, the auditor must decide whether he can serve as the principal auditor and issue a report on the financial statements. The decision should be based on (1) the materiality of the financial statement components audited, (2) how much the auditor knows about the financial statements to be reported on, and (3) the relative importance of the component he audited.

An auditor who decides to serve as the principal auditor must next decide whether or not to refer in the audit report to the work performed by the other auditor. If the principal auditor decides to assume responsibility for the work of the other auditor, no reference should be made. If, however, the principal auditor decides not to assume that responsibility, his report should refer to both (1) the work of the other auditor and (2) the division of responsibility.

DECISION NOT TO MAKE REFERENCE

A principal auditor may decide not to refer to the work of another auditor if the auditor is satisfied as to the other auditor's independence, reputation, and audit work. That decision is generally appropriate in the following circumstances:

1. There is an association between the principal auditor and the other auditor.
2. The principal auditor engaged and supervised the other auditor.
3. The principal auditor reviewed the work of the other auditor and was satisfied with the work.
4. The portion of the financial statements audited by the other auditor is not material in relation to the financial statements taken as a whole.

DECISION TO MAKE REFERENCE

If the principal auditor decides to refer to the work of the other auditor, the audit report should make the division of responsibility clear in the introductory, scope, and opinion paragraphs. The introductory paragraph should also indicate the magnitude of the portion of the financial statements audited by the other auditor. Magnitude may be expressed as dollar amounts or percentages of total assets and total revenues. The name of the other auditor may be disclosed in the introductory paragraph only if the other auditor's permission has been given and the other auditor's report is presented along with the report of the principal auditor. Reference to the other auditor should not be interpreted as a qualification of the audit report.

Sample Language for Reference to Another Auditor

A sample report to be used when the principal auditor decides to make reference to the work of another auditor is presented below.

Independent Auditor's Report

We have audited the consolidated balance sheet of X Company and subsidiaries as of December 31, 20XX, and the related consolidated statements of Income, retained earnings, and cash flows for the year then ended. These financial statements are the responsibility of the Company's management. Our responsibility is to express an opinion on these financial statements based on our audit. We did not audit the financial statements of B Company, a wholly-owned subsidiary, which statements reflect total assets and revenues constituting 20% and 22%, respectively, of the related consolidated totals. Those statements were audited by other auditors whose report thereon has been furnished to us, and our opinion expressed herein, insofar as it relates to the amounts included for B Company, is based solely on the report of the other auditors.

We conducted our audit in accordance with auditing standards generally accepted in the United States of America. Those standards require that we plan and perform the audit to obtain reasonable assurance about whether the financial statements are free of material misstatements. An audit includes examining, on a test basis, evidence supporting the amounts and disclosures in the financial statements. An audit also includes assessing the accounting principles used and significant estimates made by management, as well as evaluating the overall financial statement presentation. We believe that our audit and the report of the other auditors provide a reasonable basis for our opinion.

In our opinion, based on our audit and the report of the other auditors, the consolidated financial statements referred to above present fairly in all material respects, the financial position of X Company as of (at) December 31, 20XX, and the results of its operations and its cash flows for the year then ended in conformity with accounting principles generally accepted in the United States of America.

PROCEDURES APPLYING WHETHER OR NOT ANOTHER AUDITOR IS REFERRED TO

The following procedures apply whether or not the principal auditor decides to refer to the other auditor:

1. Determine the professional reputation and independence of the other auditor by contacting the American Institute of Certified Public Accountants, state and local societies of CPAs, other CPAs, and bankers.
2. Obtain a representation letter from the other auditor that clearly indicates the auditor's independence.
3. Communicate with the other auditor to ensure that the auditor

   a.   Is aware that the financial statements that he audited will be included in the statements to be reported on by the principal auditor and that the other auditor's report will be relied upon.

   b.   Is familiar with accounting principles and auditing standards generally accepted in the United States of America.

4.   Coordinate the activities of the other auditor to ensure proper review of items affecting the consolidation or combination of financial statement accounts.

ADDITIONAL PROCEDURES WHEN NO REFERENCE TO ANOTHER AUDITOR IS MADE

The principal auditor who decides not to refer to the work of the other auditor should consider performing one or more of the following additional procedures:

1.   Visit the other auditor to discuss audit procedures and the results.
2.   Review the audit programs of the other auditor.
3.   Review the other auditor's documentation (working papers).
4.   Discuss with management financial statement components audited by the other auditor.

The principal auditor may conclude that supplemental tests of accounts included in the financial statements reported on by the other auditor are necessary.

DEPARTURE OF OTHER AUDITOR'S REPORT FROM STANDARD REPORT

If the other auditor's report is not standard, the principal auditor should determine how significant the departure is to the financial statements the principal auditor is reporting on. If the reason for the departure is not significant and the other auditor's report is not presented, the principal auditor should not refer to the departure in the audit report.

If the reason for the departure is significant and the other auditor's report is presented, the principal auditor may, but is not required to, refer to the departure and its disposition in the audit report.

AUDITING INTERPRETATIONS

SPECIFIC PROCEDURES PERFORMED BY THE OTHER AUDITOR AT THE PRINCIPAL AUDITOR'S REQUEST (ISSUED IN APRIL 1979 AND REVISED IN NOVEMBER 1996)

The principal auditor is responsible for providing instructions on procedures, materiality guidelines, and other pertinent information to the other auditor when the principal auditor asks the other auditor to perform specific procedures. The other auditor should perform the requested procedures based on the information furnished and report his findings solely for the use of the principal auditor.

544 LACK OF CONFORMITY WITH GENERALLY ACCEPTED ACCOUNTING PRINCIPLES

SOURCE OF STANDARDS

SAS 1, *Codification of Auditing Standards and Procedures*

SUMMARY

This section applies to regulated companies, which may be defined as entities whose accounting policies and practices are prescribed by a governmental regulatory authority. Among these are public utilities and insurance companies. This section discusses the reporting requirements for regulated companies that prepare financial statements that conform to the accounting principles of the regulatory body but that depart from GAAP when the financial statements are presented to parties other than the regulatory body.

RULES OF REPORTING

When the financial statements of a regulated entity are to be presented only to a regulatory body and the financial statements conform to the accounting principles of the regulatory body (a comprehensive basis of accounting other than GAAP), the auditor should issue a special report as defined in AU Section 623.

When the financial statements of a regulated entity are to be presented to parties other than a regulatory body and they conform to the accounting principles of the regulatory body but depart from GAAP, the auditor should generally express a qualified or an adverse opinion. In addition to the explanatory language necessary for a qualified or an adverse opinion, the auditor may, but is not required to, include a paragraph expressing an opinion on whether the financial statements conform to the prescribed basis of accounting.

550 OTHER INFORMATION IN DOCUMENTS CONTAINING AUDITED FINANCIAL STATEMENTS

SOURCES OF STANDARDS

SAS 8, *Other Information in Documents Containing Audited Financial Statements*
SAS 98, *Omnibus Statement on Auditing Standards—2002*

SUMMARY

This section describes the auditor's responsibilities when other information is included in documents that contain the audited financial statements and the auditor's report. Such documents might be annual reports to holders of securities or beneficial interests, annual reports of charitable or philanthropic entities, and annual filings required by the Securities Exchange Act of 1934. The section does not apply to (1) registration statements filed pursuant to the Securities Act of 1933 and (2) engagements to express an opinion on the other information (see AU Sections 551 and 623).

PROCEDURES TO APPLY

1. The auditor should read the other information in the document to determine whether it is consistent with the financial statements but is under no obligation to corroborate it. If the auditor determines that there are material inconsistencies between the audited financial statements and the other information, the auditor should determine whether the financial statements or the audit report needs to be revised. If neither requires revision, the auditor should ask that the client revise the additional information. If the client fails to revise the additional information, the auditor should consider

   a. Adding an explanatory paragraph to the audit report in which the material inconsistency is clearly described (the opinion in the audit report does not need to be modified),
   b. Withholding use of the report in the document, or
   c. Withdrawing from the engagement.

2. An auditor who identifies a material misstatement of fact rather than just a material inconsistency should consider that

   a. The matter might need to be discussed with the client,
   b. The auditor may lack the expertise necessary to assess the validity of the fact,
   c. There may be a lack of standards by which to assess its presentation,
   d. There may be valid differences of judgment or opinion,

e. The client might be well advised to seek legal advice,

f. The auditor's concerns should be communicated to the client in writing, and

g. The auditor should perhaps consult with his own legal counsel.

AUDITING INTERPRETATIONS

REPORTS BY MANAGEMENT ON INTERNAL CONTROL OVER FINANCIAL REPORTING (ISSUED IN MAY 1994; REVISED IN JANUARY 2001)

If the other information is in the form of an assertion by management about the effectiveness of internal controls over financial reporting and the auditor has been engaged to examine and report on the assertion, the auditor should follow the guidance in AU Section 501, *Reporting on an Entity's Internal Control over Financial Reporting.*

If the auditor has not been engaged to examine and report on it, the management assertion should be treated as "other information" and the auditor should apply the procedures discussed in AU Section 550.

At the auditor's discretion, the following paragraph may be added to the standard report:

> We were not engaged to examine management's assertion about the effectiveness of [*name of entity*] internal control over financial reporting as of [*date*] included in the accompanying [*title of management's report*] and, accordingly, do not express an opinion thereon.

OTHER REFERENCES BY MANAGEMENT TO INTERNAL CONTROL OVER FINANCIAL REPORTING, INCLUDING REFERENCES TO THE INDEPENDENT AUDITOR (ISSUED IN MAY 1994; REVISED IN JANUARY 2001)

Besides following the general guidance already discussed, the auditor should determine whether management's reference to the auditor would lead a reader to conclude that the auditor

1. Performed more work than is required in an audit of financial statements,

2. Is providing assurance about the effectiveness of internal control over financial reporting, or

3. Is more involved than is supported by the facts. The auditor may therefore conclude that there is a material misstatement of fact.

If the auditor has been engaged simply to audit the financial statements but not to examine and report on management's assertion about the effectiveness of internal control over financial reporting, the other information should not refer to the auditor's communication that there are no material weaknesses in internal control. Any such reference would necessitate

1. Requesting that management omit the reference,

2. Advising management that the auditor has not consented to the use of the auditor's name, and

3. Considering other actions, such as consulting with legal counsel.

OTHER INFORMATION IN ELECTRONIC SITES CONTAINING AUDITED FINANCIAL STATEMENTS (ISSUED IN MARCH 1997; REVISED IN JANUARY 2001)

Electronic sites (e.g., World Wide Web area of the internet, electronic bulletin boards, the SEC's EDGAR system) are not "documents." They are means of distributing information, including documents. With respect to other information contained in electronic sites, the auditor does not have to apply any of the procedures described in this section.

551 REPORTING ON INFORMATION ACCOMPANYING THE BASIC FINANCIAL STATEMENTS IN AUDITOR-SUBMITTED DOCUMENTS

SOURCES OF STANDARDS

SAS 29, *Reporting on Information Accompanying the Basic Financial Statements in Auditor-Submitted Documents*
SAS 98, *Omnibus Statement on Auditing Standards—2002*

SUMMARY

This section offers guidance for when an auditor submits to a client or others a document containing the financial statements and other information (client representations) outside the basic financial statements. Examples of such information are additional details or explanations of items related to the financial statements (e.g., schedules of expenses by cost center), consolidating information, historical summaries derived from the financial statements (e.g., a presentation detailing trend analysis), statistical data, and other data that may be from sources outside the accounting system or outside the entity. The general rule requires that the auditor report on all client representations in the document.

REPORTING RESPONSIBILITY

An auditor must report on all information in auditor-submitted documents. (An auditor's responsibilities are different when the audit report is included in a client-prepared document; see AU Section 550.)

The auditor's report must conform to the following guidelines:

1. State that the purpose of the audit was to report on the basic financial statements.
2. Identify the accompanying information.
3. State that the accompanying information is for purposes of analysis and is not a required part of the basic financial statements.
4. Either express an opinion on whether the accompanying information is stated fairly, in all material respects, in relation to the financial statements taken as a whole, or disclaim an opinion. (Partial opinions and disclaimers for different portions of the information are permissible.)

Misstated accompanying information should be discussed with and revised by the client. If the revision is not made, the auditor should modify his report or refuse to include the information in the document.

STANDARD REPORTING OPTIONS

The report on the accompanying information may be added to the auditor's standard report after the opinion paragraph or may be presented elsewhere in an auditor-submitted document. The following illustrates the appropriate wording for both reporting options.

Sample Language on Accompanying Information

Our audit was conducted for the purpose of forming an opinion on the financial statements taken as a whole. The [*identify the accompanying information*] is presented for purposes of additional analysis and is not a required part of the basic financial statements. The information has been subjected to the procedures applied in the audit of the financial statements and, in our opinion, is fairly stated in all material respects in relation to the financial statements taken as a whole.

DISCLAIMING AN OPINION

The auditor may disclaim an opinion on all or part of the accompanying information. In either circumstance, the auditor should mark the information as "unaudited." Alternatively, the auditor may refer to it in the disclaimer of opinion. The form of the disclaimer will vary, depending on whether it applies to all or only part of the accompanying information.

Disclaimer on All Accompanying Information

Our audit was conducted for the purpose of forming an opinion on the basic financial statements taken as a whole. The [*identify the accompanying information*] is presented for purposes of additional analysis and is not a required part of the basic financial statements. Such information has not been subjected to the auditing procedures applied in the audit of the basic financial statements, and, accordingly, we express no opinion on it.

Disclaimer on Part of the Accompanying Information

Our audit was conducted for the purpose of forming an opinion on the basic financial statements taken as a whole. The information on pages XX-YY is presented for purposes of additional analysis and is not a required part of the basic financial statements. Such information, except for that portion marked "unaudited," on which we express no opinion, has been subjected to the auditing procedures applied in the audit of the basic financial statements; and, in our opinion, the information is fairly stated in all material respects in relation to the basic financial statements taken as a whole.

WHEN THE OPINION ON THE BASIC FINANCIAL STATEMENTS IS QUALIFIED

If a qualified opinion is rendered on the basic financial statements, the effect on the accompanying information should be made clear in an explanatory paragraph.

Sample Explanatory Paragraph

Our audit was conducted for the purpose of forming an opinion on the basic financial statements taken as a whole. The schedules of investments (page XX) and property (page YY) as of December 31, 20XX, are presented for purposes of additional analysis and are not a required part of the basic financial statements. The information in these schedules has been subjected to the auditing procedures applied in the audit of the basic financial statements, and, in our opinion, except for the effects of the schedule of investments not accounting for the investments in certain companies by the equity method as explained in the second preceding paragraph (second paragraph of our report on page 1), such information is fairly stated in all material respects in relation to the basic financial statements taken as a whole.

SUPPLEMENTARY INFORMATION REQUIRED BY GAAP

If supplementary information required by US GAAP is presented outside the basic financial statements, the auditor should disclaim any opinion thereon unless specifically engaged to do so.

Sample Disclaimer on Supplementary Information

The [*identify the supplementary information*] on page XX is not a required part of the basic financial statements but is supplementary information required by accounting principles generally accepted in the United States of America. We have applied certain limited procedures, which consisted principally of inquiries of management regarding the methods of measurement and presentation of the supplementary information. However, we did not audit the information and express no opinion on it.

If the auditor concludes that the supplementary information required by US GAAP is omitted or departs from GAAP, or the auditor encounters a scope limitation with respect to the supplementary information, the auditor should follow the guidelines in AU Section 558, *Required Supplementary Information*.

CONSOLIDATING INFORMATION

An auditor who is engaged to express an opinion only on consolidated statements but consolidating information is also presented should verify that the consolidating information is suitably identified.

If the consolidating information has not been audited, the auditor might phrase the report as follows:

Our audit was conducted for the purpose of forming an opinion on the consolidated financial statements taken as a whole. The consolidating information is presented for purposes of additional analysis of the consolidated financial statements rather than to present the financial position, results of operations, and cash flows of the individual companies. The consolidating information has been subjected to the auditing procedures applied in the audit of the consolidated financial statements and, in our opinion, is fairly stated in all material respects in relation to the consolidated financial statements taken as a whole.

ADDITIONAL COMMENTARY ABOUT THE AUDIT

Typical other information might be a description of the audit procedures applied to specific financial statement items. The description should not contradict or detract from the auditor's standard audit report and be separated from the accompanying information, not interspersed with it.

COEXISTING FINANCIAL STATEMENTS

An auditor needs to be satisfied that "accompanying information" in an auditor-submitted document would not lead a reader to conclude that the basic financial statements in a client-prepared document depart from GAAP.

552 REPORTING ON CONDENSED FINANCIAL STATEMENTS AND SELECTED FINANCIAL DATA

SOURCES OF STANDARDS

SAS 42, *Reporting on Condensed Financial Statements and Selected Financial Data*
SAS 100, *Interim Financial Information*

SUMMARY

This section deals with reporting in a client-prepared document on condensed financial statements derived from the audited financial statements of a public entity; and selected financial data derived from audited financial statements of either a public or a nonpublic entity presented in a document that includes audited financial statements.

CONDENSED FINANCIAL STATEMENTS

Because condensed financial statements do not constitute fair presentation under GAAP, to avoid misleading users, the auditor should not report on them in the same way as on the complete financial statements. It is further recommended that condensed statements be marked as such. The auditor's report should indicate

1. That the financial statements were audited and that the auditor expressed an opinion on the complete set of financial statements,
2. The date thereof,
3. The type of opinion expressed, and
4. An opinion as to whether the condensed financial statements are fairly stated in all material respects in relation to the complete financial statements from which they were derived.

Sample Auditor's Report on Condensed Financial Statements

Independent Auditor's Report

We have audited, in accordance with auditing standards generally accepted in the United States of America, the consolidated balance sheet of X Company and subsidiaries as of December 31, 20X3, and the related consolidated statements of income, retained earnings, and cash flows for the year then ended (not presented herein); and in our report dated February 15, 20X4, we expressed an unqualified opinion on those consolidated financial statements.

In our opinion, the information set forth in the accompanying condensed financial statements is fairly stated, in all material respects, in relation to the consolidated financial statements from which it has been derived.

If a statement in a client-prepared document names the auditor and states that the condensed financial statements have been derived from audited financial statements, the auditor is not required to report on the condensed financial statements if the document either (1) includes audited financial statements or (2) incorporates the statements by reference to information filed with a regulatory agency.

However, the auditor should not permit his or her name to be used, or should include a report on the condensed financial statements, if (1) the client-prepared document does not include audited financial statements or fails to incorporate them by reference to information filed with a regulatory agency, and (2) the company is a publicly traded entity subject to annual filing requirements.

INTERIM INFORMATION

If condensed financial statements are presented for comparative purposes with reviewed interim financial information of a subsequent period, the report on the condensed financial statements may be combined with the report on the reviewed financial information.

SELECTED FINANCIAL DATA

The entity's management is responsible for determining the specific financial data presented. An auditor engaged to report on those data should limit the report to data derived from audited financial statements. If a combination of audited and other information (e.g., number of employees) is presented, the report should identify the data on which the auditor is reporting. The auditor's report should indicate

1. That the financial statements were audited and that the auditor expressed an opinion on the complete financial statements,
2. The date thereof,
3. The type of opinion expressed, and
4. An opinion as to whether the selected financial data are fairly stated in all material respects in relation to the complete financial statements from which they were derived.

The report on selected financial data is generally presented as a paragraph added to the auditor's standard report after the opinion paragraph:

> We have also previously audited, in accordance with auditing standards generally accepted in the United States of America, the consolidated balance sheets as of December 31, 20X3, 20X2, and 20X1, and the related statements of income, retained earnings, and cash flows for the years ended December 31, 20X2, and 20X1 (none of which are presented herein); and we expressed unqualified opinions on those consolidated financial statements. In our opinion, the information set forth in the selected financial data for each of the five years in the period ended December 31, 20X5, appearing on page xx, is fairly stated, in all material respects, in relation to the consolidated financial statements from which it is derived.

If a statement in a client-prepared document names the auditor and states that the selected financial data have been derived from audited financial statements, the auditor is not required to report on the selected financial data if the document either includes audited financial statements or incorporates the statements by reference to information filed with a regulatory agency.

However, the auditor should not permit the auditor's name to be used or should include a disclaimer of opinion on the selected financial data if the client-prepared document does not include audited financial statements or fails to incorporate the statements by reference to information filed with a regulatory agency, and if the company is a publicly traded entity subject to annual filing requirements.

558 REQUIRED SUPPLEMENTARY INFORMATION

SOURCES OF STANDARDS

SAS 52, *Required Supplementary Information*
SAS 98, *Omnibus Statement on Auditing Standards—2002*

SUMMARY

This section provides guidance in connection with the procedures the auditor should apply to supplementary information required by GAAP when the auditor is not engaged to audit such information. This section also applies to documents a client voluntarily includes as a supplement to the financial statements or in an unaudited note to the statements certain information that is not required of the reporting entity but is required of other entities.

However, this section does not apply when the entity indicates that procedures described in this section have not been applied or the auditor in the audit report has a paragraph disclaiming an opinion on the supplementary information. When the auditor does not apply the procedures described in this section to a voluntary presentation, the auditor should follow AU Section 550, *Other Information Included in Documents Containing Audited Financial Statements*.

INVOLVEMENT WITH INFORMATION OUTSIDE BASIC FINANCIAL STATEMENTS

In general, an auditor is not required to audit information that is outside the basic financial statements. If the auditor must submit to a client or another party a document that includes information outside the basic financial statements that is not required supplementary information, the auditor should follow AU Section 551, *Reporting on Information Accompanying the Basic Financial Statements in Auditor-Submitted Documents*.

The auditor's responsibility for required supplementary information is specified in this section and discussed below.

INVOLVEMENT WITH REQUIRED SUPPLEMENTARY INFORMATION

Required supplementary information is information that FASB, GASB, or FASAB considers essential to the reporting process of certain entities. In these cases the auditor must

1. Consider whether supplementary information is required,
2. Apply certain limited procedures if it is, and
3. Report deficiencies in, or omissions of, the required supplementary information.

APPLICATION OF PROCEDURES

An auditor who concludes that supplementary information is required should proceed as follows:

1. Inquire of management about

    a. Whether it measured and presented the required information within GAAP guidelines,
    b. Any changes, and reasons therefor, in measurement or presentation, and
    c. Significant assumptions or interpretations on which measurement or presentation is based.

2. For consistency, compare the required information with

    a. Management's responses to the auditor's inquiries,
    b. The audited financial statements, and
    c. Other relevant information obtained during the audit.

3. Determine whether representations concerning the required supplementary information need to be included in the management representation letter (see AU Section 333).
4. Apply other procedures required by relevant pronouncements.
5. Make additional inquiries if, based on use of the procedures mentioned, the auditor believes that the required supplementary information is not measured or presented properly.

Reporting Requirements

Because supplementary information is not considered a required part of basic financial statements, it is not audited, so it is not necessary for the auditor to add an explanatory paragraph referring to the information to the report on the audited financial statements unless

1. Though required, the information is omitted,
2. The information materially departs from GAAP guidelines,
3. The auditor cannot complete the procedures relating to the method of preparation and consistency, or
4. The auditor has substantial doubt about whether the information conforms to prescribed guidelines. Addition of an explanatory paragraph has no effect on the auditor's opinion on fairness of presentation of the financial statements in conformity with GAAP. If the required supplementary information is omitted, the auditor has no responsibility to present it.

The explanatory paragraph will vary depending on the circumstances

Omission of Required Supplementary Information

The [*company or governmental unit*] has not presented [*describe the supplementary information required by (1) GAAP or (2) the body requiring the information*] that accounting principles generally accepted in the United States of America has determined is necessary to supplement, although not required to be part of, the basic financial statements.

Material Departures from GAAP Guidelines

The [*specifically identify the supplementary information*] on page XX is not a required part of the basic financial statements, and we did not audit and do not express an opinion on such information. However, we have applied certain limited procedures, which consisted principally of inquiries of management regarding the methods of measurement and presentation of the supplementary information. As a result of such limited procedures, we believe that the [*specifically identify the supplementary information*] is not in conformity with accounting principles generally accepted in the United States of America because [*describe the material departure(s) from the (1) GAAP or (2) the body requiring the information*].

Prescribed Procedures Not Completed

The [*specifically identify the supplementary information*] on page XX is not a required part of the basic financial statements, and we did not audit and do not express an opinion on such information. Further, we were unable to apply to the information certain procedures prescribed by professional standards because [*state the reasons*].

Substantial Doubt about Adherence to Prescribed Guidelines

The [*specifically identify the supplementary information*] on page XX is not a required part of the basic financial statements, and we did not audit and do not express an opinion on such information. However, we have applied certain limited procedures prescribed by professional standards that raised doubts that we were unable to resolve regarding whether material modifications should be made to the information for it to conform with guidelines established by accounting principles generally accepted in the United States. [*The auditor should consider including in the report the reason(s) why these substantial doubts could not be resolved.*]

Additional Reporting Considerations

Even if the auditor cannot complete the prescribed procedures discussed, the auditor should suggest that the client revise the required supplementary information if it is clear that the measurement or presentation of the information does not conform with prescribed guidelines.

If the auditor has subjected the required supplementary information to auditing procedures sufficient to express an opinion on the fairness of its presentation, the report on the basic financial statements may be expanded to cover the supplementary information (see AU Section 550).

The auditor's report on the basic financial statements should include an opinion or a disclaimer of opinion on the supplementary information if the client includes with the supplementary information an indication that the auditor performed any procedures related to the information and if the client fails to indicate that the auditor does not express an opinion on the information.

Finally, if required supplementary information is included in the basic financial statements (possibly as a note to the financial statements), the auditor should disclaim an opinion on the information unless it is clearly marked as "unaudited."

560 SUBSEQUENT EVENTS

SOURCESOF STANDARDS

SAS 1, *Codification of Auditing Standards and Procedures*
SAS 12, *Inquiry of a Client's Lawyer Concerning Litigation, Claims, and Assessments*
SAS 98, *Omnibus Statement on Auditing Standards—2002*
SAS 113, *Omnibus Statement on Auditing Standards—2006*

SUMMARY

Subsequent events may be defined as events or transactions that materially affect the financial statements that occur after the balance sheet date but before the issuance of the financial statements. Subsequent events therefore require adjustment or disclosure in the financial statements.

TYPES OF SUBSEQUENT EVENTS

There are two basic types of subsequent events:

1. Subsequent events requiring adjustment (type I) are those events that

    a. Provide additional evidence about conditions that existed at the balance sheet date, and
    b. Affect estimates included in the financial statements.

    Among such events are events that affect the realization of assets or the settlement of estimated liabilities; they are generally the culmination of conditions that existed over a relatively long period of time. Examples of type I subsequent events are settlement of litigation for an amount materially different from the amount listed in the financial statements as an accrued liability or a loss on an uncollectible account receivable due to the customer's bankruptcy after the balance sheet date.

2. Subsequent events requiring disclosure (type II) are those events that

    a. Provide evidence relating to conditions that did not exist at the balance-sheet date,
    b. Arose after the balance sheet date, and
    c. Might render the financial statements misleading if not disclosed.

    Type II subsequent events usually result from something sudden. Examples of type II subsequent events are

    (1) Destruction of inventory or plant assets as a result of a flood, fire, or earthquake;
    (2) Purchase of a business;
    (3) Sale of a debt or equity issue;

(4) Loss on an uncollectible trade account receivable as a result of a customer's sudden financial deterioration; and

(5) Settlement of a lawsuit that arose after the balance-sheet date. Sometimes the event is so material that the auditor may wish to discuss it in a separate paragraph of the audit report.

AUDITING PROCEDURES IN THE SUBSEQUENT PERIOD

The subsequent period may be defined as the time period between the balance-sheet date and the issuance of the audit report. At or near the date of the auditor's report, the auditor should perform the following procedures:

1. Examine data for proper cutoffs.
2. Review the latest available interim financial statements to see if they have been prepared on the same basis as the audited financial statements were.
3. Ask officers and other executives who have financial statement and accounting oversight about

   a. Substantial contingent liabilities or commitments;
   b. Significant changes in capital stock, long-term debt, or working capital;
   c. Current status of items previously accounted for on a tentative or preliminary basis or based on inconclusive data; and
   d. Unusual adjustments made during the subsequent-events period.

4. Review the minutes of meetings of directors, stockholders, and relevant committees.
5. Ask the client's legal counsel about litigation, claims, and assessments (see AU Section 337).
6. Obtain a management representation letter (see AU Section 333) ensuring that information relevant to subsequent events is included.
7. To eliminate any questions resulting from these procedures, make additional inquiries or perform any additional procedures deemed necessary.

561 SUBSEQUENT DISCOVERY OF FACTS EXISTING AT THE DATE OF THE AUDITOR'S REPORT

SOURCES OF STANDARDS

SAS 1, *Subsequent Discovery of Facts Existing at the Date of the Auditor's Report*
SAS 98, *Omnibus Statement on Auditing Standards—2002*

SUMMARY

This section comes into play when the auditor, after the date of the audit report, becomes aware of facts that may have existed at the date of the report that might have affected it had he been aware of them. As a protective measure the auditor should consult with legal counsel if circumstances covered by this section are identified. Unless the auditor becomes aware of new information that may affect the report, the auditor is not required to perform any procedures or make additional inquiries after the date of the audit report.

WHEN ACTION IS NECESSARY

The auditor should determine the existence and reliability of the facts at the date of his report. The auditor should take further action if

1. The audit report would have been affected had the auditor known about the facts at the audit-report date, and
2. The auditor believes that persons in possession of the financial statements would attach importance to the facts.

TYPE OF ACTION

There are a number of options available to the auditor who learns of such facts:

1. Advise the client to make appropriate disclosure to actual and potential users of the financial statements.
2. Consider issuing revised financial statements accompanied by a revised audit report.
3. If the issuance of subsequent period financial statements is imminent, as an alternative to item 2, ensure that suitable disclosure is made in those financial statements.
4. If the effects on the financial statements will take time to determine, the auditor should advise the client to notify actual or potential users that

   a. They should not rely on the financial statements and the related audit report, and
   b. Revised financial statements and an auditor's report will follow after the matter is thoroughly investigated.

5. If the client refuses to make the necessary disclosures, the auditor should

    a. Notify the client that the audit report no longer holds; and
    b. Undertake to notify all actual and potential users, including regulatory bodies, that the audit report should not be relied on.

CONTENT OF AUDITOR DISCLOSURE

If the auditor determines that the information affecting the financial statements is reliable and the client refuses to make the appropriate disclosure, the auditor's disclosure should describe the effect the information would have had on the audit report had the auditor been aware of it before issuing the audit report. Appropriate disclosure would include a description of the subsequently identified information and its likely effects on the financial statements. The auditor should be careful to ensure that the disclosure is precise and factual; it should not include comments about any person's motives or conduct.

If a client does not make the necessary disclosures and refuses to cooperate in the investigation, the auditor may not be able to perform a satisfactory audit. In that case the auditor need not disclose the specific information but can simply indicate that information has come to the auditor's attention that cannot be substantiated because the client has not cooperated. The auditor should consider disclosing the belief that if the information is true, the audit report should no longer be relied on or associated with the financial statements.

AUDITING INTERPRETATION

AUDITOR ASSOCIATION WITH SUBSEQUENTLY DISCOVERED INFORMATION WHEN THE AUDITOR HAS RESIGNED OR BEEN DISCHARGED (ISSUED IN FEBRUARY 1989).

If the auditor has resigned or been discharged, his responsibility with respect to subsequently discovered information remains unchanged; he should therefore determine whether the information is reliable and existed at the audit report date.

623 SPECIAL REPORTS

SOURCES OF STANDARDS

SAS 62, *Special Reports*
SAS 77, *Amendments to Statements on Auditing Standards No. 22, Planning and Supervision*; *No. 59, The Auditor's Consideration of an Entity's Ability to Continue as a Going Concern*; and *No. 62, Special Reports*

SUMMARY

Special reports are auditors' reports issued in connection with the following:

1. Financial statements using a comprehensive basis of accounting other than GAAP.
2. Specified elements, accounts, or items of financial statements.
3. Compliance with contracts or regulations related to audited financial statements.
4. Financial presentations to comply with contracts or regulations that are incomplete or not in conformity with US GAAP or another comprehensive basis of accounting.
5. Financial information in prescribed forms or schedules that require an auditor's report to be presented in a prescribed format.

BASIC FINANCIAL STATEMENTS

By definition, a financial statement is a presentation of financial data, including any necessary notes. The basis for a financial statement is accounting records. A financial statement should be designed to effectively communicate the economic resources or obligations of an entity at a specific point in time. A financial statement alternative may communicate the changes in economic resources or obligations of an entity over a specified period.

Presentations of financial data that constitute financial statements include

1. Balance sheet,
2. Statement of income or statement of operations,
3. Statement of retained earnings,
4. Statement of cash flows,
5. Statement of changes in owners' equity,
6. Statement of assets and liabilities that do not include owners' equity accounts,
7. Statement of revenue and expenses,
8. Summary of operations,
9. Statement of operations by product lines, and
10. Statement of cash receipts and disbursements.

GAAS apply to audits of all financial statements, regardless of the basis of accounting. However, in reports on financial statements prepared in conformity with a comprehensive basis of accounting, this section applies rather than AU Section 508, which applies to audit reports issued in connection with financial statements prepared in conformity with GAAP.

COMPREHENSIVE BASIS OF ACCOUNTING OTHER THAN GAAP

A comprehensive basis of accounting other than GAAP may be any basis of accounting that is

1. Used to comply with the requirements of a government agency, such as the basis of accounting used by a state-regulated insurance company;
2. Used for income-tax purposes;
3. The cash basis (i.e., cash receipts and disbursements) or, where substantial support exists, a modified cash basis. Financial statements based on a modified cash basis of accounting might include such noncash items as depreciation on property, plant, and equipment and accrued income taxes.
4. Based on definite criteria that have substantial support, such as the price-level basis.

REPORTS ON FINANCIAL STATEMENTS USING OTHER COMPREHENSIVE BASIS OF ACCOUNTING (OCBOA)

An auditor's special report issued in connection with OCBOA financial statements should contain the following elements:

1. A title that includes the word *independent*.
2. An introductory paragraph that states that

    a. The financial statements identified in the report were audited,
    b. The financial statements are the responsibility of management, and
    c. The auditor is responsible for expressing an opinion based on the audit.

3. A scope paragraph that states that

    a. The audit was conducted in accordance with GAAS;
    b. The auditor is required to plan and perform the audit to obtain reasonable assurance that financial statements are free of material misstatement;
    c. An audit includes examining on a test basis evidence supporting the amounts and disclosures in the financial statements, assessing accounting principles used and significant estimates made by management, and evaluating the overall presentation of the financial statements; and
    d. The auditor believes that the audit provides a reasonable basis for his opinion.

4. A paragraph, placed before the opinion paragraph, that

    a. Makes reference to the note in the financial statements describing the basis of accounting, and
    b. States that the basis of accounting is a comprehensive basis of accounting other than GAAP.
    c. An opinion paragraph in which the auditor expresses or disclaims an opinion on whether the financial statements are presented fairly, in all material respects, in conformity with the basis of accounting described in the note to the financial statements.

5. A signature of the auditor's firm, which may be manual or printed.
6. The date of the special report.
7. In connection with these report elements, the following should be noted:

    a. The introductory paragraph of the special report is similar to the introductory paragraph of an audit report on financial statements that conform to GAAP, but because the basis of accounting is different, the titles of the financial statements identified in the report will change.

b.   The scope paragraph of the special report is identical to the scope paragraph of an audit report on GAAP-conforming financial statements.

c.   If the auditor is reporting on financial statements prepared on a basis of accounting prescribed by a governmental regulatory agency solely for filing with that agency, the report should contain a paragraph placed after the opinion paragraph that restricts the use of the report to that agency. This restriction on distribution is necessary even when the auditor's report is by law a matter of public record.

Sample Special Report for Income Tax Basis of Accounting

Independent Auditor's Report

We have audited the accompanying statements of assets, liabilities, and capital-income tax basis of XYZ Partnership as of December 31, 20X2, and 20X1, and the related statements of revenue and expenses-income tax basis and of changes in partners' capital accounts-income tax basis for the years then ended. These financial statements are the responsibility of the Partnership's management. Our responsibility is to express an opinion on these financial statements based on our audits.

We conducted our audits in accordance with auditing standards generally accepted in the United States of America. Those standards require that we plan and perform the audit to obtain reasonable assurance about whether the financial statements are free of material misstatement. An audit includes examining, on a test basis, evidence supporting the amounts and disclosures in the financial statements. An audit also includes assessing the accounting principles used and significant estimates made by management, as well as evaluating the overall financial statement presentation. We believe that our audits provide a reasonable basis for our opinion.

As described in Note X, these financial statements were prepared on the basis of accounting the Partnership uses for income tax purposes, which is a comprehensive basis of accounting other than generally accepted accounting principles.

In our opinion, the financial statements referred to above present fairly, in all material respects, the assets, liabilities, and capital of XYZ Partnership as of December 31, 20X2, and 20X1, and its revenue and expenses and changes in partners' capital accounts for the years then ended, on the basis of accounting described in Note X.

[*Signature*]

[*Date*]

Sample Special Report for Cash Basis of Accounting

Independent Auditor's Report

We have audited the accompanying statements of assets and liabilities arising from cash transactions of XYZ Company as of December 31, 20X2, and 20X1, and the related statements of revenue collected and expenses paid for the years then ended. These financial statements are the responsibility of the Company's management. Our responsibility is to express an opinion on these financial statements based on our audits.

We conducted our audits in accordance with auditing standards generally accepted in the United States of America. Those standards require that we plan and perform the audit to obtain reasonable assurance about whether the financial statements are free of material misstatement. An audit includes examining, on a test basis, evidence supporting the amounts and disclosures in the financial statements. An audit also includes assessing the accounting principles used and significant estimates made by management, as well as evaluating the overall financial statement presentation. We believe that our audits provide a reasonable basis for our opinion.

As described in Note X, these financial statements were prepared on the basis of cash receipts and disbursements, which is a comprehensive basis of accounting other than generally accepted accounting principles.

In our opinion, the financial statements referred to above present fairly, in all material respects, the assets and liabilities arising from cash transactions of XYZ Company as of December 31, 20X2, and 20X1, and its revenue collected and expenses paid during the years then ended, on the basis of accounting described in Note X.

[*Signature*]

[*Date*]

Sample Special Report for Regulatory Basis of Accounting

Independent Auditor's Report

We have audited the accompanying statements of admitted assets, liabilities, and surplus—statutory basis of XYZ Insurance Company as of December 31, 20X2, and 20X1, and the related statements of income and cash flows—statutory basis and changes in surplus—statutory basis for the years then ended. These financial statements are the responsibility of the Company's management. Our responsibility is to express an opinion on these financial statements based on our audits.

We conducted our audits in accordance with auditing standards generally accepted in the United States of America. Those standards require that we plan and perform the audit to obtain reasonable assurance about whether the financial statements are free of material misstatement. An audit includes examining, on a test basis, evidence supporting the amounts and disclosures in the financial statements. An audit also includes assessing the accounting principles used and significant estimates made by management, as well as evaluating the overall financial statement presentation. We believe that our audits provide a reasonable basis for our opinion.

As described in Note X, these financial statements were prepared in conformity with the accounting practices prescribed or permitted by the Insurance Department of [*State*], which is a comprehensive basis of accounting other than generally accepted accounting principles.

In our opinion, the financial statements referred to above present fairly, in all material respects, the admitted assets, liabilities, and surplus of XYZ Insurance Company as of December 31, 20X2, and 20X1, and the results of its operations and its cash flows for the years then ended, on the basis of accounting described in Note X.

This report is intended solely for the information and use of the board of directors and management of XYZ Insurance Company and [name of regulatory agency] and is not intended to be used and should not be used by anyone other than these specified parties.

[*Signature*]

[*Date*]

MODIFICATIONS TO THE STANDARD REPORT

Because GAAS apply to audits of all financial statements, regardless of the basis of accounting, an auditor may modify his report on OCBOA financial statements for a variety of circumstances including, but not limited to, improper titling of the financial statements, lack of adequate disclosures (e.g., omission of a summary of significant accounting policies), and restrictions on the scope of the audit. Therefore, in modifying his report, the auditor should be guided by AU Section 508, *Reports on Audited Financial Statements*.

SPECIFIED ELEMENTS, ACCOUNTS, OR ITEMS

An auditor may express an opinion on a specified element, account, or item (hereinafter "element" for all three) in financial statements that is presented in the report containing the expressed opinion or a separate document that will accompany the auditor's report on the element.

Specified elements of financial statements that auditors are often requested to report on include

1. Rental income,
2. Royalty income,
3. Contributions to retirement plans,
4. Provisions for income taxes,
5. Receivables,
6. Inventory, and
7. Investments.

Since GAAP may not apply to a specified element, the first standard of reporting under GAAS may not apply. Therefore, the report need not necessarily refer to conformity with GAAP.

An engagement to report on a specified element of a financial statement may be

1. Performed in combination with an audit of an entity's financial statements, or
2. Undertaken as a separate engagement.

For both types of engagements, materiality should relate to each element covered by the auditor's report. Accordingly the scope of an audit of an element is usually more extensive than if it were considered part of a total financial statement audit.

As a rule, no report should be issued on specified elements when the auditor has either expressed an adverse opinion or disclaimed one when such reporting might be considered the equivalent of issuing a piecemeal opinion, which an auditor may never do. However, the auditor may express an opinion on one or more elements if the matter to be reported on and the scope of the audit were not intended to and did not encompass so many elements as to constitute a major portion of the financial statements. An auditor who has disclaimed an opinion on the financial statements taken as a whole may still express an opinion, for instance, on an entity's royalty income but only if the report on the royalty income is presented separately from the disclaimer of opinion on the financial statements.

REPORTS ON SPECIFIED ELEMENTS OF A FINANCIAL STATEMENT

An auditor's special report issued in connection with a specified element, account, or item of a financial statement should incorporate the following:

1. A title that includes the word independent.
2. An introductory paragraph that states

   a. That the specified element identified in the report was audited;
   b. If the audit was made in conjunction with a financial statement audit, the date of the audit report and any relevant departures from the standard report;
   c. That the specified element is the responsibility of management; and
   d. That the auditor is responsible for expressing an opinion based on his audit.

3. A scope paragraph that states that

   a. The audit was conducted in accordance with US GAAS;
   b. The auditor is required to plan and perform the audit to obtain reasonable assurance that the specified element is free of material misstatement;
   c. An audit includes examining on a test basis evidence supporting the amounts and disclosures in the presentation of the specified element, assessing the accounting principles used and significant estimates made by management, and evaluating the presentation of the specified element; and

    d.   The auditor believes that the audit provides a reasonable basis for his opinion.

4.   A paragraph, placed before the opinion paragraph, that

    a.   Describes the basis of presentation of the specified element,

    b.   Describes any agreements specifying such basis if not presented in conformity with GAAP, and

    c.   Describes any significant management interpretations of provisions of a relevant agreement.

5.   A paragraph in which the auditor expresses or disclaims an opinion on whether the specified element is presented fairly, in all material respects, in conformity with the basis of accounting described.

6.   If necessary, a separate paragraph before the opinion paragraph that describes substantive reasons for

    a.   A conclusion that the specified element is not presented fairly on the basis of accounting described, and

    b.   A scope limitation.

7.   Modification of the opinion paragraph for either item referenced in 5. above.

8.   A restriction on distribution if the specified element is prepared pursuant to a contract or other agreement but the presentation is not in conformity with GAAP or another comprehensive basis of accounting.

9.   A signature of the auditor's firm, which may be manual or printed.

10.   The date of the special report.

In order for an auditor to report on net income or stockholders' equity, or its equivalent, or another specified element based thereon, the auditor must first audit the complete financial statements.

Sample Standard Report Relating to Accounts Receivable

Independent Auditor's Report

We have audited the accompanying schedule of accounts receivable of ABC Company as of December 31, 20X2. This schedule is the responsibility of the Company's management. Our responsibility is to express an opinion on this schedule based on our audit.

We conducted our audit in accordance with auditing standards generally accepted in the United States of America. Those standards require that we plan and perform the audit to obtain reasonable assurance about whether the schedule of accounts receivable is free of material misstatement. An audit includes examining, on a test basis, evidence supporting the amounts and disclosures in the schedule of accounts receivable. An audit also includes assessing the accounting principles used and significant estimates made by management, as well as evaluating the overall schedule presentation. We believe that our audit provides a reasonable basis for our opinion.

In our opinion, the schedule of accounts receivable referred to above presents fairly, in all material respects, the accounts receivable of ABC Company as of December 31, 20X2, in conformity with accounting principles generally accepted in the United States of America.

[*Signature*]

[*Date*]

REPORTS ON COMPLIANCE WITH CONTRACTS OR REGULATIONS

Contracts, such as a loan agreement, or regulatory agencies may require that compliance reports be audited. An auditor's compliance report may provide negative assurance relating to covenants of an agreement, but even that requires the audit of the financial statements to which they relate.

The auditor's negative assurance may be provided

1. As a modification to the auditor's report accompanying the financial statements, or
2. In a separate report.

Negative assurance should not be provided if the auditor

1. Has not audited the financial statements to which the contract or regulation relates or
2. Has expressed an adverse opinion or disclaimed an opinion on those financial statements.

Nor should negative assurance be provided with respect to matters that have not been subjected to relevant auditing procedures.

REPORT CONTENTS

An auditor's separate special report issued in connection with compliance with a contract or regulation should include the following seven elements:

1. A title that includes the word *independent.*
2. A paragraph that states
   a. That the financial statements were audited in accordance with US GAAS, and
   b. The date of the standard audit report and any relevant departures from it.
3. A paragraph that
   a. Refers to the specific covenants or paragraphs of the agreement,
   b. Expresses negative assurance regarding compliance with the agreement as it relates to accounting matters,
   c. States that the negative assurance is provided in connection with the financial statement audit, and
   d. Clearly indicates that the audit was not directed primarily to obtaining knowledge about compliance.
4. If necessary, a paragraph that describes significant management interpretations of provisions of the agreement.
5. A paragraph that restricts distribution and use of the report to those within the entity and parties to the contract or agreement or the regulatory agency with which the report is being filed.
6. A signature of the auditor's firm, which may be manual or printed.
7. The date of the special report.

Sample Report on Compliance

Independent Auditor's Report

We have audited, in accordance with auditing standards generally accepted in the United States of America, the balance sheet of XYZ Company as of December 31, 20X2, and the related statements of income, retained earnings, and cash flows for the year then ended, and have issued our report thereon dated February 16, 20X3.

In connection with our audit, nothing came to our attention that caused us to believe that the Company failed to comply with the terms, covenants, provisions, or conditions of Sections XX to YY, inclusive, of the indenture dated July 21, 20X0, with ABC Bank insofar as they relate to accounting matters. However, our audit was not directed primarily toward obtaining knowledge of such noncompliance.

This report is intended solely for the information and use of the boards of directors and management of XYZ Company and ABC Bank and is not intended to be and should not be used by anyone other than these specified parties.

[*Signature*]

[*Date*]

In lieu of a separate report, an auditor may report on compliance with contracts or regulations as part of the report accompanying the audited financial statements by adding a paragraph after the opinion paragraph that includes the information described in items 3., 4., and 5. above.

SPECIAL-PURPOSE FINANCIAL PRESENTATIONS

An auditor may report on special-purpose financial presentations prepared to comply with contracts or regulations, among them those that

1. Constitute incomplete presentations prepared in conformity with GAAP or another comprehensive basis of accounting; or
2. May be a complete set of financial statements, or a single financial statement, prepared on a basis of accounting prescribed in an agreement but not in conformity with GAAP or another comprehensive basis of accounting.

Incomplete Presentations

Incomplete presentations, as contemplated by this section, should differ from complete financial statements only to the extent necessary. Presentations should be appropriately titled and include, for example

1. A real estate entity's schedule of gross income and expenses exclusive of interest, depreciation, and provision for income taxes; and
2. An entity's schedule of gross assets sold and liabilities transferred pursuant to a buy-sell agreement.

An incomplete presentation should generally be treated as a financial statement, and materiality should relate to the presentation taken as a whole.

An incomplete presentation containing items that are the same as or similar to those included in a complete set of financial statements prepared in conformity with GAAP should also contain similar informative disclosures.

Reporting

An auditor's special report issued in connection with an incomplete presentation prepared in conformity with GAAP or another comprehensive basis of accounting should contain the following eight elements:

1. A title that includes the word independent.
2. A paragraph identical to the introductory paragraph in a standard audit report on a complete set of financial statements.
3. A paragraph identical to the standard scope paragraph.
4. A paragraph that

    a. Explains what the presentation is intended for and refers to the note to the special-purpose financial statements that describes the basis of presentation; and

b. Clearly indicates that the presentation is not intended to be complete as to the entity's assets, liabilities, revenues and expenses, but only if the basis of presentation is in conformity with GAAP.

5. A paragraph wherein the auditor expresses or disclaims an opinion on the fairness of presentation, in all material respects, of the information the presentation is intended to present in conformity with GAAP or another comprehensive basis of accounting. If necessary, this paragraph should identify the United States of America as the country or origin of the GAAP. This opinion paragraph should be modified if the auditor

a. Concludes that the information is not presented fairly on the basis of the accounting described, or
b. Encounters a scope limitation.

The modification should include the proper type of opinion or disclaimer and refer to an explanation preceding the opinion paragraph in which the auditor discloses all substantive reasons for his conclusion.

6. A final paragraph that restricts distribution and use of the report to specified parties. This paragraph should not be included if the report and related financial presentation are to be filed with a regulatory agency and the document will be available to the general public.
7. A signature of the auditor's firm, which may be manual or printed.
8. The date of the report.

Sample Report on a Statement of Assets Sold and Liabilities Transferred to Comply with a Contractual Agreement

Independent Auditor's Report

We have audited the accompanying statement of net assets sold of ABC Company as of June 8, 20XX. This statement of net assets sold is the responsibility of ABC Company's management. Our responsibility is to express an opinion on the statement of net assets sold based on our audit.

We conducted our audits in accordance with auditing standards generally accepted in the United States of America. Those standards require that we plan and perform the audit to obtain reasonable assurance about whether the statement of net assets sold is free of material misstatement. An audit includes examining, on a test basis, evidence supporting the amounts and disclosures in the statement. An audit also includes assessing the accounting principles used and significant estimates made by management, as well as evaluating the overall presentation of the statement of net assets sold. We believe that our audit provides a reasonable basis for our opinion.

The accompanying statement was prepared to present the net assets of ABC Company sold to XYZ Corporation pursuant to the purchase agreement described in Note X, and is not intended to be a complete presentation of ABC Company's assets and liabilities.

In our opinion, the accompanying statement of net assets sold presents fairly, in all material respects, the net assets of ABC Company as of June 8, 20XX sold pursuant to the purchase agreement referred to in Note X, in conformity with accounting principles generally accepted in the United States of America.

This report is intended solely for the information and use of the boards of directors and managements of ABC Company and XYZ Corporation and is not intended to be and should not be used by anyone other than these specified parties.

[*Signature*]

[*Date*]

Presentations Not in Conformity with GAAP or an OCBOA

Examples of presentations contemplated by this section are as follows:

1. Consolidated financial statements prepared pursuant to a loan agreement that include certain assets, such as inventory, that do not conform to GAAP or an OCBOA.
2. Financial statements of an entity being acquired that are prepared in conformity with GAAP but that, pursuant to an acquisition agreement, include certain assets (such as accounts receivable and inventory) whose value is predicated on a basis specified in the acquisition agreement.

These types of presentations are not considered to conform to a "comprehensive basis of accounting."

Reporting

A special report issued in connection with nonconforming presentations should contain the following number of elements:

1. A title that includes the word *independent.*
2. A paragraph identical to the introductory paragraph in a standard audit report on a complete set of financial statements.
3. A paragraph identical to the standard scope paragraph.
4. A paragraph that

    a. Explains what the presentation is intended to present and refers to the note to the special-purpose financial statements that describes the basis of the presentation, and
    b. Clearly indicates that the presentation is not intended to be in conformity with GAAP.

5. If necessary, a paragraph that describes any significant management interpretations of provisions of a relevant agreement.
6. A paragraph in which the auditor expresses or disclaims an opinion about the fairness of presentation, in all material respects, of the information the presentation is intended to present in conformity with the basis of accounting specified. This opinion paragraph should be modified if the auditor

    a. Concludes that the information is not presented fairly on the basis of the accounting described, or
    b. Encounters a scope limitation.

    The modification should include the proper type of opinion or disclaimer of opinion and refer to an explanation preceding the opinion paragraph in which all substantive reasons for the auditor's conclusion are disclosed.

7. A final paragraph that restricts distribution and use of the report to specified parties.
8. A signature of the auditor's firm, which may be manual or printed.
9. The date of the report.

Presented next is a sample report on a statement of assets and liabilities designed to illustrate the inclusion of these report elements.

Sample Report on a Nonconforming Statement of Assets and Liabilities

Independent Auditor's Report

We have audited the special-purpose statement of assets and liabilities of ABC Company as of December 31, 20X2 and 20X1, and the related special-purpose statements of revenue and expenses and of cash flows for the years then ended. These financial statements are the responsibility of the Company's management. Our responsibility is to express an opinion on these financial statements based on our audits.

We conducted our audits in accordance with auditing standards generally accepted in the United States of America. Those standards require that we plan and perform the audit to obtain reasonable assurance about whether the statement of net assets sold is free of material misstatement. An audit includes examining, on a test basis, evidence supporting the amounts and disclosures in the statement. An audit also includes assessing the accounting principles used and significant estimates made by management, as well as evaluating the overall presentation of the statement of net assets sold. We believe that our audits provide a reasonable basis for our opinion.

The accompanying special-purpose financial statements were prepared for the purpose of complying with Section 4 of a loan agreement between DEF Bank and the Company as discussed in Note X, and are not intended to be a presentation in conformity with generally accepted accounting principles.

In our opinion, the special-purpose financial statements referred to above present fairly, in all material respects, the assets and liabilities of ABC Company as at December 31, 20X2 and 20X1, and the revenues, expenses, and cash flows for the years then ended, on the basis of accounting described in Note X.

This report is intended solely for the information and use of the boards of directors and managements of ABC Company and DEF Bank and is not intended to be and should not be used by anyone other than these specified parties.

[*Signature*]

[*Date*]

REPORT MODIFICATIONS

Circumstances that require modifying the report but that do not negate the unqualified opinion include

1. A lack of consistency in accounting principles,
2. Going-concern uncertainties,
3. Involvement of other auditors,
4. Comparative financial statements, and
5. Need to emphasize a matter.

Financial Information Presented in Prescribed Ways

When a printed form or schedule requires an auditor to assert something that the auditor believes is not justified, the auditor should reword the report or attach a separate report.

625 REPORTS ON THE APPLICATION OF ACCOUNTING PRINCIPLES

SOURCES OF STANDARDS

SAS 50, *Reports on the Application of Accounting Principles*
SAS 97, *Amendment to Statement on Auditing Standards No. 50*

SUMMARY

Consultations with accountants commonly concern

1. The application of accounting principles (whether GAAP or OCBOA) to completed or proposed audits, and
2. The type of opinion that may be expressed on an entity's financial statements.

These consultations, which may involve members of management or others, such as attorneys and investment bankers, are often requested to increase knowledge of specific financial reporting issues.

This section provides guidance to the reporting accountant about such consultations. A reporting accountant is any accountant in public practice who is asked to provide a report in writing or orally on the application of accounting principles to specific transactions that involve facts and circumstances of a specific entity, or the type of opinion that may be rendered on a specific entity's financial statements.

An accountant should not accept an engagement to provide a written report on application of accounting principles to a hypothetical transaction that is not based on actual facts and circumstances.

PERFORMANCE STANDARDS

The reporting accountant has the following responsibilities:

1. Exercise due professional care and have adequate technical training and proficiency.
2. Adequately plan the engagement, supervise assistants, and accumulate enough evidence to obtain a reasonable basis for the professional judgment rendered.
3. Understand the transaction, review the applicable GAAP, and perform other appropriate procedures.
4. Consult with the entity's continuing accountant (the one who was engaged to report on the financial statements of a party to the transaction) to identify all the facts needed to form a professional judgment.

REPORTING STANDARDS

The reporting accountant's report should

1. Be addressed to the requesting entity (e.g., management or the board of directors).

2. Briefly describe the nature of the engagement and state that the engagement was performed in accordance with applicable AICPA standards.
3. Identify the specific entity; describe the transaction; state the facts, circumstances, and assumptions; and state the sources of information.
4. Describe the accounting principles (with the country of origin) to be applied or the type of opinion that may be rendered on the financial statements and, if appropriate, describe the reasons for the reporting accountant's conclusion.
5. State that the responsibility for proper accounting treatment rests with the preparers of the financial statements, who should consult with their continuing accountants.
6. State that any difference in the facts, circumstances, or assumptions presented may change the report.
7. Include a separate paragraph that

   a. States that the report is intended solely for the information and use of specified parties,
   b. Specifies the parties to whom use is restricted, and
   c. States that the report is not intended to be and should not be used by anyone other than those parties.

Sample Report on the Application of Accounting Principles

A reporting accountant may use the following sample report format.

Introduction

We have been engaged to report on the appropriate application of accounting principles generally accepted in [*country of origin of such principles*] to the specific transaction described below. This report is being issued to ABC Company for assistance in evaluating accounting principles for the described specific transaction. Our engagement has been conducted in accordance with standards established by the American Institute of Certified Public Accountants.

Description of Transaction

The facts, circumstances, and assumptions relevant to the specific transaction as provided to us by the management of ABC Company are as follows:

Appropriate Accounting Principles

[*Text discussing generally accepted accounting principles*]

Concluding Comments

The ultimate responsibility for the decision on the appropriate application of accounting principles generally accepted in [*country of origin of accounting principles*] for an actual transaction rests with the preparers of financial statements, who should consult with their continuing accountant. Our judgment on the appropriate application of accounting principles generally accepted in [*country of origin of such principles*] for the described specific transaction is based solely on the facts provided to us as described above; should these facts and circumstances differ, our conclusion may change.

Restricted Use

This report is intended solely for the information and use of the board of directors and management of ABC Company and is not intended to be and should not be used by anyone other than these specified parties.

AUDITING INTERPRETATION

REQUIREMENT TO CONSULT WITH THE CONTINUING ACCOUNTANT (ISSUED IN JANUARY 2005)

The requirement to consult with the continuing accountant is a presumptively mandatory requirement. The advisory accountant may overcome the presumptive requirement if the accountant

1. Believes that a second opinion is not being requested, and
2. Has obtained from management all relevant information necessary to provide requested written or oral guidance concerning the application of accounting principles to the specific client transactions.

It may be easier to overcome the presumptively mandatory requirement in a recurring engagement as opposed to a periodic engagement. A recurring engagement may involve the outsourcing of a controllership function, which generally would not be representative of opinion shopping and would not permit the advisory accountant to have complete access to management information. Before undertaking this type of engagement, the advisory accountant should establish an understanding with the client as to the nature and terms of the engagement. In addition to following the other requirements in AU Section 625, the advisory accountant should document how he or she overcame the presumptively mandatory requirement to consult with the continuing accountant.

634 LETTERS FOR UNDERWRITERS AND CERTAIN OTHER REQUESTING PARTIES

SOURCE OF STANDARDS

SAS 72, *Letters for Underwriters and Certain Other Requesting Parties*

SAS 76, *Amendments to Statement on Auditing Standards No. 72,* "Letters for Underwriters and Certain Other Requesting Parties"

SAS 86, *Amendment to Statement on Auditing Standards No. 72,* "Letters for Underwriters and Certain Other Requesting Parties"

See section 9634 for interpretations.

INTRODUCTION/SUMMARY

Accountants may be asked to provide "comfort letters" to underwriters and certain other parties. These letters are issued in connection with financial statements and financial statement schedules contained in registration statements. The registration statements are filed with the Securities and Exchange Commission (SEC) under the Securities Act of 1933 (the Act). Section 11 of the Act provides that underwriters, among others, could be liable if any part of a registration statement contains material omissions or misstatements.

The Act provides an affirmative defense for underwriters. The underwriters must demonstrate that the underwriter had reasonable grounds to believe that there were no material omissions or misstatements. Underwriters may show that a reasonable investigation was performed by asking an accountant to issue a comfort letter.

PARTIES TO WHOM A COMFORT LETTER MAY BE ISSUED

Accountants may provide a comfort letter to

1. Underwriters, or
2. Other parties with a statutory due diligence defense under Section 11 of the Act.

Other than a named underwriter, accountants are allowed to provide comfort letters only to parties with a statutory due diligence defense under Section 11 of the Act. It is required that a law firm or attorney for the requesting party issue a written opinion to the accountants that states that such party has a due diligence defense under Section 11 of the Act. Anything less would not be sufficient. For instance, AU 634.03 states that

> *An attorney's letter indicating that a party "may" be deemed to be an underwriter or has liability substantially equivalent to that of an underwriter under the securities laws would not meet this requirement. Letter is provided by the broker-dealer or other financial intermediary, and the letter contains the following wording (AU 634.06):*

This review process, applied to the information relating to the issuer, is (will be) substantially consistent with the due diligence review process that we would perform if this placement of securities (or issuance of securities in an acquisition transaction) were being registered pursuant to the Securities Act of 1933 (the Act) . We are knowledgeable with respect to the due diligence review process that would be performed if this placement of securities were being registered pursuant to the Act.

AU 634.07 provides the following example of a letter containing the required elements from a party requesting a comfort letter:

[*Date*]

Dear ABC Accountants:

[*Name of financial intermediary*], as principal or agent, in the placement of [*identify securities*] to be issued by [*name of issuer*], [*Name of Financial Intermediary*]

Accountants may also provide a comfort letter in connection with acquisition transactions in which there is an exchange of stock. A representation letter meeting the conditions specified above would be required before the accountant may issue the requested comfort letter. An accountant providing agreed-upon procedures in connection with a proposed transaction such as a merger, an acquisition, or a financing is not covered by AU 634.

When a party other than an underwriter or a party with a due diligence defense under Section 11 of the Act requests a comfort letter but does not provide the representation letter, the accountant should not issue a comfort letter. Instead the accountant may provide them with another type of letter. Such a letter should include the following statements (AU 634.09):

It should be understood that we have no responsibility for establishing (and did not establish) the scope and nature of the procedures enumerated in the paragraphs above; rather, the procedures enumerated therein are those the requesting party asked us to perform. Accordingly we make no representations regarding questions of legal interpretation or regarding the sufficiency for your purposes of the procedures enumerated in the preceding paragraphs; also such procedures would not necessarily reveal any material misstatement of the amounts or percentages listed above as set forth in the offering circular. Further we have addressed ourselves solely to the foregoing data and make no representations regarding the adequacy of disclosures or whether any material facts have been omitted. This letter relates only to the financial statement items specified above and does not extend to any financial statement of the company taken as a whole.

The foregoing procedures do not constitute an audit conducted in accordance with generally accepted auditing standards. Had we performed additional procedures or had we conducted an audit or a review of the company's [*give dates of any interim financial statements*] consolidated financial statements in accordance with standards established by the American Institute of Certified Public Accountants, other matters might have come to our attention that would have been reported to you.

These procedures should not be taken to supplant any additional inquiries or procedures that you would undertake in your consideration of the proposed offering.

This letter is solely for your information and to assist you in your inquiries in connection with the offering of the securities covered by the offering circular, and it is not to be used, circulated, quoted, or otherwise referred to for any other purpose, including but not limited to the registration, purchase, or sale of securities, nor is it to be filed with or referred to in whole or in part in the offering document or any other document, except that reference may be made to it in any list of closing documents pertaining to the offering of the securities covered by the offering document.

We have no responsibility to update this letter for events and circumstances occurring after [*cutoff date*].

LIMITATIONS OF COMFORT LETTERS

There are certain limitations concerning comfort letters and level of assistance accountants can provide.

1. Accountants can only comment on matters on which they have professional expertise.
2. Accountants can only, at best, provide negative assurance unless they conduct an audit.

Procedures typically contemplated in a comfort letter are limited in scope. While such procedures may alert the accountant to significant matters, they do not provide any assurance that all significant matters would come to the accountant's attention. There exists additional risk that the accountants may have provided negative assurance on the absence of conditions or matters when in fact such conditions or matters actually exist.

Comfort letters are not required under the Act. Copies of the comfort letters are not filed with the SEC. However, it is generally required in an underwriting agreement in connection with the offering for sale of securities registered with the SEC under the Act, and the underwriter will expect the accountants to furnish a comfort letter.

The scope of the comfort letter should be specified in the underwriting agreement. A draft of the underwriting agreement should be furnished to the accountant to ensure that the accountant will be able to comply with the underwriter's request and will be able to furnish the comfort letter in an acceptable form.

Upon receiving a draft of the agreement, it is recommended that the accountant prepare a draft of the comfort letter for the underwriter's review. The draft should attempt to deal with all matters expected to be covered in the final letter and should use exactly the same terms as those to be used in the final letter. It should, of course, be understood that actual comments contained in the final comfort letter cannot be determined without performing the required accounting procedures. The draft comfort letter should be clearly marked as draft to avoid giving the impression that the procedures described therein have been performed and that this is the actual comfort letter.

Providing the draft of the comfort letter to the client and the underwriter at an early stage reduces misunderstandings. It lets the client and underwriter know what to expect from the accountant's comfort letter. It also gives them the opportunity to discuss relevant issues and concerns with the accountant. For instance, the underwriter may request that additional procedures be performed. If additional procedures are performed, a revised draft should be sent to the client and underwriter.

Accountants should refrain from making statements or implying that the accountants are carrying out such procedures as they consider necessary. This may lead to misunderstandings about the accountant's responsibility for the sufficiency of the procedures. Instead the following should be placed on the draft letter to identify and explain the purpose of the comfort letter (AU 364.16):

> This draft is furnished solely for the purpose of indicating the form of letter that we would expect to be able to furnish [*name of underwriter*] in response to their request, the matters expected to be covered in the letter, and the nature of the procedures that we would expect to carry out with respect to such matters. Based on our discussions with [*name of underwriter*], it is our understanding that the procedures outlined in this draft letter are those they wish us to follow. Unless [*name of underwriter*] informs us otherwise, we shall assume that there are no additional procedures they wish us to follow. The text of the letter itself will depend, of course, on the results of the procedures, which we would not expect to complete until shortly before the letter is given and in no event before the cutoff date indicated therein.

COMFORT LETTERS REQUESTED FROM MULTIPLE ACCOUNTANTS

Occasionally, comfort letters are requested from more than one accountant. The client should inform other accountants about their responsibility at the earliest possible date. The client should ensure that the other accountant has received a draft of the underwriting agreement. A draft copy of the secondary accountant's comfort letter should be provided to the principal accountant. The principal accountant should read the secondary accountant's comfort letter. The secondary accountant's comfort letter should contain statements similar to those contained in the comfort letter prepared by the principal accountant, including statements about their independence. The principal accountants should state in their comfort letters that (AU 364.18)

1. Reading letters of the other accountants was one of the procedures followed, and
2. The procedures performed by the principal accountants (other than reading the letters of the other accountants) relate solely to companies audited by the principal accountants and to the consolidated financial statements.

ISSUING COMFORT LETTERS AT THE EFFECTIVE DATE OF SHELF REGISTRATION

The Act permits companies, in certain circumstances, to register a designated amount of securities for continuous or delayed offerings for an extended period by filing a "shelf" registration statement. The registrant may not have selected an underwriter at the effective date of a shelf registration statement. In such a situation the client or the legal counsel designated to represent the underwriting group might request a comfort letter. The accountant should not provide a comfort letter addressed to the client, legal counsel, or a nonspecific addressee such as "any or all underwriters to be selected."

However, the accountants may agree to provide the client or legal counsel for the underwriting group with a draft comfort letter. In the draft comfort letter, the accountant may describe the procedures that he or she has performed and the results of the procedures. The draft comfort letter should include a legend similar to the following (AU 634.19):

> This draft describes the procedures that we have performed and represents a letter we would be prepared to sign as of the effective date of the registration statement if the managing underwriter had been chosen at that date and requested such a letter. Based on our discussions with [*name of client or legal counsel*], the procedures set forth are similar to those that experience indicates underwriters often request in such circumstances. The text of the final letter will depend, of course, on whether the managing underwriter who is selected requests that other procedures be performed to meet his or her needs and whether the managing underwriter requests that any of the procedures be updated to the date of issuance of the signed letter.

The accountant may issue a comfort letter to the underwriter selected for the portion of the issue then being offered when the underwriting agreement for an offering is signed and on each closing date.

FORMAT AND CONTENTS OF COMFORT LETTERS

The following subjects may be covered in a comfort letter (AU 634.22):

1. The independence of the accountants.
2. Whether the audited financial statements and financial statement schedules included (incorporated by reference) in the registration statement comply as to form in all material respects with the applicable accounting requirements of the Act and the related rules and regulations adopted by the SEC.

3. Unaudited financial statements, condensed interim financial information, capsule financial information, pro forma financial information, financial forecasts, management's discussion and analysis (MD&A), and changes in selected financial statement items during a period subsequent to the date and period of the latest financial statements included (incorporated by reference) in the registration statement.
4. Tables, statistics, and other financial information included (incorporated by reference) in the registration statement.
5. Negative assurance as to whether certain nonfinancial statement information, included (incorporated by reference) in the registration statement complies as to form in all material respects with Regulation S-K.

DATING

The comfort letter is generally dated on or just before the effective date of the registration statement. Sometimes, the letters may be dated at the date on which the registration statement is filed with the SEC. A "cutoff" date for procedures performed is typically specified in the underwriting agreement. The cutoff date may be a few days before the date of the letter. In such a situation the letter should clearly state that the inquiries and other procedures described in the letter do not cover the period from the cutoff date to the date of the letter.

ADDRESSEE

The letter should only be addressed to the client and a named party such as the underwriter, broker-dealer, financial intermediary, or buyer or seller.

INTRODUCTORY PARAGRAPH

AU 634.26 suggests an introductory paragraph similar to the following:

> We have audited the [*identify the financial statements and financial statement schedules*] included (incorporated by reference) in the registration statement (no. 33-00000) on Form _____ filed by the company under the Securities Act of 1933 (the Act); our reports with respect thereto are also included (incorporated by reference) in that registration statement. The registration statement, as amended as of _____, is herein referred to as the registration statement.

When the report on audited financial statements (and schedules incorporated by reference) departs from the standard report, the accountant should refer to that fact in the comfort letter. Similarly, if the SEC accepts a qualified opinion on financial statements, the accountant should refer to it in the introductory paragraph of the comfort letter.

The accountant should NOT do the following in the comfort letter:

1. Repeat the opinion issued on audited financial statements in the comfort letter.
2. Give negative assurance regarding the accountant's report.
3. Give negative assurance about audited financial statements that are reported on in the registration statement by other accountants.

The accountants may refer in the introductory paragraphs of the comfort letter that they have issued reports on (AU 634.29)

1. Condensed financial statements that are derived from audited financial statement,
2. Selected financial data,
3. Interim financial information,
4. Pro forma financial information,
5. A financial forecast, and
6. Management's discussion and analysis.

INDEPENDENCE

The accountant will normally make a statement reflecting independence. AU 634.31 suggests the following:

> We are independent certified public accountants with respect to The Blank Company, Inc., within the meaning of the Act and the applicable rules and regulations thereunder adopted by the SEC.

In a non-SEC filing the accountants may refer to the AICPA's Code of Professional Conduct as follows:

> We are independent certified public accountants with respect to The Blank Company, Inc., under rule 101 of the AICPA's Code of Professional Conduct and its interpretations and rulings.

KNOWLEDGE OF INTERNAL CONTROL

The accountants should not comment in a comfort letter on (AU 634.36)

1. Unaudited condensed interim financial information;
2. Capsule financial information;
3. Financial forecast when historical financial statements provide a basis for one or more significant assumptions for the forecast; or
4. Changes in capital stock, increases in long-term debt and decreases in selected financial statement items, unless they have obtained knowledge of a client's internal control as it relates to the preparation of both annual and interim financial information.

If the accountant has not audited the entity's most recent annual financial statements, the auditor should perform procedures to obtain that knowledge.

UNAUDITED CONDENSED INTERIM FINANCIAL INFORMATION

Accountants may comment on unaudited condensed interim financial information in the form of negative assurance only when a review of the interim financial information has been conducted. Moreover the comfort letter should specifically identify any unaudited condensed interim financial information, and the accountant should state that no opinion is being expressed on such information.

PRO FORMA FINANCIAL INFORMATION

Accountants should not comment in a comfort letter on pro forma financial information unless they have appropriate accounting and financial knowledge of the entity. Such knowledge would ordinarily be obtained by the accountants auditing or reviewing historical financial statements of the entity.

CONCLUDING PARAGRAPH

AU 634.61 recommends that the comfort letter should conclude with a paragraph similar to the following:

> This letter is solely for the information of the addressees and to assist the underwriters in conducting and documenting their investigation of the affairs of the company in connection with the offering of the securities covered by the registration statement, and it is not to be used, circulated, quoted, or otherwise referred to within or without the underwriting group for any other purpose, including, but not limited to, the registration, purchase, or sale of securities, nor is it to be filed with or referred to in whole or in part in the registration statement or any other document, except that reference may be made to it in the underwriting agreement or in any list of closing documents pertaining to the offering of the securities covered by the registration statement.

711 FILINGS UNDER FEDERAL SECURITIES STATUTES

SOURCE OF STANDARDS

SAS 37, *Filings under Federal Securities Statutes*

See section 9711 for interpretations of this section

INTRODUCTION/SUMMARY

The independent accountant's responsibility for reports filed under the federal securities statutes is essentially the same as in other types of reporting. However, Section 11(a) of the Securities Act of 1933 imposes responsibility for false or misleading statements.

Section 11(b) provides a defense for the accountant if

1. The accountant had conducted a reasonable investigation (using the prudent man standard) and believed that the statements were true and that there was no material omission that would make the statements misleading, or
2. The registration statement did not fairly represent his statement or was not a fair copy of his report.

The independent accountant should make sure that the prospectus does not imply the accountant's responsibility is greater than intended. In particular, the "experts" section should be worded such that it is not implied that the financial statements were prepared by the independent accountant or that the financial statements are a direct representation of the accountant (instead of management).

Under rules of the Securities and Exchange Commission (SEC), the accountant does not have a statutory responsibility for review of interim financial information reports. The SEC requires that when an independent accountant's report based on a review of interim financial information is presented or incorporated by reference in a registration statement, wording such as the following should be included (AU 711.09):

Independent Public Accountants

The consolidated balance sheets as of December 31, 20X2 and 20X1, and the consolidated statements of income, retained earnings, and cash flows for each of the three years in the period ended December 31, 20X2, incorporated by reference in this prospectus, have been included herein in reliance on the report of _____ independent public accountants, given on the authority of that firm as experts in auditing and accounting.

With respect to the unaudited interim financial information for the periods ended March 31, 20X3 and 20X2, incorporated by reference in this prospectus, the independent public accountants have reported that they have applied limited procedures in accordance with professional standards for a review of such information. However, their separate report included in the company's quarterly report on Form 10-Q for the quarter ended March 31, 20X3, and incorporated by reference herein, states that they did not audit and they do not express an opinion on that interim financial information. Accordingly, the degree of reliance on their report on such information should be restricted in light of the limited nature of the review procedures applied. The accountants are not subject to the liability provisions of section 11 of the Securities Act of 1933 for their report on the unaudited interim financial information because that report is not a "report" or a "part" of the registration statement prepared or certified by the accountants within the meaning of sections 7 and 11 of the Act.

SUBSEQUENT EVENTS PROCEDURES IN 1933 ACT FILINGS

A "reasonable investigation," as required under the Securities Act of 1933, requires the auditor to perform subsequent event procedures from the date of the audit report up to the effective date (or as close as possible) . The auditor should make sure that the client updates the auditor on the progress of the registration proceedings. From a practical perspective, generally the auditor will discover subsequent events by making inquiries of client. In addition, the auditor should

1. Read the prospectus.
2. Read the registration statement.
3. Inquire of and obtain written representations from officers and other executives.

If a registration statement contains the reports of two or more independent auditors for audits in different periods, the auditor for the prior period is responsible for subsequent events from the date of the prior period financial statements to the effective date.

If the auditor discovers subsequent events, the auditor should follow the guidance given in AU Section 560, *Subsequent Events,* AU Section 561, *Subsequent Discovery of Facts Existing at the Date of the Auditor's Report,* and AU Section 530, *Dating of the Independent Auditor's Report.*

If an accountant believes that *unaudited* financial statements or unaudited interim financial information presented or incorporated by reference in a registration statement are not in conformity with GAAP, the accountant should insist that management revise it. If the management does not cooperate

1. If the accountant has reported on a review of this financial information, the accountant should follow the guidance of AU section 561.
2. If the accountant has not yet reported on a review of the unaudited financial statements or interim financial information, the accountant should modify his report to describe the departure from GAAP.

The accountant should also consider withdrawing from the engagement and withholding his consent to using the report.

722 INTERIM FINANCIAL INFORMATION

SOURCE OF STANDARDS

SAS 100, *Interim Financial Information.*

INTRODUCTION/SUMMARY

This section provides guidance on conducting a review of interim financial information. Interim financial information means (AU 722.02)

Financial information or statements covering a period less than a full year or for a 12-month period ending on a date other than the entity's fiscal year end.

The Securities and Exchange Commission (SEC) requires registrants to use independent accountants to review interim financial information before filing quarterly reports on Form 10-Q or Form 10-QSB. The SEC also requires that a review report be filed with the interim financial information if, in any filing, the entity states that the interim financial information has been reviewed by an independent public accountant.

If the entity's latest annual financial statements have been audited, an accountant may review interim financial information of an SEC registrant or of a non-SEC registrant that is filing with a regulatory agency for a public offering or listing. The interim financial information may be presented either as financial statements or as condensed information conforming with generally accepted accounting principles and applicable regulatory requirements.

OBJECTIVE OF A REVIEW OF INTERIM FINANCIAL INFORMATION

The objective of a review is to provide the accountant with a basis for communicating whether the accountant is (AU 722.07)

Aware of any material modifications that should be made to the interim financial information for it to conform with generally accepted accounting principles.

A review differs significantly from an audit. A review is not a sufficient basis for expressing an opinion about the fairness of financial statements. A review (AU 722.07) consists principally of performing analytical procedures and making inquiries of persons responsible for financial and accounting matters, and does not contemplate

1. Tests of accounting records through inspection, observation, or confirmation.
2. Tests of controls to evaluate their effectiveness.
3. Obtaining corroborating evidence in response to inquiries.
4. Performing certain other procedures ordinarily performed in an audit.

The purpose of a review is to bring significant matters to the accountant's attention. However, it does not provide any assurance that the accountant will become aware of all significant matters that would generally be discovered with an audit.

ESTABLISHING AN UNDERSTANDING WITH THE CLIENT

An understanding should be established with the client about the services that will be performed to reduce the risk that either side misunderstands the needs or expectations of the other party. This understanding should be documented, preferably through written communication with the client.

THE ACCOUNTANT'S KNOWLEDGE OF THE ENTITY'S BUSINESS AND ITS INTERNAL CONTROL

The accountant should have knowledge of the entity's business and its internal control. Generally, an accountant who has audited the entity's most recent financial statements would have sufficient knowledge of an entity's internal control. If the accountant has not audited the most recent annual financial statements, procedures should be performed to acquire such knowledge.

The accountant should be able to identify the types of potential material misstatements to determine the likelihood of their occurrence. The accountant should inquire and perform analytical procedures to learn about material modifications to the interim financial information that may be necessary. Common procedures include

1. Reading prior year's audit documentation.
2. Reading most recent annual financial information.
3. Considering prior year's audit procedures.
4. Inquiring of management about significant changes in business activities and internal controls.

ANALYTICAL PROCEDURES, INQUIRIES, AND OTHER REVIEW PROCEDURES

Analytical procedures, for reviewing interim financial statements, include

1. Comparing quarterly interim financial information with information from comparable preceding periods.
2. Considering plausible relationships among both financial and relevant nonfinancial data.
3. Comparing recorded amounts, or ratios to expectations.
4. Comparing disaggregated revenue data with data of comparable prior periods.

REPRESENTATIONS FROM MANAGEMENT

Written representations from management should be obtained. Specifically, the following representations should be furnished:

1. Management acknowledges its responsibility for fair presentation of financial information in conformity with GAAP.
2. Management has disclosed all significant deficiencies and material weaknesses in the design or operation of relevant internal controls.
3. Management's knowledge of fraud or suspected fraud, or allegations of fraud.
4. Completeness and availability of all information, including minutes of meetings of stockholders, directors, and committees of directors.
5. There are no unrecorded transactions.
6. Information concerning related-party transactions.
7. Guarantees, whether written or oral, under which the entity is contingently liable.
8. Violations or possible violations of laws or regulations.

9. Unasserted claims or assessments and other gain or loss contingencies.
10. Satisfactory title to all owned assets, liens or encumbrances on such assets, and assets pledged as collateral.
11. Compliance with contractual agreements.
12. Information concerning subsequent events.

COMMUNICATIONS TO MANAGEMENT, AUDIT COMMITTEES, AND OTHERS

Based on the review procedures, the accountant may learn of likely misstatements. Such misstatements should be evaluated both individually and in the aggregate. The accountant should communicate these matter(s) to the appropriate level of management.

If management does not respond appropriately to the accountant's communication, the accountant should inform the audit committee or others with equivalent authority and responsibility.

If the audit committee does not respond appropriately to the accountant's communication, the accountant should consider resigning from the engagement.

THE ACCOUNTANT'S REPORT

The accountant's review report accompanying interim financial information should consist of (AU 722.37)

1. Includes the word *independent* in the title.
2. A statement that the interim financial information was *reviewed.*
3. A statement that the interim financial information is the responsibility of the entity's management.
4. A statement that the review was conducted in accordance with standards established by the AICPA.
5. A description of the procedures used for a review.
6. A statement explaining that a review is substantially less in scope than an audit.
7. A statement about the accountant awareness of no necessary material modifications.
8. Accountant's signature.
9. Date of the review report.
10. Each page should be marked as unaudited.

The following is an example of a review report (AU 722.38):

Independent Accountant's Report

We have reviewed the accompanying [*describe the interim financial information or statements reviewed*] of ABC Company and consolidated subsidiaries as of September 30, 20X1, and for the three-month and nine-month periods then ended. This (These) interim financial information (statements) is (are) the responsibility of the company's management.

We conducted our review in accordance with standards established by the American Institute of Certified Public Accountants. A review of interim financial information consists principally of applying analytical procedures and making inquiries of persons responsible for financial and accounting matters. It is substantially less in scope than an audit conducted in accordance with generally accepted auditing standards, the objective of which is the expression of an opinion regarding the financial statements taken as a whole. Accordingly, we do not express such an opinion.

Based on our review, we are not aware of any material modifications that should be made to the accompanying interim financial information (statements) for it (them) to be in conformity with accounting principles generally accepted in the United States of America.

[*Signature*]

[*Date*]

Modification of the Accountant's Review Report

The accountant's report should be modified for departures from GAAP. An additional paragraph is not required if substantial doubt about the entity's ability to continue as a going concern or a lack of consistency in the application of accounting principles has been appropriately disclosed.

The accountant should describe the departure from GAAP and, if practicable, should state the effects on the interim financial information. Following is an example of such a modification of the accountant's review report:

[*Explanatory third paragraph*]

Based on information furnished to us by management, we believe that the company has excluded from property and debt in the accompanying balance sheet certain lease obligations that we believe should be capitalized to conform with accounting principles generally accepted in the United States of America. This information indicates that if these lease obligations were capitalized at September 30, 20X1, property would be increased by $ _____, long-term debt by $ _____, and net income and earnings per share would be increased (decreased) by $_____, $_____, $_____, and $_____, respectively, for the three-month and nine-month periods then ended.

[*Concluding paragraph*]

Based on our review, with the exception of the matter(s) described in the preceding paragraph(s), we are not aware of any material modifications that should be made to the accompanying interim financial information (statements) for it (them) to be in conformity with accounting principles generally accepted in the United States of America.

If the accountant believes that there is inadequate disclosure, the accountant should modify the report and, if practicable, include the necessary information in the report. An example of such a modification follows:

[*Explanatory third paragraph*]

Management has informed us that the company is presently contesting deficiencies in federal income taxes proposed by the Internal Revenue Service for the years 20X1 through 20X3 in the aggregate amount of approximately $_____, and that the extent of the company's liability, if any, and the effect on the accompanying information (statements) is not determinable at this time. The information (statements) fail(s) to disclose these matters, which we believe are required to be disclosed in conformity with accounting principles generally accepted in the United States of America.

[*Concluding paragraph*]

Based on our review, with the exception of the matter(s) described in the preceding paragraph(s), we are not aware of any material modifications that should be made to the accompanying interim financial information (statements) for it (them) to be in conformity with accounting principles generally accepted in the United States of America.

For going-concern considerations, the accountant may add an explanatory paragraph to the review report after the concluding paragraph as follows:

As indicated in Note 3, certain conditions indicate that the company may be unable to continue as a going concern. The accompanying interim financial information does not include any adjustments that might result from the outcome of this uncertainty.

801 COMPLIANCE AUDITING CONSIDERATIONS IN AUDITS OF GOVERNMENTAL ENTITIES AND RECIPIENTS OF GOVERNMENTAL FINANCIAL ASSISTANCE

SOURCE OF STANDARDS

SAS 74, *Compliance Auditing Considerations in Audits of Governmental Entities and Recipients of Governmental Financial Assistance*

INTRODUCTION/SUMMARY

This section provides guidance for auditing governmental entities under generally accepted auditing standards (GAAS) for testing and reporting on compliance under Government Auditing Standards (the Yellow Book), or in certain circumstances for governmental financial assistance, such as single or organization-wide audits or program-specific audits under certain federal or state audit regulations. It provides guidance on

1. Applying the provisions of Section 317, *Illegal Acts by Clients.*
2. Performing a financial audit in accordance with Government Auditing Standards, issued by the Comptroller General of the United States.
3. Performing a single or organization-wide audit or a program-specific audit in accordance with federal audit requirements.
4. Communicating with management if the auditor learns that the entity is subject to certain audit requirements that were not encompassed in the terms of engagement.

EFFECTS OF LAWS ON FINANCIAL STATEMENTS

Financial statements of governmental entities are affected by the entity's compliance with a variety of laws and regulations. Generally accepted accounting principles (GAAP) for governmental entities recognize the variety of legal and contractual considerations typical in the government environment. These legal and contractual considerations are a distinguishing factor between governmental accounting versus commercial accounting. For instance, the laws and regulations may specify the fund structure, bond covenants, debt limitations, and legal authority for transactions.

Frequently, federal, state, and local governmental entities provide financial assistance to other entities.

Many not-for-profit organizations and business enterprises are primary recipients, subrecipients, or beneficiaries of

1. Governmental grants of cash and other assets
2. Loans
3. Loan guarantees
4. Interest-rate subsidies

By accepting financial assistance, both governmental and nongovernmental entities may become subject to laws and regulations that may have a direct and material effect on the financial statements. Management is responsible for ensuring compliance with laws and regulations.

The auditor's responsibility is to design the audit to provide reasonable assurance that the financial statements are free of material misstatements resulting from violations of laws and regulations that have a direct and material effect on the determination of financial statement amounts.

The following procedures may assist the auditor in assessing compliance with laws and regulations and in obtaining an understanding of their possible effects on the financial statements (AU 801.07):

1. Consider knowledge about such laws and regulations obtained from prior years' audits.
2. Discuss such laws and regulations with the entity's chief financial officer, legal counsel, or grant administrators.
3. Obtain written representation from management regarding the completeness of management's identification.
4. Review the relevant portions of any directly related agreements, such as those related to grants and loans.
5. Review the minutes of meetings of the legislative body and governing board of the governmental entity being audited for the enactment of laws and regulations that have a direct and material effect on the determination of amounts in the governmental entity's financial statements.
6. Inquire of the office of the federal, state, or local auditor, or other appropriate audit oversight organization about the laws and regulations applicable to entities within their jurisdiction, including statutes and uniform reporting requirements.
7. Review information about compliance requirements, such as the information included in the Compliance Supplements: Compliance Supplement for Single Audits of State and Local Governments and Compliance Supplement for Audits of Institutions of Higher Learning and Other Non-Profit Institutions, Catalog of Federal Domestic Assistance, issued by the Government Printing Office, and state and local policies and procedures.

FEDERAL AUDIT REQUIREMENTS

The scope and reporting requirements of an audit of a recipient of federal financial assistance generally include the following factors:

1. The audit is conducted in accordance with GAAS and Government Auditing Standards.
2. The auditor's consideration of internal control, including obtaining an understanding of internal control, and documenting the understanding and testing controls to evaluate the effectiveness.
3. Issuance of a report on the consideration of internal controls.
4. A determination and report on whether there has been compliance with federal financial assistance.

The recipient of federal financial assistance may be subject to a single or organization-wide audit or to a program-specific audit. Sometimes, a recipient may "elect" to have a program-specific audit. In other instances, the federal regulations require a program-specific audit.

COMPLIANCE REQUIREMENTS FOR FEDERAL FINANCIAL ASSISTANCE PROGRAMS

There are two types of compliance requirements for federal financial assistance programs. General requirements are based on national policy and almost all federal financial assistance programs must meet the general requirements. Specific requirements are particular to a specific federal program and are based on statutory requirements or regulations.

The OMB's Compliance Supplements contain the general and specific requirements for most of the federal programs. The Compliance Supplement also contains recommended audit procedures for testing compliance. In addition, for program-specific audits, federal grantor agency audit guides should be consulted for programs-specific compliance requirements and audit tests. The auditor should also consult grant agreements or contracts for additional specific requirements.

EVALUATING RESULTS OF COMPLIANCE AUDIT PROCEDURES ON MAJOR FEDERAL FINANCIAL ASSISTANCE PROGRAMS

To evaluate compliance, the auditor should consider

1. The frequency of noncompliance.
2. How well can the primary recipient monitor the subrecipients? What are the possible effects on the program due to noncompliance?
3. Did noncompliance result in questioned costs (i.e., auditor's best estimate of total costs questioned for each major federal financial assistance program)? Were the questioned costs material to the program?

The auditor should be aware that regardless of his opinion on compliance, the federal regulations may require him to report individual instances of noncompliance discovered, as well as associated questioned costs.

Noncompliance should be reported following the Government Auditing Standards. When reporting questioned costs, the auditor is required to report only *known* questioned costs. *Likely* questioned costs do not have to be reported.

COMMUNICATIONS REGARDING APPLICABLE AUDIT REQUIREMENTS

While management is responsible for obtaining audits that satisfy the legal requirements, auditors should ensure that management understands the type of engagement being performed and whether that engagement would meet the needs of management. An engagement letter is recommended and the letter should contain a statement about the type of engagement and what specific audit requirements will be met.

GAAS require the auditor to perform procedures to obtain sufficient competent evidential matter to form an opinion on the financial statements. While the auditor is not required to perform additional procedures in a GAAS audit, the auditor should communicate with the client if the auditor becomes aware that the entity is subject to an audit requirement that was not in the terms of the engagement.

The management, the audit committee, or others with equivalent authority, should be notified that a GAAS audit is not sufficient for relevant regulatory or contractual purposes.

The auditor may notify the appropriate party either orally or in writing. Oral communication should be documented in the working papers. Management's response to such communication should also be noted. The auditor should consider management's response in evaluating the potential effect on financial statements as well as the auditor's report.

901 PUBLIC WAREHOUSES: CONTROLS AND AUDITING PROCEDURES FOR GOODS HELD

SOURCE OF STANDARDS

SAS 1, *Codification of Auditing Standards and Procedures*
SAS 43, *Omnibus Statement on Auditing Standards*

INTRODUCTION/SUMMARY

The independent auditor of the warehouse employee should (AU 901.03)

1. Obtain an understanding of controls and perform a test of controls;
2. Test the warehouse employee's records for goods in custody;
3. Test accountability for outstanding warehouse receipts;
4. Observe physical counts of goods in custody, and when possible reconcile such counts with records of stored goods;
5. Confirm accountability by direct communication with the holders of warehouse receipts; and
6. Apply other procedures as considered necessary.

TYPES OF WAREHOUSES

A warehouse is a facility that maintains custody of goods for others. Warehouses can be classified functionally as *terminal warehouses* or *field warehouses:*

1. *Terminal Warehouse.* A terminal warehouse's primary function is storage. Sometimes the employees perform other functions such as packaging and billing.
2. *Field Warehouse.* Field warehousing is basically a financing arrangement, rather than a storage operation. A field warehouse is set up on space leased by the warehouse employee on the premises of the owner of the goods or the premises of a customer of the owner. Generally, most of the warehouse employees are hired by the warehouse operator from among the employees of the owner (or customer). A field warehouse is set up primarily to allow the warehouse operator to take and maintain custody of goods and issue warehouse receipts, which may be used as collateral for a loan.

Warehouses can also be classified according to the types of goods stored. For instance

1. A refrigerated warehouse may be used to store food or other perishables; and
2. A commodity warehouse may be used to store bulk commodities such as agricultural products (often these warehouses store only one commodity, and fungible goods are commingled without regard to ownership); and

3. A general merchandise warehouse may be used to store a variety of general merchandise.

WAREHOUSE RECEIPTS

A warehouse receipt is a basic document used in warehousing. Uniform Commercial Code (UCC) Article 7 regulates the issuance of warehouse receipts. The code

1. Prescribes terms that should be contained in such receipts,
2. Provides for their negotiation and transfer, and
3. Establishes the rights of receipt holders.

The warehouse receipt may be used as evidence of collateral for loans or other types of credit. The warehouse receipts may be in negotiable form or nonnegotiable form. A negotiable warehouse receipt must be surrendered for goods to be released. A nonnegotiable receipt does not need to be surrendered for goods to be released. A nonnegotiable receipt does not provide any evidence of ownership. It also does not indicate any accountability on the part of the warehouse operator. Since goods may be taken a few items at a time, the warehouse operator's accountability is for the total quantity of goods for which receipts have been issued less authorized withdrawals.

THE WAREHOUSE OPERATOR

AUDITOR'S EVALUATION OF CONTROLS

The warehouse operator only has custody of goods. The goods do not appear as assets and the related custodial responsibility does not appear as a liability in the financial statements.

The warehouse operator has potential liability for faulty performance. Examples of risk of loss for faulty performance include

1. Loss or improper release of goods,
2. Improper issuance of warehouse receipts, and
3. Failure to maintain effective custody of goods so that lenders' preferential liens are lost.

Auditors of a warehouseman should be aware of the potential liability of their client. Auditors of the warehouse operator must

1. Obtain an understanding of relevant controls, and
2. Perform tests of controls to evaluate their effectiveness.

The controls related to the custodial nature of the business must be evaluated even though they are not directly related to the financial statements. The warehouse operator can incur significant liabilities if the warehouse operator's custodial responsibility is not discharged adequately.

RECEIVING, STORING, AND DELIVERING GOODS

1. A receipt should be given for all goods received for storage.
2. A receiving report should be prepared for all goods received. The quantities showing on the receiving report should be compared with quantities shown on bills of lading or other documents generated by outside sources.
3. Goods received should be inspected, counted, weighed, measured, or graded as necessary. Periodically the accuracy of mechanical facilities used for these purposes should be checked.

4. Unless the goods stored are fungible goods, they should be stored separately and clearly marked with identifying data. Electronic or paper records should show the location of the goods for each issued and outstanding warehouse receipt.

5. Goods represented by nonnegotiable receipt should only be released after proper authorization.

6. Goods represented by a negotiable receipt should only be released after surrender of the receipt.

7. Goods should be released from the warehouse only on the basis of written authorization from an authorized employee independent of the storage function.

8. Access to storage areas should be limited to authorized individuals. Controls should be in place to prevent unauthorized access to key areas of the storage facility.

9. Statements identifying the goods held should be provided to customers. Customers should be requested to report any discrepancy to an independent individual or department. This individual or department should not be involved with receiving, storing, or delivering goods.

10. Goods should be physically counted on a periodic basis. The counted quantities should be reconciled to storage records by someone independent of the storage function.

11. Perishable goods should be inspected on a regular basis to ensure conditions for their storage are as intended.

12. Protective devices such as burglar alarms, fire alarms, sprinkler systems, and temperature and humidity controls should be installed and inspected on a periodic basis.

13. An independent count of goods should be made before goods are released and the independent count should be compared before the goods are released.

WAREHOUSE RECEIPTS

1. Only prenumbered warehouse receipts should be issued. The numerical sequence of the receipts should be accounted for periodically. Negotiable receipts should be canceled after goods are released.

2. Unused receipt forms should be stored in a secure location. An individual not authorized to prepare or sign the receipt should have custody of the forms.

3. Receipts should be prepared and completed completely to prevent unauthorized alterations.

4. Authorized signers should ensure that receipts are supported by receiving records or other underlying documents.

INSURANCE

Insurance coverage should be reviewed periodically to ensure that both the amount and type of coverage is adequate.

ADDITIONAL CONTROLS FOR FIELD WAREHOUSES

The purpose of a field warehouse is different from a terminal warehouse. A field warehouse operator may typically manage a large number of locations. The controls for a field warehouse are needed at both the field location and the warehouse operator's central office. Only nonnegotiable warehouse receipts should be issued from field locations. The receipt forms should be provided to the field locations by the central office in limited quantities, as appropriate.

The following controls are suggested by AU 901.18 for the central office:

1. Review of the business reputation and financial standing of the depositor.
2. Preparation of a field warehouse contract in accordance with the particular requirements of the depositor and the lender.
3. Determination that the leased warehouse premises meet the physical requirements for segregation and effective custody of goods.
4. Satisfaction as to legal matters relative to the lease of the warehouse premises.
5. Investigation and bonding of the employees at the field locations.
6. Providing employees at field locations with written instructions covering their duties and responsibilities.
7. Maintenance of inventory records at the central office showing the quantity (and stated value, where applicable) of goods represented by each outstanding warehouse receipt.
8. Examination of the field warehouse by representatives of the central office.

Examinations of the field warehouse should include inspection of the facilities, observation as to adherence to prescribed procedures, physical counts or tests of goods in custody and reconcilement of quantities to records at the central office and at field locations, accounting for all receipt forms furnished to the field locations, and confirmation (on a test basis, where appropriate) of outstanding warehouse receipts with the registered holders.

PROCEDURES OF THE INDEPENDENT AUDITOR

AU 901.19 recommends that the independent auditor apply the following procedures when considered necessary under the circumstances:

1. Obtain an understanding of controls relating to the accountability and custody of goods in the warehouse and perform tests of controls to evaluate their effectiveness.
2. Test the warehouse operator's records concerning accountability for goods in custody.
3. Test the warehouse operator's accountability for recorded outstanding warehouse receipts.
4. Observe physical counts of the goods in custody, and reconcile with records of goods stored.
5. Confirm accountability as necessary by direct communication with the holders of warehouse receipts.

CONTROLS AND AUDITING PROCEDURES FOR OWNER'S GOODS STORED IN PUBLIC WAREHOUSES

The owner should conduct an investigation of the warehouse operator before the goods are placed in the operator's custody.

The performance of the warehouse operator should be evaluated on a periodic basis. The owner should ensure that controls over the goods in a warehouse operator's custody provide reasonable safeguards. AU 901.26 suggests the following be considered when investigating the warehouse operator:

1. Review of the business reputation and financial standing of the warehouse operator.
2. Inspection of the physical facilities.
3. Inquiries as to the warehouse operator's controls and whether the warehouse operator holds goods for a personal account.
4. Inquiries as to type and adequacy of the warehouse operator's insurance.
5. Inquiries as to government or other licensing and bonding requirements and the nature, extent, and results of any inspection by government or other agencies.

6. Review of the warehouse operator's financial statements and related reports of independent auditors.

AU 901.27 suggests the following for periodically evaluating the warehouse operator's performance:

1. Review and update the information described above.
2. Physical counts or test counts of the goods.
3. Reconcilement of quantities shown on statements received from the warehouse operator with the owners records.
4. Review of insurance on goods in the custody of the warehouse operator.

PART 3

ATTESTATION

20 DEFINING PROFESSIONAL REQUIREMENTS IN STATEMENTS ON STANDARDS FOR ATTESTATION ENGAGEMENTS

SOURCE OF STANDARDS

SSAE 13, *Defining Professional Requirements in Statements on Standards for Attestation Engagements*

INTRODUCTION/SUMMARY

This section clarifies terminology concerning "requirements" in attestation engagements.

PROFESSIONAL REQUIREMENTS

An *unconditional requirement,* included in a Statement on Standards for Attestation Engagements, means that the practitioner is required to comply with the requirement in all cases. The phrases *"must"* and *"is required"* are indicative of an unconditional requirement.

A *presumptively mandatory requirement,* on the other hand, means that, under normal conditions, the practitioner is required to comply with the requirement. However, in rare circumstances, the practitioner may depart from a presumptively mandatory requirement, provided the practitioner documents the justification for the departure and how alternative procedures performed were sufficient. The phrase *"should"* indicates a presumptively mandatory requirement.

EXPLANATORY MATERIAL

Explanatory material is text included in a Statement on Standards for Attestation Engagements that

1. Provides additional explanation and guidance on a professional requirement, or
2. Identifies and describes other attest procedures or actions. It should be noted that the words *may, might,* and *could* are used in the context of explanatory material.

50 SSAE HIERARCHY

SOURCE OF STANDARDS

SSAE 14, *SSAE Hierarchy*

INTRODUCTION/SUMMARY

This section revises the attestation standards in AT Section 101, *Attestation Engagements*. In addition this section clarifies that attestation standards represent a measure of quality and the objectives to be achieved in an attestation engagement, while attestation procedures represent acts performed during an attestation engagement to comply with the attestation standards. Finally, the use of attestation interpretations and other attestation publications is addressed.

ATTESTATION STANDARDS

Refer to AT Section 101, *Attestation Engagements,* for a discussion of the revised attestation standards.

ATTESTATION INTERPRETATIONS

Attestation interpretations represent recommendations on the application of Statements on Standards for Attestation Engagements in specific circumstances and include

1. Interpretations of the SSAEs,
2. Appendixes included in SSAEs,
3. Attestation guidance contained in Audit and Accounting Guides issued by the AICPA, and
4. Statements of Position issued by the AICPA.

If a practitioner does not follow an applicable attestation interpretation, the practitioner should be prepared to explain how the SSAE provisions were otherwise complied with.

OTHER ATTESTATION PUBLICATIONS

While not authoritative, other attestation publications may assist in the understanding and application of the SSAEs. Other attestation applications include

1. Articles in professional journals such as the *Journal of Accountancy,*
2. Articles in the *CPA Letter* published by the AICPA,
3. Materials contained in continuing professional education courses,
4. Textbooks, and
5. Attestation programs and checklists.

101 ATTEST ENGAGEMENTS

SOURCE OF STANDARDS

SSAE 10, *Attest Standards: Revision and Recodification*
SSAE 11, *Attest Documentation*
SSAE 12, *Amendments to Statements on Standards for Attestation Engagements No. 10: Revision and Recodification*
SSAE 14, *SSAE Hierarchy*

SUMMARY

This section provides guidance concerning the performance and reporting for attest engagements, wherein a CPA is engaged to issue or does issue an examination, a review, or an agreed-upon procedures report on subject matter, or an assertion about the subject matter (assertion) that is the responsibility of another party. The practitioner is not required to follow the provisions contained in this section if engaged to

1. Perform an audit in connection with historical financial statements, to which Statements on Auditing Standards (SAS) are applicable;
2. Perform a compilation or review of historical financial statements, to which Statements on Standards for Accounting and Review Services (SSARS) are applicable;
3. Conduct a consulting engagement involving management, to which Statements on Standards for Consulting Services (SSCS) are applicable;
4. Serve as an expert witness;
5. Provide tax advice or prepare tax returns; or
6. Serve as a client's authorized representative at an income tax audit.

In order to reduce the risk of misinterpretation by the practitioner or the client, the CPA should establish an understanding with the client regarding the services to be performed. The understanding should include

1. The objectives of the engagement,
2. The responsibilities of management, and
3. The limitations of the engagement.

The practitioner should document the understanding in the working papers, preferably by means of a written communication with the client. (An engagement letter is highly suggested.) A practitioner should not accept an engagement unless an understanding with the client has been established.

DEFINITIONS AND UNDERLYING CONCEPTS

The *subject matter,* which may be as of a point in time or for a period of time, may be in many forms, including the following:

1. Historical or prospective performance or condition; for example, the latest annual rate of return on a stock fund.
2. Physical characteristics; for example, square footage of a storage facility.
3. Historical events, such as the price of a commodity at a specific date.
4. Analyses; for example, break-even analysis for a particular product.
5. Systems and processes; for example, a client's internal control (see AT Section 501).
6. Behavior; for example, compliance with applicable laws and regulations (see AT Section 601).

An *assertion* may be any declaration or set of declarations about whether the specific subject matter is based on or in conformity with the selected criteria. It should be noted that a CPA may be engaged to report on a written assertion or directly on the subject matter. In either case, in an examination or a review engagement (discussed below), a CPA should ordinarily obtain a written assertion, which may be presented in a narrative description, within a schedule, or as part of a representation letter.

The responsible party may be the person or persons responsible for the subject matter. It is important to remember that the practitioner CPA serving as an attester cannot be the responsible party.

ATTESTATION STANDARDS AND THEIR RELATIONSHIP TO QUALITY CONTROL STANDARDS

An accounting practitioner or a firm of accounting practitioners must set up and adhere to a system of quality control if the practitioner or the firm of practitioners performs any attest service to which SSAEs apply. However, by itself, a deficiency in or lack of compliance with a system of quality control should not be interpreted to mean that a particular attest engagement was not in compliance with the attestation standards.

ATTESTATION STANDARDS

General Standards

1. The practitioner must have adequate technical training and proficiency.
2. The practitioner must possess adequate knowledge of the subject matter.
3. The practitioner must have reason to believe that the subject matter is capable of evaluation against criteria that are suitable and available to users. Suitability of criteria should be based on the objectivity, measurability, completeness, and relevance of the criteria.
4. Throughout the conduct of an attest engagement, a practitioner must maintain mental independence, as detailed in Rule 101 of the AICPA Code of Professional Conduct.
5. In planning and performing an attest engagement, and preparing the report, the practitioner must exercise due professional care. Accordingly there must be a critical review of the work performed at all levels of supervision.

Standards of Fieldwork

1. The engagement must be adequately planned, and if assistants are utilized, they must be properly supervised. To adequately plan an attest engagement, a practitioner should consider:

    a. The criteria to be used.
    b. Preliminary judgments regarding materiality and attestation risk.

    c.   Conditions likely to cause modification or addition to attest procedures.

    d.   The nature of the subject matter.

    e.   Items with the assertion about the subject matter that are likely to need adjustment.

    f.   The nature of the report expected to be issued by the practitioner.

       In planning the engagement, the practitioner should establish an understanding with the client regarding the services to be performed.

2. The practitioner must obtain sufficient evidence in order to support the conclusion expressed in his or her report.

As in an audit of financial statements, the following should be understood:

1. Evidence generated from independent external sources is more reliable than evidence obtained from within the client entity.

2. Information is more persuasive if derived from the practitioner's direct personal knowledge. Accordingly the practitioner should consider selecting procedures that include, where appropriate, physical examination, observation, operating tests, and inspection.

3. More assurance regarding the subject matter or the assertion about the subject matter is provided if internal controls over the subject matter are effective.

The practitioner should keep in mind that the objective of an "examination" engagement is to express a high level of assurance. Thus the practitioner should select a combination of procedures from all those available. However, the objective of a "review" engagement is to express a moderate level of assurance. Thus the practitioner should select a combination of procedures based only on inquiry and analytical procedures.

In an examination or a review engagement, a CPA should consider obtaining, from the responsible party, a representation letter that covers both oral and written representations made in response to specific inquiries or through the presentation of the subject matter or the assertion.

Standards of Reporting

The practitioner's report must include the following:

1. Identification of the subject matter and the character of the engagement.

2. A conclusion regarding the subject matter or the assertion in relation to the criteria against which the subject matter was evaluated. If the engagement was an examination, an opinion should be expressed; if the engagement was a review, negative assurance should be expressed.

3. All significant reservations (i.e., unresolved problems and/or scope limitations) about the engagement, the subject matter, and if applicable, the related assertion.

4. A statement that the report is intended solely for the information and use of the specified parties when

    a.   The practitioner determines that the criteria used to evaluate the subject matter are appropriate for a limited number of parties who either participated in their establishment or can be presumed to possess an adequate understanding of the criteria,

    b.   The criteria used to evaluate the subject matter are available only to specified parties,

    c.   Reporting on subject matter and a written assertion has not been provided by a responsible party, or

    d.   The report is based on the application of agreed-upon procedures.

REPORTS BASED ON AN EXAMINATION TO EXPRESS AN OPINION

Conclusions should be expressed in the form of an opinion about whether the subject matter is based on (or in conformity with) the criteria in all material respects, or whether the assertion is presented (or fairly stated), in all material respects, based on the criteria. Reports may be qualified, modified (e.g., as in the case of emphasizing a matter), or contain a disclaimer.

If the examination results in the identification of conditions that result in one or more material misstatements or departures from the criteria, then the practitioner should modify the report, and ordinarily express a conclusion directly on the subject matter, rather than on the assertion.

An examination report generally should include

1. A title that includes the word *independent.*
2. An identification of the subject matter or an identification of the assertion (or a statement of the assertion, if the assertion does not accompany the examination report) and the responsible party.
3. A statement that the subject matter (or the assertion) is the responsibility of the responsible party.
4. A statement that the practitioner's responsibility is to express an opinion on the subject matter (or the assertion) based on his or her examination.
5. A statement that the examination was conducted in accordance with attestation standards established by the American Institute of Certified Public Accountants, and, accordingly, included procedures that the practitioner considered necessary in the circumstances.
6. A statement that the practitioner believes the examination provides a reasonable basis for his or her opinion.
7. The practitioner's opinion on whether

   a. The subject matter is based on (or in conformity with) the criteria in all material respects, or
   b. The assertion is presented (or fairly stated), in all material respects, based on the criteria.

8. A statement restricting the use of the report to specified parties when

   a. The criteria used to evaluate the subject matter are determined by the practitioner to be appropriate only for a limited number of parties who either participated in their establishment or can be presumed to have an adequate understanding of the criteria;
   b. The criteria used to evaluate the subject matter are available only to the specified parties; or
   c. A written assertion has not been provided by the responsible party (a statement to that effect should also be included in the explanatory paragraph of the report).

9. A signature of the practitioner's firm, which may be manual or printed.
10. The date of the examination report.

The form and content of a standard examination report on subject matter for general use follows.

Independent Accountant's Report

We have examined the [*identify the subject matter; e.g., the accompanying schedule of investment returns of XYZ Company for the year ended December 31, 20XX*]. XYZ Company's management is responsible for the schedule of investment returns. Our responsibility is to express an opinion based on our examination.

Our examination was conducted in accordance with attestation standards established by the American Institute of Certified Public Accountants and, accordingly, included examining on a test basis, evidence supporting the [*identify the subject matter; e.g., XYZ Company's schedule of investment returns*] and performing such other procedures as we considered necessary in the circumstances. We believe that our examination provides a reasonable basis for our opinion.

[*Additional paragraph(s) may be added to emphasize certain matters relating to the attest engagement or the subject matter.*]

In our opinion, the schedule referred to above presents, in all material respects, [*identify the subject matter; e.g., the investment returns of XYZ Company for the year ended December 31, 20XX*] based on [*identify criteria; e.g., the ABC criteria set forth in Note 1*].

[*Signature*]

[*Date*]

The form and content of a standard examination report on an assertion for general use follows.

Independent Accountant's Report

We have examined management's assertion that [*identify the subject matter; e.g., the accompanying schedule of investment returns of XYZ Company for the year ended December 31, 20XX is presented in accordance with ABC criteria set forth in Note 1*]. XYZ Company's management is responsible for the assertion. Our responsibility is to express an opinion on the assertion based on our examination.

Our examination was conducted in accordance with attestation standards established by the American Institute of Certified Public Accountants and, accordingly, included examining, on a test basis, evidence supporting management's assertion and performing such other procedures as we considered necessary in the circumstances. We believe that our examination provides a reasonable basis for our opinion.

[*Additional paragraph(s) may be added to emphasize certain matters relating to the attest engagement or the assertion.*]

In our opinion, management's assertion referred to above is fairly stated, in all material respects, based on [*identify established or stated criteria; e.g., the ABC criteria set forth in Note 1*].

[*Signature*]

[*Date*]

REPORTS BASED ON A REVIEW TO EXPRESS NEGATIVE ASSURANCE

Conclusions should be expressed in the form of negative assurance. A review report generally should include

1. A title that includes the word *independent.*
2. An identification of the subject matter or an identification of the assertion (or a statement of the assertion, if the assertion does not accompany the examination report) and the responsible party.
3. A statement that the subject matter (or the assertion) is the responsibility of the responsible party.

4. A statement that the review was conducted in accordance with attestation standards established by the American Institute of Certified Public Accountants.
5. A statement that a review is substantially less in scope than an examination, the objective of which is the expression of opinion on the subject matter (or the assertion), and accordingly, no such opinion is expressed.
6. Negative assurance, which is a statement about whether the practitioner is aware of any material modifications that should be made to

    a. The subject matter in order for it to be based on (or in conformity with), in all material respects, the criteria, other than those modifications, if any, indicated in the review report, or
    b. The assertion in order for it to be presented (or fairly stated), in all material respects, based on (or in conformity with) the criteria, other than those modifications, if any, indicated in the review report.

7. A statement restricting the use of the report to specified parties when

    a. The criteria used to evaluate the subject matter are determined by the practitioner to be appropriate only for a limited number of parties who either participated in their establishment or can be presumed to have an adequate understanding of the criteria;
    b. The criteria used to evaluate the subject matter are available only to the specified parties; or
    c. A written assertion has not been provided by the responsible party (a statement to that effect should also be included in the explanatory paragraph of the report).

8. A signature of the practitioner's firm, which may be manual or printed.
9. The date of the review report.

The form and content of a standard review report on subject matter for general use follows.

Independent Accountant's Report

We have reviewed the [*identify the subject matter; e.g., the accompanying schedule of investment returns of XYZ Company for the year ended December 31, 20XX*]. XYZ Company's management is responsible for the schedule of investment returns.

Our review was conducted in accordance with attestation standards established by the American Institute of Certified Public Accountants. A review is substantially less in scope than an examination, the objective of which is the expression of an opinion on [*identify the subject matter; e.g., XYZ Company's schedule of investment returns*]. Accordingly we do not express such an opinion.

[*Additional paragraph(s) maybe added to emphasize certain matters relating to the attest engagement or the subject matter.*]

Based on our review, nothing came to our attention that caused us to believe that the [identify the subject matter; e.g., schedule of investment returns of XYZ Company for the year ended December 31, 20XX] is not presented, in all material respects, in conformity with [*identify the criteria; e.g., the ABC criteria set forth in Note 1*].

[*Signature*]

[*Date*]

The form and content of a standard review report on an assertion for general use follows.

Independent Accountant's Report

We have reviewed management's assertion that [*identify the assertion e.g., the accompanying schedule of investment returns of XYZ Company for the year ended December 31, 20XX, is presented in accordance with the ABC criteria referred to in Note 1*]. XYZ Company's management is responsible for the assertion.

Our review was conducted in accordance with attestation standards established by the American Institute of Certified Public Accountants. A review is substantially less in scope than an examination, the objective of which is the expression of an opinion on management's assertion. Accordingly we do not express such an opinion.

[*Additional paragraph(s) may be added to emphasize certain matters relating to the attest engagement or the assertion.*]

Based on our review, nothing came to our attention that caused us to believe that management's assertion referred to above is not fairly stated, in all material respects, based on [*identify the criteria; e.g., the ABC criteria referred to in the investment management agreement between XYZ Company and DEF Investment Managers, Ltd., dated November 15, 20XX*].

[*Signature*]

[*Date*]

ENGAGEMENTS TO PERFORM AGREED-UPON PROCEDURES

If the practitioner is requested to perform an "Agreed-upon Procedures Engagement," the guidance to follow is in AT Section 201.

OTHER INFORMATION IN A CLIENT-PREPARED DOCUMENT CONTAINING THE PRACTITIONER'S ATTEST REPORT

The practitioner's responsibility for other information in a client-prepared document containing the attest report is similar to an auditor's responsibility for other information in a client-prepared document containing audited financial statements and the audit report, as discussed in AU Section 550. In an attest engagement the practitioner essentially should read the other information to identify material inconsistencies between the other information and the information in the practitioner's report.

CONSIDERATION OF SUBSEQUENT EVENTS AND SUBSEQUENT DISCOVERY OF FACTS IN ANATTEST ENGAGEMENT

The practitioner's responsibility for subsequent events and subsequent discovery of facts in an attest engagement is similar to an auditor's responsibility for these items in an audit of financial statements. Accordingly the practitioner should follow the guidance in AU Sections 560 and 561.

ATTEST DOCUMENTATION

The form and content of attest documentation, which may be referred to as working papers, should be designed to meet the circumstances of the engagement. The quantity, type, and content of attest documentation are matters of the practitioner's professional judgment.

Attest documentation may be in paper form, electronic form, or other media. Attest documentation should

1. Enable supervisory and review personnel to understand

   a. The procedures performed,
   b. The results obtained, and
   c. The information obtained.

2. Indicate the engagement team member(s) who performed and reviewed the work.

Attest documentation is the property of the practitioner. Accordingly the practitioner should adopt reasonable retention procedures to meet the needs of professional practice and to satisfy applicable legal and regulatory retention requirements.

The practitioner should adopt reasonable procedures to ensure confidentiality of attest documentation and to prevent unauthorized access to attest documentation.

Attest documentation may sometimes serve as a reference source for a client, but is not part of, or a substitute for, a client's accounting records.

ATTEST SERVICES RELATED TO CONSULTING SERVICE (CS) ENGAGEMENTS

When a practitioner performs an attest service as part of a CS engagement, the Statements on Standards for Attestation Engagements apply only to the attest service. Statements on Standards for Consulting Services apply to the balance of the CS engagement. Accordingly separate reports should be issued for the attest engagement and the CS engagement.

An attest service may involve written assertions, evaluation criteria, or evidential matter developed during a concurrent or prior CS engagement. Furthermore, the evaluation of statements contained in a written assertion of another party when performing a CS engagement does not in and of itself constitute the performance of an attest service.

201 AGREED-UPON PROCEDURES ENGAGEMENTS

SOURCES OF STANDARDS

SSAE 10, *Attest Standards: Revision and Recodification*
SSAE 11, *Attest Documentation*

SUMMARY

This section provides guidance for the performance of and reporting on all agreed-upon procedures engagements, except for the following:

1. Reporting on specified compliance requirements based solely on an audit of financial statements (AU Section 523).
2. Reporting in certain government audits (AU Section 801).
3. Reporting on the processing of transactions by service organizations for use by other auditors (AU Section 324).
4. Letters for underwriters (AU Section 634).

This section also applies to engagements involving financial forecasts and projections (AT Section 301) and compliance attestation (AT Section 601).

AGREED-UPON PROCEDURES ENGAGEMENTS

An agreed-upon procedures engagement is an engagement in which a practitioner is engaged by a client to issue a report of findings based on specific procedures performed on the subject matter or on an assertion about the subject matter. The goal of such an engagement is to help parties evaluate a specific assertion; its underlying premise is that specified parties and the practitioner agree upon the procedures to be performed. In this type of engagement the specified parties assume responsibility for the sufficiency of the procedures the practitioner is to perform.

In an agreed-upon procedures engagement, because the practitioner does not perform an examination or review, the practitioner should not express an opinion or provide negative assurance about the assertion. Rather, the report should simply state procedures and findings. It should also clearly state that its use is restricted to the specified parties.

ASSERTIONS AND RELATED SUBJECT MATTER

An assertion is any declaration, or set of related declarations, about whether the subject matter as a whole is based on or in conformity with the criteria selected by a party responsible for it. It is the specific subject matter of the assertion to which the agreed-upon procedures are to be applied. Examples of assertions are

1. A statement of investment performance statistics of a mutual fund,
2. A statement of claims of creditors,

3. A statement by management about the effectiveness of its internal control over financial reporting, and
4. A statement by management about the effectiveness of its internal control over compliance with the laws and regulations.

A written assertion is generally not required in an agreed-upon procedures engagement.

CONDITIONS FOR PERFORMING THE ENGAGEMENT

A practitioner may perform an agreed-upon procedures attestation engagement provided that the following conditions are met:

1. Independence is maintained throughout the engagement.
2. The party engaging the practitioner either

    a. Is responsible for the subject matter or has a reasonable basis for providing a written assertion about the subject matter when the subject matter is such that a responsible party does not otherwise exist; or
    b. Is not responsible for the subject matter but is able to provide the practitioner, or have a third party who is responsible for the subject matter provide the practitioner, with evidence of the third party's responsibility for the subject matter.

3. The specific procedures to be performed are agreed upon by the practitioner and the specified parties.
4. The sufficiency of the agreed-upon procedures is the responsibility of the specified parties.
5. The subject matter of the agreed-upon procedures engagement is subject to reasonably consistent estimation or measurement.
6. The practitioner and the specified parties agree on the criteria to be used to determine findings.

Reasonably consistent findings are expected based on the procedures to be applied.

1. It is expected that evidential matter is expected to exist to provide a reasonable basis for expressing the findings in the report.
2. Where needed, materiality limits for reporting purposes are agreed upon.
3. Use of the report is restricted to the specified parties.
4. In connection with engagements on prospective financial information, a summary of significant assumptions is included in the prospective financial statements.

It should be readily apparent that before undertaking an agreed-upon procedures engagement, the practitioner should reach an understanding with the client as to the services to be rendered. It is preferable that the understanding be documented in writing, as in an engagement letter.

PROCEDURES TO BE PERFORMED

The procedures to be performed may be as limited or as extensive as the specified parties desire. The practitioner should be careful not to perform procedures that are overly subjective and possibly subject to more than one interpretation, and to avoid terms of uncertain meaning (e.g., limited review).

While the procedures agreed upon are generally to be performed entirely by the independent practitioner, it may be appropriate in some cases to use the services of a specialist. If so, the report should describe the nature of the specialist's involvement.

Although internal auditors and others may prepare data for the practitioner's use, it would be inappropriate for the practitioner to

1. Agree to merely read the reports of internal auditors in order to describe or repeat their findings, or
2. Report anything that could lead a reader to conclude that the practitioner shares responsibility for the procedures with the internal auditors.

FINDINGS

The results of applying agreed-upon procedures should be presented in the form of findings. It is inappropriate for the practitioner to make a negative statement about whether the subject matter or the assertion is fairly stated.

The practitioner's report should include all findings. In general, materiality does not apply to the findings to be reported. However, the specified parties may agree to the definition of materiality, but this definition must be described in the report.

REPORTING

REQUIRED ELEMENTS

The practitioner's report should

1. Have a title that includes the word *independent.*
2. Identify the specified parties.
3. Identify the subject matter and the character of the engagement.
4. Identify the responsible party.
5. State that the subject matter is the responsibility of the responsible party.
6. State that the procedures performed were those agreed to by the parties specified in the report.
7. State that the agreed-upon procedures engagement was conducted in accordance with attestation standards established by the AICPA.
8. State that the sufficiency of the procedures is solely the responsibility of the specified parties and disclaim responsibility for the sufficiency of those procedures.
9. List or otherwise refer to the procedures performed and the related findings. (Negative assurance should not be provided.)
10. State any agreed-upon materiality limits.
11. State that the practitioner was not engaged to, and did not, examine the subject matter.
12. Disclaim an opinion, and state that if the practitioner had performed additional procedures, other matters might have arisen that would have been reported.
13. State the restrictions on the use of the report and that it is intended to be used solely by the specified parties.
14. Identify any reservations or restrictions concerning the procedures or findings.
15. For engagements on prospective financial information, include all relevant items as discussed in AT Section 301.
16. Describe the nature of any assistance provided by a specialist.
17. Be signed by the practitioner's firm; the signature may be manual or printed.
18. Be dated with the date of completion of the agreed-upon procedures.

ILLUSTRATIVE REPORT

Independent Accountant's Report on Applying Agreed-upon Procedures

To the Audit Committees and Managements of ABC, Inc., and XYZ Fund:

We have performed the procedures enumerated below, which were agreed to by the audit committees and managements of ABC, Inc., and XYZ Fund, solely to assist you in evaluating the accompanying Statement of Investment Performance Statistics of XYZ Fund [*prepared in accor-*

dance with the criteria specified therein] for the year ended December 31, 20X3. XYZ Fund's management is responsible for the statement of investment performance statistics. This agreed-upon procedures engagement was conducted in accordance with attestation standards established by the American Institute of Certified Public Accountants. The sufficiency of these procedures is solely the responsibility of those parties specified in this report. Consequently, we make no representation regarding the sufficiency of the procedures described below, either for the purpose for which this report has been requested or for any other purpose.

[*Include paragraphs to enumerate procedures and findings.*]

We were not engaged to and did not conduct an examination, the objective of which would be the expression of an opinion on the accompanying Statement of Investment Performance Statistics of XYZ Fund. Accordingly, we do not express such an opinion. Had we performed additional procedures, other matters might have come to our attention that would have been reported to you.

This report is intended solely for the information and use of the audit committees and managements of ABC, Inc., and XYZ Fund, and is not intended to be and should not be used by anyone other than these specified parties.

[*Signature*]

[*Date*]

EXPLANATORY LANGUAGE

The practitioner may explain in the report a variety of matters, including any restrictions on the performance of procedures.

REPRESENTATION LETTER

A representation letter may be a useful and practical means of obtaining representations from the responsible party, depending on the nature of the engagement and the specified parties. While the practitioner is generally not required to obtain a representation letter as part of an agreed-upon procedures engagement, a letter is required if the engagement relates to compliance with specified requirements (AT Section 601).

The refusal of a responsible party to furnish a representation letter is tantamount to a limitation on performance of the engagement. In such circumstances the practitioner should

1. Modify the report to disclose the inability to obtain the representations,
2. Withdraw from the engagement, or
3. Change the engagement to another form of engagement.

KNOWLEDGE OF MATTERS OUTSIDE THE AGREED-UPON PROCEDURES

The practitioner should modify the report to reflect matters that were identified through means other than applying the agreed-upon procedures only if the matters significantly contradict the subject matter or a related written assertion that is referenced in the report.

CHANGE TO AN AGREED-UPON PROCEDURES ENGAGEMENT

In an attest situation, a practitioner may be asked to change the level of service to an agreed-upon procedures engagement. Before making the change, the practitioner should consider the reasons for the request and the additional effort that may be necessary to complete the original engagement. Clearly, changes in client circumstances and misunderstandings about the type of engagement are valid reasons for a change in the level of service.

If the change in the level of service is appropriate, the report should not refer in any way to either the original engagement or the circumstances that resulted in the change.

301 FORECASTS AND PROJECTIONS

SOURCES OF STANDARDS

SSAE 10, *Attest Standards: Revision and Recodification*
SSAE 11, *Attest Documentation*

SUMMARY

This section provides guidance to practitioners who are engaged to issue or do issue examination, compilation, or agreed-upon procedures reports in connection with prospective financial statements or partial presentations of prospective financial information.

This section does not apply to engagements in which prospective financial information is used solely in conjunction with litigation support services.

Prospective financial statements should be in the format of the historical financial statements that would be issued for the periods covered unless there is an agreement to the contrary between the responsible party and the potential users. Prospective financial statements may be in the form of complete basic financial statements or of presentations containing the following minimum number of items:

1. Sales or gross revenues.
2. Gross profit or cost of sales.
3. Unusual items or those that occur infrequently.
4. Provision for income taxes.
5. Discontinued operations or extraordinary items.
6. Income from continuing operations.
7. Net income.
8. Basic and diluted earnings per share, if these apply.
9. Significant changes in financial position.
10. Summary of significant assumptions.
11. Summary of significant accounting policies.
12. Description of what the responsible party intends the prospective financial statements to present.
13. A statement that the assumptions are based on the responsible party's judgment at the time of preparation.
14. A warning that the prospective results may not be achieved.

The omission of any one of items 1 through 9 results in a partial presentation (discussed below). Omission of any one of items 10 through 14 does not result in a partial presentation.

An accountant may generally accept an engagement to compile, examine, or apply agreed-upon procedures to prospective financial statements so long as the prospective financial statements do not omit a summary of significant assumptions. It should be readily apparent that under no circumstances may an accountant review prospective financial statements.

DEFINITIONS

Prospective financial statements are either financial forecasts or financial projections that include summaries of significant assumptions and accounting policies.

Financial forecasts are prospective financial statements that present, to the best of the responsible party's (usually management's) knowledge and belief, the expected financial position of an entity, results of its operations, and cash flows based on assumptions reflecting expected conditions and the course of action expected to be taken.

Financial projections are prospective financial statements that present, to the best of the responsible party's (usually management's) knowledge and belief, given one or more hypothetical assumptions (assumptions used to present a condition or course of action that is not necessarily expected to occur), the expected financial position, results of operations, and cash flows of an entity, based on assumptions reflecting expected conditions and the course of action expected to be taken. The fact that financial projections are based on "what if" assumptions that are not necessarily expected to occur distinguishes them from financial forecasts.

A responsible party is a person responsible for the assumptions underlying prospective financial statements. While this is usually management, it may be outsiders, such as a person considering acquisition of the entity.

USES OF PROSPECTIVE FINANCIAL STATEMENTS

General use refers to use by persons not negotiating directly with the responsible party, as when prospective financial statements are included in a company's prospectus for a public stock offering. Because only a financial forecast is appropriate for general use, accountants should ensure that their names are not used in connection with a financial projection intended for general use, unless the projection is a supplement to a financial forecast.

Limited use refers to use by either the responsible party alone or by the responsible party and third parties negotiating directly with the responsible party. Limited use of prospective financial statements includes use by a client in negotiations with a bank for a loan or line of credit. Both financial forecasts and financial projections are appropriate for limited use.

COMPILATION OF PROSPECTIVE FINANCIAL STATEMENTS

BACKGROUND

In a compilation of prospective financial statements, no assurance is provided regarding:

1. The prospective financial statements, including the assumptions underlying the statements, or
2. The accountant becoming aware of significant matters that might be disclosed through the application of more extensive procedures.

The accountant is precluded from compiling

1. Prospective financial statements that fail to include the summary of significant assumptions, or
2. Financial projections that fail to identify the hypothetical assumptions or fail to describe limitations on the usefulness of the presentation.

COMPILATION PROCEDURES

In addition to following the guidelines of Statements on Standards for Accounting and Review Services (AR Sections), the accountant should obtain a representation letter in which the responsible party states its responsibility for the underlying assumptions.

COMPILATION REPORTS

The compilation report on prospective financial statements should

1. Identify the prospective financial statements.
2. State that the prospective financial statements have been compiled in accordance with attestation standards established by the American Institute of Certified Public Accountants.
3. State that a compilation is limited in scope, and does not enable the accountant to express an opinion or any other form of assurance on the prospective financial statements or the underlying assumptions.
4. Include a caveat that the prospective results may not be achieved.
5. State that the accountant assumes no responsibility to update the report for events and circumstances that occur after the report date.
6. If the report is issued in connection with a projection, (a) describe the special purpose for which the projection was prepared, and (b) include a paragraph that restricts the use of the report to the specified parties.
7. If the prospective financial statements states a range, include a separate paragraph explaining that the responsible party has elected to portray the expected results as a range; for example

   > As described in the summary of significant assumptions, management of XYZ Company has elected to portray forecasted (projected) [*describe financial statement element or elements for which the expected results of one or more assumptions fall within a range, and identify the assumptions expected to fall within a range, for example, "revenue at the amounts of $X,XXX and $Y YYY, which is predicated upon occupancy rates of XX percent and YY percent of available apartments"*] rather than as a single point estimate. Accordingly, the accompanying forecast (projection) presents forecasted (projected) financial position, results of operations, and cash flows [*describe one or more assumptions expected to fall within a range, for example, "at such occupancy rates."*] However, there is no assurance that the actual results will fall within the range of [*describe one or more assumptions expected to fall within a range, for example, "occupancy rates"*] presented.

8. State the report date; generally the date when the compilation procedures are completed.
9. If the accountant lacks independence, so state at the end of the report: "We are (I am) not independent with respect to XYZ Company."
10. Identify any historical financial statements and reports thereon that are included in a document that also contains prospective financial statements.
11. Identify any presentation deficiencies or disclosure omissions (other than those relating to significant assumptions).
12. If the prospective financial statements are prepared in conformity with a comprehensive basis of accounting other than GAAP, disclose the basis of accounting if it is not disclosed in the prospective financial statements.
13. If the summary of significant accounting policies is not presented as part of the prospective financial statements, include the following separate paragraph:

    > Management has elected to omit the summary of significant accounting policies required by the guidelines for presentation of a forecast (projection) established by the American Institute of Certified Public Accountants. If the omitted disclosures were included in the forecast (projection), they might influence the user's conclusions about the Company's financial position, results of operations, and cash flows for the forecast (projection) period. Accordingly, this forecast (projection) is not designed for those who are not informed about such matters.

Standard Compilation Report—Forecast (No Range Included)

We have compiled the accompanying forecasted balance sheet, statements of income, retained earnings, and cash flows of XYZ Company as of December 31, 20XX, and for the year then ending, in accordance with attestation standards established by the American Institute of Certified Public Accountants.

A compilation is limited to presenting in the form of a forecast information that is the representation of management and does not include evaluation of the support for the assumptions underlying the forecast. We have not examined the forecast and, accordingly, do not express an opinion or any other form of assurance on the accompanying statements or assumptions. Furthermore there will usually be differences between the forecasted and actual results, because events and circumstances frequently do not occur as expected, and those differences may be material. We have no responsibility to update this report for events and circumstances occurring after the date of this report.

[*Signature*]

[*Date*]

Standard Compilation Report—Projection (No Range Included)

We have compiled the accompanying projected balance sheet, statements of income, retained earnings, and cash flows of XYZ Company as of December 31, 20XX, and for the year then ending, in accordance with attestation standards established by the American Institute of Certified Public Accountants. The accompanying projection was prepared for [*state purpose; e.g., "the purpose of negotiating a loan to expand XYZ Company's plant"*].

A compilation is limited to presenting in the form of a projection information that is the representation of management and does not include evaluation of the support for the assumptions underlying the projection. We have not examined the projection and, accordingly, do not express an opinion or any other form of assurance on the accompanying statements or assumptions. Furthermore, even if [*describe hypothetical assumption; e.g., "the loan is granted and the plant is expanded"*], there will usually be differences between the projected and actual results, because events and circumstances frequently do not occur as expected, and those differences may be material. We have no responsibility to update this report for events and circumstances occurring after the date of this report.

The accompanying projection and this report are intended solely for the information and use of [*identify specified parties; e.g., "XYZ Company and DEF Bank"*] and is not intended to be and should not be used by anyone other than these specified parties.

[*Signature*]

[*Date*]

EXAMINATION OF PROSPECTIVE FINANCIAL STATEMENTS

BACKGROUND

An examination of prospective financial statements involves evaluating

1. The preparation of the prospective financial statements,
2. The support for the underlying assumptions, and
3. The presentation of the prospective financial statements for conformity with AICPA guidelines; it results in the issuance of an examination report.

Attest documentation should state that the process by which the entity developed its prospective financial statements was considered in determining the scope of the examination.

In examining prospective financial statements, the practitioner should be guided by the standards in AT Section 101, *Attest Engagements*.

EXAMINATION PROCEDURES

The practitioner should perform the procedures that generally apply to audits of historical financial statements, except that in the representation letter the responsible party should acknowledge its responsibility for both the presentation and the underlying assumptions.

EXAMINATION REPORTS

The examination report on prospective financial statements should

1. Have a title that includes the word *independent.*
2. Identify the prospective financial statements.
3. Identify the responsible party and state that the forecast or projection is that party's responsibility.
4. State that the practitioner's responsibility is to express an opinion based on the examination.
5. State that the examination (a) was conducted in accordance with attestation standards established by the AICPA and (b) included procedures the practitioner considered necessary.
6. State the belief that the examination provides a reasonable basis for the practitioner's opinion.
7. Include an opinion that
   a. The forecast or projection is presented in conformity with AICPA presentation guidelines, and
   b. The forecast's or projection's underlying assumptions provide a reasonable basis for its preparation.
8. Warn that the prospective results may not be achieved.
9. State that the practitioner has no responsibility to update the report after the date of the report.
10. Include a signature of the practitioner's firm, which may be manual or printed.
11. State the report date; generally the date the fieldwork was completed.
12. If the report is issued in connection with a projection
    a. Describe the special purpose for which the projection was prepared, and
    b. Add a paragraph that restricts use of the report to the specified parties.
13. If the prospective financial statements includes a range, add a separate paragraph to state that the responsible party has elected to portray the expected results as a range; for example:

    As described in the summary of significant assumptions, management of XYZ Company has elected to portray forecasted (projected) [*describe financial statement element or elements for which the expected results of one or more assumptions fall within a range, and identify the assumptions expected to fall within a range; e.g., "revenue at the amounts of $X,XXX and $Y,YYY which is predicated upon occupancy rates of XX percent and YY percent of available apartments"*] rather than as a single point estimate. Accordingly the accompany forecast (projection) presents forecasted (projected) financial position, results of operations, and cash flows [*describe one or more assumptions expected to fall within a range; e.g., "at such occupancy rates*]. However, there is no assurance that the actual results will fall within the range of [*describe one or more assumptions expected to fall within a range; e.g., "occupancy rate"*] presented.

Independent Accountant's Report

We have examined the accompanying forecasted balance sheet, statements of income, retained earnings, and cash flows of XYZ Company as of December 31, 20XX, and for the year then ending. XYZ Company's management is responsible for the forecast. Our responsibility is to express an opinion on the forecast based on our examination.

Our examination was conducted in accordance with attestation standards established by the American Institute of Certified Public Accountants and, accordingly, included such procedures as we considered necessary to evaluate both the assumptions used by management and the preparation and presentation of the forecast. We believe that our examination provides a reasonable basis for our opinion.

In our opinion, the accompanying forecast is presented in conformity with guidelines for presentation of a forecast established by the American Institute of Certified Public Accountants, and the underlying assumptions provide a reasonable basis for management's forecast. However, there will usually be differences between the forecasted and actual results, because events and circumstances frequently do not occur as expected, and those differences may be material. We have no responsibility to update this report for events and circumstances occurring after the date of this report.

[*Signature*]

[*Date*]

Standard Examination Report—Projection (No Range Included)

Independent Accountant's Report

We have examined the accompanying projected balance sheet, statements of income, retained earnings, and cash flows of XYZ Company as of December 31, 20XX, and for the year then ending. XYZ Company's management is responsible for the projection, which was prepared for [*state purpose; e.g., "the purpose of negotiating a loan to expand XYZ Company's plant"*]. Our responsibility is to express an opinion on the projection based on our examination.

Our examination was conducted in accordance with attestation standards established by the American Institute of Certified Public Accountants and, accordingly, included such procedures as we considered necessary to evaluate both the assumptions used by management and the preparation and presentation of the projection. We believe that our examination provides a reasonable basis for our opinion.

In our opinion, the accompanying projection is presented in conformity with guidelines for presentation of a projection established by the American Institute of Certified Public Accountants, and the underlying assumptions provide a reasonable basis for management's projection [*describe the hypothetical assumption; e.g., "assuming the granting of the requested loan for the purpose of expanding XYZ Company's plant as described in the summary of significant assumptions"*]. However, even if [*describe hypothetical assumption; e.g., "the loan is granted and the plant is expanded"*], there will usually be differences between the projected and actual results, because events and circumstances frequently do not occur as expected, and those differences may be material. We have no responsibility to update this report for events and circumstances occurring after the date of this report.

The accompanying projection and this report are intended solely for the information and use of [*identify parties; e.g., "XYZ Company and DEF National Bank"*] and is not intended to be and should not be used by anyone other than these specified parties.

[*Signature*]

[*Date*]

MODIFYING AN OPINION

QUALIFIED OPINION

A qualified opinion should be issued when there is a departure from AICPA presentation guidelines but it is not significant enough to warrant issuance of an adverse opinion. Here is an example of an examination report on a financial forecast that is qualified:

Independent Accountant's Report

We have examined the accompanying forecasted balance sheet, statements of income, retained earnings, and cash flows of XYZ Company as of December 31, 20XX, and for the year then ending. XYZ Company's management is responsible for the forecast. Our responsibility is to express an opinion on the forecast based on our examination.

Our examination was conducted in accordance with attestation standards established by the American Institute of Certified Public Accountants and, accordingly, included such procedures as we considered necessary to evaluate both the assumptions used by management and the preparation and presentation of the forecast. We believe that our examination provides a reasonable basis for our opinion.

The forecast does not disclose significant accounting policies. Disclosure of such policies is required by guidelines for presentation of a forecast established by the American Institute of Certified Public Accountants.

In our opinion, except for the omission of the disclosure of the significant accounting policies as discussed in the preceding paragraph, the accompanying forecast is presented in conformity with guidelines for presentation of a forecast established by the American Institute of Certified Public Accountants, and the underlying assumptions provide a reasonable basis for management's forecast. However, there will usually be differences between the forecasted and actual results, because events and circumstances frequently do not occur as expected, and those differences may be material. We have no responsibility to update this report for events and circumstances occurring after the date of this report.

[*Signature*]

[*Date*]

ADVERSE OPINION

An adverse opinion should be issued in situations where any one of three conditions exist:

1. A severe departure from AICPA presentation guidelines and a qualified opinion being not warranted.
2. A failure to disclose assumptions that appear to be significant.
3. Lack of a reasonable basis for the forecast or projection.

Here is an example of an examination report on a financial forecast that expresses an adverse opinion for reason 1:

Independent Accountant's Report

We have examined the accompanying forecasted balance sheet, statements of income, retained earnings, and cash flows of XYZ Company as of December 31, 20XX, and for the year then ending. XYZ Company's management is responsible for the forecast. Our responsibility is to express an opinion on the forecast based on our examination.

Our examination was conducted in accordance with attestation standards established by the American Institute of Certified Public Accountants and, accordingly, included such procedures as we considered necessary to evaluate both the assumptions used by management and the preparation and presentation of the forecast. We believe that our examination provides a reasonable basis for our opinion.

As discussed under the caption "Sales" in the summary of significant forecast assumptions, the forecasted sales include, among other things, revenue from the Company's federal defense contracts continuing at the current level. The Company's present federal defense contracts will expire in March 20XX. No new contracts have been signed and no negotiations are under way for new federal defense contracts. Furthermore the federal government has entered into contracts with another company to supply the items being manufactured under the Company's present contracts.

In our opinion, the accompanying forecast is not presented in conformity with guidelines for presentation of a forecast established by the American Institute of Certified Public Accountants because management's assumptions, as discussed in the preceding paragraph, do not provide a reasonable basis for management's forecast. We have no responsibility to update this report for events and circumstances occurring after the date of this report.

[*Signature*]

[*Date*]

There are some important points to note here:

1. If the prospective financial statements omit assumptions that the practitioner considers significant, an adverse opinion is appropriate and the omitted assumptions should be included in the practitioner's report.
2. If prospective financial presentations fail to disclose all assumptions, the practitioner should not undertake an examination engagement.
3. If a financial projection fails either to identify the hypothetical assumptions or to describe limitations on the usefulness of the projection, the practitioner should not undertake an examination engagement.

DISCLAIMER OF OPINION

A disclaimer of opinion should

1. Be issued whenever the scope of the examination is not sufficient to enable the expression of an opinion.
2. Specifically state that the scope of the examination was not sufficient to make it possible to express an opinion.
3. Refer directly to the additional explanatory paragraph.
4. Omit any reference to the practitioner's responsibility to express an opinion on the presentation based on the audit.
5. Omit the standard scope paragraph.

Here is an example of an examination report on a financial forecast containing a disclaimer of opinion because a significant assumption could not be evaluated.

Independent Accountant's Report

We were engaged to examine the accompanying forecasted balance sheet, statements of income, retained earnings, and cash flows of XYZ Company as of December 31, 20XX, and for the year then ending. XYZ Company's management is responsible for the forecast.

As discussed under the caption "Income from Investee" in the summary of significant forecast assumptions, the forecast includes income from an equity investee constituting 23 percent of forecasted net income, which is management's estimate of the Company's share of the investee's income to be accrued for 20XX. The investee has not prepared a forecast for the year ending December 31, 20XX, and we were therefore unable to obtain suitable support for this assumption.

Because, as described in the preceding paragraph, we are unable to evaluate management's assumption regarding income from an equity investee and other assumptions that depend thereon, the scope of our work was not sufficient to express, and we do not express, an opinion with respect to the presentation or assumptions underlying the accompanying forecast. We have no responsibility to update this report for events and circumstances occurring after the date of this report.

[*Signature*]

[*Date*]

OTHER REPORT MODIFICATIONS

Emphasis of a Matter

A practitioner may emphasize a matter regarding the prospective financial statements by including an additional paragraph in the report. In no way is emphasis of a matter intended to negate an unqualified opinion on prospective financial statements.

Part of Examination Performed by Another Practitioner

When part of the examination of prospective financial statements is performed by another practitioner, the principal practitioner should follow the guidance in AU Section 543, *Part of Audit Performed by Other Independent Auditors.*

Comparative Historical Financial Information

When prospective financial statements are presented in a document that also includes historical financial statements with their related accountant's report, the practitioner should add the following to the last sentence of the final paragraph of the report on the prospective financial statements:

> The historical financial statements for the year ended December 31, 20XX, and our report thereon are set forth on pages XX-XX of this document.

Examination Part of a Larger Engagement

The report should be expanded to describe the entire engagement when the examination of the prospective financial statements is part of a larger engagement, such as a feasibility or business acquisition study.

APPLYING AGREED-UPON PROCEDURES TO PROSPECTIVE FINANCIAL STATEMENTS

An agreed-upon procedures attestation engagement may be performed on prospective financial statements provided that the following conditions exist:

1. The accountant maintains independence throughout the engagement.
2. The accountant and the specified parties agree on the procedures to be performed.
3. The sufficiency of the agreed-upon procedures is the responsibility of the specified parties.
4. Significant assumptions are summarized in the prospective financial statements.
5. The prospective financial statements are subject to reasonably consistent estimation or measurement.
6. The accountant and the specified parties agree on the criteria to be used in determining the findings.
7. Reasonably consistent findings are expected based on the procedures to be applied to the prospective financial statements.
8. Evidential matter is expected to exist to provide a reasonable basis for expressing the findings in the report.

9. Any materiality limits for reporting purposes are agreed on by the practitioner and the specified parties.
10. Use of the report is restricted to the specified parties.

In an engagement to apply agreed-upon procedures to prospective financial statements, the accountant should follow the guidance in AT Section 201, *Agreed-upon Procedures.*

REPORTING

Required Elements

The practitioner's report on the results of applying agreed-upon procedures to prospective financial statements should

1. Have a title that includes the word *independent.*
2. Identify the specified parties.
3. Identify the prospective financial statements and the character of the engagement.
4. State that the procedures performed were agreed to by the specified parties identified in the report.
5. Identify the responsible party.
6. State that the prospective financial statements are the responsibility of the responsible party.
7. State that the agreed-upon procedures engagement was conducted in accordance with attestation standards established by AICPA.
8. State that the sufficiency of the procedures is solely the responsibility of the specified parties and disclaim responsibility for the sufficiency of those procedures.
9. List or refer to the procedures performed and the related findings. (Negative assurance should not be provided.)
10. State any agreed-upon materiality limits.
11. State that the practitioner was not engaged to, and did not perform an examination of the prospective financial statements; disclaim an opinion; and state that if additional procedures had been performed, other matters might have come to the practitioner's attention that would have been reported.
12. State restrictions on the use of the report because it is intended to be used solely by the specified parties.
13. Identify any reservations or restrictions concerning the procedures or findings.
14. Include a caveat that the prospective results may not be achieved.
15. State that the practitioner assumes no responsibility to update the report for events and changes in circumstance after the report date.
16. Describe the nature of any assistance provided by a specialist.
17. Include a signature of the practitioner's firm, which may be manual or printed.
18. Be dated for the date of completion of the agreed-upon procedures.

Illustrative Report

Independent Accountant's Report on Applying Agreed-upon Procedures

Board of Directors—XYZ Corporation
Board of Directors—ABC Company

At your request we have performed certain agreed-upon procedures, as enumerated below, with respect to the forecasted balance sheet and the related forecasted statements of income, retained earnings, and cash flows of DEF Company, a subsidiary of ABC Company, as of December 31, 20XX, and for the year then ending. These procedures, which were agreed to by the Boards of Directors of XYZ Corporation and ABC Company, were performed solely to assist you in evaluating the forecast in connection with the proposed sale of DEF Company to XYZ Corporation. DEF Company's management is responsible for the forecast.

This agreed-upon procedures engagement was conducted in accordance with attestation standards established by the American Institute of Certified Public Accountants. The sufficiency of these procedures is solely the responsibility of those parties specified in this report. Consequently we make no representation regarding the sufficiency of the procedures described below, either for the purpose for which this report has been requested or for any other purpose.

[*Include paragraphs to enumerate procedures and findings.*]

We were not engaged to and did not conduct an examination, the objective of which would be the expression of an opinion on the accompanying prospective financial statements. Accordingly we do not express such an opinion on whether the prospective financial statements are presented in conformity with AICPA presentation guidelines or on whether the underlying assumptions provide a reasonable basis for the presentation. Had we performed additional procedures, other matters might have come to our attention that would have been reported to you. Furthermore there will usually be differences between the forecasted and actual results, because events and circumstances frequently do not occur as expected, and those differences may be material. We have no responsibility to update this report for events and circumstances occurring after the date of this report.

This report is intended solely for the information and use of the Boards of Directors of ABC, Inc., and XYZ Corporation and is not intended to be and should not be used by anyone other than these specified parties.

[*Signature*]

[*Date*]

PARTIAL PRESENTATIONS

When reporting on partial presentations of prospective financial information based on agreed-upon procedures, the practitioner should keep in mind that

1. Partial presentations are generally appropriate only for limited use, and
2. The report should include a description of any limitations on the usefulness of the presentation.

OTHER INFORMATION

Practitioner-Submitted Documents

When a practitioner's report on historical financial statements is included in a practitioner-submitted document containing prospective financial statements, the practitioner should either compile, examine, or apply agreed-upon procedures to the prospective statements unless

1. The prospective statements are labeled as a "budget,"
2. The budget does not extend beyond the end of the current year, and
3. The budget is presented with current year interim financial statements.

In such circumstances the report should state that the practitioner did not examine or compile the budget and disclaim an opinion or any other form of assurance on it.

Client-Prepared Documents

When a practitioner's report on historical financial statements is included in a client-prepared document containing prospective financial statements, the practitioner should not allow the use of the practitioner's name in the document unless the practitioner has examined, compiled, or applied agreed-upon procedures to the prospective financial statements. If the document contains information other than historical and prospective financial statements, the practitioner's responsibility is to look for inconsistencies and suggest their elimination. For additional guidance, the practitioner should consult AU Section 550, *Other Information in Documents Containing Audited Financial Statements.*

When an entity publishes a document containing information other than historical financial statements along with compiled or examined prospective financial statements (and the related practitioner's report), the practitioner should read the other information to determine whether it is consistent with the prospective financial statements. The practitioner is under no obligation, however, to corroborate the other information in the document.

A practitioner who after examining the prospective financial statements determines that there are material inconsistencies between the prospective financial statements and the other information should determine whether the prospective financial statements and the practitioner's report need to be revised. Other options for the practitioner are to express an adverse opinion, disclaim an opinion if a scope limitation was encountered, not allow use of the practitioner's report in the document, or withdraw from the engagement.

On the other hand, a practitioner who compiled the prospective financial statements should attempt to obtain additional or revised information. Failure to obtain it should cause the practitioner to withhold use of the report or withdraw from the engagement.

If the practitioner concludes that the other information contains a material misstatement of fact that is not an inconsistent statement, the practitioner should discuss the matter with the responsible party. If the concern is valid, the practitioner should suggest that the responsible party consult with legal counsel or another appropriate party for advice. The practitioner should also consider notifying the responsible party in writing about the concerns and seeking legal counsel.

401 REPORTING ON PRO FORMA FINANCIAL INFORMATION

SOURCE OF STANDARDS

SSAE 10, *Attest Standards: Revision and Recodification*

SUMMARY

This section provides guidance in connection with engagements to examine, review, and report on pro forma financial information.

Pro forma information is designed to portray what significant effects there might have been on historical financial statements had a consummated or proposed transaction or event occurred earlier. Common uses of pro forma information are as presentations used to show the effects of business combinations, disposal of a significant part of a business, or change in form of business. A presentation of pro forma information should include the following:

1. A description of the transaction or event on which the pro forma presentation is based.
2. A description of the significant assumptions used to develop the pro forma adjustments.
3. A list of significant uncertainties about the assumptions used.
4. A statement that pro forma information should be read in conjunction with the related historical financial information.
5. A statement that the pro forma information does not necessarily represent the actual results that might have been achieved if the transaction or event had taken place earlier.

CONDITIONS FOR REPORTING

A practitioner may accept an engagement to issue an examination or review report on pro forma information if the following conditions exist:

1. The document to be reported on includes or refers to the complete historical financial statements for the most recent year. (If the financial statements for the most recent year are not available when the document is being prepared, financial statements for the preceding year may be used.)
2. When the document to be reported on includes or refers to pro forma information of an interim period, the document includes or refers to interim financial information for the same period. (The historical information may be presented in condensed form.)
3. When the document to be reported on pertains to a business combination, the document includes or refers to the historical financial information for each of the constituent parts of the new combination.

4. The practitioner has audited or reviewed the pro forma information. The practitioner should be careful not to provide a level of assurance on the pro forma information that is greater than that provided on the historical financial information.
5. The auditor possesses sufficient knowledge of the accounting and reporting practices of the entity reported on.

ENGAGEMENT OBJECTIVES

The examination of pro forma financial information should give the practitioner reasonable assurance that three objectives are being met:

1. Management's assumptions provide a reasonable basis for presenting the significant effects that are directly attributable to the underlying transaction or event.
2. The pro forma adjustments give appropriate effect to management's assumptions.
3. The column of pro forma information reflects the proper application of the pro forma adjustments.

Ultimately the objective of an examination of pro forma financial information is to express an opinion on all three of these listed items. On the other hand, the objective of a review of pro forma financial information is to enable the practitioner to express negative assurance about the same items, stating, in effect, that nothing came to the practitioner's attention that would lead the practitioner not to believe the three items discussed above.

RELEVANT PROCEDURES

Besides performing procedures on the historical financial statements, which should be governed by the level of reporting on those statements, the following procedures should be performed in both examination and review engagements:

1. Obtain a sufficient understanding of the underlying transaction or event.
2. In the case of a business combination, obtain sufficient knowledge of each constituent part of the combined entity.
3. Discuss with management their assumptions about the effects of the transaction or event.
4. Ensure that all significant effects of the transaction or event are reflected in the pro forma adjustments.
5. Obtain enough evidence to support the pro forma adjustments.
6. Ensure that management's assumptions are clearly and comprehensively presented.
7. Ensure that there is consistency between

    a. Management's assumptions and
    b. The data underlying the assumptions.

8. Test the mathematical accuracy of the pro forma adjustments.
9. Ascertain that the pro forma column reflects the proper pro forma adjustments.
10. Obtain a representation letter from management regarding management's

    a. Responsibility for the assumptions underlying the adjustments,
    b. Assertion that the assumptions provide a reasonable basis for the presentation of all significant effects of the transaction or event,
    c. Assertion that the pro forma adjustments reflect the effects of the assumptions,
    d. Declaration that the pro forma column reflects the pro forma adjustments, and
    e. Declaration that the pro forma information adequately discloses the significant effects of the transaction or event.

11. Read the pro forma financial information to ensure that there is

a.   Adequate disclosure about the underlying transaction or event, the pro forma adjustments, the significant assumptions, and any significant uncertainties about the significant assumptions; and

b.   Proper identification of the source of the historical financial information.

REPORTING ON PRO FORMA FINANCIAL INFORMATION

The examination or review report on pro forma financial information

1.   May be presented as a separate report,
2.   May be combined with the practitioner's report on the historical financial statements, and
3.   Generally should be dated as of the completion of the practitioner's procedures.

If the review report on pro forma financial information is combined with the practitioner's report on the historical financial statements (as in the second item), dual-dating of the report is appropriate provided that the date of completion of the procedures applied to the pro forma financial information is after the date of completion of the procedures applied to the historical financial statements.

The practitioner's examination or review report may be modified for a variety of reasons. For example, as a result of an examination engagement, a practitioner may

1.   Express a qualified opinion or disclaim an opinion as a result of a scope limitation, and/or
2.   Express a qualified opinion or an adverse opinion if the practitioner has significant reservations about the propriety of the underlying assumptions or the form of presentation.

EXAMINATION REPORT

An examination report on pro forma financial information should

1.   Have a title that includes the word *independent.*
2.   Identify the pro forma financial information.
3.   Refer to the financial statements from which the historical financial information is derived, and state that they were audited. (The report on pro forma financial information should mention any modification in the practitioner's report on the historical financial information.)
4.   Identify the responsible party and state that the responsible party is responsible for the pro forma financial information.
5.   State that the practitioner's responsibility is to express an opinion on the pro forma financial information based on his examination.
6.   State that the examination of the pro forma financial information was conducted in accordance with attestation standards established by the AICPA and therefore included such procedures as the practitioner considered necessary in the circumstances.
7.   State that the practitioner believes that the examination provides a reasonable basis for an opinion.
8.   Explain in a separate paragraph the objective of pro forma financial information and its limitations.
9.   Give an opinion as to whether management's assumptions provide a reasonable basis for presenting the significant effects directly attributable to the transaction or event, whether the related pro forma adjustments give appropriate effect to those as-

sumptions, and whether the pro forma column reflects the proper application of those adjustments to the historical financial statements.

10. Be signed by the practitioner or the firm, either manually or printed.
11. Give the date of the examination report.

A sample examination report follows.

Independent Accountant's Report

We have examined the pro forma adjustments reflecting the transaction [*or event*] described in Note 1 and the application of those adjustments to the historical amounts in [*the assembly of*] the accompanying pro forma financial condensed balance sheet of X Company as of December 31, 20X3, and the pro forma condensed statement of income for the year then ended. The historical condensed financial statements are derived from the historical financial statements of X Company, which were audited by us, and of Y Company, which were audited by other accountants, appearing elsewhere herein [*or incorporated by reference*]. Such pro forma adjustments are based on management's assumptions described in Note 2. X Company's management is responsible for the pro forma financial information. Our responsibility is to express an opinion on the pro forma financial information based on our examination.

Our examination was conducted in accordance with attestation standards established by the American Institute of Certified Public Accountants and, accordingly, included such procedures as we considered necessary in the circumstances. We believe that our examination provides a reasonable basis for our opinion.

The objective of this pro forma financial information is to show what the significant effects on the historical financial information might have been had the transaction [*or event*] occurred at an earlier date. However, the pro forma condensed financial statements are not necessarily indicative of the results of operations or related effects on financial position that would have been attained had the above-mentioned transaction [or event] actually occurred earlier.

[*Additional paragraph(s) may be added to emphasize certain matters relating to the attest engagement or the subject matter.*]

In our opinion, management's assumptions provide a reasonable basis for presenting the significant effects directly attributable to the above-mentioned transaction [or event] described in Note 1, the related pro forma adjustments give appropriate effect to those assumptions, and the pro forma column reflects the proper application of those adjustments to the historical financial statement amounts in the pro forma condensed balance sheet as of December 31,20X3, and the pro forma condensed statement of income for the year then ended.

[*Signature*]

[*Date*]

REVIEW REPORT

A practitioner's review report on pro forma financial information should

1. Have a title that includes the word *independent.*
2. Identify the pro forma financial information.
3. Refer to the financial statements from which the historical financial information is derived and state whether those were audited or reviewed. (The report should mention any modification in the practitioner's report on the historical financial information.)
4. Identify the responsible party and state that the responsible party is responsible for the pro forma financial information.
5. State that the review of the pro forma financial information was conducted in accordance with attestation standards established by the AICPA.

6. State that a review is substantially less in scope than an examination, the objective of which is expression of an opinion on the pro forma financial information, and the practitioner does not express such an opinion.

7. Explain in a separate paragraph the objective of pro forma financial information and its limitations.

8. Give the practitioner's conclusion about whether any information that came to his attention would cause him to believe that management's assumptions do not provide a reasonable basis for presenting the significant effects directly attributable to the transaction or event, or that the pro forma adjustments do not give appropriate effect to those assumptions, or that the pro forma column does not reflect proper application of those adjustments to the historical financial statements.

9. Be signed by the practitioner or the firm, either manually or printed.

10. Give the date of the review report.

A sample review report follows.

Independent Accountant's Report

We have reviewed the pro forma adjustments reflecting the transaction [*or event*] described in Note 1 and the application of those adjustments to the historical amounts in [*the assembly of*] the accompanying pro forma financial condensed balance sheet of X Company as of December 31, 20X3, and the pro forma condensed statement of income for the three months then ended. These historical condensed financial statements are derived from the historical unaudited financial statements of X Company, which were reviewed by us, and of Y Company, which were reviewed by other accountants, appearing elsewhere herein [*or incorporated by reference*]. Such pro forma adjustments are based on management's assumptions described in Note 2. X Company's management is responsible for the pro forma financial information.

Our review was conducted in accordance with attestation standards established by the American Institute of Certified Public Accountants. A review is substantially less in scope than an examination, the objective of which is the expression of an opinion on management's assumptions, the pro forma adjustments, and the application of those adjustments to historical financial information. Accordingly we do not express such an opinion.

The objective of this pro forma financial information is to show what the significant effects on the historical financial information might have been had the transaction [*or event*] occurred at an earlier date. However, the pro forma condensed financial statements are not necessarily indicative of the results of operations or related effects on financial position that would have been attained had the above-mentioned transaction [or event] actually occurred earlier.

[*Additional paragraph(s) may be added to emphasize certain matters relating to the attest engagement or the subject matter.*]

Based on our review, nothing came to our attention that caused us to believe that management's assumptions do not provide a reasonable basis for presenting the significant effects directly attributable to the above-mentioned transaction [or event] described in Note 1, that the related pro forma adjustments do not give appropriate effect to those assumptions, or that the pro forma column does not reflect the proper application of those adjustments to the historical financial statement amounts in the pro forma condensed balance sheet as of December 31, 20X3, and the pro forma condensed statement of income for the three months then ended.

[*Signature*]

[*Date*]

501 REPORTING ON AN ENTITY'S INTERNAL CONTROL OVER FINANCIAL REPORTING

SOURCE OF STANDARDS

SSAE 10, *Attest Standards: Revision and Recodification*
(Reflects conforming amendments from SAS 112, *Communicating Internal Control Related Matters Identified in an Audit*

SUMMARY

This section is intended to guide a practitioner who is requested to issue or does issue an examination report on the effectiveness of an entity's internal control over financial reporting at a point in time or during a period of time.

CONDITIONS FOR ENGAGEMENT PERFORMANCE

A practitioner may examine the effectiveness of an entity's internal control if the following conditions are met:

1. Management accepts responsibility for the effectiveness of internal control over financial reporting. (For purposes of this section, the members of management who are responsible for the effectiveness of internal control over financial reporting are referred to as the responsible party.)
2. The responsible party evaluates the effectiveness of internal control using suitable criteria (i.e., "control criteria") that need not necessarily be established by the American Institute of Certified Public Accountants.
3. Sufficient evidential matter exists or could be developed to support the responsible party's evaluation.

A practitioner who accepts an engagement to report on the effectiveness of internal control over financial reporting must obtain from the responsible party a written assertion regarding the internal control to be reported on. The responsible party may present its written assertion about the effectiveness of the entity's internal control as

1. A separate report that will accompany the practitioner's report, or
2. A representation letter to the practitioner.

The practitioner should not consent to the use of the examination report in a general-use document unless a separate report format is used. The practitioner should also ensure that the responsible party's assertion is not so subjective that others may not form the same conclusion.

The practitioner should generally withdraw from an examination engagement if the responsible party fails to provide a written assertion; however, if the examination is required by law or regulation, the practitioner need not withdraw from the engagement, but should issue a disclaimer of opinion unless evidential matter supports an adverse opinion.

In lieu of an examination engagement, a practitioner may accept an engagement to perform agreed-upon procedures relating to the effectiveness of the entity's internal control. The practitioner should perform such an engagement in accordance with the guidance provided in AT Section 201, *Agreed-upon Procedures Engagements.*

A practitioner should not accept an engagement to review either the effectiveness of the entity's internal control or a written assertion about such subject matter. However, a practitioner may accept an engagement to provide suggestions to the responsible party in order to improve internal control over financial reporting. Guidance for such engagements may be found in CS Section 100, *Consulting Services: Definitions and Standards.*

EXAMINATION ENGAGEMENT

The objective of an engagement to examine the effectiveness of an entity's internal control is to enable a practitioner to express an opinion on

1. The effectiveness of an entity's internal control, in all material respects, based on the control criteria, or
2. Whether the responsible party's assertion about the effectiveness of internal control is fairly stated in all material respects, based on the control criteria.

An engagement to examine the effectiveness of an entity's internal control over financial reporting requires the practitioner to

1. Plan the scope of the engagement;
2. Obtain an understanding of the internal controls within each component of internal control (see AU Section 319);
3. Evaluate the design effectiveness of the controls;
4. Perform tests of relevant controls and evaluate the operating effectiveness of the controls; and
5. Form an opinion on the effectiveness of the entity's internal control, or the responsible party's assertion thereon, based on the control criteria.

DEFICIENCIES IN AN ENTITY'S INTERNAL CONTROL

The presence of a material weakness will preclude the practitioner from concluding that the entity has effective internal control. In these circumstances the practitioner should express a qualified opinion (i.e., express an opinion that the internal control is effective "except for" the material weakness noted) or express an adverse opinion, depending on the significance of the material weakness.

A practitioner is required to communicate in writing, significant deficiencies and material weaknesses (see AU Section 325) to management and those charged with governance.

MANAGEMENT'S WRITTEN REPRESENTATIONS

As part of the engagement, the practitioner should obtain the following written representations from management:

1. Acknowledgment of the responsible party's responsibility for establishing and maintaining internal control.
2. A statement that the responsible party has performed an evaluation of the effectiveness of the internal control and specification of the control criteria used.

3. The responsible party's assertion about the effectiveness of internal control based on the control criteria as of a specified date (or during a period of time).
4. A statement that all significant deficiencies have been disclosed and material weaknesses identified.
5. Description of any significant fraud by management or employees.
6. Description of any changes or corrective actions subsequent to the date being reported on that might significantly affect internal control.

It is important to recognize that the responsible party's refusal to furnish all appropriate written representations is tantamount to a severe restriction on the scope of the examination ordinarily sufficient to preclude the issuance of an unqualified opinion; a disclaimer of opinion may be issued or the practitioner may withdraw from the engagement.

REPORTING STANDARDS

A practitioner may report

1. Directly on the effectiveness of an entity's internal control over financial reporting, or
2. On the responsible party's assertion about the effectiveness of the entity's internal control over financial reporting.

In either reporting situation, the practitioner's report should include the following:

1. A title that includes the word *independent*.
2. Identification of the subject matter (i.e., internal control over financial reporting) (or the written assertion thereon) and the responsible party.
3. A statement that the responsible party is responsible for maintaining effective internal control over financial reporting (or the assertion thereon).
4. A statement that the practitioner's responsibility is to express an opinion on the effectiveness of an entity's internal control (or management's assertion) based on the examination.
5. A statement that the examination was conducted in accordance with attestation standards established by the American Institute of Certified Public Accountants and, accordingly, included obtaining an understanding of internal control over financial reporting, testing and evaluating the design and operating effectiveness of internal control, and performing such other procedures as the practitioner considered necessary in the circumstances.
6. A statement that the practitioner believes the examination provides a reasonable basis for the opinion.
7. A paragraph stating that, because of inherent limitations of any internal control, misstatements due to error or fraud may occur and not be detected. (In addition the paragraph should state that projections of any evaluation of internal control over financial reporting to future periods are subject to the risk that internal control may become inadequate because of changes in conditions, or that the degree of compliance with the policies or procedures may deteriorate.)
8. An opinion on whether
   a. The entity has maintained, in all material respects, effective internal control as of the specified date, or during a period of time, based on the control criteria; or
   b. Management's assertion about the effectiveness of the entity's internal control over financial reporting is fairly stated, in all material respects, based on the control criteria.
9. A statement restricting the use of the report to the specified parties under the following circumstances:

a. When the criteria used to evaluate internal control over financial reporting are determined by the practitioner to be appropriate only for a limited number of parties who either participated in their establishment or can be presumed to have an adequate understanding of the criteria.
b. When the criteria used to evaluate internal control over financial reporting are available only to specified parties.

10. A signature of the practitioner's firm, which may be manual or printed.
11. The date of the examination report.

Presented below is the standard form to be used when the practitioner is reporting directly on the effectiveness of an entity's internal control as of a specified date.

Independent Accountant's Report

[Introductory paragraph]

We have examined the effectiveness of W Company's internal control over financial reporting as of December 31, 20XX, based on *[identify criteria]*. W Company's management is responsible for maintaining effective internal control over financial reporting. Our responsibility is to express an opinion on the effectiveness of internal control based on our examination.

[Scope paragraph]

Our examination was conducted in accordance with attestation standards established by the American Institute of Certified Public Accountants and, accordingly, included obtaining an understanding of internal control over financial reporting, testing, and evaluating the design and operating effectiveness of internal control, and performing such other procedures as we considered necessary in the circumstances. We believe that our examination provides a reasonable basis for our opinion.

[Inherent limitations paragraph]

Because of inherent limitations in any internal control, misstatements due to error or fraud may occur and not be detected. Also, projections of any evaluation of internal control over financial reporting to future periods are subject to the risk that the internal control may become inadequate because of changes in conditions, or that the degree of compliance with the policies or procedures may deteriorate.

[Opinion paragraph]

In our opinion, W Company maintained, in all material respects, effective internal control over financial reporting as of December 31, 20XX, based on *[identify criteria]*.

[Signature]

[Date]

If the practitioner is reporting on the responsible party's assertion about the effectiveness of an entity's internal control, then the following standard form should be used.

Independent Accountant's Report

[Introductory paragraph]

We have examined management's assertion, included in the accompanying *[title of management report]*, that W Company maintained effective internal control over financial reporting as of December 31, 20XX, based on *[identify criteria]*. W Company's management is responsible for maintaining effective internal control over financial reporting. Our responsibility is to express an opinion on management's assertion based on our examination.

[Standard scope and inherent limitations paragraphs]

[Opinion paragraph]

In our opinion, management's assertion that W Company maintained effective internal control over financial reporting as of December 31, 20XX, is fairly stated, in all material respects, based on *[identify criteria]*.

[Signature]

[Date]

REPORT MODIFICATIONS

MATERIAL WEAKNESSES

If conditions are identified that result in one or more material weaknesses, the practitioner's report should be modified and should express an opinion directly on the effectiveness of internal control, and not on the assertion.

The practitioner may express a qualified opinion or express an adverse opinion if the material weakness(es) is(are) so pervasive that the entity's internal control over financial reporting does not achieve the control objectives.

If a qualified opinion is justified, the following is representative of the report that should be issued.

Independent Accountant's Report

[*Introductory paragraph*]
We have examined the effectiveness of W Company's internal control over financial reporting as of December 31, 20XX, based on [*identify criteria*]. W Company's management is responsible for maintaining effective internal control over financial reporting. Our responsibility is to express an opinion on management's assertion based on our examination.

[*Standard scope and inherent limitations paragraphs*]

[*Explanatory paragraph*]
A material weakness is a significant deficiency or combination of significant deficiencies, that results in more than a remote likelihood that a material mis-statement of the financial statements will not be prevented or detected. A significant deficiency is a control deficiency or combination of control deficiencies, that adversely affects the entity's ability to initiate, authorize, record, process, or report financial data reliably in accordance with generally accepted accounting principles such that there is more than a remote likelihood that a misstatement of the entity's financial statements that is more than inconsequential will not be prevented or detected. The following material weakness has been identified.

[*Include a description of the material weakness and its effect on the achievement of the objectives of the control criteria.*]

[*Opinion paragraph*]
In our opinion, except for the effect of the material weakness described in the preceding paragraph on the achievement of the objectives of the control criteria, W Company maintained effective internal control over financial reporting as of December 31, 20XX, in all material respects, based on [*identify criteria*].

[*Signature*]

[*Date*]

If an adverse opinion is justified, the following is representative of the report that should be issued.

Independent Accountant's Report

[*Introductory paragraph*]
We have examined the effectiveness of W Company's internal control over financial reporting as of December 31, 20XX, based on [*identify criteria*]. W Company's management is responsible for maintaining effective internal control over financial reporting. Our responsibility is to express an opinion on management's assertion based on our examination.

[*Standard scope and inherent limitations paragraphs*]

[*Explanatory paragraph*]
A material weakness is a significant deficiency or combination of significant deficiencies, that results in more than a remote likelihood that a material misstatement of the financial statements will not be prevented or detected. A significant deficiency is a control deficiency or combi-

nation of control deficiencies, that adversely affects the entity's ability to initiate, authorize, record, process, or report financial data reliably in accordance with generally accepted accounting principles such that there is more than a remote likelihood that a misstatement of the entity's financial statements that is more than inconsequential will not be prevented or detected. The following material weakness has been identified.

[*Include a description of the material weakness and its effect on the achievement of the objectives of the control criteria.*]

[*Opinion paragraph*]

In our opinion, because of the effect of the material weakness described above on the achievement of the objectives of the control criteria, W Company has not maintained effective internal control over financial reporting as of December 31, 20XX, based on [*identify criteria*].

[*Signature*]

[*Date*]

SCOPE LIMITATIONS

Depending on the significance of a limitation on the scope of an engagement, a practitioner may

1. Express a qualified opinion;
2. Disclaim an opinion; or
3. In extreme circumstances, withdraw from the engagement.

If a qualified opinion is justified, the following is representative of the report that should be issued.

Independent Accountant's Report

[*Standard introductory paragraph*]
[*Scope paragraph*]
Except as described below, our examination was conducted in accordance with attestation standards established by the American Institute of Certified Public Accountants and, accordingly, included obtaining an understanding of the internal control over financial reporting, testing and evaluating the design and operating effectiveness of the internal control, and performing such other procedures as we considered necessary in the circumstances. We believe that our examination provides a reasonable basis for our opinion.

[*Explanatory paragraph*]
A material weakness is a significant deficiency or a combination of significant deficiencies that results in more than a remote likelihood that a material misstatement of the financial statements will not be prevented or detected. A significant deficiency is a control deficiency or combination of control deficiencies, that adversely affects the entity's ability to initiate, authorize, record, process, or report financial data reliably in accordance with generally accepted accounting principles such that there is more than a remote likelihood that a misstatement of the entity's financial statements that is more than inconsequential will not be prevented or detected. The following material weakness has been identified prior to December 20, 20XX, W Company had an inadequate system for recording cash receipts, which could have prevented the Company from recording cash receipts on accounts receivable completely and properly. Therefore cash received could have been diverted for unauthorized use, lost, or otherwise not properly recorded to accounts receivable. We believe this condition was a material weakness in the design or operation of the internal control of W Company in effect prior to December 20, 20XX. Although the Company implemented a new cash receipts system on December 20, 20XX, the system has not been in operation for a sufficient period of time to enable us to obtain sufficient evidence about its operating effectiveness.

[*Standard inherent limitations paragraph*]
[*Opinion paragraph*]

In our opinion, except for the effect of matters we may have discovered had we been able to examine evidence about the effectiveness of the new cash receipts system, W Company maintained effective internal control over financial reporting as of December 31,20XX based on [*identify criteria*].

[*Signature*]

[*Date*]

If a disclaimer of opinion is appropriate, the following is representative of the report that should be issued.

Independent Accountant's Report

[*Introductory paragraph*]
We were engaged to examine the effectiveness of W Company's internal control over financial reporting as of December 31,20XX, based on [*identify criteria*]. W Company's management is responsible for maintaining effective internal control over financial reporting.
[*Scope paragraph should be omitted*]
[*Explanatory paragraph*]
[*Include paragraph to describe scope restrictions*]
[*Opinion paragraph*]
Since management [*describe scope restrictions*] and we were unable to apply other procedures to satisfy ourselves as to the entity's internal control over financial reporting, the scope of our work was not sufficient to enable us express, and we do not express, an opinion on the effectiveness of the entity's internal control over financial reporting.

[*Signature*]

[*Date*]

PART OF EXAMINATION PERFORMED BY ANOTHER PRACTITIONER

When part of the examination of the effectiveness of internal control of one or more subsidiaries, divisions, branches, or components of the entity is performed by another practitioner, the principal practitioner should follow the guidance in AU Section 543, *Part of Audit Performed by Other Independent Auditors.*

If the principal practitioner concludes that it is appropriate to refer to the report of the other practitioner, the following report format is generally appropriate.

Independent Accountant's Report

[*Introductory paragraph*]
We have examined the effectiveness of W Company's internal control over financial reporting as of December 31, 20XX, based on [identify criteria]. W Company's management is responsible for maintaining effective internal control over financial reporting. Our responsibility is to express an opinion on the effectiveness of internal control based on our examination. We did not examine the effectiveness of internal control over financial reporting of B Company, a wholly owned subsidiary, whose financial statements reflect 20 and 30 percent, respectively, of the related consolidated financial statements as of and for the year ended December 31, 20XX. The effectiveness of B Company's internal control over financial reporting was examined by other accountants whose report has been furnished to us, and our opinion, insofar as it relates to the effectiveness of B Company's internal control over financial reporting, is based solely on the report of the other accountants.
[*Scope paragraph*]
Our examination was conducted in accordance with attestation standards established by the American Institute of Certified Public Accountants and, accordingly, included obtaining an understanding of internal control over financial reporting, testing, and evaluating the design and oper-

ating effectiveness of internal control, and performing such other procedures as we considered necessary in the circumstances. We believe that our examination and the report of the other accountants provides a reasonable basis for our opinion.

[*Standard inherent limitations paragraph*]

[*Opinion paragraph*]

In our opinion, based on our examination and the report of the other accountants, W Company maintained, in all material respects, effective internal control over financial reporting as of December 31, 20XX, based on [*identify criteria*].

[*Signature*]

[*Date*]

SUBSEQUENT EVENTS

If a practitioner becomes aware of subsequent events that have a significant effect on the effectiveness of internal control over financial reporting as of the assertion date, the practitioner should report directly on the internal control's effectiveness and qualify the opinion or express an adverse opinion. However, a disclaimer of opinion is appropriate in circumstances where the practitioner experiences an inability to determine the effects of the subsequent events.

The practitioner should be aware that a subsequent event may have a prospective effect on the entity's internal control over financial reporting. If such an event has a material effect on the entity, the practitioner may elect to include an explanatory paragraph in the subsequent report in order to describe the event and its effects or bring it to the attention of the readers.

There is no responsibility to keep informed of events after the report date. If, however, the practitioner becomes aware of conditions that existed at the date of the report, the practitioner should follow the guidance in AU Section 561, *Subsequent Discovery of Facts Existing at the Date of the Auditor's Report.*

REPORTING ON THE EFFECTIVENESS OF A SEGMENT OF THE ENTITY'S INTERNAL CONTROL

An opinion may be expressed on a segment of an entity's internal control. In this situation the following report format is generally appropriate.

Independent Accountant's Report

[*Introductory paragraph*]

We have examined the effectiveness of W Company's internal control over financial reporting for its retail division as of December 31, 20XX, based on [*identify criteria*]. W Company's management is responsible for maintaining effective internal control over financial reporting. Our responsibility is to express an opinion on the effectiveness of internal control based on our examination.

[*Standard scope and inherent limitations paragraphs*]

[*Opinion paragraph*]

In our opinion, W Company's retail division maintained, in all material respects, effective internal control over financial reporting as of December 31, 20XX, based on [*identify criteria*].

[*Signature*]

[*Date*]

REPORTING ON THE SUITABILITY OF DESIGN OF INTERNAL CONTROL

A practitioner is permitted to express an opinion on the suitability of the design, rather than on the effectiveness, of the entity's internal control. A suggested report format is presented below.

Independent Accountant's Report

[*Introductory paragraph*]

We have examined the suitability of W Company's design of internal control over financial reporting to prevent or detect material misstatements in the financial statements on a timely basis as of December 31, 20XX, based on [*identify criteria*]. W Company's management is responsible for the suitable design of internal control over financial reporting. Our responsibility is to express an opinion on the design of internal control based on our examination.

[*Scope paragraph*]

Our examination was conducted in accordance with attestation standards established by the American Institute of Certified Public Accountants and, accordingly, included obtaining an understanding of internal control over financial reporting, evaluating the design of internal control, and performing such other procedures as we considered necessary in the circumstances. We believe that our examination provides a reasonable basis for our opinion.

[*Standard inherent limitations paragraph*]

[*Opinion paragraph*]

In our opinion, W Company's internal control over financial reporting is suitably designed, in all material respects, to prevent or detect material misstatements in the financial statements on a timely basis as of December 31, 20XX, based on [*identify criteria*].

[*Signature*]

[*Date*]

If the internal control is already in operation, the following wording should be added to the scope paragraph:

We were not engaged to examine and report on the operating effectiveness of W Company's internal control over financial reporting as of December 31, 20XX, and, accordingly, we express no opinion on operating effectiveness.

RELATIONSHIP OF THE EXAMINATION OF AN ENTITY'S INTERNAL CONTROL TO THE OPINION OBTAINED IN AN AUDIT

An auditor's consideration of internal control in a financial statement audit is more limited than that of a practitioner engaged to examine management's assertion about the effectiveness of the entity's internal control. However, the practitioner may, in performing an audit of the entity's financial statements

1. Use the knowledge obtained about the entity's internal control as part of such an examination as the basis for the understanding of internal control required in the audit of the financial statements, and
2. Consider the results of tests of controls performed in connection with an examination of management's assertion as well as any material weaknesses identified when assessing control risk.

601 COMPLIANCE ATTESTATION

SOURCE OF STANDARDS

SSAE 10, *Attest Standards: Revision and Recodification*

SUMMARY

This section is designed to guide a practitioner in the performance of engagements related to

1. An entity's compliance with requirements of specified laws, regulations, rules, contracts, or grants (referred to as compliance with specified requirements); and
2. The effectiveness of an entity's internal control over compliance with specified requirements (referred to as internal control over compliance).

Compliance attestation engagements should comply with the standards set forth in AT Section 101, *Attest Engagements*.

TYPES OF SERVICES

Depending on the needs of users, a practitioner may be engaged to perform agreed-upon procedures in order to assist users to evaluate

1. The entity's compliance with specified requirements,
2. The effectiveness of the entity's internal control over compliance,
3. The entity's compliance with specified requirements (or a written assertion thereon), or
4. The effectiveness of the entity's internal control over compliance (or a written assertion thereon).

A practitioner, however, should not accept an engagement to perform a review of an entity's compliance with specified requirements or the effectiveness of an entity's internal control over compliance or an assertion thereon.

A practitioner is permitted to accept an engagement to provide suggestions to the responsible party in order to improve internal control over compliance. Guidance for this type of engagement can be found in CS Section 100, *Consulting Services: Definitions and Standards.*

CONDITIONS FOR ENGAGEMENT PERFORMANCE

An engagement related to an entity's compliance with specified requirements or the effectiveness of internal control over compliance may be performed if the following conditions are met:

1. The responsible party accepts responsibility for compliance with specified requirements and the effectiveness of internal control over compliance.

2. The responsible party evaluates the compliance with specified requirements or the effectiveness of internal control over compliance.

3. For an examination engagement only, sufficient evidential matter exists or could be developed to support the responsible party's evaluations.

4. The responsible party provides to the practitioner its written assertion concerning

   a. The entity's compliance with specified requirements, or

   b. The effectiveness of the entity's internal control over compliance.

The written assertion may be presented in either a separate report that will accompany the practitioner's report or a representation letter to the practitioner. A practitioner ordinarily should withdraw from an examination engagement if the responsible party refuses to provide a written assertion to the practitioner.

REPRESENTATION LETTER

The responsible party is responsible for ensuring that the entity complies with the requirements applicable to its activities. In both an agreed-upon procedures engagement and an examination engagement, the practitioner should obtain the responsible party's written representations that

1. Acknowledge the responsible party's responsibility for complying with the specified requirements.

2. Acknowledge the responsible party's responsibility for establishing and maintaining effective internal control over compliance.

3. The responsible party has performed an evaluation of (a) the entity's compliance with specified requirements or (b) the entity's internal controls for ensuring compliance and detecting noncompliance with requirements, as applicable.

4. The responsible party's assertion about the entity's compliance with the specified requirements or about the effectiveness of internal control over compliance, as applicable, is based on the stated or established criteria.

5. The responsible party has disclosed to the practitioner all known noncompliance.

6. The responsible party has made available all documentation related to compliance with the specified requirements.

7. Provide the responsible party's interpretation of any compliance requirements that have varying interpretations.

8. The responsible party has disclosed any communications from regulatory agencies, internal auditors, and other practitioners concerning possible noncompliance with the specified requirements, including communications received between the end of the period addressed in the written assertion and the date of the practitioner's report.

9. The responsible party has disclosed any known noncompliance occurring subsequent to the period for which, or the date as of which, the responsible party selects to make its assertion.

The refusal of the responsible party to furnish all appropriate written representations is tantamount to a restriction on the scope of the engagement sufficient to require

1. In an agreed-upon procedures engagement, the practitioner's withdrawal if the client is the responsible party, (If the client is not the responsible party, the effects of the refusal on the practitioner's report should be considered carefully.)

2. In an examination engagement, the practitioner's withdrawal, the expression of a qualified opinion, or the issuance of a disclaimer of opinion.

3. In either an agreed-upon-procedures engagement or an examination engagement, the practitioner to consider the effects of the responsible party's refusal on his or her ability to rely on other representations made by the responsible party.

AGREED-UPON PROCEDURES ENGAGEMENT

The purpose of an agreed-upon procedures engagement is to provide specified parties with a report containing specific findings to be used in evaluating an entity's compliance with specified requirements or the effectiveness of an entity's internal control over compliance. The report prepared by the practitioner is based on procedures agreed upon by the users of the report. Accordingly, the practitioner is required to perform only the procedures that have been agreed to by specified parties (users).

Before performing the agreed-upon procedures, the practitioner should do the following:

1. Obtain a sufficient understanding of the specified compliance requirements by considering

    a. Relevant laws, regulations, rules, contracts, and grants;
    b. Related knowledge obtained through prior engagements and regulatory reports; and
    c. Related knowledge obtained through discussions with appropriate individuals within the entity and outside the entity.

2. Properly plan the engagement.

When the practitioner encounters a restriction on the scope of the engagement, the practitioner should obtain permission from the specified users to modify the agreed-upon procedures. In the absence of the requested permission, the practitioner should either describe the scope restriction in the engagement report or consider withdrawing from the engagement.

The practitioner has no performance obligation beyond the procedures that were agreed upon. However, if instances of noncompliance are identified by the practitioner by other means, the practitioner ordinarily should modify his or her report to include disclosure of the instances of noncompliance.

REPORT ON AGREED-UPON PROCEDURES

Depending on the engagement, the practitioner may issue a report on either the entity's compliance with specified requirements or the effectiveness of the entity's internal control over compliance. The report issued by the practitioner should contain the following:

1. A title that includes the word *independent.*
2. Identification of the specified parties.
3. Identification of the subject matter of the engagement (or management's assertion), including the period or point in time addressed and a reference to the character of the engagement.
4. Identification of the responsible party.
5. A statement that the subject matter is the responsibility of the responsible party.
6. A statement that the procedures, which were agreed to by the specified parties identified in the report, were performed to assist the specified parties in evaluating the entity's compliance with specified requirements or the effectiveness of its internal control over compliance.
7. A statement that the agreed-upon procedures engagement was conducted in accordance with attestation standards established by the American Institute of Certified Public Accountants.

8. A statement that the sufficiency of the procedures is solely the responsibility of the specified parties and a disclaimer of responsibility for the sufficiency of those procedures.
9. A list of the procedures performed (or reference thereto) and related findings.
10. A description of any agreed-upon materiality limits, if applicable.
11. A statement that the practitioner was not engaged to and did not conduct an examination of the entity's compliance with specified requirements (or the effectiveness of an entity's internal control over compliance), a disclaimer of opinion thereon, and a statement that if the practitioner had performed additional procedures, other matters might have come to his or her attention that would have been reported.
12. A restriction on the use of the report to the specified parties.
13. Reservations or restrictions concerning procedures or findings, if applicable.
14. Description of the nature of the assistance provided by a specialist, if applicable.
15. A signature of the practitioner's firm, which may be manual or printed.
16. The date of the agreed-upon procedures report, which should be the date on which the agreed-upon procedures were completed.

The report based on the application of agreed-upon procedures should not contain the expression of an opinion or negative assurance regarding the subject matter (or the written assertion thereon).

Presented below is a sample agreed-upon procedures report based on an engagement relating to an entity's compliance with specified requirements in which the practitioner's procedures and findings are listed rather than referenced.

Independent Accountant's Report on Applying Agreed-Upon Procedures

We have performed the procedures enumerated below, which were agreed to by [*list specified parties*] solely to assist the specified parties in evaluating [*name of entity's*] compliance with [*list specified requirements*] during the [*period*] ended [*date*]. Management is responsible for [*name of entity*]'s compliance with those requirements. This agreed-upon procedures engagement was conducted in accordance with attestation standards established by the American Institute of Certified Public Accountants. The sufficiency of these procedures is solely the responsibility of those parties specified in this report. Consequently we make no representation regarding the sufficiency of the procedures described below either for the purpose for which this report has been requested or for any other purpose.

[*Include paragraphs to enumerate procedures and findings*]

We were not engaged to and did not conduct an examination, the objective of which would be the expression of an opinion on compliance. Accordingly we do not express such an opinion. Had we performed additional procedures, other matters might have come to our attention that would have been reported to you.

This report is intended solely for the information and use of [*list or refer to specified parties*] and is not intended to be used and should not be used by anyone other than these specified parties.

[*Signature*]

[*Date*]

Presented below is a sample agreed-upon procedures report based on an engagement relating to the effectiveness of an entity's internal control over compliance with specified requirements in which the practitioner's procedures and findings are listed rather than referenced.

Independent Accountant's Report on Applying Agreed-Upon Procedures

We have performed the procedures enumerated below, which were agreed to by [*list specified parties*], solely to assist the specified parties in evaluating the effectiveness of [*name of entity*]'s internal control over compliance with [*list specified requirements*] as of [*date*]. Management is responsible for [*name of entity*]'s internal control over compliance with those requirements. This agreed-upon procedures engagement was conducted in accordance with attestation standards established by the American Institute of Certified Public Accountants. The sufficiency of these procedures is solely the responsibility of those parties specified in this report. Consequently we make no representation regarding the sufficiency of the procedures described below either for the purpose for which this report has been requested or for any other purpose.

[*Include paragraphs to enumerate procedures and findings*]

We were not engaged to and did not conduct an examination, the objective of which would be the expression of an opinion on the effectiveness of internal control over compliance. Accordingly we do not express such an opinion. Had we performed additional procedures, other matters might have come to our attention that would have been reported to you.

This report is intended solely for the information and use of [*list or refer to specified parties*] and is not intended to be used and should not be used by anyone other than these specified parties.

[*Signature*]

[*Date*]

If the practitioner was engaged to report on both the compliance with specified requirements and the effectiveness of an entity's internal control over compliance with specified requirements, he or she may issue separate reports. The practitioner may, however, issue a combined report by modifying the introductory paragraph as follows:

We have performed the procedures enumerated below, which were agreed to by [*list users of report*], solely to assist the users in evaluating [*name of entity*]'s compliance with [*list specified requirements*] during the [*period*] ended [*date*] and the effectiveness of [*name of entity*]'s internal control over compliance with the aforementioned compliance requirements as of [*date*]. Management is responsible for [*name of entity*]'s internal control over compliance with those requirements.

EXAMINATION ENGAGEMENT

The purpose of an examination engagement applied to compliance with specified requirements is to express an opinion on an entity's compliance (or assertion related thereto) based on specified criteria. In an examination engagement the practitioner should obtain reasonable assurance that the entity complied with the specified requirements in all material respects. This may be accomplished by designing the examination to detect both intentional and unintentional instances of material noncompliance.

During the examination engagement the practitioner should attempt to minimize attestation risk. Attestation risk may be defined as the risk that the practitioner may unknowingly fail to appropriately modify the opinion. It is composed of inherent risk, control risk, and detection risk.

In assessing attestation risk (and its related components), the practitioner may follow the guidance in AU Section 312, since attestation risk (and its related components) is similar to audit risk (and its related components) applicable to an audit of historical financial statements. In an attestation engagement, however, the relevant risks relate to material noncompliance rather than material misstatement.

The consideration of materiality in a compliance examination differs from the consideration of materiality in an audit of financial statements. The practitioner's consideration of materiality in a compliance examination depends on

1. The nature of the compliance requirements, which may or may not be quantifiable in monetary terms;
2. The nature and frequency of instances of noncompliance identified with appropriate consideration of sampling risk; and

3. Qualitative considerations, such as the needs and expectations of the report's users.

In performing an examination engagement the practitioner should proceed as follows:

1. Obtain a sufficient understanding of the specified compliance requirements.
2. Properly plan the engagement.
3. Consider relevant portions of the entity's internal control over compliance.
4. Obtain sufficient evidence, including testing compliance with specified requirements.
5. Consider subsequent events.
6. Express an opinion about whether the entity complied, in all material respects, with specified requirements (or whether the responsible party's assertion about such compliance is fairly stated in all material respects) based on the specified criteria.

In planning the engagement, the practitioner may use the work of

1. A specialist when the specified compliance requirements call for specialized skill or knowledge other than accounting or auditing, or
2. Internal auditors.

Before contacting a specialist, the practitioner should consider the guidance in AU Section 336, *Using the Work of a Specialist*. Likewise the guidance in AU Section 322, *the Auditor's Consideration of the Internal Audit Function in an Audit of Financial Statements*, provides useful information on internal auditors.

In considering internal control over compliance, the practitioner should proceed as follows:

1. Obtain a sufficient understanding in order to properly plan the engagement and to assess control risk for compliance with specified requirements.
2. Obtain an understanding of the design of specific internal controls by means of inquiries, inspection, and observation.
3. In a manner similar to that in a financial statement audit, communicate significant deficiencies of which the practitioner becomes aware. These deficiencies would concern the design or operation of internal control over compliance that could have an adverse effect on the entity's ability to comply with specified requirements. (Additional guidance on communicating these deficiencies may be found in AU Section 325, *Communication of Internal Control Related Matters Noted in an Audit*.)

In order to obtain sufficient evidence, the practitioner should apply procedures to provide reasonable assurance of detecting material noncompliance. If engaged to report on compliance with regulatory requirements, the practitioner's procedures should include reviewing reports of significant examinations and related communications between regulatory agencies and the entity.

In a manner similar to that in an audit of financial statements, a practitioner's examination of an entity's compliance with specified requirements must consider subsequent events.

One type of subsequent event provides additional information about compliance during the period addressed by the practitioner's report that may affect the practitioner's report. The procedures that the practitioner should perform to identify this type of event include reviewing reports of internal auditors, other practitioners, and regulatory agencies, which were issued during the subsequent period.

The second type of subsequent event is noncompliance that occurs subsequent to the period being reported on but before the date of the practitioner's report. The practitioner has no responsibility to detect such noncompliance. However, if the practitioner becomes aware of such noncompliance, it may be of such a nature and significance that disclosure of it is required to keep management's assertion from being misleading,

REPORT BASED ON AN EXAMINATION

The report based on an examination should

1. Express an opinion on whether the entity has complied, in all material respects (or whether the responsible party's assertion about such compliance is fairly stated in all material respects), and
2. Be based on the nature, frequency, and materiality of any instances of noncompliance.

The practitioner's examination report, which is ordinarily addressed to the entity, should contain the following:

1. A title that includes the word *independent*.
2. Identification of the specified compliance requirements (or the assertion thereon), including the period covered, and the responsible party. When the responsible party's assertion does not accompany the practitioner's report, the first paragraph of the report should also contain a statement of the responsible party's assertion.
3. A statement that compliance with the specified requirements is the responsibility of the entity's management.
4. A statement that the practitioner's responsibility is to express an opinion on the entity's compliance with those requirements or on the responsible party's assertion about such compliance based on a thorough examination.
5. A statement that the examination was conducted in accordance with attestation standards established by the American Institute of Certified Public Accountants and, accordingly, included examining, on a test basis, evidence about the entity's compliance with those requirements and performing such other procedures as the practitioner considered necessary in the circumstances.
6. A statement that the practitioner believes the examination provides a reasonable basis for the opinion.
7. A statement that the examination does not provide a legal determination on the entity's compliance.
8. An opinion on whether the entity complied, in all material respects, with specified requirements (or whether the responsible party's assertion about such compliance is fairly stated in all material respects) based on the specified criteria.
9. A restriction on the use of the report to the specified parties under the following circumstances:

   a. When the criteria used to evaluate compliance are determined by the practitioner to be appropriate only for a limited number of parties who either participated in their establishment or can be presumed to have an adequate understanding of the criteria, and

   b. When the criteria used to evaluate compliance are available only to the specified parties.

10. A signature of the practitioner's firm which may be manual or printed.
11. The date of the examination report, which should be the date on which the examination procedures were completed.

In the event that the responsible party presents its written assertion about compliance in a representation letter to the practitioner, rather than in a separate report, the introductory paragraph of the report should state the responsible party's assertion, and the opinion paragraph should report on the entity's compliance with the specified requirements.

Presented below is a sample examination report in which the practitioner is expressing an opinion on an entity's compliance with specified requirements.

Independent Accountant's Report

[*Introductory paragraph*]

We have examined [*name of entity*]'s compliance with [*list specified compliance requirements*] during the [*period*] ended [*date*]. Management is responsible for [*name of entity*]'s compliance with those requirements. Our responsibility is to express an opinion on [*name of entity*]'s compliance based on our examination.

[*Scope paragraph*]

Our examination was conducted in accordance with attestation standards established by the American Institute of Certified Public Accountants and, accordingly, included examining, on a test basis, evidence about [*name of entity*]'s compliance with those requirements and performing such other procedures as we considered necessary in the circumstances. We believe that our examination provides a reasonable basis for our opinion. Our examination does not provide a legal determination on [*name of entity*]'s compliance with specified requirements.

[*Opinion paragraph*]

In our opinion, [*name of entity*] complied, in all material respects, with the aforementioned requirements for the year ended December 31, 20XX.

[*Signature*]

[*Date*]

Presented below is a sample examination report in which the practitioner is expressing an opinion on management's assertion about compliance with specified requirements.

Independent Accountant's Report

[*Introductory paragraph*]

We have examined management's assertion, included in the accompanying [*title of management report*], that [*name of entity*] complied with [*list specified compliance requirements*] during the [*period*] ended [*date*]. Management is responsible for [*name of entity*]'s compliance with those requirements. Our responsibility is to express an opinion on management's assertion about [*name of entity*]'s compliance based on our examination.

[*Standard scope paragraph*]

[*Opinion paragraph*]

In our opinion, management's assertion that [*name of entity*] complied with the aforementioned requirements during the [*period*] ended [*date*] is fairly stated, in all material respects.

[*Signature*]

[*Date*]

REPORT MODIFICATIONS

The practitioner's report should be modified if any of the following conditions exist:

1. There is material noncompliance with specified requirements.
2. There is a restriction on the scope of the engagement.
3. The practitioner decides to refer to the report of another practitioner as the basis, in part, for the practitioner's report.

When instances of material noncompliance are identified, the practitioner should

1. Modify the report and express an opinion on the entity's specified compliance requirements, rather than on the responsible party's assertion;
2. Modify the opinion paragraph to include a reference to the noncompliance and include an explanatory paragraph before the opinion paragraph that describes the noncompliance if the responsible party discloses the noncompliance and modifies the assertion; and/or
3. Depending on materiality, express either a qualified or adverse opinion on the responsible party's assertion.

Presented below is a sample report in which the practitioner has expressed a qualified opinion because of material noncompliance with applicable requirements.

Independent Accountant's Report

[Introductory paragraph]

We have examined *[name of entity]*'s compliance with *[list specified compliance requirements]* for the *[period]* ended *[date]*. Management is responsible for compliance with those requirements. Our responsibility is to express an opinion on *[name of entity]*'s compliance based on our examination.

[Standard scope paragraph]

[Explanatory paragraph]

Our examination disclosed the following material noncompliance with *[type of compliance requirement]* applicable to *[name of entity]* during the *[period]* ended *[date]*. *[Describe noncompliance]*

[Opinion paragraph]

In our opinion, except for the material noncompliance described in the third paragraph, *[name of entity]* complied, in all material respects, with the aforementioned requirements for the *[period]* ended *[date]*.

[Signature]

[Date]

If the practitioner determines that an adverse opinion is appropriate, the following report form may be utilized.

Independent Accountant's Report

[Introductory paragraph]

We have examined *[name of entity]*'s compliance with *[list specified compliance requirements]* for the *[period]* ended *[date]*. Management is responsible for compliance with those requirements. Our responsibility is to express an opinion on *[name of entity]*'s compliance based on our examination.

[Standard scope paragraph]

[Explanatory paragraph]

Our examination disclosed the following material noncompliance with *[type of compliance requirement]* applicable to *[name of entity]* during the *[period]* ended *[date]*. *[Describe noncompliance]*

[Opinion paragraph]

In our opinion, because of the effect of the noncompliance described in the third paragraph, *[name of entity]* has not complied with the aforementioned requirements for the *[period]* ended *[date]*.

[Signature]

[Date]

OTHER INFORMATION IN A CLIENT-PREPARED DOCUMENT

An entity may publish various documents that include other information in addition to the practitioner's report on either compliance with specified requirements or the effectiveness of internal control over compliance and the practitioner's report thereon. The practitioner's responsibility with respect to other information in such a document is governed by the guidance in AT Section 101. Accordingly the practitioner's responsibility does not extend beyond information included in the report, and the practitioner is not required to perform any procedures in order to corroborate the other information included in the document. However, the practitioner should read the other information and consider whether such information, or the manner of its presentation, is materially inconsistent with the information appearing in the practitioner's report or whether such information contains a material misstatement of fact.

701 MANAGEMENT'S DISCUSSION AND ANALYSIS

SOURCE OF STANDARDS

SSAE 10, *Attest Standards: Revision and Recodification*

SUMMARY

This section provides guidance concerning attestation engagements to examine or review Management's Discussion and Analysis (MD&A) prepared in accordance with SEC rules and regulations, which are presented in annual reports to shareholders and in other documents.

MD&A is an SEC-required document that generally covers three years of audited financial statements and any interim-period financial statements. MD&A should be designed to provide a useful analysis of significant changes in financial condition and results of operations.

If a practitioner is engaged to apply agreed-upon procedures to MD&A, the practitioner should follow the provisions in AT Section 201, *Agreed-upon Procedures Engagements,* rather than follow the provisions in this section.

Since an engagement to examine or review MD&A is considered an attestation engagement, in addition to complying with the provisions contained in this section, the practitioner must also comply with the provisions contained in the AT Section 101, *Attest Engagements.*

CONDITIONS FOR ENGAGEMENT PERFORMANCE

EXAMINATION

The objective of an examination of MD&A is to express an opinion as to whether the presentation of MD&A taken as a whole

1. Presents, in all material respects, the required elements of the SEC rules and regulations;
2. Ensures that the historical financial amounts have been accurately derived, in all material respects, from the entity's financial statements; and
3. Presents the underlying information, determinations, estimates, and assumptions that provide a reasonable basis for the disclosures contained therein.

A practitioner is permitted to accept an engagement to examine MD&A if the practitioner audits the financial statements for at least the latest period to which the MD&A relates and the practitioner or a predecessor auditor has audited the financial statements of the other periods covered by the MD&A.

REVIEW

The objective of a review of MD&A is to report whether any information came to the practitioner's attention to cause the practitioner to believe that

1. The MD&A does not include, in all material respects, the elements required by the SEC;
2. The historical financial amounts have not been accurately derived, in all material respects, from the financial statements; and
3. The underlying information, determinations, estimates, and assumptions do not provide a reasonable basis for the disclosures contained therein.

A review consists principally of performing analytical procedures and making inquiries of persons responsible for financial, accounting, and operational matters. Accordingly a review, which is substantially less in scope than an examination, does not include the performance of substantive tests or obtaining corroborating evidential matter.

A practitioner is permitted to accept an engagement to review MD&A if the practitioner audits the financial statements for at least the latest period to which the MD&A relates, and the practitioner or a predecessor practitioner has audited the financial statements of the other periods covered by the MD&A.

EXAMINATION ENGAGEMENT

In examining MD&A, a practitioner should limit attestation risk to an acceptably low level. Attestation risk, like audit risk, is a combination of inherent risk, control risk, and detection risk.

In general, a practitioner should properly plan the engagement and perform procedures in order to obtain reasonable assurance of detecting material misstatements to the MD&A presentation taken as a whole and express an opinion.

EXAMINATION PROCEDURES

A practitioner examining MD&A should proceed as follows:

1. Obtain an understanding of the SEC rules and regulations for MD&A and the methods used by management in its preparation.
2. Properly plan the engagement.
3. Consider the relevant internal controls applicable to the preparation of MD&A.
4. Obtain sufficient evidence regarding the assertions embodied in MD&A (i.e., completeness, occurrence, consistency with the financial statements, and presentation and disclosure).
5. Take into account the effect of events subsequent to the balance sheet date.
6. Obtain written representations from management concerning its responsibility for MD&A, completeness of minutes, events subsequent to the balance sheet date, and other relevant matters.
7. Express an opinion about whether MD&A is presented in all material respects in accordance with required elements of the SEC rules and regulations.

REPORT CONTENTS

The practitioner's examination report on MD&A should include the following:

1. A title that includes the word *independent*.
2. Identification of the MD&A presentation, including the period covered.

3. A statement that management is responsible for the preparation of the MD&A pursuant to SEC rules and regulations, and a statement that the practitioner's responsibility is to express an opinion on the presentation based on the examination.
4. Reference to the auditor's report on the related financial statements and, if other than a standard report, the reasons therefor.
5. A statement that the examination was made in accordance with attestation standards established by the AICPA and a description of the scope of the examination.
6. A statement that the practitioner believes the examination provides a reasonable basis for the opinion.
7. A paragraph stating that

   a. The preparation of MD&A requires management to interpret the criteria, make determinations as to the relevancy of information to be included, and make estimates and assumptions that affect reported information; and
   b. Actual future results may differ materially from management's present assessment of information regarding the estimated future impact of transactions and events that have occurred or are expected to occur, expected sources of liquidity and capital resources, operating trends, commitments, and uncertainties.

8. In the case of a nonpublic entity, a statement that, although not subject to the SEC rules and regulations, the MD&A is intended to be a presentation in accordance with the SEC rules and regulations.
9. An opinion on whether

   a. The presentation includes, in all material respects, the required elements of the SEC rules and regulations;
   b. The historical financial amounts have been accurately derived, in all material respects, from the entity's financial statements; and
   c. The underlying information, determinations, estimates, and assumptions provide a reasonable basis for the disclosures contained therein.

10. Any necessary report modifications.
11. A signature of the practitioner's firm, which may be manual or printed signature.
12. The date of the examination report, which should coincide with the completion of the examination procedures.

SAMPLE EXAMINATION REPORT

Presented below is an illustration of a standard examination report.

Independent Accountant's Report

[Introductory paragraph]

We have examined XYZ Company's Management's Discussion and Analysis taken as a whole, included *[incorporated by reference]* in the Company's *[insert description of registration statement or document]*. Management is responsible for the preparation of the Company's Management's Discussion and Analysis pursuant to the rules and regulations adopted by the Securities and Exchange Commission. Our responsibility is to express an opinion on the presentation based on our examination. We have audited, in accordance with auditing standards generally accepted in the United States of America, the financial statements of XYZ Company as of December 31, 20XY and 20XX, and for each of the years in the three-year period ended December 31, 20XY, and in our report dated [month] XX, 20XZ, we expressed an unqualified opinion on those financial statements.

[Scope paragraph]

Our examination of Management's Discussion and Analysis was conducted in accordance with attestation standards established by the American Institute of Certified Public Accountants and, accordingly, included examining, on a test basis, evidence supporting the historical amounts and disclosures in the presentation. An examination also includes assessing the significant determinations made by management as to the relevancy of the information to be included and the estimates and assumptions that affect reported information. We believe that our examination provides a reasonable basis for our opinion.

[*Explanatory paragraph*]

The preparation of Management's Discussion and Analysis requires management to interpret the criteria, make determinations as to the relevancy of information to be included, and make estimates and assumptions that affect reported information. Management's Discussion and Analysis includes information regarding the estimated future impact of transactions and events that have occurred or are expected to occur, expected sources of liquidity and capital resources, operating trends, commitments, and uncertainties. Actual results in the future may differ materially from management's present assessment of this information because events and circumstances frequently do not occur as expected.

[*Opinion paragraph*]

In our opinion, the Company's presentation of Management's Discussion and Analysis includes, in ail material respects, the required elements of the rules and regulations adopted by the Securities and Exchange Commission; the historical financial amounts included therein have been accurately derived, in all material respects, from the Company's financial statements; and the underlying information, determinations, estimates, and assumptions of the Company provide a reasonable basis for the disclosures contained therein.

[*Signature*]

[*Date*]

REVIEW ENGAGEMENT

In general, a practitioner should properly plan the engagement and perform procedures in order to obtain sufficient evidence to provide a basis for forming a conclusion about whether any information came to his or her attention that would lead to the conclusion that MD&A reporting objectives were not achieved.

REVIEW PROCEDURES

A practitioner reviewing MD&A should proceed as follows:

1. Obtain an understanding of the SEC rules and regulations for MD&A and management's method of its preparation.
2. Properly plan the engagement.
3. Consider the relevant internal controls applicable to the preparation of MD&A.
4. Apply analytical procedures and make inquiries of management and others having responsibility for operational areas and financial and accounting matters.
5. Take into account the effect of events subsequent to the balance sheet date.
6. Obtain written representations from management concerning its responsibility for MD&A, completeness of minutes, events subsequent to the balance sheet date, and other relevant matters.
7. Form a conclusion as to whether any information came to the practitioner's attention to cause the practitioner to believe that

    a. The MD&A does not include, in all material respects, the elements required by the SEC;
    b. The historical financial amounts have not been accurately derived, in all material respects, from the financial statements; and

    c.   The underlying information, determinations, estimates, and assumptions do not provide a reasonable basis for the disclosures contained therein.

REPORTING

In general, in order to issue a review report on MD&A, the financial statements for the periods covered and the related auditor's report(s) should accompany the MD&A (or, in the case of a public entity, be incorporated in the document containing the MD&A by reference to information filed with a regulatory agency).

REPORT CONTENTS

The practitioner's review report on MD&A should include the following:

1. A title that includes the word *independent*.
2. Identification of the MD&A presentation, including the period covered.
3. A statement that management is responsible for the preparation of the MD&A pursuant to SEC rules and regulations.
4. Reference to the auditor's report on the related financial statements and, if other than a standard report, the reasons therefor.
5. A statement that the review was conducted in accordance with attestation standards established by the AICPA.
6. A description of the procedures for a review of MD&A.
7. A statement that a review of MD&A is substantially less in scope than an examination, the objective of which is an expression of opinion regarding the MD&A presentation, and, accordingly, no such opinion is expressed.
8. A paragraph stating that

    a.   The preparation of MD&A requires management to interpret the criteria, make determinations as to the relevancy of information to be included, and make estimates and assumptions that affect reported information; and

    b.   Actual future results may differ materially from management's present assessment of information regarding the estimated future impact of transactions and events that have occurred or are expected to occur, expected sources of liquidity and capital resources, operating trends, commitments, and uncertainties.

9. In the case of a nonpublic entity, a statement that, although not subject to the SEC rules and regulations, the MD&A is intended to be a presentation in accordance with the SEC rules and regulations.
10. A statement about whether any information came to the practitioner's attention that caused the practitioner to believe that the

    a.   Presentation does not include, in all material respects, the required elements of the SEC rules and regulations;

    b.   Historical financial amounts have not been accurately derived, in all material respects, from the entity's financial statements; and/or

    c.   Underlying information, determinations, estimates, and assumptions do not provide a reasonable basis for the disclosures contained therein.

11. Any necessary report modifications.
12. In general, a statement of restrictions on the use of the report to specified parties, because it is not intended to be filed with the SEC as a report under the 1933 or 1934 Act.
13. A signature of the practitioner's firm, which may be manual or printed.

14. The date of the review report, which should coincide with the completion of the review procedures.

SAMPLE REVIEW REPORT

Presented below is an illustration of a standard review report.

Independent Accountant's Report

[Introductory paragraph]

We have reviewed XYZ Company's Management's Discussion and Analysis taken as a whole, included *[incorporated by reference]* in the Company's *[insert description of registration statement or document]*. Management is responsible for the preparation of the Company's Management's Discussion and Analysis pursuant to the rules and regulations adopted by the Securities and Exchange Commission. We have audited, in accordance with auditing standards, generally accepted in the United States of America, the financial statements of XYZ Company as of December 31, 20XY and 20XX, and for each of the years in the three-year period ended December 31, 20XY, and in our report dated *[month]* XX, 20X2, we expressed an unqualified opinion on those financial statements.

[Scope paragraph]

We conducted our review of Management's Discussion and Analysis in accordance with attestation standards established by the American Institute of Certified Public Accountants. A review of Management's Discussion and Analysis consists principally of applying analytical procedures and making inquiries of persons responsible for financial, accounting, and operational matters. It is substantially less in scope than an examination, the objective of which is the expression of an opinion on the presentation. Accordingly, we do not express such an opinion.

[Explanatory paragraph]

The preparation of Management's Discussion and Analysis requires management to interpret the criteria, make determinations as to the relevancy of information to be included, and make estimates and assumptions that affect reported information. Management's Discussion and Analysis includes information regarding the estimated future impact of transactions and events that have occurred or are expected to occur, expected sources of liquidity and capital resources, operating trends, commitments, and uncertainties. Actual results in the future may differ materially from management's present assessment of this information because events and circumstances frequently do not occur as expected.

[Concluding paragraph]

Based on our review, nothing came to our attention that caused us to believe that the Company's presentation of Management's Discussion and Analysis does not include, in all material respects, the required elements of the rules and regulations adopted by the Securities and Exchange Commission, that the historical financial amounts included therein have not been accurately derived, in all material respects, from the Company's financial statements, or that the underlying information, determinations, estimates, and assumptions of the Company do not provide a reasonable basis for the disclosures contained therein.

[Restricted use paragraph]

This report is intended solely for the information and use of *[list or refer to specified parties]* and is not intended to be and should not be used by anyone other than the specified parties.

[Signature]

[Date]

COMMUNICATIONS WITH THE AUDIT COMMITTEE

If the practitioner concludes that the MD&A includes material inconsistencies with other information included in the document containing the MD&A or with the historical financial statements, material omissions, or material misstatement of facts, and management refuses to take appropriate corrective action, the practitioner should inform the audit committee or its equivalent.

If the MD&A is not revised, the practitioner should consider withdrawing from the MD&A engagement and any future audit engagements. As a protective measure the practitioner may wish to consult with legal counsel when considering withdrawal from the engagement.

If during the MD&A examination or review engagement, the practitioner concludes that there is evidence indicative of possible fraud, the matter (even if inconsequential) should be brought to the attention of an appropriate level of management. If the evidence of possible fraud relates to the audited financial statements, the practitioner should follow the guidance contained in AU Section 316, *Consideration of Fraud in a Financial Statement Audit.*

PART 4

ACCOUNTING AND REVIEW SERVICES

50 STANDARDS FOR ACCOUNTING AND REVIEW SERVICES

SOURCE OF STANDARDS

SSARS 11, *Standards for Accounting and Review Services*

SUMMARY

SSARS provide a measure of quality and the desired objectives in compilation and review engagements. While an accountant should have sufficient knowledge of SSARS to determine their applicability to a particular engagement, the application of SSARS requires the exercise of professional judgment.

INTERPRETIVE PUBLICATIONS

When performing a compilation or a review engagement, an accountant should be familiar with and consider applying guidance found in interpretive publications. Failure to apply the guidance in interpretive publications may require the accountant to explain how he or she otherwise complied with the provisions in SSARS.

Interpretive publications are recommendations for the application of SSARS, but by themselves do not constitute performance standards.

Examples of interpretive publications include the following:

1. Interpretations of SSARS issued by the Accounting and Review Service Committee.
2. Appendixes to the SSARS.
3. AICPA Statements of Position.
4. Compilation and Review Guidance included in AICPA Audit and Accounting Guides.

OTHER COMPILATION AND REVIEW PUBLICATIONS

While other compilation and review publications do not have authoritative status, they may be used by an accountant to facilitate understanding and applying SSARS.

Examples of other compilation and review publications include the following:

1. AICPA annual Compilation and Review Alerts.
2. Professional journal articles.
3. Articles in the AICPA CPA Letter.
4. Continuing professional education (CPE) programs.
5. Textbooks and guidebooks.
6. Compilation and Review programs and checklists.

100 COMPILATION AND REVIEW OF FINANCIAL STATEMENTS

SOURCES OF STANDARDS

SSARS 1, *Compilation and Review of Financial Statements*
SSARS 10, *Performance of Review Engagements*
SSARS 15, *Elimination of Certain References to Statements on Auditing Standards and Incorporation of Appropriate Guidance into Statements on Standards for Accounting & Review Services*

SUMMARY

Accountants should not submit unaudited financial statements of a nonpublic entity to a client or a third party, unless the accountant has at least complied with the provisions that apply to a compilation engagement. When more than one service has been performed, the report to be used is the one that relates to the highest level of service rendered.

Accountants should not allow their names to be used in any written document containing the unaudited financial statements of a nonpublic entity unless

1. They have compiled or reviewed the statements pursuant to Statements on Standards for Accounting and Review Services; or
2. The financial statements are accompanied by a statement indicating that the accountant has not compiled or reviewed the financial statements and assumes no responsibility for the financial statements.

An acceptable statement would be

> The accompanying balance sheet of X Company as of December 31, 20XX, and the related statements of income, retained earnings, and cash flows for the year then ended were not audited, reviewed, or compiled by us, and accordingly we do not express an opinion or any other form of assurance on them.

Accountants who become aware that their names are being used improperly in a client-prepared document that includes unaudited financial statements should notify the client promptly and determine whether other action might be appropriate and necessary, such as obtaining legal counsel.

DEFINITIONS

Nonpublic entity. An entity other than one

1. Whose debt or equity securities trade in a public market.
2. That makes a filing with a regulatory agency in preparation of a public sale, or
3. A subsidiary, corporate joint venture, or other entity controlled by an entity described in the two items above.

Compilation. Preparation of financial statements from information supplied by management without the accountant expressing any assurance on them.

Review. Inquiry and analytical procedures intended to provide a reasonable basis for expressing limited assurance that the accountant is not aware of any material modifications that should be made to the financial statements to make them conform to generally accepted accounting principles (GAAP) or other comprehensive basis of accounting (OCBOA).

Third party. All parties except members of management who are knowledgeable about the nature of the procedures applied and the basis of the accounting and assumptions used to prepare the financial statements.

Submission. Presenting to a client or third parties, financial statements that the accountant has prepared, either manually or by computer software.

Other Comprehensive Basis of Accounting (OCBOA). A definite set of criteria, other than GAAP, that has substantial support for use in preparing financial statements. A comprehensive basis of accounting may be any basis of accounting

1. Used to comply with the requirements of a government agency, such as a basis of accounting used by a state-regulated insurance company.
2. Used for income-tax purposes.
3. Used as a cash basis (i.e., cash receipts and disbursements) or, where substantial support exists, a modified-cash basis.
4. Based on definite criteria that has substantial support, such as price-level basis

Financial statement. A presentation of financial data, including related notes, derived from accounting records and intended to convey the financial resources or obligations of an entity at a point in time, or the changes therein for a specified period, in accordance with GAAP or OCBOA. For purposes of AR Section 100, prospective financial statements and financial presentations included in tax returns do not constitute financial statements.

UNDERSTANDING WITH THE ENTITY

Accountants should establish an understanding of the services to be performed with the entity, preferably in writing. A written communication is required if the accountant is engaged to compile financial statements not expected to be used by a third party. The understanding should

1. Describe the nature and limitations of the services to be performed.
2. Describe any report that is to be issued.
3. Specify that the engagement cannot be relied upon to disclose errors, fraud, or illegal acts.
4. State the accountant will inform the appropriate level of management of

    a. Any material errors found; and
    b. Any fraud or illegal acts identified, unless clearly inconsequential.

COMPILATION PERFORMANCE REQUIREMENTS

The accountant should understand the following:

1. The accounting principles and practices of the industry in which the entity operates.
2. The nature of the entity's business transactions.
3. The form of the entity's accounting records.
4. The qualifications of the entity's accounting personnel.
5. The accounting basis on which the financial statements are to be presented.
6. The form and content of the financial statements.

The accountant also is required to

1. Read the compiled financial statements, considering their form and any obvious material errors.
2. Request that management consider the effect on the financial statements of evidence or information concerning fraud or illegal acts that came to the accountant's attention.
3. Consider the effect on the compilation report of evidence or information concerning fraud or illegal acts that came to the accountant's attention.
4. Document any written or oral communication to management concerning fraud or illegal acts that came to the accountant's attention.
5. Consider resigning from the engagement if the owner of the business is involved in fraud or illegal acts that came to the accountant's attention.
6. Consider contacting the accountant's legal counsel and insurance provider when evidence or information concerning fraud or illegal acts come to the accountant's attention; and
7. Realize that while bound by confidentiality, disclosure of evidence or information concerning fraud or illegal acts that came to the accountant's attention may be required in order to comply with legal or regulatory requirements, respond to a subpoena, or communicate with a successor auditor under AR Section 400.

It is important to note that the accountant is *not* required to make inquiries or perform procedures to verify or review information supplied by management.

REPORTING ON THE FINANCIAL STATEMENTS

Financial statements that are reasonably expected to be used by a third party should be accompanied by a report. The basic elements of the report are as follows:

1. A statement that a compilation was performed in accordance with Statements on Standards for Accounting and Review Services, issued by the American Institute of Certified Public Accountants (AICPA).
2. A statement that the report is limited to presenting in the form of financial statements information that is the representation by of management.
3. A statement that no audit or review has taken place and the accountant therefore does not express an opinion or any assurance on the financial statements.
4. A signature of the accounting firm or the accountant, which may be manual, stamped, electronic, or typed.
5. The date on which the compilation was completed.

Each page of the financial statements should be marked, "See Accountant's Compilation Report."

The form and content of a standard compilation report applicable to GAAP financial statements are as follows:

I (we) have compiled the accompanying balance sheet of XYZ Company as of December 31, 20X1, and the related statements of income, retained earnings, and cash flows for the year then ended, in accordance with Statements on Standards for Accounting and Review Services, issued by the American Institute of Certified Public Accountants.

A compilation is limited to presenting in the form of financial statements information that is the representation of management (owners). I (we) have not audited or reviewed the accompanying financial statements and, accordingly, do not express an opinion or any other form of assurance on them.

The form and content of a standard compilation report applicable to OCBOA financial statements (in this case, prepared using the cash basis of accounting) are as follows:

> I (we) have compiled the accompanying statement of assets and liabilities arising from cash transactions of XYZ Company as of December 31, 20X1, and the related statement of revenue collected and expenses paid for the year then ended, in accordance with Statements on Standards for Accounting and Review Services issued by the American Institute of Certified Public Accountants. A compilation is limited to presenting in the form of financial statements information that is the representation of management (owners). I (we) have not audited or reviewed the accompanying financial statements and, accordingly, do not express an opinion or any other form of assurance on them.

SPECIAL REPORTING SITUATIONS

Financial Statements That Omit Substantially All Disclosures

An accountant is permitted to compile financial statements that omit substantially all of the disclosures and/or the statement of cash flows required by GAAP if the omission is clearly stated in the report and there is no intention on the part of the client to mislead actual and potential users of the financial statements. Under these circumstances it is appropriate to add a final paragraph:

> Management has elected to omit substantially all of the disclosures (and the statement of cash flows) required by generally accepted accounting principles. If the omitted disclosures were included in the financial statements, they might influence the user's conclusions about the company's financial position, results of operations, and cash flows. Accordingly these financial statements are not designed for those who are not informed about such matters.

If some disclosures are made, they should be labeled "Selected Information—Not All Disclosures Required by Generally Accepted Accounting Principles Are Included."

If an accountant compiles OCBOA financial statements that omit substantially all disclosures, it is appropriate to add a final paragraph:

> Management has elected to omit substantially all the disclosures ordinarily included in financial statements prepared on [*insert basis of accounting; for example, the income tax basis of accounting*]. If the omitted disclosures were included in the financial statements, they might influence the user's conclusions about the company's assets, liabilities, equity, revenue, and expenses. Accordingly, these financial statements are not designed for those who are not informed about such matters.

Lack of Independence

An accountant who lacks independence may still issue a compilation report. The lack of independence should be disclosed as the last paragraph of the report:

> I am (we are) not independent with respect to XYZ Company.

The reason for the lack of independence should never be disclosed.

ACCOUNTANT'S COMMUNICATIONS WITH THE CLIENT WHEN THE COMPILED FINANCIAL STATEMENTS ARE NOT EXPECTED TO BE USED BY A THIRD PARTY

An accountant who submits unaudited financial statements to a client that are not expected to be used by a third party should either issue a compilation report or document an understanding with the entity in an engagement letter, preferably signed by management, regarding the services to be performed and the limitations on use of the financial statements.

The documentation should incorporate statements

1. About the nature and limitations of the services to be performed; that a compilation is limited to presenting in the form of financial statements information that is the representation of management.
2. That the financial statements will not be audited or reviewed.
3. That no opinion or any other form of assurance on the financial statements will be provided.
4. That management has knowledge about the nature of the procedures performed and the basis of accounting and assumptions used in preparing the financial statements.
5. That acknowledge management's representation and agreement that the financial statements are not to be used by third parties.
6. That the engagement cannot be relied upon to disclose errors, fraud, or illegal acts.
7. If applicable, that there may be material departures from US GAAP or OCBOA and their effects on the financial statements may not be disclosed.
8. If applicable, that

   a. Substantially all disclosures (and the statement of cash flows) required by US GAAP or OCBOA may be omitted.
   b. The accountant lacks independence.
   c. Supplementary information may be available.

If a written understanding with the client has not been established, the accountant should not accept or perform the engagement.

It is important that each page of the financial statements be marked "Restricted for management's use only" or "Solely for the information and use by the management of (*name of entity*) and not intended to be and should not be used by any third party."

An accountant who learns that the financial statements have been distributed to third parties should discuss this with the client and ask that the statements be returned. A client's failure to comply should cause the accountant to take steps to notify known third parties that the financial statements are not intended for use by third parties.

REVIEW PERFORMANCE STANDARDS

To review financial statements, an accountant should have a general understanding of the entity's business—its organization, operations, resources, obligations, revenues, and expenses. This will require general knowledge of the entity's production, distribution, and compensation methods; products and services sold; operating locations; and material transactions with related parties. The inquiries and analytical procedures that apply to a review cover the following areas:

1. Accounting principles and practices.
2. Financial recording and financial statement preparation practices.
3. Procedures designed to identify items that appear to be unusual (e.g., comparisons with financial statements of prior periods, budgets and forecasts, predictable patterns, and intraindustry ratio analysis).
4. Minutes of stockholders' and directors' meetings.
5. Evaluation of the financial statements to see whether they appear to conform with GAAP.
6. Any applicable reports from other accountants.
7. Interviews with persons responsible for financial matters.
8. Management's knowledge of any fraud or suspected fraud involving management or others where the fraud could materially affect the financial statements.

Review procedures are not designed to corroborate assertions explicitly or implicitly embodied in the financial statements. Accordingly review procedures do not include obtaining an understanding of internal control, assessing control risk, assessing fraud risks, or the performance of tests designed to detect material misstatements caused by error, fraud or illegal acts. However, the accountant should proceed as follows:

1. Request that management consider the effect on the financial statements of evidence or information concerning fraud or illegal acts that come to the accountant's attention.
2. Consider the effect on the review report of evidence or information concerning fraud or illegal acts that come to the accountant's attention.
3. Document any written or oral communication to management concerning fraud or illegal acts that come to the accountant's attention.
4. Consider resigning from the engagement if the owner of the business is involved in fraud or illegal acts that come to the accountant's attention.
5. Consider contacting the accountant's legal counsel and insurance provider when evidence or information concerning fraud or illegal acts come to the accountant's attention.
6. While bound by confidentiality, realize that disclosure of evidence or information concerning fraud or illegal acts that come to the accountant's attention may be required in order to

   a. Comply with legal or regulatory requirements,
   b. Respond to a subpoena, or
   c. Communicate with a successor auditor under AR Section 400.

THE REPRESENTATION LETTER

The accountant must obtain a representation letter from those members of management the accountant believes to be responsible for and knowledgeable about (directly or through others in the organization) matters covered in the letter. Normally the chief executive officer and chief financial officer should sign the letter, which should be dated no earlier than the date of the review report. The letter should cover all financial statements and periods covered by the review report. If the accountant has reviewed comparative financial statements and current management differs from management in prior periods, the representation letter should be signed by the appropriate current members of management.

In the letter there should be specific representations related to the following matter:

1. Management's acknowledgment of its responsibility for fair presentation of the financial statements.
2. Management's belief that the financial statements are fairly presented in conformity with GAAP.
3. Management's full and truthful response to all inquiries.
4. Completeness of the information.
5. Information about any subsequent events that may affect the financial statements.

The accountant should consider obtaining an updating representation letter from management when any of the following happens:

1. The accountant obtains a representation letter after completion of the review procedures but does not issue the review report for a significant period of time thereafter.
2. A material subsequent event occurs after the completion of the review procedures.

3. A predecessor accountant is requested by a former client to reissue the report on the financial statements of a prior period that are to be presented on a comparative basis with reviewed financial statements of a subsequent period.

The updating management representation letter should state the following:

1. Whether any information has come to management's attention that would cause management to believe that modifications should be made to previous representations.

2. Whether any events have occurred subsequent to the balancesheet date of the latest financial statements reported on by the accountant that would require adjustment to or disclosure in those financial statements.

REPORTING ON THE FINANCIAL STATEMENTS

The accountant's report accompanying financial statements that have been reviewed should contain the following basic elements:

1. A statement that a review has been performed in accordance with Statements on Standards for Accounting and Review Services issued by the AICPA.

2. A statement that all information included in the financial statements is the representation of the management of the entity.

3. A statement that a review consists principally of inquiries of company personnel and analytical procedures applied to financial data.

4. A statement that a review is substantially less in scope than an audit, the objective of which is to express an opinion regarding the financial statements taken as a whole; accordingly, no such opinion is expressed.

5. A statement that the accountant is not aware of any material modifications (other than any that might be indicated in the report) that should be made in order for the financial statements to conform to GAAP.

6. A signature of the accounting firm or the accountant, which may be manual, stamped, electronic, or typed.

7. The date of the review report, which is the date on which the accountant's review procedures are completed.

Each page of the financial statements should be clearly marked "See Accountant's Review Report."

The form and content of a standard review report applicable to GAAP financial statements are as follows:

> I (we) have reviewed the accompanying balance sheet of XYZ Company as of December 31, and the related statements of income, retained earnings, and cash flows for the year then ended, in accordance with the Statements on Standards for Accounting and Review Services issued by the American Institute of Certified Public Accountants. All information included in these financial statements is the representation of the management (owners) of XYZ Company.
>
> A review consists principally of inquiries of company personnel and analytical procedures applied to financial data. It is substantially less in scope than an audit in accordance with generally accepted auditing standards, the objective of which is to express an opinion regarding the financial statements taken as a whole. Accordingly I (we) do not express such an opinion.
>
> Based on my (our) review, I am (we are) not aware of any material modifications that should be made to the accompanying financial statements in order for them to be in conformity with generally accepted accounting principles.

The form and content of a standard review report applicable to OCBOA financial statements (in this case, prepared using the income tax basis of accounting) are as follows:

> I (we) have reviewed the accompanying statement of assets, liabilities, and equity—income tax basis of XYZ Company as of December 31, 20X1, and the related statement of revenue and

expenses—income tax basis for the year then ended, in accordance with Statements on Standards for Accounting and Review Services issued by the American Institute of Certified Public Accountants. All information included in these financial statements is the representation of the management (owners) of XYZ Company.

A review consists principally of inquiries of company personnel and analytical procedures applied to financial data. It is substantially less in scope than an audit in accordance with generally accepted auditing standards, the objective of which is the expression of an opinion regarding the financial statements taken as a whole. Accordingly I (we) do not express such an opinion.

Based on my (our) review, I am (we are) not aware of any material modifications that should be made to the accompanying financial statements in order for them to be in conformity with the income tax basis of accounting, as described in Note X.

When the accountant is unable to perform the inquiry and analytical procedures considered necessary to achieve the limited assurance contemplated by a review, or the client does not provide a representation letter, the review is incomplete and is therefore an inadequate basis for issuing a review report. In such a situation the accountant should consider whether it is appropriate to issue a compilation report on the financial statements.

EMPHASIS OF A MATTER

In general, an accountant may, but is not required to, include a separate paragraph in either a compilation report or a review report in order to emphasize a matter already disclosed in financial statements. It is important to note that an emphasis paragraph should never be added to a compilation report on financial statements that omit substantially all disclosures.

Matters that the accountant may choose to emphasize include

1. Uncertainties concerning litigation, claims and assessments,
2. Significant related-party transactions,
3. Type II subsequent events, and
4. Significant accounting matters having an effect on comparable financial statements.

SPECIAL REPORTING SITUATIONS

Departures from GAAP

An accountant who becomes aware of a material departure from GAAP must decide whether it is necessary to modify the standard report. If modification is appropriate, the accountant should disclose the effects of departures determined by management (or known as the result of the accountant's procedures) or state that such determination has not been made.

In this case the third (*but no longer final*) paragraph of the standard report would be revised as follows:

Based on my (our) review, with the exception of the matters described in the following paragraphs, I am (we are) not aware of any material modification that should be made to the accompanying financial statements in order for them to be in conformity with generally accepted accounting principles.

In separate paragraphs, describe the nature of each departure and disclose its dollar effects, if known, or state that no determination of the effects of the departure has been made.

These are separate sample paragraphs:

Effects of Departure from GAAP Have Been Determined

As disclosed in Note X to the financial statements, generally accepted accounting principles require that land be stated at cost. Management has informed me (us) that the company stated its land at appraised value and that, if generally accepted accounting principles had been followed, the land account and stockholders' equity would have decreased by $500,000.

Effects of Departure from GAAP Have Not Been Determined

As disclosed in Note X to the financial statements, generally accepted accounting principles require that inventory costs consist of material, labor, and overhead. Management has informed me (us) that the inventory of finished goods and work in process is stated in the accompanying financial statements at material and labor costs only, and that the effects of the departure from generally accepted accounting principles on financial position, results of operations, and cash flows have not been determined.

An accountant who believes that modifying the report is not enough to prevent users from being misled should consider withdrawing from the engagement, not providing any additional services, and/or conferring with legal counsel.

RESTRICTING THE USE OF AN ACCOUNTANT'S COMPILATION OR REVIEW REPORT

General use applies to an accountant's reports that are not restricted to specified parties. GAAP or OCBOA financial statements ordinarily are not restricted regarding use.

Restricted use applies to an accountant's reports intended only for one or more specified third parties.

A report should be restricted as to use when the subject matter of the report or the presentation being reported on is based on measurement or disclosure criteria contained in contractual agreements or regulatory provisions not in conformity with GAAP or OCBOA. Combined reports covering both restricted-use and general-use subject matter or presentation should be restricted to the specified parties.

The accountant should consider informing a client that restricted-use reports are not intended for distribution to nonspecified parties. An accountant is not responsible for controlling a client's distribution of such reports.

A restricted-use report should include a separate paragraph at the end of the report that includes the following:

1. A statement indicating that the report is intended solely for the information and use of the specified parties.
2. An identification of the specified parties to whom use is restricted.
3. A statement that the report is not intended to be and should not be used by anyone other than the specified parties. For example

> This report is intended solely for the information and use of [*the specified parties*] and is not intended to be and should not be used by anyone other than these specified parties.

SUBSEQUENT DISCOVERY OF FACTS EXISTING AT THE REPORT DATE

After the date of the report the accountant may become aware of facts that existed at the report date that might have led to the conclusion that information furnished by management was incorrect or incomplete if these facts had been available earlier. In general, the accountant is not required to perform any procedures after the date of the compilation or review report. However, if new information relating to previously issued financial statements comes to the accountant's attention, which was not known at the report date, the accountant should proceed as follows:

1. Consider the nature and source of the information.
2. Determine whether the information is reliable and existed at the date of the report.
3. Ascertain whether the information would have had an effect on the compilation report or the financial statements. If so, determine whether there are persons currently using or likely to use the financial statements who might attach importance to the information.

4. In a compilation engagement, obtain additional or revised information.
5. In a review engagement, perform procedures to obtain limited assurance that no material modifications should be made to the financial statements in order for them to be in conformity with the basis of accounting utilized.

During this process the accountant should discuss the matter with the appropriate level of management and request cooperation in resolving the matter.

If the accountant determines that the previously issued compilation report or financial statements should no longer be used, the accountant should advise the client to make the appropriate disclosure of the new information along with the related effect on the financial statements and take other requisite action as follows:

1. If the effects of the new information on the financial statements or accountant's report can be determined promptly, advise the client to issue revised financial statements as soon as practicable, and if applicable, the accountant should issue a revised report.
2. If subsequent-period financial statements are about to be issued, disclosure may be made in such financial statements instead.
3. If the effects of the new information cannot be determined promptly, advise the client to notify those users who are known to be using or are likely to use the financial statements that

    a. The financial statements should no longer be used,
    b. Revised financial statements will be forthcoming, and
    c. If applicable, a revised accountant's report will be issued.

If a client refuses to make the appropriate disclosure, the accountant should notify top-level management that unless disclosure is made, the accountant will take the appropriate action to preclude future use of the financial statements and, if applicable, the accountant's report. Appropriate action to preclude continued use includes the following:

1. Notifying the client that the accountant's report is no longer to be associated with the financial statements.
2. Notifying relevant regulatory agencies that the accountant's report may no longer be used.
3. Notifying each person known to be using the financial statements that the financial statements and the accountant's report may no longer be used.
4. Consulting with legal counsel before the above action is taken.

If the accountant is forced to disclose the information because the client refuses to, the disclosure should precisely describe the factual nature of the information and its related effects on the financial statements.

If necessary, because of a lack of client cooperation, the accountant's disclosure may be limited to a statement that information has come to the accountant's attention which the client has not cooperated in attempting to substantiate and that, if the information is true, the accountant believes that the ensuing report must no longer be used or associated with the financial statements.

INFORMATION PRESENTED FOR SUPPLEMENTARY ANALYSIS

When additional information is presented for supplementary analysis, how much responsibility the accountant is taking with respect to such information should be clearly indicated in the report or in a separate report on the additional data. The accountant should state the following:

1. The review has been made primarily to express limited assurance that no material modifications to the financial statements are necessary for them to be in conformity with GAAP.
2. The accompanying data are presented for supplementary analysis purposes and

    a. Have been subjected to the inquiry and analytical procedures applied in the review of the financial statements (in which case the accountant may then express limited assurance concerning the other data), or
    b. Have not been subjected to the inquiry and analytical procedures applied in the review of the financial statements (in which case the accountant should indicate that the other data have been compiled from management representations, without audit or review, and the accountant does not express an opinion or any other form of assurance on the data).

ACCOUNTANT LACKS INDEPENDENCE

Accountants cannot issue a review report with respect to entities of which they are not independent.

CHANGE IN ENGAGEMENT

Before agreeing to a change in the level of service from audit to review or compilation, or from review to compilation, an accountant should consider

1. The client's reasons for requesting the change;
2. The implications of a restriction on the scope of the service, whether imposed by circumstances or by the client; and
3. The additional audit or review effort, and the cost to complete a higher level of service.

Changes in circumstances or misunderstandings about the nature of the original engagement are ordinarily reasonable bases for changing the engagement.

When an engagement is changed from an audit because of scope limitations, the accountant should consider the possibility that the information provided may be unsatisfactory.

When engaged to perform an audit and prohibited from corresponding with the client's legal counsel, ordinarily the accountant is precluded from issuing a review or compilation report.

If, in an audit or a review engagement, a client does not provide a signed representation letter, the accountant is precluded from issuing a review report and ordinarily also a compilation report.

In all circumstances, if the engagement procedures are substantially completed, or the cost to complete the engagement is relatively insignificant, the accountant should consider the propriety of accepting the change in the engagement.

After concluding that there is reasonable justification to change the level of service, the accountant should comply with the standards applying to the new level and issue the appropriate report. The report should not refer to the original level of service, any auditing or review procedures that may have been performed, or any scope limitations that resulted in the changed level of service.

RELATIONSHIP OF STATEMENTS ON STANDARDS FOR ACCOUNTING AND REVIEW SERVICES TO QUALITY CONTROL STANDARDS

An accounting firm should have in place quality control policies and procedures that reasonably assure compliance with Statements on Standards for Accounting and Review Services (SSARS), but deficiencies in or instances of noncompliance with a CPA firm's quality control policies and procedures do not by themselves indicate that a particular compilation or review engagement was not performed in accordance with SSARS.

ADDITIONAL NOTES

If the statement of comprehensive income is presented, then the compilation or review report should include references thereto.

A separate statement of retained earnings is not required under GAAP. Accordingly, if it is not presented, it is not necessary to refer to it in the compilation or review report.

INTERPRETATIONS OF AR SECTION 100

OMISSION OF DISCLOSURES IN REVIEWED FINANCIAL STATEMENTS (ISSUED IN DECEMBER 1979; REVISED IN NOVEMBER 2002)

An accountant should not accept an engagement to review financial statements that omit substantially all of the disclosures required by GAAP. If, during a review engagement, a client declines to make substantially all required disclosures, the accountant should modify the report, if practicable, to include the omitted disclosures.

FINANCIAL STATEMENTS INCLUDED IN SEC FILINGS (ISSUED IN DECEMBER 1979)

In general, compilation and review reports should not be included in filings with the SEC.

REPORTING ON THE HIGHEST LEVEL OF SERVICE (ISSUED IN DECEMBER 1979; REVISED IN OCTOBER 2000)

The report need not be upgraded merely because the accountant has performed other accounting services. For example, an accountant should not issue an audit report when engaged to compile financial statements and reconcile the client's accounts receivable balances by confirming the balances.

An accountant may issue a compilation report on monthly financial statements and a review report on quarterly or annual financial statements for a period ending on the same date as one of the monthly financial statements, provided compilation and review standards are followed.

An accountant may accept an engagement to perform a higher level of service in connection with financial statements that have already been compiled or reviewed.

PLANNING AND SUPERVISION (ISSUED IN AUGUST 1981; REVISED IN NOVEMBER 2002)

In planning and supervising a compilation or review engagement, accountants are not required to follow the Statements on Auditing Standards.

WITHDRAWAL FROM COMPILATION OR REVIEW ENGAGEMENT (ISSUED IN AUGUST 1981; REVISED IN NOVEMBER 2002)

An accountant who believes that GAAP were departed from to mislead users of the financial statements should consider withdrawing from the engagement. Withdrawal is not normally necessary, however, if the client agrees that the effects of the departures should be determined and disclosed in the accountant's report. Withdrawal is appropriate when the financial statements containing departures from GAAP are not revised and the client refuses to accept a modified accountant's report.

REPORTING WHEN THERE ARE SIGNIFICANT DEPARTURES FROM GAAP (ISSUED IN AUGUST 1981; REVISED IN NOVEMBER 2002)

An accountant may not modify a compilation or review report to state that the financial statements are not in conformity with GAAP or OCBOA because to do so would be equivalent to expressing an adverse opinion, which is only appropriate in an audit engagement.

An accountant is, however, permitted to emphasize the pervasiveness of departures from GAAP or OCBOA by modifying the compilation or review report to include a separate explanatory paragraph like this:

> Because the significance and pervasiveness of the matters discussed above make it difficult to assess their impact on the financial statements taken as a whole, users of the financial statements should recognize that they may reach different conclusions about the company's financial position, results of operations, and cash flows if they had access to revised financial statements prepared in conformity with generally accepted accounting principles [*or state the other comprehensive basis of accounting other than GAAP*].

Besides adding such a paragraph, the accountant's report should, if practicable, disclose the departures or the effects of the departures.

REPORTING WHEN MANAGEMENT HAS ELECTED TO OMIT SUBSTANTIALLY ALL DISCLOSURES (ISSUED IN MAY 1982)

This interpretation emphasizes the importance of modifying the accountant's report to stress that the omission of substantially all disclosures is the decision of management, not that of the accountant. It is well to be cautious in modifying the phrase "Management has elected to omit," which is not required but is normally included in the explanatory paragraph.

REPORTING ON TAX RETURNS (ISSUED IN NOVEMBER 1982)

An accountant is not required to issue a report based on an engagement to prepare a client's tax return, but may accept an engagement to issue a compilation or review report on the return.

REPORTING ON UNCERTAINTIES (ISSUED IN DECEMBER 1982; REVISED IN NOVEMBER 2002)

A compilation or review report need not be modified if an uncertainty is adequately disclosed in the financial statements. However, an accountant who wishes to emphasize the uncertainty may modify the report using language like the following:

> As discussed in Note X, certain conditions indicate that the Company may be unable to continue as a going concern. The accompanying financial statements do not include any adjustments to the financial statements that might be necessary should the Company be unable to continue as a going concern.

Disclosure of an uncertainty is not considered so significant that it may never be omitted. Such language in the accountant's report is considered sufficient to warn users of the limitations of the financial statements in a compilation or review engagement.

ADDITIONAL PROCEDURES (ISSUED IN MARCH 1983; REVISED IN OCTOBER 2000 AND NOVEMBER 2002)

An accountant may, at the client's request or based on professional judgment, perform additional procedures ordinarily considered relevant to an audit. The performance of these procedures does not elevate the level of service to an audit.

DIFFERENTIATING A FINANCIAL STATEMENT PRESENTATION FROM A TRIAL BALANCE (ISSUED IN SEPTEMBER 1990; REVISED ON OCTOBER 2000)

An accountant should exercise judgment to differentiate a trial balance from a financial statement. Engagements in connection with the former do not require compliance with SSARS; those in connection with the latter do. Attributes of a financial statement include classifications or account groupings and titles that identify the presentation.

SUBMITTING DRAFT FINANCIAL STATEMENTS (ISSUED IN SEPTEMBER 1990; REVISED IN OCTOBER 2000)

An accountant who intends to submit financial statements in final form may submit draft financial statements without complying with SSARS, as long as those statements are clearly marked to indicate that they are not in final form. Sample wording might be "Draft," "Preliminary Draft," "Draft—Subject to Changes," or "Working Draft."

REPORTING WHEN FINANCIAL STATEMENTS CONTAIN A DEPARTURE FROM PROMULGATED ACCOUNTING PRINCIPLES THAT PREVENT THE FINANCIAL STATEMENTS FROM BEING MISLEADING (ISSUED IN FEBRUARY 1991; REVISED IN OCTOBER 2000 AND NOVEMBER 2002)

In a review engagement, as in an audit engagement, an accountant may conclude that the financial statements contain a departure from GAAP that is necessary to prevent the financial statements from being misleading. In this circumstance the review report should only be modified to include an additional paragraph that states the departure from the principle, its principal effects on the financial statements (if practicable), and the reasons why compliance with the principle would result in misleading financial statements.

This interpretation does not apply to compilation engagements, which should be guided by the general provisions of AR Section 100.

APPLICABILITY OF SSARS TO LITIGATION SERVICES (ISSUED IN MAY 1991; REVISED IN OCTOBER 2000)

In general, SSARS does not apply to financial statements submitted in connection with services involving pending or potential litigation or regulatory proceedings:

1. If the accountant is serving as an expert witness or the "trier of fact,"
2. The accountant's work product may be subjected to analysis and dispute by the parties, or
3. The accountant has been engaged by a lawyer to produce a work product that will be covered by the attorney's work product privilege.

APPLICABILITY OF SSARS NO. 1 TO CONTROLLERSHIP OR OTHER MANAGEMENT SERVICES (ISSUED IN JULY 2002)

An accountant who practices public accounting and is not a shareholder, partner, director, officer, or employee of the entity must comply with SSARS 1 when performing controllership or other managerial services.

An accountant who is a shareholder, partner, director, officer, or employee of the entity does not have to comply with SSARS 1 so long as his or her relationship to the entity is communicated, preferably in writing. For example

> The accompanying balance sheet of X Company as of December 31, 20X1, and the related statements of income and cash flows for the year then ended have been prepared by [*name of accountant*], CPA. I have prepared such financial statements in my capacity [*describe capacity; e.g., as a director*] of X Company.

This phrasing may also be used by an accountant who is not in the practice of public accounting, but the accountant should not issue a report under SSARS.

USE OF "SELECTED INFORMATION—SUBSTANTIALLY ALL DISCLOSURES REQUIRED BY GENERALLY ACCEPTED ACCOUNTING PRINCIPLES ARE NOT INCLUDED" (ISSUED IN DECEMBER 2002)

If a client's financial statements includes more than a few disclosures required by GAAP, the disclosures should not be labeled "Selected Information—Substantially All Disclosures Required by Generally Accepted Accounting Principles Are Not Included."

The omission of one or more notes, when substantially all other disclosures have been made, should generally be treated as a departure from GAAP, causing the accountant's report to be modified.

HOW SSARS APPLIES WHEN AN ACCOUNTANT ENGAGED TO PERFORM A BUSINESS VALUATION DERIVES INFORMATION FROM AN ENTITY'S TAX RETURN (ISSUED IN AUGUST 2003)

SSARS does not apply to engagements in which an accountant is engaged to perform a business valuation, even if information is derived from a tax return that the accountant has prepared. The accountant should, however, include the following wording in the business valuation report:

> In preparing our business valuation report, we have relied upon historical financial information provided to us by management and derived from [*refer to the appropriate source of the information: tax return, audit report issued by another auditor, etc.*]. This financial information has not been audited, reviewed or compiled by us and accordingly we do not express an opinion or any other form of assurance on this financial information.

The submission of financial statements in connection with a business valuation should be treated as an engagement governed by SSARS; at a minimum, the accountant must adhere to the standards applicable to a compilation of financial statements.

110 COMPILATION OF SPECIFIED ELEMENTS, ACCOUNTS, OR ITEMS OF A FINANCIAL STATEMENT

SOURCE OF STANDARDS

SSARS 13, *Compilation of Specified Elements, Accounts, or Items of a Financial Statement*

INTRODUCTION/SUMMARY

While presentations of specified elements, accounts, or items of a financial statement do not constitute financial statements, Statements on Standards for Accounting and Review Services are applicable when an accountant is engaged to compile or issues a compilation report on one or more specified elements, accounts, or items of a financial statement. In these situations, the accountant does not express any form of assurance on the information. Examples of specified elements, accounts, or items of a financial statement include schedules of rental income, profit sharing and depreciation.

CONDITIONS FOR COMPILING SPECIFIED ELEMENTS, ACCOUNTS, OR ITEMS OF A FINANCIAL STATEMENT

An accountant is permitted to accept an engagement to prepare or assist a client in preparing one or more specified elements, accounts or items of a financial statement. This type of engagement may be undertaken as a separate engagement or as part of an engagement to compile financial statements.

If an accountant has prepared or assisted a client in preparing a schedule of one or more specified elements, accounts, or items of a financial statement and he or she believes that he or she will be associated with such a schedule, the accountant should consider issuing a compilation report.

UNDERSTANDING WITH THE ENTITY

Before accepting an engagement covered by this section, the accountant should establish an understanding with the entity, preferably in writing, regarding the services to be performed. The understanding should provide, among other engagement specific items, that

1. The engagement cannot be relied on to disclose errors, fraud, or illegal act, and
2. The accountant will communicate to the appropriate level of management any material errors, conditions indicative of fraud or instances of illegal acts (except those that are clearly inconsequential).

PERFORMANCE REQUIREMENTS

In general, the accountant should follow the performance requirements applicable to engagements to compile financial statements as detailed in AR Section 100.

REPORTING REQUIREMENTS

The basic elements of a compilation report on one or more specified elements, accounts, or items of a financial statement are as follows:

1. A statement that the specified elements, accounts, or items identified in the report were compiled. If the compilation was in conjunction with a compilation of the entity's financial statements, this should be stated along with the date of the report and any departure from the standard report.
2. A statement that the compilation was performed in accordance with Statements on Standards for Accounting and Review Services issued by the American Institute of Certified Public Accountants.
3. If other than generally accepted accounting principles (GAAP), a description of the basis of accounting used in preparing the specified element, account, or item of the financial statement, and a statement that the basis is a comprehensive basis of accounting other than GAAP.
4. A statement that a compilation is limited to presenting financial information that is the representation of management (owners).
5. A statement that the accountant has not audited or reviewed the specified element, account, or item of the financial statement, and, accordingly, no opinion or any other form of assurance on it is being expressed.
6. A signature, which may be manual, stamped, electronic, or typed.
7. The date of the report, which should be the date of the completion of the compilation.

Each page of the compiled schedule should include a reference, such as "See Accountant's Compilation Report."

The form and content of a standard compilation report applicable to a presentation under generally accepted accounting principles are as follows:

I have compiled the accompanying schedule of [*for example, accounts receivable*] of Due From Company as of December 31, 20XX, in accordance with Statements on Standards for Accounting and Review Services issued by the American Institute of Certified Public Accountants.

A compilation is limited to presenting financial information that is the representation of management (owners). I (we) have not audited or reviewed the accompanying schedule of [*for example, accounts receivable*] and, accordingly, do not express an opinion or any other form of assurance on it.

The form and content of a standard compilation report applicable to a presentation based on a basis of accounting other than generally accepted accounting principles are as follows:

I have compiled the accompanying schedule of [*for example, depreciation—income tax basis*] of Due From Company as of December 31, 20XX, in accordance with Statements on Standards for Accounting and Review Services issued by the American Institute of Certified Public Accountants. The schedule of [*for example, depreciation—income tax basis*] has been prepared on the accounting basis used by the Company for federal income tax purposes, which is a comprehensive basis of accounting other than generally accepted accounting principles.

A compilation is limited to presenting financial information that is the representation of management (owners). I (we) have not audited or reviewed the accompanying schedule of [*for example, depreciation—income tax basis*] and, accordingly, do not express an opinion or any other form of assurance on it.

It should be noted that if an accountant lacks independence with respect to an entity, the accountant is permitted to accept such an engagement provided that the accountant discloses the lack of independence in the compilation report. The reason for the lack of independence should not be disclosed in the compilation report. Accordingly the following should be added as the final paragraph of the report:

> I am (we are) not independent with respect to [*name of entity*].

120 COMPILATION OF PRO FORMA FINANCIAL INFORMATION

SOURCE OF STANDARDS

SSARS 14, *Compilation of Pro Forma Financial Information*

INTRODUCTION/SUMMARY

Pro forma financial information is intended to show what the significant effects on historical financial statements might have been had a consummated or proposed transaction (or event) occurred at an earlier date. Pro forma financial information is commonly used to show the effects of transactions such as business combinations, change in capitalization, and disposition of a significant portion of the business.

Pro forma financial information should be labeled as such in order to distinguish it from historical financial information. A presentation of pro forma financial information should take the following form:

1. Describe the transaction or event.
2. Describe the source of the historical financial information on which it is based.
3. Describe the significant assumptions used (including any significant uncertainties)
4. Indicate that the pro forma financial information should be read in conjunction with the related historical financial information.
5. Indicate that the pro forma financial information is not necessarily indicative of the results that would have been attained had the transaction (or event) occurred at an earlier date.

CONDITIONS FOR COMPILING PRO FORMA FINANCIAL INFORMATION

An accountant is permitted to accept an engagement to prepare (compile) or assist a client in preparing pro forma financial information. This type of engagement may be undertaken as a separate engagement or as part of an engagement to compile financial statements.

If an accountant has prepared or assisted a client in preparing pro forma financial information and the accountant believes he or she will be associated with the presentation, the accountant should consider issuing a compilation report.

In the case of a business combination, the document containing the pro forma financial information should include (or incorporate by reference) the historical financial information of the combined entity's significant components. Further, the historical financial statements must have been compiled, reviewed, or audited and the related accountant's or auditor's report should be included (or incorporated by reference).

UNDERSTANDING WITH THE ENTITY

Before accepting such an engagement, the accountant should establish an understanding with the entity, preferably in writing, regarding the services to be performed. The understanding should provide, among other engagement specific items, that the engagement cannot be relied on to disclose errors, fraud, or illegal acts, and the accountant will communicate to the appropriate level of management any material errors, conditions indicative of fraud or instances of illegal acts (except those that are clearly inconsequential).

PERFORMANCE REQUIREMENTS

In general, the accountant should follow the performance and communication requirements applicable to engagements to compile financial statements as detailed in AR Section 100.

REPORTING REQUIREMENTS

The basic elements of a compilation report on pro forma financial information are as follows:

1. A statement that the pro forma financial information identified in the report was compiled. If the compilation was in conjunction with a compilation of the entity's financial statements, this should be stated along with the date of the report, and any departure from the standard report.
2. A statement that the compilation was performed in accordance with Statements on Standards for Accounting and Review Services issued by the American Institute of Certified Public Accountants.
3. A reference to the financial statements from which the historical financial information is derived and a statement as to whether such financial statements were compiled, reviewed, or audited (including a reference to any report modifications).
4. If other than generally accepted accounting principles (GAAP), a description of the basis of accounting used in preparing the pro forma financial information, and a statement that the basis is a comprehensive basis of accounting other than GAAP.
5. A statement that a compilation is limited to presenting financial information that is the representation of management (owners).
6. A statement that the accountant has not audited or reviewed the pro forma financial information and, accordingly, that no opinion or any other form of assurance on it is being expressed.
7. A separate paragraph explaining the objective and limitations of pro forma financial information.
8. A signature, which may be manual, stamped, electronic, or typed.
9. The date of the report, which should be the date of the completion of the compilation.

Each page of the compiled pro forma financial information should include a reference, such as "See Accountant's Compilation Report."

The form and content of a standard compilation report applicable to a presentation of pro forma financial information are as follows:

I (we) have compiled the accompanying pro forma financial information as of and for the year ended December 31, 20XX, reflecting the business combination of the Company and Blendin Company in accordance with Statements on Standards for Accounting and Review Services issued by the American Institute of Certified Public Accountants. The historical condensed financial statements are derived from the historical unaudited financial statements of Mergin Company, which were compiled by me (us), and of Blendin Company, which were compiled by another (other) accountant(s).

A compilation is limited to presenting pro forma financial information that is the representation of management (owners). I (we) have not audited or reviewed the accompanying pro forma financial information and, accordingly, do not express an opinion or any other form of assurance on it.

The objective of this pro forma financial information is to show what the significant effects on the historical financial information might have been had the transaction (or event) occurred at an earlier date. However, the pro forma financial information is not necessarily indicative of the results of operations or related effects on financial position that would have been attained had the above-mentioned transaction (or event) actually occurred earlier.

It should be noted that if an accountant lacks independence with respect to an entity, the accountant is permitted to accept such an engagement provided the accountant discloses the lack of independence in the compilation report. The reason for the lack of independence should not be disclosed in the compilation report. Accordingly the following should be added as the final paragraph of the report:

I am (we are) not independent with respect to [*name of entity*].

200 REPORTING ON COMPARATIVE FINANCIAL STATEMENTS

SOURCE OF STANDARDS

SSARS 2 *Reporting on Comparative Financial Statements*
SSARS 15 *Elimination of Certain References to Statements on Auditing Standards and Incorporation of Appropriate Guidance into Statements on Standards for Accounting and Review Services.*

SUMMARY

This section discusses standards for reporting on comparative statements of nonpublic entities when one or more periods have either been compiled or reviewed in accordance with SSARS 1 (AR Section 100). Unaudited, unreviewed, and noncompiled client statements may be presented on separate pages of a document containing statements of other periods on which the accountant has reported, but the client must indicate that the accountant has not reported on them and assumes no responsibility for them.

If financial statements for one or more periods that omit substantially all the disclosures required by GAAP are presented with financial statements of another period that include substantially all the required disclosures, the accountant should not report on any of them because they are not comparable.

Each page of comparative statements should carry the reference, "See Accountant's Report."

DEFINITIONS

Comparative financial statements are financial statements of two or more periods presented together in columnar format.

A *continuing accountant* is an accountant who has been engaged to audit, review, or compile and issue a report on current period financial statements and financial statements of one or more consecutive periods immediately preceding the current period.

A *reissued report* is a report issued after the date of the original report but bearing the same date. A report that requires revision for the effects of specific events should be dual-dated (i.e., it should carry the original date and a separate date related to the effects of such events).

An *updated report* is a report on prior periods that considers information that an accountant becomes aware of during the current engagement. In an updated report, an accountant either reexpresses the original conclusion about a prior period or offers a different one.

CONTINUING ACCOUNTANT'S STANDARD REPORT

A continuing accountant performing the same level of service on financial statements of one or more periods that are to be presented as comparative with financial statements of the current period should update the report on the prior period financial statements.

COMPILATION FOR EACH PERIOD PRESENTED

The typical report on a compilation would read

I (we) have compiled the accompanying balance sheets of XYZ Company as of December 31, 20X3 and 20X4, and the related statements of income, retained earnings, and cash flows for the years then ended, in accordance with Statements on Standards for Accounting and Review Services issued by the American Institute of Certified Public Accountants.

A compilation is limited to presenting in the form of financial statements information that is the representation of management (owners). I (we) have not audited or reviewed the accompanying financial statements and, accordingly, do not express an opinion or any other form of assurance on them.

REVIEW FOR EACH PERIOD PRESENTED

A typical report would read:

I (we) have reviewed the accompanying balance sheets of XYZ Company as of December 31, 20X3 and 20X4, and the related statements of income, retained earnings, and cash flows for the years then ended, in accordance with Statements on Standards for Accounting and Review Services issued by the American Institute of Certified Public Accountants. All information included in these financial statements is the representation of the management (owners) of XYZ Company.

A review consists principally of inquiries of company personnel and analytical procedures applied to financial data. It is substantially less in scope than an audit in accordance with generally accepted auditing standards, the objective of which is the expression of an opinion regarding the financial statements taken as a whole. Accordingly I (we) do not express such an opinion.

Based on my (our) reviews, I am (we are) not aware of any material modifications that should be made to the accompanying financial statements in order for them to be in conformity with generally accepted accounting principles.

STEP-DOWN IN LEVEL OF SERVICE

An accountant may perform a level of service with respect to the financial statements of the current period that is lower than the level of service with respect to the financial statement of one or more of the prior periods with which it is to be compared. This might be a compilation for the current period stepped down from a review for one or more prior periods.

In this circumstance the accountant may issue a compilation report on the current period, adding a paragraph to describe the responsibility assumed for the prior period. This should give the original date of the review report and state that no review procedures were performed after that date. The paragraph, appended to the compilation report on the financial statements of the current period, may be worded as follows:

The accompanying 20X3 financial statements of XYZ Company were previously reviewed by me (us) and my (our) report dated March 1, 20X4, stated that I was (we were) not aware of any material modifications that should be made to those statements in order for them to be in conformity with generally accepted accounting principles. I (we) have not performed any procedures in connection with that review engagement after the date of my (our) report on the 20X3 financial statements.

Alternatively, the accountant may combine a compilation report with a reissued review report on the prior period. If this is done, the combined report should state that no review procedures were performed after the original review date. A combined report may be worded as follows:

I (we) have reviewed the accompanying balance sheet of XYZ Company as of December 31, 20X3, and the related statements of income, retained earnings, and cash flows for the year then ended, in accordance with Statements on Standards for Accounting and Review Services issued by the American Institute of Certified Public Accountants. All information included in these financial statements is the representation of the management (owners) of XYZ Company.

A review consists principally of inquiries of company personnel and analytical procedures applied to financial data. It is substantially less in scope than an audit in accordance with generally accepted auditing standards, the objective of which is the expression of an opinion regarding the financial statements taken as a whole. Accordingly I (we) do not express such an opinion.

Based on my (our) review, I am (we are) not aware of any material modifications that should be made to the accompanying 20X3 financial statements in order for them to be in conformity with generally accepted accounting principles.

The accompanying 20X4 financial statements were compiled by me (us). A compilation is limited to presenting in the form of financial statements Information that is the representation of management (owners). I (we) have not audited or reviewed the 20X4 financial statements and, accordingly, do not express an opinion or any other form of assurance on them.

STEP-UP IN LEVEL OF SERVICE

An accountant may perform a level of service with respect to the financial statements of the current period that is higher than the level of service with respect to the financial statement of one or more prior periods with which the current financial statements are being compared. This step-up might be from a compilation for a prior period to a review for the current period. In this circumstance, the accountant may issue a review report on the current period, adding a paragraph to describe the responsibility assumed for the prior period.

A review report on the current period, modified to reflect the compilation of a prior period, might read:

I (we) have reviewed the accompanying balance sheet of XYZ Company as of December 31, 20X3, and the related statements of income, retained earnings, and cash flows for the year then ended, in accordance with Statements on Standards for Accounting and Review Services issued by the American Institute of Certified Public Accountants. All information included in these financial statements is the representation of the management (owners) of XYZ Company.

A review consists principally of inquiries of company personnel and analytical procedures applied to financial data. It is substantially less in scope than an audit In accordance with generally accepted auditing standards, the objective of which is the expression of an opinion regarding the financial statements taken as a whole. Accordingly I (we) do not express such an opinion.

Based on my (our) review, I am (we are) not aware of any material modifications that should be made to the accompanying 20X3 financial statements in order for them to be in conformity with generally accepted accounting principles.

The accompanying 20X2 financial statements of XYZ Company were compiled by me (us). A compilation is limited to presenting in the form of financial statements information that is the representation of management (owners). I (we) have not audited or reviewed the 20X2 financial statements and, accordingly, do not express an opinion or any other form of assurance on them.

CONTINUING ACCOUNTANT'S CHANGED REFERENCE TO A DEPARTURE FROM GAAP

During an engagement related to current period financial statements, an accountant may become aware of circumstances or events that may affect prior period financial statements. The effects of these must be analyzed because they may require a separate explanatory paragraph referring to a departure from GAAP. The explanatory paragraph should state

1.   The date of the previous report.
2.   The circumstances or events resulting in the changed reference, and

3. That the prior period financial statements have been changed, if they have been.

The following is an illustration of an explanatory paragraph.

> In my (our) previous compilation (review) report dated March 1, 20X2, on the 20X1 financial statements, I (we) referred to a departure from generally accepted accounting principles because the company carried its land at appraisal values. However, as disclosed in Note X, the company has restated its 20X1 financial statements to reflect its land at cost in accordance with generally accepted accounting principles.

PREDECESSOR'S COMPILATION OR REVIEW REPORT

When a predecessor's report is not presented, the successor accountant should incorporate the following references in an additional paragraph:

1. A statement that another accountant compiled or reviewed the prior period financial statements.
2. The date of the predecessor's report.
3. A description of the standard disclaimer (in a compilation) or limited assurance (in a review).
4. A description of any report modifications.

For example

1. For a review of the prior period by a predecessor

> The 20X1 financial statements of XYZ Company were reviewed by other accountants, whose report dated March 1, 20X2, stated that they were not aware of any material modifications that should be made to those statements in order for them to be in conformity with generally accepted accounting principles.

2. For a compilation of the prior period by a predecessor

> The 20X1 financial statements of XYZ Company were compiled by other accountants who report dated February 1, 20X2, stated that they did not express an opinion or any other form of assurance on those statements.

PREDECESSOR'S COMPILATION OR REVIEW REPORT REISSUED

A predecessor accountant is not required to reissue a report on prior period financial statements but may do so at the client's request. Before reissuing a report, the predecessor should

1. Consider whether the report is still appropriate in the light of subsequent events,
2. Read and compare the current period statements to those of the prior period, and
3. Obtain a letter from the successor indicating whether the accountant is aware of matters that might have a material effect on the prior period financial statements.

A predecessor accountant who becomes aware of information occurring subsequent to the report date that may affect the report should perform procedures similar to those that would have been done originally.

The date of the reissued report should be the date used in the original report. If a revision is made, the accountant should dual-date the report for the revised aspect. The accountant's responsibility for subsequent events is limited to the specific events disclosed. A written statement should be obtained from the former client, setting forth the new information and its effect.

A predecessor accountant who is precluded from performing the procedures that are necessary in the circumstances should not reissue the report.

RESTATED PRIOR PERIOD FINANCIAL STATEMENTS

In general, a predecessor accountant would reissue a report with respect to restated prior period financial statements. If the predecessor accountant chooses not to reissue the report, and the successor accountant is not engaged to report on prior period financial statements, the successor accountant should modify the introductory paragraph of the compilation or review report by stating that a predecessor accountant reported on the prior period financial statements before restatement. Further, if engaged to do so, the successor accountant may compile or review the restatement adjustment(s). The successor accountant's compilation or review report may then be modified to reflect this action.

The form and content of a successor accountant's compilation report when the predecessor accountant's report is not presented and the successor accountant is engaged to compile the restatement adjustment(s) follows:

> I (we) have compiled the accompanying balance sheet of XYZ Company as of December 31, 20X2, and the related statements of income, retained earnings, and cash flows for the year then ended in accordance with Statements on Standards for Accounting and Review Services issued by the American Institute of Certified Public Accountants. 1 (we) also compiled the adjustment described in Note X that was (were) applied to restate the 20X1 financial statements. The 20X1 financial statements of XYZ Company, before the adjustment(s) described in Note X[11] that was (were) applied to restate the 20X1 financial statements, were compiled by other accountants whose report dated March 31, 20X2, did not express an opinion or any other form of assurance on those financial statements.
>
> [*Same second paragraph as in the standard report*]

The form and content of a successor accountant's review report when the predecessor accountant's report is not presented and the successor accountant is engaged to review the restatement adjustment(s) follows:

> I (we) have reviewed the accompanying balance sheet of XYZ Company as of December 31, 20X2, and the related statements of income, retained earnings, and cash flows for the year then ended in accordance with Statements on Standards for Accounting and Review Services issued by the American Institute of Certified Public Accountants. All information included in these financial statements is the representation of the management (owners) of XYZ Company. The 20X1 financial statements of XYZ before the adjustment(s) described in Note X that was (were) applied to restate the 20X1 financial statements were reviewed by other accountants whose report dated March 31, 20X2, stated that they were not aware of any material modifications that should be made to those financial statements in order for them to be in conformity with generally accepted accounting principles.
>
> [*Same second and third paragraphs as in the standard report*]
>
> I (we) also reviewed the adjustment(s) as described in Note X that was (were) applied to restate the 20X1 financial statements. Based on my (our) review, nothing came to my (our) attention to indicate that the adjustment(s) is (are) not appropriate and properly applied.

WHEN ONE PERIOD IS AUDITED

When reporting on compiled or reviewed current period financial statements that are being compared with audited prior-period statements and the accountant decides not to reissue the prior period audit report, the accountant's current period compilation or review report should have a separate explanatory paragraph stating

1. That the prior period financial statements were audited,
2. The date of the previous audit report,
3. The type of opinion expressed,
4. The substantive reasons for any other-than-unqualified opinion, and

5. That since the date of the previous report no additional auditing procedures have been performed.

The paragraph might read like this.

> The financial statements for the year ended December 31, 20X1, were audited by us (other accountants) and we (they) expressed an unqualified opinion on them in our (their) report dated March 1, 20X2, but we (they) have not performed any auditing procedures since that date.

FINANCIAL STATEMENTS THAT PREVIOUSLY DID NOT OMIT SUBSTANTIALLY ALL DISCLOSURES

An accountant who, based on an audit, a review, or a compilation, has reported on financial statements that did not omit substantially all of the disclosures required by GAAP may later be requested to compile financial statements for the same period that do omit these disclosures when they are presented in comparative financial statements. The accountant may report on such comparative financial statements if there is added to the report a paragraph like the following, indicating the nature of the previous service rendered and the date of the previous report:

> The accompanying 20X2 financial statements were compiled by me (us) from financial statements that did not omit substantially all of the disclosures required by generally accepted accounting principles and that I (we) previously reviewed as indicated in my (our) report dated 20X3.

CHANGE OF STATUS FROM PUBLIC TO NONPUBLIC ENTITY

The current status of an entity governs whether Statements on Auditing Standards (AU Sections) or Statements on Standards for Accounting and Review Services (AR Sections) apply.

A previous report that is no longer appropriate should not be reissued or referred to in the current report.

300 COMPILATION REPORTS ON FINANCIAL STATEMENTS INCLUDED IN CERTAIN PRESCRIBED FORMS

SOURCE OF STANDARDS

SSARS 3, *Compilation Reports on Financial Statements Included in Certain Prescribed Forms*

SSARS 15, *Elimination of Certain References to Statements on Auditing Standards and Incorporation of Appropriate Guidance into Statements on Standards for Accounting and Review Services.*

SUMMARY

This section provides for an alternative compilation report format when a prescribed form calls for a departure from GAAP or OCBOA. A prescribed form is any preprinted standard form designed or adopted by the body (other than the entity whose statements are to be compiled) to which it is to be submitted.

GENERAL REPORTING RULE

Because it is generally presumed that the needs of the body (e.g., a bank or credit agency) that designed or adopted the prescribed form will be satisfied by the contents of the form, the accountant does not usually need to communicate to the body departures from GAAP required by the form or the instructions related to it. The following is an acceptable standard compilation report on a prescribed form:

> I (we) have compiled the [*identify financial statements, including period covered and name of entity*] included in the accompanying prescribed form in accordance with Statements on Standards for Accounting and Review Services issued by the American Institute of Certified Public Accountants.
>
> My (our) compilation was limited to presenting In the form prescribed by [*name of body*] information that is the representation of management (owners). I (we) have not audited or reviewed the financial statements referred to above and, accordingly, do not express an opinion or any other form of assurance on them.
>
> These financial statements [*including related disclosures*] are presented in accordance with the requirements of [*name of body*], which differ from generally accepted accounting principles. These financial statements are therefore not designed for those who are not informed about such differences.

SPECIAL REPORTING SITUATIONS

Departures from GAAP other than those prescribed by the form or its instructions must be disclosed and their effect on the report determined. In such circumstances SSARS 1 (AR Section 100) applies.

A printed form that does not conform to SSARS 1 or SSARS 3 should not be signed. A report should be issued instead.

400 COMMUNICATION BETWEEN PREDECESSOR AND SUCCESSOR ACCOUNTANTS

SOURCE OF STANDARDS

SSARS 4, *Communication between Predecessor and Successor Accountants*
SSARS 15, *Elimination of Certain References to Statements on Auditing Standards and Incorporation of Appropriate Guidance into Statements on Standards for Accounting and Review Services*

SUMMARY

A successor is not required to communicate with a predecessor concerning acceptance of a compilation or review engagement. However, the successor may decide to do so because of such matters as frequent changes in accountants, limited information obtained from the prospective client, or the contemplated change will take place substantially after the end of the applicable accounting period. This section provides guidance on communications between a predecessor and successor accountant for such situations.

INQUIRIES REGARDING ACCEPTANCE OF AN ENGAGEMENT

If the successor accountant concludes that communication with the predecessor accountant is appropriate, the successor should request the client to permit inquiries and authorize the predecessor to respond. The implications of the client's refusal must be considered.

The successor's inquiry, which may be oral or written, would ordinarily concern the following:

1. Integrity of management.
2. Accounting disagreements between the predecessor and management.
3. Cooperation of management in providing requested information.
4. The predecessor's knowledge of any fraud or illegal acts perpetrated by the client.
5. The reasons for the change of accountants.

The predecessor should respond promptly and fully unless, due to unusual circumstances (e.g., pending litigation), such response must be limited. Under these circumstances the predecessor should state the nature of the limited response.

OTHER INQUIRIES

The successor may wish to review the predecessor's working papers. Such a review needs to be client-authorized.

The predecessor ordinarily should provide access on items of continuing accounting significance and those relating to contingencies. However, valid business reasons (including unpaid fees) may lead the predecessor to decide not to allow the requested access.

SUCCESSOR ACCOUNTANT'S USE OF COMMUNICATIONS

In general, the report of the successor accountant should not include any reference to the predecessor accountant's work or report. Exceptions exist for reporting on comparative financial statements (see AR Section 200).

DISCOVERY OF INFORMATION AFFECTING PREDECESSOR'S REPORT

When the successor accountant becomes aware of information that causes him or her to conclude that the financial statements reported on by the predecessor accountant may require revision, the successor accountant should request that the client communicate this information to the predecessor accountant. A client's subsequent refusal to communicate the information, or an inadequate response by the predecessor, should cause the successor to question its implications on the current engagement. Accordingly the successor may conclude that it is necessary to resign from the engagement and/or consult with legal counsel to determine an appropriate course of action.

INTERPRETATION OF AR SECTION 400

REPORT ON THE APPLICATION OF ACCOUNTING PRINCIPLES (ISSUED IN AUGUST 1987; REVISED IN NOVEMBER 2002)

Anytime an accountant (including a successor accountant) is requested to report on the application of accounting principles to specified transactions, or the type of opinion that may be expressed on an entity's financial statements, the accountant should follow the guidance in AU Section 625 (SAS 50, *Reports on the Application of Accounting Principles*).

600 REPORTING ON PERSONAL FINANCIAL STATEMENTS INCLUDED IN WRITTEN PERSONAL FINANCIAL PLANS

SOURCE OF STANDARDS

SSARS 6, *Reporting on Personal Financial Statements Included in Written Personal Financial Plans*

SUMMARY

This section provides an exemption from SSARS 1 (AR Section 100) when an accountant submits a written personal financial plan containing unaudited personal financial statements to a client without complying with the requirements of SSARS 1.

USE OF PERSONAL FINANCIAL STATEMENTS

To qualify for the exemption from SSARS 1, the personal financial statements must

1. Be used solely to assist a client and a client's advisers in developing a client's personal financial goals and objectives, and
2. Not be used to obtain credit or for any other purposes other than developing these goals and objectives.

ACCOUNTANT'S REPORT ON PERSONAL FINANCIAL STATEMENTS

The accountant's report, based on the exemption from SSAS 1, should include statements indicating that the financial statements

1. Are designed solely to assist in the development of the financial plan;
2. May be incomplete or contain departures from GAAP;
3. Should not be used to obtain credit or for any purpose other than to assist in the development of the financial plan; and
4. Have not been audited, reviewed, or compiled.

An illustrative report follows.

The accompanying Statement of Financial Condition of ABC, as of December 31, 20XX, was prepared solely to help you develop your personal financial plan. Accordingly it may be incomplete or contain other departures from generally accepted accounting principles and should not be used to obtain credit or for any other purposes other than developing your financial plan. We have not audited, reviewed, or compiled the statement.

It should be noted that each page of the personal financial statements should contain a reference to the accountant's report.

INTERPRETATION OF AR SECTION 600

SUBMITTING A PERSONAL FINANCIAL PLAN TO A CLIENT'S ADVISERS (ISSUED IN MAY 1991)

The development of a client's personal financial goals and objectives includes the actual implementation of the plan by a client and/or the client's advisers. As a result an accountant is permitted to submit a written personal financial plan containing unaudited financial statements to a client and/or the client's advisers, without complying with the provisions of SSARS 1. The written personal financial plan may be used, for example, by a stockbroker who will recommend specific investment vehicles, or by an attorney engaged to prepare trust documents or a will.

PART 5

CONSULTING SERVICES

100 CONSULTING SERVICES: DEFINITIONS AND STANDARDS

SOURCE OF STANDARDS

SSCS 1, *Consulting Services: Definitions and Standards*

INTRODUCTION

CPAs have become more than specialists in accounting, auditing, attestation, and tax-related matters. Clients have come to rely on CPAs as business advisors in many diverse areas such as mergers and acquisitions, information technology, and controllership activities. The American Institute of Certified Public Accountants has long recognized the involvement of CPAs in nontraditional services and had previously issued Statements on Standards for Management Advisory Services. In 1992, those statements were superseded by a Statement on Standards for Consulting Services to indicate a broader range of professional services and provide standards for the practitioner to follow.

DEFINITIONS

Consulting services are professional services involving the application of technical skills, education, observations, and experiences.

Consulting services include the following:

1. *Consultations,* in which the CPA provides counsel, based on existing knowledge of the client. This service usually spans a short time period; for example, providing guidance in connection with a client-prepared business plan.
2. *Advisory services,* in which the CPA formulates findings, conclusions, and recommendations; for example, analysis of an information technology based accounting system.
3. *Implementation services,* in which the CPA alone, or with client assistance, puts an action plan into effect; for example, actual installation of a computer system.
4. *Transaction services,* which involve providing services applicable to a specific client transaction, typically with an outside party; for example, insolvency services.
5. *Staff and other support services,* in which the CPA provides staff and other support to perform client-specified tasks; for example, computer programming and controllership activities.
6. *Product services,* in which the CPA sells a product to a client, along with related support; for example, the sale and training of computer programs.

Consulting services exclude, however, among other services: tax return preparation, tax planning and tax advisory services, financial planning, bookkeeping services, and financial statement services governed by SASs, SSAEs, and SSARSs.

STANDARDS FOR CONSULTING SERVICES

The practitioner should comply with the general standards of the profession, which may be found in Rule 201 of the AICPA Code of Conduct. In addition the practitioner should adhere to the following general standards specifically applicable to consulting services:

1. *Client interest.* While maintaining integrity and objectivity, the CPA should serve the client's best interest and accordingly attempt to achieve client objectives.
2. *Understanding with client.* Before accepting an engagement, the CPA should establish a written or oral understanding with the applicable parties concerning the nature, scope, and limitations of the services to be performed.
3. *Communication with client.* The CPA should notify the client of conflicts of interest that arise, significant reservations concerning the engagement, and significant findings.

CONSULTING SERVICES FOR ATTEST CLIENTS

A CPA should be cautious when considering the performance of a consulting service for an attest client. By itself, performance of a consulting service does not impair an accountant's independence. A CPA should take steps to comply with independence requirements of the AICPA, applicable regulatory agencies, state boards of accountancy and state societies of CPAs.

A word of caution: The practitioner should be aware that the Public Company Accounting Oversight Board for the most part precludes an auditor of a publicly traded entity from performing any additional services other than preparation of the entity's tax returns, which requires approval of the entity's audit committee.

PART 6

QUALITY CONTROL

20 SYSTEM OF QUALITY CONTROL FOR A CPA FIRM'S ACCOUNTING AND AUDITING PRACTICE

SOURCE OF STANDARDS

SQCS 2, *System of Quality Control for a CPA Firm's Accounting and Auditing Practice.*

INTRODUCTION

In 1979 the Auditing Standards Board of the American Institute of Certified Public Accountants issued SAS 25, *The Relationship of Generally Accepted Auditing Standards to Quality Control Standards.* As indicated in the pronouncement, generally accepted auditing standards relate to the conduct of an audit whereas quality controls relate to the conduct of the accounting firm's practice.

Subsequent to the issuance of SAS 25 the Auditing Standards Board began issuing a series of pronouncements titled Statements on Quality Control Standards (SQCS). Firms enrolled in the AICPA practice-monitoring program are required to comply with the provisions in these statements. Firms not enrolled in the AICPA practice-monitoring program are encouraged to comply with the provisions in the SQCS.

A word of caution: SQCS do not specify guidance for quality control considerations of the Public Company Accounting Oversight Board, which regulates the audits of publicly traded entities (i.e., issuers).

SYSTEM OF QUALITY CONTROL

A system of quality control is a process, consisting of policies and procedures, designed to provide reasonable, but not absolute assurance that CPA firm personnel comply with professional standards and the standards of quality established by the firm.

A system of quality control should be established for a CPA firm that performs any of the following services:

1. Auditing (governed by SASs).
2. Attest engagements (governed by SSAEs).
3. Accounting and review services (governed by SSARSs).
4. Other services for which there are professional standards (e.g., consulting services).

In designing a system of quality control, the CPA firm should take into account

1. The size of the firm;
2. The number of offices the firm maintains;

3. The qualifications and experience of its personnel and the authority granted the personnel;
4. The nature and complexity of the practice, including the types of services performed; and
5. Cost–benefit considerations.

QUALITY CONTROL POLICIES AND PROCEDURES

ELEMENTS OF QUALITY CONTROL

A system of quality control should consist of the following interrelated elements:

1. Independence, integrity, and objectivity.
2. Personnel management.
3. Acceptance and continuance of clients and engagements.
4. Engagement performance.
5. Monitoring.

INDEPENDENCE, INTEGRITY, AND OBJECTIVITY

A CPA firm should design and implement policies and procedures to maintain independence in fact and in appearance in circumstances requiring independence. A CPA firm should take steps necessary to ensure that firm personnel possess integrity (i.e., honesty) and are capable of making professional decisions objectively (i.e., with an unbiased mental attitude). For example, a CPA firm may periodically require personnel to complete a checklist indicating ownership interests in clients.

PERSONNEL MANAGEMENT

"Personnel management" should include policies and procedures relating to the following:

1. Hiring staff, including resume and application submission followed by the interview process.
2. Assignment of staff to specific engagements, based on experience and other qualifications.
3. Professional development, including continuing professional education.
4. Advancement (i.e., promotion).
5. Competency of supervisory personnel in such areas as the Code of Professional Conduct, the specific service to be performed, the industry in which the client is operating, and the client's information technology systems.

ACCEPTANCE AND CONTINUANCE OF CLIENTS AND ENGAGEMENTS

Whether or not a firm accepts or continues a client relationship or a specific engagement is of course based on professional judgment. Professional judgment should take into account the following:

1. The integrity of the client.
2. Whether the CPA firm reasonably expects to complete a specific engagement.
3. Risks associated with performing specific professional services.

It is recommended that before undertaking an engagement, the CPA firm should establish, either orally or in writing, an understanding with the client regarding the needs and expectations of the client, the responsibilities of the client and the CPA firm, as well as any limitations relevant to the engagement.

ENGAGEMENT PERFORMANCE

A CPA firm needs to establish policies and procedures to provide reasonable assurance that each engagement is performed in accordance with professional, and where applicable, regulatory standards. Engagement performance must also meet the firm's standards of quality.

Policies and procedures regarding engagement performance should reasonably ensure that engagements are planned, performed properly, supervised, reviewed, and documented. Engagement results also need to be properly communicated to interested parties.

In view of the above, policies regarding engagement performance might include disseminating copies of new pronouncements and providing means for consulting with others inside and outside the CPA firm.

Monitoring

Monitoring, which should be an ongoing process, involves considering the following:

1. Relevance and adequacy of the firm's policies and procedures relevant to the other elements of quality control.
2. Appropriateness of the firm's practice aids and other materials used by firm personnel.
3. Effectiveness of the firm's professional development activities.
4. Compliance with the firm's policies and procedures.

Monitoring may be accomplished by a variety of means including, but not limited to, inspection procedures applied to personnel records, engagement workpapers, and engagement reports, and pre- and postissuance review of specific engagements. Peer review alone is not sufficient for monitoring purposes but may be a substitute for some or all inspection procedures.

A sole practitioner may monitor his or her own compliance with quality controls. However, for additional assurance regarding compliance, a sole practitioner may decide to engage another individual to perform an independent inspection.

Documentation

A CPA firm should document the quality control policies and procedures designed and implemented. Compliance with the policies and procedures should also be documented. The form and content of the documentation should be based on professional judgment.

RELATIONSHIP OF QUALITY CONTROL STANDARDS TO PROFESSIONAL STANDARDS APPLICABLE TO SPECIFIC ENGAGEMENTS

Deficiencies in or instances of noncompliance with a CPA firm's quality control policies and procedures do not, in and of themselves, indicate that a specific engagement was not performed in accordance with professional standards applicable to that engagement.

30 MONITORING A CPA FIRM'S ACCOUNTING AND AUDITING PRACTICE

SOURCE OF STANDARDS

SQCS 3, *Monitoring a CPA Firm's Accounting and Auditing Practice*

INTRODUCTION/SUMMARY

This section is designed to assist implementation of the monitoring element of a firm's system of quality control (as described in QC Section 20).

MONITORING PROCEDURES

Monitoring procedures should be designed to provide reasonable assurance that a firm's system of quality control is effective and include the following:

1. Inspection procedures, which may be performed continuously and/or at specific times during the year, include

   a. Review of administrative and personnel records,
   b. Review of engagement documentation including reports and entity financial statements,
   c. Brainstorming with CPA firm personnel,
   d. Summarizing identified deficiencies and determining areas in need of improvement, and
   e. Determining specific corrective actions to be implemented.

2. Review of selected engagements before and after issuance of reports, which should be done by a management-level individual who was not directly associated with the performance of the engagement.

3. Consideration of new pronouncements and professional development (including continuing professional education).

4. Discussions with CPA firm personnel, including communication of quality control deficiencies.

In general, the review performed by the individual with final responsibility for the engagement does not constitute a valid monitoring procedure. However, review by the individual with final responsibility for the engagement may constitute an acceptable inspection procedure in the case of small firms with a limited number of management-level individuals. Alternatively, it may be prudent to engage an individual from outside the firm to perform pertinent inspection procedures.

THE RELATIONSHIP OF PEER REVIEW TO MONITORING

While peer review is not an acceptable substitute for monitoring procedures in totality, a qualified peer review may enable elimination of some or all "inspection" procedures.

40 THE PERSONNEL MANAGEMENT ELEMENT OF A FIRM'S SYSTEM OF QUALITY CONTROL— COMPETENCIES REQUIRED BY A PRACTITIONER IN CHARGE OF AN ATTEST ENGAGEMENT

SOURCE OF STANDARDS

SQCS 4, *The Personnel Management Element of a Firm's System of Quality Control— Competencies Required by a Practitioner in-Charge of an Attest Engagement*

INTRODUCTION

This section provides guidance in connection with the element of quality control known as personnel management (see QC Section 20).

THE PERSONNEL MANAGEMENT ELEMENT OF QUALITY CONTROL

Policies and procedures pertaining to "personnel management" should reasonably ensure the following:

1. Employees have the academic requirements, maturity, integrity, and leadership skills necessary for competent performance.
2. Only individuals possessing technical training and proficiency are assigned specific tasks.
3. Staff members partake in continuing professional education and other activities that promote professional development.
4. Advancement of personnel is based on pertinent qualifications.

COMPETENCIES

An individual in charge of an engagement should possess knowledge, skills, and abilities to conduct an engagement in accordance with professional standards. Competency is based on qualitative factors rather than quantitative factors such as the number of years of experience of the individual.

GAINING COMPETENCIES

While recent experience in performing professional engagements certainly contributes to the competency of an in-charge practitioner, competency may need to be enhanced through continuing professional education and consultation.

COMPETENCIES EXPECTED IN PERFORMING ACCOUNTING, AUDITING, AND ATTESTATION ENGAGEMENTS

A CPA firm's quality controls should ensure that an in-charge practitioner is competent in the following:

1. The role of quality control.
2. The AICPA Code of Professional Conduct.
3. The performance, supervision and reporting aspects of specific engagements.
4. Applicable general and industry-specific accounting, auditing, and attest professional standards.
5. Knowledge of the industry in which the client operates, including organization and operating characteristics.
6. The exercise of professional judgment and professional skepticism.
7. The use of information technology.

PART 7

TAX SERVICES

PREFACE

Statements on Standards for Tax Services (SSTS) and related Interpretations represent the AICPA standards of tax practice and set forth AICPA members' professional responsibilities to clients, the public, the government, and the profession. Provisions in SSTS expand on many of the provisions contained in Treasury Department Circular 230, and the Internal Revenue Code and are applicable to federal, state and local tax practice.

100 TAX RETURN POSITIONS

SOURCE OF STANDARD

SSTP 1, *Tax Return Positions*

INTRODUCTION

This section is applicable to the recommendation of tax return positions and the preparation and signing of tax returns. A tax return position is a position (i.e., stance or approach) utilized on a tax return as to which the AICPA member has advised the client or as to which the AICPA member has deemed to be appropriate based on the client's knowledge of all material relevant facts and circumstances. It should be readily apparent that when preparing a tax return, a member should serve as the taxpayer's advocate.

STANDARDS

The following standards are relevant to AICPA members in connection with tax return positions:

1. Do not recommend the use of a tax return position unless there is a good-faith belief that there is a realistic possibility of it being sustained (i.e., upheld) in an administrative (e.g., audit) or judicial (i.e., court) proceeding.
2. Do not prepare or sign a tax return containing a tax return position that the member should not have recommended.
3. A tax return position may be recommended even if it does not have a realistic possibility of being sustained if it is not frivolous and the taxpayer is advised to disclose it on the tax return.
4. When relevant, the taxpayer should be advised of potential penalties in connection with a recommended tax return position and the possibility of mitigating the penalties through disclosure.

A member would violate the standards above if that member knowingly recommended a tax return position that exploits the taxing authority's audit selection process or serves as bargaining leverage in an administrative proceeding.

200 ANSWERS TO QUESTIONS ON TAX RETURNS

SOURCE OF STANDARDS

SSTP 2, *Answers to Questions on Tax Returns*

INTRODUCTION

Questions on tax returns include requests for information on the face of the return, in the instructions to the return, or in the taxing authority's regulations, and need not be in the form of a question.

STANDARD

A reasonable effort should be made to obtain relevant information from the taxpayer in order to appropriately answer all questions on a tax return before signing as the preparer.

The omission of an answer to a question on a tax return may be based on reasonable grounds such as the following:

1. Information necessary to answer the question is not available and the answer does not significantly affect either the computation of taxable income or the tax liability.
2. The meaning of the question is genuinely uncertain.
3. The answer to the question is voluminous; in this case a statement should be appended to the return clearly stating that the information will be furnished upon examination.

A tax return preparer is not required to attach an explanation to the tax return when the omission of an answer to a question is based on reasonable grounds. The preparer should, however, consider whether the tax return is incomplete.

It would be an unprofessional act to omit an answer to a question merely because it would benefit the taxpayer.

300 CERTAIN PROCEDURAL ASPECTS OF PREPARING RETURNS

SOURCE OF STANDARDS

SSTP 3, *Certain Procedural Aspects of Preparing Returns*

INTRODUCTION

This section concerns a tax preparer's obligation to examine or verify data supporting information included in a tax return and consider information of another taxpayer when preparing a tax return.

STANDARDS

A tax return preparer may generally rely on information supplied by a taxpayer or a third party. While verification of the information is not required, reasonable inquiries should be made if the information appears to be incomplete, incorrect, or inconsistent. If possible, tax returns of prior years should be referred to when preparing a tax return of the current year. For example, if a prior year tax return includes dividend income from a particular entity, the tax return preparer would generally expect dividend income to be reported in the current year; absence of dividend income in the current year should prompt the tax return preparer to inquire as to the reason for its omission, which might be disposition of the stock.

Appropriate inquiries should be made to determine a taxpayer's compliance with laws and regulations that stipulate conditions for the deductibility or tax treatment of an item. For example, if there is a legal requirement that documentation exist to support a deduction, the tax return preparer should inquire about the existence of the documentation.

A tax return preparer should consider known information from the tax return of another taxpayer that is relevant to the preparation of the tax return of the taxpayer. (*A word of caution:* Laws and rules concerning confidentiality should be adhered to.) For example, if a mortgage exists between a parent and a child, the tax return preparer should take into account the interest paid by the child to the parent when preparing the tax returns of the two taxpayers.

400 USE OF ESTIMATES

SOURCE OF STANDARDS

SSTP 4, *Use of Estimates*

INTRODUCTION

The section addresses the use of estimates in preparing tax returns. While a tax return preparer may provide advice concerning estimates to be included in a tax return, the taxpayer is ultimately responsible for furnishing the estimated data to the tax return preparer. For purposes of this section, appraisals and valuations are not deemed to be estimates.

STANDARD

A tax return preparer may use a taxpayer's estimates if

1. The use of the estimates does not violate a law or a rule.
2. It is not practical to obtain exact data.
3. The tax return preparer considers the estimates to be reasonable.

Presentation of taxpayer estimates should not imply accuracy that is greater than actually exists.

500 DEPARTURE FROM A POSITION PREVIOUSLY CONCLUDED IN AN ADMINISTRATIVE PROCEEDING OR COURT DECISION

SOURCE OF STANDARDS

SSTP 5, *Departure from a Position Previously Concluded in an Administrative Proceeding or Court Decision*

DEFINITIONS

1. An *administrative proceeding* includes an audit performed by a taxing authority as well as an appeals conference concerning a tax return or a claim for a refund.
2. A *court decision* is a decision made by any court that has tax jurisdiction.

STANDARD

A tax return preparer may generally recommend a tax return position or prepare or sign a tax return that departs from a position previously concluded in an administrative proceeding or court decision if such a position currently has a realistic possibility of being sustained in an administrative proceeding or court decision. It should be noted that a taxpayer may be required to prospectively follow the position previously concluded; for example, a formal closing agreement may impose this requirement.

600 KNOWLEDGE OF ERROR: RETURN PREPARATION

SOURCE OF STANDARDS

SSTP 6, *Knowledge of Error: Return Preparation*

DEFINITION

Error includes a tax return position, omission, or method of accounting that does not meet the standards stated in TS Section 100, *Tax Return Positions*, and a previously utilized tax return position that no longer meets the standards stated in TS Section 100, *Tax Return Positions*, because of the retroactive effect of a change in law, judicial decision, or administrative pronouncement.

STANDARD

A tax return preparer has a responsibility to inform a taxpayer promptly upon becoming aware of either an error in a tax return that was previously filed or the failure to file a required tax return. The notification, which may be oral, should include one or more recommendations for corrective action. The tax return preparer has no responsibility to communicate the error to the relevant taxing authority and should not communicate the error to any party other than the taxpayer without the taxpayer's consent.

A tax return preparer should consider a taxpayer's failure to take the appropriate action (e.g., filing an amended tax return) to correct an error on a tax return of a prior period as a basis for terminating the professional relationship with the taxpayer. Further, if a taxpayer fails to take remedial action and the taxpayer could be charged with fraud or other criminal misconduct, the tax return preparer should advise the taxpayer to consult with an attorney.

700 KNOWLEDGE OF ERROR: ADMINISTRATIVE PROCEEDING

SOURCE OF STANDARDS

SSTP 7, *Knowledge of Error: Administrative Proceeding*

DEFINITION

An *administrative proceeding* includes an audit (i.e., examination) by a taxing authority or an appeals conference. For purposes of this section, a criminal proceeding is not considered to be an administrative proceeding and the definition of an *error* is the same as the definition contained in TS Section 600.

STANDARD

If a practitioner is acting in the capacity of a taxpayer representative in an administrative proceeding with respect to a tax return that includes an error that the practitioner is aware of, the practitioner should inform the taxpayer of the error as soon as possible after discovery of the error. The notification, which may be oral, should include one or more recommendations for corrective action. The tax return preparer has no responsibility to communicate the error to the relevant taxing authority and should not communicate the error to any party other than the taxpayer without the taxpayer's consent.

The tax return preparer should also request permission from the taxpayer to disclose the error to the taxing authority. A tax return preparer should consider a taxpayer's failure to grant such permission as a basis for terminating the professional relationship with the taxpayer. Further, if a taxpayer fails to disclose the error and taxpayer could be charged with fraud or other criminal misconduct, the tax return preparer should advise the taxpayer to consult with an attorney.

800 FORM AND CONTENT OF ADVICE TO TAXPAYERS

SOURCE OF STANDARDS

SSTP 8, *Form and Content of Advice to Taxpayers*

This section addresses a tax practitioner's responsibilities in connection with advice provided to a taxpayer.

STANDARDS

In connection with providing advice to a taxpayer, a tax return preparer should proceed as follows:

1. Exercise professional judgment to reasonably ensure that the tax advice reflects professional competence and serves the taxpayer's best interests. Communication of tax advice may be oral or written and need not conform to any specific format or guidelines. A taxpayer should also be informed that the advice provided is based on stated facts and circumstances which are subject to change.
2. Follow the standards discussed in TS Section 100, *Tax Return Positions.*
3. Understand that, in general, once the tax advice is provided, there is no obligation to communicate subsequent developments. However, communication of subsequent developments is appropriate when

    a. A specific agreement exists to so communicate or
    b. The practitioner is in the process of assisting a taxpayer implement plans or procedures in connection with advice previously provided.

PART 8

PERSONAL FINANCIAL PLANNING

100 BASIC PERSONAL FINANCIAL PLANNING ENGAGEMENT FUNCTIONS AND RESPONSIBILITIES

SOURCE OF STANDARDS

SRPFP 1, *Basic Personal Financial Planning Engagement Functions and Responsibilities*

INTRODUCTION

This section specifies the types of personal financial planning engagements and their objectives and provides general guidance concerning planning and performing a personal financial planning engagement.

DEFINITION AND SCOPE OF PERSONAL FINANCIAL PLANNING

In general, personal financial planning engagements assist clients in formulating financial planning goals and strategies. Accordingly a personal financial planning engagement typically involves the following:

1. Establishing objectives of the engagement.
2. Planning the specific relevant procedures.
3. Formulating recommendations.
4. Communicating engagement results to the client.
5. Identifying tasks for implementing planning decisions.
6. Assisting clients in executing strategies.
7. Monitoring client activities.
8. Updating recommendations.

It should be noted that financial planning engagements do not include those limited to compiling personal financial statements, preparing tax projections, or providing tax advice.

GUIDANCE APPLICABLE TO PERSONAL FINANCIAL PLANNING ENGAGEMENTS

A practitioner should conduct a personal financial planning engagement in a professional and ethical manner. Accordingly it is important that the practitioner comply with the AICPA Code of Conduct.

In the event that a personal financial planning engagement involves rendering tax advice, the practitioner should also comply with the provisions contained in Statement on Responsibilities in Tax Practice 8, *Form and Content of Advice to Clients* (see TS Section 800).

A practitioner performing an engagement involving the preparation of personal financial statements should, when relevant, adhere to Statements on Standards for Accounting and Review Services (see AR Sections) and Statements on Standards for Attestation Engagements (see AT Sections).

Finally, if a business valuation service is part of a personal financial planning engagement, the practitioner should consider Statement on Standards for Consulting Services 1 (see CS Section 100) and Statement on Standards for Valuation Services 1 (see CS Section 1).

PERSONAL FINANCIAL PLANNING ENGAGEMENTS

DEFINING THE ENGAGEMENT OBJECTIVES

A personal financial planning engagement should involve all of the following:

1. Obtaining an understanding of the client, including the client's family situation, cash flow and other available resources, and financial planning goals.
2. Establishing and documenting an understanding with the client as to engagement's scope, nature, terms, objectives and limitations. Documentation, which may be in the form of an engagement letter or a memo to the file, should also indicate the degree of responsibility the practitioner is taking to assist the client's implementation of planning decisions.
3. As the engagement progresses, monitoring the appropriateness of original engagement objectives.

PLANNING THE SPECIFIC PROCEDURES APPROPRIATE TO THE ENGAGEMENT

A personal financial planning engagement should be properly planned based on the objectives of the engagement. The specific procedures performed should take into consideration materiality and the cost–benefit relationship. The procedures performed and the results obtained should be documented in order to demonstrate that the practitioner had a reasonable basis for any recommendations.

DEVELOPING A BASIS FOR RECOMMENDATIONS

Information relevant to developing a basis for recommendations includes the following:

1. Client goals.
2. Existing client financial position.
3. Available client resources.
4. External factors.
5. Reasonable estimates.
6. Client-furnished assumptions.
7. Projections.

COMMUNICATING RECOMMENDATIONS

Recommendations should generally be communicated in writing. The written communication should include the following:

1. A summary of client goals and assumptions.
2. A description of any engagement limitations.
3. Specific recommendations.
4. A caveat that projected results may not be achieved due to possible changes in facts and circumstances.

If the practitioner performs a limited engagement that involves only selected goals, the practitioner may add the following paragraph to the written communication:

> We have considered ways to achieve your goal of providing for [*insert goal; e.g., the education of your children*]. However, you have instructed us not to consider other planning areas that might have an impact on that goal. If we had done so, it is possible that different conclusions or recommendations might have resulted.

MONITORING THE CLIENT'S PROGRESS IN ACHIEVING GOALS

A practitioner has no obligation to monitor a client's progress in achieving goals unless a specific agreement to do so exists.

UPDATING RECOMMENDATIONS AND HELPING THE CLIENT REVISE PLANNING DECISIONS

A practitioner has no obligation to update recommendations and help a client revise planning decisions unless a specific agreement to do so exists.

200 WORKING WITH OTHER ADVISERS

SOURCE OF STANDARDS

SRPFP 2, *Working with Other Advisers*

INTRODUCTION

This section provides guidance for situations in which a practitioner interacts with other financial advisers, including obtaining advice and referring a client to other advisers.

WORKING WITH OTHER ADVISERS IN PERSONAL FINANCIAL PLANNING ENGAGEMENTS

When working with other advisers, a practitioner should follow existing guidance in other Statements on Responsibilities in Personal Financial Planning.

A practitioner should suggest to a client that the client engage another adviser when the practitioner encounters a scope limitation that precludes completion of the engagement. The practitioner, however, may agree with the client to continue the engagement if the client chooses not to obtain the services of another adviser. In this situation the client should be advised of any scope limitations and the potential related effects on the conclusions and recommendations the practitioner may formulate. For example, the practitioner may add the following paragraph:

> At your request, [*e.g., insert scope limitation*] an independent appraisal of your real property has not been obtained. Such an appraisal may have affected the conclusions in your personal financial plan.

RECOMMENDING OTHER ADVISERS

Before recommending another adviser, the practitioner should be satisfied as to the qualifications and reputation of the other adviser. Accordingly the following should be taken into account:

1. The practitioner's previous working relationship, if any, with the adviser.
2. The certification and licensure of the adviser.
3. The professional reputation of the adviser.
4. Any relationship between the client and the adviser.

The recommendation of another adviser should result in a written communication to the client that specifies the nature of the other adviser's service and the extent of the referring practitioner's involvement in evaluating the results. When the practitioner refers the client to an attorney, it is advisable to include the following as part of the written communication:

> As we discussed, you should consult with an attorney to [*e.g., prepare updated will provisions*]. We have provided you with the names of several attorneys whose professional credentials and reputation are familiar to us. The selection of an attorney is your decision. Our referral does not constitute an endorsement of these attorneys or any advice they may render.

USING ADVICE PROVIDED BY OTHER ADVISERS

In order to use opinions of another adviser, the practitioner should

1. Understand the procedures utilized by the adviser,
2. Understand the opinions of the adviser, and
3. Evaluate the opinions of the adviser.

The practitioner is not required to communicate to the client that the practitioner concurs with the opinions of the adviser.

If the practitioner uses the opinions of the adviser, but does not evaluate the opinions, this fact should be communicated, ordinarily in writing, to the client. The communication should include a caveat that the practitioner does not take responsibility for conclusions reached by the advisor. For example, the caveat may be worded as follows:

> We have used the ABC Company's estimate of the value of your real estate in developing your financial plan. We have not evaluated their estimate and do not accept responsibility for it. If a different value were used, different recommendations could have resulted.

300 IMPLEMENTATION ENGAGEMENT FUNCTIONS AND RESPONSIBILITIES

SOURCE OF STANDARDS

SRPFP 3, *Implementation Engagement Functions and Responsibilities*

INTRODUCTION

An implementation engagement is undertaken in order to assist a client in executing a plan of action that resulted from a personal financial planning engagement. Implementation activities include the following:

1. Choosing investment advisers.
2. Restructuring debt.
3. Creating estate documents such as wills and trust agreements.
4. Establishing cash reserves.
5. Preparing budgets.
6. Selecting and acquiring investments and insurance products.

It should be noted that this section does not apply to a practitioner who is serving in a fiduciary or an agency relationship; for example, serving as a trustee of an investment trust.

IMPLEMENTATION ENGAGEMENTS

GUIDANCE APPLICABLE TO IMPLEMENTATION ENGAGEMENTS

When undertaking an implementation engagement, a practitioner should follow existing professional standards and guidance in other Statements on Responsibilities in Personal Financial Planning.

PLANNING THE ENGAGEMENT

An understanding should be established between the practitioner and the client concerning the level of implementation assistance. In all situations responsibility for implementation decisions rests with the client. Once reached, the understanding should be documented by the practitioner in accordance with the provisions in PFP Section 100.

COMMUNICATING WITH THE CLIENT

Information and recommendations should generally be communicated in writing. The written communication should include the following:

1. A summary of planning decisions being implemented.
2. Recommendations concerning actions to be taken.
3. A description of any engagement limitations.
4. Engagement results.

If the practitioner performs a limited engagement that involves selective implementation, the practitioner may add explanatory language to a written communication. For example,

> We have evaluated investment alternatives available to fund your retirement plan. However, you have instructed us not to consider limited partnerships as an investment alternative. If we had done so, it is possible we would have recommended a different investment strategy.

IMPLEMENTING PLANNING DECISIONS DEVELOPED BY OTHERS

A practitioner is not precluded from assisting a client in implementing planning decisions developed by other advisers. In order to provide such assistance, the practitioner should obtain a sufficient understanding of the planning decisions.

400 MONITORING AND UPDATING ENGAGEMENTS—FUNCTIONS AND RESPONSIBILITIES

SOURCE OF STANDARDS

SRPFP 4, *Monitoring and Updating Engagements—Functions and Responsibilities*

INTRODUCTION

This section is applicable only to monitoring and updating engagements

DEFINITIONS

A *monitoring engagement* involves tracking a client's progress in achieving personal financial planning goals.

An *updating engagement,* which usually results from a monitoring engagement, involves changing an existing personal financial plan and related recommendations.

GUIDANCE APPLICABLE TO MONITORING AND UPDATING ENGAGEMENTS

When undertaking a monitoring or updating, a practitioner should follow existing professional standards and guidance in other Statements on Responsibilities in Personal Financial Planning.

An understanding should be established between the practitioner and the client concerning the nature and extent of services to be provided. In the case of a monitoring service, an understanding should be reached as to how frequently progress should be monitored. Once reached, the understanding should be documented by the practitioner in accordance with the provisions in PFP Section 100.

MONITORING ENGAGEMENTS

In tracking a client's progress in achieving personal financial planning goals, the practitioner should proceed as follows:

1. Determine whether all recommendations have been implemented.
2. Measure and evaluate progress toward goal achievement.
3. Identify client circumstances as well as external factors that might necessitate plan modifications.

The practitioner's progress evaluation should generally be communicated in writing. Any recommendations concerning potential plan changes should be communicated in a timely way.

UPDATING ENGAGEMENTS

When undertaking an updating engagement, the practitioner should advise the client that all plan aspects and recommendations should be reviewed and possibly updated. The practitioner and the client should establish an agreement as to the nature and extent of the updating service.

Recommendations concerning potential plan changes should generally be communicated in writing and in a timely way.

If a practitioner is engaged to update only selected aspects of a personal financial plan, the practitioner should consider communicating this fact to the client. Sample wording is as follows:

> Updating any portion of your personal financial plan may affect other aspects of the plan. All of your financial planning recommendations should be reviewed periodically as part of the updating process. You have asked us to update only those financial planning recommendations for achieving your [*indicate specific goals; e.g., estate planning*] goals. Had we addressed all aspects of your financial plan, different recommendations could have resulted.

500 DEVELOPING A BASIS FOR RECOMMENDATIONS

SOURCE OF STANDARDS

SRPFP 5, *Developing a Basis for Conclusions*

DEFINITION

Financial planning recommendations represent suggestions made to a client to facilitate achievement of specific financial planning goals.

Developing a basis for financial planning recommendations involves

1. Gathering both quantitative and qualitative information,
2. Analyzing the client's current financial situation, and
3. Developing, evaluating, and recommending pertinent strategies for goal achievement.

GUIDANCE APPLICABLE TO DEVELOPING A BASIS FOR RECOMMENDATIONS

When developing a basis for recommendations, a practitioner should follow existing professional standards and guidance in other Statements on Responsibilities in Personal Financial Planning.

COLLECTING INFORMATION

While the procedures performed by the practitioner are a matter of professional judgment, the practitioner should proceed as follows:

1. Document the nature and extent of procedures performed.
2. Obtain sufficient relevant information to afford a reasonable basis for recommendations.
3. Communicate in writing to the client any scope limitation as well as the potential effects of the scope limitation on the recommendations.
4. Consider terminating the engagement if there is insufficient information; in this case, the practitioner should provide written notice to the client.

ANALYZING INFORMATION

In part, the practitioner should evaluate estimates and assumptions in terms of reasonableness. Accordingly the following should be considered:

1. Appropriateness of assumptions.
2. Consistency between assumptions.

3. Sensitivity of estimates, assumptions, and projections in relation to the entire financial plan.
4. The appropriateness of the original engagement if the practitioner concludes that estimates, assumptions, or projections lose validity.

The practitioner should generally communicate the following in writing to the client:

1. Significant estimates and assumptions.
2. Estimates and assumptions that are highly variable.
3. A caveat that that projected results may not be achieved.
4. If applicable, the practitioner's determination that goal achievement is not possible and the need to revise original goals.

FORMULATING STRATEGIES AND RECOMMENDATIONS

A client should be notified in writing that a client-imposed constraint could affect the conclusions reached and the recommendations developed.

PART 9

STATEMENT ON STANDARDS FOR VALUATION SERVICES

1 VALUATION OF A BUSINESS, BUSINESS OWNERSHIP INTEREST, SECURITY, OR INTANGIBLE ASSETS

The American Institute of Certified Public Accountants (AICPA) Consulting Services Executive Committee has issued a Statement on Standards for Valuation Services No. 1. It covers the valuation of businesses, business ownership interest, security, or intangible assets. The Statement applies to valuation engagements accepted on or after January 1, 2008.

INTRODUCTION

The Statement on Standards for Valuation Services 1 is designed to improve the consistency and quality of practice for certified public accountants (CPAs) doing business valuations. CPAs must adhere to this Statement whenever they conduct a business valuation engagement that results in expressing a conclusion of value or a calculated value. This Statement applies to both profit and not-for-profit entities or activities. A CPA who is engaged in estimating value in a valuation engagement is referred to as a valuation analyst. The assumptions, limiting conditions, and restrictions must be disclosed in the valuation report. Valuations involve a continual process of obtaining, evaluating, and updating data.

A valuation analyst may use a client's estimates for compliance reporting to a third party if the member determines that the estimates are reasonable based on the facts known to the analyst. Business valuations may be conducted for several reasons:

1. Transactions or potential transactions such as mergers, acquisitions, initial public offerings (IPOs), employee stock ownership plans, stock redemptions, and leveraged buyouts.
2. Lawsuits associated with contractual disputes, intellectual property matters, bankruptcy, divorce actions, owner disagreements, stockholder litigation, and employee actions.
3. Compliance engagements such as that for financial reporting and tax matters.
4. Planning engagements such as that for personal financial planning, mergers and acquisitions, and tax planning.

QUALIFICATIONS

Performance of a valuation involves specialized knowledge and experience. The CPA who is to perform such an engagement must have the skill to gather and analyze the information needed to do a valuation. The CPA must be familiar with the various valuation methods and approaches. The CPA must use professional judgment in deriving the estimate, including a single amount or a range of values.

The CPA as a valuation analyst must be professionally competent. In making this decision as to competence, the valuation analyst should take into account the following factors:

1. Subject interest.
2. Subject entity.
3. Valuation date.
4. Scope of valuation engagement including purpose, assumptions, and limiting conditions.
5. Value standard to be used (e.g., fair market value).
6. Type of report to be issued.
7. Intended users of the report.
8. Restrictions to be placed on the use of the report.
9. Governmental regulations and laws, and applicable professional standards.

NATURE AND RISK OF VALUATION

In understanding the nature and risks of valuation services as well as client expectations, the valuation analyst should consider the following:

1. Identity of the client.
2. Valuation engagement terms.
3. Item(s) to be valued.
4. Circumstances beyond the control of the CPA or client.
5. Nature of the interest and ownership rights in the entity.
6. Procedural requirements of the valuation including any client restrictions on procedures to be performed.
7. Control characteristics and marketability of the interest.
8. When the valuation report must be updated.
9. Use of and limitations of the report and the conclusion of value or calculated value.

CONTRACTUAL AGREEMENT

It is preferred that there is a written understanding between the valuation analyst and client of the valuation engagement and terms. However, if the understanding is oral, the valuation analyst should document that understanding by suitable memoranda or workpaper notations. The written understanding should include client responsibilities, duties of the valuation analyst, assumptions, restrictions, standard of value, purpose and nature of engagement, and type of report to be issued.

WORK OF SPECIALISTS

In doing the business valuation, the valuation analyst may rely on the work of a third-party expert appraiser who has been hired by the valuation analyst, the client, or a legal counsel. The valuation analyst must carefully read the third-party specialist's report. If the valuation analyst concludes that the results and conclusions of the third party are unreasonable, the valuation analyst, that expert's report and valuation information cannot be relied upon.

In the event that the outside expert appraiser's work can be relied upon, the valuation analyst should appraise the expert's qualifications to determine if the specialist is duly qualified in knowledge, experience, and skill. The valuation analyst must consider the specialist's education, profession certifications, reputation and professional standing, familiarity with the subject matter and industry, and any other suitable criteria. The specialist's work can only be used if the valuation analyst is satisfied that the specialist is qualified.

CONFLICT OF INTEREST AND INDEPENDENCE

If there is a potential conflict of interest in performing the business valuation, the valuation analyst must make proper disclosures. Note that the conflict of interest may preclude the valuation analyst from undertaking the engagement because of a lack of objectivity.

The valuation analyst must satisfy the independence rules for a client such as when the valuation analyst also performs an attest engagement for the client.

ASSUMPTIONS AND LIMITING CONDITIONS FOR A BUSINESS VALUATION

Even though a valuation analyst would be expected to question data that management provides if it seems unreasonable or inconsistent, the valuation analyst does *not* audit that information.

HYPOTHETICAL CONDITIONS

Hypothetical conditions related to the subject matter may be needed in some instances such as for litigation or for comparative purposes. When hypothetical conditions are used during a valuation or calculation engagement, the valuation analyst should disclose the basis for their use and how they were used in deriving the valuation or calculation.

TYPES OF VALUATION ENGAGEMENTS

There exist two types of engagements to estimate value. They are the valuation engagement and the calculation engagement. The former requires more procedures than the latter.

A *valuation engagement* applies when the valuation analyst must ascertain a value estimate of a subject matter and applies the appropriate valuation approaches and methods to the circumstances following the guidelines of this Statement. The valuation analyst expresses the valuation results as a conclusion of value. The conclusion may be either a single dollar amount or range of dollar amounts.

A *calculation engagement* occurs when the valuation analyst and the client are in agreement on the valuation methods and approaches to be used and the degree of procedures to be conducted by the valuation analyst to derive an estimate of value of a subject interest, and the valuation analyst estimates the value in accordance with the agreement. The valuation analyst expresses the results of these procedures as a calculated value. The calculated value is usually expressed as a range but may also be a single dollar amount. A calculation agreement does not include all of the procedures needed in a valuation engagement.

SUBJECT INTEREST

The appraisal of the subject interest aids the valuation analyst in considering, planning, and applying the appropriate valuation approaches and methods to the subject interest. The nature and degree of information required and available to conduct the evaluation depends on the nature of the subject interest, scope of engagement, intended use of valuation, governmental regulations, professional standards, assumptions, restrictions and limiting conditions, valuation date, standard of value, and premise of value.

In evaluating the subject interest, consideration should be given to both financial and nonfinancial information. The type, availability, and significance of such information will vary with the subject matter.

The valuation analyst should gather and evaluate the financial information on the subject entity including historical financial information (e.g., year-end and quarter-end financial statements, financial ratios, and financial trends), prospective financial information (e.g., forecasts, projections, and budgets), comparative financial statements (e.g., five year), horizontal and vertical analysis, and tax returns.

Nonfinancial information includes history and nature of the business, management team (e.g., officers, directors, and key employees), product line, service line, organizational structure, risk, facilities, economic and political conditions, geographic markets, major suppliers and customers, degree of competition, classes of equity ownership interests and associated rights, and industry markets.

Ownership information should be obtained with respect to the subject interest so that the valuation analyst can ascertain the type of ownership interest (e.g. controlling interest), understand the legal rights (if any) associated with the intangible asset, comprehend the classes of equity ownership interests, evaluate the different ownership interests of other owners and appraise the potential impact on the value of the subject interest, and understand any other matter that may affect the value of the subject interest (e.g., security, shareholder or partnership agreement, buy–sell agreement, licensing agreement, nondisclosure agreement, voting trust arrangement, restrictions and limitations, and development rights).

VALUATION APPROACHES AND METHODS

The three most common valuation approaches are

1. The income approach,
2. The asset approach (used for businesses) or cost approach (used for intangible assets), and
3. The market approach.

The valuation analyst should use the valuation approaches and methods most suitable for the valuation engagement.

INCOME APPROACH

The two most common income valuation methods are the capitalization of earnings method and the discounted future earnings method. The *capitalization of earnings* method is where economic benefits for a representative single period are converted to value through division by a capitalization rate. A capitalization rate is any multiple or divisor (usually expressed as a percentage) used to convert anticipated economic benefits of a single period into its value. The *discounted future earnings* method is where the present value of future expected economic benefits is calculated using a discount rate. In using these methods, the valuation analyst should consider the following:

1. For the capitalization of earnings method, consider normalization adjustments, taxes, financial costs, noncash items, capital structure, expected growth rate in profitability and cash flows, nonrecurring revenue and expenses, capital investments, risks, discount rate, and capitalization rate.
2. For the discounted future earnings method, consider expected earnings and cash flows, forecast/projection assumptions, and terminal value.

In the case of an intangible asset, the valuation analyst should take into account legal rights, appropriate capital charges, relief from royalty, tax amortization benefit (if any), remaining useful life, position of intangible asset in its life cycle, allocation of income to intangible assets, and discounted and multiple-year excess earnings.

Asset Approach or Cost Approach

When using methods under the asset-based approach in business valuation, the valuation analyst should consider asset and liability valuation as well as liquidation costs. Under the cost approach a value determination of an individual asset is made by quantifying how much money would be needed to replace the future service capability of that asset.

When using methods under the cost approach to value intangible assets, the valuation analyst must consider the type of cost to be used, such as replacement cost or reproduction cost, obsolescence, depreciation, and the remaining useful life of the intangible asset.

Market Approach

The market approach involves the valuation of a business by using one or more methods that compare the subject's business to similar businesses. The three frequently used valuation methods under the market approach for business valuation are as follows:

1. Guideline public company method whereby market multiples are derived from market prices of stocks of companies that are engaged in the same or similar business lines, and that are actively traded on a free and open market.
2. Guideline company transactions method whereby market multiples are derived from the sales of entire companies that are engaged in the same or similar business lines.
3. Guideline sales of interest in the subject entity such as business ownership interests or securities.

Three market approach valuation methods for intangible assets are frequently used.

1. Comparable profit margin method (which is based on comparison of the profit earned by the subject entity that owns or operates the intangible asset to profit margins earned by guideline companies).
2. Comparable uncontrolled transactions method (which is based on arm's-length sales or licenses of guideline intangible assets).
3. Relief from royalty method (which is based on the royalty rate, usually stated as a percentage of sales or revenue), that the subject entity that owns or operates the intangible asset would be required to pay to a hypothetical third-party licensor to use the intangible asset.

It is suggested that the valuation analyst disclose the rationale and support for the valuation method selected.

In the case of the methods involving guideline intangible assets such as the comparable profit margin method, the valuation analyst should take into account the subject intangible asset's remaining life compared to the remaining life of the guideline intangible assets.

Multiples

In deriving valuation pricing multiples, the valuation analyst should take into account arm's-length transactions and prices, dates and relevance of market data, and quantification and qualitative comparisons.

Rules of Thumb

Even though it is not a valuation method, some valuation analysts use rules of thumb or industry benchmark indicators in a valuation engagement. A rule of thumb is usually a reasonableness check against other methods used and should typically not be used as the sole method to determine the value of the subject interest. A valuation analyst using a rule of thumb should use valuation methods in determining a conclusion of value.

In the event that a rule of thumb is used with the valuation methods, the valuation analyst must document in the workpapers and cite in the valuation report the information sources used and how the rule of thumb was applied.

VALUATION ADJUSTMENTS

The valuation analyst should consider if valuation adjustments (premiums or discounts) should be made to a value determination using one of the valuation approaches. Examples of valuation adjustments are a discount for lack of control or lack of marketability.

In the valuation of a controlling ownership interest under the income approach, the value of nonoperating assets or excess operating assets should be excluded from computing the value based on the operating assets and should be added to the value of the operating entity. In valuing a noncontrolling ownership interest under the income approach, the value of nonoperating assets or excess operating assets may or may not be added to the value of the operating entity, depending on the valuation analyst's evaluation of the influence exercisable by the noncontrolling interest. With the asset-based or cost-based approach, it may not be necessary to separately take into account nonoperating assets or excess operating assets.

CONCLUSION OF VALUE

In determining the conclusion of value, the valuation analyst should do the following:

1. Evaluate the reliability of the results under the different approaches and methods, using the information obtained in the valuation engagement.
2. Compare, correlate, and reconcile the results gathered under the different approaches and methods.
3. Determine whether the conclusion of value should reflect the results of one valuation approach and method or a combination of the results of one or more approaches and methods.

SUBSEQUENT EVENTS

The valuation date is the specific date at which the valuation analyst estimates the value of the subject interest. In most cases the valuation analyst should take into account just the circumstances existing at the valuation date and events taking place up to the valuation date. An event that could impact the valuation may occur after the valuation date but before the valuation report is issued. This occurrence is termed a subsequent event. The valuation analyst should consider the following two kinds of subsequent events:

1. Events reflective of conditions that were *not* known or knowable at the valuation date, including conditions that took place after the valuation date.
2. Events reflective of conditions that were known or knowable at the valuation date. The valuation should take those events and conditions into consideration.

In general, the valuation of known or knowable conditions (item 1) is *not* updated to incorporate subsequent events or conditions. Also the valuation report does not usually include a description of the conditions or events because a valuation is conducted as of a point of time—the valuation date—and the events taking place subsequent to that date are *not* relevant to the value determined as of that date. However, in cases where a valuation is meaningful to the intended user beyond the valuation date, the events may be of such nature and significance to justify disclosure in a separate section of the report in order that users are not misled. The disclosure must specify that the events are provided for informational reasons only and do not impact the determination of value.

DOCUMENTATION

Documentation is the major record of data gathered and evaluated, the procedures conducted, valuation approaches and methods used, and the conclusion of value. It is in the valuation analyst's professional judgment of the type, quantity, and content of documentation. The following should be documented:

1. Information obtained and examined affecting the value of the subject interest.
2. Work conducted to satisfy oneself as to the work of specialists.
3. Any limitation or restriction on the scope of the valuation analyst's work or the information available for analysis.
4. Valuation approaches and methods considered.
5. Assumptions and limiting conditions.
6. For any rule of thumb used in the valuation, the sources of data used, and how the rule of thumb was applied.
7. Basis for any valuation assumptions made by the valuation analyst in connection with the valuation.
8. Events and circumstances considered after the valuation date and before the issuance of the valuation report.

The valuation analyst should keep the documentation for a time period adequate to satisfy the needs of applicable regulatory, legal, or other professional mandates for records retention.

CALCULATION ENGAGEMENT

In conducting a calculation engagement, the valuation analyst should take into account the client's identity, the subject interest, purpose and expected use of the calculated value, valuation date, premise and standard of value, if or if not a business interest has ownership control characteristics and its marketability, data sources used, valuation approaches and methods used, expected users of the report, limitations on report use, and subsequent events.

VALUATION REPORT

A valuation report represents a written or oral communication to the client about the conclusion of value or the calculated value of the subject interest. Excluded from this reporting standard, however, are reports issued for certain controversy proceedings.

There are three kinds of written reports that may be used for the valuation engagement as follows:

1. *Detailed report.* This report may be used solely to report the results of a valuation engagement (conclusion of value). It should *not* be used for a calculation engagement (calculated value).
2. *Summary report.* This report may be used just to report the results of a valuation engagement (conclusion of value). It should *not* be used for a calculation engagement (calculated value). In the case of a valuation engagement, whether to issue a detailed report or a summary report is dependent on the reporting level detail desired by the valuation analyst.
3. *Calculation report.* This report should be used solely to show the results of a calculation engagement. It should not be used for a valuation engagement.

The valuation analyst should note in the written valuation report the restrictions on how the report is used including limitations on the users of the report.

The Statement on Standards for Valuation Services does not apply to the reporting provisions of a valuation conducted for a matter before an arbitrator, mediator, court, or governmental or administrative proceeding. However, the developmental provisions of the Statement do apply if the valuation analyst forms a conclusion of value or a calculated value.

DETAILED REPORT

The detailed report provides adequate information to allow intended users to sufficiently comprehend the information, reasoning, and analyses underlying the valuation analyst's conclusion of value. The following sections should be included in the detailed report:

1. Introduction.
2. Information sources.
3. Valuation approaches and methods used.
4. Financial statement analysis.
5. Valuation adjustments.
6. Appraisal of nonfinancial data.
7. Information appraisal.
8. Nonoperating assets and excess operating assets.
9. Evaluation of the subject entity.
10. Valuation analyst's representations, conclusion of value.
11. Exhibits and appendices.

Discussed next are the major sections in the detailed report.

In the *introductory section,* there is an overall description of the valuation engagement. The information provided should enable the expected user of the report to comprehend the nature and scope of the valuation engagement besides the work performed. The introduction should include

1. Valuation date,
2. Report date,
3. Client's identity,
4. Assumptions and limiting conditions,
5. Reason and intended use of the valuation,
6. Type of report issued,
7. Expected users,
8. Hypothetical conditions in the valuation including their basis for use,
9. Identity of the subject entity, if the business interest has ownership control characteristics and its marketability,
10. Subject interest description,
11. Subsequent event disclosure,
12. Premise and standard of value,
13. Restrictions in the scope of work or information available for analysis,
14. An enumeration of how a specialist's work was relied upon,
15. Any application of the jurisdictional exception, and
16. Any further information the valuation analyst considers useful so that users of the report can comprehend the work performed.

If these items are not part of the introduction, they should be presented somewhere else in the valuation report.

In the *sources of information section,* there should be an identification of the relevant information sources evaluated or otherwise used during the valuation engagement. This section includes the following:

1. For a business valuation, business ownership interest, or security, whether and to what degree the subject entity's premises visited.
2. For valuation of an intangible asset, whether there was an inspection of the contractual agreement, legal registration, or other tangible evidence.
3. Names, titles, and positions of individuals interviewed and their relationships to the subject interest.
4. Industry data.
5. Economic information.
6. Financial data
7. Tax information.
8. Marketing information.
9. Relevant documents and other sources.
10. Other empirical data.

In the event that financial information includes financial statements that were reported on (audit, review, compilation, attest engagement) by the valuation analyst's firm, there should be disclosure of this in the valuation report. If the valuation analyst's firm did not report on the financial information, such should be noted and include a statement that the valuation analyst assumes no responsibility for the financial information.

The financial information may be derived from tax returns. The valuation analyst should note the tax returns used and any relationship between the valuation analyst and the tax preparer.

In the situation where the financial data was derived from financial statements prepared by management that were not subject to an audit, review, compilation, or attest engagement, the valuation analyst should identify the financial statements, and state that the valuation analyst did *not* undertake an audit, review, compilation, or attest function.

In the *financial statement/information analysis section,* there should be a description of the rationale associated with any normalization or control adjustments to the financial information, comparison of performance with the industry trends and norms, and comparison of current with historical performance.

In the *valuation approaches and methods used section,* the valuation analyst should present the valuation methods used under each valuation approach and the reason(s) for their use. This section should disclose the following for each of the three approaches (if used):

1. *Income approach.* Identify the method(s) used, risk factors taken into account in choosing the discount rate and/or capitalization rate, composition of the representative benefit stream, and any other pertinent factors.
2. *Asset-based approach or cost approach.* For the asset-based approach, note any adjustments made to the balance sheet data. For the cost approach, identify the type of cost used, and how this cost was estimated.
3. *Market approach.* With respect to the *guideline public company method,* identify the guideline companies and how they were selected, pricing multiples used and how they were used, reason(s) for choosing the pricing multiples, and any adjustments to the pricing multiples and why. In the case of the *guideline transactions method,* identify the sales transactions and pricing multiples used, how they were used, reason for their selection, and if pricing multiples were adjusted and why. For the *guideline sales of interests in the subject entity method,* identify the sales transactions used, how they were used, and the rationale that the sales are representative of arm's-length transactions.

When a rule of thumb is used in combination with other methods, the valuation report should disclose the information sources used and how the rule of thumb was applied.

In the *valuation adjustments section,* the valuation analyst should note each valuation adjustment used, the rationale for such use, factors considered in choosing the amount or percentage used, and description of the base values to which the adjustment was applied.

If the subject interest is a business, the valuation report should identify any associated nonoperating assets or excess operating assets and their impact on the valuation.

In the *representation of the valuation analyst section,* the following representations should be included:

1. Analyses, opinions, and conclusion of value are subject to the noted assumptions and limiting conditions of the valuation analyst.
2. The information used in the valuation report is gathered from multiple printed and/or electronic reference sources that are believed to be reliable (any exceptions should be stated), although the valuation analyst has not conducted corroborating procedures to substantiate that information.
3. There is an identification of the parties who are using the valuation report, and any restrictions on the use of the report are noted.
4. An outside specialist's work was used to assist in the valuation. Such specialists should be identified. The valuation report should state that the valuation analyst has not conducted procedures to validate the specialist's work.
5. The valuation engagement was conducted in accordance with AICPA guidelines.
6. The valuation report is not updated for information coming to the valuation analyst's attention subsequent to the date of the report.
7. The valuation analyst's compensation is based on a fee or is contingent on the outcome of the valuation.
8. The valuation analyst should sign the report.

It may be advisable for the valuation analyst to receive from the subject entity's management a representation in writing of information provided for the valuation engagement.

In the *conclusion of value section,* the valuation analyst provides an estimate of the value of the subject interest. The valuation analyst should present the rationale underlying the calculation of value. This section should include the following:

1. Date of valuation report.
2. A valuation engagement was conducted, including the subject interest and the valuation date.
3. A statement that the value estimate is expressed as a conclusion of value.
4. A statement describing the value conclusion, either in a single amount or a range.
5. The appraisal was conducted only to aid in accomplishing its purpose.
6. An explanation of any limitations or restrictions in the scope of work or information available.
7. The valuation was performed based on AICPA guidelines.
8. A statement that the conclusion of value is subject to the limiting conditions and assumptions as well as the valuation analyst's representation.
9. The signature of the valuation analyst or members of the valuation analyst's firm.

The Statement provides an example of report language that may be used (but is not required) in reporting the results of a valuation engagement as follows:

We have performed a valuation engagement of DEF Company as of December 31, 20X8. This valuation was performed solely to assist in the matter of [*purpose of the valuation*] and the resulting estimate of value should not be used for any other purpose. This valuation was conducted in accordance with the Statement on Standards for Valuation Services (SSVS) of the American Institute of CPAs. The estimate of value that results from a valuation engagement is expressed as a conclusion of value.

[*If applicable*] We were restricted or limited in the scope of our work or data available for analysis as follows: [*describe restrictions or limitations*].

Based on our analysis as described in this valuation report, the estimate of value of DEF Company as of December 31, 20X8, was [*value, either a single amount or a range*]. This conclusion is subject to the Statement of Assumptions and Limiting Conditions found in [*reference to applicable section of valuation report*] and to the Valuation Analyst's Representation found in [*reference to applicable section of valuation report*].

[*Signature*]

[*Date*]

Exhibits and appendixes may be used for required information or information that supplements the detailed report. In many instances the assumptions and limiting conditions and the valuation analyst's representations are included in appendixes to the detailed report.

SUMMARY REPORT

A summary report provides an information summary that would be included in a detailed report and, in consequence, need not have the same level of data as a detailed report. However, a summary report should include the following:

1. Valuation approaches and methods used.
2. The client's identity, identity of subject entity.
3. Valuation date.
4. Valuation report date.
5. Information sources used.
6. Purpose and expected use of the valuation.
7. Description of the subject interest.
8. Type of report issued.
9. Assumptions and limiting conditions of the valuation engagement.
10. Premise and standard of value.
11. Business interest ownership control characteristics.
12. Degree of marketability.
13. Restrictions or limitations of the scope of work or data available for appraisal.
14. Description of how a specialist's work was used.
15. Subsequent event disclosures.
16. Hypothetical conditions used in the engagement (including basis for use).
17. Application of the jurisdictional exception.
18. Valuation analyst's representation.
19. Summary of the conclusion of value.

CALCULATION REPORT

A calculation report is the only report allowed to report the results of a calculation engagement. The calculation report should note any hypothetical conditions used in the calculation agreement (including the basis for their use), assumptions and limiting conditions of the engagement, how a specialist's work was used, application of the jurisdictional exception, and certain kinds of subsequent events.

In the calculation report there should be a section summarizing the calculated value. The following should be provided in this section:

1. Calculation date.
2. Identification of the subject interest.
3. Calculated value, either in a single amount or range.
4. Purpose of the calculation procedures.
5. Calculation procedures performed along with description.
6. Estimate of value derived from the calculation engagement stated as a calculated value.
7. Business interest's ownership control characteristics, and degree of marketability.
8. General description of a calculation engagement, including that a calculation engagement does not include all of the procedures mandated for a valuation engagement, and had a valuation engagement been conducted, different results may have arisen.
9. The calculation engagement was carried out under AICPA guidelines.
10. Valuation report date.
11. Signature of valuation analyst or members of the valuation analyst's firm.

There is no obligation that the valuation analyst has to update the report or value calculation for information coming to the valuation analyst's attention after the report date

The Statement on Standards for Valuation Services provides an example of report language that could be used (but is not required) in reporting a calculation engagement as follows:

> We have performed a calculation engagement. We performed certain calculation procedures on DEF Company as of December 31, 20X8. The specific calculation procedures are detailed in paragraphs [*reference to paragraph numbers*] of our Calculation Report. The calculation procedures were performed solely to assist in the matter of [*purpose of valuation procedures*] and the resulting estimate of value should not be used for any other purpose. This calculation engagement was conducted in accordance with the Statement on Standards for Valuation Services (SSVS) of the American Institute of CPAs. The estimate of value that results from a calculation engagement is expressed as a calculated value.
>
> In a calculation engagement, the valuation analyst and the client agree on the specific valuation approaches and valuation methods the valuation analyst will use and the extent of valuation procedures the valuation analyst will perform to estimate the value of the subject interest. A calculation engagement does not include all of the procedures required in a valuation engagement …. Had a valuation engagement been performed, the results might have been different.
>
> Based on our calculations in this report, which are based solely on the procedures agreed upon as referred to above, the resulting calculated value of DEF Company as of December 31, 20X8, was [*calculated value, either a single amount or a range*]. This calculated value is subject to the Statement of Assumptions and Limiting Conditions found in [*reference to applicable section of valuation report*] and to the Valuation Analyst's Representation found in [*reference to applicable section of valuation report*].
>
> [*Signature*]
>
> [*Date*]

ORAL REPORT

An oral report may be used in a valuation engagement or a calculation engagement. In an oral report the valuation analyst should document in the workpapers the substance of the oral communication and affirm that the reporting elements were orally given to the client.

APPENDIX A

CROSS-REFERENCE TO STATEMENTS ON AUDITING STANDARDS

No.	Title	Guide section
31	Evidential Matter (superseded by SAS 106)	
32	Adequacy of Disclosure of Financial Statements	431
33	Supplementary Oil and Gas Reserve Information (superseded by SAS 45)	
34	The Auditor's Considerations when a Question Arises about an Entity's Continued Existence (superseded by SAS 59)	
35	Special Reports—Applying Agreed-upon Procedures to Specified Elements, Accounts, or Items of a Financial Statement (superseded by SAS 75.)	
36	Review of Interim Financial Information (superseded by SAS 71)	
37	Filings under Federal Securities Statutes	711
38	Letters for Underwriters (superseded by SAS 49)	
39	Audit Sampling	350
40	Supplementary Mineral Reserve Information (superseded by SAS 52)	
41	Working Papers (superseded by SAS 96)	
42	Reporting on Condensed Financial Statements and Selected Financial Data	552
43	Omnibus Statement on Auditing Standards	331, 350, 420, 901
44	Special Purpose Reports on Internal Accounting Control at Service Organizations (superseded by SAS 70)	
45	Omnibus Statement on Auditing Standards—1983	313 & 334
46	Consideration of Omitted Procedures after the Report Date	390
47	Audit Risk and Materiality in Conducting an Audit (superseded by SAS 107)	
48	The Effects of Computer Processing on the Audit of Financial Statements	311 & 326
49	Letters for Underwriters (superseded by SAS 72)	
50	Reports on the Application of Accounting Principles	625
51	Reporting on Financial Statements Prepared for Use in Other Countries	534
52	Omnibus Statement on Auditing Standards—1987	558
53	The Auditor's Responsibility to Detect and Report Errors and Irregularities (superseded by SAS 82)	
54	Illegal Acts by Clients	317
55	Consideration of Internal Control in a Financial Statement Audit (superseded by SAS 109 and 110)	
56	Analytical Procedures	329
57	Auditing Accounting Estimates	342
58	Reports on Audited Financial Statements	508
59	The Auditor's Consideration of an Entity's Ability to Continue as a Going Concern	341
60	Communication of Internal Control Related Matters Noted in an Audit (superseded by SAS 112)	
61	Communication with Audit Committees (superseded by SAS 114)	
62	Special Reports	623
63	Compliance Auditing Applicable to Governmental Entities and Other Recipients of Governmental Financial Assistance (superseded by SAS 68)	
64	Omnibus Statement on Auditing Standards—1990	341, 508 & 543
65	The Auditor's Consideration of the Internal Audit Function in an Audit of Financial Statements	322
66	Communication of Matters about Interim Financial Information Filed or to Be Filed with Specified Regulatory Agencies—An Amendment to SAS No. 36, *Review of Interim Financial Information* (superseded by SAS 71)	
67	The Confirmation Process	330
68	Compliance Auditing Applicable to Governmental Entities and Other Recipients of Governmental Financial Assistance (superseded by SAS 74)	
69	The Meaning of *Present Fairly in Conformity with Generally Accepted Accounting Principles*	411

No.	Title	Guide section
70	Service Organizations	324
71	Interim Financial Information (superseded by SAS 100)	
72	Letters for Underwriters and Certain Other Requesting Parties	634
73	Using the Work of a Specialist	336
74	Compliance Auditing Considerations in Audits of Governmental Entities and Recipients of Governmental Financial Assistance	801
75	Engagements to Apply Agreed-Upon Procedures to Specified Elements, Accounts, or Items of a Financial Statement (withdrawn by SAS 93)	
76	Amendments to Statement on Auditing Standards 72, *Letters for Underwriters and Certain Other Requesting Parties*	634
77	Amendments to Statements on Auditing Standards No. 22, *Planning and Supervision;* No. 59, *The Auditor's Consideration of an Entity's Ability to Continue as a Going Concern;* and No. 62, *Special Reports*	311, 341, 544 & 623
78	Consideration of Internal Control in a Financial Statement Audit: An Amendment to Statement on Auditing Standards No. 55 (superseded by SAS 109 and 110)	
79	Amendment to Statement on Auditing Standards No. 58, *Reports on Audited Financial Statements*	508
80	Amendment to Statement on Auditing Standards No. 31, *Evidential Matter* (superseded by SAS 109 & 110)	
81	Auditing Investments (superseded by SAS 92)	
82	Consideration of Fraud in a Financial Statement Audit (superseded by SAS 99)	
83	Establishing an Understanding with the Client	310
84	Communications between Predecessor and Successor Auditors	315
85	Management Representations	333
86	Amendment to Statement on Auditing Standards No. 72, *Letters for Underwriters and Certain Other Requesting Parties*	634
87	Restricting the Use of an Auditor's Report	532
88	Service Organizations and Reporting on Consistency	324 & 420
89	Audit Adjustments	333 & 380
90	Audit Committee Communications	380
91	Federal GAAP Hierarchy	411
92	Auditing Derivative Instruments, Hedging Activities, and Investments in Securities	332
93	Omnibus Statement on Auditing Standards—2000	315, 411, 508 & 622
94	The Effect of Information Technology on the Auditor's Consideration of Internal Control in a Financial Statement Audit	319
95	Generally Accepted Auditing Standards (amended by SAS 105)	150
96	Audit Documentation (superseded by SAS 103)	
97	Amendment to Statement on Auditing Standards No. 50, *Reports on the Application of Accounting Principles*	319
98	Omnibus Statement on Auditing Standards—2002	150, 161, 312, 324, 508, 530, 550, 551, 558, 560 & 561
99	Consideration of Fraud in a Financial Statement Audit	316
100	Interim Financial Information	722
101	Auditing Fair Value Measurements and Disclosures	328
102	Defining Professional Requirements in Statements on Auditing Standards	120
103	Audit Documentation	339

APPENDIX B

CROSS-REFERENCES TO STATEMENTS ON STANDARDS FOR ATTESTATION ENGAGEMENTS

SSAE No.	Title	Guide section**
1	Attestation Standards*	101, 301, and 401
2	Reporting on an Entity's Internal Control over Financial Reporting*	501
3	Compliance Attestation*	601
4	Agreed-Upon Procedures Engagements*	201
5	Amendments to Statement on Standards for Attestation Engagements No. 1, *Attestation Standards**	101
6	Reporting on an Entity's Internal Control over Financial Reporting: Amendments to Statement on Standards for Attestation Engagements No. 2*	501
7	Establishing an Understanding with the Client*	101
8	Management's Discussion and Analysis*	701
9	Amendments to Statement on Standards for Attestation Engagements Nos. 1, 2, and 3*	101, 501, 601
10	Attestation Standards: Revision and Recodification	101-701
11	Attest Documentation	101-301
12	Amendment to Statement on Standards for Attestation Engagements No. 10, *Attestation Standards, Revision and Recodification*	101
13	Defining Professional Requirements in Statements on Standards for Attestation Engagements	20
14	SSAE Hierarchy	50

*Revised and Recodified by SSAE 10
**Sections affected by SSAE 10 and/or containing provisions from SSAEs 11 and 12.

APPENDIX C

CROSS-REFERENCE TO STATEMENTS ON STANDARDS FOR ACCOUNTING AND REVIEW SERVICES

SSARS No.	Title	Guide section
1	Compilation and Review of Financial Statements	100
2	Reporting on Comparative Financial Statements (amends and supersedes parts of AR Section 100)	200
3	Compilation Reports on Financial Statements Included in Certain Prescribed Forms (amends parts of AR Sections 100 and 200)	300
4	Communications between Predecessor and Successor Accountants (amends part of AR Section 200)	400
5	Reporting on Compiled Financial Statements (deleted by SSARS 7)	-
6	Reporting on Personal Financial Statements Included in Written Personal Financial Plans	600
7	Omnibus Statement on Standards for Accounting and Review Services—1992 (amends parts of AR Sections 100-400)	-
8	Amendment to Statement on Standards for Accounting and Review Services No. 1, *Compilation and Review of Financial Statements* (amends parts of AR Section 100)	-
9	Omnibus Statement on Standards for Accounting and Review Services—2002 (amends parts of AR Sections 100 and 400)	-
10	Performance of Review Engagements (amends parts of AR Section 100)	-
11	Standards for Accounting and Review Services (amends part of AR Section 200)	-
12	Omnibus Statement on Standards for Accounting and Review Services—2005 (amends parts of AR Sections 100 and 200)	-
13	Compilation of Specified Elements, Accounts, or Items of a Financial Statement	110
14	Compilation of Pro Forma Financial Information	120
15	Elimination of Certain References to Statements on Auditing Standards and Incorporation of Appropriate Guidance into Statement on Standards for Accounting and Review Services (amends parts of AR Sections 100-400)	-